READINGS AND CASES IN THE MANAGEMENT OF NEW TECHNOLOGY

An Operations Perspective

Hamid Noori
Wilfrid Laurier University

Russell W. Radford
University of Western Ontario

PRENTICE HALL, Englewood Cliffs, New Jersey 07632

Library of Congress Cataloging-in-Publication Data

Readings and cases in management of new technology : an operations perspective / [edited by] Hamid Noori, Russell W. Radford.

p. cm.

ISBN 0-13-552142-4

1. Technological innovations—Management. 2. Technological innovations—Management—Case studies. 3. Production management. 4. Production management—Case studies. I. Noori, Hamid. II. Radford, Russell W.

HD45.R29 1990

658.5—dc20 89-26546
CIP

Editorial/production supervision: Robert C. Walters
Interior design: Ann Lutz
Cover design: Ben Santora
Cover photo: Nubar Alexanian/Woodfin Camp & Associates
Manufacturing buyer: Peter Havens

Case material in this book is made possible by the cooperation of business firms who may wish to remain anonymous by having names, quantities, and other identifying details disguised while basic relationships are maintained. Cases are prepared for class discussion rather than to illustrate either effective or ineffective handling of administrative situations.

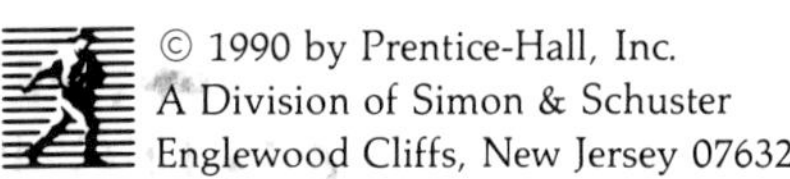

A Division of Simon & Schuster
Englewood Cliffs, New Jersey 07632

Printed in the United States of America

10 9 8 7 6 5 4 3 2 1

ISBN 0-13-552142-4

Prentice-Hall International (UK) Limited, *London*
Prentice-Hall of Australia Pty. Limited, *Sydney*
Prentice-Hall Canada Inc., *Toronto*
Prentice-Hall Hispanoamericana, S.A., *Mexico*
Prentice-Hall of India, Private Limited, *New Delhi*
Prentice-Hall of Japan, Inc., *Tokyo*
Prentice-Hall of Sutheast Asia Pte. Ltd., *Singapore*
Editora Prentice-Hall do Brasil, Ltda, *Rio de Janeiro*

To Annie and Barbara-Ann

CONTENTS

Chapter Twelve
A DYNAMIC ANALYSIS OF ADOPTING NEW TECHNOLOGY 477

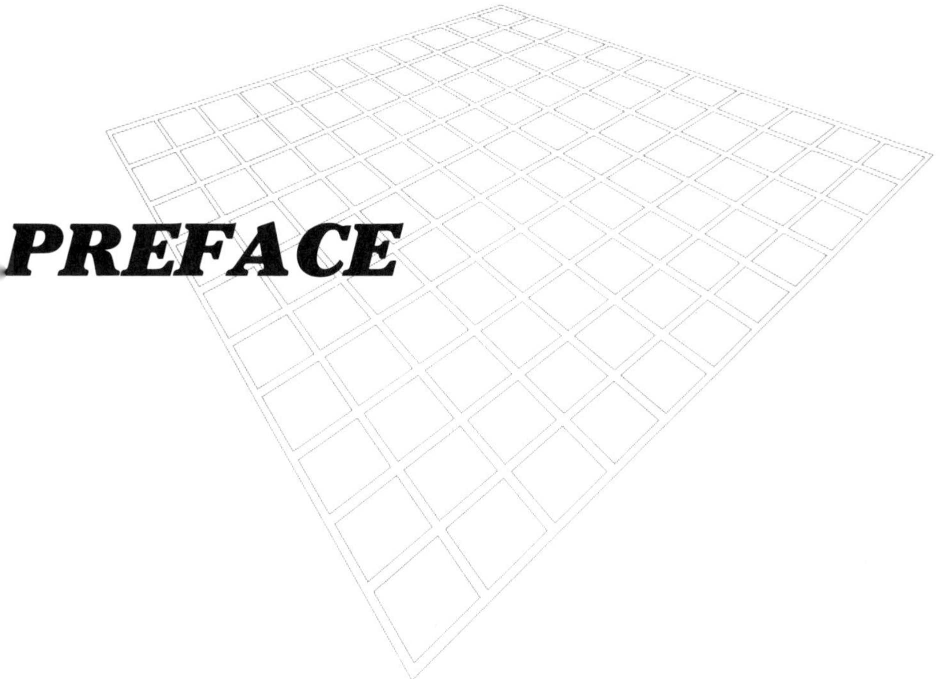

PREFACE

This collection of readings and cases has been assembled to bring a managerial perspective to new technology adoption and implementation. For many years after the Second World War, US manufacturing was an unchallenged force in driving global prosperity. The US was, in fact, a solid manufacturing force which used to dictate the direction and the tune for the rest of the world.

But things change. The economic strengths and the technological capabilities of other countries began to have a marked impact on global competition. The nature of manufacturing, the size and the source of inventions, and the quality of basic education have been shifting in favor of countries outside North America. Today, for manufacturing, the question of change and the future is more than a distant, strategic issue to be discussed at leisure in closed corporate boardrooms. It is an issue of immediate, critical importance, an issue of survival of global magnitude. In this context, operating and general managers are now faced with new challenges in the form of an environment which has dramatically changed in scope. The need is to assume a variety of professional roles and to address, understand, and manage an arsenal of new tools in the form of advanced technologies; all at a time in which ideas about how work should actually be accomplished are continually changing. In this environment managers must focus on INTEGRATION.

This book has been prepared to complement *Managing the Dynamics of New Technology: Issues in Manufacturing Management,* also published by Prentice Hall, Inc. However, the book can also stand alone; it will support any general course in Operations Management or Engineering Management, a course focused on technology, or a course in General Management. The book is not a technical manual; it is intended to help generalist managers, not merely technical specialists, understand the process and the implications of new technology acquisition *for the whole of the adopting organization.* Subsequently, the perspective chosen for the readings and cases are not only global but functionally broad. The material covers many issues from acquisition to implementation, and deals with matters of importance from the individual to the economy at large.

The book has been organized in twelve sections, beginning with general issues concerning the factory of the future. The other sections cover topics from characteristics and potential of new technology through a dynamic analysis of adopting new technology. The readings run, roughly, from fairly focused problems to broad managerial issues. The cases in all sections contain a variety of management concerns that need to be taken into account. The situation presented at the beginning of each chapter provides a brief description of a real case as experienced and resolved in real life. This is a very helpful starting point for individual and/or group analysis of the teaching cases. In addition, the epilogue provided after the readings in each chapter gives a sense of direction and a focal point on the important issues that should be considered when reading and thinking through the cases.

Acknowledgments

We have had considerable help and support in making this book a reality. All the cases used in the book that have not been written by us have been written by colleagues at Wilfrid Laurier University and The University of Western Ontario. Case writing is a time-consuming and arduous task, yet everyone we asked immediately consented to the use of their case or cases in this book. We owe them all a debt of thanks. We also received support in our own case writing efforts from several people who gathered the initial data during site visits to some of the companies involved, or from library research. These individuals, and the cases with which they were involved, are Brian Burlacoff and Debbie Dunn (The Mitchell Drug Company), John McDade (Zepf Technologies Inc. A and B), Alex Stirling (Eastern National Bank), Glen Bell (Electronic Craftsmen Limited A), Cathy Foy and Thomas Foran (World Wide Industries), Scott Murray (Hand Tools Inc.), Mike Smith (UWO Voice/Telephone Registration), Peter Cummins (City Central Hospital—Pharmacy Department), and Chris Schnarr.

The cases could not have been written without the support of the managements of the companies involved, and to all who gave time and valuable insight we give sincere thanks. None of the teaching cases used in this book have been written to describe either effective or ineffective management practice, but to describe a decision point in an operating organization, and the context within which a managerial decision has to be made. Some of the companies have chosen to remain anonymous; that in no way diminishes their contribution or our gratitude.

Our institutions have provided moral and financial support for some case writing as well as some administrative support. At Laurier, this has come through the office of University Research, and at UWO this has come from the School of Business Administration's Fund For Excellence, administered by Prof. James E. Hatch, Director of Research. Support in all conceivable ways also has come from Alison Reeves, our editor at Prentice Hall, and her staff. Without her help this preface would have been prepared at a later date. We were helped by those of our colleagues who found time to read the manuscript in its various guises, particularly John Haywood-Farmer, and two anonymous referees whose many helpful comments they will find reflected in the final document.

But nothing gets done without someone actually massaging the thoughts into a presentable form on paper. And our final, and greatest, debt of gratitude is to our secretaries, Carole Litwiller and Sue LeMoine, for their perseverence in word processing the complete manuscript, and for themselves adopting a new technology while being involved in this undertaking.

We are fortunate to have been able to work with all these people, and for having families who allowed us the pleasure of agonizing over this book. Theirs is the credit; any errors of judgment or fact are ours alone.

Hamid Noori
Russell W. Radford

"By the year 2000, fewer than 15 years off, most of the major manufacturers of goods will have replaced all their machinery. All of it. That's the rate of change we are going through."

Alex Maier,
Vice President, Technical Staff Group,
General Motors, U.S.A.

"Manufacturing may replace finance as a profitable career path; but first, management personnel need a basic education in technology and production."

Lester Thurow,
Dean, Sloan School of Management, MIT.

Chapter One

TOWARDS THE FACTORY OF THE FUTURE

SITUATION 1.1

IBM: Making the Chips Fly[1]

INTRODUCTION

In the lightning-paced computer business, getting a new machine to market quickly is critical to staying on top; the window of opportunity for any new product is breathtakingly brief. But despite its size, IBM has managed to deliver new products as fast as its smaller and theoretically more nimble competitors. Much of the credit for this quick turnaround is due to an advanced integrated circuit (IC) production plant at IBM's semiconductor manufacturing center in East Fishkill, New York.

Appropriately called the Quick Turn-Around Time (QTAT) facility, it routinely produces new circuits in 18 days; in a pinch, it can turn out a circuit in as little as three days. By contrast, most semiconductor production facilities require at least six weeks to produce a new chip.

QTAT serves as both a high-speed prototyping facility and an initial volume-production facility, giving IBM a significant edge over its competitors in product development time, says Donald T. Mozer, QTAT's senior engineering manager. For its wide product line, IBM designs about 5,000 new chips each year. Other companies cannot go into volume production of a new computer until chip designs have been transferred from a prototype facility to a volume-production facility—a procedure that normally takes a couple of months. But with QTAT, IBM can begin production immediately.

QTAT's remarkable ability to quickly turn out small quantities of high-quality chips results, in part, from the use of advanced processing techniques. For example, it

[1]P Kinnucan, *High Technology*, May, 1985. © 1985 *High Technology*. Reprinted with permission.

starts from master slices—rectangular arrays of transistors, diodes, resistors, and other circuit elements—prefabricated on a wafer of silicon crystal, and then adds three wiring layers that customize them for performing specific logic functions. The use of master slices eliminates the numerous steps required to build the circuit elements and thereby cuts production time significantly. The use of electron beam lithography to add the wiring layers also results in sizable time savings, because it eliminates the usual mask-making steps and permits multiple designs on the same wafer.

ONE-AT-A-TIME PROCESSING

In the QTAT line, wafers typically move through a sequence of processing steps one at a time. In contrast, most IC fabrication facilities process wafers in batches of similar design so as to reduce delays resulting from wafer transport and tool setup; hence an individual wafer can move through a facility only as fast as its batch. With QTAT's serial mode of processing, the turnaround time for a wafer is limited only by the time required to process a single wafer. Moreover, it is easy to change the priority of processing for a part. But the key to QTAT's performance, says Mozer, is automation. The facility uses computer-controlled equipment for almost every processing step—from wafer cleaning to pattern exposure.

Most conventional facilities employ human workers to transport wafers from tool to tool and to load and unload tools. In contrast, QTAT uses automatic systems for these tasks. Its 100 automatic tools are grouped into eight processing lines, or sectors. and the tools in each sector are interconnected by an automatic transport system that can move wafers much faster than human operators can. Therefore, transport and setup delays are reduced significantly. And by eliminating the handling of wafers between tools, the system lessens the risk of contamination, which can ruin a wafer and increase turnaround time.

In the transport system, jets of air propel wafers along enclosed tracks between tools within each sector. Because each tool is connected to the air track by a T-shaped junction, a wafer may bypass tools not needed for its fabrication. In normal operation, the wafer moves along the air track to each of the process tools specified and is finally returned to a receiver buffer. There it is batched into a sealed cartridge with other wafers, ready for manual transport to the next process sector in the line.

The QTAT facility is controlled by dozens of computers interlinked by data communications lines. These computers handle the routing of master slices through the sectors, and the monitoring and control of operations. Tools that read a serial number inscribed on a wafer's edge enable the QTAT line to identify, route, and process wafers automatically.

The computers are organized in a four-level control hierarchy. At the top level is an IBM mainframe computer that serves as the central controller. This system is responsible for the logistics, measurements, and IC-processing functions, as well as data communications throughout the network. It distributes, collects, analyzes, and reports data for the entire QTAT line. The second level consists of a factory logistics system—based on an IBM System/7 minicomputer—for routing wafers from sector to sector. At the third level, System/7 minicomputers route wafers within each sector. The fourth level, also based on System/7 minicomputers, comprises individual tool controllers.

Information flows both up and down this hierarchy. Downward, the central computer passes an overall plan for manufacturing a chip to the factory logistics system, which then passes the information required to process the wafers to the sector controllers; these in turn pass process parameters to the individual tools in a sector. Upward, the tool controllers pass data collected during the process to the sector controller, and ultimately the information reaches the central computer, where it is stored for analysis.

Some information is also passed laterally, from tool to tool and from sector to sector. For example, a machine that measures the thickness of insulating layers on a wafer passes this information forward to etching machines so they can determine the amount of time the wafer must spend in an acid bath.

CUSTOM TOOLS FOR CUSTOM CHIPS

When QTAT was designed in the early 1970s, automatic tools did not exist for many of its innovative processes. The automatic tools that did exist were designed to process wafers in batches, as in conventional facilities. But QTAT was intended for producing custom chips, one wafer at a time and in a hurry. Thus IBM had to develop every automatic tool in the factory, says John R. Ohrvall, the facility's project engineer, even though the company's usual policy is to buy tools off-the-shelf.

QTAT's wet processor tools are an example. They are used for cleaning, developing, photoresist stripping, and etching patterns on wafers, with robotic arms picking up and dipping the wafers into chemical tanks. These tools automatically perform such functions as wafer orientation, multiple chemical processing, and filling and draining chemicals after each series of processing operations. In conventional facilities, these functions are done manually.

But not all the custom-designed tools were successful. For example, a single wafer metal evaporation tool developed by IBM was not reliable. "It was down more than it was up," recalls Mozer. As a result, IBM replaced it with a commercial batch tool that was more dependable. The company learned from this experience that strict adherence to the serial processing ideal is not always technologically feasible. "We got a little carried away with the single wafer concept," he observes.

Like the automatic tools, the air track system was developed by IBM. The line's designers chose it as a method of transport because it minimizes friction and hence damage to the wafers. In addition, the use of a sealed track allows the air quality in the area surrounding the sectors to remain relatively uncontrolled. In conventional facilities, clean air must be pumped through the entire processing area to sweep away contaminating particles that might ruin a circuit, and workers must wear special garb and refrain from wearing makeup.

But the air track has been a mixed blessing for IBM. For one thing, it cannot handle wafers larger than 82 millimeters (3 inches) in diameter, explains H. Owen Hill, manager of management systems development at QTAT. This capacity was ample when the facility was designed, because wafers could not be built larger than 52 millimeters (2 inches) in diameter. Now, however, silicon crystal growers are able to produce 6-inch wafers, and QTAT cannot take advantage of this development. Therefore IBM has been exploring other modes of wafer transport, such as robots.

Because of its heavy use of automation, the IBM facility requires very few workers. Indeed, the designers originally "envisioned a line with no people," says Hill. But the company subsequently discovered that human workers are needed even in the automated portions of the facility for cleaning and repairing tools.

Because IBM had to design virtually all of QTAT's equipment, the plant costs much more than conventional facilities (although IBM refuses to give figures). Nevertheless, the investment quickly proved worthwhile in the development of the current line of large- and medium-sized mainframe computers, the 3080 and the 4300 series. "We could not have survived without it," says Hill.

When QTAT went into operation in 1979, IBM was facing a serious challenge to its dominance in the mainframe market. A group of "plug-compatible" computer makers led by Amdahl were using readily available advanced ICs to make imitations of IBM's 370 series computers (the predecessors to the current line) that were faster, cheaper, and more reliable than the IBM products. And because they could run the same software as IBM machines, it was easy for the company's customers to replace their current machines with the plug-compatible ones. As a result, the contenders were taking a significant business away from IBM, and many believed that they had broken IBM's hegemony in the industry for good.

Before the QTAT facility, it would not have been easy for IBM to respond to this challenge. In contrast to the plug-compatible makers, who used standard off-the-shelf circuits, IBM designed all of its own circuitry. Custom circuits have an advantage over standard circuits in that they can be made denser, but without QTAT it would have taken years to get the new chips designed and tested.

QTAT enabled IBM to quickly complete new designs, taking advantage of the latest processes (which allowed 2-micron line widths) for packing more devices on a chip. IBM's new generation computers were just as reliable as the plug-compatible machines, yet they used fewer chips and were cheaper to build. Consequently, the company was able to sell its new series at a competitive price, and IBM customers who had been lured away by the plug-compatible machines returned to the fold. As for the challengers, many of them collapsed under the force of IBM's rebound or were absorbed by bigger companies.

Besides helping IBM regain its standing in the market, the QTAT facility has given the company a new capability in developing and operating automated manufacturing systems. "It has been a valuable learning experience," says Hill. "We educated a whole set of people who can now consult on other automation projects within IBM."

Ironically, the QTAT facility, despite being only five years old, is rapidly becoming obsolete. New silicon crystal-growing techniques have allowed wafer size to double since the facility was completed. And new processing techniques such as dry etching are shrinking circuit geometries to the 1-micron level, allowing more circuits to be put on a chip. Meanwhile, the semiconductor equipment industry has developed automated processing equipment and materials-handling machines that are cheaper and faster than those on the QTAT line. As a result, IBM has already begun designing a replacement facility.

"In retrospect, QTAT amply served its purpose," says Hill. "It taught us when it was right to do wafer processing one at a time. It kicked off a whole series of tool developments. And it proved we cannot afford to live without such a facility in an era when response time is critical."

SITUATION 1.2

General Motor's AUTOPLEX[2]

INTRODUCTION

The General Motors (GM) AUTOPLEX in Oshawa is altering the traditional concept and design of auto assembly plants. When the plant is finally at full production, new manufacturing techniques will have replaced the outdated concepts of labor-intensive line assembly supported by large inventories.

GM has created a multibillion dollar integrated manufacturing complex. This system will link computers, robots, automated guided vehicles (AGVs), other GM plants, and the network of auto part manufacturers in Ontario and Quebec. AUTOPLEX will produce 500,000+ of the 730,000 GM-10 vehicles made annually in North America. The technology and knowledge used in the plant has been gathered world-wide—a steel stamping press from Germany, computer programs from the United States, and management styles from Japan. These, and an excellent Canadian work force will make the AUTOPLEX one of the most advanced plants in the world.

Hugh Holland, director of manufacturing, planning and engineering is accredited with the vision behind the AUTOPLEX concept, in which efficiency is the key issue. A product development team works at designing easy-to-handle assembly materials and techniques, taking advantage of detailed analysis of layouts, the work to be performed at each work station, and the impact of a work station on downstream operations.

[2]This case example was prepared using the following sources:
1. Materials Management and Distribution June, 1987, Galila Turkienicz.
2. AUTOPLEX—supplement to Financial Times, March 20, 1987.

THE OPERATION

AGVs are at the heart of the new manufacturing concept "parallel" build rather than the "linear" build of the assembly line. Parallel build differs from the assembly line in three important respects: workers are organized as small interdependent teams; at each work station a number of assembly operations are performed; and in most instances, at least two work stations perform identical operations allowing AGVs to be routed by computer from a buffer area to any available station. The AGV is released from the work station by the work group only when all members of the team feel all operations have been satisfactorily completed. One benefit of this has been a heightened focus on quality on the shop floor, with resultant pressure on designers to design for assembly, as the assembly is not forced through the system by the pressure upstream and the inexorable pull of the chain.

In cooperation with suppliers, AUTOPLEX uses the Just-In-Time (JIT) philosophy. Suppliers provide guaranteed-quality parts in four to eight hour lots. The number of docks has increased so that suppliers deliver parts at or near point-of-use for immediate installation (increasing the number of trucks with parts for delivery from 290 to 450 per day), allowing GM to maintain lower inventories and smaller inventory areas. Higher buffer stocks must be maintained in areas where the free flow of vehicles can increase the need for certain parts. If major components are being resequenced due to problems with the work team, product designs, or parts, higher inventories are required, as well as excellent communication and response time from suppliers. The computer-based communication system aids in this process. It links AUTOPLEX to its thousands of suppliers and allows for an average response time of one-and-one-half hours from order time to delivery. Suppliers in return are paid more quickly through the same electronic monitoring system. Some suppliers have even set up satellite supply facilities and laboratories within the AUTOPLEX complex.

Internal changes have also helped to reduce inventories. A $228 million steel stamping plant has been built to support GM's AGVs assembly system. Inventories of stampings have therefore been reduced to two days of assembly, down from the previous norm of 30 days. Because die changes now take only eight minutes or less (as opposed to eight hours under the old method), smaller press runs are economically justified.

Already the largest user of robots in Canada, GM wil have an even greater share as the number of robots in the AUTOPLEX is increased ten-fold to 2,300 over the next four years. Twenty-five percent of the robots will be used for welding and sealing of vehicle bodies in the body shop; 98 percent of all body welding will be done by robots. Laser and vision cameras check the accuracy of production to insure precision is maintained and quality is controlled.

The use of work teams places a heavy emphasis on the human aspects of the work place, which will lead to an improvement in labor relations. These changes in the relationship between management and labor are expected to have an even greater long-term impact on plant performance than the newly installed equipment.

AUTOPLEX combines a number of features which promise to reap long-term benefits for the company. Reduced cost of inventory, rigid worker-directed quality control, and decreased production time are the benefits of a total systems approach.

The material systems at GM in Oshawa have not only been automated, they have been simplified. This factor, combined with a synchronized assembly system, independent work teams, and JIT manufacturing techniques and technologies will provide GM with a competitive stance, a direction for future growth, and a basis for counteracting rising costs in an increasingly price-competitive marketplace.

SITUATION 1.3

High Tech is Revolutionizing the Way We Live, Work, Think[3]

INTRODUCTION

No bigger than your thumb, the microchip is revolutionizing our lives, changing the way we work, shop, bank, are educated and think. The microchip controls computers, automatic teller machines, supermarket checkouts, and the assembly lines in many manufacturing plants.

The blurring speed of technological developments based on the microchip means these wonders are just over the horizon, if not actually in use:

- The "factory of the future" is now operating in Japan, where one firm uses robots to make robots, with humans doing only maintenance chores.
- The "fifth generation" computer, boasting artificial intelligence, is only a few years away. Some say it will think. Others say it will help humans think.
- This supermachine is behind Ronald Reagan's Star Wars plan. It will have almost unlimited application in industry and will be used to translate human languages and forecast weather patterns years away.
- At a Chrysler plant in Detroit, $500,000 a year is saved by a machine that cuts cloth, vinyl, and leather to patterns set by a computer.
- The extent of miniaturization is mind-boggling. In 20 years we will be able to put the contents of a reference library into a cubic-inch device.
- The home computer explosion will likely see us banking from home and our children learning much of their basic knowledge there.

[3]G. Brett, *Toronto Star*, February 17, 1985, Section F 1, 4. Reprinted with the permission of The Toronto Star Syndicate.

- You will carry your medical records on a VISA-like card that can be read by scanners in hospitals and doctors' offices.
- Computers will come to the aid of the handicapped. Already, a Canadian device helps blind typists by reading aloud what has been typed so errors can be caught.

"What's happening today is that we are undergoing a second industrial revolution which is as transformative, if not more so, than the first," says William Hutchison, former chairman of the Canadian Advanced Technology Association. "It's going to change the way we do business, the way we educate, the way we live our lives, the way we manage and operate, and even the way we think."

But it is estimated that for every six jobs the microchip creates, it will kill 10. The counterargument: That if we do not create those six jobs they will be created elsewhere.

Nowhere is it more apparent how the new technology changes the economics of production and competition than at Chrysler Canada Limited's minivan plant in Windsor, where 128 robots paint, weld, and handle materials. On the automatic welding line, 58 robots have replaced 700 workers. The state-of-the-art plant has almost a quarter of the industrial robot "population" in Canada of about 600 compared with about 4,000 robots in the United States and 30,000 in Japan. On a smaller scale, six robots at IBM Canada Limited's Don Mills plant assemble video-display terminals. Watched over by two people each on two shifts, they do a job that would require 18 people.

Robots excel in hostile environments, and Spar Aerospace Limited of Toronto is making use of the technology it used in developing the Canadarm for the United States space shuttles in a $33 million joint venture with Ontario Hydro. A massive remote manipulator arm is being developed for retubing nuclear reactors.

The robot or computer, however, is an inanimate mass of parts that can do nothing for its human masters without a link between them, and that is the program, or software, stored as electrical pulses on a disk with a magnetic coating.

With CAD (Computer-Aided Design), specifications such as dimensions are entered into the computer, which then uses graphics to produce a three-dimensional image. The object can be "rotated" so the engineer can see it from different angles.

CAM (Computer-Aided Manufacturing) refers to software used to instruct machines what to do in the manufacturing process. One of the virtues of CAM is the flexibility to replace high-volume production of identical items with the production of goods tailored to smaller markets.

The impact of the microchip—representing the miniaturization to the nth degree of the technology that earlier produced the radio, radar and television—has been astounding.

When John Leppik joined IBM Canada Limited in 1962 as a newly-graduated electrical engineer, his first major task was supervising the installation of an IBM 7090 computer at the University of Toronto. "That was the big scientific number-cruncher in the country," he recalls. It cost about $3 million, occupied a high room and needed its own air conditioning system. "For most practical purposes," says Leppik, who left IBM Canada recently set up a computer-applications consulting business, "today's desktop computer does the same thing."

Microelectronic devices have become everyday tools in many other ways. There is the pocket calculator that makes everyday arithmetic painless; the greater reliability of "solid-state" entertainment equipment; the computers airlines use to make reservations and print out tickets; the terminals utility companies use to quickly call up information on your account when you phone with a billing query. Stockbrokers—who need to know prices now—were early and enthusiastic users of computer terminals linked to the stock exhanges.

For people with home computers, the Bank of Montreal has two projects underway aimed at gathering information for the future implementation of a home-banking service. You would pay bills and get access to other banking services with the aid of a device hooked up to your personal computer.

Many of the electromechanical control mechanisms in our machines have gone electronic—in cars, dishwashers, washers and dryers, and microwave ovens.

Amy Wohl, a well-respected Pennsylvania computer consultant, told an audience recently she thinks it is silly to suppose that in a few years we will all be carrying little computers in briefcases when we travel. "How many of you carry phones when you travel?" she asked rhetorically. Instead, Wohl said people will carry a plastic identification card which they will use to gain access to computers installed in every hotel room so they can read electronic mail and write reports that will be flashed to their offices.

A similar technology is at the heart of a service announced last fall at six Canadian airports. Ten "teleport booths"—each consisting of a specially-equipped microcomputer—allow subscribers to send and receive electronic messages.

Computers can be the equalizer for handicapped people in the job market. One example: David Kostyshyn, a Hamilton electronic consultant who is blind has developed a device that allows a blind typist to correct errors by having a speech synthesizer read back what the person has typed.

And a program known as ACT (Alternative Computer Training) was introduced in Toronto recently to provide training for the disabled in business-related computer programming.

Computer programs have paralleled the development of the machines themselves—from programs you needed a degree in computer science to understand, to today's "user-friendly" software. William Hutchison says we are now moving toward "fifth generation" software, lead by developments in Japan, the United States and Britain. "It will treat the computer more like a human," he says. "It'll say, 'Here are the facts; you decide.'"

The concept behind artificial intelligence (AI)—is that a machine with the ability to do human-like intuitive thinking in combination with enormous calculating power would give its human possessors an edge in any endeavor, industrial or military.

With industrial applications in mind, the Japanese in 1981 launched a national effort to find artificial intelligence, with $850 million (U.S.) of public money to be spent in a decade.

And in 1983, with mainly military applications in mind, the U.S. Defense Department entered the race with a $600 million, five-year research program to develop fifth generation computers. (The first four generations are computers based on the vacuum tube, the transistor, the microchip,and the very-large-scale-integration chips, now being used.)

Washington's artificial intelligence program is coordinating the efforts of universities, industry, and the government in the development of a "completely autonomous weapons/battlefield management system."

The program would likely be the key to the space-born strategic weapons in President Ronald Reagan's Star Wars program. But in addition, the report envisages a computer of less than 225 kilos (500 pounds) and enormous flexibility. In one application it could drive an unmanned land vehicle across country at up to 60 kilometers an hour for as much as 50 kilometers.

Computer scientist Douglas Lenat writes in *Scientific American* magazine that AI is likely to be developed but the challenge is tremendous. "Even a millionfold increase in computing power will not change the fact that most problems cannot be solved by brute force," he writes, "but only through the judicial application of knowledge to limit the search."

READING 1.1

High Technology Management[4]

INTRODUCTION

Newly emerging technologies, high technologies, are reintegrating workers' and managers' labor and knowledge: they represent a clear break from the past technologies, which were mostly devoted to amplifying efficiency and enhancing specialization. Consequently, the symbiosis between man and machine is emerging not as a matter of choice, but as a manifestation of the reversal of the ancient process of the division of labor and specialization of knowledge.

Instead of machines further enhancing division of labor and specialization of knowledge, high technologies (computers, robots, telecommunications, AI, DSS, CIM, and so forth) support a multifunctional worker, self-reliant customer, self-service user, and systems-oriented manager-catalyst. In short, man ceases to be dominated by machines (worker as an appendix to technology) and the continued degradation of his skills is finally being arrested.

The newly emerging and mutually enriching interdependency of man and machine will require a new science of complexity: *symbionics*. Symbionics will study the process of reintegration of labor and knowledge, transition from single-task specialization to multifunctionality, human skills and knowledge enhancement (rather than degradation), transformation from hierarchical coordination (management) to self-organization and self-management of mutually interdependent professionals.

[4]*Human Systems Management*, Volume 6, pp. 109–120. © 1986, Elsevier Science Publishers B.V. Extracted with permission.

More detailed discussion of the reversal in the process of division of labor and its implications can be found in Zeleny [1986b]. Here we attempt to explore the fundamental and novel role of high technology in this reversal.

HUMAN SYSTEMS

The systems of complex, inseparable and symbiotic relationships of men and machines are human systems. Human systems management refers to one particular and increasingly significant area of symbionics: that of management (including analysis and design) of man-machine symbiosis. The emphasis is on the symbiosis (mutually enhancing relationship), that is on the system, rather than either of its two components (men or machines) considered separately.

To use a simple metaphore: it is neither the hardware, nor the software, and not even the brainware that determines the scope and functioning of this emerging symbiosis. It is the inseparable interaction of all three aspects (hardware + software + brainware)—in its appropriate socioeconomic embedding—that represents the object matter of human systems management in particular, and symbionics in general.

We are grappling with the qustion: How do we manage human systems characterized by the symbiosis of men and machines?

DEFINING TECHNOLOGY

In defining technology for our purposes, it is quite useless to talk about applications of science, the entire body of methods and materials, or to engage in listing of characteristics or perform costs/benefits analysis.

Any technology has clearly identifiable components:

- **Hardware:** The physical/logical plant (machine, equipment, contrivance); the means of carrying out the tasks to achieve objectives or goals. Hardware refers not only to a particular physical structure of components, but to their logical layout as well.
- **Software:** The set of rules, guidelines, and algorithms necessary for using the hardware (program, covenants, rules of conduct, rules of use); the know-how: how to carry out tasks to achieve goals or pursue objectives.
- **Brainware:** The purpose (objectives and goals), the application, and the justification of hardware/software deployment, the know-what and the know-why of technology. What to employ, how, when, and why?

These three components of technology are interdependent, codeterminant, and equally important: their relationship is circular (not linear or hierarchical). In different stages of technology development and usage, the components are over- or under-emphasized by users and managers: yet the circular balance must be ultimately restored, purposefully or spontaneously. For further discussion of circularity and spontaneity in social systems see, for example, Zeleny (1985b, 1986a).

Example: An automobile has a clearly identifiable hardware: a particular physical/logical organization of components which distinguishes it from, say, a motorcycle. Its software consists of rules of how to operate it in different modes and under different conditions; driving manuals, user's manuals, maintenance schedules, road maps, and so forth. Its brainware consists of decisions, where to go, which route to take, when and why to go there; the answers can only come from human knowledge, purposes and preferences, thus: brainware.

One cannot define an automobile (as technology) without referring to all three aspects: hardware, software, and brainware at the same time.

There is however a fourth and the most important aspect of technology which still remains to be discussed. Each technology (a unity of hardware, software and brainware) is embedded in a complex network of physical, informational, and socioeconomic relationships which support the proper use and functioning of a given technology towards the stated goals and objectives. We shall refer to such a structure as technology support network (or net).

Technology support net consists of the requisite organizational, administrative, and cultural structures: work rules, task roles, requisite skills, work contents, formal and informal covenants of the workplace, systems standards and measures, management styles and culture, organizational patterns, and so on. Material, energy and information flows connect the "technology" to its support net in a symbionic (codeterminant) fashion: it is proper to speak of embedding. Any technology requires (and is determined by) the appropriate embedding in its support net of relationships. There can be no technology without its support net (there could be a piece of hardware or junk, or a software manual and documentation, or a set of lofty purposes, but there would still be no technology).

Technology is neither a thing, nor a tool or logical design: technology is a form of social relationship and only as such can it be properly understood, discussed and managed.

Example: Let us look at the automobile as technology again. Even as a triune whole of hardware, software and brainware, the definition remains incomplete and still useless, incapable of functioning. The support net of the automobile consists of the infrastructure of roads, bridges and facilities, accompanied by maintenance and emergency services, supplemented by rules and laws of conduct and institutions for their enforcement, requisite skills and education, communication linkages, style and culture of driving, behavior, and so on. An auto half buried in the desert sand or packed on wooden stumps in a Siberian village symbolizes the extreme separation from the support net, it cannot be thought of as technology anymore: a sculpture, a status symbol, a statement of sorts—perhaps. But an automobile? It is too easy and too damaging to confuse technology with hardware or equipment.

In Exhibit 1.1 we summarize the principal components of technology, their interrelationships and their embedding in the support net. We are ready to give the

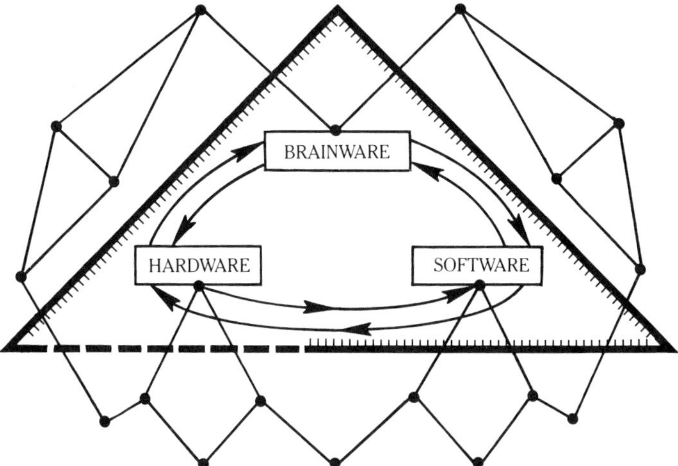

Exhibit 1.1 Technology and Its Support Net Embedding

operational definition of technology for the purposes of management: technology is a circular unity of hardware, software and brainware, embedded in its support net of requisite relationships.

The concept of support net allows us to separate (at least temporarily) the equipment from its embedding. This separation gives rise to a variety of phenomena and problems which are of interest to managers. The notion of "misplaced" technology serves as a useful metaphor: a technology embedded in the wrong support net. Similarly we speak of inadequate technology, window-dressing technology, dominating technology, technology transfer, (in)appropriate technology and, of course, high technology.

DEFINING HIGH TECHNOLOGY

What is high technology? How different is it from technology? Does the difference matter?

> **Remark:** Existing "definitions" of high technology are mostly useless. Especially popular journalism engages in the most profane (mis)use of this term, defining it either by listing (robots, computers, optical fibers, or by platitudes (leading-edge, new, future-oriented) or by attributes (electronics-based, computer-based, information-based). None of such "definitions" can be useful in business and management.

High technology is any technology (see the earlier definition) which affects the very structure and organization of the support net. That is, high technology changes the nature of tasks and their performance, interconnections and nature of physical, energy and information flows, the skills required, the roles played, the styles of management and coordination, even the organizational culture. It allows (and often requires) to do things differently and to do different things. Therefore, high technology is fundamentally different from technology and from appropriate technology:

- **Technology** affects only the flows: it allows us to perform tasks faster, more reliably, in larger quantities, or more efficiently, while preserving the qualitative nature of flows, structure of the support net, skills, styles, and culture. Technology allows us to do the same thing, in essentially the same way, but better.
- **Appropriate technology** preserves the support net as well as the flows through it; its effects are neutral with respect to the support net. It allows us to do the same thing in the same way as before. Appropriate technology is extremely important in situations where the preservation of the support net (say for the purpose of maintaining social stability) takes precedence.

In Exhibit 1.2 we represent the impacts of the three different technology embeddings. Compared to the invariance of appropriate technology, we should not fail to see the flow effects of technology and the organizational/structural effects of high technology.

Example: Introducing the electric typewriter into the support net of the manual typewriter affects the flows but not the support net structure: we speak of technology. Introducing a PC word processor into the net of the electric (or manual) typewriter changes the net itself; the tasks, the skills, the culture. In this case we speak of high technology. Obviously, not every new (or leading-edge) technology is high technology.

To summarize our definitions: while technology improves the functioning of a given system with respect to at least one criterion of performance, high technology breaks the direct comparability by changing the system itself, requiring new measures and new assessments of its productivity. Appropriate technology indicates that rather than improving the measures of performance, it is the preservation of the support net itself which is the main purpose of technology implementation.

Exhibit 1.2 Three Fundamental Types of Technology

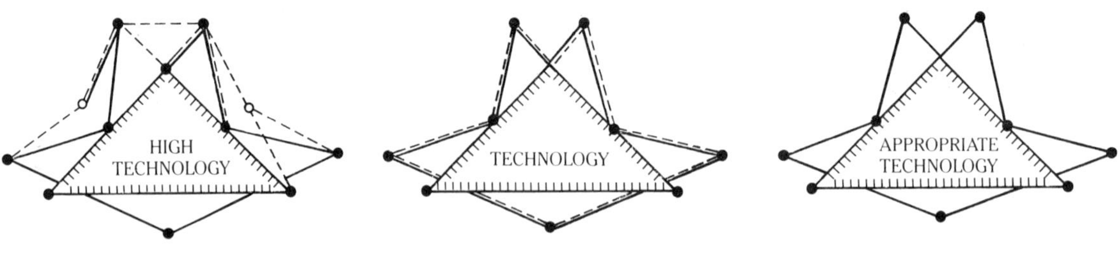

Example: Certain options and functions on a machine may be "locked" or "disconnected" in order to preserve manual tasks and functions of the previous technology. Potentially high technology is thus purposefully degraded to appropriate (or even to inappropriate) technology. Administration, bureaucracy and management (support net) might resent the introduction of technology which would "restructure" it, even though the task (production of a product, performance of a scientific project) would be enhanced on all performance criteria. This process often ends in pathological states of scientists supporting administrators, workers supporting managers, and professors supporting assorted deans in (much too common) "reversed" institutions.

Misplacement of technology is usually fatal. For example, introducing farm mechanization and automation into systems lacking adequate fuel distribution, maintenance and repair facilities, sufficient parts supplies, requisite skills, education, motivation and self-reliance, could lead to lower and less reliable performance than an appropriately embedded low technology, animal-powered system. High technology can become degraded even below appropriate technology—to misplaced (inappropriate) technology and thus cause direct system deterioration.

Problems of so-called "technology transfer" must be viewed from the above vantage point. ("High technology" trucks standing unused in the desert sun are not high technology; they are not even a technology—they are a potent symbol of something. . . .)

In order to avoid the simple notion that technology and high technology are essentially the same, if not identical, we summarize useful metaphors of the essential (if not revolutionary) differences between the two concepts in Exhibit 1.3.

Exhibit 1.3 Comparative Metaphors for Technology and High Technology

Technology	High Technology
Efficiency	Effectiveness and explicability
Economies of scale	Economies of scope
Know-how	Know-what and know-why
Data and information	Knowledge and wisdom
Standards, quotas, targets	Continuous improvement
Status quo, given systems	Innovation, creativity, and change
Specialization	Systems view and integration
Optimize given systems	Design optimal systems
Same thing, same way, but better	Same thing differently, or different (better) thing
Working harder	Working smarter

HIGH TECHNOLOGY MANAGEMENT

The effects of technologies on their respective technology support nets are in the domain of management of human systems. The nature of management tasks is different for the three major kinds of technology:

1. **Appropriate technology:** management as caretaking—administration, continuity maintenance, political and bureaucratic skills, dependency, habits, customs, traditions, etc.
2. **Technology:** management as performance—productivity improvement, standards and measures, goals, motivational skills, hierarchy of command, attention to detail, market-reliance, equilibrium, etc.
3. **High technology:** management as catalysis—knowledge and innovation, organizational and leadership skills, diffusion of hierarchy, self-management, self-reliance, discontinuity and disequilibrium, etc.

High technology must not only be managed, but it must be managed differently. Discontinuities, breakthroughs, structural transformations, redefinitions of tasks and skills, reorganization, multifunctionality, integration (not atomization) of labor and knowledge—all these require managerial attention and skills which are fundamentally different from those of the recent past. High technology management is a qualitative step, not an evolutionary process which simply builds upon or extends the previous practices. It requires the skills of creativity, knowledge, leadership, flexibility, competence, and self-reliance which were previously unnecessary.

Buying and marketing high technology is not the same as buying and marketing dog food. Acquisition of high technology implies acquisition of new organizations, new tasks, new styles, new cultures—new ways of doing business. This is often more than the buyer expected and "bargained for." Yet, it is unavoidable.

It is one thing to manage a status quo. It is quite another thing to manage short-term performance improvements within a given system. It is a fundamentally different thing to manage new systems, previously tested, towards goals not previously stated and explicated; the latter constitutes the task and challenge of high technology management.

HISTORICAL PERSPECTIVE ON TECHNOLOGY

High technology is obviously a relative term. No technology is ever fixed, and, being a form of social relationship, it evolves; it starts, develops, persists, stagnates, and declines. So does high technology.

High technology emerges, its support net is evolved. New versions of it become technologies capable of exploiting the existing niche—a given support net; finally, technologies become appropriate technologies, assuring continuity, preserving organizations—until new high technology appears and the new cycle is started. This recycling of technology is schematically outlined in Exhibit 1.4.

We trace the example of a cycle ($A \rightarrow B \rightarrow B_1 \rightarrow B_2 \rightarrow C \rightarrow$), where A and B_2 are "appropriate," B and C are "high," and B_1 is "technology."

There always were high technologies in the past. But only during the Industrial Revolution they emerged simultaneously in almost all areas of human endeavor. So it is today: robots or word processors, taken in isolation, would not amount to a "revolution," but combined with lasers, optical fibers, satellite communications, AI, DSS, CIM, biotechnology, solar energy, and so forth, amounts to a "high-technology revolution"

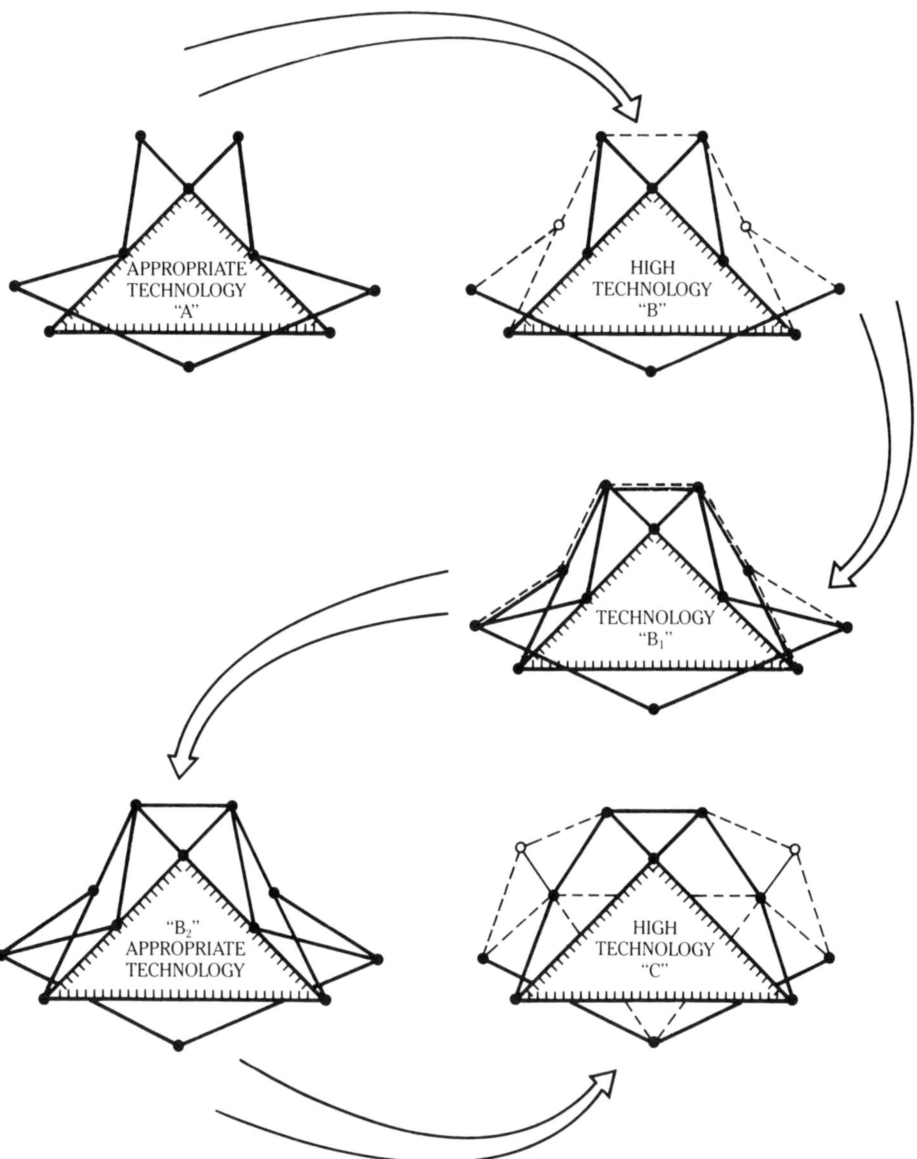

Exhibit 1.4 Cyclical Stages of Technology Evolution

because of its special characteristics to managerial revolution in the last two decades of this century. A more detailed discussion of some high technology impacts is in Zeleny [1985a].

Today's high technology, in addition to the described support net effects is also distinguished by additional and previously not encountered features: high technology is integrative, multifunctional and multipurpose in its nature. This trend is only now starting to be fully perceived and its implications realized: the ancient process of the division of labor (and specialization of knowledge) is slowing down and is reversing itself—for the first time in history. Modern high technologies allow us not to do one (or smaller) task better, but to do more (or larger) tasks. The impacts of this labor/knowledge reintegration are so vast and so fundamental that they deserve a separate treatment (Zeleny 1986b).

CONCLUDING REMARKS

A space shuttle (such as was the Challenger), is one of the most complex high technologies in existence. It consists of hardware and software (equipment), and more importantly; of human brainware and the requisite support network. The two latter components of technology must never be ignored. If there is an inadequate, inappropriate or out-of-date support network, then the technology is misplaced and is bound to fail.

Technology may be administered, but "high technology" must be managed. In the era of high technology, any failure must be traceable to the inadequate brainware and inappropriate support net—not to the equipment.

It is the flawed decision making, incompetent management, the can-do managerial (sub)culture, less-than-professional conduct, politically motivated expediencies, diffused responsibilities, clogged lines of (mis)communication, suffocating layers of the hierarchy of command, fuzzy goals and objectives, the multitude of stakeholders—in short, the support net: the stuff modern tragedies are made of. There is too much of know-how, too little of know-what, and appalling absence of know-why.

High technology management must now be taught, studied and applied. Current support nets must be redesigned: organizations, structures, practices, people, skills, competencies, education, style, and culture of management and be in harmony with the high technologies of modern era.

Human beings (like the astronauts) cannot be kept in the dark about the functioning of the support net, about the risks involved, and about the decision-making processes affecting them: they are not machine cogs. Being human beings, they have to participate.

Once we understand technology as a form of social relationships (hardware + software + brainware + support net) and not narrowly as equipment (hardware + software), we shall also begin to understand that at certain levels of complexity, significance and riskiness, the equipment can never fail. Only humans can.

REFERENCES AND BIBLIOGRAPHY

TAYLOR, J. R. [1983]. *Conceptual Impediments to Productivity, Optimum 14,* pp. 19–42.

ZELENY, M. [1986a]. "Les ordres sociaux spontanes." In: *Science et pratique de lacomplexite.* Actes du colloque de Montpellier, Mai 1984. IDATE/UNU (La Documentation Francaise, Paris), pp. 357–378.

ZELENY, M. [1986b]. "Management of human systems." Erhvervs okonomisk Tidsskrift 50, pp. 107–116.

ZELENY, M. [1985a]. "La gestione a tecnologia superiore e la gestione della tecnologia superiore." In Gianluca Bocchi and Mauro Cerute (eds.), *La sfida della complessita* (Feltrinelli, Milano) pp. 401–413.

ZENELY, M. [1985b]. "Spontaneous social orders." In The Science and Praxis of Complexity (The United National University, Tokyo) pp. 312–328. Also: General Systems 11, pp. 117–132.

READING 1.2

Factory of the Future[5]

THE CHALLENGE

Imagine, if you will, an engineer sitting at a computer terminal punching in data for the design of a new product and sketching freely with a light pen on the screen before him. Happy with the design, he presses a button and the details are passed electronically to another computer running software that checks to see whether the design's stresses and strains are within prescribed limits. The information then zips along to a third computer which generates instructions that command the tools in the workshop to machine, assemble and store the engineer's product ready for distribution—all done automatically, without hassle, delay or hefty manhandling, and all before the morning's coffee break. One more satisfied customer.

Welcome to the "factory of the future." For the first time in three-quarters of a century, the factory is being reinvented from scratch. Long, narrow production lines with men crawling all over them—a feature of manufacturing everywhere since the early days of the car making dynasties—are being ripped apart and replaced with clusters of all-purpose machines huddled in cells, run by comptuers, and served by nimble-fingered robots. The whole shape of the industrial landscape is changing in the process.

The name of the game in manufacturing has become, not simply quality or low cost, but "flexibility"—the quest to give the customer his or her own personalized design, but with the cheapness and availability of mass-produced items. Saville Row at High Street prices. In short, nothing less than a whole new style of manufacturing is in the process of being defined. As firms seek to add extra value by customizing their products,

[5]*The Economist*, May 30, 1987. © 1987, The Economist Newspaper Ltd. Extracted with permission.

while somehow managing to make them at affordable prices, the concept of "economy of scale" is being transformed into an idea best expressed as "economy of variety."

Exhibit 1.5 shows where this technological path is leading —into a magic kingdom where elements of the mass production of Henry Ford and the craftsmanship of Peter Faberge coexist. More than anything attempted so far, more than any amount of retooling, more than all the brave efforts to solve manufacturing problems by hurling raw technology at them—this finally is what the ephemeral factory of the future is really all about.

The catchall title for the set of technologies involved is CIM (Computer-Integrated Manufacturing). Popularizers portray CIM as a plant that pools all its data—whether from manufacturing, marketing, planning, personnel, and finance departments —so that the factory's machine tools may be reprogrammed instantly, and as often as necessary, in order to make whatever customers demand or the business forecasts suggest. Want a new left-handed double-threaded widget in pink plastic? Whiz-bang, you've got one. This is how the factory of the future is supposed to function.

Actually, a few heroic attempts come pretty close. All told, there are now 30 or so factories working in the United States that exploit CIM extensively; many of them (like LTV's Vought plant that produces the B-1B bomber) are veiled heavily in secrecy. In Europe, perhaps half that number are in operation. And in Japan, almost none.

None? Few Japanese manufacturers have as yet anything like enough software savvy to crunch the numbers for a CIM plant. And that may be a blessing in disguise. Many American firms have found that the factory of the future can be as disaster-prone as anything conjured up by Charlie Chaplin or Fritz Lang. Even so, CIM has become

Exhibit 1.5 Best of Both Worlds

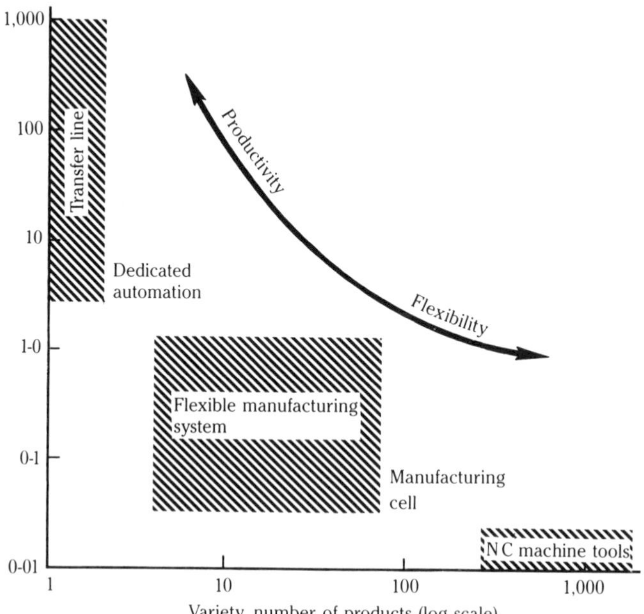

a kind of holy grail. With all the trappings of an industrial crusade, CIM (or something much like it) is the big stick America is going to be wielding in the coming battle for global competitiveness.

At stake, says the Department of Commerce in Washington, is nothing less than the future of the country's manufacturing base, worth $300 billion a year and employing 20 million Americans. Determined not to be left too far behind are the Europeans, with 27 million people employed in a manufacturing sector that contributes $240 billion to the community's economy. And then there are the Japanese, possessors of the most productive manufacturing industry of all, where 15 million workers generate $350 billion a year. With a different perspective on manufaturing, the Japanese have their own ideas about how to build a factory of the future. Who, then, is the most likely to survive in these difficult, promising, challenging, modern times?

WHEN MARKETS GO INTO OVERDRIVE

In the early 1980s, the product life of most manufactured goods was still averaging around six years. Big-ticket items like cars stayed in production (with minor face lifts) far longer—even a dozen years or more. Domestic appliances such as refrigerators and washing machines lasted about five years. Four years separated successive generations of microchips. Even in consumer electronics, product life cycles rarely dipped below three years.

That has all changed—for which we can blame consumers as well as manufacturers. Since the last recession, many of the young now have better paying jobs; and the wealth has spread to new markets—in East Asia particularly. With it has gone the voracious consumption habits of young westerners. Rich, cocky, and acquisitive teenagers in Tokyo are demanding instant gratification, too. The "me now" generation has arrived with a vengeance in Japan.

But it is not all demand pull. Many manufacturers searching for a way out of the recession marched their troops blindly into the same market niches. Large Japanese manufacturers have been arguably among the blindest—and certainly the quickest to cannibalize their own businesses. So much so that in Japan's leading manufacturing industries (semiconductors, home electronics, appliances, clothing, and so on) there are nowadays at least a half dozen leading brand names, each with a big investment in shiny new production equipment that requires a market share of anything from 25 percent to 40 percent to get its money back. With that kind of overcapacity, the manufacturers need markets twice as large as they have just to break even. Such a level of demand is not around—neither at home nor in the now soft currency markets abroad. So ritual *seppuku* occurs in boardrooms across Japan as famous firms go bust or withdraw from the business?

Don't you believe it. In image conscious Japan, to admit defeat would mean unspeakable loss of corporate face. Besides, many of Japan's leading manufacturers belong to big diversified groups, so most can (just about) afford to stay in the game for the time being and raise the stakes. This means launching the next generation of products long before the factories making the present ones have moved out of the red. At the same time, each competitor is being forced to put up even more money for the next cycle of investment, in an urgent attempt to caputre the market share needed the next time around.

Product life cycles are therefore being shortened, in some cases to months instead of years. Retailers reckon that the average life of an electronic gizmo on the streets of Tokyo today is indeed no more than three months.

WHAT WOULD HENRY THINK?

The need for greater responsiveness to consumer tastes means becoming more flexible in terms of what you can make and how. That, in turn, means achieving a better balance between the cost of building new plants on one hand and the unit cost of the goods produced by them on the other.

This is an age-old dilemma. It has bothered every factory planner since Adam Smith. A pragmatist ever, Henry Ford deemed flexibility impossible (correct at the time) and plumped instead for the most inflexible manufacturing process ever devised—which came to be known as the transfer line. The production notions forged in Detroit over the past three-quarters of a century have been adopted around the world, and not just in motor manufacturing. Today, the sound is the same everywhere as production lines rumble along to the clank and roar of dedicated tools cranking out a single model in vast numbers.

Manufacturers today refer to this as "hard automation," meaning it cannot be reprogrammed but must be ripped out and scrapped whenever a new model is to be made. The motor industry is still the biggest fritterer on such dedicated automation. Car makers get little change out of $300 million when rejigging a plant to produce a new model. Whatever they may say, they are still hostage to the twin tyrannies of conventional manufacturing: economies of scale and standardized products.

Not so are the firms nearer the other end of the manufacturing spectrum—in the batch-production business. Every week, a company making, say, roller bearings may need to produce hundreds turned to a half dozen different diameters, thousands of a more popular size, and just a handful of special ones for particular customers. Here the use of a flexible machining center (FMC) or tools with computerized numerical control (CNC) are a far better choice than any dedicated transfer line (TL). There is a snag, of course. The unit costs of parts produced in a flexible plant are substantially higher than those of a production line running flat out. Against that, the investment is far less. More to the point, flexible tooling allows additional models to be added to the company's product range at only marginal cost.

Flexibility also confers a curious bonus—one which, if ever exploited to the fullest, could have a remarkable impact on manufacturing economics. This concerns the way a flexible factory's output can be more easily turned to meet demand on a daily, weekly, or seasonal basis. The implication is that a highly flexible plant, operated in a CIM-like manner, would be able to take customers' orders direct from a showroom's terminals and use them to drive the machine tools—the customer, so to speak, as manufacturer.

That day is still a long way off. Outside a few craft industries, no one (not even Toyota) has managed to "build to order;" everyone else "builds for stock." A few charmed suppliers (mainly in the food business) manufacture for the next day or two's demand. Though their orders may be firm, they are nevertheless forecasts based on statistical guesswork. The impact of "build to order" on car makers—let along on firms producing more personalized items like clothing, consumer gadgets or even publications—would shake up such businesses dramatically.

That, however, would be nothing compared with the impact of an innovation that leading machine tool makers are trying to accomplish. They are looking for ways of pushing flexible machining systems (FMS) more into the domain of the simple but even more adaptable CNC tools at the low-volume/high-variety end of the manufacturing spectrum. At the same time, they are trying to turn FMS into a competitor to the transfer line used in high-volume/low-variety factories around the world. Their ultimate ambition, of course, is to develop flexible manufacturing processes that offer the best of both worlds—the customization possible with CNC machines, but with the unit costs that today can be achieved only on dedicated transfer lines.

MARCH OF THE IRON MEN

Iron men have been on the march for more than a quarter of a century now. Since the first industrial robot joined the prodution line at General Motors in 1961, American manufacturers have recruited 20,000 steel-collar workers, replacing many times that number of blue-collar equivalents. In western Europe, the robot population has propagated even more—to an estimated 28,000 units today. But where western manufacturers seem to prefer their robots sprinkled lightly through their work forces (around six per 10,000 industrial workers), Japanese firms have embraced them (36 robots per 10,000 industrial workers). In modern Japan, more than 80,000 industrial robots are flexing their muscles around the clock.

Building robots has become a $1 billion business. Until recently, the biggest customers for them were the motor manufacturers, who have used robots mainly for spot welding and spraying paint. Now the electrical and electronics industries, especially in Japan, are the biggest buyers. In the process, the way robots are being used is becoming more complex. Car makers were happy to have them wielding tools (such as spray guns) and working on parts clamped to an assembly line; electronics firms want robots to be able to pick up fiddly bits (like microchips and circuit boards) and join them together. Robots are therefore graduating to the far trickier tasks involved in light assembly.

To do so, they need to be a good deal smarter than their "senseless" predecessors. The second generation robots now joining production lines are being equipped with such senses as touch and sight. They cannot, of course, see or feel with anything like the subtlety of a human. But their sensors at least let them pick up misplaced parts or make adjustments for inaccuracies in the objects they handle. For the first time, they can start doing rudimentary inspection jobs.

Another first for the new breed of clever robots is an ability to tackle manipulative tasks that are not supposed to arise on carefully laid-out production lines, but do so in the messy human world where components come higgledy-piggledy together before being assembled. Such jobs include peering into, say, a bin of assorted electronic bits and picking out the correct resistor or diode from the jumbled pile, then inserting its leads into tiny holes in a printed circuit board.

All this technological wizardry has really been conjured up in order to endow robots with the priceless, most human-like capacity of all: the ability to communicate with other members of their tribe. Chattering among themselves, the robots and machinery used in a flexible factory can now report the minutest of details about things like deterioration of their cutting edges or backlash building up in their bearings. That allows the computerized supervisors to make automatic compensations for such errors, thereby keeping the products being manufactured within even tighter tolerances.

As well as arms and fingers, eyes and ears, a tongue to talk with and a rudimentary brain, it would be handy if some members of the robot brigade were also endowed with feet—better still, a set of wheels. This is what the mobile cousin of the smart robot has been given. The AGV (Automated Guided Vehicle) is a little unmanned truck that follows a cable buried beneath the gangway to ferry components throughout a plant. The significant point is that, without AGVs trundling around the factory floor, the whole concept of "just-in-time" delivery would never have got out of the storeroom door.

ISLANDS OF AUTOMATION

Using fleets of little robot trucks to fetch and carry parts from the warehouse in small batches, even in single units at a time, puts an end to the pallets and binloads of half-finished widgets lettering the factory floor. Thus, with machine tools fed just-in-time, components are not allowed to stack up anywhere around the plant, wasting time and clocking up interest charges while nothing is happening to them. With just-in-time delivery inside the plant itself (traditionally it has been used to schedule deliveries from outside suppliers), big savings can then be made to what manufacturers call work-in-progress—half-finished components winding their way through the various manufacturing stages. For the company, economies here have a direct effect on the bottom line; for customers, they mean much faster deliveries.

Just-in-time allows engineers to start clustering their flexible machine tools into compact "cells" where all the tools needed to make a particular product line within easy reach. Once a component arrives at a manufacturing cell, all the machining operations happen on the spot—so no time is wasted moving it to the next machine tool, adding to its work-in-progress bill. At its simplest, a cell may contain just a single CNC (Computerized Numerical Control) machine tool. This offers the greatest flexibility of all, allowing a manufacturer to make as many different types of components as he or she has programs for driving his or her CNC machine. Inevitably there is a catch: CNC machines are not the cheapest way of making things; and the more of any one product which is turned out in this way, the higher the overall cost.

In more sophisticated cells, the metal cutting is done on a machining center—a kind of universal CNC machine capable of carrying out most workshop tasks (including drilling, milling, boring, tapping, and threading) without having to change its grip on the work piece. The trade-off with such a flexible machining cell is the loss of a little of CNC's instant adaptability in return for a bit more efficiency in manufacturing. The full power of this approach comes, however, only when AGVs and smart robots are allowed to joint in—linking cells organically into a collection of machine tools under the supervision of a computer.

This is big boys' stuff: it is what production engineers mean when they refer to FMS (Flexible Manufacturing Systems). As FMS equipment clusters into cells around the factory, "islands of automation" arise like volcanic eruptions from the shop floor. This is still a far cry from full-blooded CIM; before it can qualify as such, the "islands" have to be linked together into a computerized archipelago of machining centers, all communicating with one another and with computers in other departments of the firm. Even so, FMS units—costing anything from $5 million to $20 million to install—are the building blocks out of which the factories of the future are constructed. And the number of them being installed around the world is doubling every two years.

DESIGNER TOOLS

Having intelligent machines capable of making anything is one thing. Getting a picture into their mind's eye of what to make—and a recipe for how to produce it—is quite another. To accomplish this, improvements have to be made in the process by which components are designed. So start first in the drawing office.

Walk into any design shop and if you see dozens of draftsmen at drawing boards, the company has yet to join the CAD/CAM generation. Computer-aided design/computer-aided manufacturing started life more than a decade ago, mainly as an ambitious first attempt to provide some of the benefits of CIM. At the heart of a CAD/CAM work station is a powerful desktop computer that can manipulate complex geometrical shapes rather than the simple numbers and words handled by the more common personal computers seen around offices today. The designer makes sketches either on the terminal's screen with a "light pen" or traces out shapes by steering a marker around the screen using a tiny "mouse." The wiggly lines produced manually are straightened automatically by the computer.

If all CAD/CAM had ever done was to telescope design tasks that took weeks or months with pencil and T-square down to just several days in front of a computer terminal, it would have earned its keep. But CAD/CAM does much more. The software used can turn the geometrical data about the widget's shape and function into computerized instructions for driving the machine tools that will make it. So designs whipped up by the firm's engineers to meet, say, a customer's order or a modification of an existing product can be down in the workshop being made within days instead of the weeks or months it took when everything had to be drawn by hand.

COMMON LINGO

One thing is missing: a means for communicating instructions to the machines on the factory floor from, say, the design office and scheduling department. Equally important, the "islands of automation" need to be able to communicate with one another if the flexible machining centers are to be allowed to graduate into CIM and so eventually usher in the factory of the future.

The task itself is not difficult; indeed, many communications networks have been installed in factories around the world. Their one snag is that, so far, they have been proprietary systems that let just individual brands of equipment talk among themselves. Manufacturers want to be able to hook all their machines together, irrespective of who supplied them, into a single gossiping network. And they want to be able to wire up their factories just like telephone companies wire up office blocks—with standardized cables, sockets, and switchboards, installed if necessary by a host of different suppliers, but all conforming to one international convention. Noble aims, but tricky.

Tired of waiting for the International Standards Organization to come up with a common lingo, the world's biggest user of computerized machine tools, General Motors of Detroit, has imposed its own "manufaturing automation protocol" (known simply as MAP) on the rest of the industry. MAP is a set of rules that govern how, in an ideal world, machines of any make should communicate with one another. Nevertheless, such rules, backed by GM's clout in the marketplace, have brought a margin of sanity to the business. Not only have firms making industrial communications and computers begun to embrace MAP, so too have the big users of machine tools in other industries. All told, more than 1,000 manufacturers have rallied to the MAP crusade.

General Motors has a lot riding on MAP. Over the past eight years, it has spent $40 billion on new manufacturing equipment and factories in an effort to turn itself into the cheapest car maker in America. General Motors knows that time is running out; that without MAP many of the benefits of factory automation will be squandered. All its clever high tech tools will remain deaf and dumb—capable of doing an honest day's work, but unable to use their time intelligently. A year ago, GM started wiring up its first factory, a truck assembly plant in Pontiac, Michigan, containing 21 types of machines from 13 different suppliers. Since then, it has connected up machines in several more factories to its computers, and has set a deadline of 1990 for having all its new flexible manufacturing plants communicating via MAP to the corporate planning and marketing departments.

To help it achieve this, GM has forged a strategic alliance with Boeing. While keeping tabs on the 30,000 nuts, bolts, bits and pieces that go into a modern motor car is difficult enough, the problem involved in tracking the 3.5 million individual parts used in building an airliner are horrendous. Like GM in the motor industry, Boeing has been forced within the aircraft industry to take the initiative, too. But unlike a car maker that cranks out vehicles at a rate of one or more a minute, building big civil jets involves almost as much painstaking inspection as construction, with a production rate that rarely exceeds half a dozen aircraft a month. Not surprisingly, where GM's approach is to get its "islands of automation" to talk to one another, Boeing's is to build bridges between the "islands of information" that spring up wherever computers are used to automate the flow of documents. For that reason, Boeing calls its communications standard TOP (Technical and Office Protocol).

Because of their different approaches, MAP and TOP turn out to be complementary rather than competitive. Engineers from the two firms have spent the past three years pooling efforts to make the two protocols compatible. They are now five-sevenths of the way there.

WHERE THE SLOW LANE IS QUICKER

Japan may have few, if any, factories of the future, but it is a bigger user of flexible machine tools than any other manufacturing nation. Since the early 1980s, Japan has been spending twice as much as the United States or Europe on factory automation. More than half the equipment it has bought have been computerized numerically controlled (CNC) machine tools—one of the essential ingredients for flexible manufacturing. The result today is that 40 percent of the world's nifty "make-anything" machines are busy beavering away in Japan. More to the point , two out of three are in small- to medium-sized firms.

That is not all. Japanese manufacturers are getting more out of their computerized tools than firms in the West. Mr. Ramchandran Jaikumar (1986), a researcher at Harvard Business School, reports that two out of five workers in Japanese factories using computerized tools are engineering graduates who have been trained to use such equipment at a university. Similar firms in the United States have one college-trained engineer for every dozen workers. Compared with American plants, Mr. Jaikumar says:

> Japanese factories have an average of 2.5 times as many CNC machines, five times as many engineers, and four times as many people trained to use the machines.

Moreover, their utilization rate (the percentage of time the machines are actually cutting metal) is 84 percent compared with 52 percent in the United States. the difference, believes Mr. Jaikumar, can be summed up in a single word: reliability.

Reliability is crucial if you want to run a workshop with no men around and the lights turned out. And most Japanese manufacturers want to do precisely that. In one recent survey, no fewer than 18 out of a sample of 60 FMS installations in Japan were found to be running unattended throughout the night. To do this, their designers had anticipated the more obvious glitches, solving production problems long before machines had come grinding to a halt. More important still, the machines themselves had been built stronger than comparable units elsewhere.

How is it that Japanese firms have embraced the FMS part of flexible manufacturing more readily—and more pragmatically—than rivals in the West, and yet have largely failed where American companies have succeeded in mastering the intricacies of CIM? Certainly, the shortage of software skills in Japan has had some effect, though this is not the problem today that it was a decade ago. What passes for scheduling here is just a rough list of orders, materials, and time slots on various machines. The manufacturer then spends most of the week on the telephone tracking down supplies, while trying to keep the machines running and new orders flowing in. It is the way that "job shops" have functioned everywhere for age. But job shops live on more vigorously in Japan than anywhere in the United States or Europe (save perhaps Italy). And inside every Matsushita or Toshiba, despite their modern flexible factories, reigns a long and honored tradition of jobbing, too.

Unlike their counterparts in the United States or Europe, most firms in Japan are not bound by fixed ideas about the rules of mass production. Without the strong "Fordism" traditions of the United States and (by imitation) Europe, Japanese production managers view the challenge of flexible manufacturing more as a matter of simply automating a job shop—rather than trying vainly to make a rigid transfer line somehow become flexible. And they have learned to appreciate the value of making frequent incremental improvements to their processes rather than the occasional giant leaps favored by American firms.

The differences are enormous. For a start, a Japanese firm converting to FMS tooling will spend roughly a third more money doing so than is common among competitors elsewhere. The extra cash goes on equipment to make the changing of dies and cutting edges quicker, the handling of materials easier, warehouse operations slicker, and addition robots visibly everywhere to ensure that, if necessary, the plant can be run unattended. The extra cost is more than paid for by these benefits alone. All the other advantages of unmanned manufacturing—including even higher quality and still lower inventories—are thrown in free.

TOYOTA-ISM MEANS WAR ON WASTE

"Ford-ism" had its day—though to a lesser extent—in Japan, too. But it is "Toyota-ism" that is propelling Japanese firms into the new era of flexible manufacturing. The reasons go far deeper than the attractions of the fashionable *kanban* method for ordering supplies when—and only when—they are needed. Important, yes, but Japanese managers have been able to see, first hand, just what a modest role kanban has played in Toyota's overall success.

Essentially, kanban (which translates literally as "shop sign") is the same as the American "chit" system for arranging just-in-time deliveries of components. Both are ideally suited for repetitive mass production jobs, where cars, television sets or washing machines are made in large volumes but with little variety. However, when it comes to the flexible factory, neither is actually as useful as the American technique known as MRPII (Manufacturing Resources Planning). The only problem with MRP today is that it has become embedded in cumbersome computer programs.

For all their problems, the attraction of just-in-time methods for ordering parts is that they dispense with a good deal of the paperwork. No magic is needed, just a card or chit which travels with a container of thingummies. When the last gets used up, the card is returned to the thingummy supplier where it simply becomes a document authorizing the release of yet another batch of thingummies, which are dispatched to the customer along with the same (or identical) card.

Two things happen as a result: First, manufacturers quickly learn that the fewer the number of cards in circulation, the less likely are thingummies to pile up at machining stations, gumming up the works and clocking up inventory charges. Second, the battle to reduce the number of cards encourages shop floor managers to be especially vigilant, hunting down and removing production bottlenecks in their departments. All of which translates into less time and money spent making thingummies.

But one of the bigger mistakes outsiders make is to believe that mastering the mysteries of kanban is all there is to Toyota's wizardry on the shop floor. Nothing could be further from the truth. Mr. John Hartley (1986), an industrial commentator based in Tokyo, likens it to the top of an iceberg:

> Kanban represents only about 10 percent of the whole (Toyota) system, and companies that omit to do anything about the other 90 percent of their processes are doomed to fail.

In developing their production system, Toyota's engineers went on the warpath against waste. Apart from scrap and overproduction, everything else that did not add value to a product was considered waste—from unprocessed material waiting to be machined to components that had been made too soon. Above all, idle operators were singled out as especially wasteful. With equipment depreciated over time and labor a fixed overhead, idle men were clearly far more expensive to have around than idle machines. Toyota estimated that the cost ratio of men to machines was three-to-one and rising.

So, rule one at Toyota: don't bother "balancing" the machines in a production line (getting them all to complete their tasks within the time taken by the slowest), but focus instead on how workers spend their time. Nowadays, the machines in Toyota's factories are arranged so that operators can handle several at once, even if it means leaving one or two idle while man moves among them.

Rule two emerged from studies of the time material spent gathering dust—apparently 60 percent or more of its total duration in the workshop. Make savings here, said Toyota, of hours or days (say, by using kanban internally to abolish storerooms) instead of trying to save seconds by speeding up individual production processes.

Rule three concerned ways of getting a greater variety of parts, quicker, from existing machinery—in short, by reducing the batch size. The biggest problem with most machine tools is setting them up (getting their shaping surfaces or cutting edges mounted and adjusted) ready to start working on a particular batch of jobs. Because changing dies (the "male" and "female" shapes used to press sheets of metal into contoured parts) can take up to a day to complete, press shops have traditionally been run to provide a month's worth of components for the production lines. The same goes for die-casting machines and forges. Obvious answer: lick the problem of setup time. Then dies can be changed hourly instead of monthly, batch sizes brought down to dozens instead of thousands, and variety mixed in along the way.

Here, again, Toyota's approach has been characteristically creative. Its engineers redesigned the dies so all of them now have standard fittings and the same height—hence no calibration is needed when they are being installed in a press. They then redesigned the presses, so that the old dies are slid out while the new ones are slid in. Finally, they invented various quick-release fasteners to save operators from having to tighten dozens of nuts and bolts. Mr. Hartley reports cases of dies being changed on 1,000-ton presses at Toyota in 10 minutes, compared with at least four to six hours elsewhere. On one particular forge for making bolts, Toyota cut the time taken to change the dies from eight hours to less than one minute.

Imagine the implications of such a production process. The amount of stock carried internally gets slashed from (typically) 30,000 sets of pressings, forgings, or die castings to 1,000 of each at most. Practically all the parts that go to make the finished product (the model of car in Toyota's case) are themselves now manufactured on the same day that the product is assembled and moved out of the factory.

For Toyota, that means no more financing of large batches of finished vehicles of different shapes, sizes, and colors to meet its dealers' requests. Instead, it holds a small assortment but with enough variety to meet all but the finickiest of tastes—and, for the rare exceptions, the factor can turn out a car of the buyer's own choosing and deliver it to him within five days rather than five weeks.

With that kind of service, few customers have the time—let alone the inclination—to change their minds and go elsewhere. The way Toyota does it, flexible manufacturing is a far cry from any CIM-based factory of the future—but, for all that, it is an awesome competitive weapon.

AUTOMATE OR LIQUIDATE

Japan has a competitive advantage here. It annually graduates twice as many engineers per one million people as the United States, nearly three times as many as Britain or France. In company after company, in Japan, says Mr. Jaikumar, systems engineers with a thorough knowledge of several disciplines have been decisive in bringing flexible manufacturing to fruition. Contrast that with factories in the West, where managers spend so much time trying to solve routine problems concerning quality and delivery that they scarcely have any time to think about how to improve the production process itself.

But the Japanese are not 10 feet tall. The strength of Japanese manufacturers today is rooted in their traditional seiban approach to running a job shop. Up until now, its limitations have, ironically, been a blessing. Scheduling of materials and machines is done in the production manager's office on pieces of foolscap pinned to the wall. No reams here of printout spewed from MRPII programs running through the night on big mainframe computers.

Lacking the software, Japanese firms have been forced in the past to think more creatively, to be more elegant, to reduce their scheduling requirements to the base essentials. But there are limits to how far the seiban form of production control can be pushed. Already CIM is revealing glaring inadequacies in the one-side-of-foolscap approach. Meanwhile, American firms at the leading edge of manufacturing technology are learning a trick or two about getting computers to produce just the essential elements, rather than their present overwhelming volumes of information for their planning processes. Hewlett-Packard preaches the gospel: "Learn first to do what the Japanese do, then automate it."

And never discount the genius of the defense industry in the United States. Put aside $500 hammers, $1,200 toilet seats, fiascos like the $4.5 billion spent on the Divad gun, even faulty o-rings that brought the Challenger shuttle low, as lunacies tolerated or (worse) mandated by government agencies. If the rest of manufacturing in the United

States has enjoyed the benefit of, say, the American Air Force's "Get Price" or "Competition Advocacy" programs and learned to work at the same overall levels of quality assurance, performance, delivery and (yes) even price, the world today would be watching television on sets made by Sylvania, Zenith, and RCA, surrounded by appliances from Frigidaire, GE, and Westinghouse, and Detroit would be exporting cars to Japan.

America's high-tech automation firms that helped transform the country's defense contractors into the most flexible manufacturers anywhere are now busy selling their expertise to the rest of American manufacturing. Hewlett-Packard reckons that 96,000 factories in the United Statees are currently in the process of installing CIM in one form or another. In a year or two's time, many of them will be global forces to be reckoned with; some will no doubt conquer the foreign competition and become the new market leaders.

Sadly, Europe has nothing to compare. Car makers in West Germany, France, Sweden, Italy, and Britain have their "islands of automation." So does Europe's handful of world-class aerospace and computer firms. But lacking the imagination of Japanese manufacturers or the resources of American rivals, European firms tend to put their faith more in the community's multibillion dollar research programs like Esprit, Race, and Brite. Even Fiat, the Italian motor manufacturer that pioneered some of the world's most advanced car making automation, is currently lobbying Brussels for a similar "catch-up" program in CIM research. Throughout Europe, the loudest call to be heard from the manufacturers is for research handouts.

Yet nowhere else in the world could CIM have such an immediate—and more readily justifiable—impact on manufacturing. Nor are government bribes necessary. European industry is sitting on all the cash it needs to implement the latest in flexible manufacturing. Where? Gathering dust on shelves in its warehouses in the form of excess stocks and as work-in-progress on its factory floors. British industry alone is reckoned to have the equivalent of $25 billion tied up in inventories. If only a quarter of that were released through just-in-time scheduling, British firms could buy all the CIM equipment they need for the next couple of years.

When implemented correctly, just-in-time scheduling slashes inventories by, not 25 percent, but more like 75 percent. Japanese manufacturers realized that sooner than most. American firms have been getting the message for four or five years now, and are moving on from mere flexible forms of production to fully computer-integrated manufacturing. Meanwhile, the choice for the majority of mainstream manufacturers in Europe is becoming chillingly clear: either they automate using the flexible new tools that lead to CIM, or many will be left with little choice but to liquidate.

REFERENCES AND BIBLIOGRAPHY

HARTLEY, J. [1986]. "Fighting the Recession in Manufacture." *IFS*. McGraw-Hill.

JAIKUMAR, R. [1986]. "Post-industrial Manufacturing." *Harvard Business Review*, November-December, pp. 69-76.

EPILOGUE

The Competitive Challenge

Companies must prepare for the future if their survival and prosperity is to be based on more than luck. In the 1990s the competitive challenge will be the strategic integration of flexibility, productivity, and quality. Response to this challenge will be centered in manufacturing, and will almost invariably involve the collective concept of computer-integrated manufacturing (CIM).

CIM involves a number of hardware innovations (robotics, CNC, FMS, CAD/CAM) and some management philosophies (JIT) to replace the inflexible "hard automation" (transfer lines) in use today. The successful integration of these flexible technologies into an interdependent functional unit will allow rapid, flexible response to market changes, product customization, and also support quality and efficiency improvements.

Integration, however, is the key here. The full benefits of the individual technologies will not be realized if they operate as separate, noncommunicating units. To overcome this "islands of automation" problem and achieve the synergies made available by the technology, communication networks (MAP and TOP) have been developed.

This book is about the future, and how to manage towards that future by managing the whole new technology process. As the notion of CIM implies, technology involves hardware, software, and brainware, plus a technology support net of physical, informational, and socioeconomic relationships which support its effective use. New technology is any technology which alters the structure of the support net. The main purpose of technology implementation is the improvement and preservation of this support net. It is the failure to address these infrastructural issues that lies at the heart of most new technology failures.

The structural transformations, task and skill redefinitions, and reorganizations required to successfully implement new technology will place great emphasis on creativity, knowledge, leadership, flexibility, and competence in managers. When managers understand that technology is a social relationship of the hardware, software, and brainware components within the support net, rather than mere equipment, the creative symbiosis will be complete and the benefits made available by the technology can be realized.

The challenge for managers, then, is managing new technology, perhaps in non-traditional ways, and certainly with an open mind. The management process involves managing some or all of the following activities: identifying and assessing opportunities, technology adoption or innovation, technology implementation, and operating, controlling, and evaluating the implemented technology. These are common, basic, management processes, yet North American managers have been slow in applying themselves to the new competitive challenge, and to the identification and use of appropriate technological response.

The Japanese appear to have recognized the challenge, and have readily accepted and utilized the new, flexible technologies. Even though Japanese companies have not yet achieved a complete "factory-of-the-future" status, they are most certainly ahead of their North American and European competitors in the race. Some commentators suggest that North American companies must either "automate or liquidate" in the face of the Asian competition. This is too strong, and almost totally wrong, for it concentrates solely on hardware. A better slogan is "innovate or imitate;" either is fine if managed properly. To do nothing is to stagnate, and in today's competitive enviroment that invariably spells disaster. And to imitate implies an acceptance of "second class" status. Our preferred alternative is to innovate; this book is concerned with managing that total, critical process.

Chapter Two

CHARACTERISTICS AND POTENTIAL OF NEW TECHNOLOGY

SITUATION 2.1

Flexible Manufacturing Systems–Seven of the World's Best[1]

INTRODUCTION

According to the best estimates, there are no more than several hundred flexible manufacturing systems throughout the world. Probably no two are exactly alike, because each takes into consideration the specific needs of the user company. Thus while numerous systems use towlines to deliver materials to machine tools, others have AGVS (Automated Guided Vehicle Systems), roller conveyors, car-on-track conveyors, and even AS/RS (Automated Storage/Retrieval Systems).

An AS/RS may be an integral part of the handling network, interfacing automatically with wire-guided carts or towcarts, for example. In a few installations, tool handling is also automated. Monorail carriers or AGVS have been used as the link between a tool room and the machine tools. Sometimes even the tool changing is automated.

People, of course, are involved in every FMS (Flexible Manufacturing System). At a minimum, they perform the setup operations—putting raw forgings or castings on fixtured pallets and removing the finished parts after machining. Frequently they also report part numbers at terminals, perform inspection operations, and drive fork trucks or other vehicles to transport parts to assembly or to shipping. Yet as vital as these functions are, the heart of the system is the automated portion, and that is where we focus our attention.

[1]*Modern Materials Handling*, September, pp. 63–71. © 1982 by Cahners Publishing, Division of Reed Publishing USA. Extracted with permission.

FLEXIBILITY FOR LESS MONEY THAN A CONVENTIONAL SYSTEM

John Deere's computer-controlled towline conveyor uses identification codes on machining pallets to control the routing of parts to the right machine tools. Mechanical devices carry the codes, which are "read" by limit switches. The system helps the firm to increase productivity, reduce work-in-process inventory, eliminate extra handling, cut lead times, and save floor space. And it does so with a capital investment significantly less than required for a conventional system, reports manufacturing manager, Troy W. McAfee.

A special make-ready operation is vital to the success of the operation at John Deere Component Works, Waterloo, Iowa. This is the mounting of parts on fixtured pallets that carry the identification codes. Towline carts arrive at palletizing stations carrying fixtures on machining pallets. Workers load parts on the fixtures, report part numbers and pallet codes at a computer terminal, and release the carts to the towline.

Electromechanical limit switches "read" the identification codes at transfer points beside machine stations. A transfer to a machine takes place automatically when the code matches instructions from the computer, and when space is available in the queue.

The layout provides two interconnected towline loops. These serve two rows of CNC (Computer Numerical Control) machines, including nine multifunction machining centers and three multispindle head indexers. Pallets are transferred from the carts to the machines. After machining, the carts "pass through" each machine for pickup on the opposite side.

A family of eight large, heavy castings, used in drive-train assemblies, are processed on the 12 CNC machine line (Kearney and Trecker Corp.). Daily production ranges from nine to 50 pieces for any one part. Total annual production is 50,000 pieces.

Selection of CNC machines is essentially on a random basis, within two categories of machines, as parts are routed to the machines having suitable tooling. Fork trucks bring incoming castings to accumulation conveyors at the palletizing stations. There, workers use hoists to transfer castings, that weigh up to 1,500 pounds, to appropriately fixtured pallets. These 31×48 inch metal pallets remain on the towline carts after finished castings have been removed.

After palletizing a part, a worker steps to a CRT keyboard terminal and enters the part number and pallet identification code. The computer already knows the operations related to this part-and-pallet combination, and which machines can do the work.

The towline conveyor system (SI Handling, Inc.) has zones defined by limited switches. Such devices report movement between zones to the computer. They also report pallet transfers that take place at each machining station. After the computer routes a part to a machine, it downfeeds an NC program to the machine. This takes place while the palletized part is on the machine shuttle, waiting to enter the machining position. Each part is usually machined on one or two machining centers, used for milling, drilling, boring, and tapping operations. It is also machined on one or two head indexers. These can work on several hole patterns with multiple spindle heads, and do precision boring. It is possible to be machining all types of parts at once, with different operations being performed at all 12 machines.

The computer routes a part from any one machine to the next machine that is available to handle the part. Cycle times range from six to 30 minutes per operation.

The machining centers use 10 to 23 tools per operation. Each has a magazine that holds 69 tools. The indexers use as many as 70 different spindles per operation.

ROBOTS LOAD MACHINE TOOLS AND FILL STORAGE BINS

Robots working in integrated manufacturing cells handle hydraulic pump-cover castings in 25 different sizes and styles, at Sperry Vickers, North American Group, Omaha, Nebraska.

Conveyors and a buffer storage tower link two cells. As a result, continuous production is possible in either cell if the other is temporarily out of service. The two robots accomplish at least as much work as three people could, performing consistently in a manner that boosts machine utilization. Each robot (Unimation Inc.) serves a cluster of work stations within a cell. It performs a total of six different functions and makes decisions. One robot is equipped with a two-part cam-actuated hand with compliant polyurethane grippers to cope with irregular surfaces on rough castings. The other robot has a special parts gripper and a vacuum gripper used to lift sheets of plastic dunnage.

Parts arrive at the first cell in pairs. The input conveyor is a two-lane gravity-feed design, with lanes that are adjustable for the different combinations of parts. The first robot transfers parts from the input conveyors to a six-station dial index machine. There, several operations are performed, including the drilling of clearance holes in the cover. The robot unloads the machine tool, and places two semifinished castings in a wash station. Next, it reloads the machine tool with two more castings, picked up from the set-down stand at the machine, and starts the machining cycle. The robot then goes back to the wash station, picks up two parts and places them on a gauge. While the parts are being gauged, it returns to a dual-lane input conveyor, picks up two more castings and places them at the set-down stand. The robot swings back to the gauge, picks up the two gauged parts, and makes a decision. It either puts the parts on a "reject" conveyor, or places each one onto an output pallet for delivery to the next cell.

The second robot has an equally complex routine and serves another machine tool. It also has to decide whether to place parts onto a conveyor that leads to additional operations, or to build bin-loads of finished parts. When the second robot has finished building the first layer of parts within a bin, its controller repositions the hydraulic lift table under the bin. The robot then picks up a sheet of dunnage and places that over the layer of parts. In this way it builds loads up to five layers high, including as many as 90 small parts or 60 larger parts.

AS/RS SYSTEM AND MONORAIL HANDLE PARTS AND TOOLS

A Czechoslovakian system, now being checked out for an industrial client of the VUOSO (SKODA) Research Institute, is like no other FMS. It uses an Automated Storage and Retrieval System (AS/RS) to store work-in-process on pallets and deliver it to machining centers. And it uses a monorail carrier to shuttle tools between a tool room and robots at the machines. The entire operation is computer controlled and operates 24 hours a day, using work on the first shift only. The system supports eight automated machining centers that work on 40 different gray iron castings.

During the first shift, workers receive batches of about 20 castings, each casting smaller than a 16-inch cube. The workers set up the castings on fixtured machining pallets. An AS/RS machine picks up these loaded pallets one by one and puts them into storage. The machining pallets are stored in racks at each machine, on both sides of the storage machine travel aisle.

While a machine center is completing an operation on one work piece, the AS/RS machine brings another from storage to the work station. The incoming machining pallet is placed at a buffer holding position. Next, a rotary shuttle unit exchanges both pallets. The rotary shuttle reloads the machine while the buffer unit transfers the machined work piece back to the AS/RS machine for storage.

First-shift workers also set up standard and specialized tools in two magazines within the tool room. As many as 144 tools are made ready in each magazine for automated delivery to tool magazines at the machine tools. The magazine at each machine holds about 48 common tools and 96 specialized tools. Each tool is protected by a plastic cartridge, used for storage and transportation.

A robot at each machining station swaps tool cartridges between the tool carrier and the machine magazine. The location and condition of all tools is actively monitored by the computer. Each tool is identified by a code, and this is "read" by an optical reader in the robot.

The robot fetches tools from the magazine and places them, one at a time, in a cartridge removal unit at the machine. This unit moves to the machine's "ready" position, where a tool exchanger does its work. The "just used" tool is removed from the machine and placed in the plastic cartridge. This is then picked up by the robot and automatically returned to the magazine.

ROLLER CONVEYOR ADAPTS TO INCREASED VARIETY

The roller conveyor system at Sundstrand Corporation's Aviation Division has proved its adaptability to a tremendous increase in the variety and total volume of job-lot production. Sundstrand's conveyor system delivers housings used in constant speed drives. The conveyor loop installed about 10 years ago is not much different today than it was then. But it now handles a family of about 150 part numbers, in lot sizes of 10 to 500, with a total of 2,200 parts per month. "This means the line processes nearly five times as many different parts, and almost twice as much total volume as in 1969," says Larry Myers, director of plant operations.

Codes on machining pallets route housings to the right machining stations around the conveyor loop. Supporting the machining line is a versatile handling and storage system. Input-output conveyor spurs hold short queues of machining pallets ahead of each machine, and link each machine to the one-way roller conveyor delivery loop. This loop also serves a special pallet loading station, where housings are manually transferred to-and-from a separate power and free system, used for work-in-process storage.

When first installed, Sundstrand's FMS system cut manufacturing time and in-process inventory by 40 percent. It was also estimated that the original 10 NC machines in their line eliminated the need for 100 conventional metal working machines. Now Sundstrand has unveiled another major change—this time in controls. The new control system made it possible to cope with demands for increased efficiency in job-lot production.

Production plans are generated by an administrative computer. The foreman then sets up daily schedules for each machine in the line. Machines are set up with the right tooling numerical-control programs, and matching pallets are set up with the right adapters for the parts and scheduled operations. A day's supply of housings can be conveniently positioned ahead of production on "free" lines of the overhead conveyor system.

At the pallet loading station, a worker mounts housings on pallets with adapters. He sets tabs on the pallets to represent the part number and operation status. He also releases palletized parts to the maching line, as required, to keep machines busy. At each machine, the code on the pallet is identified automatically. This means that proper pallets will be accepted into the machine's queue, in accordance with the CNC program assigned to the machine.

In other words, the foreman has complete control over the activity at each machine. He can even assign more than one machine to a given part and operation. He has the scheduling flexibility he needs to satisfy changes in demand.

As a rule of thumb, each part goes through a single operation at one time, and then is routed back to work-in-progress storage. This approach allows the system to cope with a tremendous variety of housings, each of which requires as many as three successive operations in the line.

All machines are self-loading and unloading, within two minutes. They are quickly set up and capable of exchanging 40 tools. Tools may be exchanged as often as once a minute, in work cycles of 15 to 50 minutes.

The bottom of each pallet has been designed to fit indexing fixtures on machine tools. A drawbar locks the pallets in place in the fixtures, after they have been precisely located by a diamond pin.

CAR-ON-TRACK SYSTEM PROVIDES PRECISE DELIVERY

A car-on-track conveyor and three robots are the key handling equipment in an automated line that includes 11 separate machine systems—welders, cutters, and grinders—at Harris Corporation's Forth Worth, Texas plant. This combination of equipment, all under computer control, produces about 700 kinds of cylindrical printing rolls in small lot sizes.

Some of these hard-to-handle parts weight more than 2,000 pounds. They range in size from 1½ inches in diameter and 18 inches long to 14 inches in diameter and 120 inches long. The robots handle rolls that weight up to 220 pounds.

Each printing roll is processed through an average of five different machines. Therefore, there are 3,500 different routing combinations which the computer stores in memory.

The automated line occupies an area about 250 feet long by 40 feet wide. The main delivery line of the car-on-track conveyor (SI Handling Systems, Inc.) provides two-way flow, with cars carrying several cylindrical parts on wooden machining "pallets." The overall layout also includes several side tracks and spurs that serve as buffers to the machines. Overall, the system has cut work-in-process inventory by 75 percent.

A host computer routes the cars to the proper machines in the sequence for each part. The computer also operates the robots and controls the machine tools. Computer control and automatic feedback provide real-time information about machining operations. This means that materials can be sent to machines before the need work.

Power is transmitted to individual cars through a constantly rotating tube in the center of the track. The tube is contacted by a drive wheel on the botton of each car. Changing the angle of the wheel changes the speed of the car. Each car is gently advanced to a mechanical stop, at each machining station.

The system runs two 10-hour shifts a day, five days a week. Direct labor consists of two operators and four technicians. The technicians oversee the operation of the system through CRT keyboard terminals. The two operators handle machine loading and unloading at two stations where robots could not be justified, because of low output. As system activity increases, these manual stations will be eliminated.

Machine setup time has been reduced to an average of less than 10 minutes by application of group technology in processing a family of parts. Each machining station is controlled by the same host computer that handles all management decisions and transactions. Data is passed through various numerical controls that provide two-way communication capability. At each work station, there is a terminal used for setup and changeover instructions, and maintenance diagnosis.

AS/RS FOR PARTS DELIVERY BOOSTS PRODUCTIVITY 270 PERCENT

Behind the Iron Curtain, in the German Democratic Republic, an FMS designed to produce small gears has brought about a 270 percent gain in productivity and a 40 percent reduction in floor space. The previous system was conventional in design. The system uses an AS/RS to store and deliver gear blanks in unusual three-tier machining pallets—like "lazy susans"—at the Zerbst plant of the "7 October" kombinat. Robots transfer the blanks between the pallets and the metal working machines.

The system is designed to produce gears in the 60 to 200 mm size range, in small- to medium-sized batches. The designers recognized that conventional machining methods for these "parts of rotation" generally experience a 30 percent to 40 percent loss of machine utilization. The design criterion was an index of "financial returns." Payback for the new system is estimated to be four or five years. It now produces over 310,000 gears per year—twice the original output.

At the start of the system, fork trucks bring empty pallets and gear blanks. Workers load gear blanks on each pallet, keeping blanks of the same size together. The AS/RS puts full pallets into centralized storage. It also serves 16 machining stations on both sides of the travel aisle. After work has been completed at a specific machine tool, the AS/RS delivers the load to the next work area. Or, if the next machine tool is not available, it puts the load into storage. When the work station is available, a pallet moves to it. The transfer equipment lifts the pallet and rotates it, as required, to locate a "zero" indexing position. Some pallets must be rotated 180 degrees. This is necessary because the AS/RS serves both sides of the aisle. A robot at the work station transfers one gear after another between the pallet and the machine tool, and handles gears on the three levels in the pallet. The machining process includes a number of operations: turning, grinding, broaching, drilling, counterboring, threading and milling, debarring, hobbing, along with washing and testing.

AGVS FORMS THE LINE WITH CNC MACHINE TOOLS

An AS/RS and AGVS combine to serve 10 machining centers 24 hours a day, at Murata Machinery, Limited, Inuyama, Japan. All parts handling is automated, from storage to the metal working machines that produce a variety of machinery components.

A 12-hour supply of parts is stored on fixtured machining pallets, suitable for pallet transfers at machining centers and for machining operations. Parts not needed for production within the next 12 hours are on conventional pallets. Setting up parts on the fixtured pallets is a daytime operation in a work piece setup area, beside the storage racks. This is where raw materials are transferred from storage pallets to machining pallets. This approach makes automatic storage and delivery of parts practical, without an excessive investment in pallets or fixtures. As a result, handling has cut machine time and boosted productivity.

Driving this FMS sytem is a hierarchy of computers, including: a host computer at the company's head office, a plant computer that controls inventory and sets up machining schedules, and a minicomputer that controls the FMS. The minicomputer is linked to controllers for the metal working machines and pallet transfers, for guided vehicles, for a single aisle AS/RS and other equipment.

Along one side of the storage system is a special purpose AS/RS. It works in and out of rack delivery stations—conveyorized rack openings, transferring loads between storage and the work piece area.

Following schedules, the minicomputer controls the output of machining pallets, from storage to wire-guided vehicles and deliveries by the vehicles to automatic pallet exchanges at machines. These guided vehicles reach a maximum speed of 197 fpm and declerate gently to a stop. Positioning accuracy at the machines is within plus or minus 1 mm.

More than one type of pallet transfer is used. Each provides two pallet positions: one for an unmachined part, and one for a machined part. Pinions extend from the device toward a guided vehicle, then engage in a rack under the incoming pallet and remove the pallet from the vehicle.

As soon as the machining cycle is over, the machined part, on its pallet, is also moved to the device. It then reloads the machine and transfers the finished work to the guided vehicle. After this, the traffic controller for the guided vehicle system can dispatch the palletized part to another metal working machine, or back to the AS/RS. Workers remove finished components from pallets during the day shift.

READING 2.1

Flexibility: A Strategic Response in Changing Times[2]

INTRODUCTION

Survival in a business environment characterized by a pace of change unwitnessed in history mandates that every facet of our business operation be flexible. Today's business environment is so dynamic that:

- The half-life of many products has decreased to the point that 50 percent of the sales of a product often occur in less than 18 months.
- New competitors enter our markets almost overnight and from almost everywhere.
- Engineering changes are demanded at an increasing rate.
- New products, materials and processes are introduced almost daily.

Labor management, facilities, manufacturing processes and information systems must all be able to adapt to new circumstances quickly and inexpensively in order for the firm to compete on a domestic and international basis. Those that do so, while maintaining a fundamental set of business values, will flourish in these and coming economic times.

In that light, this article describes flexibility and how it is created and maintained in the business context. Specifically, the design of flexibility into facilities, layouts, material handling systems, manufacturing systems, labor systems and information systems is described.

[2]E. Frazelle, *Industrial Engineering*, March, 1986.

WHAT IS FLEXIBILITY?

According to Webster, flexibility is the quality of being capable of responding or conforming to changing or new situations. In a business context, flexibility might then be defined as the ability to respond or conform to changing or new situations quickly and inexpensively.

Business flexibility can also be defined in terms of long- and short-term flexibility. Long-term flexibility is described as:

> ...reduced effort required to reconfigure for new production tasks and business strategies because of changes in the production program and business plan and changes in the quantitative and qualitative capacity requirements on the business.

Short-term flexiblity is described as:

> ...reduced effort necessary to reset between known production tasks within the scope of an existing production program or business plan.

In the face of ever decreasing product life cycles, manufacturing facilities must be designed to outlive the product they were originally designed to manufacture. Likewise, office facilities must be designed to adapt to a pace of change even greater than that found in manufacturing facilities. Designing for change and longevity mandates that flexibility be the principal functional design attribute of the facility.

Flexibility is best designed into office and manufaturing facilities via the spine concept. Estimates are that the concept may reduce the cost of change as much as 50 percent. The concept is characterized as follows:

- All facility services (electricity, compressed air, heating, plumbing, and so forth) are routed through the spine and then into the modules via feeder connections.
- All personnel travel moves from one module into the spine, and then to other modules.
- All material handling takes place via a feeder system, through the primary handling, identification and storage systems in the spine.

The expansion of a spine facility requires no alterations to the primary facility services, personnel travel patterns or material/information handling and storage systems.

Modularity is designed into the facility through the shape and size attributes of the models. The modules act as small factories or offices, and create a "close-knit" working environment conducive to high productivity.

THE OPEN PLAN

Recently, to improve flexibility, the popular open plan office concept has been taken into the factory. There, brightly colored modular and flexible work stations are applicable for light assembly inspection and testing operations. The work stations are designed to be disassembled with as few tools as a screwdriver and a $\frac{1}{4}$-inch hex head wrench or allen wrenches. The panels are then easily reconfigured into new layouts.

FLEXIBLE WAREHOUSE FACILITIES

The traditional warehouse design is a box. Namely, it is a rectangularly shaped building with a uniform roof profile. Unfortunately, the degrees of freedom for expansion are reduced with a box warehouse having docks along just one or two walls. Since disruption of receiving and shipping should be avoided, expansion is limited to those walls without docks.

In contrast, a flexible warehouse would include high-bay modules for high-bay functions and low-bay modules for low-bay functions, all connected by a flexible handling system. In some cases, the "interface module" that houses receiving, in-bound inspection, order accumulation, shipping administrative offices, and computer systems support is a multi-story module.

PARTS MANUFACTURING FLEXIBILITY

Flexible parts manufacturing requires that changes in product mix, volume, routing and design be absorbed quickly and at minimal cost.

PRODUCT MIX FLEXIBILITY

Product mix flexibility requires the processing at any one time of a mix of different parts loosely related to each other by shape or routing. The relationships are defined by group technology analysis, and placed into part families. The parts are then manufactured in a flexible manufacturing system where programmable, flexible machine tools, with the necessary tools and fixtures close at hand, adapt quickly to the variety of products.

VOLUME FLEXIBILITY

Volume flexibility is the accommodation of shifts in volume for a given part. It requires flexible layouts which adapt easily to additions and subtractions of machine tools. Volume flexibility also requires a modular and flexible material handling system. Automated guided vehicles (AGVs) and towline conveyors are excellent examples of modular material handling equipment. When the volume of manufacturing activity increases, vehicles are simply added to the existing fleet. Variable speed conveyors also respond well to volume changes, the speed modified to reflect the change in volume.

ROUTING FLEXIBILITY

Routing flexibility is the ability to dynamically assign parts to machines quickly and inexpensively. Clearly, routing flexibility requires a high degree of material handling flexibility. Such flexibility is characterized by the functional attributes of an AGV—programmability, bi-directional capability and quickly and inexpensively modified guide paths.

DESIGN CHANGE FLEXIBILITY

Design change flexibility is the rapid and inexpensive implementation of engineering design changes for a particular part. It is achieved when the product design, process planning and manufacturing functions are integrated. Design change flexibility is characterized by a minimum of documentation and time required to implement design changes. Computer-integrated manufacturing (CIM), featuring programmable machine tools, computer-aided process planing (CAPP), and computer-aided design (CAD), offers the highest degree of design change flexibility.

FLEXIBLE INFORMATION SYSTEMS

Flexible information systems respond easily to the changing demands which are placed on the system. A flexible information system requires that the system hardware and software be flexible individually and as a whole.

An example of a flexible hardware system is a local area network (LAN) with manufacturing automation protocol (MAP) specified for information transfer. Depending on the type of LAN topology, cabling is easily modified to accommodate facility and operation modifications. Different types of equipment are simply plugged into the data highway.

CONCLUSION

As managers and engineers in manufacturing and office operations, how should we respond to a business enviornment which is more dynamic than any other that has been witnessed in history? Our only effective response is to design flexibility into every facet of our business operations. Doing so will require designing flexibility into our manufacturing, office and warehouse facilities, layouts, and work stations. It will require flexible manufacturing systems, flexible material handling systems, flexible information systems and flexible labor systems. It will also require flexible management systems, characterized by shorter strategic planning review windows and a participative approach which relishes the knowledge of the persons closest to and most affected by the change.

READING 2.2

CIM and the Flexible Automated Factory of the Future[3]

INTRODUCTION

In this article we offer some insights about how the technology and practice of CIM will affect the development of flexible automation in the future.

TRENDS IN MANUFACTURING

We believe that American manufacturing industries are working towards such fully computer-integrated systems, and so are several other countries throughout the world. Manufacturing, for so long given little attention in the United States, has finally been recognized as having strategic importance, not only in a corporate sense but also in a national sense.

Implementing CIM stands as perhaps the brightest hope that the United States has for competing against foreign manufacturing firms with their traditionally lower labor rates. It also represents the best current approach for continuing the long historical trend toward increased productivity in manufacturing.

Let us examine some of the other trends that characterize manufacturing today. They include:

1. *Shorter product life cycles* and associated need to accomplish the design/production

[3]M. Groover and J. Wiginton, *Industrial Engineering* magazine, January, 1986. © Institute of Industrial Engineers, 25 Technology Park, Atlanta, Norcross, Georgia 30092. Reprinted with permission.

cycle in less time. Increased levels of competition are forcing companies to release products that are more complex in less time than ever before.

2. *Increased emphasis on product quality.* This is especially prevalent in the automotive industry, where foreign competition has demonstrated that higher quality and lower cost can be achieved simultaneously, an apparent revelation to many American producers.
3. *Pressure to reduce inventory.* Companies have discovered that maintaining inventories represents a significant investment that can be avoided. Reduction of inventories, particularly work-in-process, is being identified as a primary goal of manufacturing companies.
4. *Outsourcing.* Many large companies today are deciding to subcontract the manufacturing of the components for their products rather than perform this function themselves. In most cases final assembly of the product is remaining in-house. Instead of becoming specialists in manufacturing the variety of component parts required in a complex product, the large companies are relinquishing that role to the smaller companies who serve as suppliers to a number of large firms.
5. *Just-In-Time production.* This is related to the outsourcing trend. Just-In-Time production means that suppliers are required to deliver components within a certain time interval (for example, same day) of when the items will be needed for final assembly of the product. This keeps inventories much lower, but requires very close coordination between the company and its suppliers.
6. *Ever greater use of computer technologies in manufacturing.* Examples include CAD/CAM for product design and manufacturing planning, programmable logic controllers for manufacturing process control, microprocessors for control of robots and machine tools, and personal computers to solve problems for manufacturing personnel at all levels.
7. *Focused factories.* Wickham Skinner's (1974) concept of the focused factory is being employed with greater frequency in newly installed manufacturing plants. The concept of the focused factory is that a single manufacturing plant (approximately 600 or fewer employees) should be organized around a limited set of products and processes, and it should become expert in those areas. In effect, the concept reflects the principle of specialization of labor practiced on a plant-wide basis. The size and organization of the plant permits flexibility and rapid changeover of product to accommodate changes in the market.

FLEXIBLE AUTOMATION AT THE WORK CELL LEVEL

Flexible automation is an important concept that is closely associated with computer-integrated manufacturing (CIM). Indeed, the development of flexible automated production systems is dependent on the implementation of CIM.

Flexible automation denotes an automated manufacturing system that is capable of producing a variety of products (that is, parts or assemblies) with virtually no time losses to change over from one product to the next. This permits the system to produce variable combinations and schedules of products, rather than requiring the different models to be made in batches.

Flexible automation is similar to and often confused with programmable automation. We are only beginning to realize the importance of the conceptual distinctions between these two types of automated systems. In programmable automation, the two features described previously are not included. Although programmable automation is driven by a program corresponding to the product, time is required to perform the programming procedure, or portions of it, on the production system. This results in interruptions in operations when a changeover is made from one product to the next. Not only is time lost to change the program, but additional time is required to change the physical setup for the next product.

What these distinctions mean in a practical way is that programmable automation is best utilized in batch manufacturing situations where the cost of the downtime (for reprogramming and changing the setup) can be spread over the number of units in the batch. Using a programmable automation to produce one-of-a-kind parts is costly, because the downtime must be born by the single product.

By contrast, because flexible automation provides for no changeover losses, it becomes the most economical method for producing single units of product. To be sure, the time required to accomplish the product programming (for example, the part program in numerical control) must still be charged to the product even though it is done off-line, but the flexible production system continues in operation with no time losses between products.

TWO PRODUCTION SITUATIONS

It is instructive to define two types of product situations and to examine how programmable and flexible automation relate to these situations. The two product cases are:

Case 1: *Limited product variety.* A limited number of different products (or models) are to be made on the system, and the configurations of the products are known in advance.

Case 2: *Unlimited product variety.* The number of different products (or models) is large (perhaps unlimited) and not defined in advance; the general configurations of the products are known, but the exact configurations are not known.

In Case 1, it is possible to design a production system based on programmable automation. The programs for the limited number of different models can be prepared and tested before production begins. This permits the system to avoid stopping to reprogram for each different product during regular operation. If the physical changeover to accommodate the different products can be minimized (this is done by minimizing the model variations), the production system can be operated continuously.

The automobile industry provides an excellent example of this type of automation. Car body welding lines that use industrial robots to perform the spot welding can deal with two or three different body styles (sedans, coupes, or wagons) operating in a continuous flow manner without stopping to reprogram or change physical setups for each different model.

The programming for the different models is done in advance, and the correct spot welding program for each robot is activated by a central control unit according to the particular body style located at the work station. This first case might be called pseudo-flexible automation; in reality, it is programmable automation organized in a very efficient way.

In Case 2 (unlimited product variety), the preceding application of pseudo-flexible automation does not work. Since the model variations are large and unknown in advance of production, the programming of the system for all model variations cannot be done before production begins. Unless the reprogramming can be accomplished entirely off-line, there will be interruptions for changing the product programs between models.

It may be possible to minimize the consequences of this downtime, perhaps by changing and testing the program during nonproductive periods (for example, on the third shift in a regular two-shift operation). However, this procedure will force the production system to operate in a batch mode rather than in a continuous mixed model fashion. For truly continuous operations and true flexible automation, there must be the capability for full off-line programming of the system.

More difficult than the reprogramming problem is the problem of changing the physical setup of the production system for each new model. The setup consists of the fixturing to position and orient the product during processing, tooling to perform the processing (or assembly), and other physical apparatus used in the work place that must be altered for each different product made on the system. The strategies for solving this physical changeover problem include:

1. *Minimize model variations.* This strategy goes against the whole notion of a flexible production system that can deal with the large (or unlimited) product variations in Case 2.
2. *Off-line changeovers.* This refers to the procedure of performing the physical changeover off-line, and then moving it into place at the work station simultaneously with the introduction of the next new model.
3. *Generic fixturing.* This term refers to fixtures that are designed to accommodate the variety of product made. This is a difficult design problem when the configurations of the different models are unlimited and unknown in advance.
4. *Mechanized adaptable fixturing.* This might be viewed as a special case of generic fixturing. It represents the strategy of using mechanized fixturing that is capable of changing itself to accommodate new product configurations in response to instructions downloaded from the system controller. These instructions are correlated with (perhaps contained in) the product program for the new model.
5. *Intelligent self-adaptive fixturing.* Similarly, this is a special case of mechanized adaptable fixturing. In this strategy, the fixture is endowed with sufficient sensor capabilities and intelligence that it is capable of determining its own physical configuration so as to adapt itself to the next product without instructions from the system controller.

All of these strategies are applicable to the case of limited product variety (Case 1). Strategies 2 through 5 are more likely to be applicable to the case of unlimited variety (Case 2). Clearly, strategies 4 and 5 are somewhat futuristic.

FLEXIBLE AUTOMATED FACTORY

Our discussion has focused on applications of flexible automation to a single production system, perhaps a machine cell or a production line in the factory. In order to extend the concept of flexible automation to the entire plant, two significant issues must be addressed. These are:

- Factory information and communications
- Material handling

The first issue involves the plant-wide information and communication system that distributes product programs and other instructions to the individual production systems throughout the factory and collects data on shop floor performance. Material handling is concerned with the movement, storage and control of materials (raw materials, work-in-process, final product and other materials to support the manufacture of the product) in the factory.

In a very real sense, these two issues parallel the two problems encountered in the design and operation of an indvidual flexible automated production system (reprogramming and changing the physical setup).

FACTORY INFORMATION AND COMMUNICATIONS SYSTEMS

To achieve flexible automation at the plant level, there is a need to deal with the problem of communicating the large amounts of data and information between the different systems in the factory. Let us consider the current state of and future prospects for database management systems and data communications networks in the future factory environment.

The importance of the factory information and communication systems is highlighted by an observation of Wickham Skinner:

> In the old days, we thought of the factory as a place where you transformed materials. It was a physical environment where people performed with their hands or with machines. Now, only about one-eighth of the people in the factory are directly involved with changing materials. The other seven are handling and processing information (Skinner 1985).

THE FACTORY DATABASE

Malkanoff (1984) presents a summary of the difficulties that are faced in providing a CIM database system. The difficulties arise from a variety of requirements and constraints on the design and operation of a manufacturing database.

First, there is the problem of multiple databases. Many firms have been attempting to provide some form of computer support for various manufacturing activities using currently available technologies. The result has been a proliferation of heterogeneous hardware, software and data models, with each application being optimized locally. The complexity and cost of converting so many systems and data to a common database may be prohibitive.

The second set of problems is concerned with the sheer size of the databases that will be needed to fully support true CIM. Estimates are that such databases will be serveral orders of magnitude larger than the largest databases in use today (see Appleton 1984).

This implies that these databases are unlikely to be the centralized monolithic structures of the type typically assumed in the current literature. On the contrary, the databases are more likely to be distributed of necessity.

It is not enough for a database management system to manage data passively on behalf of appliation programs. Rather, it must be aware of the inherent meaning of the data being managed. This implies that the database must model the nature of the enterprise, and the database management system based on this model must make decisions and initiate actions appropriate to maintain the consistency and integrity of the database and insure timely and orderly execution of the procedures that occur during the product life cycle. An example would be the automatic propagation of an engineering change throughout the various data files that are affected by the change.

The resulting system with these capabilities is no longer a database management system. Instead, it is more appropriately described as a "knowledge base management" system which merges artificial intelligence (AI) and database management technologies through extensions of databases which add intelligence.

For example, a knowledge base system would use AI (an expert system) to generate the processing program based on product geometry data for downloading to the flexible automated system.

MAP

This observation was partly responsible for the decision by General Motors, in conjunction with McDonnell-Douglas, to initiate the development and standardization of MAP (manufacturing automation protocol). This development is based directly on the International Standards Organization (ISO), Open System Interconnection (OSI) model of data communication, described in Gross (1984).

The initial success of the MAP program is due partly to the fact that it employs standards from national and international organizations at the appropriate layers of the ISO/OSI model. This makes it easier for automation equipment vendors to make their devises MAP-compatible. It is also in the best interests of such vendors to develop products which conform to the MAP specifications, and in turn for their component suppliers to produce MAP-compliant pieces.

The main benefit to the manufacturing community of the MAP initiative is that it has expedited development of local area networking technology for the factory environment by several years, with concomitant cost reductions. We do not wish to imply that the manufacturing automated protocol (MAP) is the complete answer and that all the problems have been solved.

On the contrary, MAP merely defines a set of rules for the movement of data between points such that the content of the message transmitted from one point can be extracted at another, and for moving such data at reasonably high speeds with small probability of loss in message integrity. MAP does not deal with semantics—the meaning of the messages.

MATERIAL HANDLING

As we proceed toward the future automated factory, the material handling function looms as a substantial hurdle. As indicated above, material handling in a production plant is concerned with the movement, storage and control of the raw materials, the work-in-process, the final product and the various suppiles (for example, tooling, spare parts for equipment, and so forth) that support the manufacture of the product. The relationship between material handling and CIM was discussed by White and Applie (1985).

There are several issues related to the material handling function that must be considered when implementing the computer-integrated flexible automated factory. These issues include:

1. Control of work-in-process
2. Compuer automation of material handling

WORK-IN-PROCESS PROBLEM

Several of the trends in manufacturing that were previously mentioned relate to the work-in-process (WIP) problem. One important objective of manufacturing managers today is to reduce their levels of inventory, particularly WIP. Outsourcing and just-in-time production are two approaches that are currently being taken. Design of an automated storage system to control WIP is another approach.

Outsourcing is an approach used by many companies today to reduce the burden of managing their manufacturing operations. The benefits they see in this approach include reduction of inventory, elimination of labor problems in manufacturing, consolidation of operations, disposing of production equipment that is poorly utilized, avoidance of major investments to modernize their manufacturing facilities, opportunity to implement a just-in-time production system, and purchase of components from companies that have developed expertise in specific areas of manufacturing rather than maintaining that expertise in-house. With specific reference to the inventory benefits, outsourcing permits the company to avoid the need to store raw materials, tooling, spare parts and work-in-process for the components.

There is an opposite side to the coin. By transferring the burden of producing its components to outside vendors, the company runs the risk of losing control over these components in terms of quality and delivery. Unless outsourcing is done with great attention to detail, problems are created in assembly when attempts are made to put the final product together using poor quality or missing parts.

An approach closely related to outsourcing is just-in-time (JIT) production. JIT refers to an arrangement between the final product assembly company and its component suppliers in which the suppliers agree to deliver the components to the assembly plant immediately before they are needed (that is, "just in time"). By means of just-in-time deliveries, inventories of these components are kept at very low levels.

This is in contrast to the typical operation of most assemby plants in the past where quantities equivalent of several days' (sometimes several weeks') usage were kept in inventory awaiting final assembly. As in the outsourcing approach, a successful JIT policy requires careful control and coordination between the final assembly company and its suppliers.

Principles of just-in-time can be applied internally, within a given manufacturing plant. Instead of making large quantities of components and putting them into storage before final assembly, the JIT approach calls for parts to be made either close to or immediately adjacent to the assembly line, so that the components feed into the appropriate assembly stations as they are needed.

In addition to these approaches for dealing with the WIP problem, another technique involves the use of automated storage/retrieval systems and storage carousels to automate (or semiautomate) the storage function in manufacturing. The justification of these systems by the companies installing them is based on the premise that keeping the inventories is a requirement and what is needed is a better way to manage the inventories. Reasons for installing automated storage systems include:

- Buffer storage between two processes with different production rates
- Use in conjunction with a JIT system
- Use if kitting of parts for assembly

Other companies are attacking the premise that inventories (raw materials and work-in-process) are required nearly to the extent that has been thought necessary in the past. These companies are adopting the viewpoint that it is possible to reduce inventories to an absolute minimum so that whatever work-in-process remains in the plant can be maintained on the assembly line or within the production system.

COMPUTER AUTOMATION OF MATERIAL HANDLING

A second issue is concerned with computer control of the material handling equipment. Material handling equipment has traditionally been operated manually. The first fork lift trucks, cranes, hoists and many other pieces of handling equipment were designed well before any consideration was given to factory automation.

In order to achieve full automation of the factory, handling equipment must be selected that possesses the following attributes: First, the handling system must be capable of dealing with product variations. The different products will have variations in geometry, and the handling system must be able to hold and transport the products in spite of these variations. Second, because the different products will require different processing operations, the handling system must be capable of alternate routings throughout the factory. Finally, the handling system must be compatible with computer control. It must be capable of receiving instructions from the central controller, and it must be able to report back to the controller about its status and actions.

The material handling system that seems most compatible with these attributes today is an automated guided vehicle system (AGVS). An AGVS consists of independently operated, battery-powered vehicles that follow pathways defined in the factory or warehouse floor. The pathways are defined typically by means of a guide wire embedded in the floor or a chemical paint strip marked on the surface of the floor. Sensors on board the vehicles track the pathways and make deliveries between various stations in the buildings. AGVS are capable of variable routings; they can carry a variety of loads (products, parts assemblies, and so forth) by using standard pallets to hold the loads; and they can be operated under computer control. We envision that automated guided vehicle systems will constitute the central handling system in the future flexible automated factory, with other handling systems (for example, industrial robots, conveyor systems) used within individual production cells and lines.

REFERENCES AND BIBLIOGRAPHY

APPLETON, D. [1984]. "The State of CIM." *Datamation,* December 15, pp. 66–72.

GROSS, J. L. [1984]. "Components Can Be Added Gradually by Logically Mapping Out Present, Future Uses." *Industrial Engineering,* June, pp. 28–37.

MELKANOFF, M. [1984]. "The CIMS Database: Goals, Problems, Case Studies and Proposed Approaches Outlined." *Industrial Engineering,* November, pp. 78–93.

SAUL, G. [1985]. "Flexible Manufacturing System is CIM Implemented at the Shop Floor Level." *Industrial Engineering,* June, pp. 35–39.

SKINNER, W. [1985]. *Manufacturing: The Formidable Competitive Weapon.* John Wiley & Sons, New York.

SKINNER, W. [1974]. "The Focused Factory." *Harvard Business Review,* May–June, pp. 113–121.

WHITE, J. A., and J. M. APPLIE, JR. [1985]. "Material Handling Requirements are Altered Dramatically by CIM Information Links." *Industrial Engineering,* February, pp. 36–41.

WOLFE, P. M. [1985]. "Computer-Aided Process Planning is Link Between CAD and CAM." *Industrial Engineering,* August, pp. 72–77.

YOUNG, R. E., and R. MAYER [1984]. "The Information Dilemma: To Conceptualize Manufacturing as Information Process." *Industrial Engineering,* September, pp. 28–34.

EPILOGUE

Trends in Manufacturing Leading to Flexible Automated Factories

The 1980s have seen several major competitive trends (or themes) pushing for action. They include: (1) a trend towards shorter product lives, requiring firms to keep ahead of, rather than merely abreast of, market demands; (2) an increased demand on quality, compounded by increasing numbers of international competitors, requiring a rethinking of traditional approaches to quality; (3) outsourcing and utilization of JIT to improve quality and reduce inventory costs; (4) focusing of factories—as manufacturers become more concerned with quality and individual products within the process it makes sense to limit the products each factory produces; and (5) the introduction and utilization of computer technologies, such as CAD/CAM and CAPP, that speed up processes and allow for greater flexibility of the firm as a whole.

There is a need and desire for greater flexibility throughout the factory. Flexibility is required in the warehouse, to accommodate the expansion and contraction that coincide with more frequent market changes. Production planners, controllers, and supervisors desire flexibility in the following areas:

- Product mix
- Volume
- Design changes
- Routing

Without flexibility in these areas managers cannot effectively control the process, and may be unable to respond rapidly enough to environmental changes, to remain competitive.

Labor flexibility is another important concept, currently used mainly by the

Japanese, but increasingly evident in North America. It implies that workers have the ability to do multiple jobs, as well as the initiative to help in problem areas when required. Overall this leads to increased responsibility and autonomy for the workers.

Total integration and flexibility cannot be achieved until flexible management systems are in place. Management must have the information to allow short lead-time response to operate in a participative environment. Further, managers must be able to understand and utilize the variables necessary to enact frequent changes. This need can be met with the help of CIM. Cim gives managers the edge necessary to remain flexible, and options can be increased. Communication and information systems combined in one source or "brain" is the ultimate goal.

Unfortunately the multi-database systems necessary to support CIM currently have some problems. Combining different types of hardware, software and data models have proven to be the most challenging aspect; the cost and complexity of assimilating many systems into a common database may be simply too restrictive.

The second hurdle to CIM stems from the fact that databases needed to adequately support CIM will be extremely large. These databases in fact will be larger than all databases used today. At the present time, no database management system exists that displays the intelligence necessary to manage a fully operational CIM system.

The need for communication devices to integrate the components of CIM lies in attempts at designing standardized data communication systems. For example, General Motors has developed manufacturing automation protocol (MAP). This program outlines the standard tasks individual data systems must be able to perform in order to facilitate integration. The standardization at national and international levels thus enables automated equipment vendors to make their products more compatible. MAP defines rules for the movement of data between points, it does not deal with the meaning of the message being transmitted, only the messages themselves.

Furthermore, to implement CIM, companies must be concerned with not just information and data flows, but also actual material flows. This puts emphasis on the material handling function. Traditionally, material handling has been manually performed. In a fully automated factory, however, computers will control work-in-process, materials in general, and the overall interfacing of different systems.

Work-in-process problems are being solved with the use of the following methods:

- Outsourcing
- Just-In-Time
- Buffer storage between two processes with different production rates
- Kitting of parts for assembly

AGVs are being used to overcome material flow problems throughout the automated process, with the additional help of industrial robots and conveyor systems. The integration of systems to achieve a smooth flow of operations requires a careful evaluation of the plant, the goods it produces and its future requirements. Solutions include standardized pallets, lift and carry devices, push-pull devices, and deflectors.

These systems must tie the entire factory so that the individual processes combine together to maximize the efficiency of the total manufacturing operation.

If companies can achieve all of the prerequisites for CIM, have flexibility throughout the factory and compatibility of all information systems, they can hope to ultimaely achieve a flexible automated factory. To attain this flexibility, many companies are turning to expert systems. Expert systems are those that allow computers to make decisions, and in fact virtually think for themselves; they organize information in a way that gives the computers the ability to reason out problems. At present, however, there are several obstacles to the widespread use of expert systems. They include: a limited ability to test every contingency, compromised security of information, lack of information about day-to-day corporate operations, and the typical inertia and resistance to change in established companies. The value of expert systems for those companies who have successfully used them is often overwhelming. However, problems and difficulties do remain, and alterations are likely to occur in the future, as companies gain experience with the technology. The following provides a perspective summary of the points discussed.

Summary Framework Trends in Manufacturing Leading to Flexible Operations

Trends in Manufacturing	Need for Flexibility Throughout the Factory	Dynamic Options With CIM (Flexible Automated Factories)
• Shorter product life cycle • Quality emphasis • Outsourcing • Computer technologies • Rationalization of factories	• In the warehouse • When manufacturing parts –productive –volume –design change –routing • Work force • Information systems • Management systems	• Communication and information systems –database –MAP • Materials handling systems • Expert systems • Advanced manufacturing technologies

CASE 2.1

Zepf Technologies Inc. (A)[4]

INTRODUCTION

"Well, do we buy it, or don't we?" asked Larry Zepf, co-founder and CEO of Zepf Technologies Inc. (ZTI) of Waterloo, Ontario, in October 1984. "Given our recent successes, can we afford a nightmarish repetition of our last major equipment experience? On the other hand, can we afford *not* to take the step right now?"

"It" was a new, advanced, and expensive computer-aided design (CAD) system, which Larry felt ZTI would need to support the design and manufacture of the company's expanding range of products for the packaging industry. Given the lead time for obtaining the equipment, and the training required for the operators, the decision would have to be made before the coming Christmas if the equipment was going to be useful at all in the following year.

BACKGROUND

ZTI was founded in 1972 by Larry Zepf and his son Paul. Larry had always dreamed of owning a family-run business, so when Paul graduated from the University of Waterloo in engineering, the pair took the opportunity to open a small machine shop. Drawing on Larry's 25 years in Seagram Distilleries' packaging division, ZTI began by rebuilding, servicing, and selling change parts to the packaging industry.

In 1972, ZTI was a very small company—"a garage operation just trying to

[4]This case was written by Professor Hamid Noori and John McDade, 1987.

establish some rapport with customers," according to Larry—but by 1979 annual sales had reached $900,000, primarily due to ZTI's developing reputation for producing high quality products, and for custom designing solutions to customer's problems. Sales growth led to increases in staff, and to the purchase in 1979 of new machining equipment which was thought would give ZTI a manufacturing edge in its industry. By the beginning of 1982 ZTI had expanded from its initial two employees to a total staff of 48, including seven sales representatives.

1982 was a difficult year for the packaging industry in general. For ZTI it was potentially disastrous, as the company had borrowed heavily three years earlier in order to buy the new machinery. The highly leveraged company could not expect help or sympathy from any outside source as sales fell, least of all its bankers and other creditors. Faced with bankruptcy, Larry had reluctantly cleaned house; by the end of 1983 ZTI's staff had been reduced to a total of 32, and even the newly-hired general manager had not survived (see Exhibits 2.1 and 2.2). Although the belt-tightening had averted the

Exhibit 2.1 ZTI Organization Chart

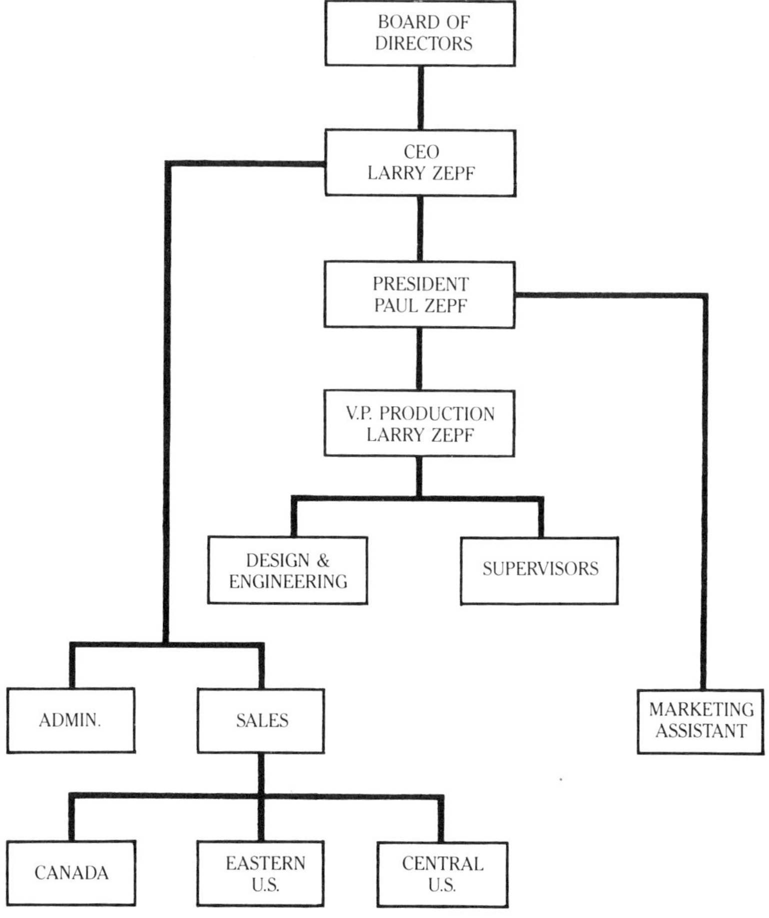

Exhibit 2.2 Support Staff (1983)

Job Title	No. Employed
Design engineers	3
Tradesmen (including 5 supervisors)	23
Sales representatives	2
Marketing assistant	1
Receptionist	1
Secretary	1
Accountant	1
Purchaser	1
Shipper	1

immediate crisis, Larry and Paul both knew that continued operation depended on increased sales. Increases in sales volume in the existing economic climate could only come (at the expense of competitors) through increases in market share: that, in turn, would mean concentrating not only on existing products, but also on expanding the product portfolio.

PRODUCTS AND MARKETS

In 1982 ZTI's custom-designed products fell into three main categories: changeover parts for packaging machinery which would enable the machines to handle different sizes and shapes of containers; timing screws which determined the spacing of containers on conveyor belts; and high precision cams for activating levers in packaging machines. 1983 brought the development of ZTI's first line of stand-alone packaging machinery—converger/diverger machines. Exhibit 2.3 details the 1985 sales forecast by product.

Exhibit 2.3 Product/Service Sales Forecast by Product for the Period September 1984 to August 1985

	Sales	Cost of Sales	Gross Profit	G.P. %
Change parts	$1,003,989	$ 514,467	$485,922	48.8
Timing screws	525,942	277,369	248,573	47.3
Cams	187,884	123,666	64,218	43.1
New equipment	320,598	219,783	100,815	34.1
Used equipment	195,511	143,668	51,843	26.5
Service	36,110	11,792	24,318	67.3
Other	22,640	17,532	15,108	22.5
Total	$2,292,674	$1,308,277	$948,397	42.9

In 1984 there were five major (approximately $2 million in annual sales) and 24 minor (approximately $200,000 in annual sales) companies specializing in the production of timing screws in North America. The total market for the plastic screws was estimated at 24 million units, with the specialty companies accounting for 75 percent of total sales. Larry Zepf estimated that ZTI held a 13 percent share of the market for timing screws in North America, which covered as disparate a group as the household products industry, the oil industry, and the distilling industry.

The entry into the original equipment manufacturer (OEM) occurred in typical ZTI fashion. Breathing easier following the easing of the 1982 crisis, and armed with the knowledge that new products were a necessity, Larry and Paul spent long hours with large multinational packaging firms trying to determine what products were really needed by the industry. They were convinced that more effective converger/divergers were required and, more importantly, that ZTI already had the resources which could make design and manufacture of specialized equipment of this type practicable. With this confidence, Larry approached Lever Bros. and offered to build a prototype machine to Lever's specifications. If the machine met the specifications, Lever would order another machine to go with the prototype, which ZTI would donate to Lever Bros. If the machine did not work to Lever's satisfaction ZTI would absorb the loss.

ZTI spent nine months and $70,000 developing the prototype, which was tested by Lever Bros.'s R&D and engineering departments in the United States. The machine passed all tests with ease. Lever Bros. ordered two new machines, allowing ZTI to claim OEM status. When asked if ZTI would be willing to take on this type of risk again, Larry replied, "We are not your average passive Canadian company. We are very active, high risk takers."

The converger/diverger machine developed by ZTI had caused a breakthrough in the packing industry. Before its development bottlenecks had been a common frustration in packaging operations. It was dificult to accurately match the speeds of adjacent conveyors, and this caused the packaging machines to be either backed up with, or waiting for, goods to be packaged. The adjustable speed of the ZTI converger/diverger machines made packaging flows more consistent, and effectively allowed conveyor lines to be combined or divided at twice the rate previously possible.

The technical advance was not in the converger/diverger machines, but rather in the complex timing screws which enables ZTI to give guarantees of 98–99 percent performance to specification. The performance guarantee allowed ZTI to bid 40–100 percent higher on contracts than its competitors in many instances, with only minimal impact on ZTI's chance of winning the particular contract. This strong position also enabled the company to ask for, and receive, an advance of up to 50 percent of the full price of the equipment at the time the contract was signed; this made it considerably easier to finance the larger projects.

The majority of timing screws produced by ZTI were very sophisticated, and reproduction by competitors was very difficult, if not impossible. Only 40 percent of the timing screws produced by ZTI could be duplicated by the competition, and this 40 percent did not include the timing screws used in the converger/diverger machines. Although there were several full-line packaging equipment companies capable of producing converger/divergers, none possessed the technology necessary to produce the timing screws, and, therefore, the machines that could operate with the speed and consistency guaranteed by ZTI.

INTERNAL OPERATIONS

If the key to the converger/diverger machines was the timing screws, the keys to the timing screws were ZTI's design and manufacturing operations. ZTI's complement of design engineers and draftsmen had grown with the company, and Larry considered he had one of the best mechanical design offices available. The group could take a customer's problem and quickly design an innovative timing screw to overcome the perceived problem—and, sometimes, to solve problems the customer was not aware existed. These custom solutions often became standard products.

Design competence was matched by manufacturing competence, augmented by two highly specialized computer numerical control (CNC) machines used to manufacture the screws. The machines, one a standard machining center and one a custom-built lathe, were purchased from a West German firm in 1979 and 1980 for a total cost of $750,000. The CNC machines were capable of producing both timing screws and cams. Although some of the timing screws could be produced by most competitors using 40-year-old technology and a skilled machinist, the quality and accuracy of the parts produced was not comparable to that achieved on the CNC machines. In addition, a typical setup using the old technology could only produce eight timing screws in an eight-hour period while the CNC technology had three times as much capacity. Another benefit of the CNC technology was a reduction in the machined parts rejection rate from 10 percent to only 1 percent. At average, materials cost $80 per meter, this translated into a significant savings for ZTI. (See Exhibit 2.4 for financial details.)

Exhibit 2.4 Zepf Technologies Inc.
Balance Sheet as of August 31, 1984

	1984 $	1983 $
CURRENT ASSETS		
Bank	170	2,227
Accounts Receivable	274,299	259,596
Inventory	371,618	327,308
Prepaid expenses and deposits	14,973	9,756
Current portion of note receivable	23,236	—
	684,296	598,887
NOTE RECEIVABLE	26,990	53,792
ADVANCES TO AFFILIATE	—	24,363
FIXED	439,124	582,911
TOTAL ASSETS	1,150,410	1,259,953
CURRENT LIABILITIES		
Bank loan	182,000	240,000
Accounts payable and accrued liabilities	166,584	156,159
Customer deposits	16,200	10,507
Current portion of long-term liabilities	118,548	74,904
	483,332	481,570

Exhibit 2.4 Zepf Technologies Inc. (*continued*)

	1984	1983
LONG-TERM LIABILITIES	432,247	549,481
SHAREHOLDERS' ADVANCES	20,183	93,274
	935,762	1,124,325
SHAREHOLDERS' EQUITY		
Capital Stock	224,631	159,521
	(9,983)	(23,893)
DEFICIT	214,648	135,628
TOTAL LIABILITY	1,150,410	1,259,953

Statement of Income as of August 31, 1984

	1984		1983	
SALES	$1,808,825	(100%)	$1,790,010	(100%)
COST OF SALES				
Inventory of finished goods				
• beginning of year	92,280		141,659	
Cost of goods manufactured				
• per schedule	1,157,108		1,029,199	
	1,249,388		1,170,858	
Inventory of finished goods				
• end of year	126,083		92,280	
	1,123,305	62.1	1,078,578	60.3
GROSS MARGIN	685,520	37.9	711,432	39.7
SELLING AND ADMINISTRATIVE EXPENSES				
• per schedule	682,100	37.7	700,693	39.1
INCOME FROM OPERATIONS	3,420	0.2	10,739	0.6
OTHER INCOMES				
Interest	7,963		4,460	
Miscellaneous	556		2,947	
Gain on sale of fixed assets	1,971		—	
	10,490	0.6	7,407	0.4
INCOME BEFORE EXTRAORDINARY ITEMS	13,910	0.8	18,146	1.0
• Gain on sale of development property	—		89,589	5.0
• Allowance on advance to affiliated company	—		(15,000)	(0.8)
NET INCOME	13,910	0.8	92,735	5.2

Exhibit 2.4 Zepf Technologies Inc. (*continued*)
Statement of Deficit as of August 31, 1984

	1984 $	1983 $
DEFICIT—beginning of year	23,893	116,628
NET INCOME	13,910	92,735
DEFICIT—end of year	9,983	23,893

"We could design and build a better car if we really wanted to," proclaimed Larry Zepf enthusiastically while discussing his company with a group of visitors. "We have the people, the organization, the team work, the talent, and the intense desire to seek out and master challenges." The confidence Larry had in the work force and the management team at ZTI was transparent. The management team consisted of Larry and his seven sons: Paul, Larry, William, Stephen, Frank, James and Peter as well as his son-in-law Herb Friedrich. The eight Zepfs and Friedrich were the sole owners of ZTI, and as Larry put it, "No one but the Zepfs will ever own Zepf Technologies Inc."

This family-oriented approach seemed to work well at ZTI, and the organization was very tight-knit and informal. According to Larry, "We're an information organization based on collective responsibility; everybody is hands-on. We want everyone involved. And right now we have to decide how to be even better at what we do well if we are going to take full advantage of the growth opportunities that are sitting out there for the taking."

THE CAD DECISION

Larry was confident that one way of taking advantage was to purchase a CAD system, and the sooner the better. He remembered his father's philosophy that, "When we want something, we go and get it. We can't afford to waste time and let our competitors catch up." Control and coordination of the drafting office was becoming difficult, and the documentation of designs and design changes was questionable. ZTI had a superb core of draftsmen and engineers, but Larry felt that they would be even more valuable if they could be given access to a good CAD system. Over the past few years Larry had been keeping an eye on the progress of CAD technology, and he had been waiting for prices to come down before committing ZTI to the purchase of a system. Right now a United States built system that would have cost $500,000 in 1980 could be purchased for $200,000, and Larry felt the time had come to take the plunge.

"To pass up the opportunity would be foolish," said Larry. "Among other advantages, CAD allows more dimensioning, more views and more options than manual drafting. It also provides built-in quality control, as it can catch design errors before they reached the production process. A CAD system allows the same drawing to be shown on many different scales, and provides exploded and color coded views of a drawing. One of the other major advantages of CAD is the capability to quickly reproduce a similar drawing with minor changes. And the ability to keep our drawings in electronic files means we can avoid the trap we frequently run into of wasting our time designing a special component when we already have a design which will fit the bill."

Paul was much more cautious. "We had tremendous difficulties with the CNC machines, starting with our inability to quantify their advantages over our existing equipment. Had we been the subsidiary of a larger company I am sure our request for the machines would have been laughed out of the board room. As it was, we were turned down by our own bankers, even after we secured an Ontario Development Corporation loan for $400,000. We had to go to another bank with a more sympathetic and risk-taking manager for the other $300,000 we needed."

"And it wasn't long after we received the machines, especially the second one, that we began wondering if our banker hadn't been right after all. We received some in-house training from the West German supplier, but after that we were on our own. All further problems had to be resolved by telephone and/or telex, or sorted out by us. It took almost three years to get the programming correct on the machines, and only then would they work at what we considered to be reasonable rates of operation. And these were items of equipment with whose basic nature of operation we were pretty comfortable. I concede that, in the long run, the lack of support was actually beneficial to ZTI, as it forced us to become thoroughly familiar with every aspect of the technology. But we don't want to take the hair shirt approach to major investment again."

Paul was also concerned about not having qualified people to operate the CAD system, although past experience had shown that ZTI's engineers and staff adapted quickly to technological changes. He remembered that early on no one was able to operate the simplest Apple computer, but now several of the key people were heavily involved with the computer technology associated with the CNC machines. What training would be required for the people immediately affected by any new system, and for those involved on the periphery? And how might that training be accomplished?

CONCLUSION

"Don't think I'm being bloody narrow-minded about the idea of a CAD system," said Paul. "I'm all in favor of the purchase. But we have to be very clear what we are going to get ourselves into, and that means doing a much better job of assessing the impact of the technology than we did with the CNC machines. What we really need is to be able to quantify the benefits and drawbacks of the system , but how do you put numbers to notions such as flexibility, even if we see flexibility as one of our key success factors and as something a CAD system can augment? And how do you think through changes you are not even aware of? It will be difficult, for example, to assess the impact on relationships in the design team, and between the design office and the rest of the organization."

"In short, how might we convince a conservative outsider of the benefits of something which will affect most aspects of the organization? And where should we go to get the answers to the questions we don't even know how to ask?"

CASE 2.2

The Mitchell Drug Company[5]

INTRODUCTION

"So now its Just-In-Time is it?" mused Maria Craigs, production manager of Mitchell Drug Company (MDC). "Doesn't head office have anything better to do than endorse each new management technique that shows up, and expect us to immediately show benefits for these imposed solutions to perceived problems? And do these people understand what it is they want us to do anyway?" Craigs was reacting to a directive that MDC investigate implementing Just-In-Time (JIT) as a means of significantly reducing inventories. Maria conceded that inventories were high, but in MDC's business—non-prescription drugs—that was almost inevitable. And how would JIT influence inventories anyhow?," she wondered.

COMPANY BACKGROUND

The Mitchell Drug Company, located in Sydney, Australia, was a wholly-owned subsidiary of International Pharmaceutical Inc. (IP), headquartered in New York City. IP was over a century old and operated worldwide. Both MDC in Australia, and IP worldwide, had excellent reputations and were leaders in their industries.

International Pharmaceutical employed over 77,000 people in the manufacture and sales of a broad range of health care and related products. Product lines outside

[5]This case was written by Professor Hamid Noori with the assistance of Brain Burlacioff and Debbie Dunn, 1988.

the health care field had been developed from the application of resources, technology and products originally designed for the health care field. IP competed internationally against companies of all sizes. Competition was strong in all lines and in all markets, regardless of the number and size of competing companies. The development of new and improved products and processes was deemed important to the company's success, requiring substantial ongoing investments in research and develoment. In addition, gaining and retaining consumer acceptance of new products meant heavy expenditures on advertising, promotion and selling.

IP controlled a number of decentralized operating subsidiaries and divisions which were, for the most part, self-contained and autonomous. Responsibility for each subsidiary or division lay with its operating management, headed by a president, general manager or managing director, who reported either directly or through a company group chairman to a member of the executive committee in New York. IP's international (non-U.S.) business was conducted by subsidiaries which manufactured IP's products in 47 countries outside the United States; these products were then sold in most countries of the world. International subsidiaries were, with few exceptions, managed by citizens of the country in which they were located.

Each of IP's diversified businesses could be placed in one of three semgnets:

1. The consumer segment (43.0 percent of total sales) which marketed toiletries and hygienic products including baby care items, first aid products, and nonprescription drugs. These products were marketed to the general public and distributed either through wholesalers or direct to independent and chain retail outlets.
2. The professional segment (32.3 percent of total sales) which marketed ligatures and sutures, mechanical wound closure products, diagnostic products, dental products, medical equipment and devices, surgical dressings, surgical apparel and accessories, surgical instruments and related items. These items were used principally in professional fields by physicians, dentists, nurses, therapists, hospitals,diagnostic laboratories and clinics. Products were distributed to these markets directly or through surgical supply and other dealers.
3. The pharmaceutical segment (24.7 percent of total sales) which marketed prescription drugs, contraceptives, therapeutics, and antifungal and veterinary products. These products were distributed directly or through wholesalers for use by health care professionals and the general public.

MITCHELL DRUG COMPANY

MDC, part of IP's international consumer segment, was based in Sydney, Australia. MDC marketed four groups of nonprescription drugs:

1. Pediatric analgesics (pain killers) in the form of caplets, tablets, drops and elixir (syrup)
2. Regular strength adult analgesics in the form of tablets and caplets
3. Extra strength adult analgesics in the form of tablets and caplets
4. Analgesics for sinus conditions in regular and extra strengths, in the form of caplets.

MDC held a 20 percent share of the Australasian (Australila and New Zealand) adult nonprescription analgesic markets, and a 50 percent share of the Australasian pediatric nonprescription analgesic markets. Total unit sales were about 800 million single doses annually; this included sales to the South Pacific and Southeast Asian markets.

MARKETING

The marketing philosophy at MDC, and most other pharmaceutical suppliers, involved a "push" strategy. The marketing department pushed MDC's products by offering discounts to retailers for volume purchases; in turn, the retailers, now having large quantities in inventory pushed the product to the end-customer. A common attitude among retailers was "I have a large inventory, and since I paid for it, I have to sell it." The company offered immediate supply of any drug in its catalogue from one of its distribution centers in each Australian state capital, and in Auckland, Wellington, and Christchurch in New Zealand. Most sales were the result of a call by a sales representative on a customer; on rare occasions a customer rang a distribution center to initiate a purchase.

PRODUCTION

IP produced about 2 billion single dose analgesics in the United States each year to satisfy domestic demand. MDC currently produced about 800 million single doses per year. Because of the Australian import control policies the same range of IP product lines was manufactured in both the United States and Australia. In the United States the relatively large prodution volumes allowed production facilities to be dedicated to single products; economies of scale were the toal in these cases, with high speed, high volume and high efficiency production runs. Australasia's smaller markets made the dedication of production facilities to specific products impractical, and economies of scope were felt to be better suited to this production environment. MDC's equipment therefore operated at lower volumes and slower speeds than that in any United States plant, emphasizing quick changeovers between the many production runs.

MDC's solid dose pharmaceuticals were all manufactured in the same general production sequence: formulation, granulation, compression, coating if required, and packaging. Formulation involved measuring, combining and mixing raw materials in the proper proportions to ensure that the particular pharmaceutical had the correct medicinal properties. Formulation was currently labor intensive and nonautomated.

Following formulation, the batch of dry chemicals was mechanically mixed to combine the ingredients into small granules about the size of sugar grains. This granulation process enabled the raw materials to be better compressed into single dose tablets during the ensuing compression process. After compression, some single dose pharmaceuticals were coated, making them easier to swallow. The final step in the production process involved packaging, which was fully automated except for loading packaging materials and pharmaceuticals into hoppers on the packaging equipment.

Raw materials were mixed in numbered lots, thus allowing pharmaceuticals to be recalled immediately if the raw materials were subsequently found to be of substandard quality. Lots normally consisted of a total of 600 kg of raw materials, because the quality of granules from the granulation process peaked at this level. 600 kg lots were produced even if that amount of product represented several weeks' or months' sales. As a consequence, the average age of finished goods inventories at the Sydney plant was six weeks.

In addition to the high average age of finished goods, the anticipated time a manufacturing order would spend in process through the plant was 22 days. Of this time, actual processing normally took 14-20 hours: formulation two hours, granulation four hours, compression six hours, coating six hours, and packaging two hours. There were two obvious reasons for this time difference. The prodution line was not balanced; bottlenecks occurred between steps in the production process, and these bottlenecks created large WIP inventories averaging $120,000, equivalent to three weeks of inventories. Also, otherwise-finished goods were sometimes stored for days until quality control released them for shipment to the distribution centers. Quality control had also been known to hold up materials in process after any of the intermediate operations.

PRODUCTION SCHEDULING AND CONTROL

The basis of all production planning and the more detailed schedules was the series of marketing forecasts. Marketing forecasts, aggregations of regional forecasts made by sales representatives, were made 12 months out, and updated monthly. The monthly forecast update was used by the production planners to generate a block schedule for production for the next three months. These block schedules were themselves updated each Wednesday, as the following week's manufacturing orders were released. Release notes were sent to both manufacturing and the raw materials storehouse. In the storehouse ingredients for a production run were placed together on the floor, and any materials shortages were notified to purchasing. No production materials for an order were released until the ingredient list was complete and the quality of the ingredients approved by quality control.

Purchasing used the block schedule as the basis for buying chemicals and packaging materials. All suppliers of chemicals had to be approved by the head office in New York; once approved, all purchases from a vendor were tested by quality control. MDC tried to use several vendors for each chemical purchased, although this was not always possible. Blanket orders were not used for chemicals (although they were for packaging materials), but each vendor was given an indication every six months of what MDC would require from them.

Because costs were important, MDC's purchasing department took anticipated raw material price movements into account in deciding when to order. Other order timing criteria included market shortages, vendor delivery data reliability, and the lead time required for completion of the prescribed incoming quality checks. Raw materials generally did not deteriorate in store, and the company policy was to hold sufficient raw materials on hand to allow for possible last-minute schedule changes.

Once in the manufacturing process, materials were tightly controlled. Each production lot was tracked using the company's computer, and the production controllers were able to check quickly the status of each lot. Information on location in the plant, status (that is, in-process, in quality hold, or available for processing) and yield allowed the controllers to reschedule operations at any work center almost as soon as production problems were identified.

THE JUST-IN-TIME REQUEST

The request to investigate Just-In-Time (JIT) was accompanied by an article describing the system. The head office wanted inventories reduced, and Craigs noted the 50 percent reduction in WIP the article implied was a reasonable expectation. Would that be feasible at MDC? More importantly, would the head office consider 50 percent reasonable? And wasn't WIP reduction only part of the JIT system? The article talked of inventory reduction, cost reduction, dramatic increases in quality, and a company attuned to the realities of the marketplace. What did all this mean?

Several points were made in the article. Companies adopting JIT would need to build closer relationships with suppliers and customers. Ideally, goods would be produced only in time to meet the customers' needs. Similarly, supplies would arrive only at the time necessary, and would spend little more time in the plant than the time being worked on or moved between work centers. If the plant was to produce the same range of products in the future, minimizing inventory yet retaining the same response time to customer demands, something would have to give. That "something" appeared to be lot sizes. And if lot sizes were reduced there would be more setups. What would that do to the effective plant capacity?

One problem right now would be the length of time required to complete a setup; if costly downtime was to be controlled, setup times would have to be reduced. Faster production equipment required longer setup times because finer adjustments had to be made before the equipment ran effectively. As an example, the three existing compression machines each had an output of 4,000–6,000 tablets per minute, but had setup times of approximately 16 hours. Machines were available on the market that ran at 2,000 tablets per minute; these machines had setup times of only three hours.

The packaging line consisted of 12 pieces of equipment, each with setup times of approximately 1 to 1½ hours, resulting in a total average setup time of 16 hours because of MDS's policy of having one setup crew (of two people) complete the entire changeover. The production manager noted that, if smaller lot sizes were to prove economical, changeover times would have to be reduced. Hopefully, new packaging equipment would not be required. To maintain quality in smaller lot sizes, however, a new granulator would be necessary, particularly if lots were to be as small as 50 kg (which equated to 150,000 tablets) for drugs with really low volume sales.

If MDC was to purchase new equipment, how automated should it be? Technology was currently available to generate and read bar codes; if this equipment was bought and integrated into the central database it would be possible to reduce the flow of paperwork in the plant—and the number of employees in stores, shipping, and traffic control. And on the plant floor, for example, the existing coating machine needed an operator to ensure that constant air volumes, air temperatures and spray rates were maintained. These manual skills could be replaced by computers right now. It was IP's international policy to find jobs within the company for those individuals who lost their jobs as a result of new technologies.

In addition, because labor costs were a small percentage of the total cost of goods sold, it was unlikely that further reduction of the nonunionized labor force would be undertaken for the prupose of controlling costs. If labor was to be reduced, it was MDC's goal that this be accomplished through labor attrition. Currently, the costs for $1 of sales were estimated according to Exhibit 2.5.

Exhibit 2.5 Costs for One Dollar of Sales

Cost of Goods Sold	= 25%	- 4% labor -50% material -45% overhead - 1% other
Marketing	= 40%	
General and Administration	= 20%	
Tax	= 5%	
Income	= 10%	

Labor and material variances from standards were recorded using computer software (developed in-house) for costing and production control. At present, labor and material variances were recorded for each lot after each step in the production process. Maria wondered if, in a JIT environment, the current finely detailed variance reports would be necessary. Labor and material variances from standard for each lot would still need to be recorded, of course, but if the cause of variances could be easily observed by noting where bottlenecks occurred in the production process, why not formally record variances only for the overall production process? The only variances required by law were total material variances, and these were required for government health and inspection audits because of the sensitive nature of the active ingredients.

The article mentioned the "stream and rocks" analogy. Reducing the level of inventory would be like lowering the water level in a stream, for just as lowering water levels would expose rocks and impede navigation, so lowering inventory levels would expose process problems and impede production. Maria knew, too, that progressive lowering of inventory levels would expose progressively more problems. And, she admitted, she had no idea what those problems would be.

CONCLUSION

As she prepared for her first visit to the plant floor that day, Maria reviewed the implications of JIT and the corporate reality. How did you maintain close to 100 percent customer service levels, and at the same time reduce inventory levels, reduce operating and product costs, and maintain quality standards? Corporate policy stipulated that no employee would be laid off if new equipment was purchased; labor costs would therefore adjust only slowly to technical change.

And where did you start? Internally? With suppliers? With customers? Withe the head office? What were the steps required to implement a scheme such as this? It seemed as though the essence of JIT was cooperation, not confrontation. How did you set about developing a cooperative, almost collaborative, series of relationships throughout the chain? What would that do to expectations? With a sigh, Maria opened her door—all those were tomorrow's problems. She still had to face the realities of today's new crises as she headed into the plant.

Chapter Three

THE DRIVE FOR NEW TECHNOLOGY

SITUATION 3.1

Rolls Royce

Computer-integrated manufacturing (CIM), with its connotations of high-tech wizardry, does not fit every manufacturing situation. There are situations in which integrated manufacturing is appropriate, however, and where systems have become more productive and effective. The keys, as always, are integrated planning and integrated implementation if the integrated system is to be successful.

Rolls Royce's Derby plant is one example of a successful small batch CIM system—the $8 million advanced integrated manufacturing system, or AIMS. AIMS integrates 12 of the plants metal working machines and associated materials handling systems which are devoted to the manufacture of very expensive discs and rings for jet aircraft engines. Rethinking and retooling the complete process has allowed Rolls Royce to reduce product lead times by 50 percent, inventories by 25 percent, and scrap by 39 percent.

The manufacture of discs and rings is straightforward. Forgings, purchased from outside suppliers, are turned (on lathes), milled, broached and ground on specialized machines, and shipped after a final inspection. Internal operations add value of up to $100,000 per component. Forgings account for about 76 percent of final unit cost; the manufacturing processes removed almost 60 percent of the forged metal.

Components spent 95 percent of their time in the shop (up to 26 weeks) in queues waiting to be processed. Of the 5 percent machining time, only 30 percent was physical machining, the remainder being required for machine loading and unloading and gauging the parts. One contributing element was long setup times on machines. Typical setups took three hours for turning, four hours for milling, 21 hours for broaching, and 15 hours for grinding machines. Economics dictated minimum lot sizes of 10, even though only one item may have been needed. Finished goods and work in process (WIP) inventories were therefore high, and inevitably bore little relationship to demand. Another high inventory consisted of highly specialized cutting tools and machining fixtures, over 2,000 of the former and 500 of the latter.

Before integration makes sense, organizations should rethink their processes, simplifying and eliminating where possible. One area where this pays dividends is in the product range, and Rolls Royce was no exception. Through standardizing the product, the number of cutting tools was reduced to 100 and the number of fixtures to 200. This reduced the tooling inventory; it also helped reduce setup times because the likelihood of fitters selecting the correct parts from the tool room were dramatically increased.

A concerted effort was made to reduce setup times on machines, and the combination of new machines and improved setup techniques slashed setup times to two hours for turning, 3.5 hours for milling, eight hours for broaching, and 13 hours for grinding. Batch sizes were able to be reduced to one or two items. Machining operations themselves were reduced by purchasing slimline forgings, with less metal to be machined away.

The last element needed to physically integrate manufacturing was a material handling system. A computer-controlled automated guided vehicle (AGV) system was installed, with eight wire guided, battery powered AGVs transporting all products throughout the factory. Forty-five AGV docking locations and 21 traffic control microcomputers were placed in machining areas. These computers tell AGVs where and when to go (using a local scheduling system), and report to the plants central control computer on the location of all AGVs.

Each machine center consists of one type of metal working machine. Operators do not need to leave a center for work-related reasons; AGVs move all required materials to and from the work cell, and each cell has a computer terminal allowing communications with the plant's control center. All work instructions are sent to the local terminals, and the introduction of in-cycle inspection means that few outsiders need visit the machine center. The physical separation of machine centers, the isolation of each machine center from production control and middle management, and the ability of the machine center crew to negotiate and control output and quality, has created a mini-factory atmosphere within each machine center.

IBM 8100 computers lie at the heart of AIMS. The Derby plant is controlled by an IBM 8100 computer which is linked to Rolls Royce's mainframe computer. Two minicomputers work to the IBM 8100; these computers control work flow through the machine centers and, with the traffic control microcomputers, control all material handling. Ten shop floor data collection terminals are used in the in-cycle inspection process. Computers also allowed Rolls Royce to test the entire system before it was even installed. In-house specialists designed a comprehensive simulation program. The simulation allowed AIMS to be tested, with the specialists varying machine center and machine layouts and testing AGV routings and scheduling sequences in order to obtain the best system possible before any equipment was moved.

The AIMS program at Rolls Royce required an examination of all aspects of manufacturing, from design to packaging. Implementation took six years, from 1978 to 1984. Results have, however, been impressive. Production times have been reduced on average to six weeks, inventories have been cut by $8 to $12 million, and annual interest charges reduced by $1.4 million. By purchasing slimline forgings, the number of machines has been reduced from 57 to 26, and the variety of machines from 17 to eight. This resulted in $1.6 million annual saving. At the end, the entire project had a remarkable two-year payback.

READING 3.1

The Strategic Advantages of New Manufacturing Technologies for Small Firms[1]

INTRODUCTION

A deluge of material has hit the American public concerning the factory-of-the-future, high technology, and computerized automation. Stories and descriptions abound of the firms that have invested millions of dollars into computer-aided manufacturing, flexible manufacturing systems, robotized factories, and other such advanced manufacturing technologies. For example:

1. General Electric spent in the neighborhood of $40 million gutting and automating their dishwasher plant in Louisville.
2. IBM spent almost 10 times this amount, a third of a billion dollars, automating their typewriter plant in Lexington, Kentucky.
3. General Motors' newly announced Saturn plant promises to top even these staggering investments in factory automation.

Undoubtedly some of these expenditures were more in preparation for automation than for the equipment itself: product redesign, rerouting of utilities, relayout of the plant, and so on. Nevertheless, from the stories it would appear to planners and managers of small businesses that high technology automation is an expenseive business that only the giants in our industrial economy can afford to chance. What's more, the message seems even more pointed: that only the very large firms can benefit from these

[1]J. Meredith, adapted for length from *Strategic Management Journal*, 1987, Volume 8, pp. 249–258. Reproduced by permission of John Wiley and Sons Limited.

advanced manufacturing systems, thereby leaving small firms even further disadvantaged in the future.

Based on our studies of the management of factory automation we are coming to another conclusion. These advanced manufacturing technologies may have as much, if not more, to offer the small firm as the large firm. We are seeing small firms employ these technologies in novel, creative ways to gain significant advantages over their competitors, including large firms. They are especially capitalizing on the flexibility, quality, lead-time reductions, and other benefits the new technologies offer.

THE NEW MANUFACTURING TECHNOLOGIES

There are a large variety of new manufacturing technologies, not all of which are computerized. The major ones are listed, along with their acronyms and descriptions, in Exhibit 3.1. Less common technologies such as computer-aided testing (CAT), vision systems, and computer-aided inspection (CAI) are still being developed, but promise to become more prominent in the future. The discussion below further describes the major new technologies and identifies those characteristics that offer advantages over existing manufacturing processes.

Exhibit 3.1 New Manufacturing Technologies

Technology	Acronym	Description
Numerical control	NC	A tape-driven machine tool
Direct numerical control	DNC	Multiple machine tools controlled by a central computer
Computer numerical control	CNC	A machine tool controlled by a dedicated computer
Robots	—	A flexible reprogrammable manipulator
Group technology	GT	Cellular production of part-families
Computer-aided design	CAD	Computerized software for product design
Computer-aided engineering	CAE	Computerized software for engineering analysis
Computer-aided process planning	CAPP	Computerized software for manufacturing routings, operations, and so forth
Automated storage/retrieval systems	AS/RS	Computerized warehousing and materials handling
Flexible manufacturing systems	FMS	Large cells of computerized machine tools and conveyors
Manufacturing resource planning	MRP II	Interconnected computer software systems for manufacturing planning and control
Computer-integrated manufacturing	CIM	Integration of all functions of the firm with manufacturing

Numerically controlled machine tools (NC) have been around for decades. At first controlled by punched tape, many of these machines are now controlled directly by a computer. If a computer is directly attached and dedicated to the machine tool, it is called computer numerical control (CNC). If the computer is centralized and directing the operations of a number of machines it is called direct numerical control (DNC); the latest technology is NC machining. The primary advantages of such equipment are their machining flexibility, the consistent quality of their product, and the reduction in skilled labor required. Though more expensive than regular machine tools, they replace such tools and thus, on a capacity basis, are not necessarily more expensive than standard equipment. Because of the years of documented experience with these machines, their risks are typically minimal, though problems may arise for those firms still unfamiliar with the technology.

Robots have received a considerable amount of press coverage lately. There are sophisticated, reprogrammable robots as well as simplistic robots with very limited abilities—the Japanese have even defined six different levels of robot sophistication. Depending on the situation, robots can offer significant advantages in flexibility, quality, labor, image (of the firm in the eyes of its customers, competitors, and employees), and safety (from their use in otherwise hazardous situations). Also, as with NC, enough knowledge of their application is being accumulated to be fairly confident of the success of future applications.

Group technology is a noncomputerized process of reorganization of the plant into cells to do in-line processing of part-families. It holds significant advantages for lead time (product design through production) and cycle time (production time) reductions, frequently on the order of one-tenth as much time as previously required. Because of this time reduction, work-in-process inventories are substantially reduced and capacity is significantly increased.

Computer-aided design (CAD) is the use of a computerized software package to design new products, modify existing produts, and do the required drafting to produce them. CAD systems are extremely flexible and can considerably enhance the quality and reduce the required lead time of new products. Because of their ease of use they multiply an engineer's productivity substantially and thus save on the need for this limited skill (classified as "less labor" in the table). Perhaps of even greater importance, CAD systems provide the foundation for linking design with manufacturing. Not only does this result in designs that can be more automatically manufactured (see CAPP) but the products are better designed for manufacturability.

Computer-aided engineering (CAE) allows the engineer to examine and test a design from a structural and engineering viewpoint. These packages are often tied to, or built into, CAD software, and exhibit largely the same characteristics.

Computer-aided process planning (CAPP) works with part-families and allows the manufacturing engineer to quickly design the production process for the product. Again, the benefits are similar to CAD and CAE, but CAPP has only a minimal effect on the product quality itself.

Computer-aided manufacturing (CAM) is often a misnomer, being used with CAD (as in CAD/CAM) when only CAD exists. Originally the term was meant to include the tape production for NC machines, or now the computer instructions for CNC or DNC machining. However, CAM has progressed beyond the point of being considered to constitute only numerically controlled machining, and now includes such aspects of laser cutting, water-jet cutting, robot control, and, in some interpretations, all computerized plant floor operations. Being an aggregation of many of the previously described systems, as well as some of those that follow, CAM exhibits many of their advantages and costs. Being such a complex of systems, and lacking a broad base of experience, the risk of failure is higher here than for simple, stand-alone equipment or software.

Automated storage and retrieval systems (AS/RS) use high-rise stacker cranes, automated guided vehicle systems (AGVS), computerized conveyors, computerized carousels, and other such systems to store and retrieve materials. These systems are particularly advantageous where space is at a premium, or simply unavailable. Compared to a standard warehouse or storage and retrieval system, an AS/RS can be very expensive.

Flexible manufacturing systems (FMS) have also been receiving a lot of press lately. These are systems of NC machines, robots, material conveyors, and other such computer-driven equipment that can be grouped into cells to handle various prismatic or turned parts in random order. Although confined largely to machine tools, these systems exhibit many of the benefits, and disadvantages, of CAM. In some ways to show their cost as a negative factor is unfair because the cost of general-purpose tooling to do the same job could be considerably more. However, their image is that of a very large, and therefore expensive, aggregation of machines (which is true).

Manufacturing resource planning (MRP II) systems are interconnected software packages that include forecasting, master scheduling, order entry, engineering data, production data, inventory control, resource requirements planning, product cost tracking, manufacturing activity planning, plant monitoring and control, plant maintenance, purchasing, receiving, distribution, and sometimes even other functions. These are information systems for the manufacturing function, meant to be tied in with the engineering, accounting, finance, and marketing data and information systems. Their benefits are the coordination they bring to the plant floor, and thus the cycle time reduction and capacity increases. Their success rate, in terms of completely operational systems, has not been high, however.

COMPETITIVE ADVANTAGE AND TECHNOLOGICAL INNOVATION

One common way that small firms often compete is through new products. In terms of the product life cycle theory (Exhibit 3.2), they start by introducing a new, highly profitable product and proceed to the growth stage. In the growth stage, new forms and variants of the product are offered to the public. Eventually the product design stabilizes, at which point the product enters the maturity stage. But this is also where large follower or me-too firms frequently pursue the market aggressively, reducing the margin for the small firm by producing the now-stable product design in volume at low cost. In doing so they take advantage of the expensive start-up hurdles overcome by the small firm in gaining market acceptance of the product. The larger firms then continue to battle for market share with the small firm, sometimes driving out the start-up firm and other times sharing the final market with them.

The new manufacturing technologies allow a drastic shortening of this life cycle in both the design and the production stages. The result is the possibility of a faster product introduction by the start-up firm and then a much quicker replacement of the product with a new product or variant, as illustrated in Exhibit 3.2.

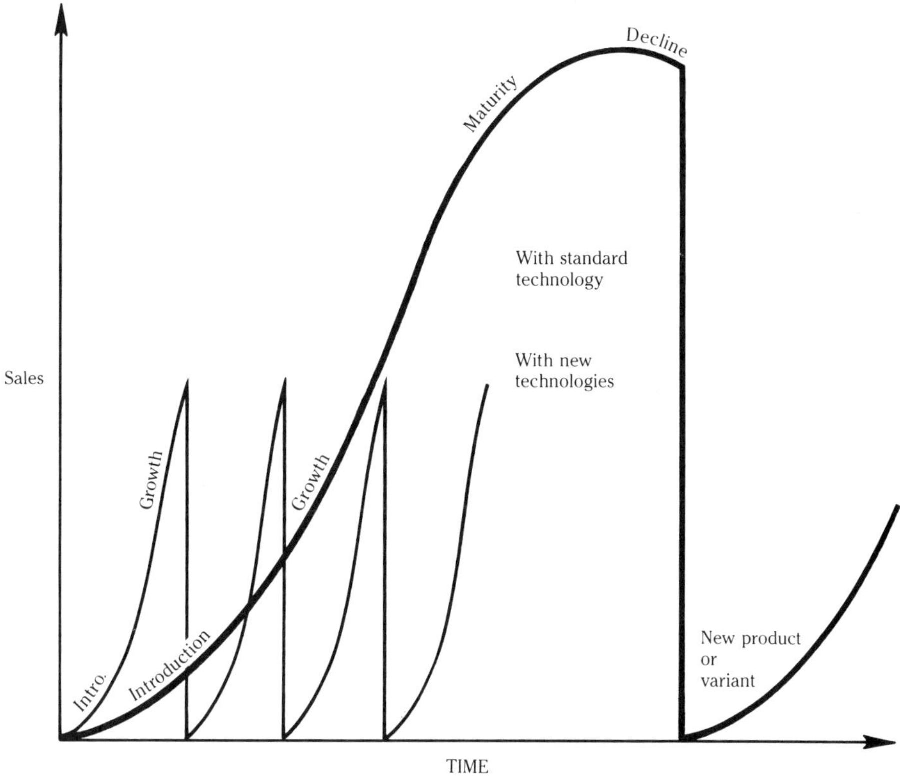

Exhibit 3.2 The Product Life Cycle Reduction Due to New Technology

Exhibit 3.3 summarizes the technology-relevant characteristics of innovator and follower strategies under the old and new technologies. Under the old standard technologies the small start-up firms had to compete on the basis of being local, offering

Exhibit 3.3 Size-Technology Matrix of Characteristics

	Large firm (follower strategy)	Small firm (innovator strategy)
Old technologies	Low cost Volume	Innovator Service Local supply Speed Variety
New technologies	Less time at maturity Lower volumes Shorter lead times for mass production	Faster innovation Shorter lead time Variety proliferation Quicker growth Earlier new product/variant introductions

better service, being innovative, responding quicker, or providing customization and variety, whereas the larger follower firms could use their capital strength to invest in high-efficiency production processes that produced a large volume of standard products at low unit cost. With the new technologies the small firm can innovate faster, produce faster, and cheaply proliferate their product line. This leaves less time for follower firms to cherry-pick their product line since there will be less time to put high-volume equipment in place and, more important, less time to produce in volume at maturity to recoup their capital investment.

Another perspective of the competition between firms is illustrated in Hayes and Wheelwright's (1979) product-process matrix of Exhibit 3.4. This exhibit depicts the four major types of production processes—large scale projects, job shops, flow shops, and continuous processes—in terms of their batch size and product variety. At the extreme of a single, custom product for every customer is the project firm producing buildings,

Exhibit 3.4 Effect of the New Technology on the Product-Process Matrix of Production Possibilities

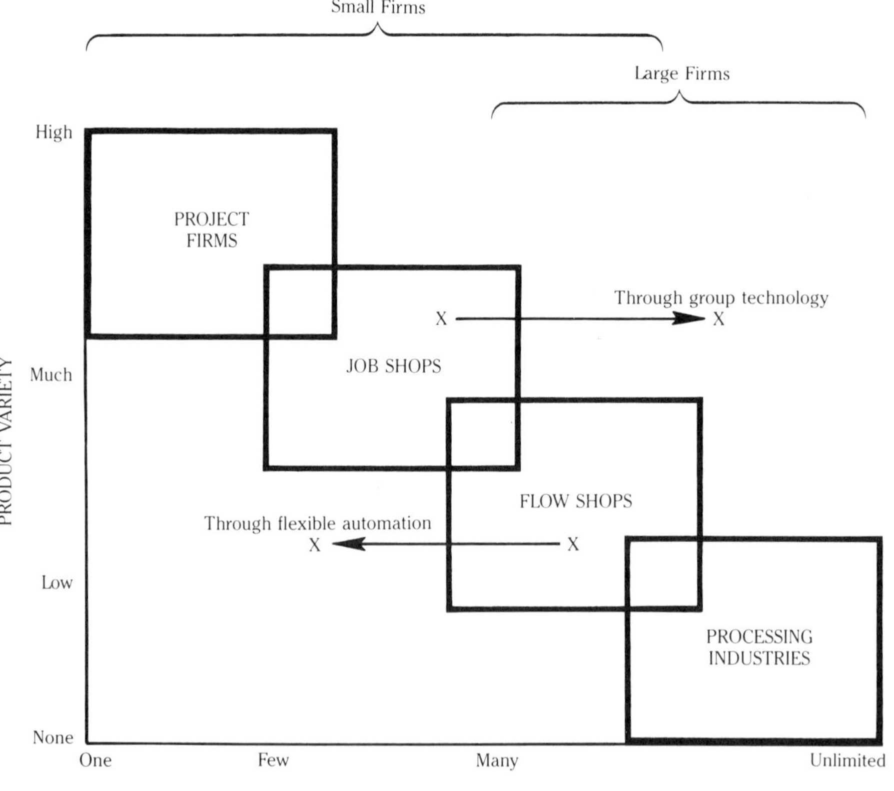

dams, and so on. At the other extreme of infinite batch size of identical molecular products is the processing firm producing gasoline, coal, or wheat, for example.

Previously, firms were largely limited to strategies that lay on the diagonal. For example, job shops produced small volumes with some variety and flow shops produced large volumes with little variety. But, as noted by Goldhar and Jelinek (1983), the new technologies are allowing firms to move off this diagonal. As illustrated in Exhibit 3.4, firms can, and are (Suresh and Meredith 1985), producing larger volumes at low cost in their job shops through group technology and smaller volumes at low cost in their flow shops through flexible automation.

However, research by Jaikumar (1984) indicates that the large firms are finding it difficult to take advantage of this flexibility, preferring to maximize the utility of the complex, expensive equipment, once the bugs have been laboriously worked out, rather than further experimenting with it to see what it can do. This leaves smaller firms the opportunity to capitalize on the flexibility and labor, space, inventory, and other cost-reduction opportunities available from the new technologies. What's more, because the computer tracks the jobs with these new technologies, the historical complexity and confusion that is commonly rampant in job shops is largely eliminated, allowing the small firm to better compete on the basis of cost, lead time, quality, and other such characteristics.

HOW TECHNOLOGY IS CHANGING THE COMPETITIVE EQUATION

As noted earlier, it would seem from the public media that high technology is only appropriate for large firms. First, they are able to afford the often extreme expense of these computerized technologies, and the cost of failure should the investment fail. Also, they are more likely to have the skill and manpower it takes to understand, implement, and manage these technologies. Finally, they are making a large enough number of products, in both depth and breadth, to benefit from the technologies. But, as just previously described, there are also a number of reasons why these technologies may be even more appropriate for small firms. The following sections reconsider and elaborate some of these reasons.

Organizational Inertia

A technologically important aspect of large firms compared to small firms is their apparent (Voss 1984) organizational inertia. As Dowling (1985) states, "many corporations are too large to get along in a world of dynamic change." This relates directly to a major characteristic of the new manufacturing technologies, their extensive shortening effect of product life cycles and lead times. Many small firms have competed successfully against larger firms because they could respond and react faster, both in the marketplace and within their own facilities (Nichols 1984; Kotkin 1985). The large firms can employ the new technologies to reduce their response time but the small firm, using the same technologies, can also speed up the pace even more.

Long-Range View

A number of authors (Hayes and Abernathy 1980; Ginzberg and Vojta 1985) have castigated American management, particularly of large firms, for their short-term perspective and musical-chairs management. A current extreme in the perspective is the concept of the disposable plant, described by Sepehri (1985). In contrast the new technologies are largely flexible, computerized systems that are meant to be reprogrammed and used over an extended time frame. With the apparently longer-term perspective of small firm managers, these reusable technologies are clearly a better fit to their strategies.

Another aspect of long-range planning is the approach taken by firms to approving investments in the new technologies. There currently seem to be two primary ways that automation investment decisions are made (Meredith 1985c). The large firms appear to examine a product line and decide whether or not to even stay in that line. If they decide to stay in (for example, dishwashers or typewriters), they simultaneously agree to pump in enough capital to make the entire plant extremely competitive. And once they have made the investment they tend not to alter it for some time (Jaikumar 1984).

Small firms, on the other hand, usually cannot afford a greenfield investment. Rather, they must carefully scrutinize any investment at all, evaluating its compatibility with present equipment, its cost, its payback, its advantages, and its risk. Because of this more limited incremental investment, and because they are closer to the application, small business managers often can see more clearly the benefits and problems of their automation decisions and be more effective in their implementation.

Competitive Basis

Rather than investing for volume-based cost advantages or capacity increases, as larger firms are prone to do, the small firm appears to invest for faster turnaround, quality, or some other such advantage (Meredith 1985c). Being used to competing on the basis of being local, providing service, customizing, or expediting, the small firm uses the new technologies to further extend and increase this selected competitive advantage.

In terms of foreign competition the point is even more significant. As described by Kotkin (1985), offshore production is hindered by transportation time and cost, distance from the customer, inability to respond to customization requests, and quality/design change problems. The small domestic firm attempts to capitalize on these disadvantages of offshore competitors and uses automation to further enhance its own advantages.

Human Resource Stability

The musical-chairs syndrome was previously mentioned as a distinct liability of larger firms with their constantly mobile managers, fast-track executives, and merry-go-round rotation programs (Dowling 1985). Shop workers with 15 to 20 years seniority in such firms commonly see a new manager every two or three years, each with his or her own favorite new "project" to help the company, so there is little incentive for them to make another (temporary) change. The small firm, often still being managed by its founding managers, thus has a better chance of educating its employees in the new automation technologies and reusing and extending their talents later when more automation is added. This further adds to the likelihood of successfully implementing the new technologies.

Technology Implementation

A number of crucial aspects of implementation (Meredith 1981) are aided by being a small firm. First, the project team often has a broader perspective rather than a narrow one (for example, that of the large firm's data processing department) due to their closer contact with all other members of the firm. Second, the users will probably be heavily involved in the implementation process and better understand its need and use. Finally, since top management is closer to the project, it is more likely that the required top management project "champion" (Meredith 1985a) will emerge to ensure its success. The major disadvantage the small firm faces, of course, is that if implementation problems develop, it will not have the resource base to fall back on that the large firm has.

CONCLUSION

Most of the publicity surrounding automation, high technology, and computerization concerns large firms and investments of many millions of dollars. However, this is because such large investments in computerized equipment are newsworthy, not because they are successful. Though they may still be successful, our research seems to indicate that these new technologies offer substantial potential for small firms also, and possibly even more.

Though both large and small firms can obtain these new technologies, smaller firms seem better able to capitalize on their benefits. Furthermore, the new technologies seem to offer the types of benefits that small firms are already used to competing with: fast customer response, quick production, more customization, greater variety, and so on. Yet these technologies are a major commitment for small firms, in terms of their managerial skill requirements as well as their capital requirements.

Wherever it is applied, the small firm must be able to capitalize on the new technology's benefits to provide a significant competitive advantage over others in its market, or the market it is entering. The factory of the future, we are convinced, can be a small factory.

REFERENCES AND BIBLIOGRAPHY

DOWLING, R. [1985]. "Is the Big Corporation Its Own Worst Enemy?" *Business Week*, April 22, pp. 12-13.

FROST, C. [1984]. "Integrated Automation Programs at Frost, Inc." *P&IM Review and APICS News*, April, pp. 32-36.

GINZBERG, E., and G. VOJTA [1985]. "Beyond Human Scale: The Large Corporation at Risk." *Basic Books*, New York.

GOLDHAR, J. P., and M. JELINEK [1983]. "Plan for Economies of Scope." *Harvard Business Review*, November-December, pp. 141-148.

HAYES, R. H., and W. J. ABERNATHY [1982]. "Managing our Way to Economic Decline." *Harvard Business Review,* July–August, pp. 67–77.

HAYES, R. H., and S. G. WHEELLWRIGHT [1979]. "The Dynamics of Process-Product Life Cycles." *Harvard Business Review,* March–April, pp. 127–136.

JAIKUMAR, R. [1984]. "Flexible Manufacturing Systems: A Managerial Perspective." *Working Paper 1-784-078,* Harvard Business School, Boston, Massachusetts.

KOTKIN, J. [1985]. "The Case for Manufacturing in America." *Inc,* March, pp. 49–62.

MEREDITH, J. R. [1985b]. "Peerless Saw Co." *Case Study,* University of Cincinnati, Cincinnati, Ohio.

MEREDITH, J. R. [1985c]. "Results of the Manufacturing Management Council Study of Justification Procedures." *Manufacturing Management Industry,* University Consortium, Society of Manufacturing Engineers, Dearborn, Michigan.

MEREDITH, J. R. [1981]. "The Implementation of Computer Based Systems." *Journal of Operations Management,* October, pp. 11–21.

NICHOLS, J. D. [1984]. "How Customer Needs are Shaping the 'Factory of the Future'." *Management Review,* December, pp. 29, 35–36.

SEPEHRI, M. [1985]. "A Machine Builds Machines at Apple Computer's Highly Automated Macintosh Manufacturing Facility." *Industrial Engineering,* April, pp. 60–67.

SURESH, N. C., and J. R. MEREDITH [1985]. "Achieving Factory Automation Through Group Technology Principles." *Journal of Operations Management,* 5(2), pp. 151–182.

VOSS, C. [1984]. "The Management of New Manufacturing Technology." *Working Paper,* London Business School, London, England.

READING 3.2

Technology Transfer: Challenges Facing Smaller Companies

INTRODUCTION

Whole segments of industries in North America are now threatened by offshore competition. The reflex response in the 1980s has been to either promise or actually undertake to modernize individual processes or whole plants; in return, companies operating in these segments have sought government intervention. Protection against some low cost steel imports was granted to United States integrated steelmakers on the grounds that time was required for the large steelmakers to recapitalize, and thus save their markets. This protection was not sought by specialty steelmakers (who were essentially niche players), or by the small steelmakers who employed fundamentally different steelmaking technology than the integrated producers—the mini-mill (or more properly market mill) producers. The mini-mills, in fact, were as much a threat to the integrated producers as were the Japanese and Koreans. The process technologies used by the mini-mill manufacturers were not brand new, nor were the products they were able to produce and effectively market. What some mini-mill operators discovered was a niche which the integrated producers would not be able to protect; what was necessary was an investment in innovation.

That small firms can adopt new technologies, and not only survive but grow in the process, is graphically demonstrated by the success story of the mini-mill. This success has been repeated in other industries (perhaps in not as spectacular a manner); machine-tool building (the adoption of CAD/CAM technology), medicine (the adoption of new practice management techniques in family medicine), and agriculture (the adoption of new varieties and species by fruit growers) are just three further examples of this phenomenon. Each of these latter three is different, and provides an example of the three different types of technology; process, managerial, and product respectively. But each example is similar in two respects; in every (or almost every) case, by definition the technology must have been adopted or transferred in by the small firms in the industry, and the majority of adopters would not have been start-ups. Contrast this with steel, where all the early mini-mills were greenfield sites, and nearly all first installations in companies were in firms making their first move into steelmaking; either as start-ups or through backward vertical integration.

FOCUS

The observations previously made indicate the importance of technology transfer to, and the adoption of new technology by, small firms. This note discusses what small firms might consider and ask questions about before adopting new technology, and looks at the characteristics a small firm should possess in order to improve the success rate of new technology adoption.

THE SMALL FIRM

The archetypical small firm was started up by one or a small number of entrepreneurs to take advantage of an observed opportunity in the market in which the entrepreneur had recent experience. The owner perceived a product/market opportunity that was not being adequately addressed by existing firms in the industry. Relatively low barriers to entry allowed the firm to be established, with the firm's focus firmly on surviving by getting the product into the market, and developing some competitive advantage. In industries with low barriers to entry it is highly probable that the start-up firm will use general purpose manufacturing technologies with which the management is familiar. This is in keeping with the probable strategy; it is highly unlikely that the small firm will be able to sustain a low-cost strategy, especially as it tries to grow, and will therefore have to differentiate itself from its competitors by satisfying other market needs.

The majority of small firms have gaps in management skills. This is true even of spinoffs or leveraged buyouts, where staff functions and managements will not exist because of their cost and their lack of contribution to cash generation. It is likely that small firms will be more involved in organizing and controlling essential activities than in planning (Wallender 1979, 50). Any planning will likely be rudimentary, reactive, and fine tuning in nature. Development activities, where they occur, will almost certainly be product focused and aimed to expand the product line to move into new markets or take advantage of new opportunities discovered in existing markets. Changes to process technologies will probably come from outside the firm. Whatever the focus of development activities, they will probably be allocated few resources (Craig and Noori 1985), and the search process will be local and incremental (Cyert and March 1963).

TECHNOLOGY ADOPTION

The literature on adoption of technology at the level of the firm generally agrees that the adoption process, more properly called the innovation-decision process (for the firm must have the ability to temporarily or permanently reject an innovation) is multiphased. Rogers and Shoemaker (1971, 103) describe a four stage process; knowledge, persuasion, decision, and confirmation. Nabseth and Ray's (1974, 7) eight stage model is substantively the same as Rogers'; interestingly, both models imply that adoption after initial rejection will occur without a new search being undertaken. This is curious, for most studies point out the need for up-to-the-minute information on the state of technology before proceeding further through the adoption process (see, for example, Gasse 1984, 60).

Foregoing subsequent search is valid only if the time interval between initial rejection and later adoption is very short, or where it is known that the rate of technological change in and expansion of the set of appropriate technologies is very slow. Both conditions may well apply to the small firm considering adopting new technology; an ability to make and change decisions rapidly, and a reluctance to seriously consider new technologies until they are well-understood—which implies maturity. Any firm choosing to become a world-class manufacturer has been enjoined to adopt proven rather than radically different manufacturing technologies (Gunn 1987, 27); being a late adopter or even a laggard (Rogers 1971). This applies to the small firm as well, for the cost of searching for information when a technology is unproven is significantly higher than when the technology is well-understood and documented.

CHARACTERISTICS OF SMALL FIRMS

From the aspect of decision-making and implementation small firms are different from large firms. Small firms are generally able to reduce the time between information gathering and decision-making, and the decision makers typically have greater awareness of risk and therefore show a greater commitment to any decision made. A lack of resources significantly increases the risks of the technology not performing as anticipated; technical risk is accompanied by financial, business, and personal risk—and the risks are high. Small firms normally do not have the knowledge or time to evaluate technology potential; while there is a greater awareness of risk in the small firm, there is likely to be less understanding of the risk. And even if there is an ability to evaluate a technology, there is likely to be a lack of adequate management skills to support implementation of new process technology.

INFORMATION NEEDS

But what information is required? And is all the information required at the beginning of the process, or are different parcels of information required at different points through the process? The answer seems to lie in understanding the factors that facilitate, and the fators that inhibit, technology adoption. One study (Ounjian and Carne 1987, 197) suggests that characteristics in the technology, characteristics in the receiver, and the relationship between the receiver and the donor will influence the ability to successfully transfer technology.

TECHNOLOGY

Perhaps the element focused on most, and the element analyzed and understood the least, is the technology itself. The keyword in discussing the adoption of technology is fit—fit of the technology with the adopting firm, and fit of the technology with the other technologies in the firm. The three forms of technology mentioned are product, process, and managerial. This is not necessarily the same as Zeleny's (1986) typology of hardware, software, and brainware, although in information-intensive industries the typologies converge. Regardless of the typology, adopting firms must satisfy themselves of the consistency of fit and mutual support among the various technologies and the firm's strategy; or, if there is no immediate fit, of the ability of the firm to make the necessary adjustments in order to properly accommodate the new technology.

Noori (1987, 14–15) develops a framework by which to analyze the technology under review. His four dimensions of merit—inventive, embodiment, operational, and market—collapse into two dimensions, technology potency and marketing advantage. This is practically the same as the two dimensions in Abernathy's transilience matrix (Abernathy 1983, 110), which are impact on market linkages and impact on productive systems. Noori, however, is more concerned with adoption and implementation, as his specific questions indicate; Abernathy is concerned with strategic impact on market structure, and relating the technology to the firm's strategy.

Firms can adopt one of two generic strategies, cost-focused or differentiation-focused (Porter 1980, 35.)[2] For the small, and growing firm, overall cost leadership is probably out of the question, and another sustainable competitive advantage has to be found. The differentiation from industry norms may either be embodied in the uniqueness of the firm's product(s), or come from operating attributes such as quality or the ability to respond flexibly and rapidly to customer requirements. These abilities are reflected in structural and infrastructural policies (Hayes and Wheelwright 1984, 31). For any firm, selection of new technologies which do not support the enacted strategy or its bundle of supporting policies is fraught with danger—especially if the firm does not have the capability of recognizing the sometimes subtle changes in strategy forced by the new technology.

The questions thus become:

1. What is the firm's current strategy? What is the firm's existing competitive advantage? What does the firm have to do to do well and survive profitably?

[2]Porter actually indicates three generic strategies; overall cost leadership, differentiation, and focus. Focus is, however, more properly a second dimension on a matrix with the two generic strategies as factors on the strategy dimension. Thus a firm can choose to be a global cost leader, or may choose to have different strategies for different segments of the business. For the small firm this is a moot point initially, but need to be kept in mind as the firm contemplates expansion.

2. Where do we want the firm to go in the next few years? Is our current strategy consistent with the strategy we will need to have in place in five years?
3. Is the technology under review able to support our current strategy? Will it help us attain our future goals?
4. Does the technology fit with the other technologies we have in place? What will be the impact on our other structural policies in the areas of capacity, facilities, vertical integration?
5. Does the technology fit with our managerial technologies and philosophies? What impact will the new technology have on our infrastructural policies in the areas of the work force, quality, organization, and operations planning and control?
6. What impact will the technology have on our products? What impact will the technology have on our relationships with our customers, current and potential?
7. What impact will the technology have on our cost structures? What impact will the new technology have on our ability to understand our costs?
8. Do we have the capability to successfully assimilate the technology? What will the negative implementation effects be, internally and externally?

RECEIVER

The last question focuses on the characteristics of the receiver of the technology. Any technology which cannot be properly assimilated is of extremely limited value, and small firms are vulnerable in this regard because of their lack of resources. Firms need to be aware of their financial, organizational, personnel (direct, indirect and support), and managerial strengths in order to gauge their ability to assimilate, and the best ways by which to assimilate, the new technology.

Because of the paucity of financial resources, a lack of skills appropriate to the technology, and the inability to conduct a detailed information search, small firms intent on adopting new technology should consider taking a series of small steps rather than one bold (and perhaps fatal) step. These steps should allow the financing to be spread over a longer period, thus helping cash flows, and should allow for a move by increments into the new technology, allowing learning and adjustment inside and outside the firm to occur in a planned fashion. Archer (1984) suggests that a planned approach and a real understanding of the value of each incremental step also allows a firm to see if a lower level of technology might be as appropriate as the "higher" technology initially felt to be necessary.

MANAGEMENT

The literature on innovation suggests several key individual roles, such as gatekeeping (Allen 1977), and championing (Meredith 1988). The role of the gatekeeper is to keep abreast of developments and ideas outside the firm, and to allow into the firm only a subset of the total set of ideas that may be useful. Championing has four roles; creative originator, entrepreneur, sponsor, and project manager (Meredith 1988, 6–7). The originator is the source of the innovation, and is not normally within the adopting organization; the entrepreneur adopts and sells the idea within the organization; the sponsor is a senior manager who provides resources and protection for the entrepreneur, and the project manager is the day-to-day administrator of the project. The gatekeeper therefore comes between the originator and the entrepreneur. In a small firm it is not unusual to find one manager performing the gatekeeping through project management functions; importantly, if any one of these roles is not played the chances of successful implementation are not high.

RELATIONSHIP BETWEEN THE GIVER AND RECEIVER

For any firm the chances of successful innovation are improved if the innovation itself is accompanied by personnel prepared and able to install, start up, operate, and train people on the innovation. This is more critical in small firms, where slack resources within the firm are relatively rare. What is required is an "arms around" rather than an "arms length" relationship between giver and receiver; in football parlance better a handoff to a running back for a guaranteed few yards on the ground than a long, spectacular, but risky pass into double coverage. The transition phase is the most tricky part, and both parties must plan this phase carefully. More (1989), writing from the seller's perspective, is adamant that managing the seller/buyer relationship so that the seller can utilize the buyer's capabilities is critical to the success of the transfer process.

In addition to managing the physical transfer, both parties have to be clear about what constitutes a successful implementation, the time within which the demonstration of success has to occur, and the actions to be taken if the implementation is a partial or total failure. The greater the degree of uncertainty, the greater the responsibility of the giver, all other things being equal.

PUBLIC POLICY

Observation of these phenomena raises the public policy issue of support to small business. What, if any, support should governments provide for small business to help them manage the innovation-decision process? The answer is "not much," and should be aimed at the most critical part of the decision process, information search. Reducing the extent of the search pattern allows the small firm to better utilize scarce resources; all other things being equal, the better understood the information, the better the decision.

The availability of funds from financial institutions will be important for any firm seeking to adopt new technology. Perhaps more important is the attitude of the financial institution to lending for the acquisition of new technology, and while governments may not (or should not) be lenders even of last resort, they can play an important role in fostering a supportive attitude in the lending agencies. This is, incidentally, another reason for adopting technology late; financial analysis supportive of technology acquisition is likely to be more sympathetically received by a lending institution when the relationships are clear, and that is more likely with incremental than with radically new technology.

CONCLUSION

Change is always risky, and for the small firm which lacks resources innovating can be traumatic. Provided the process is planned, and provided reasonable precautions are taken, however, implementation of innovation can be made into a reasonable challenge, not a gamble or a chore. The keywords are consistency, caution, common sense, champion, and communication. Clear leadership from the top for an innovation consistent with the strategy and the other technology and manufacturing policies that involves the minimum possible technological change, installed in as deliberate and incremental a fashion as possible, is the key to success. And if, at the end of the planning process, the notion of adopting new technology does not make sense, don't do it. After all, you only get one chance to bet the whole company—and lose.

REFERENCES AND BIBLIOGRAPHY

ABERNATHY, W. J. et al. [1983]. *Industrial Renaissance.* Books, New York.

ALLEN, J. [1977]. *Managing the Flow of Technology.* MIT Press, Cambridge, Massachusetts.

ARCHER, J. [1984]. "Is There A Low Cost Route to Flexible Automation?" *Proceedings, 3rd International Conference on Flexible Manufacturing Systems,* pp. 491–499.

CRAIG, R., and H. NOORI [1985]. "Recognition and Use of Automation." *Journal of Small Business and Entrepreneurship.* Volume 3, No. 1, Summer, pp. 37–44.

CYERT, R. M., and J. G. MARCH [1963]. *A Behavioral Theory of the Firm.* Prentice-Hall, Englewood Cliffs, New Jersey.

HAYES, R. H., and S. C. WHEELWRIGHT [1984]. *Restoring Our Competitive Edge.* John Wiley & Sons, New York.

GASSE, Y. [1984]. "A Model of Adoption Process of New Technologies for Small and Medium Firms." *Proceedings, Administrative Sciences Association of Canada.* Volume 5, Part 6, pp. 57–70.

GUNN. T. G. [1987]. *Manufacturing for Competitive Advantage.* Ballinger, Cambridge, Massachusetts.

MEREDITH, J. [1988]. "The Role of Manufacturing Technology in Competitiveness: Peerless Laser Processors." *IEEE Transactions in Engineering Management.* Volume EM-35, No. 1, February, pp. 3–10.

MORE, R. [1989]. "The Impact of Buyer/Seller Relationships on the Adoption of New Technologies: Exploratory Empirical Application of a Decision-Interdependency Network." Working Paper NC 89-01. School of Business Administration, The University of Western Ontario, January.

NABSETH, L., and G. F. RAY (eds.) [1974]. *The Diffusion of New Industrial Processes.* Cambridge University Press, Cambridge.

NOORI, H. [1987]. "Benefits Arising From New Technology Adoption: Small versus Large Firms." *Journal of Small Business and Entrepreneurship.* Volume 5, No. 1, Summer, pp. 8–16.

OUNJIAN, M. L., and E. B. CRANE [1987]. "A Study of the Factors Which Affect Technology Transfer in a Multilocation Multibusiness Unit Corporation." *IEEE Translation in Engineering Management.* Volume EM-34, No. 3, August, pp. 194–201.

PORTER, M. E. [1980]. *Competitive Strategy.* The Free Press, New York, New York.

ROGERS, E. M. with F. F. SHOEMAKER [1971]. *Communication of Innovations* (2nd ed.). The Free Press, New York, New York.

WALLENDER, H. W. III [1979]. *Technology Transfer and Management in Developing Countries.* Ballinger, Cambridge, Massachusetts.

ZELENY, M. [1986]. "High Technology Transfer." *Human Systems Management.* Volume 6, pp. 109–120.

EPILOGUE

The Impetus for New Technology

Throughout history, man has continually pursued and promoted technological advancement. The advances achieved have never reached the magnitude of those we have witnessed over the last few decades, yet even the pace and magnitude of recent change may pale in comparison to that which lies ahead. Firms the world over are faced with the challenge of reacting and adapting to this change.

Several major environmental changes are catalysts for the adoption of new technologies. The incidence and magnitude of international (even global) competition in many products has markedly increased. Faced with intensified competition, firms are pursuing many means to gain advantage, and the means often chosen first is the application of new technology, and there is a "snowballing" effect. As a result, the need for and rate of technology adoption accelerates.

Perhaps the most significant feature of the technology invasion in manufacturing today is that it is universal. It affects many industries, and both large and small firms. Much consideration has been given to who is affected more and in what ways, but as yet no true consensus has been reached.

It is generally agreed that small firms can realize significant advantages through new technology, but that the time and resources required for a successful application are often prohibitive. Some of these constraints include inadequate financial resources, and lack of in-house expertise, time, and knowledge. Yet a growing number of small firms have successfully applied the new technology, and taken advantage of its flexibility and cost and quality gains to compete quite successfully (and sometimes more successfully) with larger firms.

Does this mean then, that small firms that cannot (and large firms that do not) adopt new technology, will falter and fail? The answer to this question is a resounding

No! New technology cannot and will not replace good planning and strategy, sound management, and a capable and dedicated work force. Examples abound of firms who do not have any of the new technologies in operation, yet who consistently outperform some of their more rapidly adopting competitors. It is important for firms to realize that, although potentially an extremely powerful and effective competitive weapon, new technology is not a cure-all. For those well-managed firms that do match their technology applications to the needs of their process and their market, however, new technology may hold the key to the future.

Should the management of a smaller firm decide that it makes good strategic sense to adopt a new technology, though, the onus is on the managers to develop a thorough plan for investigating, deciding upon, and implementing the appropriate technology. A sound plan is essential, as the smaller company will not normally be able to afford the luxury of a technology which does not live up to expectations. And, as the smaller company will often be short of critical resources, it will have to rely on suppliers and others for information and assistance with implementation.

Managers in this situation must therefore be very clear about what they are trying to achieve, what the relationships with outside agencies should be, what the outside agencies are to provide, and how to measure the performance of each party to the technology transfer project. Obtaining commitment inside the small firm is relatively straightforward, especially if a small management group champions the project from the start. That counts for nought, however, if external parties are not obliged to commit themselves fully to the project.

CASE 3.1

Doka (Sweden)[3]

In mid-January, 1986, Mr. Lindstrom, factory manager of the Doka plant in Stockholm, was reviewing a capital expenditure proposal. The Doka plant had started manufacturing Kelno blocks in the summer of 1984 and the proposal called for replacing some of the Kelno equipment.

DOKA (SWEDEN)

Doka (Sweden) was a subsidiary of Doka Corporation (U.S.), a large multinational corporation with 32 plants worldwide. Doka specialized in the soap and detergent field and had a reputation as a high quality and innovative producer and aggressive marketer of consumer brands. Doka (Sweden) was responsible for the manufacture and sale of Doka products in Finland, Sweden, Norway and Denmark. Other major Doka plants in Europe were situated in England, West Germany, France, Italy and Spain. Although each national subsidiary had considerable local autonomy, major investment proposals (those exceeding $200,000) had to be approved by Doka International, headquartered in New York.

MR. LINDSTROM

Mr. Lindstrom had been appointed the new factory manager for the Swedish operation as of January 1, 1986. He had worked as a technical director about a decade earlier at the Stockholm plant, but had since worked in a variety of capacities in other Doka sub-

[3]This case was written by Professor M. R. Leenders and Ir. B. A. A. M. van Baren. © 1986 Erasmus Universiteit, The Rotterdam School of Management and the School of Business Administration, The University of Western Ontario.

sidiaries in Europe. Mr. Lindstrom had looked forward to taking over the Stockholm plant. This new position afforded him an opportunity to return to the country of his birth. Moreover, the Swedish plant had an excellent reputation within Doka International as an active and technically sophisticated operation in which opportunities for cost and product improvement were aggressively pursued. The Swedish operation had strongly performing cost improvement and value analysis programs which generated substantial savings both for Swedish as well as other Doka plants where similar products were made.

KELNO BLOCKS

In 1982 Doka (Germany) acquired Mueller S. A., a relatively small West German manufacturer of specialty products. One of the Mueller products was the Kelno block, a toilet bowl deodorizer and disinfectant which was hung on the rim of the toilet bowl. With each flushing, the water flowed over the block and dissolved a small amount of the block. The block itself was held in a small plastic cage. Thus, when the block was fully dissolved, the empty case could be thrown away and a new one hung in its place. Blocks retailed at about 70 cents each.

One of the Doka (Sweden) marketing specialists believed a Scandinavian market opportunity existed for Kelno blocks and requested a market test. Kelno blocks turned out to sell well and Doka (Sweden) imported substantial amounts from West Germany. When it became obvious that the Scandinavian market was large enough to warrant local production, Doka (Sweden) prepared a capital request for manufacture in Sweden. Since the project would provide additional employment, Doka (Sweden) received government support of about $400,000 for this $2 million investment. Space for Kelno block manufacture was available in the Stockholm plant, but almost all of the equipment had to be purchased. Moreover, a large room had to be built with air-controlling equipment, to contain the vapors and perfume of the Doka blocks. The Swedish Kelno block facility started operation in the summer of 1984.

THE NEW KELNO FORMULATION

By the spring of 1985 the West German plant had completed development work on a newly formulated Kelno block. Environmental authorities had raised questions about the impact of Kelno block discharge on water quality. Particular concerns centered on the disinfectant (DI) component, one of the seven raw materials included in the original Kelno block formulation. Part of the difficulty was that even a minor change in any of the Kelno block components had a major impact on the physical and chemical characteristics of the product. Thus, the change in disinfectant developed by the German team required a new block manufacturing process. Whereas the previous process (and the one currently employed by Doka (Sweden)) mixed the ingredients at about 70°C and poured the liquid mix into molds, the new formulation required a kneading/mixing operation and extrusion of the blocks. It was Doka policy that environmental issues should always be attended to promptly. Even though no real proof of environmental damage existed, the German subsidiary switched to the new formulation in mid-1985. The Doka (Sweden) executives had followed the German developments closely and decided that they should also reformulate. Even though no environmental concerns had been raised in any of the Scandinavian countries, the executives believed it wise to reformulate Kelno blocks and asked Mr. Lindstrom's predecessor to start the planning process.

A member of the plant engineering group had worked with a member of the plant's process development group to investigate various process options. Both men had tried to find a way to manufacture Kelno blocks by a continuous process rather than the batch process adopted by the German plant. Mr. Lindstrom was aware from his predecessor that this investigation had taken place. He also knew that his predecessor had not had a chance to read the capital expenditure proposal prepared by the project team. Thus, after having spent most of his first two weeks on the new job on urgent matters, Mr. Lindstrom read the proposal carefully. (See Exhibit 3.5 for excerpts from this proposal.) He had already scheduled a meeting with the Kelno process team members for the following day and wanted to understand what they were proposing.

FURTHER CONSIDERATIONS

Mr. Lindstrom knew that capital proposals were very carefully examined by staff members in New York. Normally, capital projects should show a return on investment of at least 25 percent and preferably, pay for themselves within three years. Mr. Lindstrom also knew that Kelno blocks had already captured a substantial market share in Scandinavia and that marketing forecasts of the demand had been much too low in the past. In Mr. Lindstrom's opinion, a product like Kelno blocks was substantially different from the soap and detergent products produced in the Stockholm factory. Records of costs and productivity of other products, due to extensive automation, had labor productivity figures of about eight tons per labor day. Kelno blocks were accounted for in individual units. Current capacity was rated at 80 blocks per minute, but actual production was close to 70 percent of this figure, primarily due to significant problems with the blister pack machine. Kelno labor productivity, if translated into traditional plant figures, would be close to 0.2 tons/labor day.

Mr. Lindstrom also knew that the current Kelno facility was operated at three shifts per day, whereas, almost the whole Stockholm plant was on two shifts. Swedish law required that people working three shifts be paid at least a 25 percent premium and two shifts at 12 percent premium. Current finished goods inventory levels of Kelno blocks were only at the one week level, whereas a three to four week period would usually be considered normal.

Mr. Lindstrom had also found out that it would be possible to purchase the new blocks from an Italian supplier. However, if Sweden stopped production of Kelno blocks in the plant, he expected the government would require the return of its grant. Apparently, the mold line for the existing blocks had little or no scrap value.

Mr. Lindstrom visited the current Kelno block manufacturing unit and noted that the blister pack machine was down during his visit. He had heard that this par-

Exhibit 3.5 Doka (Sweden)

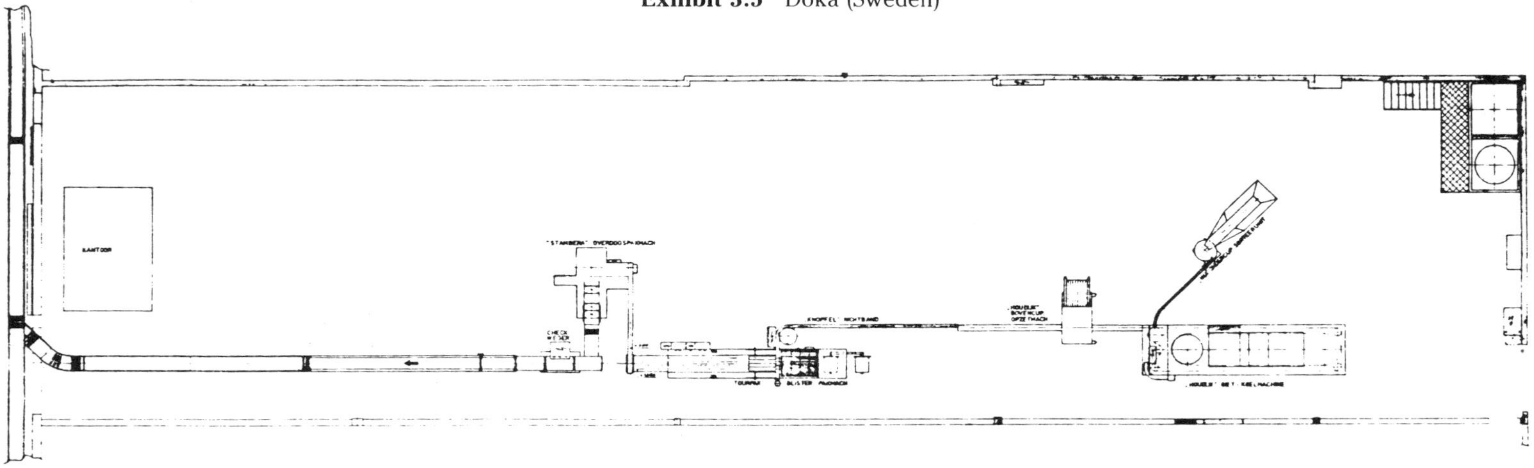

EXISTING SITUATION

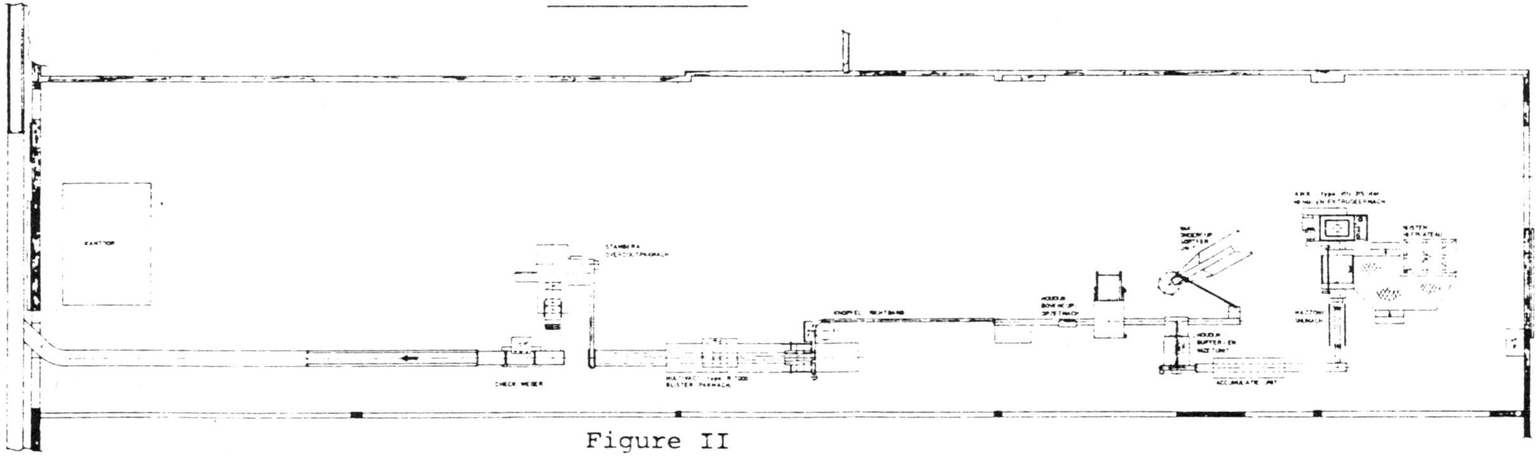

Figure II

PROPOSED SITUATION

0 1 2 3 4 5 meter

Note: Actual plans included in the proposal.

ticular machine had been relatively inexpensive at a price of about $70,000, but that a more reliable machine would cost at least $140,000 and a larger model with 50 percent more capacity would cost $175,000. There were currently six workers in the department on each shift, including a lead hand, and two persons who manually placed the top cages on the bottom ones. Including all fringe benefits Doka's (Sweden) labor cost per person averaged about $28,000.

Mr. Lindstrom had some reservations about the proposal. He had a high regard for the German subsidiary and believed they would have chosen a continuous process, if they had believed it technically and economically feasible. The Swedish proposal was for a much larger sum than originally envisaged in the capital budget for 1986. Mr. Lindstrom believed that, therefore, the arguments for the higher investment would have to be particularly strong. He also knew that company policy favored standardization of processes for identical products between subsidiaries. The Swedish proposal was, therefore, out of line with the German plant. At Doka it was normal to have fast and frequent changes in product formulations. These stemmed from value analysis and product improvement programs as well as ongoing research and development. In Mr. Lindstrom's opinion the continuous process proposed was probably less flexible and less reliable than the batch technology chosen in Germany. He did, however, agree that, in prinicple, a continuous process was more desirable than a batch process.

CAPITAL EXPENDITURE PROPOSAL

Narrative
Proposal No. 1986–051

1. General Description and Justification

Consumer testing in Sweden showed that the acceptance of the new block compared satisfactorily with that of the current block. The new formula gives a raw materials cost saving of approximately 5 percent. The total capital investment amounts to $500,000. $330,000 associated with the exiting block molding process will be written off. The main justification of the proposal is to abandon the old formula so as to avoid having to defend against a potential environmentally-based attack. It is a key company objective to avoid environmental threats before they can arise rather than defend subsequently.

Secondly, there are savings in raw materials costs and a decrease in personnel employed from 18 to 15. Further advantages will arise in the areas of:

- Innovation and cost savings will focus on the new block.
- Harmonization of production between the two sites provides the best international production base.
- Total volume requirements out of Sweden and peak demands for other European countries require a fall back in Germany.
- Germany obtains a higher output from their extrusion line than their molding line. This has not been taken into account but could increase savings if achieved in Sweden.

2. Differences with Budget

The sum included in the 1986 capital budget was $140,000. This amount was based on the first indications from Germany and corresponded to that made in order to get started quickly with the production of new blocks. This was a nonautomated route and significantly increased labor requirements. Inclusion in the capital budget was also intended to signal the need for the investment rather than the amount.

The present proposed amount of $500,000 results from the following arguments:

- In order to achieve continuous operation and avoid large buffers of extruded blocks, continuous extrusion as is practiced in toilet soap production has been chosen.
- The present in-cage block molding machine automatically places blocks into the case halves without hook. The extruded block, however, has to be inserted into the cage half without hook afterwards either by hand or automatically.
- In Sweden this operation will be automated on the basis of savings.
- A new cage assembling machine will be purchased and the new process built up in parallel to the present so that the production does not need to undergo a long downtime and the new process can be operationally tested before discontinuing the present molded block production.

3. Alternatives

A molded block formulation that is not liable to lead to environmental discussions is not available and is no longer being worked on due to other priorities for R&D expenditure. In the past, Germany has searched unsuccessfully for other formulations that could be manufactured using the molding system. Total German production has switched over to the extruded block. Several arrangements of mixer/kneaders and buffering systems have been considered.

Single RTS-Type Mixer/Kneader (German Setup). In Germany a discontinuous working RTS machine produces batches of 95 kg (1,696 blocks). The extruded blocks fall onto a slow moving conveyor which is used as a buffer. From the buffer blocks the blocks are manually placed into cages and assembled further requiring four operators per shift.

The Germans are undertaking an in-house development of a block buffering machine together with a block insertion to change the discontinuous block production to a continuous supply to the packing line. The upper cage halves will, however, still be assembled manually.

The estimated cost of $65,000 for the buffer machine and cage filler cannot be compared with quotations from third party manufacturers.

Continuous Extrusion. Germany also considered arrangements of two RTS mixers/kneaders to achieve a continuous output of 80 blocks/minute and examined Johnston and Blass and Louzon's continuous extrusion processes, undertaking trials at Johnston.

Investments were similar to the proposed arrangement with a continuous extruder. Having already committed to the RTS single mixer and production pressure, Germany decided not to follow continuous extrusion further.

Due to the continuous extrusion route being more compatible with total automation of the line while avoiding larger areas for buffers and more laborious cleaning of the machines associated with the discontinuous German approach, Sweden took over the German continuous extrusion work.

4. Advisory-Service Departments Consulted

Several consultative talks with German staff and engineering were held. Also corporate technical groups were consulted.

5. Environmental Consequences

The block production department is already well-ventilated to ensure acceptable levels of disinfectant vapors and perfume. The manufacturing of the new block introduces handling of ATL-flakes in bags. ATL flakes produce a fine dust that needs to be extracted. Therefore, a dust ventilation and filter system is included in the proposal.

6. Employment

One mixing operator in day shift for the production of molten product for the existing melt/mold process will be saved. After implementation, the line will require a manning of five per shift giving a total of 15 persons in three shifts against 18 in the present situation. During the startup of the extrusion process, it is foreseen that two extra operators per shift, four in total, will be required for the first four months.

7. Timing

The delivery time of the continuous extruder is approximately six months after ordering. If ordered in March, 1986, production of extruded blocks could be commissioned in the fourth quarter of 1986.

CAPITAL EXPENDITURE PROPOSAL

Technical Appendix

1. General

The new block must be manufactured by an extrusion process as opposed to the melt/mold process applied for blocks.

Germany started production of extruded new blocks at the end of August, 1985 on a discontinuous extruder. The choice of this machine was based on immediate availability to meet sudden demand but accepting increased manning.

The main objective for Sweden is to keep manning as low as is economical and a continuous extrusion system is more in line with an automated system. Based on successful trials by staff from Germany and after consultation with corporate/technical groups, Sweden proposed to choose a twin-screw-type continuous extruder.

Powders will be premixed in batches of approximately 100 kg in a powder blender with dust extraction, situated in the packing department. The powder mix will be transported via a belt or a screw to the powder dosing station. Perfume and water will be dosed by metering pumps.

The extruded material is then cut into blocks and transported to the newly designed machine for placement in cages. The cage halves with blocks are then assembled on the existing assembly machine and subsequently packed on the existing blister machine and casepacker.

2. Capital Investment

		CAPITAL		REPAIRS II
1.	Extruder Johnston type PT160 Material: steel	$145,000		
2.	Plodder head including electric heating	7,000		
3.	Platform	14,500		
4.	Transport belt between mixer and extruder	5,500		
5.	Pallet life for sacks	5,500		
6.	Weighing scale (maximum 250 kg) with transport containers	7,000		
7.	Dust extraction including filter	36,000		
8.	Block cutting machine (Italian)	29,000		
9.	Block insertion machine (German)	136,000		
10.	Adjustments to unscrambler			$ 1,800
11.	Insatallation	18,000		
12.	Electrical	18,000		9,000
13.	Piping	9,000		3,700
14.	Removal existing equipment			1,800
15.	Building provisions incuding painting			3,700
16.	Safety provisions	9,500		
17.	Contingencies	50,000		
		$480,000		$20,000
	TOTAL		$500,000	

3. Remarks on Machinery

Our Extrusion Machine. Germany based the choice of machines on immediate availability because production of new blocks had to start at very short notice. A discontinuous working mixing/kneading machine happened to be the option that was immediately available and gave the greatest chance of successful, if labor intensive, production.

The main objective for Sweden is to have a continuous output of W. C. blocks at a rate of at least 80 per minute, so that the filling of cages can be done automatically without large and complicated buffering systems at a low manning. This can be achieved either by:

1. Installing two AMK-type discontinuous mixing/kneading machines. The first machine for mixing and kneading feeds, the second machine for buffering and extrusion of blocks.
2. Installing a continuous working twin screw extruder machine fed by a set of dosing pumps and a powder feeder. The powder needs to be premixed in a blender.

After consultations with Germany and corporate technical groups, it was decided to choose the continuous twin screw extruder. Also, this option requires less space which would be fairly limited if a second line should ever be installed. However, the final decision on actual supplier has not yet been made and is dependent on an ongoing examination of Johnston and Blass and Louzon alternatives. The budget is based on Johnston as this has been demonstrated successfully with the new block composition.

Block Cutting Machine. Sweden has a long established experience with Italian cutting machines in the soap packing department. They have proven to be very reliable. Cutting speed and blade distance are variable.

Germany uses a German cutter machine. A final choice will be made based on price/performance considerations.

Insertion of Blocks in Cage Halves. In Germany the insertion of blocks in the cage half without hook is undertaken manually. Two ladies per shift fill the cages at a rate of 80 per minute. Germany is developing an automatic insertion system together with a buffering system for intermediate storage of blocks. These machines are especially designed for their local situation starting with a discontinuous mixing/kneading machine.

In Sweden the automation of the assembling of the upper cage halves with hook has been very successful. Therefore, the same machine manufacturer has been asked to design and construct a machine for insertion of extruded blocks into the cage halves without hook. This automation thus avoids extending the manning by four persons. This part of the investment can be seen as a cost saving proposal in relation to the current approach. $100,000 is associated with this part and the yield is 600 percent in constant terms, payback 1.1 years.

Cage Assembling Machine. In order to lose a minimum of production time, the extrusion machine and the block insertion machine will be installed alongside the present block molding machine.

The existing cage assembly machine is closely integrated with the block molding machine. In order to save on downtime (approximately six weeks) it has been decided to build a new cage assembly machine and install it in line with the block insertion machine. This approach increases investment by $34,000.

The old machine would be available for a second production line if ever required.

Capacity. Line capacity of finished product is not affected by the extrusion process since this is dependent on the blister pack machine.

Some of the equipment being purchased could be sufficient to supply two packing lines (power mixing, pallet lift, weighing scale and dust extraction—$67,000 in total).

The output of the extruder is at least 400 kg/hour (equivalent to 105 blocks/minute). Actual output will have to be determined in practice.

Location. Exhibit 3.6 shows the first phase in the changeover to block extrusion in the W. C. block department.

Exhibit 3.6 The Current Kelno Block Manufacturing Process

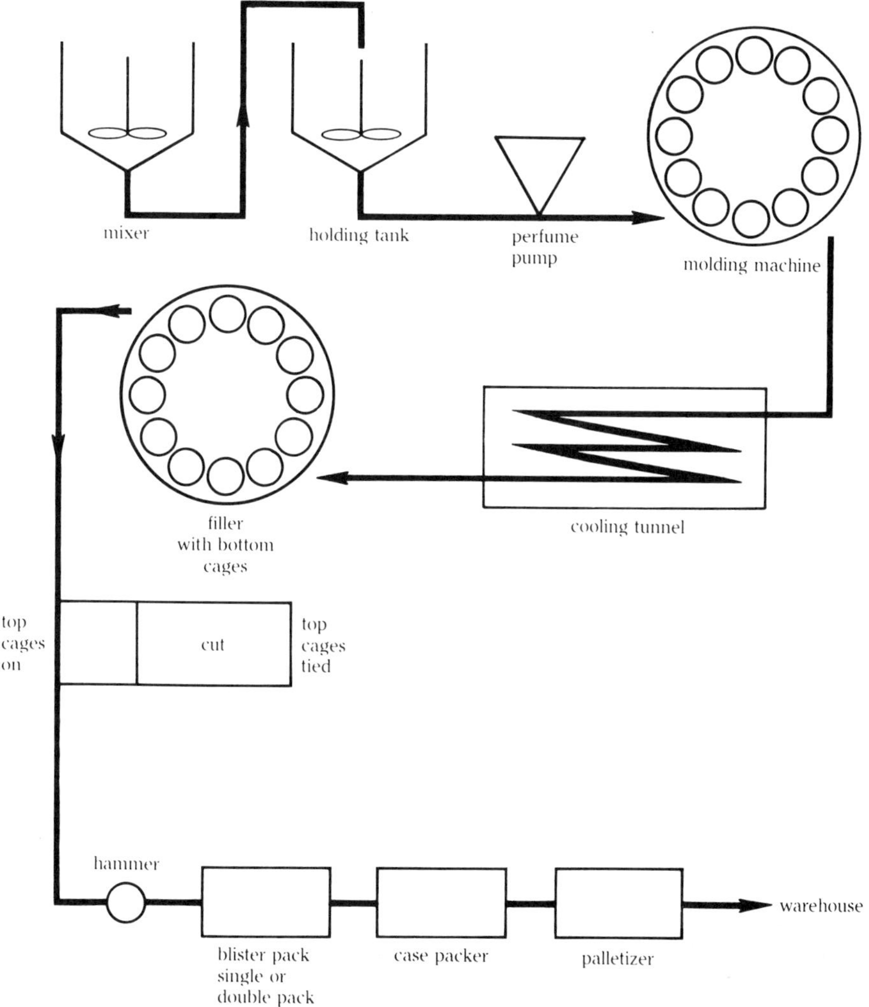

The extrusion machine, the insertion, and the assembly machines are located next to the existing block molding machine. The latter is connected to the blister machine by an extended conveyor.

CAPITAL EXPENDITURE PROPOSAL

Marketing Appendix

1. Ecological aspects can force us to introduce a new block with a very short lead time. The existing problems in Germany (that is, limitations on promotion) can cause similar problems in Scandinavia. We as a market leader would suffer most.
2. Performance-wise the new block is better than the present one in the areas of disinfection, enough foaming and longer lasting cleaning. Also on perfume aspects the new block is better than the current formula. Only in wearing properties are there variable results. *Source:* Teltest Product Test 13:11,85°.
3. Changeover to the new block gives a saving on raw materials of approximately 5 percent, based on the same block weight.
4. A reformulation of the block gives the possibility to draw attention anew to the brand.

CASE 3.2

Power Motion Manufacturing Limited[4]

"Pierre, we've squeezed as much production out of this plant as we can. The time has come to decide how we will expand." Joe Ebner, general manager of Power Motion, was telling his assistant general manager, Pierre Ravary, that he had just learned about unexpectedly large increases in the company's probable sales for the next two years. Power Motion was a London, Ontario, manufacturer of small electronic motors for the automotive industry and in the six years since its formation had enjoyed steadily increasing demand for its products. Now, in July, 1984, projections showed a probable 50 percent increase in sales within two years, volumes that would exceed existing production capacity. Mr. Ebner knew that a small plant atmosphere had been a considerable factor in the company's success to this point. Meeting the forecast sales level might jeopardize that success unless he could devise some way to increase output without creating a "large-plant" atmosphere. In order to meet the increased demand expected the following summer, Mr. Ebner had to decide within a few months how this could best be done.

POWER MOTION

Power Motion was a subsidiary of Magna International Inc., a diversified Canadian auto parts manufacturer. Magna had grown rapidly since the late 1960s by acquiring or establishing many small, independently operated firms, each of which specialized in a particular function or product line. Power Motion had been set up in 1978 and was

[4]This case was prepared by D. McCutcheon under the direction of Professor A. R. Wood.

grouped along with several other companies in Magna's electrical components division, one of the company's five major divisions. The other divisions produced metal stampings, plastic trim parts, belts, assemblies (such as door latches) and a variety of other components and accessories. These products were sold directly to North American automobile manufacturing companies, to other suppliers (including other Magna subsidiaries), or to automotive aftermarket suppliers.

Magna based its organizational philosophy on the principles of its founder and chairman, Frank Stronach, who believed that success depended on instilling a sense of ownership in a company's managers and employees, as well as on the managers' thorough knowledge of their specific businesses. To instill the motivational sense of ownership, hourly-paid employees were given bonuses from a profit-sharing scheme based on Magna's overall profitability, while managers received bonuses based on the profitability of their particular subsidiary firms. To insure managers' intimate familiarity with all facets of their operations, each company was designed to be small. Individual product lines were usually handled by separate companies. Each of the subsidiary firms was given financial and technical support by the parent corporation, usually through its divisional office, but was allowed a great deal of latitude to operate as independently as possible. One of the chairman's rough guidelines was that each company should be small enough to keep the number of shop floor employees below 100. This would help insure that a "small company" atmosphere was maintained and allow a lean management structure to handle the administrative requirements within the subsidiary.

Magna operated a substantial corporate research and development department. Many of the projects were undertaken to support individual subsidiary objectives. In this way, the subsidiaries functioned as small, independent operators while having access to financial and development resources not available to small scale competitors. The small company atmosphere and the profit-sharing scheme for the employees were cited by the chairman as primary reasons for the absence of unions in any Magna plant. This, combined with the lean management structure, gave Magna companies cost advantages when competing with larger firms in the auto supply business. Under this system, Magna had grown to operate nearly 50 small plants in Canada and the United States. In 1968, net income of $153,000 was earned on sales of $4,016,000; sales for the year ending in July, 1984 were expected to exceed $490 million, with profits of over $30 million. Financial information for Magna is shown in Exhibit 3.7.

Power Motion was the only Magna company that produced electric motors for the automotive manufactures. Its products included powered radiators, heaters and air conditioner cooling fans for a broad range of vehicles. It was the largest production company within the electrical component division. Another of the division's firms, also based in London, produced similar motors for aftermarket suppliers. Many of its motor components were identical to those used by Power Motion, and the two companies often sourced these together. However, the less stringent reliability standards needed for aftermarket sales allowed the other company to use some relatively simple manufacturing techniques. The other small firms in the division made unrelated equipment such as instrument clusters and sensing devices or produced parts required for these end products. In addition, the division included some small companies that acted as research and development cells.

Exhibit 3.7 Power Motion Manufacturing Limited

FINANCIAL SUMMARY–MAGNA INTERNATIONAL INC. (Figures in $000 except those per share)

Year	1984	1983	1982	1981	1980	1979	1978	1977	1976	1975
Operations Data										
Sales	493,559	302,451	226,534	232,114	183,456	165,738	128,189	80,953	55,010	39,415
Income from operations	57,124	25,473	9,055	12,054	9,249	15,924	12,899	8,185	5,734	2,880
Net income	31,480	14,647	6,265	6,911	5,640	8,455	6,595	4,093	2,786	1,339
Extraordinary items	—	—	—	—	(1,922)	272	795	—	—	—
Earnings per share (after extraordinary items)	1.93	1.10	0.49	0.64	0.53	0.86	0.71	0.48	0.36	0.17
Depreciation	15,044	11,267	9,325	6,154	4,506	4,506	3,349	2,210	1,416	1,118
Cash flow from operations	55,945	32,522	14,604	12,052	15,275	15,275	13,160	7,542	5,171	2,757
Dividends per share	0.31	0.26	0.25	0.36	0.36	0.28	0.19	0.12	0.06	0.03
Financial Position										
Working capital	79,804	48,291	31,792	30,792	28,223	19,174	15,351	7,412	4,925	3,233
Capital expenditures	110,239	29,806	17,434	21,052	23,630	23,085	16,231	8,584	3,456	2,016
Fixed assets (less depreciation)	179,817	87,388	70,533	74,074	62,629	47,089	30,269	19,387	8,940	6,900
Long-term debt	49,708	42,159	55,554	56,308	45,830	30,441	19,588	10,238	4,627	4,578
Equity per share	8.43	5.59	4.13	3.84	3.35	3.18	2.41	1.68	1.25	0.90

Mr. Ebner and a small staff started Power Motion in 1978. Initially, they were based in the division headquarters, located in an industrial area adjacent to the city. The first production facilities were set up in a 1,100 square meter building adjoining the headquarters. Over the following six years, the plant had been expanded three times to a total area of 5,000 square meters. The current layout reflected this piecemeal growth. Old external walls divided the plant into four roughly equal parts and limited the company's ability to develop an efficient layout. (See Exhibit 3.8.) For example, to go from the administrative offices to the engineering area required cutting through the plant and the cafeteria or going outside and re-entering the building through another door.

Because of increased volume, the work force had grown rapidly and was approaching twice the size thought to be the ideal limit within Magna. Power Motion staff believed that their company was now the largest production unit within the corporation. (However, this assumption was based on a limited amount of information. Because of the desire to foster independence in the subsidiaries, there were few systems within Magna to provide communications among the unrelated small companies.) Management currently consisted of the general manager, a plant manager, and managers for production engineering and quality assurance, quality control, accounting and administration, and purchasing.

The company had grown rapidly through its success in designing, manufacturing, and selling a series of conventional direct-current electric motors. Among Power Motion's competitive advantages were high product quality and continual improvement of motor efficiency and quietness. With the auto makers growing recognition of the necessity for improved product quality, Power Motion's excellent quality record had helped to capture the ever-increasing market shares for its products.

Although the company had one basic design for its motors, each of the dozen major customers specified different variations. As a result, over 40 models were actually assembled. Most variations were minor (differing shaft lengths, types of bearings, or mounting brackets, and so forth) and most of the assembly operations were common to all models. The units ranged in price from about $8 to $12.

Magna's research and development strengths aided Power Motion in the engineering of new or improved designs. Power Motion paid management fees for product R&D performed by the Electrical Component Division's motor development company, but performed production process improvements itself. The company had developed considerable expertise in tool making and in analyzing process operations. The consequent process improvements and jig and fixture developments resulted in increased product quality and reduced cost.

Mr. Ebner was a firm supporter of Frank Stronach's philosophy. He believed that limited plant size enabled supervisors and managers to be more aware of what was going on, to know the employees better, and to communicate more effectively. In turn, the inherent informality of the smaller plant left employees at ease and willing to participate in solving production problems. Inevitable changes in work patterns and tasks were more readily accepted. A sense of "family" was actively promoted through the encouragement of employee social and sports activities. Mr. Ebner believed that as long as informal communication existed, the company could react promptly to sources of dissatisfaction in the work force.

Exhibit 3.8 Power Motion Manufacturing Limited

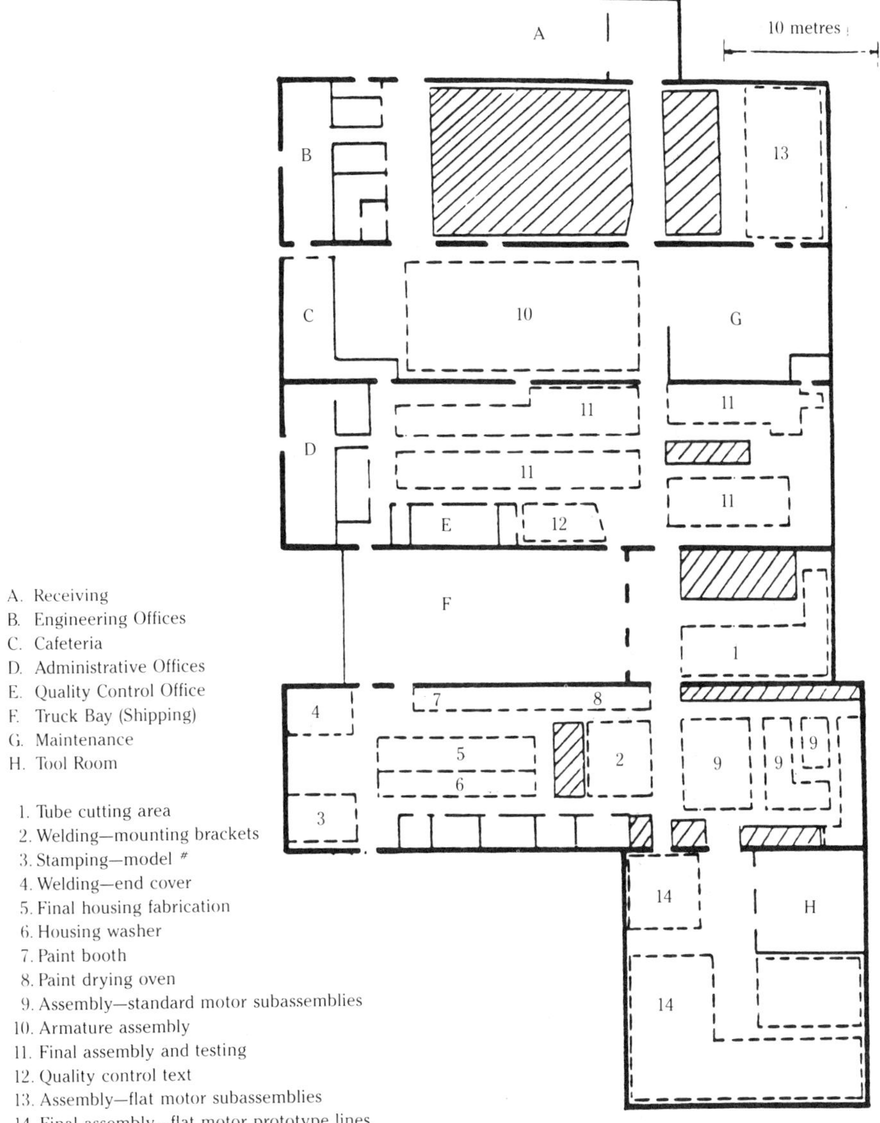

Hatching indicates areas used for storage of materials and work in process.

In keeping with the policy of maintaining a satisfied work force, the plant usually operated one shift, five days a week. Only when bottlenecks occurred or when a rush order was received would a crew work overtime or on a second shift. Mr. Ebner felt that quality suffered, supervisors were stressed, and communications were degraded when more than one shift was used.

THE AUTO PARTS INDUSTRY

For cost reasons, automobile manufacturers relied heavily on subcontracting for most of the components used in production vehicles. Although most manufacturers produced many of their parts themselves, they usually sought to have outside companies bid against their subsidiary suppliers.

If a sourced component was a standard item, the purchasing company usually dictated specifications and awarded contracts on the basis of the cost and quality of trial batches submitted by competing suppliers. However, when a component required considerable development by suppliers to create reasonable designs at acceptable prices, the auto maker was likely to enter into a cooperative arrangement with each potential supplier. The auto maker would provide technical assistance to establish each firm as a possible high-quality, low-cost producer of the component while the competing suppliers each tried to offer unique capabilities in an effort to establish a mutually beneficial relationship. The small supplier companies tended to be reactive, forced to try to meet the specifications dictated by the auto manufacturers. Larger firms, such as Magna or auto company subsidiaries, had the resources to develop new products or improve on specified designs in anticipation of customer needs. If these developments were successful, they gave the supplier the advantages of improving its position with the auto maker. It also provided a competitive edge because, in effect, the innovator established the standards for the particular component.

To insure supplier loyalty, the auto companies attempted to establish long-term relationships. To get continued support from an auto maker, each supplier was expected to show considerable "up front" commitment to the partnership. Typically, a supplier had to invest in a complete production facility, with significant technical and administrative expense, before that company would be considered even a potential source. As a result, the development process often started more than two years before a particular component would be required for the new model. If selected, a supplier would be notified of the manufacturer's intention to purchase a stated portion of the requirements for the component, usually for the following model year. When more than one supplier was selected, each could normally expect an equal proportion of the orders. If one supplier was substantially better in price or quality, however, the auto maker might allot it a larger share as an incentive to the others to improve. Frequently, the notice of intent to purchase was given shortly before the beginning of the automotive model year, which ran from August to July. Regardless of the stated purchase intentions, actual volumes ordered throughout the following year were dependent on the sales performance of the particular models that used the components. Depending on the performance of the suppliers throughout the year, the share of the volume that each was allotted might be altered, with the change announced shortly before the start of the next model year.

THE PRODUCTION PROCESS

Power Motion's manufacturing process was divided into four main operations (see Exhibit 3.9).

Exhibit 3.9 Power Motion Manufacturing Limited
Components of a Typical Standard Motor

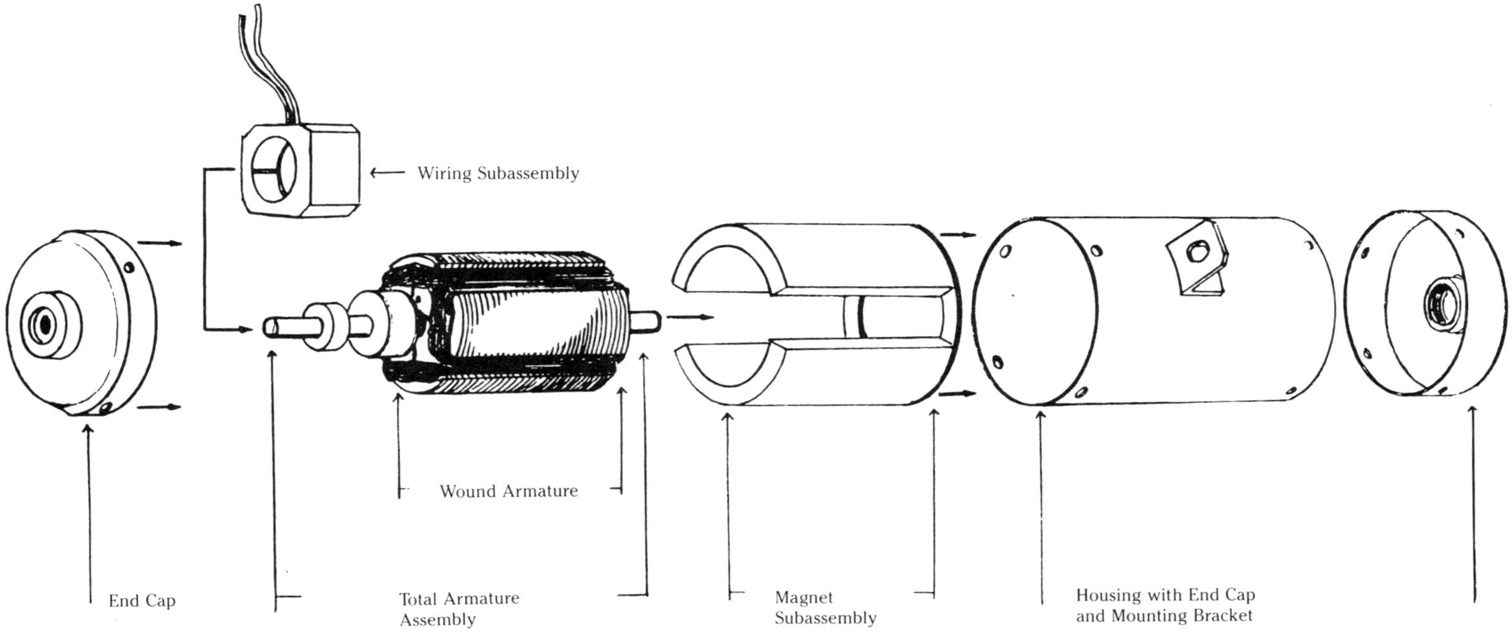

Wiring Subassembly

Wound Armature

End Cap

Total Armature Assembly

Magnet Subassembly

Housing with End Cap and Mounting Bracket

1. The motor's housing was fabricated from a section of a six-meter-long steel tube that was cut to length. External mounting brackets were then welded on. The tube section and stamped metal end covers had vent holes pierced in them. All pieces then had model numbers stamped on them.
2. The housing assembly and the end covers were washed, painted in a conveyorized spray painting system, and manually transferred to a drying oven.
3. The armature, the main internal motor component, was assembled and wound with wire on semiautomated equipment. Other shaft-mounted parts were then attached in an assembly line process.
4. The housing, the shaft-mounted assembly and other components were moved to final assembly. Here, magnet components were installed inside the housing, the shaft-mounted armature assembly and the wiring subassembly were inserted, and the end covers were attached. The completed motor was then tested and packed for shipping.

In a separate operation, bearings (which held the motor shafts in place) were installed inside the end caps and magnet and wiring subassemblies were produced for installation during final assembly. Conveyor belts moved each unit progressively through the assembly stations. Subassembly components were moved by cart between the main operation areas. Power Motion purchased stamped metal parts, electrical components and wiring, bearings, and machined pieces (such as motor shafts). Although many components were sourced from other Magna subsidiaries, the company was given complete freedom in its choice of suppliers.

The "intent to purchase" received prior to the beginning of the model year gave Power Motion an indication of the total annual volume expected for each motor model. However, no units were produced until purchase orders were received by mail or by telephone. Usually the orders specified volumes and required delivery times and were received three or four weeks in advance of the delivery dates. Order sizes were typically between 5,000 and 15,000 units. Power Motion purposely kept assembly lines flexible, a policy that put some limits on the amount of automation that could be used but one which allowed very rapid changes in production from one model to another. As a result, the order in which batches were produced or the size of a batch did not significantly affect operating efficiency. To minimize warehousing of finished goods, orders were normally scheduled to be completed as close as possible to delivery date.

The main constraint on scheduling was assembly capacity. Occasionally, rush orders were received less than a week before their required delivery dates and overtime became necessary to meet both the rush demand and the inflexible delivery commitments for the orders already scheduled.

As sales increased, production capacity had been further constrained by the emergence of a variety of bottlenecks. In some cases, the company's manufacturing engineers had improved a limiting operation by modifying machinery or automating some processes. However, recent bottlenecks had involved some automated equipment and in these cases, the only way to increase capacity had been to purchase duplicate machinery. Two such situations had arisen in the last few months when armature winding and dynamic balancing of the armature assemblies had reached capacity. Two new automated winding machines and a balancing machine had been ordered; these additions represented substantial increases to the company's manufacturing capital.

THE PRESENT CAPACITY CONSTRAINT

In a few months, once the new automated equipment on the armature assembly line was operating properly, the painting operation would become the main capacity constraint. Average production was currently running at about 7,500 motors per day; the paint booth could only handle about 5,000 housings per shift. As a result, the paint booth was operating on two shifts, with a daily capacity of 9,500–10,000 painted housings.

The existing painting capacity could not be expanded without utilizing three shifts. The painting area was cramped, limiting the options for increasing operator efficiency. An investigation had been conducted to see what equipment would be required to attain a capacity of 10,000 units per shift. It was found that such a system would normally be custom-made to suit the specific requirements. However, any painting system of that size would be too large to fit anywhere in the plant, because of the building's layout.

In addition, a system of the required size would need a larger washing system. The present site could not guarantee an adequate supply of water for a washing unit of the needed capacity. The plant was located beyond the city's water and sewage systems and it relied on its own wells and a septic tank. The company already trucked in water to meet peak demands. This requirement was likely to be constant if such a unit was installed. In addition, elaborate filtration and recirculation systems would have to be used to avoid overloading the sewage system.

THE FUTURE DEMAND

The company had been attempting to create a market for a new type of motor which the parent corporation's research and development staff had designed. The motor was flatter, quieter and more efficient than existing designs. The latest extension to the building, built in 1983, currently housed the prototype production facilities that were needed to carry out the preliminary marketing activities for the new motor. A prestigious European auto maker had already entered into negotiations with the company for the flat motors and Mr. Ebner anticipated that Power Motion would be asked to provide test batches within the next year. Small production volumes were likely to be ordered in the 1986 model year (beginning August, 1985), with possible regular production volumes of 1,500 to 2,000 per day starting the year after. He expected that the European sales would encourage the incorporation of the new type into North American-designed cars also. The flat motor design could be manufactured using the existing housing fabrication and painting operation sequences and equipment.

Mr. Ebner knew that the division's motor design engineers were also working on plans for another type of motor. This type used a recently developed material that was yet very difficult to source. Like the flat motor design, this type would require unique manufacturing procedures. Although actual production of this type was not likely for several years, it could eventually replace the standard design now being built by Power Motion.

Despite the recent plant extension, it now appeared that this last building expansion was likely to be inadequate for any growth into new lines. The company had now received its customers' purchase intentions for standard motors for the following year and Power Motion had been awarded larger shares of the projected requirements for several standard models. Total demand for all standard models was to increase by an average of 3,000 units per day, starting in August. Although there would be space for the prototype production line for flat motors, it was evident that full production of this type, plus the increased volume of standard motors, could not be housed in the existing plant.

THE ALTERNATIVES

Mr. Ebner realized that expanding the facilities this time would be a significantly larger step than the incremental changes that the plant had undergone to date. To meet the future demand for both the standard and flat motor lines, the fabrication, finishing and assembly operations all would have to be expanded. However, each of these operations had different factors that determined the best way to increase their capacity.

Some fabrication steps, such as housing fabrication, could be expanded through the addition of equipment similar to that already in use. Although such operations could be set up at more than one location, grouped, for example, to handle the different motor types, it would be more efficient to locate them centrally to handle all requirements. Armature winding and assembly, on the other hand, required unique operations for each motor type and little would be gained by grouping these activities.

Painting represented a different situation. Simple expansion of the existing system by adding equipment was not possible and replacing the existing facilities elsewhere was not attractive either. The discussions with equipment suppliers had indicated that the smallest installation that met quality, cost and automation objectives would have more than enough capacity to handle all of the company's projected painting needs. In fact, the capacity of such an installation would be great enough that Power Motion could consider offering paint services to other Magna plants.

For final assembly operations, a single expanded line per motor type was preferable, some significant labor economies could be achieved, and greater efficiencies through line balancing were possible.

These factors made one basic expansion approach infeasible. The idea of creating a second plant to handle the complete fabrication of new lines would require duplication of too many operations. Parallel, small scale housing fabrication and painting facilities made little sense. In addition, the construction of a plant designed for one type of motor that had no guaranteed customer was risky. For these reasons, the idea of building a plant specifically for the new types alone was quickly eliminated.

Moving all operations to a new site where better utilities were available would create the same problem as if the present plant were to be expanded—the size of the plant. A further problem posed by such a move was that the disruption of production by moving existing equipment to the new location would threaten Power Motion's ability to fill orders on time. One lost order could jeopardize all of its business with the affected customer.

If neither building new facilities for one of the lines nor relocating all operations was practical, a third alternative was to build new facilities for selected operations. If a new plant were to contain the main operations common to both motor types—the housing fabrication and painting—most of the remaining operations could be housed in the existing building.

With this alternative, Mr. Ebner saw two options. Power Motion could either expand through further building at the existing plant site, or build a second plant at a site where city utilities were avaialble. In either case, the new facility would contain the common operations and the full-scale flat motor assembly line. Here, all housings would be fabricated and painted. Those housings for standard motors would have magnet subassemblies and bearings installed, then would be sent to the existing plant. Flat motors would be completely assembled in the new plant, then sent to the existing facilities; with the first option, transport would be only a short distance, but with the second, it might be several kilometers from a site within the city limits.

Preliminary engineering studies indicated that the displaced operations would require an extension to the existing plant of 3,700 square meters of additional floor space or a remote facility of 6,500 square meters. Although the present site could accommodate the expansion, Mr. Ebner was very concerned about the potential problems with inadequate utilities and the risk that expanding at the present site would result in the work force becoming too large to maintain the "small company" atmosphere. Unless more operations could be automated, the number of plant employees under one roof was likely to exceed 200.

Mr. Ebner knew that there was a large industrial building site available within the city limits, about five kilometers from the plant. A facility built there would have access to the city's water and sewage systems. The site was also large enough to allow for considerable future expansion as well.

Whether Power Motion went with a one-plant or a two-plant scheme, Mr. Ebner wanted operations to be automated as much as possible and sized to have capacities adequate for the foreseeable future. With the painting and drying operations automated, he estimated that about 195 employees would be required for single-shift operation. (The only activity that would likely require second-shift operation was the tube cutting, the initial operation in housing fabrication. For this job, each of the two machines now working was capable of cutting approximately 3,000 sections per shift.) Under the two-plant scheme, about 125 people would be required for the activities in the new facility, the remainder staying at the existing plant. Of these 125, only the plant manager and a truck driver would not be needed if the decision was made to expand the existing plant to the same capacity.

Based on these guidelines, Mr. Ebner's staff estimated the investment needed for the two alternatives. The plant extension was likely to cost $600,000 for the building and services; new equipment would cost an additional $1.2 million. The second plant at a different location would cost about $1.6 million and would require the same investment for equipment plus an additional $700,000 for transportation and handling systems and for the duplication of some services and equipment already present at the existing plant.

Mr. Ebner knew that Magna relied very heavily on each general manager's judgment for operations decisions of this type. Because of Mr. Ebner's personal stake in the profitability of Power Motion, the parent company believed that his choice would best contribute to Power Motion's performance. As a result, any proposal that Mr. Ebner made to his division president was unlikely to be questioned. Financing would be arranged on request, using corporate funds channeled through the divisional head office. Either alternative was a large investment in Power Motion's terms. However, Magna had invested over $140 million in fixed assets over the past two years. Power Motion's expansion would therefore represent only a medium-sized project for the parent company and would probably not generate much comment at the corporate head office.

The expected volumes in the coming model year were likely to require more multiple-shift operation than had ever been used at Power Motion. Unless expansion was undertaken, the necessary two-shift operations in the 1986 model year would be unacceptably high. In order to have any plan implemented by August, 1985, Mr. Ebner realized that he would have to make his decision by September, 1984 to ensure that the work of planning, designing, equipment ordering and building construction could be carried out in time.

Chapter Four

MANAGING TECHNOLOGICAL INNOVATION

SITUATION 4.1

Digital Equipment Corporation

INTRODUCTION

Technical advances, especially in product development, often shape the evolution of an entire industry. There may be no better example than the computer industry, which has grown from a mere $45 million in 1952 to a mature industry of $11 billion in 1972!

To survive in this versatile industry, companies must be able to change constantly as the products evolve. Very few companies which began during the industry's growth stage are still in operation today. One company which was able to anticipate, plan and develop successfully throughout the evolution of the computer industry is Digital Equipment Corporation (DEC) and although it may only be 5 percent the size of IBM, DEC is the leader in the *minicomputer market,* with a net income of $23.5 million.

Rapid technological change during the 1960s contributed to the growth of competition and the growth of the market. The first generation computers used vacuum tubes, which were very bulky and costly and required great amounts of power. At this development stage, the market was basically confined to government applications with IBM, and Sperry-Rand dividing the business.

With the advent of the transistor, second generation computers became much smaller, faster and required less power. Computers also became less costly to build. IBM and Sperry-Rand were now joined by Burroughs, Honeywell, RCA, Philco, NCR, GE, and Control Data. But these improvements were quickly followed by the introduction of integrated circuits and silicon microchips. These two advances allowed manufacturers to produce computers that were still smaller, faster and even less expensive!

DIGITAL EQUIPMENT CORPORATION

Digital Equipment Corporation (DEC) designs, manufactures, sells and services minicomputers and associated computer accessories. The products are used in varying applications, from scientific research, education, and medical systems to industrial process controls. While DEC did not start as a "mini" manufacturer, it grew and developed into the leader of this segment to its present 45 percent market share.

DEC was founded in 1957 by Ken and Stanley Olsen, and Hurlan Anderson, who had let MIT's Lincoln labs to start their own company; building logical modules and test equipment. Since the cheapest computer at the time was about $1 million, Ken Olsen quickly perceived the need for a low-cost computer. He also realized the need for more user-friendly computers. At that time computers were used in a batch mode, meaning people would push their punch card through slots in the computer department door and would expect their results the next day.

While the research for low cost computers was being done, DEC had to start off its business selling logical modules to labs and engineers who would build their own equipment. At that time, DEC with 50 employees, badly needed financing for its computer research. This motivated the company to approach George Doriot of American Research and Development (ARD), who invested $70,000 to become the largest stockholder of DEC; an investment that in 1972 was worth $350 million.

In 1959, after years of development, DEC introduced its first computer, the PDP-1 (Programmable Digital Processor). The price tag was $120,000, yet DEC sold all the 53 machines it made to large laboratories and industrial users. By selling, and not leasing, which was the common practice at the time, DEC offered its customers only minimal support (in the way of software and service). This resource saving helped DEC fund computer reearch and development.

DEC's marketing was virtually nonexistent at this point; products were sold through salesmen/engineers and no advertising was done. Three years later, in 1962, DEC had developed and sold 50 PDP-4's; a cheaper version of the PDP-1. Like the PDP-1, the PDP-4 was also targeted to the scientific market and was still too expensive for many users.

The next step was for DEC to produce a cheaper, more affordable product. A shorter 12-bit word length and a smaller memory were the new features in DEC's PDP-5, the first minicomputer priced at $27,000. Until then, (while DEC's microcomputers were targeted to the scientific market), the end-users were not dependent on DEC for complete support. PDP-5 in effect had created its own niche, and now computers could reach a whole new market of potential customers.

CHANGING STRATEGY

This development required DEC to change its strategy and to expand out of the laboratory market and attract customers who would require much more support than before. In 1965, the new PDP's were introduced. The PDP-8 was four times faster and about two-thirds the price of the popular PDP-5.

Initially, PDP-8's were sold to scientific markets, but making some minor changes in the application programs allowed DEC to sell them to other users as well. With this realization, DEC began developing software packages, and specialized peripherals resulting in a computer system ready for special applications. Some of these systems included manufacturing systems (quality control, testing), typesetting, pulse-height analyzers for nuclear research and a radiation treatment planning system. Along with the special applications, DEC also expanded the PDP-8 family, through a number of different models. In 1972 there were over 13,000 PDP-8's installed worldwide, costing only about $4,000 each.

DEC soon realized that moving from the introduction stage to the growth/development stage in the minicomputer market required both a technical/performance differentiation from the growing number of competitors as well as increasing the importance of the marketing and service function.

In 1980 DEC introduced a major breakthrough with the PDP-11, with its Unibus feature. This feature allowed various combinations of memories and peripherals, to be used in any combination, giving consumers unlimited combination/applications. Orders for 200 machines were received within a week of the PDP-11's announcement!

Along with the introduction of the Unibus sysem, DEC began to develop its own peripherals (such as printers, disc systems, and terminals) which were previously subcontracted. This move allowed DEC to design products complementary to its new models and at the same time decrease the cost of manufacturing. Peripherals usually constitute up to 40 percent of the cost of a system, and in-house manufacturing reduces the cost to DEC which is carried onto the end users in this price-elastic market.

DEC's strategy has been to increase the money spent on software/peripheral (complementary) research and limit the development in hardware to evolutionary changes; which has been usually industry wide.

As previously mentioned, DEC's sales and service functions have become increasingly important with over 130 service offices worldwide. Traditionally, advertising, has not been an important factor in this market—for example, DEC spends only $4 million per year for advertisements in trade journals. Primarily, consumers "shop around" for a system incorporating their needs, evaluating alternatives on cost and reliability. DEC feels that with its dominance in the market and its manufaturing capabilities and efficiencies it will be able to remain on top. The company's philosophy on growth is: first, to do a quality job for the customers and the employees, and the growth comes automatically!

READING 4.1

The Discipline of Innovation[1]

Despite much discussion these days of the "entrepreneurial personality," few of the entrepreneurs with whom I have worked during the last 30 years had such personalities. But I have known many people—salespeople, surgeons, journalists, scholars, even musicians —who did have them without being the least bit "entrepreneurial." What all the successful entrepreneurs I have met have in common is not a certain kind of personality but a commitment to the systematic practice of innovation.

Innovation is the specific function of entrepreneurship, whether in an existing business, a public service institution, or a new venture started by a lone individual in the family kitchen. It is the means by which the entrepreneur either creates new wealth-producing resources or endows existing resources with enhanced potential for creating wealth.

SOURCES OF INNOVATION

There are, of course, innovations that spring from a flash of genius. Most innovations, however, especially the successful ones, result from a conscious, purposeful search for innovation opportunities, which are found only in a few situations.

Four such areas of opportunity exist within a company or industry:

Unexpected occurrences

Incongruities

[1]Peter F. Drucker, "The Discipline of Innovation." *Harvard Business Review*, May-June, pp. 67-72. © 1985 by the President and Fellows of Harvard College. Extracted with permission.

Process needs
Industry and market changes

Three additional sources of opportunity exist outside a company in its social and intellectual environment:

Demographic changes
Changes in perception
New knowledge

True, these sources overlap, different as they may be in the nature of their risk, difficulty, and complexity, and the potential for innovation may well lie in more than one area at a time. But among them, they account for the great majority of all innovation opportunities.

UNEXPECTED OCCURRENCES

Consider, first, the easiest and simplest source of innovation opportunity: the unexpected. In the early 1930s IBM developed the first modern accounting machine, which was designed for banks, but banks in 1933 did not buy new equipment. What saved the company—according to a story that Thomas Watson, Sr., the company's founder and long term CEO, often told—was its exploitation of an unexpected success: the New York Public Library wanted to buy a machine. Unlike the banks, libraries in those early New Deal days had money, and Watson sold more than 100 of his otherwise unsaleable machines to libraries.

Fifteen years later, when everyone believed that computers were designed for advanced scientific work, business unexpectedly showed an interest in a machine that could do payroll. Univac, which had the most advanced machine, spurned business applications. But IBM immediately realized it faced a possible unexpected success, redesigned what was basically Univac's machine for such mundane applications as payroll, and within five years became the leader in the computer industry, a position it has maintained to this day.

Unexpected successes and failures are such productive sources of innovation opportunities because most businesses dismiss them, disregard them, and even resent them. Corporate reporting systems further engrain this reaction, for they draw attention away from unanticipated possibilities. The typical monthly or quarterly report has on its first page a list of problems, that is, the areas where results fall short of expectations. Such information is needed, of course; it helps prevent deterioration of performance.

INCONGRUITIES

Alcan Industries was one of the great success stories of the 1960s because Bill Connor, the company's founder, exploited an incongruity in medical technology. The cataract operation is the world's third or fourth most common surgical procedure. During the last 300 years, doctors systematized it to the point that the only "old-fashioned" step left was the cutting of a ligament. Eye surgeons had learned to cut the ligament with complete success, but it was so different a procedure from the rest of the operation and so incompatible with it that they often dreaded it. It was incongruous.

Doctors had known for 50 years about an enzyme that could dissolve the ligament without cutting. All Connor did was to add a preservative to this enzyme that gave it a few months' shelf life. Eye surgeons immediately accepted the new compound, and Alcan found itself with a worldwide monopoly. Fifteen years later, Nestlé bought the company for a fancy price.

Such an incongruity within the logic or rhythm of a process is only one possibility out of which innovation opportunities may arise. Another source is incongruity between economic realities. For instance, whenever an industry has a steadily growing market but falling profit margins—as, say, in the steel industries of developed countries between 1950 and 1970—an incongruity exists. The innovative response: minimills.

PROCESS NEEDS

Around 1909, a statistician at the American Telephone & Telegraph Company projected two curves 15 years out: telephone traffic and American population. Viewed together, they showed that by 1920 or so every single female in the United States would have to work as a switchboard operator. The process need was obvious, and within two years, AT&T had developed and installed the automatic switchboard.

What we now call "media" also had their origin in two process need-based innovations around 1890. One was Mergenthaler's Linotype, which made it possible to produce a newspaper quickly and in large volume; the other was a social innovation, modern advertising, invented by the first true newspaper publishers, Adolph Ochs of the New York Times, Joseph Pulitzer of the New York World, and William Randolph Hearst. Advertising made it possible for them to distribute news practically free of charge, with the profit coming from marketing.

INDUSTRY AND MARKET CHANGES

Managers may believe that industry structures are obtained by the Good Lord, but they can—and often do—change overnight. Such change creates tremendous opportunity for innovation.

One of American business's great success stories in recent decades is the brokerage firm of Donaldson, Lufkin & Jenrette, recently acquired by the Equitable Life Assurance Society. DL&J was founded in 1961 by three young men, all graduates of the Harvard Business School, who realized that the structure of the financial industry was changing as institutional investors became dominant. These young men had practically no capital and no connections. Still, within a few years, their firm had become a leader in the move to negotiated commissions and one of Wall Street's stellar performers. It was the first to be incorporated and go public.

When an industry grows quickly—the critical figure seems to be in the neighborhood of a 40 percent growth rate over 10 years or less—its structure changes. Established companies, concentrating on defending what they already have, tend not to counterattack when a newcomer challenges them. Indeed, when market or industry structures change, traditional industry leaders again and again neglect the fastest growing market segments. New opportunities rarely fit the way the industry has always approached the market, defined it, or organized to serve it. Innovators therefore have a good chance of being left alone for a long time.

DEMOGRAPHIC CHANGES

Of the outside sources of innovation opportunity, demographics are the most reliable. Demographic events have known lead times; for instance, every person who will be in the American labor force by the year 2000 has already been born. Yet, because policy makers often neglect demographics, those who watch them and exploit them can reap great rewards.

The Japanese are ahead in robotics because they paid attention to demographics. Everyone in the developed countries around 1970 or so knew that there was both a baby bust and an education explosion going on; half or more of the young people were now staying in school beyond high school. Consequently, the number of people available for traditional blue-collar work in manufacturing was bound to decrease and become inadequate by 1990. Everyone knew this, but only the Japanese acted on it and they now have a 10 year lead in robotics.

Managers have known for a long time that demographics matter, but they have always believed that population statistics change slowly. In this century, however, they do not. Indeed, the innovation opportunities that changes in the numbers of people, and their age distribution, education, occupations, and geographic location make possible, are among the most rewarding and least risky of entrepreneurial pursuits.

CHANGES IN PERCEPTION

"The glass is half-full" and "the glass is half-empty" are descriptions of the same phenomenon but have vastly different meanings. Changing a manager's perception of a glass from half-full to half-empty opens up big innovation opportunities.

All factual evidence indicates, for instance, that in the last 20 years, American's health has improved at unprecedented speed—whether measured by mortality rates for the newborn, survival rates for the very old, the incidence of cancers (other than lung cancer), cancer cure rates, or other factors. Even so, collective hypochondria grips the nation. Never before has there been so much concern with health or so much fear about health. Suddenly everything seems to cause cancer or degenerative heart disease or premature loss of memory. The glass is clearly half-empty.

Rather than rejoicing in great improvements in health, Americans seem to be emphasizing how far away they still are from immortality. This view of things has created many opportunities for innovations: markets for new health foods, and for exercise classes and jogging equipment. The fastest growing new United States business in 1983 was a company that makes indoor exercise equipment.

A change in perception does not alter facts. It changes their meaning, though, and very quickly. It took less than two years for the computer to change from being perceived as a threat and as something only big businesses would use to something one buys for doing income tax. Economics do not necessarily dictate such a change; in fact, they may be irrelevant. What determines whether people see a glass as half-full or half-empty is mood rather than fact, and change in mood often defies quantification. But it is not exotic or intangible. It is concrete. It can be defined. It can be tested. And it can be exploited for innovation opportunity.

NEW KNOWLEDGE

Among history-making innovations, those based on new knowledge—whether scientific, technical, or social—rank high. They are the superstars of entrepreneurship; they get the publicity and the money. They are what pepole usually mean when they talk of innovation, though not all innovations based on knowledge are important. Some are trivial.

Knowledge-based innovations differ from all others in the time they take, in their casualty rates, and in their predictability, as well as in the challenges they pose to entrepreneurs. Like most superstars, they can be temperamental, capricious, and hard to direct. They have, for instance, the longest lead time of all innovations. There is a protracted span between the emergence of new knowledge and its distillation into usable technology. Then, there is another long period before this new technology appears in the marketplace in products, processes, or services. Overall, the lead time involved is something like 50 years, a figure that has not shortened appreciably throughout history.

Binary arithmetic; Charles Babbage's conception of a calculating machine in the first half of the nineteenth century; the punch card, invented by Herman Hollerith for the U.S. Census of 1890; the audion tube, an electronic switch invented in 1906; symbolic logic, which was created between 1910 and 1913 by Bertrand Russell and Alfred North Whitehead; and the concepts of programming and feedback that came out of abortive attempts during World War I to develop effective antiaircraft guns. Although all the necessary knowledge was available by 1918, the first operational computer did not appear until 1946.

Long lead times and the need for convergence among different kinds of knowledge explain the peculiar rhythm of knowledge-based innovation, its attractions, and its dangers. During a long gestation period, there is a lot of talk and little action. Then, when all the elements suddenly converge, there is tremendous excitement and activity and an enormous amount of speculation.

It may be difficult, but knowledge-based innovation can be managed. Success requires careful analysis of the various kinds of knowledge needed to make an innovation possible.

Careful analysis of the needs and, above all, the capabilities of the intended user is also essential. It may seem paradoxical, but knowledge-based innovation is more market dependent than any other kind of innovation.

De Havilland, a British company, designed and built the first passenger jet airplane, but it did not analyze what the market needed and therefore did not identify two key factors. One was configuration—that is, the right size with the right payload for the routes on which a jet would give an airline the greatest advantage. The other was equally mundane: how the airlines could finance the purchase of such an expensive plane. Because De Havilland failed to do an adequate user analysis, two American companies, Boeing and Douglas, took over the commercial jet aircraft industry.

PRINCIPLES OF INNOVATION

Purposeful, systematic innovation begins with the analysis of the sources of new opportunities. Depending on the context, sources will have different importance at different times. Demographics, for instance, may be of little concern to innovators in fundamental industrial processes like steel making, although Mergenthaler's Linotype machine became successful primarily because there were not enough skilled typesetters available to satisfy a mass market. By the same token, new knowledge may be of little relevance to someone innovating a social instrument to satisfy a need that changing demographics or tax laws have created. But, whatever the situation, innovators must analyze all opportunity sources.

Because innovation is both conceptual and perceptual, would-be innovators must also go out and look, ask, and listen. Successful innovators use both the right and left sides of their brains. They look at figures. They look at people. They work out analytically what the innovation has to be to satisfy an opportunity. Then they go out and look at potential users to study their expectations, their values, and their needs.

To be effective, an innovation has to be simple and it has to be focused. It should do only one thing; otherwise it confuses people. Indeed, the greatest praise an innovation can receive is for people to say: "This is obvious! Why didn't I think of it? It's so simple!" Even the innovation that creates new users and new markets should be directed toward a specific, clear, and carefully designed application.

Effective innovations start small. They are not grandiose. They try to do one specific thing. It may be to enable a moving vehicle to draw electric power while it runs along rails, the innovation that made possible the electric streetcar. Or it may be the elementary idea of putting the same number of matches into a matchbox (it used to be 50). This simple notion made possible the automatic filling of matchboxes and gave the Swedes a world monopoly on matches for half a century. By contrast, grandiose ideas for things that will "revolutionize an industry" are unlikely to work.

In fact, no one can foretell whether a given innovation will end up a big business or a modest achievement. But even if the results are modest, the successful innovation aims from the beginning to become the standard setter, to determine the direction of a new technology or a new industry, to create the business that is—and remains—ahead of the pack. If an innovation does not aim at leadership from the beginning, it is unlikely to be innovative enough.

Above all, innovation is work rather than genius. It requires knowledge. It often requires ingenuity. And it requires focus. There are clearly people who are more talented as innovators than others but their talents lie in well-defined areas . Indeed, innovators rarely work in more than one area. For all his systemic innovative accomplishments, Edison worked only in the electrical field. An innovator in financial areas, Citibank for example, is not likely to embark on innovations in health care.

In innovation as in any other endeavor, there is talent, there is ingenuity, and there is knowledge. But when all is said and done, what innovation requires is hard, focused, purposeful work. If diligence, persistence, and commitment are lacking, talent, ingenuity, and knowledge are of no avail.

There is, of course, far more to entrepreneurship than systematic innovation: distinct entrepreneurial strategies, for example, and the principles of entrepreneurial management, which are needed equally in the established enterprise, the public service organization, and the new venture. But the very foundation of entrepreneurship—as a practice and as a discipline—is the practice of systematic innovation.

READING 4.2

Why Innovations Fail[2]

"It was," said William Holden as the business executive in the movie *Executive Suite*, "just one attempt in a hundred to make one improvement in a hundred." The "it" was a new molding process which would presumably have improved the Tredway Corporation's furniture line. Unfortunately, a key production test failed and the innovation was delayed. A failure of technology? Perhaps. But Holden felt that the test might have succeeded had he been there to make a key management decision rather than cooling his heels in the board room waiting for a hastily called meeting. A failure of management, then? Either way it would have been called an innovation failure in the real industrial world.

The failure rate for industrial innovations is high. One study found that although the rate varies among industries and companies, on the average "it takes some 58 ideas to yield one successful new product." The vast majority of ideas fail at the outset: only 10 or 12 percent of the ideas submitted for initial screening and analysis enter the development pipeline toward commercialization.

What does this high failure rate mean? Is it simply evidence that the competitive battle insures the survival of only the fittest innovations? Or does it represent a waste of potentially useful products and therefore of scarce industrial resources? Whatever the hypothesis, such a high rate of failure calls for an effort to understand its causes. With that understanding, management can better steer its product innovations around the barriers to successful commercialization.

We conducted a study of 200 innovations that passed initial screenings but failed after entering the commercialization pipeline for the Denver Research Institute, under

[2]Adapted for length from S. Myers and E. E. Sweezy, "Why Innovations Fail." *Technology Review*, March/April, pp. 43–47. © 1978. Reprinted with permission.

the auspices of the National Science Foundation. Our results confirmed some of managements' fondly held convictions, but exploded some others:

- The greatest risk is still the marketplace. Uncontrollable market factors scuttle more new products and processes than anything else—27.5 percent of the innovations studied. Yet management often plunges ahead without trying hard enough to minimize that risk.
- Limited sales potential blocked 16 percent of the new products studied. Better research to identify new markets would help here, as would a stronger national economy. In a sagging economy, innovations start slowly and succeed with difficulty—even with good market research, shrewd management, and all the technology in the world. A booming economy, on the other hand, spurs innovation by generating the new demand that drives the innovation process.
- The inability to find buyers for somethinig developed in the public interest—a large market problem that management is often criticized for avoiding—blocked 10 percent of the innovations surveyed. Even though managers sometimes let philanthropy overwhelm good sense in choosing which innovation to develop.
- Poor management accounted for 23.5 percent of the innovations that were cancelled, shelved, or inordinately delayed. Not surprising perhaps, but disturbing—over one-third of the management errors involved market factors which management could have controlled.

MANAGEMENT ERRORS—TOO MANY "GOOFS"

Whether pulled by the market or not, too many innovations fail because of management errors that seem preventable. And too many of these errors are simply "goofs"—forgetting to do the obvious. For example, one firm spent a good deal of money to develop a special welding torch for use in repairing automobile bodies. Not one was sold. Puzzled, management representatives visited potential customers to find out why. Only then did they learn the torch could not be used on the auto body with the upholstery already in place. The torch would have been a fire hazard. Obviously, management could have avoided this failure had it checked with its potential customers before developing such a product.

In sum, failures of management and marketing together accounted for half of the 20 innovations in the sample that faltered or failed. Yet, we also find from the data that management does a good initial job of screening many innovations that would obviously fail later on:

- Only 9 percent of the innovations studied were stopped in the marketplace because the company was unable to find a market for them. Fragmented markets undoubtedly pose a larger problem, but they usually surface at the project selection stage when management can simply reject the proposed innovation.
- About 7 percent of the innovations were blocked by competition. Here, too, if management sees an overcrowded market ahead, the proposed innovation is rejected before it is developed.
- Management also tends to reject would-be products or processes obviously susceptible

> to patent and antitrust problems. Factors arising from patent and antitrust laws accounted for stopping only 3 and 2.5 percent (respectively) of the innovations studied. In short, management takes a most conservative approach which usually avoids problems that can be spotted at the outset.

Management succeeds in anticipating some types of market and legal problems, but its performance with respect to capital and technology is poor. Some 11.5 percent of our sample were adversely affected by technology, and one-quarter of these innovations stopped for technological reasons were, in effect, "scooped" by another company's superior technical approach which management had failed to anticipate.

Money was a problem for companies of all sizes, but to less of an extent than expected: management's estimates of the capital required to complete the innovation process are usually too low; lack of capital halted 15.5 percent of the blocked innovations. The costs of pilot plant, installation and changeover often overrun—so often that overruns accounted for almost one-third of the innovations blocked for capital-related reasons.

WHERE THE TROUBLE STARTS

Innovations are weeded out little by little until they enter the pilot test stage, where many more of them falter or fail entirely. Almost three quarters of the innovations entering the development pipeline made it all the way into pilot test before management decided to call a halt. Indeed, more innovations—23 percent—fail in the pilot test stage than in any other. Tht second largest number of innovations—19 percent—are stopped in the final and most expensive phase, production installation. Management must seriously consider the cost implications for companies when innovations pass the inexpensive early stages only to expire later. It is remarkable that 84 percent of all innovations in the sample continued to be funded beyond the low-cost phases of assessment and initiation—the stages where common sense dictates that products less likely to succeed should be screened out.

LEARNING FROM FAILURE

To learn how, where, and why innovations actually run into trouble, we asked management officials who were directly involved in specific failures to tell us the story of what happened. Our respondents generally were the corporations presidents, vice presidents in charge of research and development, or heads of research and development divisions within the corporations attempting the innovations who personally made the tough decisions to cancel, shelve, or delay the innovations in question.

Memories were surprisingly sharp on the details of what happened, even down to the fine points. Once an innovation is funded, the decision to drop it seems sufficiently wrenching to be remembered by those involved. In any event, while managers tended to be hazy about how an innovation was started, they were very clear about how it ended.

Our respondents' stories were straightforward enough to be classified easily into the five broad categories: market, management, capital, technology, and laws and regulations. They also yielded additional lessons for innovators. For example:

- The search for the capital necessary to develop an innovation through the marketing phase may end in a "Catch 22." One company developed a new diagnostic x-ray machine with government research and development funding. Before the machine could be produced in marketable form, extensive field trials were required. Government funds could not be used to conduct such trials, and other possible suppliers of capital were unresponsive because marketability had not been demonstrated by available data—which could be obtained only through field tests. (The barrier in this case was classified as capital.)
- A superior competing technological approach may cancel the development of a new product or process. A major metals company undertook the development of vacuum deposition of aluminum as a substitute for tin plate in cans and other containers. The process was developed through completion of a full-scale, high-speed production line—which never went into full production because the firm discovered that chrome plate was much cheaper and just as good. The entire production line for aluminum production remains mothballed by the firm. (The barrier in this case was classified as technology.)
- The public interest often fails to express itself in the marketplace. A major supplier of automobile components tried to introduce an antiskid brake-control system for passenger vehicles. The firm carried the project almost to the production phase but was unable to arouse enough public interest in voluntary adoption of the system to market it. (The barrier in this case was classified as market.)
- Lack of technical capabilities in the staff of a firm may delay the solution of a technical problem for so long that a project loses its competitive advantage by the time it becomes marketable. One firm developed some prototype engines using a piezo-electric ignition system but sold the rights to the system to another firm. The second firm had to solve some technical (noise and time-delay) problems before the system could be marketed. Because the lack of technical expertise ate into time, when the system was finally ready, the market was no longer exclusive; the opportunity to achieve economies through large-scale production techniques was lost. The product was withdrawn after the costly, two-year delay; new techniques were used to develop an acceptable low-cost ignition system. (The barrier in this case was classified as management.)
- The assumption that an innovation will violate antitrust regulations may prevent its development. A medium-sized steel company developed a process for reclaiming zinc and iron by processing pelletized dust recovered from scrubbers of exhaust gases. The quality and quantity of the zinc by-product made the process look economically promising at the pilot-plant stage, if sufficient tonnage of reclaimed dust could be obtained. This would require access to more than one plant. When a joint venture with other steel companies was explored as a feasible basis for full-scale operation, however, the objection was raised that such a venture would violate antitrust laws. The process has not been developed further in spite of its economic and ecological advantages—although the requisite joint venture might or might not violate antitrust laws: the Department of Justice will not provide this information until the process is in operation! (The barrier in this case was classified as regulatory.)

HOW TO SAVE THE GOOD ONES

The process of innovation is Darwinian, and not all innovations deserve to survive. Our respondents, therefore, were asked to judge, in a broad economic sense, whether the innovation was still "good" or "not good" in view of the events that led to its blocking. For example, although management's judgments were necessarily subjective, they were strong; when several respondents commented on the same innovation, they almost always agreed as to whether the innovation was "good" or "not good."

Ninety-two of the 200 innovations that faltered were judged by management to be ideas well worth saving. (All the innovations mentioned previously were judged to be good ones, except for the two blocked either by technology or market factors.) To save the promising innovations, management should, of course, pay more attention to factors that block "good" rather than "not good" innovations. So it is important to note that management error and government regulations accounted for 28 and 20 percent, respectively, of the 92 "good" innovations that ran into trouble. The data clearly indicate:

- Managers can save many good innovations by doing a better job of management, particularly by asking the right questions at the right time.
- Managers should press government to overhaul the regulatory processes that block so many good innovations. Government administrators could ease this problem without necessarily addressing the substantive issues of regulation—although the latter may be most desirable. For example, the government could provide advisory guidance concerning the applicability of a regulation and the means by which the items in question could be adapted to meet regulatory requirements. In the absence of such advice, firms often discover too late that their innovations must be adapted expensively to meet regulatory requirements which had been "incorrectly" interpreted.

The data also show that few, if any, innovations might be saved by loosening the federal government's stringent standards, tough tests, and so forth—most of which, in any event, are meant in the public interest. The obvious conclusion is that management should not waste its time lobbying for less stringent regulations.

While managers may hope for the unsnarling of the regulatory process and companies may lobby for simpler controls, a more pressing task for industry is to examine its own practices. These are immediately controllable. Industrial managers who do this will see obvious mistakes that could have been avoided by asking seemingly trivial questions. Does the innovation have a clearly designated manager? Are staff capabilities matched to the innovation tasks? Is the cost analysis adequate? And so on. Obvious as these questions are, management often forgets to ask them until it is too late.

The real problem is to design and adopt a system that forces management to ask the right questions at the right time. Management systems with built-in forced questioning would perform two major functions:

- They remind management to do the things that are so obvious that they are easily forgotten.

- They force an appraisal of the assumptions and ideologies that underlie every innovation. It is a rare organization whose commonly held beliefs need never be examined, and such scrutiny is the task of management.

Another good way to get the right questions asked at the right time is to broaden the membership of product development teams to include people from outside the organization. Whatever their technical qualifications, such people may be perceptive enough to sense what is missing or assumed, and disinterested enough to blow the whistle on innovations which are going to falter or fail.

EPILOGUE

Managing Innovations and Technology

As global markets become more competitive, companies wishing to remain successful will be forced to adapt. One of the main tools for this adaptation is product/process innovation. Yet many companies still consider innovations as unpredictable, happenstance occurrences in the corporate R&D lab. All too few realize that to capitalize on its innovative capabilities, a company must manage the process of innovation, much as it manages its other operations.

The first step in managing the innovation process is to conduct an "innovative capabilities audit," both at the corporate and business unit levels, to address the formulation and implementation of potential innovation strategies. These strategies are summarized in Exhibit 4.1.

Exhibit 4.1 A Summary of Political Innovation Strategies

Business Unit Level

- Timing of market entry with new products/services and/or production/delivery systems.
- Technological leadership/followership in new products/services, and/or production/delivery systems.
- Scope of innovativeness in product/market portfolio.
- Rate of innovativeness in particular categories of products/services and/or production/delivery systems.

Corporate Level

- Scope and rate of development of new product/service and/or production/delivery systems that are derived from combining innovative capabilities across existing business units.
- Scope and rate of new business development based on corporate technology development efforts.
- Timing of entry with respect to the above.

The innovative capabilities audit should give a company a starting point, and a direction, for innovation. The challenge then becomes to apply a conscious, controlled discipline to an inherently and traditionally undisciplined operation.

While there are occasionally innovations that are literally "stumbled across," a company cannot rely on this in the long term. Innovation should be purposeful, systematic and begin with a rational analysis of opportunities. As such, analysis of areas of opportunity for innovation is appropriate.

Conceptually, there are four such areas within a company or an industry:

- Unexpected occurrences
- Incongruities
- Process needs
- Industry and market changes

There are also three note sources of opportunity, in the company's social and intellectual environment:

- Demographic changes
- Changes in perception
- New knowledge

To take advantage of opportunities in these areas, companies must study the market and its needs and values, and then determine what is required from within to successfully respond. Firms that attempt to innovate without explicit consideration of these factors leave much to chance, and risk the waste of time and resources developing ineffective or inappropriate innovations.

Further prerequisites to successful innovation include raw talent, ingenuity, and knowledge. However, these must be complemented by diligent, focused, purposeful work, or else any innovation-based strategy will simply be based on luck.

Clearly then, the process of innovation is a difficult one for firms. Several studies have been done in an attempt to determine what factors within this process are the major cause of failure, in order to give firms a focal point for improvement. One revealed four major causes of innovation failure. They are:

1. The marketplace—uncontrollable market variables which increase the risk of a project and are often overlooked by management caused 27.5 percent of the failures.
2. Poor management—innovations that were cancelled, shelved or inordinately delayed by management without proper cause accounted for 23.5 percent of the sample.
3. Limited sales potential—the market acceptance was often not sufficiently evaluated in assessing projects in the early stages. 16 percent of the projects were blocked at some stage by the realization that the sales potential of the innovation was not sufficient.
4. Inability to find buyers—10 percent of the innovations in the survey were stymied by the inability to find actual buyers of something that was (supposedly) developed in the public interest.

These difficulties point to the need for a formal innovation planning and control system. Ideally, these systems should screen out poor ideas early, and force managers to consider the realities of the marketplace and make the difficult business decision to drop a project when the potential is poor. In this way, a more organized approach minimizes both the chance that poor ideas are conceived, and more importantly the chance that valuable corporate resources are inappropriately allocated to poor projects.

CASE 4.1

Northern Telecom Canada Limited: Harmony (B)[3]

The atmosphere in the office of the Harmony project manager Northern Telecom's Station Apparatus Division (SAD)[4] plant was tense. Jim Retallack's weekly meeting with project staff was due to begin in less than an hour, and Retallack was only half-way through the stack of progress reports and milestone sheets piled on his desk. Jim rapidly scanned each report, looking for critical information to help him gauge the stage of completion of each component of the total project.

The Harmony telephone was slated to be in full production in eight months, and Retallack was determined to meet that deadline. In the face of criticism from some detractors, Jim wondered if he should be doing something differently in order to complete the project on time and under budget. As he scrutinized the reports, he thought, "I'm certain that project teams are the best way to organize . . . but how can I make team efforts more integrated, more productive?"

Retallack was aware that differences of opinion existed among certain members of the 10 working groups (teams) which constituted the Harmony project staff. Many urgent issues were awaiting his immediate decision, including the thorny problem of whether to build or buy the Electret transmitter. The Harmony project would significantly affect the lives and livelihoods of many plant employees.

HARMONY'S HISTORY

Doug Clark, new product manager for the division, had been named acting eBasic project manager 15 months earlier by Alan Lutz, general manager of the plant. (The eBasic name—"e" for electronic—was used to identify the new basic residential telephone prior

[3]This case was prepared by Eileen D. Watson under the direction of Professor James C. Rush. © 1987, The Unviersity of Western Ontario.

[4]The name of the division was changed to Telecom Terminals Division (TTD).

to the creation of the "Harmony" name.) The project involved building the Harmony prototype and manufacturing the finished product. Automated manufacturing and assembly processes were assumed from the beginning.

Clark became the driving force behind extensive market research which was used to formulate NTC's strategy vis-à-vis the new product:

> To design, develop and introduce a new family of high quality electronic single-line telesets which will be low cost, have wide consumer appeal, have high volume sales, employ flexible, common technologies and manufacturing processes, have low labor content, and be introduced by January 1984 for global rollout.

As a result of intensive study and research by Clark and other key staff, the best design was chosen for the first member of the family. This was the Harmony telephone, a basic residential set. It was to be the first of the complete eBasic (800) line of Northern Telecom products, which would also include a partially featured residential telephone (Signature), a basic business telephone (Unity I), and a featured business telephone (Unity II). It was proposed that Harmony be in production by November 1983, for introduction in January 1984.

Corporate approval had to be sought for the recommended expenditure of $12 million in additional research and development and capital investment. At first, the corporation questioned the project. For an organization which for two decades had mainly concerned itself for one basic model, the idea of a massive change from a serial, technology based, product development process to an iterative, market-focused integrated team approach was greeted with skepticism by some. Also, many engineers tended to believe that NTC should be in the switching business, not the terminal business.

Other objections were raised: the product was wrong; the market had been improperly read; basic phones were not needed; sales projections were too optimistic; other sets (Contempora) would be cannibalized; the London plant would be unable to deliver on time; the product would cost too much; and the project did not fit the corporate strategy.

Within the plant itself, morale was low—"doom and gloom" prevailed. Concerns were expressed about probable effects of automation on the 1,300-member work force. The union executive was concerned about new manufacturing processes that might adversely affect experienced workers, and which surely would reduce the number of jobs available.

The proposal finally was accepted on the basis of establishing a cost-effective manufacturing process for all NTC terminals. The project was given a "do or die" mandate. Lack of success at any stage ultimately could result in plant closure, affecting 1,300 employees.

Official approval had the effect of silencing objections inside and outside the London plant. When it was made clear to workers and management alike that the only alternative to introducing new products and manufacturing processes was to close down the London operation entirely, the union and management agreed to work together toward a successful Harmony launch. The plant would continue producing the old 500 line throughout the developmental period for the new model.

STAFFING THE PROJECT

Doug Clark, acting project manager, brought engineering manager Jim Baker on board shortly after his own appointment. Controller Kathy Flanagan and technology manager M. Alikhan were added later, completiong the core group of four.

When official approval of the project seemed only a matter of time, general manager Alan Lutz was considering going outside the plant to hire a full-time project manager. He talked with Jim Retallack (a Ph.D. in Electrical Engineering who was working at BNR in Ottawa) about the job. Retallack recalled the circumstances of his move to the London plant:

> After three and a half years in R&D, I wanted to broaden my experience in the business side of NTC, and to get some production under my belt. I called the general manager in London, to tell him I was interested in moving—he and I had talked together in the past. The outcome of this was an interview with Al, and an offer to head up the Harmony project team!
>
> As I thought about the opportunity, I sought the advice of John Roth, then president of BNR and former general manager in London. He suggested, "If you think you can succeed at the job, you should do it." So, I wound up my Ottawa job in a month or so, and arrived in London early in December.

Retallack immediately began a campaign to establish the definition of the Harmony project team as a unique, high-status group composed of dedicated people with exceptional talent and motivation. One of his first acts was to acquire separate office space reserved for the use of the Harmony project group only. He was successful in commandeering an area which came to be known throughout the plant as the "eBasic office."

He got to know the people already assigned to the Harmony project, and came to appreciate the initial personnel selection. Divisional general manager Al Lutz had put new people into positions of responsibility; and Doug Clark and Jim Baker had handpicked the best group of "maverick nonconformists" they could find within the division. They felt that special talents and skills were needed for such a unique and innovative project.

Speaking about his early days in his new position, Jim Retallack recalled:

> My first week on the job, I attended an important value analysis session where we discussed a significant cost reduction. We were talking $20.00 minimum to $27.00 maximum to produce Harmony—almost 60 percent less than the old basic 500 set. It seemed to me that $23.000 was the number to shoot at.
>
> And I relied heavily on Doug in the beginning—so much so, that I was only there

for a short time before I took off for six weeks of previously scheduled vacation. Some people never quite figured out how I could do that . . . but I had made a point of working with them quite intensively before I went away.

ORGANIZATIONAL STRUCTURE

Al Lutz made it clear from the beginning that the new project manager was to be given people and resources from other departments who would be dedicated to the Harmony project full-time as required. (See Exhibit 4.2 for a partial divisional organization chart.) Jim was to have the freedom and the authority to structure every aspect of the project his way. Talking about his early impressions of the organization already in place when he arrived, Retallack said:

The financial and marketing aspects seemed to be in good shape when I took over—I needed only to ensure that Clark and Flanagan and their people were kept informed

Exhibit 4.2 Managing Change at NTC(B): Team Play Partial Organizational Chart, SAD Plant

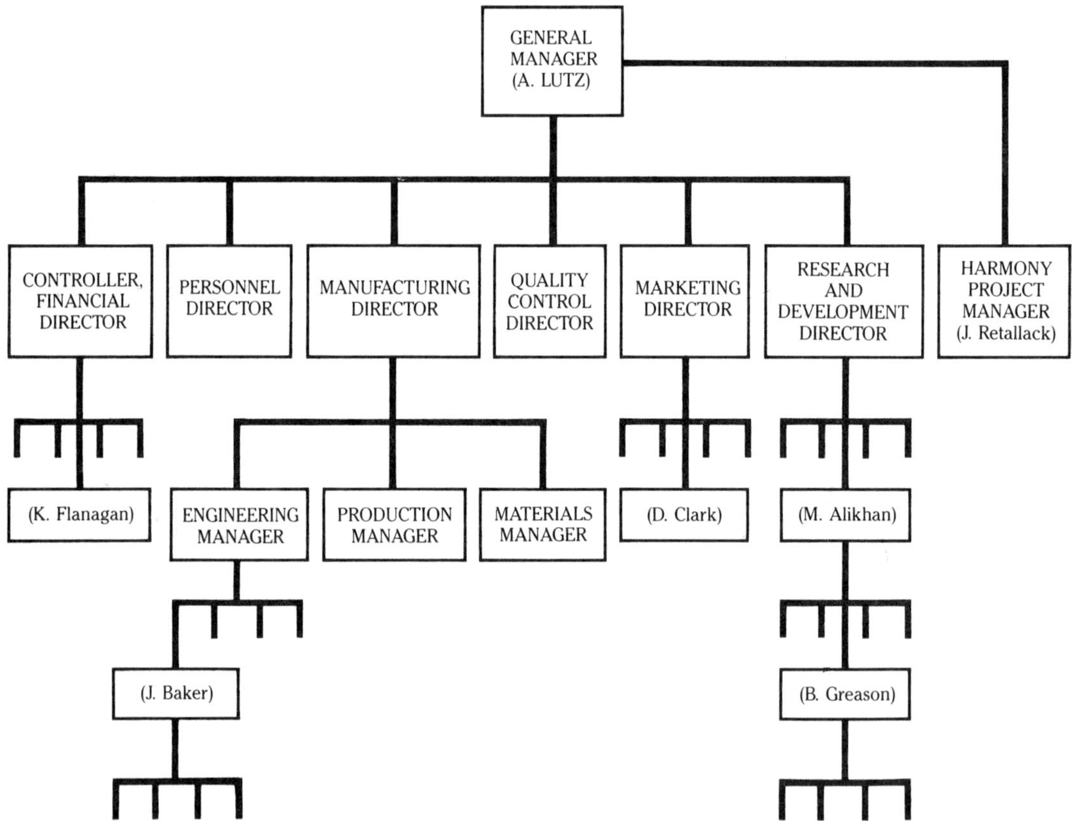

and involved. Alikhan had just come on board, replacing the former design head; and both he and Baker had chosen excellent people for their teams starting with Jim's key man, Jim Kilpatrick. However, I felt that their functionaL roles should be more sharply focused, making for greater accountability and increased effectiveness.

Retallack believed that, in order to design and develop every component and complete the final assembly simultaneously within severe time and cost constraints, cross-functional teams were necessary. So, responsibility for product development was broken down among 10 teams, each comprising technology (design) and manufacturing (engineering) people (see Exhibit 4.3). Test staff, quality control, and materials control people were to be added later, as needed.

Exhibit 4.3 Managing Change at NTC(B): Team Play

HARMONY TEAM CHART

Project Manager:	Jim Retallack
Manufacturing/Engineering Manager:	Jim Baker
Design/Technology Manager:	M. Alikhan
Controller:	Kathy Flanagan

Team	Responsible for	
	Design	Manufacturing
1. Base and Housing Assembly	Kuhfus Charchanko	McGowan
2. Circuit Board	Turner	Darling
3. Alerter	Hayward	McGowan
4. Keypad	Kuhfus	Neate
5. Line Switch	Walker	Kilpatrick Romano
6. Jacks	Walker	McAlpine
7. Cords	Walker	McAlpine
8. Handset Assembly	Kuhfus	Robinson
9. Transmitter	Gumb Freeman	Foster
10. Receiver	Freeman	Foster

Each team was responsible for one key component of the product, and for meeting the following objectives:

1. Developing a reliable design that could be manufactured within cost objectives.
2. Maintaining a close liaison with other cross-functional teams.

3. Maintaining close liaison with marketing, quality control, production control, and purchasing.
4. Producing a design that would lend itself to automation.

Retallack's strategy was to nail down a well thought out, uncomprising structure and comprehensive reporting system. He said:

> To get the product to market quickly on time and on budget means getting it right the first time! I know we can do it. . . but it's going to take a lot of discipline, and strong control and leadership from the top.

Jim was aware of the strength of his position as a dedicated full-time project manager reporting directly to the general manager. He thought it was advantageous that he has been brought in from outside the plant, so he had no prior reputation in the plant to contend with. "However," Jim remarked, "it helps that the common assumption is that I am a good personal friend of Al Lutz, a popular and competent GM. This isn't the case; but I'll never tell that to anyone!"

Jim believed that effective management of change was critical to the project's success. He felt that a key success factor was having superior personnel on the Harmony team, representing the major functions. About half of the team members were dedicated to the Harmony project; but Jim remarked, "I had to fight very hard with some other guys to keep these people dedicated. Some other managers tried to steal them back; and I could not allow that to happen."

Negative reactions to various aspects of the project were being expressed by skeptical directors throughout the division, including a few members of the existing Harmony team. As one manager recalled, "We had many nonbelievers in our midst." Retallack faced a severe attitude problem—"Here's another new boy—he'll soon learn! Harmony will never be completed on time, and costs will escalate out of sight."

REPORTING PROCEDURES

From the beginning of his tenure, Retallack insisted on a strict reporting schedule involving report forms, regular meetings, sign-off procedures, memos, work orders, and other means of tracking the progress of every Harmony component toward completion. Initially, each team was asked to produce a detailed schedule of the tasks or steps required to develop and source their assigned component (see Exhibit 4.4). These steps were then listed on the team's "milestone chart," giving planned start and completion dates. Actual start and completion dates were added when known, and any slippage was monitored (see Exhibit 4.5).

By early February 1983, an overall eBasic milestone chart had been developed by manufacturing manager Jim Kilpatrick and technology manager Alikhan, and

Exhibit 4.4 Managing Change at NTC(B): Team Plan Tooling Schedule

E. FOSTER 2320
EXT 7336

DYNAMIC RECEIVER

DRAFTED: 83-01-13
REVIEW DATE 83-03-01

LOWER POLE PIECE	JUN I 83	JUN I 83		107958	N.T. 513492
UPPER POLE PIECE	JUN II 83	JUN II 83		107955	N.T. 513493
CENTER POLE PIECE					
CONNECTOR	JAN III 83	FEB III 83 COMP.	16K	107954	N.T. 513484
TERMINAL	FEB I 83	FEB III 83 COMP.	16K	107956	N.T. 513486
DIAPHRAGM	MAY I 83	MAY I 83	11K		N.T. 513448
ACOUSTIC RESISTANCE	USE	B.A.R.	MACHINE		
FERRULE	JUN III 83	JUN III 83		107957	N.T. 513485
ENCAPSULATION	83-05-05 83-09-	MAY II 83 SEP 83	106K		N.T. 513481-1 " -2
COVER	MAY III 83	MAY III 83	36K		N.T. 513499
HOUSING	83-05-16	MAY IV 83	41K		N.T. 513494

distributed by Jim Retallack. Because all of the Harmony components were interrelated, no single team could complete its job alone, without reference to the others' work. To keep all teams fully informed, Retallack kept up a constant stream of communication—information updates, deadline reminders, announcements, program reports, and so forth (see Exhibit 4.6). Retallack's ongoing preoccupation was with prodding everyone to complete each step on time, on or under budget.

Jim believed in written commitments, "enforced personally," to engender a high realization of personal responsibility. Every team was required to make a formal report once a week on its progress to date, based on a report form outlining:

1. Status to date with respect to scheduled milestones (including outstanding, current, and future milestones).
2. Problems and suggested solutions.
3. Interaction with other teams.

These were delivered to Jim each Thursday morning, and formed the basis of "in person" reporting at weekly Harmony team meetings.

Exhibit 4.5 Managing Change at NTC(B): Team Play First Page of Team 9's Milestone Chart, March 10, 1983

First Page of Team 9's Milestone Chart, March 10, 1983

DATE: MAR II SUB PROJECT: TRANSMITTER (9)
PAGE 1 OF 6

TECHNOLOGY B. GUMB
E of M E. FOSTER
TEST R. MILLER

LINE	ITEM: ACTIVITY	WEEKS	RESP.	J	F	M	A	M	J	J	A	S	O	N
				BASIC SINGLE LINE TELEPHONE (800 SERIES) 1983										
1	DESIGN CONCEP.	3	B.G.	▼ ▲										
2	DESIGN	10	B.G.			Δ - - Δ								
3	ALUMINUM VS. GRAPHITE	3	B.G.	▲										
4	LINER VS. GASKET	4	B.G.	▲										
5	MODEL	2	B.G.	▲▼			∇ Δ							
6	PRINTING PROCESS DEVEL	10	T.R.		▼		Δ							
7	PROTOTYPE TOOLING	14	E.F.		▼				Δ					
8	FIELD TRIAL PIECE PARTS	6	E.F.					∇	Δ - -	Δ				
9														
10	FIELD TRIAL SAMPLES (500)	6	E.F.						∇	Δ - -	Δ			
11														
12														
13	PRINTED CIRCUIT BOARD													
14	JACK FOOT PRINT		G.K.			Δ Δ								
15	DESIGN	13	B.G.	▲			Δ							
16	ARTWORK DESIGN		S.L.	▼ ▲				Δ						
17	PROTOTYPE		B.G.	▼	▲									
18	FIELD TRIAL BOARDS	3	E.F.						Δ					
19	PRODUCTION TOOLING	23	E.F.				∇					Δ		
20	PROCURE P.C.B.	22	2170					∇						Δ
21														
22	CAN													
23	DESIGN		B.G.	Δ -	▲									
24	FIELD TRIAL PARTS	13	O.S.		▼			Δ						
25	PRODUCTION TOOL													
26	DESIGN	10	O.S.		▼		Δ							
27	ORDER	2	O.S.				∇	Δ						
28	BUILD	17						∇				Δ		

LEGEND ∇ PLANNED START Δ PLANNED COMPLETION ◊ PLANNED SLIP ▼▲◆ ACTUAL

Exhibit 4.6 Managing Change at NTC(B): Team Play

MEMORANDUM

83-02-02

To: eBASIC Project Team

From: L. J. Retallack

Subject: eBASIC Schedules

"The time has come, the Walrus said, to talk of many things", and the most painful of all is schedules. Attached is the preliminary version of the eBASIC schedule generated by Jim Kilpatrick and Alikhan. A number beside some of the entries references them to sub-projects as defined in my recent memorandum. Note primarily that Development MDA*** sign-offs scheduled for March/April (with the Dynamic already completed in January) are in agreement with our original schedules, and hence we are on track with respect to the overall Product Plan.

It is extremely important that we meet the MDA sign-off dates in order to meet January 1984 shipment comitments. I am proposing that we complete the MDAs to their full extent even if we have not fully optimized the design. EofM can then use the MDAs to start production planning and the Technology team can step back to iterate the design as required to further improve cost/performance.

Over the next week, ie. by February 11, 1983, each team must meet with Jim Kilpatrick and Alikhan to finalize detailed schedules for each sub-project. We are getting off the ground and now is the time to consolidate our activities into a solid team effort.

L. J. Retallack

LJR/Ms
att.

***Manufacturing Design Authority = design OK'd for manufacturing the prototype.

MEETINGS, MEETINGS, MEETINGS

Weekly project review meetings were held Thursdays at 3:00 PM. Retallack demanded strict punctuality at every session, and anyone who was late was reprimanded publicly by his colleagues. The meetings were opened by the project manager with some overview statements ("I tried to inject some humor," Jim said), and then were chaired by either the engineering manager or the technology manager. This freed Retallack to track progress manually on a master chronological grid chart, and to focus on the issues raised by each team.

Project review meetings also included reports from the product manager and the controller on market issues and the financial status of the project. There were generally 30 or more people in attendance, from the level of manager down to the working levels. Directors were not permitted at these meetings. Other meetings were held on a regular basis, implemented later in the project development as they became necessary.

1. Senior Management Status Reviews, Mondays at 8:15 AM—information sessions for managers of project staff.
2. Production Reviews, Tuesdays at 1:00 PM—status reviews for production, material control and engineering of manufacture personnel not directly involved in the cross-functional teams.
3. Field Trial Reviews, Mondays at 9:30 AM—status reviews, focusing on short-term action required as a result of new information.

DECISIONS, DECISIONS, DECISIONS

Among the many urgent issues competing for Jim Retallack's attention was the Electret transmitter "build or buy" decision. The electroaccoustics manager in charge of transducers for the Harmony project was Bill Greason, an electrical engineer and five year Northern employee. Bill was responsible for two key handset components (the Dynamic receiver and the Electret transmitter) and for the tone alerter which was to be installed in the base assembly.

Bill Greason's reputation as an excellent manager was well-established. His team had been successful in developing the new Dynamic receiver prototype, to be manufactured in Penang; but how to install it in the plastic handset package was a problem. Greason's people maintained that a difference of 1/10 inch diameter in the plastic cup size would improve acoustical properties of the Dynamic receiver. The BNR industrial design crew adamantly refused to change their specs, which were optimized for appearance. (Eventually, a satisfactory installation method was worked out, leaving both sides satisfied.)

However, this was a relatively simple decision compared to the human and other issues surrounding the pending decision about the Electret transmitter. Greason summarized his concerns as follows:

> I've got the team that built the first Electret. Originally, this type of transmitter component was BNR's idea, but BNR needed us to build it—and we did! I'm proud of my team; and I envision delivering the "perfect Electret" as our quality contribution to the Harmony project.
>
> However, at our last value analysis session, our preliminary cost estimates came in at $1.00 over our original goal. When Jim Retallack asked what else we could do to lower costs, the Electret was singled out.
>
> And an alternative exists. One Japanese supplier manufactures prepackaged microphones by the billions, at $.25 each—much below our cost. We've run a "shake

and bake" analysis[5] on samples we purchased from the Japanese supplier, and they seem OK.

But talking with my people, I find reluctance to go with the imported Electret. They worry about jobs being lost in the plant. Also, it would seem a slap in the face of a good team to reject our own product, particularly when the common perception is that Japanese quality and reliability will be uncertain. My team has voiced the concern that "we're selling out to the Japanese"... and yet Retallack keeps pushing cost constraints, and insisting on an answer today, if not sooner!

Other pending decisions involved the resolution of differences between and among the varous teams, each of which depended on one or more of the others to complete its own work satisfactorily. For example, the jacks were to be built in the London plant (it had been ascertained that no alternative source existed); but absolute cooperation was essential between the jacks team and the teams for the circuit board and transmitter. Only one model of jack would be produced, and it would end up on the modules for both the transmitter and the printed circuit board; and problems had surfaced when two different teams with two different philosophies tried to come to some mutually acceptable conclusions. While the original jack design satisfied the needs of one, the needs of the other were not satisfied. For instance, the holes drilled in the circuit boards to make contact with the jacks were different sizes than those for the transmitter—the transmitter team wanted a larger opening than the circuit board team's requirements.

Another issue dealt with the installation of the new piezo-electric alerter which had been built by one of Greason's teams (Team 3). It tested as a good product, and was already being manufactured in the London plant. However, certain problems were awaiting resolution with the base assembly team (Team 1). Modification in the design of the alerter or of the Harmony base might be needed to complete the assembled "fit" of the two components. Also, Team 1 was insisting that one of the four pedestal feet supporting the base be installed in the back of the acoustic cavity. Team 3 was resisting the placement; the quality and volume of alerter sound might be adversely affected.

Occasionally, differences of opinion surfaced between the design and manufacturing elements within the Harmony teams. When design engineers submitted a new design, the "knee jerk" reaction of some manufacturing people tended to be, "It can't be done that way!" Where any of the technology was already in production, the temptation was to "just take it and put it in, as is," in the new set. However, the existing manufacturing technology had not been built to be automated; and automation of all possible Harmony processes was an absolute necessity.

As he thought about the many issues which needed to be resolved, Jim Retallack wondered how to dispel the unsettled atmosphere he kept encountering. He was aware, uncomfortably, that old patterns of noncommunication between professional management and the rest of the plant had exacerbated the anxieties of people throughout the organization. The plant grapevine was rife with rumors of production changes, layoffs, and even a possible plant closing. Jim wondered what could be done to improve morale

[5]Tests indicating the product's reaction to extremes of temperature and different types of impact.

and develop a positive spirit of cooperation and commitment to a successful Harmony launch.

THE NEXT STEP

Jim Retallack scanned the last report, noted that team's progress toward its goals for the week, and plotted its current status on his master chart. He was pleased to see that the cords group had achieved its "on time, under budget" goal; and the keyboard and line switch teams appeared to be on target for next week's deadline. The upcoming Electret transmitter decision was a major source of concern, however.

His mind still grappling with aspects of the Electret issue, the project manager strode purposefully through the office area of the plant to the eBasic meeting room, bulging file folders in hand. It was precisely three minutes to the hour. The weekly meeting was about to begin.

CASE 4.2

Eastern National Bank[6]

INTRODUCTION

"Well, it's been fun dragging the bank kicking and screaming into the 1980s, and getting them to recognize computer-aided banking exists. Now the hard part begins, getting the recognition turned into banking reality." The speaker was Ada Noseworthy, senior vice president (Operations) at Eastern National Bank's head office. Noseworthy had just received the February 1987 progress report on Eastern's 'electronic banking' pilot project—a computer-based expert system to support the bank's loans officers—and the results looked encouraging. The start date of November 1, 1987 Ada had set herself for introducing the first operational units still looked feasible, provided the Board gave its approval at its March meeting, just two weeks away.

A convincing demonstration would help sway the Board, which up to now had been noncommittal. The only reason grudging approval had been given was the Board's recognition that something drastic had to be done to reduce Eastern's loan exposure in the face of increasing competition and falling margins. Favorable results would encourage the Board; even more crucial, however, would be a sound plan for implementing the system across the whole Canadian operation.

EASTERN NATIONAL BANK

Banks in Canada organized around the branch banking principle, with national or multi-provincial banks operating a large number of branches throughout their very large geographical markets. As a consequence of their national charters, some banks had grown very large, and had gained a major role in a very concentrated industry. Eastern National

[6]This case was written by Professor Hamid Noori and Alex Striling, 1988.

Bank (Eastern) was one example of this growth. Founded as a merchants' bank in the Atlantic provinces in the mid 1850s, Eastern had grown through a series of mergers and acquisitions to be one of the largest banks in Canada. In March 1987 Eastern operated approximately 1,100 bank branches throughout Canada, and had subsidiaries and representative offices in 30 other countries. Approximately 27,000 employees were on the payroll; most served in branches, but about 10 percent performed various support functions in regional and head offices.

Eastern had a history of profitability and slow but steady growth in earnings (see Exhibit 4.7).

Exhibit 4.7 Financial Statements (millions of dollars)

INCOME STATEMENT	1982	1983	1984	1985	1986
INTEREST INCOME					
Income from loans, excluding leases	$ 8,137	$ 6,050	$ 5,985	$ 6,033	$ 6,103
Income from lease financing	30	29	25	28	30
Income from securities	570	480	480	563	615
Income from deposits with banks	550	393	588	539	444
Total interest income, including dividends	9,287	6,952	7,078	7,163	7,192
INTEREST EXPENSE					
Interest on deposits	7,650	5,199	5,339	5,189	5,025
Interest on bank debentures	88	103	109	118	141
Interest on liabilities other than deposits	15	3	1	15	15
Total interest expense	7,753	5,305	5,449	5,322	5,181
Net interest income	1,534	1,647	1,629	1,841	2,011
Provision for loan losses	303	376	404	489	636
Net interest income after loan loss provision	1,231	1,271	1,225	1,332	1,375
Other income	430	460	515	599	708
Net interest and other income	1,661	1,731	1,740	1,951	2,083
NON-INTEREST EXPENSES					
Salaries	749	760	779	850	907
Pension contributions and other staff benefits	59	54	54	58	58
Premises and equipment expenses, including depreciation	220	222	238	255	273
Other expenses	230	245	261	308	374
Total noninterest expenses	1,258	1,281	1,332	1,471	1,612
Net income before provision for income taxes	403	450	408	480	471
Provision for income taxes	70	159	120	183	130
Net income before minority interest in subsidiaries	333	291	288	297	341
Minority interests in subsidiaries	1	3	3	3	0
Net income for the year	$ 332	$ 288	$ 285	$ 294	$ 341

Exhibit 4.7 Financial Statements (*continued*)

BALANCE SHEET	1982	1983	1984	1985	1986
ASSETS					
CASH RESOURCES					
Cash and deposits with Bank of Canada	$ 1,498	$ 1,530	$ 1,400	$ 1,653	$ 1,191
Deposits with other banks	3,087	5,859	5,208	5,175	7,523
Checks and other items in transit, net	719	931	173	5	427
	5,304	8,320	6,781	6,833	9,141
SECURITIES					
Issued or guaranteed by Canada	2,029	3,383	2,279	3,583	2,619
Issued or guaranteed by provinces and municipal or school corporations	23	26	349	560	279
Other securities	2,699	2,598	2,954	3,517	4,029
	4,751	6,007	5,582	7,660	6,927
LOANS					
Day, call and short loans to investment dealers and brokers, secured	569	109	724	496	100
Loans to banks	1,610	1,528	1,763	1,645	1,529
Mortgage loans	7,059	8,049	8,749	10,269	12,500
Other loans	44,319	39,401	39,811	43,009	42,998
	53,557	49,087	51,047	55,419	57,127
OTHER					
Customers' liability under acceptances	2,969	3,019	3,081	4,185	5,453
Land, buildings and equipment	633	630	643	671	698
Other assets	1,145	984	1,099	1,017	1,424
	4,747	4,633	4,823	5,873	7,575
	$68,359	$68,047	$68,233	$75,785	$80,770
LIABILITIES					
DEPOSITS					
Payable on demand	$ 5,336	$ 6,349	$ 5,727	$ 6,247	$ 5,330
Payable after notice	14,977	16,490	17,019	19,199	21,851
Payabale on a fixed date	39,943	37,235	36,569	39,619	40,311
	60,256	60,074	59,315	65,065	67,492
OTHER					
Checks and other items in transit, net	2	2	4	115	1
Acceptances	2,969	3,019	3,079	4,185	5,450
Liabilities of subsidiaries, other than deposits	59	6	70	59	4
Other liabilities	1,809	1,405	1,819	1,698	2,503
Minority interests in subsidiaries	26	26	1	1	1
	4,865	4,458	4,973	6,058	7,959
SUBORDINATED DEBT					
Bank debentures	895	899	885	1,300	1,627

Exhibit 4.7 Financial Statements *(continued)*

BALANCE SHEET (cont'd)	1982	1983	1984	1985	1986
CAPITAL AND RESERVES					
Appropriations for contingencies	143	29	108	137	223
Shareholders' equity					
Capital stock	727	883	1,208	1,451	1,668
Contributed surplus	0	0	0	0	0
Retained earnings	1,473	1,704	1,744	1,774	1,801
	2,343	2,616	3,060	3,362	3,692
	$68,359	$68,047	$68,233	$75,785	$80,770
Average number of common shares outstanding (in thousands)					
Basic	79,107	80,401	82,094	92,084	116,478
Fully diluted	98,848	100,234	104,821	115,913	133,613
Net income per common share (in dollars)					
Basic	$4.20	$3.58	$3.47	$3.19	$2.93
Fully diluted	$3.36	$2.87	$2.80	$2.54	$2.55

CONSOLIDATED STATEMENT OF APPROPRIATIONS FOR CONTINGENCIES
For the year ended October 31 (millions of dollars)

	1982	1983	1984	1985	1986
Balance at beginning of year	$150	$143	$ 29	$108	$137
Deduct net loss experience on loans	(480)	(730)	(485)	(535)	(680)
Add provision for loan losses included in consolidated statement of income	303	376	404	489	636
Transfer from retained earnings	170	240	160	75	130
Balance at end of year	$143	$ 29	$108	$137	$223

Corporate culture was very conservative, with every effort being made to maintain the long-time public image of stability and respectability. Employees were expected to act and dress conservatively in the work place; as one employee noted, "We are, after all, looking after people's life savings, and they have a right to expect that somebody responsible is in charge."

The conservatism extended to technology. Eastern was one of the last banks to adopt computers within its branches, and few branches had small computers for their staff to use. The rationale for the slow progress was the capital cost involved in equipping some 1,100 branches and the additional expense of training both line and support staff. The typewriter was still, therefore, the principal means of communication, with all correspondence being prepared on a typewriter and then checked and signed by the writer.

ORGANIZATION

Historically, the company had been organized geographically, with senior executives in charge of each region. In an effort to better allocate its resources, Eastern had reorganized itself in 1981. (See Exhibit 4.8.)

Exhibit 4.8 Typical Branch Structure

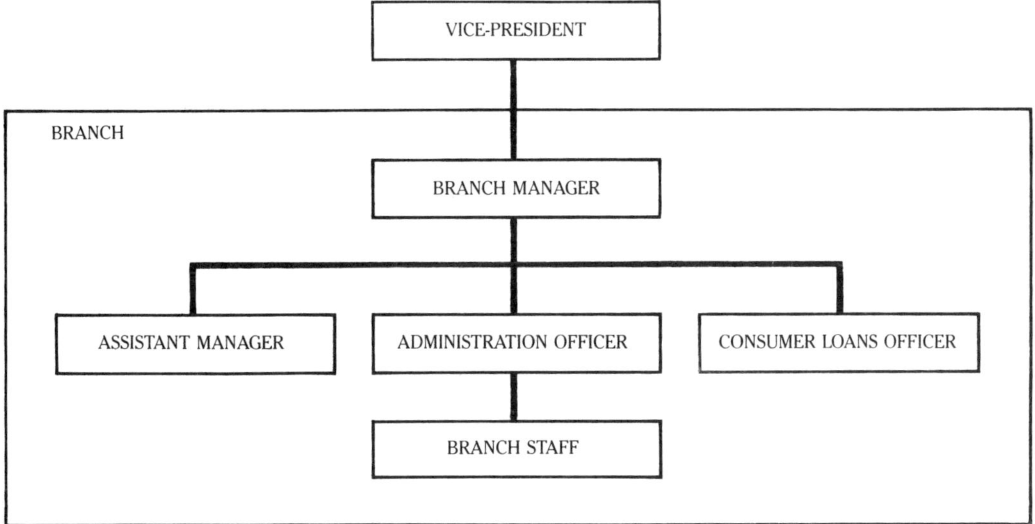

Essentially, Eastern now consisted of three strategic operational groups under the head office and regional offices; a commercial bank, a consumer bank, and a support bank.

COMMERCIAL BANK

The commercial bank's mandate was to deal with corporations with sales in excess of $5 million or loan requirements in excess of $500,000. These loans required particular expertise, and, because of the amounts involved, much closer scrutiny and frequent contact with the customer. Business development was also a major part of the bank's duties, and in addition to being treated lenders, bank personnel were also skilled sales people. Large corporate borrowing was not at present a growth industry in Canada, and most new borrowers had to be stolen from the competition, which was simultaneously making an effort to solicit Eastern's customers.

The principal source of product differentiation lay in a bank's personnel; since banking services and pricing were largely identical from bank to bank, service was a critical issue. A large part of the perceived service was in the relationship between the customer and the bank staff. If differentiation did not work, however, pesonnel could always accept applications from higher risk customers.

Aside from the head office support staff, personnel from the commercial bank were located in about 100 commercial centers (see Exhibit 4.9) across Canada, almost all of them in major centers of at least 100,000 people. Within these centers account managers, who were responsible for about 100 borrowing accounts each, completely evaluated each of their accounts at least once a year on receiving their clients' latest financial statements. Additional reviews might be necessary should the customer request new loan arrangements or if an account shows signs of financial difficulty.

CONSUMER BANK

The consumer bank's purpose was to provide banking services to the general population; basically, this was the nationwide network of branches with which the public associated the banks. With the reorganization, all branches had become part of the consumer bank, and their function had changed very little. A typical small branch with a staff of about 15 had some 2,000 bank accounts, 100 small business loans, 500 consumer loans, and 500 mortgages on its books. Branch personnel also had well-developed lending skills, but the dollar amounts tended to be smaller (below $500,000), and the overall complexity of the accounts was lower than that of commercial loans. In addition, the manager was still responsible for all aspects of branch operations, including day-to-day administration. Although the commercial account managers could concern themselves with only the lending aspects of their customer bases, the consumer managers dealt with a much wider range of issues. Consumer managers therefore had considerably less time for the lending function.

SUPPORT BANK

The support bank supervised nearly all support services, including computer services, treasury functions, audit, legal matters, human resources, and public relations. The other two banks did not involve themselves in these matters, relying instead upon the support bank for such activities. The support bank had no customer contact, nor any customer-generated revenues.

PERSONNEL

Eastern had always expected much of its employees, particularly career officers. While the work week was at present nominally 37.5 hours it was normal for the average manager to log 45 or 50 hours per week in order to complete all essential work. This had been the case for many years, and was an ingrained part of the corporate culture. Many

Exhibit 4.9 Typical Commercial Center Structure

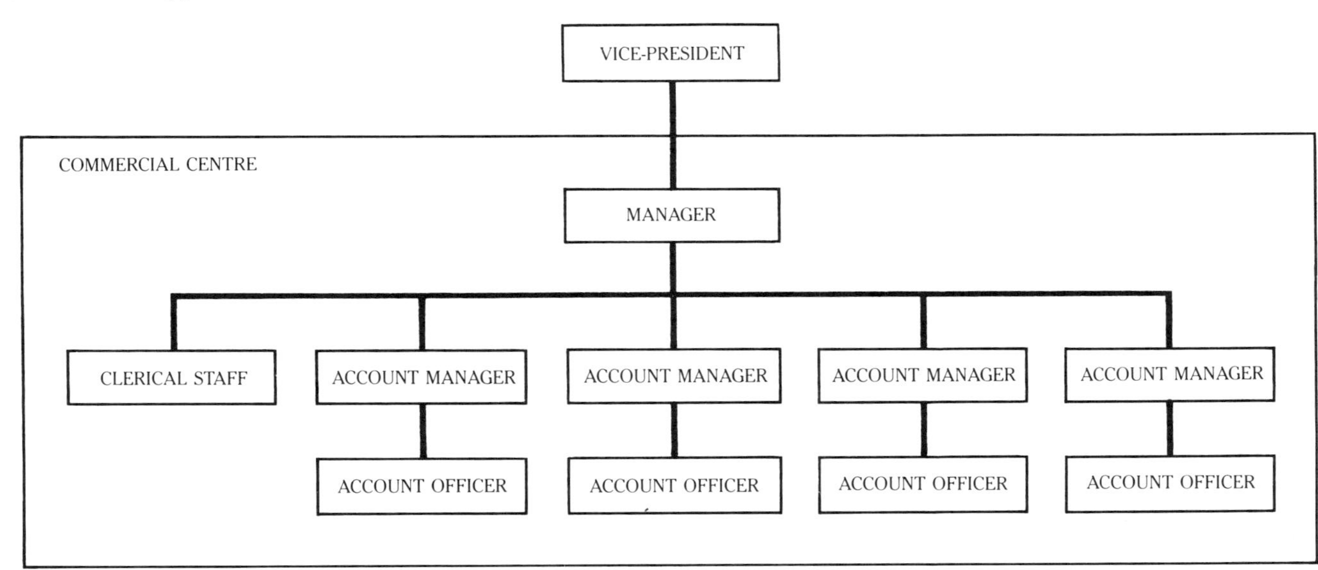

employees claimed that the organization was so obsessed with tradition that new ideas were sometimes suppressed simply because they were not congruent with the established methods of operation. A large percentage of employees who had left cited an inability to operate within established procedures as the principal reason for quitting.

Nearly all Eastern's management personnel had been employees of the bank for most of their working lives. Until 1970, most new hires were made straight from the high schools. Between 1970 and 1974, community college graduates were sought, with university graduates hired thereafter. Around 1980, an effort was made to hire MBA graduates; however, most of these persons stayed for only a year or two, and then moved on to other occupations. Most MBA's complained that opportunities for advancement were inadequate, and many left for higher-paying jobs. The situation was further complicated by the recession in the early 1980s; as the job market dried up, personnel turnover reduced dramatically and opportunities for advancement within Eastern dropped. In conjunction with this, the bank enthusiastically embraced the federal government's "6 and 5" anti-inflation policy, and wage increases were curtailed.

In 1985, Eastern again began to hire MBA's, this time with the intention of putting them through an intensive, six month long training program, then slotting them into commercial account managers' positions. Of the 500 or so commercial account managers currently in the commercial banking centers, about 10 percent of them were young MBA's; the balance were employees of longer service who had worked their way up to their current positions. More than half of the existing management team had less than a community college education, about 15 percent had completed community college, and 25 percent had a university degree, although not necessarily in business.

As part of the ongoing training and development of personnel, Eastern had traditionally encouraged its staff to take relevant outside educational courses. To encourage such activities the bank paid the tuition of any employee who passed a course, and reimbursed textbook costs. For many years Eastern had supported a professional development program supervised by the Institute of Canadian Bankers, an intercompany organization. Besides providing a solid background in accounting, economics, and business administration, the program provided training in banking management, international banking and banking law. New technologies were not addressed anywhere in the program, and no effort was made to have students consider the implications of computers on banking operations.

THE LENDING ENVIRONMENT

The collapse of the energy sector in the early 1980s, coupled with increasing pressure from competitors (often resulting in price cutting to gain or retain large borrowing customers) had put considerable pressure on Eastern's margins. Loan losses had also been higher than normal, largely due to weaknesses in various sectors of the economy. (See Exhibits 4.10 and 4.11.)

Compounding this cyclical problem was the structural phenomenon of the gradual change of the Canadian economy away from a resource base to a service industries base. There was a major difference from the banker's point of view between

Exhibit 4.10 Loan Portfolio (as at October 31, 1986)

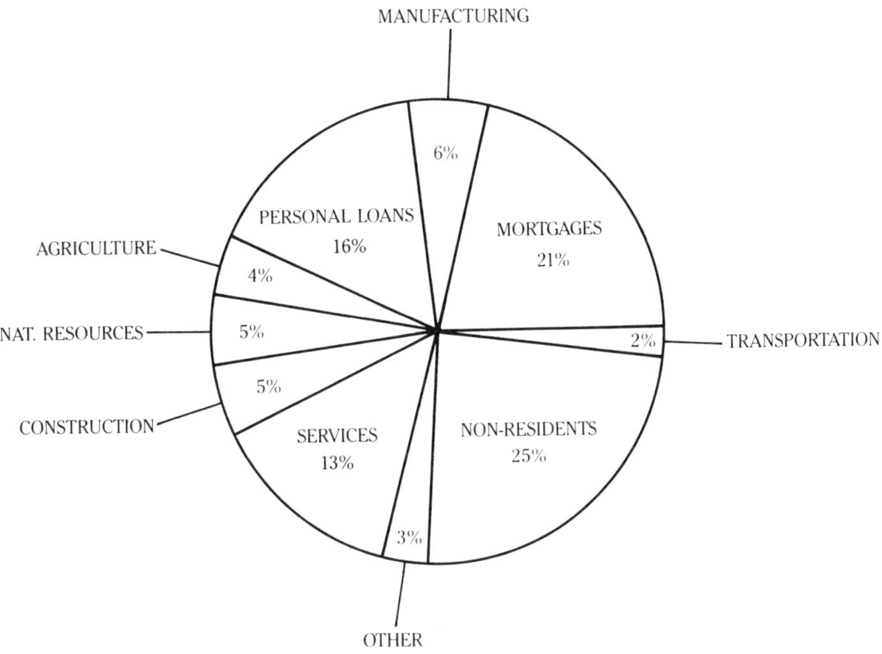

Exhibit 4.11 Loan Loss Experience (1982–1986)

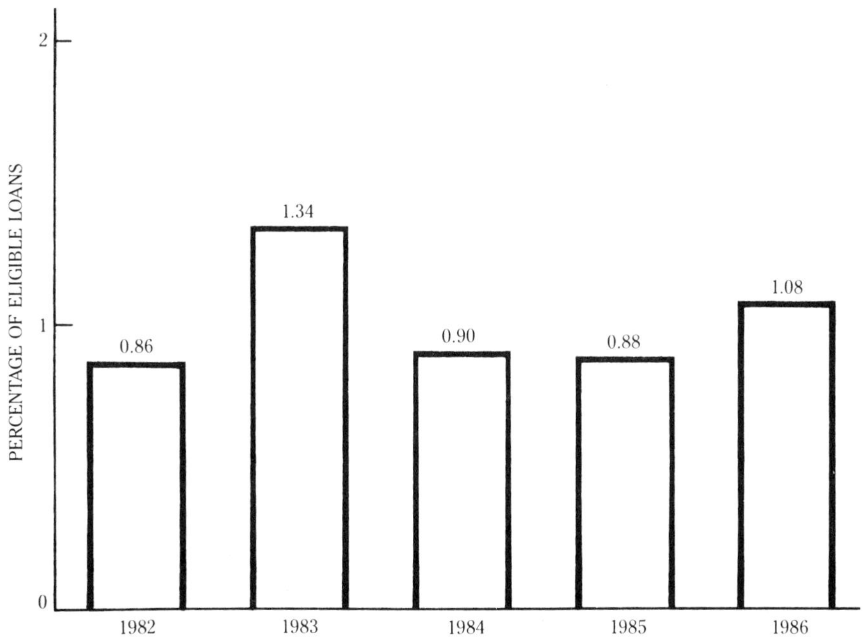

the two; a resource-based company typically had inventory and assets, both of which could be seized if necessary to liquidate outstanding debt to the bank. On the other hand, a service company often has little but its expertise and goodwill as assets, and in the event of loan default there might be little or nothing with which to reduce the bank loans. In the commercial lending centers there was the possibility of very large write-offs, and hence the need to make accurate, effective long-term lending decisions, or profitability would be affected.

The consumer sector (personal loans and mortgages) had traditionally generated very few losses; not only did personal loans tend to be fairly small (typically less than $20,000), but mortgages were by their very nature fully secured, and posed little risk for the lender. On the other hand, the commercial sector had been a source of difficulty in recent years, with losses peaking at 1.34 percent of loans outstanding in 1983. In certain sectors of the economy, "bad" loans were quite common; Exhibits 4.11 and 4.12 provide some detail. While manufacturing accounted for 6 percent of loans outstanding, it accounted for 16 percent of unproductive loans (no interest being earned due to inability to pay). At the same time, natural resources accounted for 5 percent of loans outstanding, and 32 percent of these loans earned nothing for the bank, and might ultimately have to be written-off. It was clear to Eastern's Board that certain sectors were in difficulty; if the bank chose to do business with those sectors, loans officers had to be able to assess risk accurately or be faced with substantial write-offs.

The problem was further compounded from the bank's perspective by the fact that a loan was not a short-term "in and out" transaction; very often, a loan represented a commitment for several or many years, and a loan which was good the day it was approved might not necessarily be good the next year, or five years later. Loan officers

Exhibit 4.12 Nonperforming Loans (After Deduction for Losses)

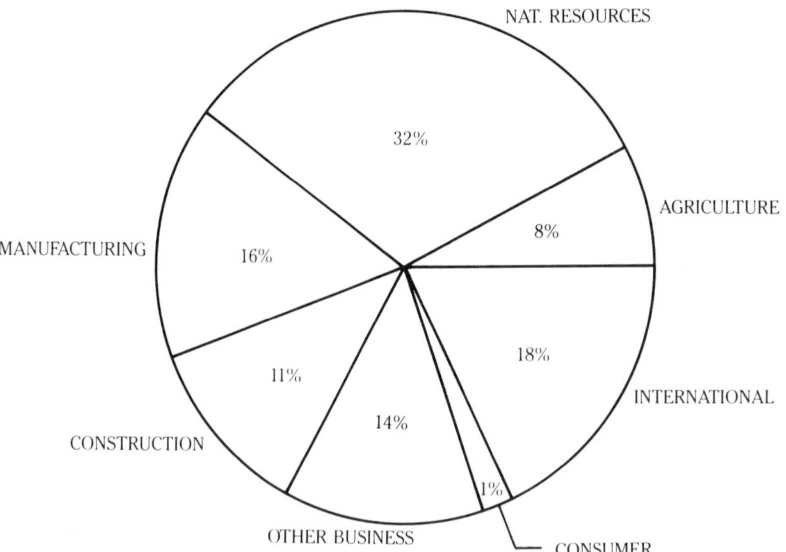

therefore had to assess not only a prospect's current situation, but also the long-term implications of such a loan.

THE LENDING PROCESS

Each of Eastern's commercial centers and branches had a manager's lending limit; the sum of money which that manager was permitted to lend without reference to superiors. In the branch setting, this ranged from a low of some $25,000 in the case of a new manager in a smaller branch to several million in the case of a senior manager in a large commercial center. Each manager's limit increased over time as competence in lending was developed and demonstrated.

Any loan application in excess of the manager's discretionary limit had to be referred to the credit department in the regional office; these departments were staffed by experienced lenders who reviewed the application in great detail and either authorized the loan, declined it, or referred it back to the manager for further explanation and consideration. Since these decision-makers rarely met face-to-face with the applicant, it was the manager's job to present the application in a detailed, concise format to the credit department. The decision would be made on the basis of the manager's application.

A series of standard forms had been developed in order to ensure consistency of presentation; while they required certain standard details (particularly of a financial nature), there was considerable leeway for the manager to add comments and explanations. The reviewer played devil's advocate with the application to ensure that the manager had taken all the relevant issues into account when recommending the loan.

There were basically two sources of new loans: either an application was initiated by the customer (existing or new) or the loan was solicited by an employee as part of the Bank's ongoing sales efforts. Loans to existing customers, particularly those who had borrowed recently, usually required much less work, since the applicant was already known. A thorough financial analysis to determine the applicant's current credit worthiness was in order, but previous experience with the customer meant that an in-depth investigation was probably not necessary. Should a borrowing account demonstrate weakness, the bank would probably require the customer to provide additional security; additionally, interest rates might be raised to reflect Eastern's increased risk.

Loans to new customers were a different matter. Even if the application had been solicited by bank employees, there was no guarantee that the prospect was financially sound; often a company under pressure from its current banker was more than happy to consider an offer from another bank.

THE EXPERT SYSTEM

Faced with the need to reduce loan exposure in the face of falling margins, the Board had reluctantly agreed to investigate the use of an expert system to help officers make lending decisions. A software company had approached Eastern and other large banks in 1985 with a system which, its developers claimed, would allow an easier and more objective review of loan applications.

An expert system is a computer program which attempts to duplicate the thought processes of an "expert" in a given area of knowledge. In essence, it is a series of rules and "if-then" statements which analyze a situation and provide a series of observations and recommendations about the data provided. The rules are entered by the program, having been created from observation about the thought processes of one or more experts in the particular field.

Ada Noseworthy, who had brought the concept to the Board's notice, thought the product offered by the software house was too general for Eastern's use, and recommended Eastern develop its own expert system in-house. The Board agreed, and Noseworthy gave Systems Division in the support bank the task of producing the tailor-made expert system.

The software manufacturer had hinted that three other banks were interested in the available product. Although Ada was skeptical about the number of banks actually purchasing systems right now, and the rate at which the expert system would penetrate the banking world, she knew that at least one of the banks had signed a contract in 1986 to purchase the available expert system and install it nationwide. With no development time involved, it would be reasonable to expect any bank purchasing the "canned" system to be ahead of Eastern in introducing the first units, and in establishing the system nationwide. What that lead would be, and what market advantage the leading bank would have, Ada did not know.

SYSTEM DEVELOPMENT

A number of skilled lenders from the commercial and consumer banks detailed the process of loan evaluation to the programming team, which then created a system (see Exhibit 4.13 for an overview). The system was evaluated by the experts, who provided additional comments and recommendations. After several iterations the lenders were satisfied that the system effectively duplicated the loan evaluation process. The expert system was more than a computer-based checklist for the loan officer; it also contained a spreadsheet for situation analysis, a database to hold several years financial results and an analysis of customer strategy, in an effort to examine the long-term implications of a loan. All the information resided in one database, which could be imported into each of the modules for use.

The system made no effort to allow for variances across industries, focusing rather upon general financial analysis and strategic issues; it was left to the loan officer to deal with those case-specific issues. When the lending experts declared themselves satisfied with the product, the development task force was disbanded and the programming team moved on to other projects.

The developed product impressed the presidents of the lending banks, who agreed to support Ada's request for a two-site pilot test of the system. The presidents demanded that the expert system run in parallel with the current credit analysis process. Parallel operation would give Systems Division a chance to observe what routine sup-

Exhibit 4.13 The Proposed Expert System

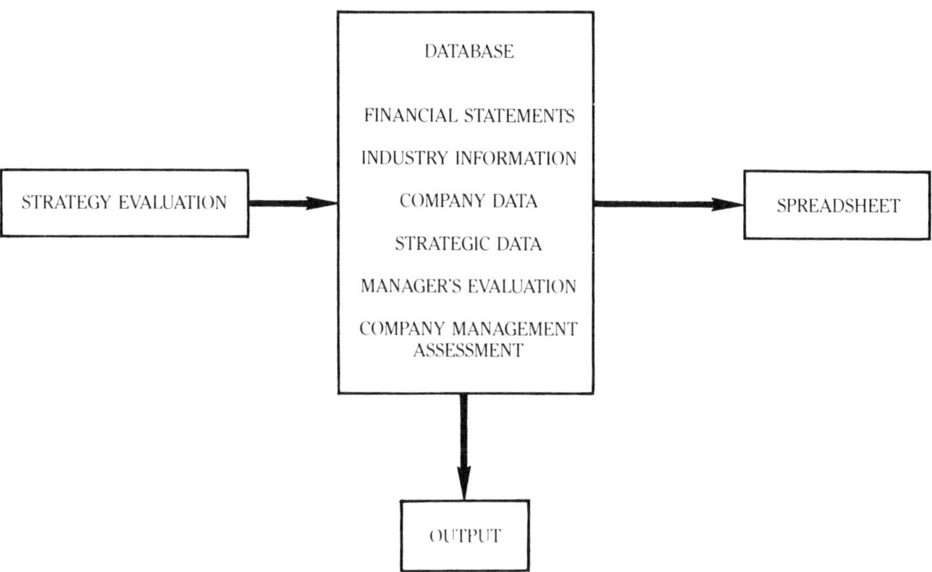

port the system required, especially as contact between the loan officers and systems division programmers was currently a rare and complicated event. The pilot might also give Noseworthy a chance to decide how the system might be implemented, and in which circumstances it would best be used. If the three month pilot studies were successful, the presidents of the lending banks would support Ada's request to fully implement the system.

Full implementation depended in large part on the availability of appropriate computer hardware within Eastern. Systems division estimated that, by mid-1988, each of the branches and commercial centers would have at least one microcomputer. The machine would be utilized primarily for word processing and financial analysis, although capacity would be available for the recently-developed expert system.

Implementation depended also on the lending banks attitude towards the system. At present neither bank intended the expert system would replace the existing process of credit evaluation. Rather, the expert system would supplement current practice, with no changes being made, for example, to the existing system of referring problematic loan applications to higher authorities. Employees would use the expert system and submit its results in conjunction with the existing application forms for review by more senior personnel.

The test results showed Noseworthy that the system required a minimum of one and one-half hours for data entry, analysis, and printing of the results for each application. This time would be added to that already required to prepare and submit a loan application. Neither lending bank was prepared to hire additional personnel or reduce the workload of personnel to accommodate this new procedure, since it was experimental and might be abandoned should it prove ineffective. In addition, the Board's desire to cut costs was placing considerable pressure on management to reduce personnel levels, even though staff complained frequently of overwork and a lack of head office support.

CONCLUSION

As she reread the results, Ada was convinced the expert system would prove itself, and rapidly repay its $200,000 development costs. First, she had to get the expert system installed in the pilot sites (which had yet to be selected) and then throughout the bank. That required initial Board approval and lending bank support. The needs of each of the banks were very different, and would probably influence the implementation plan. Ada also knew that the Board was not wholeheartedly behind her, and would withdraw support at any time they felt circumstances or costs were getting out of control.

With the recent reduction in profitability, and the consequent drop in the bank's share price, Ada conceded she would do much the same if she was on the Board. But the greatest costs were behind them now; what other substantial costs could possibly lie ahead? The greatest cost was surely that of failure; how should the system be implemented to reduce that risk? First, how should the first sites be chosen?

Chapter Five

STRATEGIC IMPLICATIONS OF NEW TECHNOLOGY

SITUATION 5.1

Strategy in the High Tech Business of Semiconductors[1]

In firms where innovation and rapid technological changes occur with regularity, engaging in business strategy, which requires planning, would appear to be contradictory. An industry where flexibility and change are the keys to survival would only be held back by maintaining an established strategy. In fact, many managers argue that in high technology firms strategic planning will not work. To establish a strategy in advance, indicate that the results can be predetermined. The semiconductor industry has been compared to the job of a securities analyst, where planning for the future is generally only a prediction.

While managers, scholars and professors believe that the planning and creation of strategies in high technology industries are an impossibility, that undermines a companies creativity and in turn its flexibility. Dr. Claudia Schoonhoven's research indicates that this is not true. High technology firms, according to her studies need and use strategies perhaps unknowingly, to reap financial and performance rewards. Strategy creation is a matter of identifying the companies objectives and then to proceed from there. Schoonhoven found that strategies of successful semiconductor companies were specific and consistent, where strategies of other less successful firms in the semiconductor industry were widespread and inconsistent. This indicates that specific strategies in this industry result in higher returns on equity assets and sales.

The semiconductor firms are a good example of an industry that experiences rapid growth, declining prices, innovations, and technical changes. Manufacturing

[1]Claudia B. Schoonhoven, "High Technology Firms: Where Strategy Really Pays Off." *Columbia Journal of World Business,* Winter. © 1984 by The Trustees of Columbia University in the City of New York. Extracted with permission.

semiconductors is a complex process involving many precise operations, yet it has been adapted to mass production. As the complexity of the product has increased, manufacturers have relied more heavily on sophisticated manufacturing and testing devices. These factors, combined with the difficulty of maintaining technology advances, due to the mobility of scientists and technicians, and delays in patent protection, makes the semiconductor industry a turbulent and ever changing environment. The competitiveness of the environment demands price and cost reductions, constant innovation in processes and machinery, and dependence on suppliers for quality products.

Contrary to popular belief, strategic decision making is evident in the semicondutor industry. It is widely realized that not all strategies are deliberate. Some aspects of original strategies in all industries are achieved, while other strategies emerge over time, as the company matures and adjust their plans to suit particular needs.

Overall strategies in the semicondutor industry fall into two major categories, broad line suppliers or narrow niche specialists. Broad line suppliers generally utilize little R&D, preferring a second source strategy. These firms adopt or buy other firms technology. Narrow niche companies such as Intel, Analog Devices, and Advanced Micro Devices (AMD) rely heavily on R&D to maintain their commpetitive edge.

In terms of performance, broad line suppliers such as Motorola and Texas Instrument, have in the past dominated the market. However, these companies have a mature set of products and are losing ground to narrow niche firms which specialize in integrated circuits. This indicates that the decision to maintain one of these strategies is crucial to the firm's profits and market share.

Research by Schoonhoven indicates that employing resources towards research and development, increases the company's performance. High end pricing also results in positive returns on equity, which helps to explain Intel's success. On the other hand, capital expenditures and aggressive cost cutting strategies do not result in healthy returns on equity and assets. A company that utilizes these strategies may be misdirecting company resources, time, and energy.

The hierarchy of a company may be influenced by these strategies. Strategies are influenced by those people in positions of major responsibility. If scientists and entrepreneurs are in these positions after the firm has begun to mature, they may not have the financial and managerial skills necessary to move the company forward in a stable, but competitive environment. However, for a firm which employs a narrow niche strategy where proactive responses are necessary, entrepreneurs and scientists would be an asset in areas of responsibility.

Proactive strategies in the semicondutor industry, and other high technology fields, allow a company to control the marketplace with unique products. These products enable companies to charge a premium price, that can be pumped back into R&D, and future unique products. In contrast if a firm adopts low R&D expenditures in favor of second sourcing, the company is reactive. Firms using this strategy must constantly adjust to an environment that is in a continual state of change. Pressures of decreasing prices and costs may influence the quality of the product, further reducing the customer base. Low cost, high quality Japanese suppliers also diminish the market for these products. These factors indicate that in North America, high tech firms, given the Japanese expertise in the low cost, high quality area of prodution, require strategy. Without strategies, production and focus becomes ad hoc, and pushes the firm out of the marketplace almost entirely, as there is little or no room for low quality, low cost suppliers.

To counteract these effects, North American firms in the semicondutor industry must use strategies to enable firms to focus on a narrow niche market, so that maximum profits and returns can be achieved.

High technology firms need to evaluate the market requirements to determine the best strategies to employ. Without strategies, returns are reduced. Strategies do allow flexibility in these industries. Firms must acquire a different attitude towards strategies or returns are reduced. Strategies do allow flexibility in these industries. Firms must acquire a different attitude towards strategies in the high tech industry. Strategies are more general, and there are fewer choices. They are also necessary. Without strategies firms cannot deal effectively with marketplace competition.

READING 5.1

Breakthrough Manufacturing[2]

INTRODUCTION

Is the decay of American manufacturing really incurable? Massive capital investment has failed to check it. The $200 billion that United States companies poured into new domestic facilities and equipment between 1980 and 1985 scarcely slowed the erosion of our global competitiveness. The United States auto industry, which alone invested $40 billion in capital improvements in that period, continues to lose ground. Six years ago, Japan's auto makers were turning out subcompacts at a cost $1,500 less than Detroit's; today the gap has widened to $1,800. Cost is not our only problem. Last year, American-made cars were still three times as likely as their Japanese counterparts to need repair in the first 12 months of ownership. Comparable cost and quality problems continue to plague nearly every corner of the United States manufacturing industry.

It is my conviction that the world competitiveness of the United States industry could be lost for good, well before the end of this century, unless American top managers can learn to think and act in a radically different way in their everyday manufacturing decisions.

By and large, United States manufacturers are still the slaves of operational necessity. When need dictates—when a new product is introduced, when volume fluctuates, or when costs have to be cut—they make operational changes. Over time, these changes may marginally enhance a company's competitiveness or at least slow its erosion.

[2]Elizabeth A. Haas, "Breakthrough Manufacturing," March-April, pp. 75–81.

Rarely, if ever, do they add up to a coherent strategy for gaining an edge over the competition.

The difference between an operational and a strategic perspective is immense. It is the difference between a focus on operational improvement—"How can we do it better than before?"—and a focus on strategic advantage—"How can we use it to beat the competition?" Managers who are preoccupied with optimizing the operational bits and pieces—reducing machining time here, paring labor costs there—will typically be blind to the big strategic opportunities. It is only by managing the operational components as an integrated system that manufacturers can exploit their full potential for delivering added value to customers through lower prices, greater service responsiveness, or higher quality.

Typically, manufacturing decisions are still taken in an operational framework defined by internal performance standards, machine downtime, scrap rate, work-in-process inventories, and the like. But the real test of manufacturing decisions is their impact on the company's performance in the dog-eat-dog world of global competition. Strategic decision-making aims to put the company ahead of its competitors and keep it there through positive differentiation, sometimes in defiance of operational logic.

A manufacturing decision that might be downright stupid in operational terms alone may look very different when seen from a strategic perspective. Consider a simple example. An appliance maker found that it could extend the life of its product and save $1.75 per unit in warranty costs by substituting a newly designed part. Against expectation, it turned out that the new part would add more than $2 to the cost of each unit—hardly an attractive proposition, operationally speaking. But on strategic grounds the move still made excellent sense. By sparing the end-user cost and inconvenience over the product's lifetime, it would strengthen the company's sales message and increase the product's value in the customer's eye. Management's decision to go ahead has since been rewarded by a hefty gain in market share.

THE STRATEGIC BREAKPOINT

How much must a company differentiate its products to gain a decisive competitive advantage? Experience indicates that there is a definable point at which the market will respond to a change in value—a point where an incremental improvement in some value parameter (price, quality, or service) will trigger a disproportionate volume increase and tilt the competitive balance. We call this the strategic breakpoint.

The success of Japanese cars in the United States auto market is a case in point. When Toyotas had to go in for repair every eight weeks on average and American cars every six weeks, few buyers noticed the difference. But when Toyiotas began to average six months, the gap was too big to miss. Using noticeably higher quality, at competitive prices, as a lever to gain market share, the Japanese had reached a strategic breakpoint. All at once, it seemed customers en masse were choosing Japan's product over Detroit's.

United States manufacturers have habitually thought of cost, quality, and service in terms of trade-offs. They have taken it for granted that higher quality means higher manufacturing cost or longer throughput time. Sometimes it does take that kind of trade-off to achieve a strategic breakpoint, but it usually does not. Quite often, it proves possible to achieve substantial improvement along two or three of these dimensions at once.

CRITICAL DECISIONS

Broadly speaking, there ae eight kinds of manufacturing decisions; product design, process design, facility and plant configuration, information and control systems, human resources, research and development, suppliers' roles and relationships, and organization. Changes in any of these areas can initially affect some or all of the others, and understanding the interrelationships is basic to achieving a strategic breakpoint.

Product Design

A primary driver of cost, quality, and factory throughput is product design. Shrewdly leveraged, the design process can lead to a strategic breakpoint—one that may even alter the company's entire business strategy. Faced with rising competition from the Far East, one American consumer electronics manufacturer found that moving production offshore could save 10 percent to 15 percent on costs. Not only did suppliers in Southeast Asia have the necessary engineering expertise, but also components, labor, and capital would be cheaper and delivery times shorter. But recent advances in the material properties of plastics, which happened to be 20 percent cheaper in the United States than in the Far East, offered management an opportunity to reduce the cost of materials and assembly by radically redesigning the product. Today, the company makes its product in the United States at a cost lower than any of its competitors.

Product design can affect parts and tooling requirements, dictate tasks for the work force, constrain or facilitate new processes and pose special scheduling or quality control problems. Thus, even when it is not the function of manufacturing strategy, design still plays a crucial role.

Process Design

Not long ago, decisions on manufacturing processes, equipment and tooling were routine. New product introductions and the need to replace worn out equipment dominated investment decisions. Except for incremental changes in equipment and systems, process innovation was rarely at the top of management's agenda.

All that is changing. Today, manufacturing executives are more alert to the strategic potential of process design. Significant process design decisions do not necessarily require massive investments in new equipment and systems. An electronic equipment company had planned to build a "factory-of-the-future" by replacing three old production lines with five automated lines. When management realized that the new process would not necessarily ensure the same level of quality, it decided to think the whole project through again. In the end, it decided on a more conservative course—selectively upgrading and rearranging its existing machines and adding material-handling devices. By making these relatively minor changes in its existing plants, the company improved both throughput and quality to the point where the three renovated lines could handle the anticipated increase in volume. Customers gained through lower prices for higher quality goods.

Many companies invest heavily in process design without getting the benefits they want. They neglect to integrate changes in the other seven manufacturing areas or they fail to set clear strategic objectives. If the organizational groundwork is not properly laid out, for example, process design changes may have little lasting effect. Workers on the shop floor may drift back to their old ways of dealing with production problems. Maintenance workers may delay preventive maintenance because of time pressures created by poor organizational planning. Purchasing agents, still preoccupied with cutting costs, may undermine quality by ordering cheaper but less uniform materials. These slippages can cause the deterioration of the entire production system.

Facility and Plant Configuration

In larger companies, improved manufacturing techniques often cause excess capacity, making reconfigurations and painful plant closures inevitable. But when implemented as the first step in a manufacturing strategy rather than later, after other decisions are made, reconfiguration can be a valuable catalyst for change. Because it compels management to take a fresh look at accepted practice, reconfiguration can trigger necessary changes in other areas.

Information and Control Systems

The bewildering variety of powerful systems that can be applied to factory-floor operations often lure top managers into a trap; they invest in new systems before thinking through their strategic objectives. Systems development priorities and resource allocation should always be guided by the strategic breakpoint that management aims to achieve. If greater responsiveness to customers is the goal, then systems to eliminate unpredictable elements in processes and thereby support part and product flows should probably head the agenda. A quality breakpoint, on the other hand, may call for developing shop floor controls and feedback systems first.

Since systems decisions are inextricably tied to other operational functions, the right system decisions can alleviate bottlenecks, eliminate the unpredictability of a manufacturing process, improve product and part availability, and enhance customer service. Before management automates a process, for example, systems may have to be installed to monitor production stations or read bar codes of incoming parts. Similarly, it may not be possible to speed up product introductions or broaden the product line without first upgrading the computer-aided design and scheduling systems. In short, before other operational changes can be implemented, system development may be necessary.

Human Resources

Companies seeking a cost advantage over competitors usually zero in early on labor cost. Wage levels in particular are an obvious target. Cutting wages and benefits may gain a temporary reprieve, but they are rarely the key to a sustainable competitive advantage. Because they sour work force attitudes, wage cuts often put out of reach the productivity gains that could be obtained by more skilled, sensitive management of human resources.

Training the work force in added skills, for example, can permit more flexibility in job assignments, and that in turn can boost shop floor productivity. By paying a wage increment for each new skill learned, Sherwin-Williams gave employees at one of its automotive paint plants an incentive to broaden their job capabilities. A year after this program was launched, more than 95 percent of the work force had developed new skills. Two and a half years later, product quality had improved and labor costs were actually cut in half.

Despite their power, human resource decisions are risky. They impinge heavily on other decision areas, and their effects are often irreversible. Restructuring a company's human resource policy can have such a profound impact on attitudes and expectations that it probably should not be attempted more than once in a management generation. Hence management should carefully think through proposed changes in the other manufacturing areas before attempting to revamp its human resource policy.

Resarch and Development

Because R&D is the key to developing proprietary process and product expertise, it influences almost all other manufacturing decisions, even those involving roles and relationships with suppliers (for example, what technology suppliers will provide), facility location, and development of special organizational capabilities.

Most people credit Polaroid Corporation's preeminence in instant photography to its founder's invention of the first instant camera in the mid-1950s. But Edwin Land's breakthrough does not explain why 30 years later Polaroid still reigns supreme in its market. The real reason has more to do with superior process technology than with product innovation. Having defined its unique product feature as "developing film in air," Polaroid has focused its research on continually improving its proprietary process for finishing spreader rollers—the component controlling picture quality. High-speed, low-cost coating and assembly of multilayered film and batteries, another unique skill perfected through patient R&D, gave Polaroid the opportunity to diversify into the coating of computer disks.

When management is alert to current developments in both products and process technology, it may take a very different approach to thinking about next generation products and other manufacturing decisions. A Far East supplier offered to sell precision-cast metal turbine blades to a United States aircraft engine manufacturer for less than the company's current cost. Management hesitated, worrying that the arrangement might tempt the supplier to enter the engine business itself. But the research group came up with convincing evidence that metal blades would eventually be replaced by ceramic blades, which had the advantages of greater strength, lighter weight, and faster heat dissipation. Reassured, management decided to source its blades from the Far East and shift its R&D from improving the casting process to developing processes for working with the next generation of materials.

Had its strategic planning process not forced management to look at the implications of basic materials science, this company would have forgone significant short-term savings and missed out on an important long-term technological opportunity.

Suppliers' Roles and Relationships

Lacking the in-house expertise needed to keep up with advances in all the relevant technologies, few companies can excel in every aspect of manufacturing. For most, it is uneconomic even to try. But there is an alternative. Global competition is pushing suppliers to develop new specialized capabilities, and by tapping their technological expertise, some manufacturers have gained the flexibility needed to reach a strategic breakpoint.

Viewed strategically, decisions on suppliers' roles and relationships go beyond simple choices about what to make in-house. They are decisions about how to position the company's manufacturing capability so as to get the best value from suppliers while also maximizing the competitive value of in-house skills. And they are decisions about how to work with suppliers—by subcontracting, joint research contracts, or joint venture, for example—to establish the best long-term working relationships. As a result, decisions about how to work with suppliers become tightly linked to process design and product design decisions, organizational decisions, and sometimes systems decisions as well as, for example, when a company links its scheduilng systems with those of its suppliers.

In the highly cyclical electronics industry, manufacturers have habitually ordered from their suppliers on a very short-term basis. Hewlett-Packard took a different tack. It committed itself to firm orders six months ahead. This change enabled Hewlett-Packard's silicon suppliers to exploit economies of scale and improve their quality. In turn, Hewlett-Packard could rely on component quality and delivery even in times of industry shortage, thereby better serving its own customers and reaching a strategic breakpoint.

Organization

Rarely can a business achieve its strategic breakpoint through organizational change alone. By changing its organizational procedures, structures, skills, and style, however, management can relax operational constraints, foster coherent decision-making, and enhance its efforts to reach a strategic breakpoint.

Take the case of a domestic automotive parts supplier. To design and manufacture a new product planned as a major entry in the world market, management needed to install complex, integrated automation and computer systems. These demanded more rigorous planning and control. Management saw that if the new technology was to be effectively deployed, organizational change would be necessary.

Instead of handling the assignment to technical experts on its central advisory staff, management set up a cross-functional project team and gave it full responsibility for both planning and implementation. Lodged in separate facilities, the team was given all the resources it needed and told to carry on without regard to established practices or historical loyalties. The organizational changes have yielded hundreds of improvements in integrating process and product development along with process breakthroughs and novel applications of old technology. Engineering and marketing now work hand-in-hand. The company is meeting rigorous new cost standards, maintaining a zero-defect quality standard, and reaching its operating targets (single-unit sizes).

INTEGRATED DECISIONS

In today's environment, there are no unitary solutions. Whatever the strategic breakpoint management has targeted, it is never possible to isolate a single decision that would make everything happen. The most successful corporations not only take the interactions among the eight critical decision areas into account; they also continually reevaluate and reorchestrate their manufacturing decisions to support their strategic goals.

Western Electric (now AT&T Technologies) also encountered problems when it installed new computer-integrated equipment to remedy a quality problem that was dragging output down. Because management failed to integrate this change with other manufacturing decisions, a host of minor troubles frustrated implementation. When the equipment needed maintenance, workers hesitated to touch it for fear of distorting data in the system. When an atypical circuit board came down the line, workers would stop the line until they had checked the records to make sure it was not the result of a computer error. When materials ran short, the purchasing people hesitated to use the established rules for parts substitution because they were not sure that the new system was compatible with the old procedures.

Success came only after Western Electric built a plant to house the new equipment and processes, established a full-time, high-level team to oversee the installation, and set about changing people's habits and assumptions. Incentives were introduced to encourage risk taking. Factory operators were trained to work with the computer system, and communication programs were launched to convert the organization to new ways of thinking about production. Western Electric's management learned that manufacturing changes cannot be made in isolation. To work effectively, the new computer-integrated equipment required a whole array of unanticipated adjustments, innovations, and leadership initiatives.

Properly linked, decisions in the eight manufacturing areas can deliver strategic breakpoints, but their interdependencies, if not taken into account, can also pose strategic barriers. Because these interrelationships are complex, what seems an obvious move may sometimes be neither feasible nor effective. At other times, an obvious move may be needlessly risky compared with a less dramatic alternative that could do the job with less disruption or at lower cost.

Technology's dramatic transformation of the factory has strengthened the link between manufacturing strategy and business strategy, and thereby invalidated a host of time-tested operational principles and decision criteria. More and more, competitive advantage will go to the companies that seek strategic breakpoints through the integration of decisions in every area of manufacturing.

Many American manufacturing companies cannot hope to be competitive unless they increase productivity by 10 percent to 15 percent annually during the next four to five years. Companies that move now to expoit the full power of manufacturing as a competitive weapon should find a commanding strategic advantage within their reach. But for those that continue to seek salvation in operational improvements, the long-term outlook is bleak.

READING 5.2

Towards Economies of Integration

INTRODUCTION

Companies have dabbled with automation for decades; but the challenge today is to choose the technology that improves quality, reduces the materials and overhead costs, and above all makes factories more *flexible.* More flexibility is viewed as a way to spread common costs over more output units. It is also considered as the key to respond to changes that have taken place in the global market, some of which are:

- The market life cycles for products are getting shorter, so now designs must follow one another more frequently.
- The marketplace is demanding a greater variety of products without increasing the volume desired. This means that a factory must produce smaller quantities of each product.
- The marketplace is time sensitive. Hence, factories are expected to produce in smaller batches on closely time-controlled schedules.
- The marketplace is cost sensitive. Hence, highly efficient production capabilities are required with high quality and reliability.

One frequently criticized manufacturing practice is the use, or the abuse of "economies of scale." Specifically, the sole pursuit of economies of scale, it is argued, can lead to the adoption of huge and inefficient plants with no strategic focus (Skinner 1974; 1985) or specialized processes, whose inflexibility critically limits a company's ability to be product innovative in changing markets (Abernathy and Kenneth 1984). Additionally, it is shown that new technological capabilities will present opportunities for a successful utilization of a different manufacturing strategy based on economies of scope (Goldhar and Jelinek 1983; 1985).

This paper maintains that there is potential with the new technology to realize both scope and scale economies simultaneously, making their relationship *interdependent.* Furthermore, firms achieving this synergy (snyergy referred to, hereafter, as *economies of integration*) will attain strategic advantage over those who focus on only one of these two dimensions.

TECHNOLOGICAL CHARACTERISTICS OF SCALE AND SCOPE ECONOMIES

The Principle of Scale

Economies of scale are realized when specialized machinery is utilized to produce a large volume of product, the process flow is continuous, and the variety of products is limited. If we denote the firm's product mix by $P=(p_1, p_2, \ldots p_n)$ and its total cost function of $C(P)$, then the following relationship

$$C(\lambda P) \leq \lambda C(P) \text{ for } \lambda \geq 1,$$

displays economies of scale. Exhibit 5.1 is modeled on this definition and is based on unit (average) costs.

With conventional technology, this form of process was the only viable way of increasing volume while maintaining strategic focus and minimizing complexity. With these technological characteristics, high volume and a smooth flowing process, a company is able to move down its long run average cost curve (LRAC), increase throughput times, and perhaps demand price breaks from suppliers. Herein, lies the true economies of scale.

Scale economies confer obvious and perhaps significant cost advantages. However, technologies for achieving economies of scale have one overriding drawback—they are product inflexible.

The Principle of Scope

The inflexibility inherent with technologies exhibiting economies of scale can be contrasted with the concept of economies of scope. Economies of scope come with the technology that allows for product variety, rather than high volume (Goldhar and Jelinek 1983). Economies of scope are realized where it is less or equally costly to combine two or more product lines in one plant than to produce them separately. Using our previous notation, this, in the case of two products p_1 and p_2 implies that:

$$C(p_1,p_2) \leq C(p_1,0) + C(0,p_2).$$

Exhibit 5.1 also demonstrates the implication of this definition with respect to unit (average) costs. The specific cost benefits of scope economies are derived from shared costs and/or the usage of excess capacity—that is, by reducing the cost penalty of product diversity.

Scope economies have been recognized by economists for years as a characteristic for multiproduct firms. See (Panzar and Willig 1985; and Baumol et al. 1982) for an extensive coverage of this topic. However, the advent of new manufacturing technology has given the concept of economies of scope a new life and has made its usefulness more apparent. The need for adequate flexibility makes the capability to adapt to the market (economies of scope) much more important than economies of scale. It is argued that economies of scope are quite compatible with competitive, monopolistic or oligopolistic market structure (see Panzar and Willig 1975, 30).

To expand the manufacturing strategic options, it is important to assess the relationship between economies of scale and economies of scope. As a prerequisite to this discussion, a cognizance of "levels of automation" is important (see page 190).

In practice, flexible automation has effectively eliminated those technological barriers that have, to date, kept scale and scope economies apart by:

1. Allowing the specialization normally built into the production hardware to be built into the computer software. This significantly reduces the inflexibility of a dedicated production process because general purpose machines with specialized software can be used in place of specialized hardware.
2. Eliminating learning curve effects through software that can perform the required operations perfectly every time.

Exhibit 5.1 Cost Implications of Scale and Scope

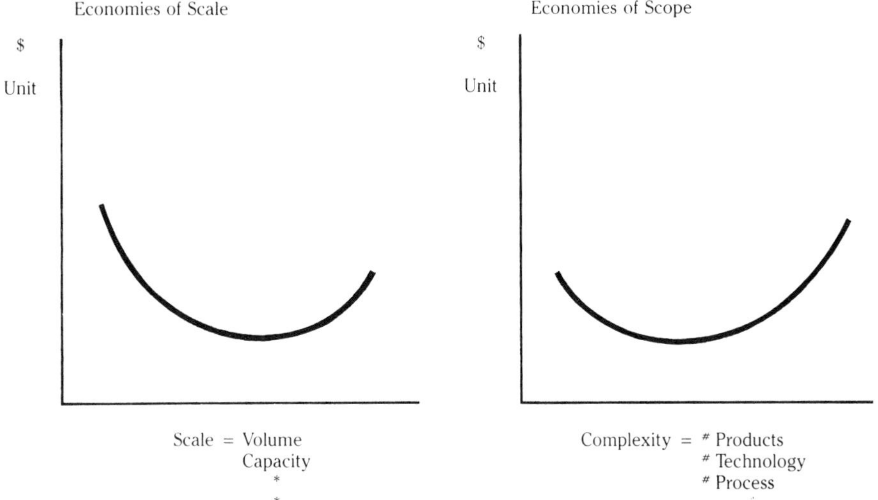

Adopted from Cohen and Lee (1985), p. 161.

3. Eliminating the confusion of an unfocused factory through the computer direction of scheduling, machinery, materials flow, and tooling.
4. Allowing setup changes that can be accomplished with no significant time loss—this along with point 2 previously mentioned, effectively reduces the Economic Batch Quantity (EBQ) to one.

This implies that the traditional relationship of independence between scale and scope economies has now changed to one of interdependence—it is possible for a plant to have the capabilities associated with the two economies simultaneously.

THE PRINCIPLE OF INTEGRATION

While the notion of integration is not new (Teece 1980, 241), economies of integration is a concept we introduce here as a synergy whose dependence relies on the coexistence of scale and scope economies. Integration economies usually stems from characteristics of scale and scope which possess the greatest flexibility along the volume, variety, and value dimensions. Conceptually, we expect economies of integration will encourage firms to maintain a medium-sized plant operation. As Starr (1988) points out, "with technological innovation, the production cost curve is lowered, . . . , the minimum total per unit cost point moves left, indicating a smaller size organization is warranated."

Justifying Economies of Integration

Economies of integration can be realized only at a level of automation sufficiently sophisticated to allow for the operation of CIM systems (see Appendix). Integration economies encourage customized production as well as standardized consumer goods. Software can be programmed with the information needed to perform the operation each and every time. This effectively allows any benefits gained by producing large batches to be realized also by the production of small batches. Exhibit 5.2 outlines the various technological and strategic characteristics of integration economies and compares them with those of scope and scale economies.

Technological developments in product designs are the keys in reshaping the factory-of-the-future. Novel approaches in designing new products have led to end products having fewer components and a much lower proportion of total added value. In the manufacture of sewing machines, for example, the microprocessor has replaced 350 mechanical parts. Similar changes have occurred in the manufacture of electronic goods.

As documented by Kumpe and Bolwijn (1987), this evolution is having a fundamental impact on final assembly, the manufacturing of subassemblies, and the production of parts. Because of the integration of components, the end products require less time and hence automation will have a relatively lower impact in improving price/performance ratio. In contrast, the manufacture of subassemblies, particularly the component area, can now possess much more added value and "know-how" within the final product and hence automation can play a more significant role in improving the price/performance ratio. In this situation, manufacturing of parts can be performed with a high degree of automation (to produce similar parts in large volume), and the manufacturing of subassemblies can benefit from high flexible automation (to produce various subcomponents in different quantities and configurations). This implies that the notion of economies of integration is best suited to the subassembly area.

The achievement of economies of integration, which requires flexible automation, is most appropriately pursued in situations where a range of different products are to be produced under circumstances where *general* rather than *exact* configurations are known. An example of this type of situation is GM's recently completed AUTOPLEX in Oshawa, Ontario where the conventional assembly line principle has been replaced by a new system called "Tracking Signal;" cars are completed with all of the various options, colors, and specific parts ordered by customers.

Economies of integration are an attractive option for companies that want to obtain the cost effectiveness of economies of scale and the flexibility of economies of scope. In short, economies of integration reflect the highest degree of *aggregate manufacturing flexibility* because the technology makes it possible to switch the production process with no significant cost thereby allowing both flexibility in output and low per unit costs.

Exhibit 5.2 Principal Characteristics of the Three Economies

Characteristics:	Scale (Volume)	Scope (Variety)	Integration (Variety and Volume)
Process	Continuous flow	Jumbled flow, batch	Continuous flow
	Special purpose machinery	General purpose machinery	Specialized software, computer integrated multipurpose machinery
Product	Standardized-commodity	Customized-multi-products	Customized-commodity
Facility	Centralized	Decentralized	Moderately decentralized
	Large (in size)	Small (in size)	Medium (in size)
Level of Automation	Low (hard to programmable automation)	High	Highest (flexible automation)
Total Added Flexibility	Low	High	Highest
Relative Costs:			
• Fixed	Low	High	Highest
• Variable	High	Low	Lowest
Experience Curve	Not too flat	Flat	Flatter and lower
Organization	Process focus	Product focus	Product focus
Managerial Characteristics	Technical	Entrepreneurial	Entrepreneurial-technical
Marketing	Low cost, dependability	Flexibility, product innovation	Low cost, dependable product innovation, flexibility

LINKING ECONOMIES OF INTEGRATION TO MANUFACTURING STRATEGY

Economies of integration offers the potential for a new and revitalized manufacturing strategy. Its adoption increases machine utilization and scheduling flexibility, reduces direct and indirect labor costs, and decreases manufacturing lead-time and in-process inventory. In short, it has a fundamental impact on the product-process (P-P) life cycle matrix, introduced by Hayes and Wheelright (1979), which assumes long life cycles for products. The existence of multipurpose machinery allows for the excess capacity of one product's production run to be made available for another's production run—an effective way to address possible excess demand (for certain products) and under capacity problems. It is no longer necessary to focus the manufacturing strategy on one or two competitive axioms. Attempting to be competitive on all four axioms—cost, dependability, flexibility, and quality—is not at all inconsistent with the concept of economies of integration. By eliminating these explicit trade-offs, imagination and strategic foresight become the new constraining factors.

No Need for the Process to Enter Into the Product Life Cycle

One key principle in the P-P matrix is that the production process must change as the products do. This process evolution is deemed necessary because as a product moves through its life cycle, different demands which vary from high flexibility to more cost efficiency and standards are placed on the process. Obviously, when the technology permits both flexibility and efficiency, process change or evolution is not required because it serves no purpose.

The notion of integration economies is also consistent with manufacturing strategic flexibility. Traditionally, flexibility and efficiency have been viewed as two opposite ways of evaluating the economies of capital-equipment design (see Fuss and McFadden 1978, Ch. II:4), and any variations in corporate direction is viewed as being very expensive with conventional technology. Flexibility which comes with the application of new technology (and CIM in particular) can indeed eliminate many of the costs associated with a change of direction. In addition, as batch sizes approach one with CIM, the choice as to whether to stock an item or make it to order, is greatly simplified. Producing to order allows for reduced inventory costs and increased product alteration.

Strategic Possibilities of Economies of Integration

The P-P matrix assumes that the lower left-hand corner is nonattainable because of the physical limitations inherent in conventional technology. With flexible automation, these limitations are no longer evident and hence this region should be considered as a viable part of the strategic options available to companies. In fact, a revised P-P matrix, such as the one suggested in Exhibit 5.3, can be developed to account for all of the new technological capabilities and changes. Such a framework could then be used as a basis for developing a new manufacturing strategy.

Exhibit 5.3 Revised Product-Process Matrix

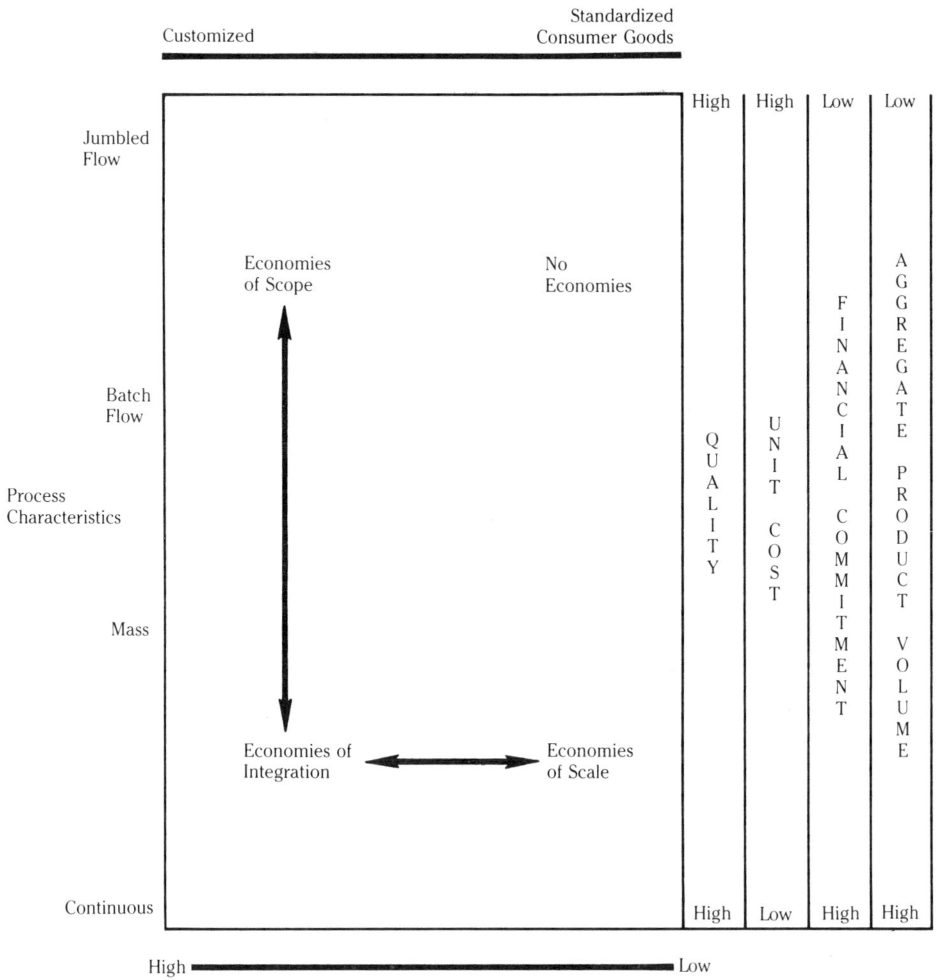

In the "revised" matrix, the left vertical axis characterizes the production process in a way similar to that of the original P-P matrix. However, notice that while economies of integration and economies of scale require a mass/continuous *type process,* they are characterized by a different level of automation. The top horizontal axis of the revised P-P matrix is left relatively untouched when compared to the original P-P matrix. The only difference is that the traditional product life cycle element was eliminated because of its contemporary questionable validity.

The bottom horizontal axis indicated that greater production flexibility is required not only when the products are customized, but also when the degree of market segmentation and dynamics are high. Note that the revised P-P matrix does not assume that costs decline or dependability increases as one moves rightward in the matrix. Finally, the right vertical axis indicates that high quality (defined as the degree of conformance) is possible at either end of the matrix. It further illustrates that per unit cost declines as one moves down the matrix, and that the financial commitment must increase together with aggregate product volume.

IMPLICATIONS

There are several salient points that should be noted when determining a position on the revised P-P matrix. A general rule of thumb is that the best strategic option for a company is to maintain a position to the left and below most competitors. This will enable the company to compete along the four surrogate criteria previously mentioned. The advantages of such a position will encourage many producers toward the left-hand corner of the revised P-P matrix in the future. This trend should be considered when determining future positioning direction. Furthermore, financial constraints are important considerations with respect to positioning. New technology, in general, changes the balance between fixed cost, capital cost, and overhead cost. In particular, CIM requires enormous capital investments. If, by adopting a higher level of automation, the company is financially strapped for a number of years to come, it should consider a more moderate position. Another consideration when weighing the costs and benefits of locating right or left of the competition is flexibility requirements. What kind, and what degree of flexibility is required for a given market objectives, market characteristics, and marketing strategy? Flexibility not used is a wasted resource. However, a lack of flexibility can stifle the company's growth, and limits its future opportunities.

REFERENCES AND BIBLIOGRAPHY

ABERNATHY, W. J., and K. WAYNE [1984]. "Limits of the Learning Curve." *Harvard Business Review*, September-October, pp. 66-76.

BAUMOL. W., J. PANZER, and R. WILLIG [1982]. *Contestable Markets and the Theory of Industry Structure*. Harcourt Brace Jovanovich, Inc., New York.

BROWNE, J. ET AL. [1984]. "Classification of Flexible Manufacturing Systems." *The FMS Magazines*, April.

COHEN, M., and H. L. LEE [1985]. "Manufacturiung Strategy." In P. Kleindorfer (ed.), *The Management of Productivity and Technology in Manufacturing*. Plenum Press, New York, Chapter 5, pp. 153-188.

DAY, G. S., and D. B. MONTGOMERY [1983]. "Diagnosing the Experience Curve." *Journal of Marketing*, Volume 47, Spring, pp. 44-58.

FUSS, M., and D. McFADDEN [1978]. "Flexibility Versus Efficiency in Ex Ante Plant Design." In M. Fuss and D. McFadden (eds.), *Production Economies: A Dual Approach to Theory and Applications*, Volume 1, North Holland Publishing Co., New York, pp. 311-364.

GOLDHAR, J. D., and M. JELINEK [1985]. "Computer Integrated Flexible Manufacturing: Organizational, Economic, and Strategic Implications." *Interfaces*, Volume 15, No. 3, May-June, pp. 94-105.

GOLDHAR, J. D., and M. JELINEK [1983]. "Plan for Economies of Scope." *Harvard Business Review*, November-December, pp. 141-148.

GORMAN, I. E. [1985]. "Conditions for Economies of Scope in the Presence of Fixed Costs." *Rand Journal of Economics,* Volume 16, No. 3, pp. 431–436.

HAYES, R. H., and S. C. WHEELRIGHT [1979]. "Link Manufacturing Process and Product Life Cycles." *Harvard Business Review,* January–February, pp. 133–140.

KUMAR, V., and U. KUMAR [1987]. "Manufacturing Flexibility: A New Approach to Its Flexibility." In *The Proceedings of World Productivity Forum,* International Industrial Engineering Conference, Washington, D. C., May 17–20, pp. 469–475.

KUMPE, T., and P. T. BOLWIJN [1987]. "Trends and Issues in Improving Productivity of Industrial Organizations Engaged in Medium to High-Volume Manufacture of Discrete Products." In the *Proceedings of World Productivity Forum,* International Industrial Engineering Conference, Washington, D. C., May 17–20, pp. 48–50.

LAWRENCE, J. [1984]. "Levels of Automation." *Systems International,* March.

PANZAR, J. C., and R. D. WILLIG [1981]. "Economies of Scope." *American Economic Review Papers and Proceedings,* Volume 71, May, pp. 268–272.

PANZAR, J. C., and R. D. WILLIG [1975]. "Economies of Scale and Economies of Scope in Multi-Output Production. *Economic Discussion Paper No. 33,* Bell Laboratories, August.

SKINNER. W. [1985]. "The Taming of Lions." In K. B. Clark, R. H. Hayes, and C. Lorenz (eds.), *The Uneasy Alliance: Managing the Productivity-Technology Dilemma.* Harvard Business School Press, pp. 63–110.

SKINNER, W. [1974]. "The Focused Factory." *Harvard Business Review,* May–June, pp. 113–121.

STARR, M. K. [1984]. "The Effects of New Technology on Optional Size for Productivity." Research Working Paper No. 439A, Graduate School of Business, Columbia University, October.

TECE, D. J. [1980]. "Economies of Scope and the Scope of the Enterprise." *Journal of Economic Behavior and Organization,* pp. 223–247.

WILLIG, R. [1979]. 'Multiproduct Technology and Market Share." *American Economic Review,* Volume 69, No. 2, pp. 346–351.

APPENDIX

Levels of Automation

We briefly discuss levels of (soft) automation. There is a four-tier of soft automation depending on the complexity of processors (Lawrence 1984). These are:

Level One:	Application of control systems for use within the production process, for example, NC machines and robots.
Level Two:	Application of supervisory systems for providing the control for the production process. They monitor and control the production lines.
Level Three:	Application of integrated systems to fully integrate and control different aspects of the design and production processes. These are combinations of level one and level two automation. Examples include CAD and CAE.
Level Four:	Application of large-scale systems which link control and supervisory systems to corporate information systems. This is known as a global concept and is usually referred to as Computer-Integrated Manufacturing (CIM) systems.

Obviously, each of these levels of automation provides a certain degree and type of manufacturing flexibility to companies. (See Browne et al. 1984; and Kumar and Kumar 1987 for more detail on flexibility.) For example, level four automation allows for close-to-zero-time factory concept (Goldhar and Jelinek 1985). This implies that a shift to higher levels of automation results in a gradual increase in the fixed costs portion and a relative decline in the variable costs part of the total cost. Furthermore, the cost of dealing with uncertainty in the marketplace is reduced due to the added flexibility of higher levels of automation which increase the ability of the firm to adjust immediately to changes in demand.

A move toward a higher level of automation also implies a shift in the experience curve defined as a combination of: (a) learning experience, (b) technological advances, and (c) economies of scale (Day and Montgomery 1983). As we move to a higher degree of automation, the learning portion of this equation becomes more and more level and other components remain equal, this alone would shift the experience curve lower and would make it flat.

EPILOGUE

Towards an Integration Strategy

Just as new technology has changed the manufacturing function, it has also changed the approach which companies must take to formulate strategy. Many North American firms either do not realize this or are unwilling to take it into account. Unless they do (and soon), they risk further and more dramatic erosion of their competitive position.

Some of the traditional manufacturing theories are being brought into question, and are being modified. For example, traditional operations trade-offs between cost, quality and service may no longer hold. It is now possible to achieve substantial improvements along several of these dimensions simultaneously. Perhaps the best example of this comes through the recent availability of economies of integration. Traditional manufacturing theory has pointed to two different strategies: economies of scale and economies of scope.

Under scale economies, the decline in unit cost with cumulative output provides the largest (volume wise) firm in the industry with a competitive cost advantage. However, the dedicated production systems needed to realize these economies make a firm extremely product inflexible.

Economies of scope, on the other hand, exist where it is cheaper to produce several products within one facility than to produce them separately. Scope economies however are primarily for multiproduct firms, and limit the size a firm may attain in any one product market, as well as the technology it may economically utilize.

Economies of integration, finally, exist where scope and scale economies coexist. New technology provides the potential to pursue such a strategy and in effect have the best of both worlds; high volume, high variety, and reasonable cost all at once. Thus integration economies provide the highest degree of aggregate manufacturing flexibility, and increase the number of feasible strategic options available to firms.

In a general sense, there are eight specific areas of manufacturing decison making: product design, process design, facility and plant configuration, information and control systems, human resources, research and development, suppliers' roles and relationships, and organization. To fully realize the potential benefits available in these areas, it is necessary for firms to stop viewing them as distinct and separate manufacturing decisions, and begin to consider them in a strategic perspective. If managed correctly, through new technology adoption and explicit consideration in the strategy formulation process, firms can gain significant competitive advantage in these areas. If this is not done, the firm may well fall prey to the typical trade-offs and thus vastly underutilize available resources, and fall rapidly behind those firms who have progressed beyond this outmoded approach.

However, it is not enough merely to consider these decision areas once. They must continually be reevaluated in the context of the business strategy, particularly given the dynamic environment created by new technology.

CASE 5.1

Electronic Craftsmen Limited (A)[3]

INTRODUCTION

"It appears everything is going great," Glen Bell said, "but I have concerns about the increase in orders and their impact on our backlog and deliveries. Even though we turn down orders, delivery delays continue to increase, and unless something is done quickly we will lose customers. A few are already talking of going offshore to reduce costs, and we have to show them that we can produce what they want, when they want it, and at a reasonable cost. Today we have to decide for ourselves how we are going to do that."

The occasion was a November, 1984 meeting arranged by Glen Bell, vice president of operations at Electronic Craftsmen Limited (ECL), with the company's treasurer Audrey Stoddart. Deterioration in customer confidence, created by ECL's growing inability to deliver on time, had been apparent for some time. Glen realized that one option was to increase capacity, in which case automation might provide a reasonable solution. None of the trade shows Glen Bell had visited had shown equipment fully compatible with ECL's needs, and besides, the impact of automation on ECL would be difficult to assess.

BACKGROUND

ECL was a small Canadian company wholly-owned by a large Toronto-based holding company which had total sales exceeding $150 million. The ECL operation was self-financing and required basic approvals only on major proposals. Once approval had

[3]This case was written by Professor Hamid Noori and Glen Bell, 1987.

been given, ECL had full autonomy to execute plans. The ECL facilities were located in Waterloo, Ontario and occupied 2,500 square meters of manufacturing and office facilities, which could be expanded to 4,000 square meters. Space for any additional equipment did not pose any problems. The company specialized in the design and manufacture of high quality custom magnetics (transformers and coils). (See Appendix A for details on the types of products.) These magnetics ranged from large power transformers weighing up to 50 kilograms and costing several hundred dollars, to audio transformers weighing a few grams and selling for less than $3.00 each. Sales in 1984 were in the $3–$4 million range with net profit approximately 15 percent. The smaller to mid-range transformers made up 70 percent of the total volume.

PRODUCT DESCRIPTION

A transformer is an electrical device which changes an input voltage and current to a different desired level. These devices generally have at least two windings of insultated magnet wire wound on a coil form. Coil forms can be either electrical grade paper tubes or bobbins made from plastic or phenolic material. The individual windings are usually separated by an insulating material (such as mylar tape or electrical grade papers). The windings are coil finished, which means they have either flexible lead wire, terminals or printed circuit board pins attached to the free ends of the magnet wire. An insulating layer of material is placed over the winding, and a magnetic core added to the coil of the transformer.

CURRENT PRODUCTION TECHNIQUES

Several standard production techniques existed for winding transformers, the size, type and cost factor of the transformer generally dictating the method used. As a rule of thumb, the material/labor ratio could be as high as 80/20 for large power transformers to as low as 30/70 for audio transformers.

Stick or multiple winding was used for mid-sized power transformers. This was considered the least expensive method of manufacturing, since up to 25 units at one time could be wound on a paper tube. After winding, the transformers were slit into individual units and sent on to have the magnet wires picked out and coil finished. The main disadvantage of this technique was the fact that the transformers tended to be larger than they would be by using other techniques. This could take away valuable space needed for other components in the overall design of the production in which such transformers were used.

Unit or hand winding was used for large power transformers or transformers which may have complicated winding patterns. This was the most expensive winding technique as the units were wound one at a time either on a paper tube or on bobbin coil forms. The method was usually reserved for transformers with very heavy wire and relatively few turns.

Bobbin winding was used for the smaller power transformer coils and audio transformers. The transformers could usually be wound one or two at a time (depending on the number of turns) using a preformed bobbin. This bobbin might have prepinned terminations molded into the form or may have required either leads or terminals to be attached at a later process station. Bobbin winding could be used for any number of turns as was considered a moderately cost effective method of manufacture.

TRANSFORMER INDUSTRY IN CANADA

Advances in silicon technology in the 1970s brought disaster to the transformer industry. The commercial use of the transistor and integrated circuit resulted in drastic changes to the design and use of the transformer. Higher frequency switching power supplies were being increasingly adopted by a market which was interested in smaller size and more efficient products. This advance in technology also created newer magnetic materials and design concepts.

The trend to offshore manufacturing for consumer products also had an impact on the transformer industry. Manufacturers of transformers supplying companies in the radio and TV industry found themselves in an awkward position. Their customers, such as Admiral or Electrohome, were either facing bankruptcy or forced to buy from offshore sources due to cost advantages. At the time, many of the magnetic manufacturers believed the trend to manufacture offshore was just temporary. There was a general belief that North American consumers would not tolerate the offshore inferior products for very long. It was also believed that offshore companies could not continue to "gouge" the market with completed products which in some cases were below North American cost.

The Canadian Industry as a whole was very slow to adapt to the newer technology. Of the 20 companies in the magnetics industry in Canada, only four appeared to recognize the technological change in the market. ECL was one of those companies and later became noted as a leader in innovative design techniques in the industry.

ECL'S STRATEGY

With the drastic downturn in the industry in the mid to late 1970s, ECL had recognized that some type of change was required. The type of change and direction was not realized until Glen Bell prepared ECL's first formal marketing study in the early 1980s (see Exhibit 5.4). The report verified that consumer products were declining while telecommunications products were increasing. It was hence concluced that ECL would benefit by concentrating on servicing the telecommunication industry.

The first thing to be done was to establish design credibility. This was accomplished by hiring Alec Leslie, a professional engineer in electronics specializing in magnetic components. A fully-equipped laboratory and technical library was built up under his direction using the latest and best equipment available. Next, ECL concentrated on leading companies in the telecommunications industry. ECL became known as specialists in the field of telecommunication magnetics, and the larger customer base, generated a steady increase in sales at the rate of 25 percent per year.

Exhibit 5.4 Summary of Domestic Consumption of Electronic Products*
(In Millions of Dollars)

		1974	1975	1976	1977	1978
Telecommunications Equipment	Canadian Shipments	655.3	806.1	814.0	850.0	960.0
	Imports	201.9	236.7	278.6	348.1	376.3
	Exports	173.6	210.9	248.5	220.7	272.4
	Consumption	683.6	831.9	844.1	977.4	1,063.9
Components and Assembly Through Distribution	Canadian Shipments	368.1	246.4	277.2	289.0	326.0
	Imports					
	Exports	175.0	152.5	153.4	163.0	226.9
	Consumption	192.0	460.5	555.4	606.3	728.0
Office Machinery	Canadian Shipments	99.4	139.4	152.1	110.1	135.0
	Imports	148.9	170.9	174.4	95.1	60.6
	Exports	53.3	88.7	111.7	56.1	63.9
	Consumption	195.0	221.6	214.8	149.0	131.7
Instruments	Canadian Shipments	121.6	132.6	127.8	133.0	144.0
	Imports	91.2	107.6	109.0	125.0	154.2
	Exports	45.7	51.0	60.4	68.8	67.9
	Consumption	167.1	189.2	176.4	189.2	230.3
Consumer Products	Canadian Shipments	317.9	264.0	243.2	163.5	188.0
	Imports	324.8	268.9	418.5	463.5	568.7
	Exports	34.8	31.2	31.6	55.9	95.4
	Consumption	607.9	501.7	630.1	571.1	661.3
Total	Consumption	2,475.0	2,393.8	2,658.0	2,789.3	3,362.6

*Mclean-Hunter Research Bureau Estimates

NOTE: It is estimated that since magnetics are present in most electronic devices and constitute a major portion of the cost of the item then allow for potential market to be 5 percent of total consumption. Also note that in-house manufacturing takes up to 50–60 pecent of total potential market.

The new strategy put a strain on some of the production equipment. In the past, the largest percentage of transformers made were manufactured on the four stick winding machines that were available. Newer techniques required more unit winding and bobbin winding. The unit winding area was increased from three machines to six, at a cost of $6,000 each, the bobbin winding area being increased by four $10,000 machines to a total of 12 machines. To try and ease some of the production overload, a partial night shift was placed on both unit and bobbin windings. This, however, turned out to be a disaster due to absenteeism (six times the daily average), quality problems, and a shortage of skilled labor.

OPERATIONS AT ECL

In 1984, there were 13 salaried employees on staff, the remaining 75 nonunion employees being paid by the hour. Generally, the hourly-paid employees had no secondary education. Job skills were usually acquired through company training which could take anywhere from one to two weeks for basic training and three months for extensive training. Labor-management relationships at ECL had always been good and management encouraged employees to update their educational and technical training. (See Organizational Chart–Exhibit 5.5.)

ECL's transformers were custom designed for individual customers. In a typical year there could be over 300 new designs, with over 1,000 designs actively being manufactured. Manufacturing was done on a job basis. Parts were only started on the "make-to-order" policy after a confirmed purchase order was received. There may be up to 40 new purchase orders each week while running over 500 different jobs on the floor at one time. Job quantities could vary from one piece to 50,000 pieces, however the typical jobs varied from 250 pieces to 2,500 pieces. The variety of raw materials for such a range of products could cause potential problems since most materials were only replenished after the orders are confirmed.

Once an order had been taken and the part was processed for the shop floor, the production manager released the part for manufacturing and monitored the produc-

Exhibit 5.5 Organizational Structure of ECL

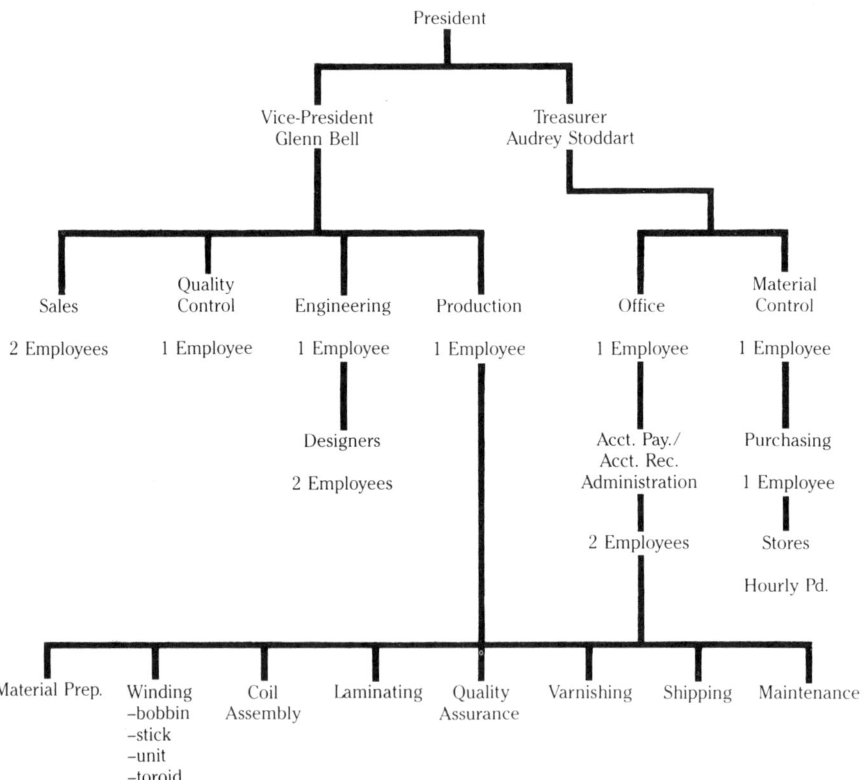

tion flow. The individual group leaders were responsible for the setup and running of the department.

PRELIMINARY INVESTIGATION INTO AUTOMATED WINDING EQUIPMENT

Bell felt that the industry appeared to be automating in some areas, but no equipment that he knew of would be likely to do a satisfactory job for ECL. The technology currently in use in the industry was either hard automation (that is, specifically setup to do one type of job) or where flexibility was required, was crudely "piecemealed" together with some type of material handling system. In either case, Bell felt that neither approach would be appropriate to address ECL's needs.

The most logical place that Bell believed would be appropriate to look for information regarding automation was North American manufacturers of existing coil winding equipment, who Bell thought, would be developing updated equipment as technology advanced. To Bell's surprise, this was not the case. Of the eight identified North American manufacturers of coil winding equipment, only one (Backi Inc.) was actually manufacturing the equipment and one other (Amicoil) was representing a European coil manufacturing company (Meteor) and modifying the equipment to meet their customers' needs.

During his search for the right technology, Bell also became aware that those United States coil transformer manufacturers which had some type of automated equipment installed were unwilling to share their experience with ECL management. In all cases, they were large comapnies doing their own coil winding in-house and to whom ECL posed no competitive threat.

Bell next attended a large coil winding show in London, England, at which three manufacturers of automated winding equipment were identified and contacted. An unanticipated problem was uncovered during their discussion; construction techniques used for placing insulating materials between the primary and secondary windings in hand manufacturing could not be duplicated by machine. To rectify the problem, 80 percent of all the bobbin coil forms in use would eventually have to be retooled at a cost of between $3,000 and $6,000 U.S. each. Ten of the coil forms would require immediate action. Furthermore, selecting the appropriate equipment could be tricky, since ECL's engineers were not familiar with the machine capabilities, and the machine designers were not aware of all ECL's design requirements.

The next issue was flexibility, and the costs associated changeovers. In most cases, the base machine had the capabilities of doing any job, but at $10,000–$15,000 for the tool set required for each bobbin type the expense associated with each increment in product flexibility was high. On his return from Europe Bell asked the production department to investigate the options and to simulate the production differences between the techniques then in use and possible automated manufacturing (see Exhibits 5.6, 5.7, 5.8 and 5.9).

Exhibit 5.6 Description of Operations Required for Winding and Audio Transformer Specification: Custom Audio Transformer 600:600 OHM (ECL) Part No. 2322–80109)

General Material:		
	Bobbin 3/16 × 3/16:	#02–335 or #02–378
	Primary Wire:	36 SPN Bifilar
	Secondary Wire:	41 SPN
	Insulating Tape:	3M #56
	Core:	186EL–8014

Comparison for Possible Construction Techniques and Times

Operations/Techniques		Present Technique	Time (seconds)	Modified Technique (Newly tooled bobbins)	Time (seconds)	Automated Technique	Time (seconds)
Coil Form Used		02–335 One Up		02–378 One Up		02–378 Six Up	
Set-Up							
Primary	Load bobbin	Place on arbor	10	Place on arbor	10	Place on arbor	
	Anchor start	Wrap on pin	35	Wrap on pin	35	Machine anchor	
	Insulate	Crossover	25	Not required	N/A	Not required	
	Wind	145T Bifilar 36	60	145T Bifilar 36	60	Winds	6
	Anchor finish	Wrap on pin	35	Wrap on pin	35	Anchors	
	Insulate	Tape winding	36	Tape winding	36	Insulate	
	Unload bobbin	Unload bobbin	10	Unload bobbin	10	Unload bobbin	

Exhibit 5.6 (continued)

Operations/Techniques		Present Technique	Time (seconds)	Modified Technique (Newly tooled bobbins)	Time (seconds)	Automated Technique	Time (seconds)
Coil Form Used		02–335 One Up		02–378 One Up		02–378 Six Up	
Set-Up Secondary	Load bobbin	Place on arbor	10	Place on arbor	10	Place on arbor	
	Anchor start	Wrap on pin	25	Wrap on pin	25	Machine anchor	
	Insulate	Crossover	25	Not required	N/A	Not required	
	Wind	725T #45SPN	60	725T #45SPN	60	Winds	7
	Anchor finish	Wrap on pin	25	Wrap on pin	25	Anchors	
	Insulate	Tape Winding	36	Tape Winding	36	Imsulate	
	Unload bobbin	Unload bobbin	10	Unload bobbin	10	Not applicable	
Coil Assembly	Flux	Dip in flux	36	Dip in flux	36	Auto Dip	
	Solder	Dip in solder	72	Dip in solder	72	Auto solder	
	Unload	Not applicable		Not applicable		Unload	
Total Time per part			510 seconds		460 seconds		13 seconds
			8.5 minutes		7.67 minutes		0.21 minutes
Time/100 parts			14.2 hours		12.8 hours		0.36 hours

Exhibit 5.7 Comparison Guide for Present Techniques Versus Automated Production System
SITUATION 1—PART HAS NEVER BEEN MANUFACTURED BEFORE—TOOLING AND SET-UP COST REQUIRED

Event/Operation	Present Production Techniques	Time/Cost	Automated Production System	Time/Cost
Order Taken for Part	—Check for arbor		—Check for winding arbor	
	If Yes	N/C	If Yes	N/C
	If No—Tooling	$125–$200	If No—Tooling	$2,000–$5,000
	—Check for bobbin		—Check for bobbin	
	If Yes	N/C	If Yes	N/C
	If No—Tooling	$10,000	If No—Tooling	$10,000
Part Released For Production	—Raw material brought to machine from stores	N/A	—Raw material brought to machine from stores	N/A
	—Single or double winding Arbor located	5 minutes	—Multiple 24 set winding Arbor 6 winding chucks, tape arbor soldering/fluxing arbor located. This is a complete set.	
Machine Set-Up or Program (Winding #1)	—Place arbor on machine	5 minutes	—Place 24 arbors on machine	10 minutes
	—Program or set turns	2 minutes	—Place in #1 winding chuck	5 minutes
	—Set winding pitch	10 minutes	—"Teach In" program to wind	2–4 hours
	—Set winding length: 1 Up*	5 minutes*		
	2 Up*	7 minutes*	—Place in tape arbor Set and program	15–30 minutes
	—Wind first off to check set up and adjust	5–10 minutes	—Place on solder flux arbor Set and program	15–30 minutes
			—Place on next 5 winding chucks	10 minutes
			—Place wire on machine: 6 Up*	15 minutes
			6×2 Up*	20 minutes
			—Function and adjust where necessary	30–60 minutes
	Estimated set up for first off	30–60 minutes	Estimate set up for first off	4–8 hours

Exhibit 5.7 (continued)
SITUATION 1—PART HAS NEVER BEENMANUFACTURED BEFORE—TOOLING AND SET-UP COST REQUIRED

Event/Operation	Present Production Techniques	Time/Cost	Automated Production System	Time/Cost
Production Wind	See Comparison Guide		See Comparison Guide	
Machine Set Up or Program (Winding #2)	—Program or set turns	2 minutes	—Remove 5 winding chucks for set up	10 minutes
	—Set winding pitch	10 minutes		
	—Set winding length	10 minutes	—"Teach In" program for second winding	2–4 hours
	—Place in second wire: 1 Up*	5 minutes*		
	—Size & Tension 2 Up*	7 minutes*	(Note: Tape and soldering are set up from before)	
	—Wind first off to check Set up and adjust	5–10 minutes		
			—Place on 5 winding chucks	10 minutes
			—Place wire on machine: 2 Up*	15 minutes*
			6×2 Up*	20 minutes*
			—Function and adjust where necessary	30–60 minutes
	Estimated set up for first off	15–45 minutes	Estimated set up for first off	3–6 hours
Production Windings	See Comparison Chart		See Comparison Chart	

*Note: 1 up means winding one bobbin at a time.
2 up means winding two bobbins at a time.
6×2 up means winding 6 bobbins at a time with two separate windings.

Exhibit 5.8 Comparison Guide for Present Techniques Versus Automated Production System
SITUATION 2—PART HAS BEEN MANUFACTURED BEFORE—TOOLING AND SET-UP COSTS HAVE BEEN ACCOUNTED FOR

Event/Operation	Present Production Techniques	Time/Cost	Automated Production System	Time/Cost
Part Released for Production	—Raw material brought to machine from stores	N/A	—Raw material brought to machine from stores	N/A
	—Single or double winding arbor located	5 minutes	—Multiple 24 set winding arbor 6 winding chucks, tape arbor soldering/flux arbor located. This is a complete set.	5 minutes
Machine Set-Up (Winding #1)	—Place arbor on machine	5 minutes	—Place 24 arbors on machine	10 minutes
	—Program or set turns	2 minutes	—Place 6 winding chucks on machine	15 minutes
	—Set winding pitch	10 minutes	—Place tape arbor on machine	5 minutes
	—Set winding length	10 minutes	—Place solder/flux arbor on machine	10 minutes
	—Place in wire & tension: 1 Up*	5 minutes	—Place in winding program disc and call up/load	5 minutes
	2 Up*	7 minutes		
	—Wind first off to check set up and adjust	5–10 minutes	—Place wire on machine 6 Up*	15 minutes
			6×2 Up*	20 minutes
			—Wind first off using step function and adjust where necessary	15–30 minutes
	Estimated set up for first off	30–60 minutes	Estimated set up for first off	60–120 minutes

Exhibit 5.8 (continued)

SITUATION 2—PART HAS BEEN MANUFACTURED BEFORE—TOOLING AND SET-UP COSTS HAVE BEEN ACCOUNTED FOR

Event/Operation	Present Production Techniques	Time/Cost	Automated Production System	Time/Cost
Production Wind	See Comparison Guide		See Comparison Guide	
Machine Set-Up (Winding #2)	—Program or set turns	2 minutes	—Call up second winding	5minutes
	—Set winding pitch (continued)	10 minutes	—Program/load	
	—Set winding length	10 minutes	—Place wire on machine 6 Up*	15 minutes
	—Place in second wire 1 Up*	5 minutes	6×2 Up*	20 minutes
	—Size & tension 2 Up*	7 minutes	—Wind first off using step function and adjust where necessary	15–30 minutes
	—Wind first off to check set-up and adjust	5–10 minutes		
	Estimated set up for first off	15–45 minutes	Estimated set up for first off	30–60 minutes
Production Wind	See Comparison Chart		See Comparison Chart	

Note: 1 up means winding one bobbin at a time.
2 up means winding two bobbins at a time.
6×2 means winding 6 bobbins at a time with two separate windings.

Exhibit 5.9 Comparison of Typical In-House Jobs

ECL Part No.	Quantity	Unit Selling Price ($)	Estimated Winding Time Exist/Equip Hours/100	Estimated Winding Time Auto/Equip Hours/100	Estimated Remaining Processing Time Hours/100	Material Cost/Unit ($)
2322–80109	5,000	6.75	14.2	0.36	11	1.75
	65,000	5.35	14.2	0.36	11	1.35
2321–80143	2,500	5.95	8	0.30	10	1.25
	30,000	4.75	8	0.30	10	1.05
2322–82273	30,000	3.25	8.5	0.25	11	0.79
2322–82322	12,000	3.85	8	0.30	11	1.05

Average Labor Rate = $ 5.75/hour
Average Department Foreman = $ 8.75/hour
Skilled Labor (for equipment maintenance = $10.00–$14.75/hour

For costing purposes:
- Allow 20% additional time for rework and scrap on labor.
- Allow 10% additional material for scrap.
- Allow 7% transportation and handling on material.

Armed with the data he brought back from Europe, and the results of the local simulations, Bell requested quotes for an automated winding machine to ECL's specifications. It was hoped that the manufacturers could either modify their existing equipment to meet the needs, or design and build a new piece of equipment. Of the six respondents to the request (see Exhibit 5.10) only two could be seriously considered based on their interest and apparent ability. The Siemens quote came in at $325,000 Canadian, while the Amicoil quote was equivalent to $365,000 Canadian.

AN OPPORTUNITY ARISES

In November 1984, Bell faced his biggest challenge yet. In a routine sales call to one of ECL's customers, Bell learned that ECL had been chosen as the only approved coil supplier and that the customer was prepared to increase its orders for two specific parts (Part No. 2322–80109 and Part No. 2321–80143) to 65,000 and 30,000 units respectively, instead of a typical 5,000 and 2,500 units (see Exhibit 5.9). ECL had to react quickly as the customer needed an answer to their request within two days. Before a firm commitment was given to the customer, price and delivery of raw materials had to be confirmed. As well, verification from ECL's production department was needed on the availability of equipment required to meet the requested delivery dates.

At the time ECL was operating at nearly full capacity. Bell felt that if the order

Exhibit 5.10 Comparison of Specifications

Manufacturer	Country of Origin	Cost	Capability	Deviation	Comments
Meteor	Switzerland	280,000U	Yes	Yes	Compare
Aumann	Germany	185,000U	No	—	No Support
Bachi	U.S.A.	200,000U	No	Yes	Flywinding
Nittaker	Japan	280,000U	Yes	No	Copy of Meteor
Siemens	Germany	325,000C	Yes	Yes	Compare
Tumaka	Japan	250,000U	Yes	No	Copy of Meteor

Note: 'U' indicates US funds, 'C' indicates Canadian funds.

	ECL Requested	Siemens Proposed	Meteor/Amacoil Proposed
Wire Size	#44–$20 Bifilar	#44 to #23	#44 to #23
Termination	Horizontal Vertical	#44 to #26 #44 to #23	#44 to #30 #44 to #23
Coil Size	4–5 in Diameter 3″ Winding Length	3 in Diameter 2″ Winding Length	2.5 in Diameter 2″ Winding Length
Speed	Not specified	0–10,999 RPM	0–12,000 RPM
Programming		Teach in HP9816 Floppy Disc	Tape
Winding Method	Rotating Spindle	Rotating Spindle	Rotating Spindle
Wire Termination	Within 1/32	1.32	Separate Cutter 1/16
Tooling	Change over 2 hours	Wire Change over 12 minutes Tooling Change over 1 hour	2 Hours
Transportation System	36 Tool Holder	24 Tool Holder	12 Tool Holder
Coil Taping	1, 2, or 3 layer	1, 2, or 3 layer Must tool for different widths	2 turns only
Fluxing	Horizontal or Vertical	WMW STD Unit, Horizontal or Vertical	Electrovert
Soldering	Horizontal Vertizal	Wave solder as above	Electrovert

was refused, then ECL would lose credibility, the market niche might be lost. If the order was accepted, it would outstrip existing capacity and other customers and orders would suffer. Since there had been increases in the number of requests for ECL to quote on larger production volumes, this problem was likely to become worse, not better.

ALTERNATIVES EXAMINED

To present the situation to all the key individuals at ECL, Bell called the management team together. The first and most common suggestion was use of a night shift. Bell remembered, however, that when a second shift had been used in the past, the effects were generally unpleasant. There were two main concerns. The first was the need for a highly skilled and trained individual to constantly monitor and test the components during the production process. In the past, individuals with these qualifications had been difficult to hire even for daytime work, and it would be very difficult to find the right people for the night shift. The second concern lay with the actual machine operators. Typically, the machine operators required very high dexterity for handling very fine wires. The best people were females, and most of them were the second income earner in their family units. Unemployment levels in the area were among the lowest in Canada and attracting and retraining the sufficient number for the night shift would be extremely difficult.

The next alternative considered was purchasing additional winding machines. These machines would cost approximately $8,000 each with delivery in three to four months. One concern was hiring and training the extra operators needed, especially as Bell esimtated up to six machines would be needed. And finding space for the machines in an already overcrowded plant would be a problem.

Selective reduction of the customer base was also considered. But how, Bell wondered, would you determine which would be dropped, as well as a future potential in a rapidly growing area. And if the market kept on growing rapidly, would ECL need to keep dropping customers? This could surely only be an extreme response.

Purchase of an automated winding machine would be attractive as capacity and flexibility would be increased with no increase in space requirements. This, however, would be delivered only after a one to two year lead time, and in the meantime the technolgy would probably change. And if ECL did nothing about the short term, there would be no longer term to worry about.

There had been rumors in the industry that certain competitors were having difficult times, and a merger or an acquisition was theoretically attractive. All the resources required would come with the purchase. No one could estimate how long negotiations would take, however, and the possibility of getting into a "can of worms" with a newly acquired unprofitable company was high. What unique strengths could ECL bring to such a marriage.

The last alternative was outsourcing some of the overload winding to a competitor who may not be as busy as ECL. How could quality and performance be guaranteed under these circumstances? And how could ECL stop the competition from permanently "poaching" the customer? As with all the other alternatives, short-term relief carried with it potential longer term problems.

CONCLUSION

Glen Bell ended the meeting in somewhat of a dilemma. "I realize that ECL must act immediately to relieve the growing backlog situation. If we decide to go the conventional route and increase our capacity with existing equipment, we may never be able to effectively respond to subsequent changes in the marketplace and we will not gain any edge on our existing competition. On the other hand, if we decide to promote some type of automation, we will not solve our immediate backlog problem. I also know that it will be extremely difficult to justify, let alone introduce, any type of fully automated equipment. The future growth and even the survival of ECL depends on the direction we decide to take, I have a feeling that automation is the way to go, but I still have some serious concerns. How do we economically justify a piece of equipment that exists as an idea only? How far do we automate? What capacity should we have and what are the market implications? What impact will automation have on the people and how do we introduce the idea to the employees? Will they feel threatened? I know it is going to be difficult, but we have to make a decision very quickly. I just hope that we can cover all the angles."

CASE 5.2

Krug Furniture Inc.—The Cutoff Saw[4]

By early June 1985, David Uffelmann, vice president, production at Krug Furniture Inc., had heard a great deal of strong criticism about the Stratford plants new computer controlled cutoff saw—enough to know that almost everyone in the company who had been involved with it wanted the saw removed. Despite the concerted efforts of the firm's engineering staff and the saw's European manufacturer to get it running smoothly, the new device had failed to reach its specified output. Mr. Uffelmann had given the ultimatum to the equipment sales representatives who had sold Krug the saw: unless the system achieved a specified, reduced standard within a designated time period , the vendors would have to take back the saw, and with a considerable additional financial penalty. The time limit had just expired without the saw reaching the required goal. Mr. Uffelmann now had to decide whether to make good his threat or to continue to sort out the problems with the saw.

Krug Furniture Inc. (Krug) was a privately-owned office furniture manufacturer. The Kitchener, Ontario-based company produced chairs and small tables of solid hardwood as well as large tables and desks of veneered particleboard with hardwood frames and extensive solid wood trim. Krug was one of the largest producers of wood office furniture in Canada.

An old company, Krug had remained a relatively small family firm into the mid-1970s. The company had begun to expand rapidly, however, when its new president, Brian Ruby, began focusing the firm's efforts on improving production efficiency and the marketing on the office furniture business. Production facilities had expanded

[4]This case was prepared by David A. McCutcheon under the direction of Assistant Professor R. W. Radford. © 1986, The University of Western Ontario.

beyond the company's old Kitchener plant to include a plant in Stratford, about 40 km away, and a warehouse and assembly area at another location in Kitchener. Since 1981, the range of products had been steadily broadened and sales had increased significantly with the penetration of the American market. Sales had jumped more than 30 percent in each of the past two years, totaling $18 million in 1984.

David Uffelmann joined Krug in 1977 at a time when the president was looking for members to expand his senior management team in the growing company. Mr. Uffelmann, with a degree in business administration, had just qualified as a chartered accountant when he entered the firm. Mr. Ruby often brought in managers and supervisors who had little or no experience in the furniture business, since he considered that having a background in the business tended to perpetuate the inferior systems prevalent in the industry. Mr. Uffelmann proved highly suitable and rose to become vice president, production in 1981.

Mr. Ruby had kept the management staff small, with most of the decision making being handled by himself, the vice presidents of production and sales, and the secretary-treasurer. In the last two years, the middle management group had begun to expand significantly. However, the senior management team continued to handle everything from the design of new products to long-range planning for the firm.

THE PRODUCTION SYSTSEM

Krug produced over 60 series of chairs, many with two or three models each, 12 series of lounge chairs and sofas, eight series of solid wood tables, four desk lines and a broad range of conference tables. Most chairs had some exposed wood surfaces; all finished wood on chairs, lounge furnishings and tables was oak or walnut, while some frame components that would be completely hidden by upholstery were made of maple. To simplify the fabrication of the broad product lines, frame components of similar series were designed to have common rough dimensions. In this way, the efficiency of rough-cut frame part production was improved by reducing variety.

The company built "white frame" products to forecast, usually in large batches. (A furniture product is at the "white frame" stage when it is complete except for wood staining, finishing and, if required, upholstery.) The frames were held in a separate white frame inventory until an order was processed that specified the particular model, wood finish, and upholstery material. With this system, fabrication was generally decoupled from variations in demand and most framing operations could be set up for large batch production methods.

Using solid wood as the frame material meant that problems with warpage and wood blemishes had to be eliminated. To prevent sections from warping (and to maximize lumber yield), Krug used the standard practice of making components out of pieces cut from laminated "panels." Panels were produced by cutting the lumber into the specific panel lengths, ripping (sawing in the direction of the grain) the sections into strips a few inches wide, then gluing the strips together edge-to-edge. This practically eliminated warping across the width of the panel and allowed better yields. The panels were then cut along their lengths to provide blocks of laminated wood of appropriate widths for the rough-cut frame components. As a result, a chair arm could be fashioned from a section of panel made from several laminated strips of oak or walnut. Krug made panels in a variety of lengths and widths to suit the dimensional requirements of its wood components. Panel production was carried out in large batches, with volumes based on the white frame production forecast.

While panel production could be accurately planned, the amount of rough lumber needed for a particular panel production run was not completely predictable because of variations in yield from the rough boards. This was affected by the number of blemishes (knots, grain irregularities or gouges) in the lumber, and the mixture of required panel lengths compared to the lengths that could be cut between the blemishes in the rough lumber. The standard method for cutting the lumber involved examining each piece for blemishes and eliminating the blemished sections as the board was cut to provide pieces in the six to eight different lengths required for each batch. These pieces were sorted by length into groups, then ripped to produce the narrow strips for the panels. Usually, any good wood removed when the blemishes were cut out was wasted. Inevitably, there was also considerable waste in the form of underlength offcuts, produced as the random lengths of lumber were cut to fit an arbitrary set of panel lengths. Exhibit 5.11 shows the cutting stages for this operation.

Krug's rough mill operation used nine saw operators under the control of a supervisor. The setup was near capacity for Krug's recent volume requirements, producing about 20,000 board feet of strips weekly; increasing capacity would entail incremental increases in the number of saw operators or the use of a night shift, something the firm preferred to avoid.

The plants used a piecework labor incentive system extensively. Workers were paid according to the types and numbers of pieces put through their operations each week. Most production employees worked under the piecework system, with some, such as the finishing department personnel, being paid on group, rather than individual performance systems. All plants operated on a four-day, 10-hour-per-day week.

The piecework system was an important aspect of the company's management. The 280-person work force was nonunionized and enjoyed better pay than unionized workers in similar plants in the area. The company constantly updated the rates as required and guaranteed a minimum wage equivalent to that achieved at 100 percent-of-standard. The work force was loyal and performed well: Krug management believed that the company had one of the lowest ratios of labor costs to total direct costs of any furniture manufacturer in Canada. Management also thought that the incentive system simplified the tasks of supervisors and managers, as workers were motivated to find improved work methods, and to regulate the work flow very efficiently, in order to improve their earnings.

Although Krug's production system had served the company well, the recent rapid expansion in volume and product variety was beginning to create problems. The company had traditionally met orders by backlogging and promising six to eight week deliveries. This helped smooth the production flow considerably and boosted the efficiency of the operations that were carried out after orders were received. However, production rates were falling behind the increasing volume of orders and the resultng delays in deliveries had begun to affect sales. Recently, a major competitor had started offering

Exhibit 5.11 Krug Furniture, Inc.—The Cutoff Saw
SEQUENCE OF CUTS FOR CONVENTIONAL ROUGH MILL OPERATION

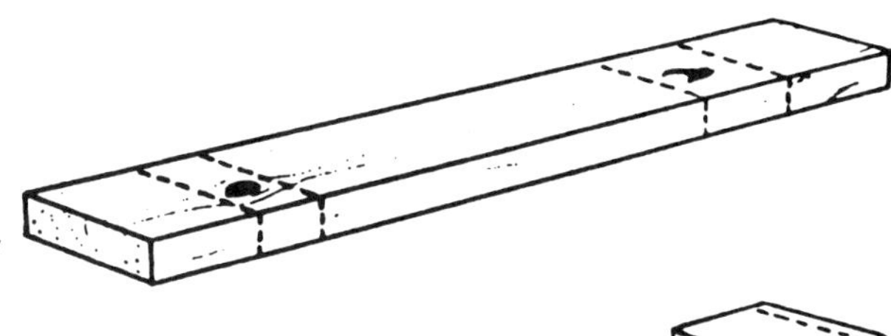

Rough lumber has blemishes removed by crosscutting, creating a number of boards of random length

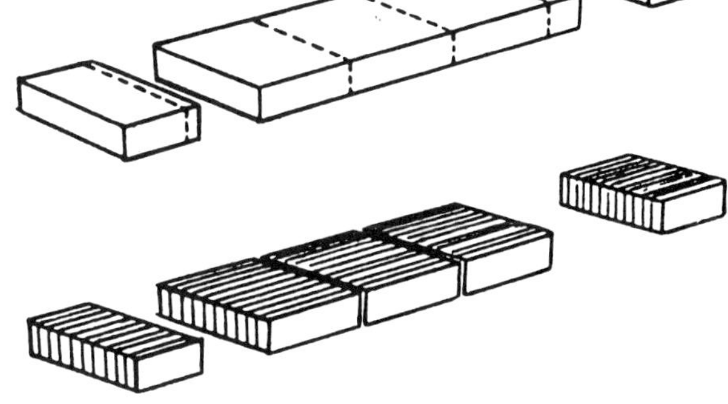

Random lengths are cut into lengths corresponding to those needed for panels. Choice of lengths to be derived is at supervisor's discretion.

Panel-length sections are ripsawn into narrow strips.

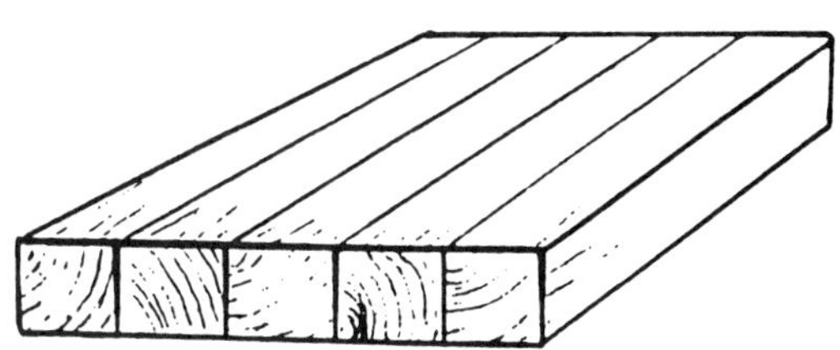

In the panel fabricating department, the strips are glued together such that the grain pattern is alternated.

four week deliveries, increasing the pressure for Krug to improve its own order turnaround. While changes to the company's computerized planning and inventory control systems promised to reduce the average lead time of orders, they were unlikely to improve delivery times to allow the company to match the competitor's quick delivery promises for any sizable part of their lines.

Mr. Ruby and Mr. Uffelmann knew that European furniture manufacturers were the world leaders in developing the industry's technology and that the trend in Europe was toward automating manufacturing processes to improve their flexibility. One German furniture manufacturer had installed a computer-controlled automated transfer line that fabricated table tops. Through the programming of the controllers, the equipment on the line was capable of being quickly reset to perform the operations for alternative designs. The setup time for switching to another table design was so short that the German company considered production runs of as few as five units economically practical. The basic equipment was available from machinery manufacturers; however, much of the automated line had been developed in-house by the furniture company.

Mr. Uffelmann recognized that the system's flexibility would allow a firm to process orders virtually in the sequence in which they were received. As long as raw material inventories could be economically maintained, a company could provide both quicker deliveries and a wider range of finished products, features not found jointly in either high-volume, limited-range operations or the slow-turnaround, wide-variety operation at Krug. It appeared quite likely that the flexible automated systems would be a basic competitive factor in the furniture manufacturing industry within the foreseeable future.

After examining the new systems in Europe, Krug's senior management team resolved that the company would have to begin moving toward the use of computer-controlled, reprogrammable automated equipment. The team was concerned about how this move would affect the company's operating and operations support policies. Quick reaction, short-run production would be difficult to fit into the piecework incentive program, which was a cornerstone of the company's management system. However, it was considered better to make a controlled, evolutionary change rather than ignore these new technologies until forced to act precipitously when the nature of the business changed around the company.

THE NEW EQUIPMENT

In late 1984 and early 1985, Krug management undertook the first steps toward flexible automated manufacturing processes. The company purchased three new pieces of CNC (computer numerical controlled) equipment: an optimizing panel saw, a boring machine, and an optimizing cutoff saw. The panel saw, which could be programmed to cut specific patterns in sheet material, was set up in the second Kitchener plant to cut sheets of particle-board that were to be used in the company's desk and table lines. The boring equipment was installed in the Stratford plant. It was used to drill patterns of holes in framing members; like the panel saw, changes in the boring pattern could be made very quickly and accurately. Both systems were imported from Italy and were based on well-established technologies developed for the metalworking industries. The machines were installed and operated without problems and greatly simplified the operations in which they were used.

The cutoff saw was brought into the Stratford plant in September 1984. It was initially set up in parallel with the existing equipment so that the operating and maintenance staff could become familiar with it before it became the sole source of panel components. The system it was to replace was a conventional rough mill process, where rough-sawn oak, walnut and maple lumber was cut for the fabrication of panels. The Stratford rough mill supplied the solid wood requirements for all three Krug plants.

The saw was the fifth of its kind produced by its West German manufacturer, the third to be installed in North America, and the first to be used to cut narrow-width hardwoods. Its operation required significant changes in the rough mill process. (See Exhibit 5.12.)

The old operation had used the conventional method—crosscutting to remove blemishes, followed by ripsawing to create strips. Now, incoming lumber was first ripped into narrow lengths by a multiblade ripsaw. Maximum use of the variable-width rough boards was made by minimizing the waste at each edge. This was done by aligning each board independently before passing it through the "multirip." (Krug's staff had calculated that wasting an average of a quarter-inch wide strip of wood, about 5 percent of the rough board, on every piece cut in the rough mill represented $30,000 annually.) The multirip reduced the lumber to strips that ranged in lengths up to 16 feet and in widths of a few inches. The strips contained all the blemishes of the board, since none had yet been removed. The strips were moved by conveyor to an inspection and marking area. Here, operators inspected each strip for blemishes. Using special pencils, they drew lines on either side of any section that was unwanted. Once marked, the strips were fed into the intake conveyor of the cutoff saw.

The first operation of the automatic saw was the reading of the defect marks. The strips passed one at a time under a scanner that read the location of the marks while the pieces simultaneously passed through a set of rollers that recorded length. From this information, the saw's processor calculated the lengths programmed as required for panel production. The strip was then transferred to the saw feed, which moved the strip past the circular sawblade that made cuts at precise times as the strip moved by. The cutting reduced each strip to defect lengths, lengths corresponding to programmed panel lengths, and pieces of good wood that were too short to be used in any panel. The saw's final operation was the sorting of strips by length. Defects and short lengths were separated and removed. As the remaining pieces continued down the output conveyor, they were kicked off at one of the six stations that each corresponded to a programmed panel length. Workers covering the stations could gather up the identical length strips, bundle them in groups, and send them to gluing stations for the fabrication of panels.

The programming of the saw could vary the way in which lengths were selected from the sections of good wood within each strip. If set to "optimize to stock," the saw's programming would minimize waste of good wood and cut each length into the best combination of one or more sections of the preselected lengths. With this system, the number of pieces produced of each panel length would depend on the conditions of the input strips; conceivably, all of the strips could be cut into only one or two of the selected panel lengths if the strip lengths consistently favored them. More difficult to program, but more useful to Krug, was setting for "optimization for a specific order." In this case, the required number of each, up to six panel lengths, was programmed into the controller. As the strips were fed into the saw, the controller selected the cuts on the basis of the lengths of good wood available and the relative numbers of each length already cut. The priorities for length selection were altered as the numbers of cut pieces of each length were continually compared with the required numbers. The programming was flexible, allowing requirement changes to be made in the middle of a batch. If the strips were of varying widths, the saw could control the length selection by computing the requirements for the total width of each panel size needed.

In addition, the saw's processor kept track of the yield achieved with each batch.

Exhibit 5.12 Krug Furniture, Inc.—The Cutoff Saw

LAYOUT OF THE NEW ROUGHMILL, VIEWED FROM ABOVE

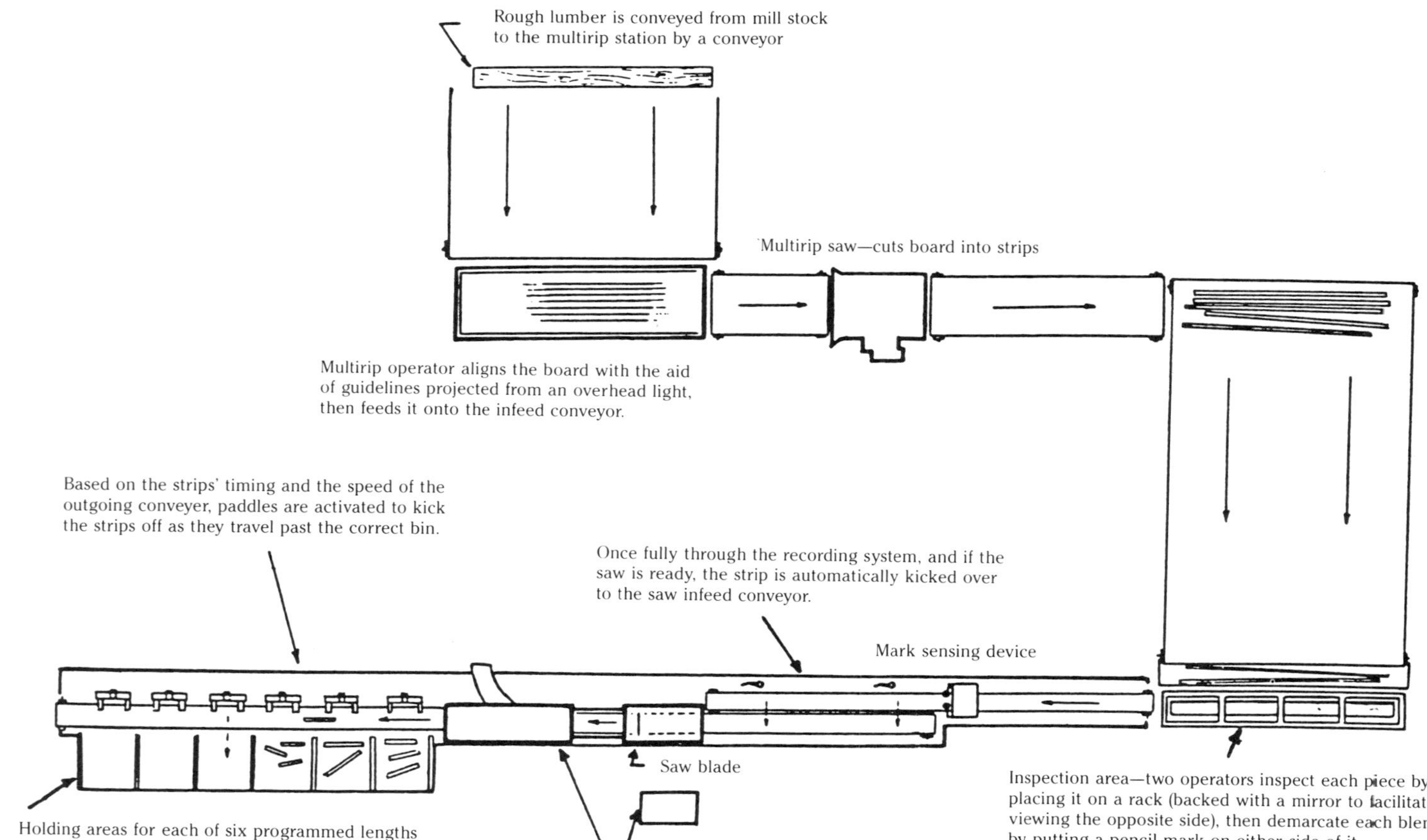
Rough lumber is conveyed from mill stock
to the multirip station by a conveyor
Multirip saw—cuts board into strips
Multirip operator aligns the board with the aid
of guidelines projected from an overhead light,
then feeds it onto the infeed conveyor.
Based on the strips' timing and the speed of the
outgoing conveyer, paddles are activated to kick
the strips off as they travel past the correct bin.
Once fully through the recording system, and if the
saw is ready, the strip is automatically kicked over
to the saw infeed conveyor.
Mark sensing device
Saw blade
Inspection area—two operators inspect each piece by
placing it on a rack (backed with a mirror to facilitate
viewing the opposite side), then demarcate each blemish
by putting a pencil mark on either side of it.
Holding areas for each of six programmed lengths
Minicomputer programmable control unit
Computer unit records strip length, sends scrap out through
a waste chute. Proper strips are sent past a sensor that
judges their timing.

By inputting various combinations of panel lengths, typical yields from each combination could be later compared. From this, the company could plan batches with combinations of panel lengths that had shown the maximum yields.

Although all strip cutting was done by a single blade, the saw worked quickly. Exhibit 5.13 shows the manufacturer's chart for the saw's rated performance. Krug's staff calculated that with their operation, an average of three cuts per meter of strip length would be required.

Exhibit 5.13 Krug Furniture, Inc.—The Cutoff Saw
SAW MANUFACTURER'S CLAIMED PERFORMANCE FOR THE CUTOFF SAW

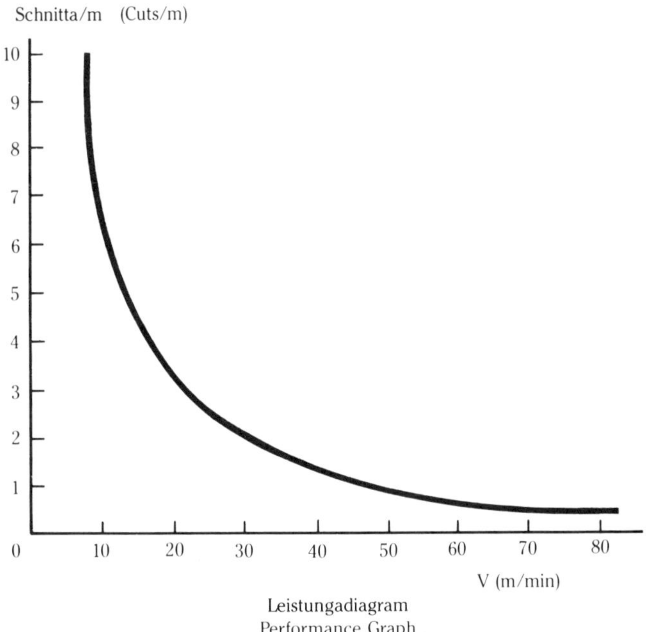

Leistungadiagram
Performance Graph

While the introduction of the cutoff saw would be a considerable change for the rough mill, change was not unknown in the Stratford plant. Krug had purchased the plant in 1980 from a household furniture company that was experiencing financial difficulty. Production had been switched from the manufacture of bedroom furniture to the making of chair components to supply Krug's Kitchener plant. The number of employees had been reduced from about 100 to 50. Rough mill operations had been shifted from the Kitchener plant to Stratford. Subsequently, the plant had become the site of the company's production of new lines of desks and conference tables and manufacturing processes had been altered to suit these products. In the process, the work force had grown to nearly 100 again. In light of the changes the plant had undergone in the previous four years, the reequipping of the rough mill was not seen as a major upheaval in the factory.

PROBLEMS WITH THE NEW EQUIPMENT

The cutoff saw had problems right from its startup. Many of the breakdowns were attributed to the use of the saw to cut the thin strips of tough oak and walnut. The four saws of this kind previously installed by the equipment manufacturere were being used to cut wide softwood boards. The hardwoods transmitted more of the vibrations imparted by the feed wheels and this damaged some of the length-sensing equipment. In addition, the strips fed into the saw were smaller in dimension than the softwood pieces typically used with the other saws and, because of the greater freedom of movement, they would sometimes kick up rather than feed smoothly into the mark reading section.

Some problems with the machine were the result of the operators' unfamiliarity with the technology. For example, the saw was shut down several times after all cut lengths ended up being sent unsorted to the last sorting station. There was no problem with the mark reading and cutting systems because all pieces were of appropriate lengths, but the sorting system woud fail in this manner at irregular intervals. Eventually, it was discovered that the photocell receptor on the sorting sensor would occasionally be blocked by sawdust. The sensor failed to detect the ends of each length as they passed through the beam. The default decision for the sorting program was to send the length to the last station. Simply dusting off the receptor and the light source solved the problem. Similarly, it was learned by trial and error that some erratic results could be traced to the way the pencil marks were interpreted by the mark reader. Once it was understood why the cutting operation was failing under these circumstance, it was easy to establish rules of thumb for marking that would avoid the problems. However, there were long periods of shutdown and erratic output before these operating problems were resolved.

Machine failure also caused lengthy delays, as even simple faults were difficult to trace. The plant's maintenance staff had one electrician who was skilled in repairing motors and more conventional control equipment; the remainder of the maintenance crew usually worked with mechanical systems. Any problem that involved the computer, sensors, controllers and many of the other cutoff saw components was beyond their experience. Troubleshooting was hampered by the lack of detail provided by the instructions and drawings. It was found that the drawings were actually inaccurate, as they did not include wiring modifications that had been made by the manufacturer as the result of its experiences with earlier models.

When stoppages were caused by a failure of some component of the complex control equipment, Krug's engineering staff would attempt to puzzle out the reason. The local equipment sales representative knew nothing about repairing and maintaining the machine and would refer Krug to the manufacturer. In a few instances, Krug contacted the firms in the United States that were the only other North American users of the saw. More often, Krug attempted to solve the problem through discussions by telephone with the West German manufacturer.

Problems were so numerous that the Krug staff expressed disappointment to the saw's manufacturer. In late November, the saw company's North American sales manager flew from Germany to look over the machine and reassured Krug that he would see to the resolution of the problems as soon as possible.

Because the new system was operated in parallel with the established rough mill, the crew used the old system to supply the panel fabricating department when the new equipment was down. After six months of trial operation, Krug's production staff decided to remove the old rough mill operation and rely solely on the system built around the cutoff saw. This would allow them to concentrate their efforts on perfecting the performance of the new operation.

To run the new system, staffing of the rough mill was altered to reflect the changes in work requirements. The supervisor remained in charge, and nine rip- and crosscut-saw operators were replaced by a multirip saw operator, an operator of the computerized saw and three lower-skilled workers who inspected and marked the infed strips and stacked the sorted strips. In recognition of the uncertainty with the equipment's performance, all members of the new rough mill crew were paid a flat rate, equivalent to the average wage each earned over the previous several weeks in their former positions, instead of an output-dependent piece rate.

By the time of the changeover, the saw had been modified to handle the hardwood strips, but the engineering staff was greatly concerned that relocating and restarting the new equipment would create even more problems. With the manufacturer's promise that the "guaranteed" rate (that indicated on the manufacturer's performance graph in the saw's sales brochure) would be achieved, the equipment maker sent a service engineer in early February to oversee the move and correct the outstanding deficiencies in the saw's hardware and programming. It was agreed that the manufacturer would be responsible for bringing the machine up to the required standard before the technician returned to Germany.

The technician arrived the second week of February and remained until mid-March, at the expense of the saw manufacturer. Although the saw was operating by the time he left, there were still constant problems and deficiencies. (Exhibit 5.14 shows

Exhibit 5.14 Krug Furniture Inc.—The Cutoff Saw
STUDY OF SAW PROBLEMS—FEBRUARY 1985

For an observed time of 271 minutes:

Average cutting speed, including all downtime ft/min	18.8
Average cutting speed, including saw downtime only ft/min	25.4
Average cutting speed without downtime ft/min	31.2

Other:
- –saw averaged one stop every 8.6 minutes
- –each "saw stop" required 1.9 minutes to fix
- –saw stoppage comprised 18.5% of saw time (controllable stops not included in saw time)

Table of Events:

Controllable items (i.e., breaks, lengths inputs, etc.)	70.5 minutes	26.0%
Uncontrollable items (saw stoppages)	37.0 minutes	13.7%
Actual saw running time	163.5 minutes	60.3%

Exhibit 5.14 (continued)
PROBLEM SUMMARY—MARCH 26 TO MAY 28, 1985
(Prepared by Stratford Plant Engineering Staff)

Date		Problem	Downtime (hours)
March	26	Computer blocked. Reprogramming did not solve. Wiggled some wires. Solution unknown.	9
	28	Infeed drive rollers loose at saw	1
April	1	Infeed light barrier intermittent	1
	1–4	First air pressure roller sticking down	22
	8–10	Replace down pressure cylinder	23
	16	Saw blade proiblems—dull?	5
	23	Outfeed air cylinder shoe fell off	0.75
May	1	Gate and width measuring cylinder out of sequence	12.5
	2	Counterbalance on paddle broke off	1
	3–6	Saw not recognizing marks—defective encoder	11.5
	8	Shoe on outfeed pressure cylinder loose	0.5
	9	Sort conveyor belt #1 starting to separate	0.5
	9	Gate in front of infeed not closing—light barrier problem	0.5
	13	Cross feed cylinder broken	1.25
	13	Paddle stuck—due to broken hinge; video display—time & date not functioning	1
	15	Hinge screws fell out—jammed drive rolls	1
	16	Hinge broke	1
	21	Computer blocked—reprogrammed	0.5
	22	Foot on outfeed clamp cylinder loose	1
	22	Set screw on encoder coupling came loose	0.75
	24	Replaced hinges on paddle with door hinges	4
	27	Computer blocked—reprogrammed	
	28	Saw would not complete stroke	0.5

RESULTS OF STUDY CARRIED OUT BY MANUFACTURING ENGINEERING STAFF, APRIL 30, 1985

Total Time Worked		600.0 minutes
Less: Downtime caused by:		
Equipment	84.4	
Us	84.9	169.3
Actual Equipment Working Time		430.7 minutes

NOTE: Equipment went down 85 times, averaging 1 stoppage each 5.1 minutes, with a duration of 1.0 minute per occurrence over the 430.7 minutes of running time. Equipment was working 72% of the time; downtime caused by equipment was 14%, by us 14%.

Output Rates:

Type of Wood	Cuts/Meter	Including Downtime	Not Including Downtime
1.25″ #2 grade Oak*	3.1	47 ft/min	54 ft/min
1.25″ #2 grade Oak	3.1	49 ft/min	56 ft/min
1.5″ #1 grade Walnut*	2.8	40 ft/min	52 ft/min

*hydraulic oil for saw not warm enough
**saw infeed drive rollers had problems gripping stock

Exhibit 5.14 (continued)

Equipment:

	Occur	Total Time	Average Time
Saw WentDown	56	29.22	0.52
Scanner Jams	18	6.45	0.36
Computer Went Down	4	38.52	9.63
Sorting Table Jams	4	8.04	2.02
Miscellaneous: Adjustments, etc.	3	2.13	0.71
Totals	85	84.36	0.99

Us:

	Occur	Total Time	Average Time
No Stock	17	3.21	1.89
Breaks, etc.	6	63.54	10.59
Changeover—Oak to Walnut	1	12.32	12.32
Misc: Scanner Not Plugged in 1.48			
Personal Accident 0.90			
Reprogramming 2.65			
Shut down 0.75	4	5.78	1.45
	28	84.85	3.03

OUTSTANDING PROBLEMS—MAY 29, 1985

Operator must assist when:

—Boards tip over.
—Light barriers become dirty.
—Boards move away from infeed paddle.
—Boards do not advance due to warpage.
—Scraps jam up.
—Hollow or vacant spot is encountered in lumber.
—Modification to programs or program blocks.

Present Difficulties:

1. Clock and date on video display incorrect.
2. Oil leaks.
3. Broken cross feed air cylinder.
4. Computer memory blocks.
5. Still missing marks, especially on thin lumber.
6. Sorter occasionally does not work.
7. Sorter conveyor belt coming apart.
8. Difficulty in changing saw blades (no lock on shaft).
9. Modifications required to keep boards from tipping.

all records kept by the manufacturing engineering department concerning the saw's performance.) In a four-week, 160-hour work period, the saw was down 37.5 hours for maintenance. With the dependence of most of the Krug operations on the output of the rough mill, the continual downtime of the saw was beginning to cause widespread disruptions throughout the plants. Stratford plant workers soon began to view the new piece of equipment with contempt. Cartoons depicting the cutoff saw being loaded into a garbage truck appeared on the factory walls. Some calendars in the shops were marked daily to show whether the saw had been working.

In early April, the saw had still not achieved the guaranteed output. In order to prompt the equipment sales company and the manufacturer into decisive action, Mr. Uffelmann negotiated that Krug would have the right to return the saw if it failed to meet a specified production rate over a four-week period. Krug would be refunded the saw's purchase price plus a $20,000 penalty fee for the disruption it had caused.

The agreement outlined conditions of infed wood and other specifics that would be considered fair for judging the saw's performance. The saw would have to cut an average of 25,000 feet of strips per 40-hour week over a four-week test period to achieve a level acceptable to Krug, based on an average of three cuts per meter of strip and 50 minutes per hour of actual saw usage. This level of output was below the specified performance of the machine but was well above that achieved with the former rough mill setup.

The test results (Exhibit 5.15) indicated that the new rough mill operation had still not reached this output by the end of May. Mr. Uffelmann was reluctant to return the saw, as he still hoped that the new equipment would achieve its production goals within a short time. However, the engineering and maintenance staffs were growing increasingly frustrated with the efforts they were expending on it and they were convinced that it would never perform as promised. He had to consider their feelings, since the cooperation of the entire work force was needed for the ultimate success of the long-range program.

Exhibit 5.15 Krug Furniture Inc.—The Cutoff Saw
RESULTS OF TEST STRIP PRODUCTION DURING TEST PERIOD

Week	Lineal ft. in day	Weekly Total
April 29–May 2	6,562	
	4,786	
	3,930	
	3,350	18,528
May 6–10	5,486	
	8,722	
	5,326	
	5,245	24,779
May 13–16	5,387	
	4,572	
	5,214	
	4,522	19,697
May 21–24	5,234	
	3,910	
	6,838	
	5,327	21,309

1 meter = 3.28 ft.

Mr. Uffelmann knew that this was a crucial step towards extensively automating the firm's operations. What impact would leaving the saw in place have on these plans? What impact would taking out the saw have? As he pondered these questions, he knew he had only a couple of days in which to make his decision, and to decide how it should be implemented.

Chapter Six

PRODUCTIVITY AND QUALITY IN THE NEW TECHNOLOGICAL AGE

SITUATION 6.1

SQC and QFD—Two Ways the Japanese Use Statistics To Improve Quality

Nothing demonstrates the contrast between traditional North American and Japanese approaches to their products and their customers than the respective attitudes to quality. The traditional approach has relied on separate inspection and customer feedback, both of which require (or allow) the manufacturing element to react; the Japanese approach has relied on designing quality in and then giving manufacturing the tools with which to guarantee that quality will be delivered.

The two main methods used by the Japanese for product design and process control are respectively quality factor deployment (QFD) and statistical quality control (SQC). Both techniques require familiarity and comfort with statistics, but there are other implications for management as well.

Statistical quality control (SQC) has at last come to be regarded as an essential technique by those progressive North American firms which acknowledge the critical importance of quality as a competitive factor. Statistical quality control enables a firm to gauge process quality—the ability of a process to operate within designed tolerances. SQC monitors this consistency by first developing specific, predetermined measurable standards and then monitoring deviations from these norms.

W. E. Deming introduced SQC to Japan some 30 years ago. From that time the majority of Japanese companies have been using the method to help produce quality products. Methods used to determine improvements in quality had been ad hoc prior to SQC. The frequently used hit-and-miss approach is slow and costly. In addition the root of the problem is not always discoverd. This means that attempts to improve ore meet quality standards are often not successful. SQC is thus a systematic method of successfully measuring and improving quality.

Deming introduced a systematic method of observing and controlling the quality of a process to Japanese and North American manufacturers. In the same vein Genichi Taguchi has introduced a systematic method of exploring experimental design techniques. The philosophy of low cost and high quality implicit in SQC applies equally as well to Taguchi's methods of improving quality and meeting standards.

Since the mid-1960s all Japanese engineers have received some training in the Taguchi method of experimental design. The Taguchi approach uncovers the variables that could cause potential problems once the product is in production. The objective is to optimize design at low cost. Nippondenso in Japan, the primary user of Taguchi methods, first introduced these methods in 1951. Today, it is known worldwide for innovation and reliability.

All new engineers at Nippondenso receive a four-day introductory course on Taguchi's methods. After three to seven years they receive a 12-day course in the use of various Taguchi techniques and the statistic techniques of orthogonal arrays. Orthongonal arrays are boxes that list the different variables that affect the design of a part or process. They also compile the number of experiments needed to achieve all combinations of variables. Linear graphs are another statistical tool used when interactions among variables affect how the part or process functions.

After five to nine years with the company, engineers partake in an advanced 11-day session on Taguchi methods. Reliable engineers take a separate course in parameter and tolerance design.

Training is an important part of Taguchi methods with emphasis placed on the ability of the trainee to produce his or her own case studies for critique. Nippondenso uses Taguchi methods primarily in optimizing product design.

QUALITY FACTOR DEPLOYMENT

Quality factor deployment (QFD) is used as a planning tool. Market research is the first step in order to identify customer wants. This is known as the "voice of the customer."

The next step is to determine specifications and manufacturing parameters on which an engineer can act. The objective at this stage is to prevent the message from the customer becoming distorted by engineers' perceptions. The house of quality is a tool used to help overcome the customers inability to explain what they want. The house of quality lists what the customer wants and matches those against how a company will meet these wants. An understanding of what the customer wants at all levels is combined with an attempt to minimize the effects of expert opinions. Each house of quality is referred to as a case study. Companies build a library of case studies. This creates a knowledge base for use in future product developments and help in training new engineers.

Quality factor deployment has been called the blueprint for product development teams. It focuses on the basics of what the customer desires and then enhances the product further. It attempts to use statistics to improve the quality of products designed to satisfy market needs.

Quality improvements in the United States have generally been achieved by fixing what the customer does not like. QFD helps companies achieve satisfication at a low cost with the finest quality in the shortest possible time by making quality products that the market wants the first time around.

Taguchi's name among North American manufacturers will soon be as well-known as Deming where a quality emphasis is the key to revitalizing businesses.

READING 6.1

Need for Change[1]

The United States continues to lose ground in the international economy. The rate of growth of our balance of trade has been negative for 17 years. The problem is quality, and, given the present system of management of most of our companies, the possibility of improvement in our position in the future is slight. For underlying the present system is the "zero sum" or "win/lose" philosophy; I CAN WIN ONLY IF YOU LOSE. That philosophy, if it ever was valid, can comfortably exist only in a truly unbounded economic environment. In the global economy of the late twentieth century every economic entity is bounded, and all resources are finite and limited. Win/lose is now a dry well.

To grow in the existing environment we must embrace a philosophy which not only allows but *expects* everyone will benefit. A shorthand notation of that philosophy is "cooperation, win, win." If we all cooperate, we all share in the rewards generated by that cooperation. That does not mean that everyone need necessarily share equally in the rewards, but everyone *will* win. Examples of the outcomes of implementing this new philosophy abound, but the new philosophy is not yet an integral element of the North American way of life. When the new system is in place everyone will have a chance to develop pride in their work, and meaning in their lives.

In order to create joy, pride, and happiness in work, and joy and pride in learning, we need first to change the reward system. Most systems of reward in North America nourish the outdated win/lose philosophy and its attendant race to be Number One. Under this system everybody ultimately loses. We must, therefore, first understand the necessity to, and then act to, abolish the merit system and its associated systems of in-

[1]W. Edwards Deming. Adapted from a note to the authors dated November 5, 1988, and from W. Deming (1986) *Out of the crisis*. Cambridge, Massachusetts, MIT Center for Advanced Engineering Study.

centive, as they choke intrinsic motivation. We must, instead, develop leadership and participation. In the process, we must create more leaders. And in order to create the leaders of tomorrow, we need to understand what attributes such leaders must exhibit.

A leader understands how the work of his or her group fits in with the aims of the company, and ensures that this understanding is shared by all group members. That understanding is enhanced when the leader and the group work with adjacent stages in the process.

A leader tries to create for everyone joy in work. This can only be achieved by optimizing everyone's education, skills, and abilities, and by the leader helping everyone to improve.

A leader, instead of being a judge, will be a colleague, counseling and leading people on a day-to-day basis, learning from them and with them. Everybody must be on a team to work for improvement of quality through controlled and planned experimentation on the job.

A leader uses figures to help gain an understanding of the individuals in the group, including him- or herself. The leader uses statistical calculation to learn who (if anybody) is outside the system on either the good or poor side, and who, therefore, is in need of special help. Ranking of people that belong to the system violates scientific logic and is ruinous as a policy; the leader uses the figures that would otherwise be used for merit ranking to help achieve overall improvement in the system (see Exhibit 6.1).

In the absence of numerical data, a leader must make subjective judgments. A leader will spend hours with every member of the group, and will know what kind

Exhibit 6.1 The Managerially Important Statistical Figures

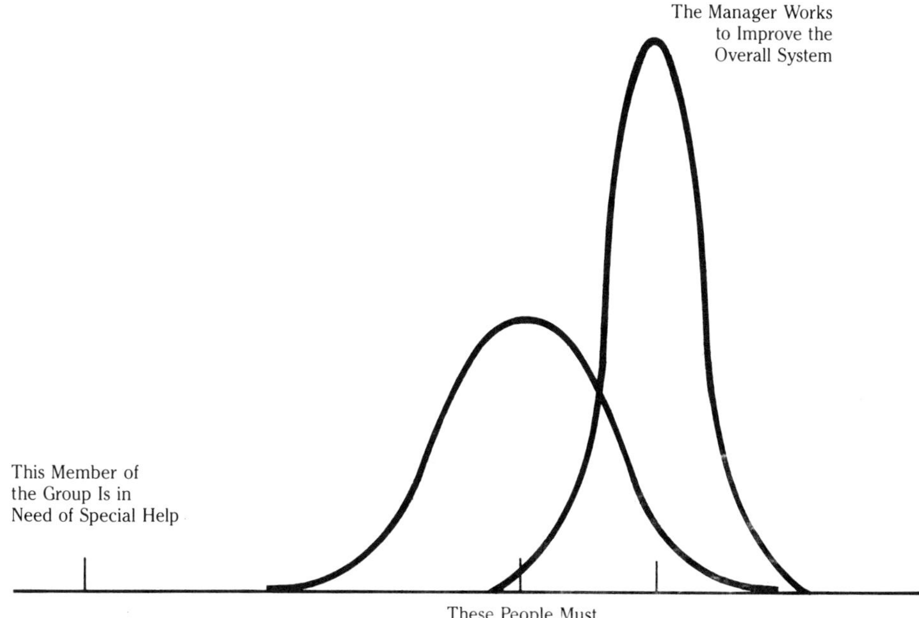

of help each individual needs. The leader will hold a long interview with each employee, three or four hours in length, at least once a year, not for criticism, but for help and better understanding on the part of everybody.

Through listening and learning, and by not expecting perfection but fostering personal and group improvement, the leader creates an atmosphere of trust. If there is one way to identify the good leader, it is this atmosphere of genuine, mutual trust and respect emanating from the group.

Management's new job will be to accomplish the necessary changes to enable the new cooperative system to be implemented. Many players will be involved, and many changes will be necessary. People naturally fear change, worrying about the personal consequences of change. A way to harness the efforts of the maximum number, and to overcome resistance to change, might be for management to deploy everyone into accomplishment of the change required. If everybody has a part in the change, and helps to paddle the canoe, fear of (and resistance to) change should vanish.

In order to deploy everyone, managers must ensure that everyone has the requisite knowledge. As the cornerstone of economic improvement is quality, efforts and investment for quality must be guided by knowlege not generally evident in the workplace. The special body of knowledge required encompasses:

1. Knowledge of variation; statistical theory.
2. Knowledge on the distinction between common causes and special causes.
3. Knowledge about tampering.
4. Knowledge of interaction of forces.
5. Knowledge of operational definitions.
6. Knowledge of psychology.

Psychology helps us to understand (predict) how uncertainty and variation in circumstances affect people. Circumstances will affect different people in different ways; one individual may react differently to two similar sets of circumstances, even if the time interval between the two experiences is small, or even if the circumstances are an unvarying element in the environment. In the environment of the firm several stable elements are desirable, and two of these are management and the reward system. Psychology might be able to predict individual changes in response through time from exposure to a stable, unchanging, set or subset of circumstances.

Even if psychology cannot always help us predict how one person's reactions will change with time, psychology can certainly help us to understand the effects of a faulty system of rewards, and can also help us to understand the change in relationship between two people, or between anybody and the system that material reward may cause. The drivers are intrinsic motivation, extrinsic motivation, and overjustification.

Intrinsic motivation drives an individual to action (such as work or study) that brings joy, self-satisfaction, and happiness. Extrinsic motivation leads an individual to action mainly for external reward (pay). Overjustificaiton is material reward for action that, of itself, brings happiness and satisfaction to the door. The result of reward is to smother the satisfaction of the doer, who ceases to carry on the action rewarded (although it may be resumed at a much later date).

Now that we have identified the attributes of the leader, and the essential knowledge required to improve quality at the individual, group, firm, and national levels, we need to identify how to actually improve the quality of a product or service? There are four ways by which improvement may be achieved:

1. Innovation in product and service.
2. Innovation in process.
3. Improvement of existing product and service.
4. Improvement of existing process.

It is a common mistake to suppose that quality is ensured solely by concentrating on improvement of existing processes, so that operations go off without a blemish on the factory floor, in the bank, in the store, in the hotel. Good operations are essential, yet they are not the decisive ingredient of quality. Quality is made in the board room.

Operations in a bank that failed last week may have had excellent operations—speed at the tellers' windows, with few mistakes; few mistakes in bank statements: likewise in the calculation of interest and of penalties on loans. The cause of failure at the bank was bad management, not operations.

Without doubt, we need improvement and innovation in one element of process—management process. Quality improvement begins with quality management, and quality management can be present only when the correct attitudes are exhibited at the top of the organization. It is wrong for senior managers to think that the people in their plants are responsible for their own product and its quality, and to expect people in the plants to act like owners. This is an abdication of the principal responsibility of senior management, to articulate and establish the norms and standards from which nobody in the organization wishes to deviate.

It is right for the people in the factories to understand their place in the overall scheme of things, to embrace the challenges of their jobs, and to willingly accept the responsibility for performance of their job; it is not right to expect them to accept responsibility for the quality of prior management decisions (or indecision), or the quality of thought displayed in upstream stages in the process.

There is an expectation in far too many firms that getting rid of the people in the plants will magically solve all the problems the firm has, particularly with its customers. In these firms nobody, of course, really tries to help the plants improve, for in the win/lose world in which we live the helpers would expect to lose as the plant performances improve. The win/lose philosophy, with its roots in rugged individualism, free land, and ever-expanding markets, is no longer viable, and must be replaced with something that will allow us to live and work in the world that now envelops us.

Transformation to the new philosophy of "cooperation, win, win" is necessary for survival in, and of, the Western World. The transformation will turn the course of Western industry sharply upward. We already have examples of cooperation, win, win in such things as international time standards, international customs documentation, and even in standaridized traffic signals. We now need to take that process to the next level, cooperation at the level of the individual and the group within the firm. Without this fundamental transformation, as Exhibit 6.2 shows, firms and countries cannot expect to make the essential commitment to quality necessary for survival in the future economy.

Exhibit 6.2 Impact Comparison: WIN/LOSE versus COOPERATION, WIN, WIN

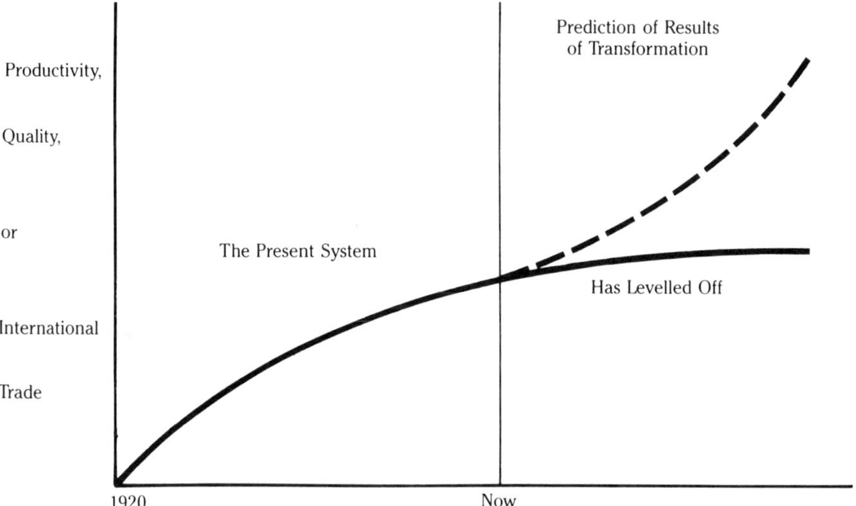

READING 6.2

Why Some Factories Are More Productive Than Others[2]

The battle for attention is over. The time for banging drums is long past. Everyone now understands that manufacturing provides an essential source of competitive leverage. No longer does anyone seriously think that domestic producers can outdo their competitors by clever marketing only—"selling the sizzle" while cheating on quality or letting deliveries slip. It is now time for concrete action on a practical level: action to change facilities, update processing technologies, adjust work force practices, and perfect information and management systems.

But when managers turn to these tasks, they quickly run up against a stumbling block. Namely, they do not have adequate measures for judging factory level performance or for comparing overall performance from one facility to the next. Of course, they can use the traditional cost accounting figures, but these figures often do not tell them what they really need to know. Worse, even the best numbers do not sufficiently reflect the important contributions that managers can make by reducing confusion in the system and promoting organizational learning.

Consider the experience of a United States auto manufacturer that discovered itself with a big cost disadvantage. The company put together a group to study its principal competitor's manufacturing operations. The study generated reams of data, but the senior executive in charge of the activity still felt uneasy. He feared that the group was getting mired in details and that things other than managerial practices—like the age of facilities and their locations—might be the primary drivers of performance. How to tell?

[2]Robert H. Hayes and Kim R. Clark, "Why Some Factories are More Productive than Others." *Harvard Business Review*, September-October, pp. 66–71. © 1986 by the President and Fellows of Harvard College. Extracted with permission.

Similarly, a vice president of manufacturing for a specialty chemical producer had misgivings about the emphasis his company's system for evaluating plant managers placed on variances from standard costs. Differences in these standards made comparisons across plants difficult. What was more troubling, the system did not easily capture the trade-offs among factors of production or consider the role played by capital equipment or materials. What to do?

Our point is simple: before managers can pinpoint what is needed to boost manufacturing performance, they must have a reliable way of ascertaining why some factories are more productive than others. They also need a dependable metric for identifying and measuring such differences and a framework for thinking about how to improve their performance—and keep it improving. This is no easy order.

These issues led us to embark on a continuing, multiyear study of 12 factories in three companies. The study's purpose is to clarify the variables that influence productivity growth at the micro level.

The first company we looked at, which employs a highly connected and automated manufacturing process, we refer to it as the Process Company. Another, which employs a batch approach based on a disconnected line flow organization of work, we refer to it as the Fab (fabrication-assembly) Company. The third, which uses several different batch processes to make components for sophisticated electronic systems, is characterized by very rapid changes in both product and process. We refer to it as the Hi-Tech Company. All five factories of the Process Company and three of the four factories of the Fab Company are in the United States (the fourth is just across the border in Canada). Of the three factories belonging to the Hi-Tech Company, one is in the United States, one in Europe, and one in Asia.

In none of these companies did the usual profit-and-loss statements, or the familiar monthly operating reports, provide adequate, up-to-date information about factory performance. Certainly, managers routinely evaluated such performance, but the metrics they used made their task like that of watching a distant activity through a thick, fogged window. Indeed, the measurement systems in place at many factories obscure and even alter the details of their performance.

A FOGGED WINDOW

Every plant we studied employed a traditional standard cost system: the controller collected and reported data each month on the actual costs incurred during the period for labor, materials, energy, and depreciation, as well as on the costs that would have been incurred had workers and equipment performed at predetermined "standard" levels. The variances from these standard costs became the basis for problem identification and performance evaluation. Other departments in the plants kept track of head counts, work-in-process inventory, engineering changes, the value of newly installed equipment, reject rates, and so forth.

In theory, this kind of measurement system should take a diverse range of activities and summarize them in a way that clarifies what is going on. It should act like a lens that brings a blurry picture into sharp focus. Yet, time and again, we found that these systems often masked critical developments in the factories and, worse, often distorted management's perspective.

Each month, most of the managers we worked with received a blizzard of variance reports but no overall measure of efficiency. Yet this measure is not hard to calculate. In our study, we took the same data generated by plant managers and combined them into a measure of the total factor productivity (TFP)—the ratio of total output to total input.

This approach helps dissipate some of the fog—especially because our TFP data are presented in constant dollars instead of the usual current dollars. Doing so cuts through the distortions produced by periods of high inflation. Consider the situation at Fab's Plant 1, where from 1974 to 1982 output fluctuated between $45 million and $70 million—in nominal (current dollar) terms. In real terms, however, there was a steep and significant decline in unit output. Several exectuives initially expressed disbelief at the magnitude of this decline because they had come to think of the plant as a "$50 million plant." Their traditional accounting measures had masked the fundamental changes taking place.

Another advantage of the TFP approach is that it integrates the contributions of all the factors of production into a single measure of total input. Traditional systems offer no such integration. Moreover, they often overlook important factors. One of the plant managers at the Process Company gauged performance in a key department by improvements in labor hours and wage costs. Our data showed that these "improvements" came largely from the substitution of capital for labor. Conscientious efforts to prune labor content by installing equipment—without developing the management skills and systems needed to realize its full potential—proved shortsighted. The plant's TFP (which, remember, takes into account both labor and capital costs) improved very little.

This preoccupation with labor costs, particularly direct labor costs, is quite common—even though direct labor now accounts for less than 15 percent of total costs in most manufacturing companies. The managers we studied focused heavily on these costs; indeed, their systems for measuring direct labor were generally more detailed and extensive than those for measuring other inputs that were several times more costly. Using sophisticated bar code scanners, Hi-Tech's managers tracked line operators by the minute but had difficulty identifying the number of manufacturing engineers in the same department. Yet these engineers accounted for 20 to 25 percent of total cost—compared with 5 percent for line operators.

Just as surprising, the companies we studied paid little attention to the effect of materials consumption or productivity. Early on, we asked managers at one of the Fab plants for data on materials consumed in production during each of a series of months. Using these data to estimate materials productivity gave us highly erratic values.

Investigation showed that this plant, like many others, kept careful records of materials purchased but not of the direct or indirect materials actually consumed in a month. (The latter, which includes things like paper forms, showed up only in a catchall manufacturing overhead account.) Further, most of the factories, recorded materials transactions only in dollars, rather than in physical terms, and did not readily adjust their standard cost figures when inflation or substitution altered material prices.

What managers at Fab plants called "materials consumed" was simply an estimate derived by multiplying a product's standard materials cost—which itself assumes a constant usage of materials—by its unit output and adding an adjustment based on the current variation from standard materials prices. Every year or half-year, managers would reconcile this estimated consumption with actual materials usage, based on a physical count. As a result, data on actual materials consumption in any one period were lost.

Finally, the TFP approach makes clear the difference between the data that managers see and what those data actually measure. In one plant, the controller argued that our numbers on engineering changes were way off base. After a brief silence, the engineering manager spoke up. He said that the controller reviewed only very large (in dollar terms) engineering changes and that our data were quite accurate. He was right. The plant had been tracking all engineering changes, not just the major changes reported to the controller.

A CLEAR VIEW

With the foglike distortions of poor measurement systems cleared away, we were able to identify the real levers for improving factory performance. Some, of course, were structural—that is, they involve things like plant location or plant size, which lie outside the control of a plants' managers. But a handful of managerial policies and practices consistently turned up as significant. Across industries, companies and plants regularly exerted a powerful influence on productivity. In short, these are the managerial actions that make a difference.

Invest Capital

Our data show unequivocally that capital investment in new equipment is essential to sustaining growth in TFP over a long time (that is, a decade or more). But they also show that capital investment all too often reduces TFP for up to a year. Simply investing money in new technology or systems guarantees nothing. What matters is how their introduction is managed, as well as the extent to which they support and reinforce continual improvement throughout a factory. Managed right, new investment supports cumulative, long-term productivity improvement and process understanding—what we refer to as "learning."

The Process Company committed itself to providing new, internally-designed equipment to meet the needs of a rapidly growing product. Over time, as the company's engineers and operating managers gained experience, they made many small changes in product design, machinery, and operating practices. These incremental adjustments added up to major growth in TFP.

Seeking new business, the Fab Company redesigned an established product and purchased the equipment needed to make it. This new equipment was similar to the plant's existing machinery, but its introduction allowed for TFP-enhancing changes in work flows (see Exhibit 6.3). Plant managers discovered how the new configuration could accommodate expanded production without a proportional increase in the work force.

Exhibit 6.3 Capital Investment Learning and Productivity Growth in Fab Company's Plant 2, 1973–1982

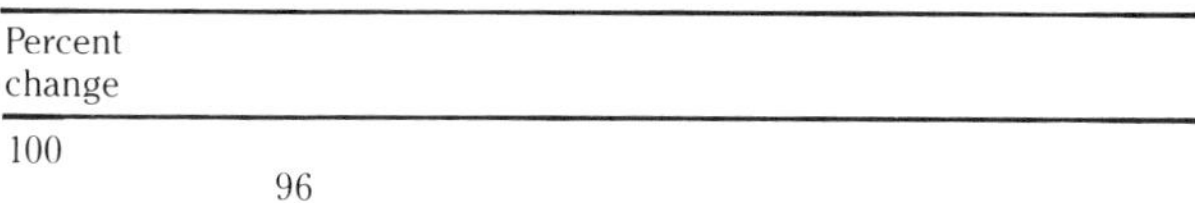

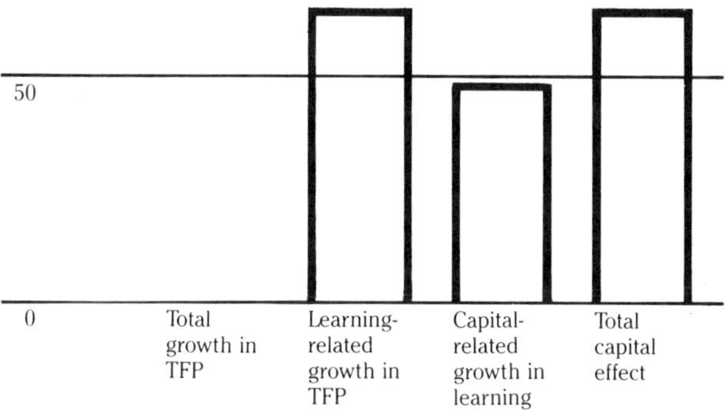

These estimates are based on a regression analysis of TFP growth. We estimated learning-related changes by using both a time trend and cumulative output. The capital-related learning effect represents the difference between the total learning effect and the effect that remained once capital was introduced into the regression. The total capital effect is composed of a learning component and a component reflecting technical advance.

These benefits spilled over: even the older machinery was made to run more efficiently.

In both cases, the real boost in TFP came not just from the equipment itself but also from the opportunities it provided to search for and apply new knowledge to the overall production process. Again, managed right, investment unfreezes old assumptions, generates more efficient concepts and designs for production systems, and expands a factory's skills and capabilities.

Exhibit 6.3 shows the importance of such learning for long-term TFP growth at one of Fab's plants between 1973 and 1982. TFP rose by 96 percent. Part of this increase, of course, reflected changes in utilization rates and the introduction of new technology. Even so, roughly two-thirds (65 percent) of TFP growth was learning-based, and fully three-fourths of that learning effect (or 49 percent of TFP growth) was related to capital investment. Without capital investment, TFP would have increased, but at a much slower rate.

Such long-term benefits incur costs; in fact, the indirect costs associated with introducing new equipment can be staggering. In Fab's Plant 1, for example, a $1 million investment in new equipment imposed $1.75 million of additional costs on the plant during its first year of operation. Had the plant cut these indirect costs by half, TFP would have grown an additional 5 percent during that year.

Everyone knows that putting in new equipment usually causes problems. Everyone expects a temporary drop in efficiency as equipment is installed and workers learn to use it. But managers often underestimate the costly ripple effects of new equipment on inventory, quality, equipment utilization, reject rates, downtime, and material waste. Indeed, these indirect costs often exceed the direct cost of new equipment and can persist for more than a year after the equipment is installed.

Here, then, is the paradox of capital investment. It is essential to long-term productivity growth, yet in the short run, if poorly managed, it can play havoc with TFP. It is risky indeed for a company to try to "invest its way" out of a productivity problem. Putting in new equipment is just as likely to create confusiuon and make things worse for a number of months. Unless the investment is made with a commitment to continual learning—and unless performance measures are chosen carefully—the benefits that finally emerge will be small and slow in coming. Still, many companies today are trying to meet their competitive problems by throwing money at them—new equipment and new plants. Our findings suggest that there are other things they ought to do first, things that take less time to show results and are much less expensive.

Reduce Waste

We were not surprised to find a negative correlation between waste rates (or the percentage of rejects) and TFP, but we were amazed by its magnitude. In the Process plants, changes in the waste rate (measured by the ratio of waste material to total cost, expressed as a percentage) led to dramatic operating improvements. As Exhibit 6.4 shows, reducing the percentage of waste in Plant 4's Department C by only one-tenth led to a 3 percent improvement in TFP, conservatively estimated.

Exhibit 6.4 Impact of Waste of TFP in Process Company Plants

Plant/ Department	Average Waste Rate	Effect of TFP of a 10% Reduction in Waste Rate	Degree of Uncertainty*
1–C	11.2%	+1.2%	.009
2–C	12.4	+1.8	.000
3–C	12.7	+2.0	.000
4–C	9.3	+3.1	.002
5–C	8.2	+0.8	.006

*The probability that waste rate reductions have a zero or negative impact of TFP.

The strength of this relationship is more surprising when we remember that a decision to boost the production throughput rate (whcih should raise TFP because of the large fixed components in labor and capital costs) also causes waste ratios to increase. In theory, therefore, TFP and waste percent should increase together. The fact that they do not indicate the truly powerful impact that waste reduction has on productivity.

Get WIP Out

The positive effect on TFP of cutting work-in-process (WIP) inventories for a given level of output was much greater than we could explain by reductions in working capital. Exhibit 6.5 documents the relationship between WIP reductions and TFP in the three companies. Although there are important plant-to-plant variations, all reductions in WIP are associated with increases in TFP. In some plants, the effect is quite powerful; in Department D of Hi-Tech's Plant 1, reducing WIP by one-tenth produced a 9 percent rise in TFP.

These data support the growing body of empirical evidence about the benefits of reducing WIP. From studies of both Japanese and American companies, we know that cutting WIP leads to faster, more reliable delivery times, lowers reject rates (faster production cycle times reduce inventory obsolescence and make possible rapid feedback when a process starts to misfunction), and cuts overhead costs. We now know it also drives up TFP.

Exhibit 6.5 Impact of Work-In-Process Reductions on TFP

Company	Plant/ Department	Effect of TFP of a 10% Reduction in WIP	Degree of Uncertainty*
Hi-Tech	1–A	+1.15%	.238
	1–B	+1.18	.306
	1–C	+3.73	.103
	1–D	+9.11	.003
Process	1–H	+1.63%	.001
	2–H	+4.01	.000
	3–H	+4.65	.000
	4–H	+3.52	.000
	5–H	+3.84	.000
Fab	1	+2.86%	.000
	2	+1.14	.000
	3	+3.59	.002

*The probability that work-in-process reductions have a zero or negative impact on TFP.

The trouble is, simply pulling work-in-process inventory out of a factory will not, by itself, lead to such improvements. More likely, it will lead to disaster. WIP is there for a reason, ususally for many reasons; it is a symptom, not the disease itself. A long-term program for reducing WIP must attack the reasons for its being there in the first place: erratic process yields, unreliable equipment, long productuon changeover and setup times, everchanging production schedules, and suppliers who do not deliver on time. Without a cure for these deeper problems, a factory's cushion of WIP is often all that stands between it and chaos.

REDUCING CONFUSION

Defective products, mismanaged equipment, and excess work-in-process inventory are not only problems in themselves. They are also sources of confusion. Many things that managers do can confuse or disrupt a factory's operation; erratically varying the rate of production, changing a production schedule at the last minute, overriding the schedule by expediting orders, changing the crews (or the workers on a specific crew) assigned to a given machine, haphazardly adding new products, altering the specifications of an existing product through an engineering change order (ECO), or monkeying with the process itself by adding to or altering the equipment used (see Exhibit 6.6).

Exhibit 6.6 Impact of Engineering Change Orders on TFP in Three Fab Company Plants

Plant	Mean Level ECOs Per Month	Number of ECOs in Lowest Month	Number of ECOs in Highest Month	Effect on TFP of Increasing Number of ECOs from 5 to 15 per Month
1	16.5	1	41	− 2.8%
2	12.2	2	43	− 4.6
3	7.0	1	19	−16.6

Much of our evidence on confusion comes from factories that belong to the same company and face the same external pressures. Some plant managers are better than others at keeping these pressures at bay. The good ones limit the number of changes introduced at any one time and carefully handle their implementation. Less able managers always seem caught by surprise, operate haphazardly, and leapfrog from one crisis to the next. Much of the confusion in their plants is internally generated.

While confusion is not the same thing as complexity, complexity in a factory's operation usually produces confusion. In general, a factory's mission becomes larger, as it adds different technologies and products, and as the number and variety of production orders increases, it must accommodate growth. Although the evidence suggests that complexity harms performance, each company's factories were too similar for us to analyze the effects of complexity on TFP. But we could see that what managers did to mitigate or fuel confusion within factories at a given level of complexity had a profound impact on TFP.

VALUE OF LEARNING

If setting up adequate measures of performance is the first step toward getting full competitive leverage out of manufacturing, identifying factory-level goals like waste or WIP reduction is the second. But without making a commitment to ongoing learning, a factory will gain no more from these first two steps than a one-time boost in performance. To sustain the leverage of plant-level operations, managers must pay close attention to—and actively plan for—learning.

We are convinced that a factory's learning rate—the rate at which its managers and operators learn to make it run better—is at least of equal importance as its current level of productivity. A factory whose TFP is lower than another's, but whose rate of learning is higher, will eventually surpass the leader. Confusion, as we have seen, is especially harmful to TFP. Thus the two essential tasks of factory management are to create clarity and order (that is, to prevent confusion) and to facilitate learning.

But doesn't learning always involve a good deal of experimentation and confusion? Isn't there an inherent conflict between creating clarity and order and facilitating learning? Not at all.

Reducing confusion and enhancing learning do not conflict. They make for a powerful combination, and a powerful lever on competitiveness. A factory that manages change poorly, that does not have its processes under control, and that is distracted by the noise in its system learns too slowly, if at all, or learns the wrong things.

In such a factory, new equipment will only create more confusion, not more productivity. Equally troubling, both managers and workers in such a factory will be slow to believe reports that a sister plant—or a competitor's plant—can do things better than they can. If the evidence is overwhelming, they will simply argue, "It can't work here. We're different." Indeed they are—and less productive too.

WHERE THE MONEY IS

Many companies have tried to solve their data processing problems by bringing in computers. They soon learned that computerizing a poorly organized and error-ridden information system simply creates more problems: garbage in, garbage out. That lesson, learned so long ago, has been largely forgotten by today's managers, who are trying to improve manufacturing performance by bringing in sophisticated new equipment without first reducing the complexity and confusion of their operations.

Spending big money on hardware fixes will not help if managers have not taken the time to simplify and clarify their factories' operations, eliminate sources of error and confusion, and boost the rate of learning. Of course, advanced technology is important, often essential. But there are many things that managers must do first to prepare their organizations for these new technologies.

When plant managers are struck with poor measures of how they are doing and when a rigit, by-the-book emphasis on standards, budgets, and exception reports discourages the kind of experimentation that leads to learning, the real levers on the factory performance remain hidden. No amount of capital investment can buy heightened competitiveness. There is no way around the importance of building clarity into the system, eliminating unnecessary disruptions and distractions, ensuring careful process control, and nurturing in-depth technical competence. The reason for understanding why some factories perform better than others is the same reason that Willie Sutton robbed banks: "That's where the money is."

EPILOGUE

Integrating Productivity and Quality Management

High productivity and quality are key for the success of any firm. North American firms and managers clearly realize this. Yet realization alone is insufficient for competitive success. Action is needed.

Productivity is considered key by virtue of its direct relationship to profitability. Productivity is the ratio of inputs to outputs. Inputs are basically costs, outputs are basically revenues; if productivity improves, it follows that profitability should also improve.

This simple concept, however, is complicated by the fact that there are several definitions for, or measurements of, productivity. First, there are single-factor productivity measurements which are based on one particular input (for example, output per labor hour). Second, there are multifactor productivity measures which are based on several inputs. Finally, there is the total-factor productivity of the firm, which considers all of its inputs (and is thus an aggregate of all the single-factor and multifactor ratios).

Many North American firms still focus too closely on specific single-factor measures (for example, labor productivity), and attempt to improve these individually. Such a narrow focus can cause management to make misguided decisions. For example, if a firm improves its throughput, or reduces rework, by purchasing higher quality raw materials, its labor productivity should rise. Since these materials will reduce material profitability however, material productivity will probably fall, and the effect on the overall productivity of the firm will be uncertain. As such, when considering productivity, management must be careful to examine all relevant and interrelated measures in order to make an informed decision.

While there are many ways, both simple and complex, to improve productivity, today many managers see the adoption of new technology as one sure-fire means. Faster, more accurate, and more flexible machinery can reduce labor requirements, scrap and rework needs, downtime, and setup time. These are only a few of the benefits available through new technology, and their effect on a firm's productivity can be dramatic. However, as we have seen in Chapter 3, without a well-planned, well-managed approach to new technology adoption many of these available gains will be forsaken.

Furthermore, if management focuses singularly on productivity (both in managing operations and also when considering the acquisition of new technologies), it may find the short-term gains it realizes come from a manufacturing infrastructure which cannot exploit longer-term potential.

It is generally thought that the main area of compromise in the productivity pursuit is product quality. As with productivity, quality is an often used, and often misunderstood, concept. Again, this stems largely from the fact that there are several definitions for, and measures of, product quality. This fundamental misunderstanding has, in North America, led to an inability to effectively respond to the higher quality demands of the market. This is often thought to be one of the main reasons for the decline in North America's competitiveness vis-à-vis the Japanese.

However, as we have seen, improving quality now and on a continual basis in the future requires a longer term outlook than is presently the norm in North American business. A short-term focus on shareholder return and cost control is not consistent with a quality philosophy.

This is so because the production of quality products carries several costs. There are *prevention costs,* such as process planning and control; *appraisal costs,* such as inspection and testing; *internal failure costs,* such as scrap and rework; and *external failure costs,* such as service and warranty costs and customer ill-will. Given the requisite for high quality in today's markets, firms are faced with the problem of improving quality while still containing costs. This has been the classic trade-off.

However, experience has shown that investments in quality at the prevention stage are by far the most cost effective. We have realized that quality has to be designed and built into a product; it cannot be inspected in. While post-process inspection, which prevents bad products from being shipped, may substantially avoid the high costs of external failure, it is not sufficient. It does not avoid at all the cost versus quality trade-off in the way that prevention investments do.

To this end, then, new technology can be utilized to improve quality in several ways. Computer-aided manufacturing (CAM) technologies enable more accurate and consistent production. Process monitoring and control technologies enable better measurement and control of the process responsible for the end-product. Automated inspection systems allow continuous 100 percent inspection for defects in given parts, and data feedback from this inspection can be used to help adjust and control the process. Finally, improved product and process design techniques enable the design of better products which will be produced by better processes.

New methods and technologies such as these are important, but not sufficient, conditions for achieving top quality. Top management must be committed to the ideal, and must work to ingrain quality as a philosophy and an unquestioned tenet of the corporate culture. In this way, the support and commitment of middle managers and line workers may be secured. Once everyone is on board, the relentless pursuit of quality, with the goal of perfection, will help the firm improve its competitive position, in both the short- and long-term.

CASE 6.1

World Wide Industries[3]

INTRODUCTION

Jim Brown, manager of quality assurance in World Wide Industries (WWI) Guelph plant, had a hectic summer in 1985, with customer plant visits in May, three weeks in Japan in June, and his own holidays in July. As July drew to a close, however, he was forced to look ahead to the 1986 model year. It was his task to analyze WWI's operations in Guelph and to determine the course of action by which the plant would earn a SPEAR II rating with General Motors (GM). This had become critical following the recent receipt from GM of the plant's current quality ratings, which were 15 percent below their supplier group average. Within the next five days Brown had to prepare, for the director of Guelph operations, concrete changes in existing operating systems and procedures which would improve the plant's quality performance.

THE GUELPH OPERATIONS

World Wide Industries/General Seating Division (WWI/GSD), one of the world's largest independent manufacturers of seating systems, had several plants in the United States and Canada. The Division produced a wide range of fully trimmed automotive seats and stampings for all the major North American auto makers.

The major Canadian operation, in Guelph, Ontario, had been in its current facility since 1962. The plant, then employing a workforce of 700 hourly and 100 salaried

[3]This case was written by Professor Hamid Noori with the assistance of Cathy Foy and Thomas Foran, 1987.

employees, was a batch producer of metal stampings and welded or riveted assemblies. Over 100 different products were produced and shipped to 40 locations in North America for GM alone. Weekly shipping volumes on the various products ranged from 25 pieces to 27,000 pieces. GM, the major customer of the Guelph plant, purchased approximately 75 percent of total production. Ford Motors accounted for a further 13 percent, with the remaining 12 percent split among intermediate suppliers.

THE INDUSTRY

The North American auto industry had been riding a boom since late 1983, when the economic recovery released pent-up consumer demand. The lean years and the continuing threat from the Japanese, whose sales were limited only by import quotas, had not been forgotten. Quality and cost efficiency were the major forces driving the revival of the North American industry. This had significant effects on automotive suppliers who had been forced into just-in-time delivery, and extensive revisions in their quality systems. All of WWI's major customers had introduced extensive supplier quality programs. These programs differed in minor details across the various companies, but the overall objectives were quite similar across GM, Ford, and Woodbridge Foam, a major supplier of seats to the automobile industry.

SPEAR PROGRAM

General Motors' Supplier Performance Evaluation and Review (SPEAR) program was implemented in 1983 with three objectives. First, it strove to provide current suppliers with the proper tools to improve quality, by providing training in statistical process control (SPC) and assisting them in preparation of written control manuals. Secondly, it hoped to avoid mid-contract quality problems by requiring suppliers to submit preproduction samples and comprehensive documentation to prove dimensional correctness and material integrity prior to shipment of any goods under contract. Finally, it provided an evaluation system, the supplier quality index (SQI), to monitor suppliers' ongoing quality performance.

Suppliers were grouped into classes with similar manufacturers for evaluation purposes. The suppliers were then rated on a quarterly basis using the SQI demerit system. The system was designed with a maximum SQI score of 145, awarded at the beginning of each quarter. This score was then driven down by both the frequency and severity of complaints from GM plants. WWI/GSD Guelph's performance was compared to that of its supplier group average. Management had been especially worried by their SQI performance, not only because they were significantly below their supplier group, but also because they were nowhere near GM's target objetives. (See Exhibit 6.7.)

Suppliers were also given an overall ranking on a scale of I to V based on demonstrated quality and reliability. A SPEAR I rating was awarded to suppliers who possessed outstanding performance in system design and execution, while SPEAR V suppliers were in danger of having their contracts discontinued. WWI Guelph currently

Exhibit 6.7 General Motor's SQI Objectives

August 2, 1984

Subject: Supplier Quality Index (SQI)

Recently General Motors of Canada developed a Five Year Quality Plan running from 1983 to 1987 inclusive.

Objective #1 of the Quality Plan states "Monitor and Report to Purchasing the supplier's progress towards reaching world class quality peformance of 145 as measured by the Supplier Quality Index, or SQI."

The target dates and expected level of SQI performance are as follows:

DATE	AVERAGE SQI
September 1, 1983	133.0
September 1, 1984	136.5
September 1, 1985	141.2
September 1, 1986	143.8
September 1, 1987	145.0

Your yearly average SQI performance ending August 31, 1983 was 108.6. To achieve the September 1, 1984 SQI target of 136.5 you will have to increase your SQI by a minimum of 29.7 percent during the 1984 Model Year.

In line with our objective of increasing the SQI performance of all suppliers to 145.0 by September 1, 1987, it will be necessary for you to plan and take positive steps for increasing your SQI to the level required.

Please make arrangements to attend a meeting in the Quality Control Building Conference Room on September 6, 1984 at 10:00 AM. Be prepared to outline your plans for increasing, as a minimum, your SQI to the September 1, 1984 target.

had a SPEAR III rating, and had set a goal to obtain a SPEAR II by the beginning of the 1987 model year. First and foremost was the improvement of the plant's SQI rating to the extent that the yearly average, based on the previous four quarters, was above the supplier group average. Once this had been achieved, an audit team from GM would visit the plant, review the in-house control systems, and could then recommend the plant for a SPEAR II based on their findings.

COMPETITION

Competition in the seating business was cutthroat, with two other large suppliers bidding directly against WWI/GSD on each contract. In addition to these existing American companies, other potential competitors were emerging. In Canada, Woodbridge Foam had been aggressively pursuing a policy of backwards integration by purchasing metal fabricating operations close to their existing foam facilities. Allen Industries was also preparing to enter into automotive seating from its operations based in Mexico. Some industry experts believed it would only be a matter of time before Magna International, a large Ontario-based firm producing a variety of auto parts, joined in the fray.

In response to these pressures placed on it by both customers and competition, WWI had made several changes to its Guelph operations. Over the past two years SPC, Just-In-Time, and a formalized sample submission program had been introduced. The plant's first two robots had been purchased the previous year. All these changes had been implemented, but with varying degrees of success. Jim decided to review the current status of each of those programs to provide some insight for his future plans.

STATISTICAL PROCESS CONTROL

An operator-oriented SPC program was started at Guelph in early 1984 by the quality assurance department. John Pitch, a metallurgical engineer with seven years experience with GM, was hired to head the program's implementation. Top management, engineering, and office staff were all sent to outside consultants for a two-day orientation in SPC. Foremen and production workers received training in-house from John Pitch and a part-time assistant from a nearby College. This classroom instruction was followed up with on-the-floor assistance for up to two weeks.

Operators were to take samples of five pieces, three times a shift, clamp them into checking fixtures, and take deviation measurements using electronic gauges. These readings were then recorded with the average and range being plotted on a control chart. Foremen were responsible for monitoring charts to ensure they were maintained correctly and to react to any out of control points. The completed control charts were then forwarded to quality assurance, where the office staff, in their spare time, entered the data into a personal computer. Software had been purchased to analyze the aggregate data for reporting purposes.

By the spring of 1985, over 200 production personnel had been trained in SPC with some 85 applications on the plant floor. Responsibility for the in-plant implementation of the program was transferred to manufacturing at this point. Nick Piron, an ex-foreman, was appointed SPC coordinator and given two assistants, one for both the evening and night shift.

After one year the early enthusiasm for the program had dissipated on the plant floor and Nick was beset by problems. Many charts ran consistently out of control, as he had insuffienct manpower to investigate the cause of most deviations. With SPC readings currently taking 200 operator hours per single-shift week, foremen were complaining that operators were spending twice the time required to take their SPC readings. In addition, Nick was swamped with damaged checking fixtures and gauges. Top management failed to make much use of the SPC information which reached their desks, as it was confusing to understand and always out-of-date.

PREPRODUCTION SAMPLES

The submission of preproduction samples on new or modified products in another area had become extremely formalized under the new quality standards. GM's bidding and submission procedure took seven months to complete (Exhibit 6.8). The sample and shipping dates were set in advance by the auto maker and considered inflexible, as delays in seating would not be allowed to hold up production of the entire car. This rigidity would often haunt product engineering if any of the frequent design changes were made to the product within three months of the sample date.

Changes to the initial blueprint supplied to WWI could occur at anytime up to the sample date. These changes originated not only from the customer, but also from WWI's own product engineers as they worked on the product. Changes were often agreed to on the phone, with written authorization and new prints arriving weeks later. While these modifications were often minor in nature, they could cause real headaches if the tooling was in an advanced stage of manufacture, or if the volume levels changed significantly. Tool and equipment contracting, debugging and product implementation placed substantial strain on engineering. During the busy season, product engineers often

Exhibit 6.8 Sample Submission Procedure

September 1	Motor company forwards request for quote (RFQ) and design drawings to Guelph's Sales Department.
September 15	After consultation with Product Engineering, Sales submits bid to auto maker quoting four specific areas: tooling dies welding equipment checking fixtures price per piece
September 30	Acceptance of bid received from auto maker. Sample submission deadline set for April 1 of the following year. The initial shipping date for productuon parts to assembly locations was estimated as April 20.
October 30	Tooling and fixture contracts are let out to local suppliers. This is done using a bidding procedure which attempts to get three bids for each contract.
NOTE:	The daily shipment volumes of the product plus the aggregate volume of the contract dictate the sophistication of tooling to be used. Higher volumes not only require more reliable equipment, but the increased costs can be more easily justified.
January 15	Industrial Engineers decide locations of new equipment and process flow. With the tooling and work flow determined, the number of operators is also decided.
January 30	Equipment arrives at the plant and is released to production for installation.
February 20	A run of 300 pieces is used to debug equipment and to satisfy sample requirements.
March 1	Quality assurance begins data collection for sample submission. Fifty sample pieces are submitted to SPC on critical dimensions to ensure capability. Failure tests are also performed. Certification of material received from suppliers is also obtained to guarantee material integrity. A control program is also designed.
March 21	The sample submission is forwarded to the auto maker's centralized purchasing function.
April 10	Sample acceptance is received.
April 18	First production run is shipped.

worked up to 10 hours overtime a week, as over 30 percent of all products would reach the shipping date without sample approval from the customer. As a result , WWI would often begin shipping to assembly plants weeks prior to receiving sample approval from GM's central purchasing office. Jim knew of one product—the C-K truck seatback assembly—which had been in production for nine months and had yet to receive sample approval. When these delays occurred, pressure mounted not only from sales, but also from the controller, as no tooling money was released by GM until sample approval was secured.

JUST-IN-TIME

WWI/GSD Guelph was operating Just-In-Time to GM in some 30 products, to GM's two Oshawa and to one of GM's Michigan assembly plants. WWI shipped a further 30 products Just-In-Time to Ford's Oakville truck plant and Woodbridge Foam's two Ontario locations. All products were produced in relatively high volumes.

Monthly orders received from customers were used to allocate manpower, material, and production time to specific departments. Actual daily shipment requirements were received five days in advance via a computer hookup. Two production clerks managed this short-term scheduling, working directly with the customer plants and WWI's own foremen to ensure proper build levels.

The system as a whole worked well since customers generally supplied accurate monthly forecasts. Problems arose, however, when stock shortages occurred due to rejection of poor quality shipments by the customer. These rejections required emergency scheduling and overtime production to supply the lost volume. With GM accounts, these rejections occurred approximately four times a month, but were far more frequent with Ford and especially Woodbridge Foam, the latter returning up to 50 percent of the stock received.

After his review of these current programs, Jim wonders how realistic the SPEAR II objective was in the one year time frame. He also wondered to what extent the problems occurring in the three programs were related and what were the key variables involved. He realized that the two most basic factors common to all the programs were the plant's current physical and human assets.

THE GUELPH PLANT

The Guelph plant's major production departments performed stamping, tube cutting and forming and welding operations. Wire forming, riveting, and painting were more minor departments. The equipment was grouped by function with open aisles for the more than 30 tow motors used to move work-in-process (WIP) from station-to-station. Ample space had also been allocated for a WIP inventory and for the isolation of parts in need of rework.

The majority of WWI tooling was sourced from small local tool shops by the engineering department. The product engineers, who were experienced personnel with some college training, were responsible for the selection of the actual tooling and the supplier. The sophistication of the equipment selected was based primarily on the volume of the contract. Higher volumes required greater reliability in equipment, as downtime had a high opportunity cost, and the increased cost of equipment being recovered over a greater number of units produced.

Product life cycles in the automotive industry ranged from three to seven years. With the introduction of a new product, any tooling specifically related to it was purchased at the customer's expense. As a result, the bulk of WWI's tooling was less than 10 years old. The generic equipment, however, used for common functions such as wire forming and tube bending, dated to the 1950s and 1960s. The updating of this equipment was difficult to justify on a cost basis, especially since any capital expenditures greater than $5,000 had to be approved by the corporate head office in California. This process took anywhere from three to six months.

The Introduction of Robotics

WWI's most significant advance in equipment was made with the acquisition of two robots in the fall of 1984 for the welding department. Two robotic welders, "Zip" and "Zap," were part of the tooling system used to meet a three year contract for 1.98 million C-K Truck seat back frames for GM's Truck and Bus Division. It was anticipated that the robots would not only increase weld integrity and achieve the tight tolerances required by the contract, but also be adaptable to a new product when the C-K contract was complete.

In preparation for the robot introduction, Keith Morison, the welding engineer, and Dave Taylor, foreman of welding maintenance, attended a one week training session on robotics offered by a consulting firm in Detroit. Other maintenance employees were introduced more gradually to the robotics by attending a training facility in Cambridge, Ontario on a rotating basis.

Coinciding with the robot introduction, the industrial engineers experimented with grouping most of the C-K tooling into one work station to reduce WIP and material handling. The export tube bender, the mat welder, and the robotic welders used to weld the final frame were all grouped in the welding department.

The implementation of Zip and Zap was not a smooth process, with the first problem arising prior to sample submission when GM increased the daily shipment volume from 2,000 units to 2,400 units. Initially, this increase was not expected to be a large problem, as engineering had ordered the robots with an assurance from the supplier that they possessed a cycle time capability of 2,600 units per day. When Zip and Zap arrived, however, it quickly became apparent that their maximum capacity was only 2,000 units and that the robotic work stations would never meet shipping requirements.

When put into operation, the robotic welders failed to place welds consistently on the proper points of the frame. Initially, it was felt that the programming or the response of the robots was faulty, but further investigation revealed that the weld jigging purchased with Zip and Zap failed to hold the seat back securely. As a result, the frames shifted out of position in the welding phase. Dave Taylor came to the conclusion that the robots were essentially "the same as the other automatic welders we have—just fancier" and placed clamps on the jigging similar to those on the automatic welders.

The higher volumes also placed extreme demands on the export tube bender, an older machine which had been overhauled prior to being placed in the robotic work station. The tube bender was unable to consistently meet the required tolerances at the volumes needed. Since the export tube bender was a problem machine, operators would shift from it as soon as another job in their classification opened up. This resulted in up to three different operators per shift.

To meet the volume requirement of the C-K contract, WWI was forced to shift some of the production flow to automatic and manual welding stations. With the increased variability introduced by three separate welders and the other factors already mentioned, quality assurance found it necessary to implement 100 percent inspection on all finished assemblies. This increaed inspection helped protect WWI's SQI from further damage, but drove rework costs to over $200,000. The next nearest rework cost on any other assembly in production was below $80,000. Material handling costs were also considerably more than anticipated, given the need to service three separate welders. Scheduling of production across the three work stations was further complicated by the "sudden" downtimes which plagued Zip and Zap.

While it usually took only a few weeks to have new equipment operating efficiently, it had taken nine months to get the C-K Truck work stations up to acceptable quality levels. Through this trial and error, however, both engineering and maintenance felt they had become well-acquainted with robotics and their operations. They were confident that they would have better experiences with the 16 robots arriving that fall as part of the W-car contract for seat backs and cushions.

Labor Force

Both the plant workers and office staff were affiliated with the United Auto Workers, one of the most powerful unions in North America. The plant had been unionized for several years, but the office staff were organized only the previous year. While WWI had some labor problems in the past, current relations had been described as "healthy." In February 1985, both employee groups signed a three year contract, following a three day strike by plant workers which was not supported by the office staff.

The bulk of the plant jobs were unskilled, consisting of feeding machines, removing finished parts, and delivering containers to the various work stations via tow motors. Two departments, maintenance and the tool room, were staffed by skilled employees. For the most part, these employees had several years seniority and had earned their "skilled" designation more through experience rather than formal training.

As a batch operation, jobs were begun at various times during a shift depending on shipping requirements and volume. The assignment of production workers to individual jobs was complicated by a complex job assignment system outlined in the union contract. As a result, an employee had a different seniority rating for each job performed in his department based on his experience in each job. When a job was run, the most senior employee in that job classification had first chance to claim it. If he was currently working on another job and wished to accept the new assignment, the resultant bumping process was a foreman's nightmare.

There has been little to no negative reaction to the plant's two robots or those proposed for the fall of 1985. In fact, a contract clause stipulating that the introduction of new technology be monitored by a committee made up of three union members and three managerial staff had never been acted on by the union. Management believed this easy acceptance was because it had equated new technology with two points—increased competitiveness and job security in all labor communications. No jobs had been eliminated as a result of the robot's arrival. Others felt the quiet was merely another example of the production employees' indifference to plant operations.

OPTIONS

The final act in Jim's analysis was interviewing people throughout the organization, in particular from sales, engineering, and manufacturing personnel.

Sales

Sales personnel lived with poor SQI ratings and missed sample dates everyday in their interactions with the customer's buyers. They knew the plant was busy, but were worried that WWI was no longer obtaining the high volume jobs they had previously attracted. They saw the SQI as a critical variable in the customer's evaluation and were worried that the effect of the current SQI performance would be felt even more severely in the medium term, as old contracts in GM's buyers were gradually replaced by new personnel.

Sales believed the short-term solution to better SQI ratings was through increased personal contact within customer plant locations. It was important to impress buyers with fast response to customer complaints and to provide advance warning of any delays in sampling or shipment. Jim was skeptical of this opinion, as currently some of his staff were spending three days a week on customer visits.

Engineering

Enginering felt the long-term solution lay in the general improvement of the plants' equipment. Robotics would allow for both high dimensional conformance and flexibility in design. Higher volume jobs would also allow for more grouped tooling stations reducing work-in-progress and material handling. In the short-term, they felt an increase in staff would relieve the pressure in their own department, which seemed to move from one crisis to another. However, this would be difficult to obtain due to an informal hiring freeze on nonproduction personnel imposed by the divisional head office.

Manufacturing

Manufacturing was by far the largest department in the organization. It was preoccupied with the need to meet production levels set by sales, with tooling selected by engineering and control systems designed by quality assurance. Manufacturing was slow to respond to any sugestions and was suspicious of any system imposed on them, knowing they would have to live with any decision on a day-to-day basis. On the plant floor, foremen were frustrated by engineering's ability to provide equipment capable of meeting requirements. The foremen were further annoyed by the tendency of individual engineers to divorce themselves from the machinery once it had been installed and made operational. Quality control was seen as one more source of nagging interruptions and paper work, hampering the foreman in his struggle to schedule production and juggle job classifications.

PLAN FOR ACTION

In late August, while the 1985 model year was drawing to a close, GM stepped up the pressure on WWI Guelph by stating no new business would be placed at the plant if it failed to achieve a SPEAR II by September 1986. In response, the plant's management began working frantically to develop a detailed action plan which would meet GM's demands. Numerous meetings were being held and considerable effort was being expended by the plant's director to ensure that the final plan would be successful.

Now, Jim Brown was carrying the torch, and it was begining to get hot. He knew that the responsibility for reaching and maintaining SPEAR II rating was his, but he was also keenly aware that several other factors would influence the impact of the procedures and systems he had to develop. How should he develop and sell his plan, he wondered. And how should the plan be implemented? Without any authority over those who would use his systems, how could he ensure they were properly applied?

But even thinking that far ahead was filled with danger, as Jim was aware he did not fully understand what impact other factors would have. What about the new robots, for instance; what impact would they have on quality, both directly and indirectly, how would they influence the new systems and procedures, and how might WWI guard against any negative impact? Should something be done in advance of the arrival of the robots; if so, what? Zip and Zap had not lived up to any of their initial expectations—would the same problems occur? Should the new procedures take account of the robots at all, at any level of efficiency?

How should the robots be integrated into the total organizational structure? Zip and Zap had been received with studied indifference, but Jim was sure that the work force was worried by the new technologies and control systems, and would upset them if at all possible. The high cost of rework was testament to that, and Jim knew that any procedures which did not have cost containment as one of their goals would not be acceptable. Relationships among departments did not help, either. And the danger in treating the new robots as the best means of attaining SPEAR II rating was that this could create even more serious longer term problems.

With a sigh, Jim reluctantly turned back to the task at hand. Knowing that the system had to suit the company's short and longer term plans was no comfort, when Jim was not even sure he knew what all the ramifications of the various sets of procedures would be. And with only a handful of days in which to develop, and then sell his boss on the plan of action, there would not be much time for relaxed contemplation.

CASE 6.2

Hand Tools Inc.[4]

John Smith, vice president and general manager of Hand Tools Inc., (HTI), had just returned from his quarterly meeting with Jim Black, president and one-third owner. It was February 1987, and HTI had just lost one of its biggest customers because the firm had not delivered its product on time. This was, John felt, largely attributable to the recent 12-month long strike at HTI.

While this was disturbing news, it was not the problem which most troubled Smith. Increasing foreign competition, shrinking North American hand tool markets, tense management-labor relations and pressure by the bank to decrease the debt load (which had worsened during the strike) all indicated that HTI was in for a rough ride in the near future.,

The plant manager, Sam Wilson, had discussed with Smith the opportunities available with some of the new technology on the market. It appeared at first glance that maybe this could be the first step towards brightening HTI's future and securing its existence over the long term.

BACKGROUND

HTI, based in Brampton, Ontario, was founded in the early 1920s by a young hand tool maker. As the business prospered, the firm began to grow both in sales and in number of employees. By the 1970s, HTI had over 130 employees and $20 million in sales.

During the 1970s the market for hand tools in North America began to level

[4]This case was written by Professor Hamid Noori and Scott Murray, 1988.

off. Simultaneously, offshore competitors, initially from Japan, and most recently, Korea, began to enter HTI's segment of the market and take market share. Customers like Canadian Tire, whose customers were largely part-time handymen, were no longer interested in high priced, high quality tools, but would instead be willing to sacrifice a degree of quality for a much lower priced tool.

Pressure from foreign competitors proved too great for some local manufacturers. By the early 1980s, the only Canadian hand tool makers left were HTI, a few small firms, and one large, multinational firm ($600 million annual sales worldwide). To remain competitive HTI had started to contract out some of its metal forming work to a Japanese firm, which then shipped the goods to HTI for finishing. HTI had also transferred its warehouse to a location closer to its main market, the United States, improving distribution and customer service. The labor force had been reduced gradually through attrition, resulting in a leaner firm. This reduction had been made necessary because labor productivity had increased at a faster rate than volume growth; the productivity increases were due principally to management's aggressive approach to process improvements and to new manufacturing machinery.

PRODUCTION FACILITIES

HTI's primary focus was on the stamping and forging of hand tools. Short production runs of the wide range of company products was the norm, and John Smith considered HTI a job shop operation.

The plant was organized into six main sections (see Exhibit 6.7):

1. Shipping and receiving/raw material holding area
2. Drilling and boring (including the automatics and the Kingsbury)
3. Polishing/grinding
4. Heat treatment
5. Plating
6. Tooling and diemaking/engineering

The areas where automation was most feasible were: drilling and boring, where several hours could be spent setting up tooling in between production runs; and tooling/engineering, since designing new products and their respective tooling was also very time consuming.

PROCESS DESCRIPTION

The production process in the plant was fairly straightforward. First raw materials were received in the form of metal bar stock. They were taken into the drilling and boring area where they were cut into small pieces and then drilled with various bits. This procedure was done either by single operators, who did a piece at a time, or by an automatic machine, where multiple holes of different widths were made. A special form of automatic

Exhibit 6.7 Hand Tools Inc. Plant Layout

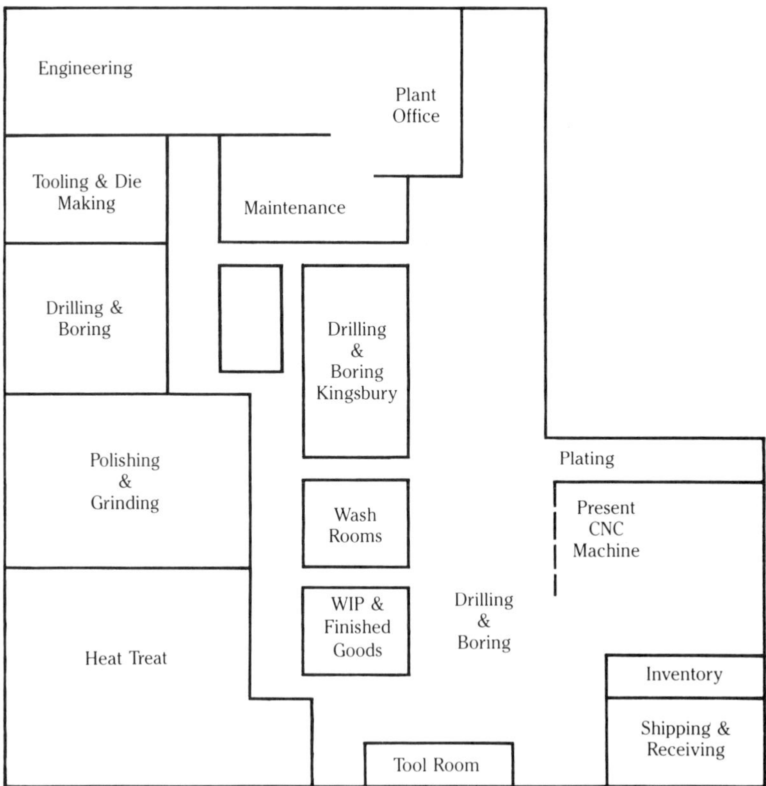

machine was used (called the Kingsbury), which, with an operator's guidance, formed the holes and pieced together various types of ratchets.

Once the drilling and boring operations were complete, the products were heat-treated in large furnaces to strengthen the metal. Then they were taken through the grinding and polishing process to ensure that the products were able to meet the very precise specifications.

From there, the tools moved to plating where, in a series of tanks, the tools were first cleaned and then chrome plated. This strengthened the tool and gave it an attractive finish. Once the tools were dried, they were packed and shipped to the warehouse in Niagara Falls.

While this represented the general flow of goods, there were many exceptions. For example, HTI contracted out much of the initial work on certain goods, only performing finishing operations. If this were the case, they would bypass many of the production steps mentioned. *Note:* The effective utilization of space in the plant was extremely important since the firm was able to rent out any unused portions of its plant. Saving space then, translated directly into rental income for HTI.

INNOVATION AT HTI

Plant management had, largely through experience and a certain degree of ingenuity, improved the production process in a number of specific areas. Since flexibility was a main priority, special tooling had been designed and built for the machines which sped up die changeovers. Product flexibility was also achieved through better production scheduling. Families of products which could be produced back-to-back were grouped together, making the changeovers between sets of products faster, and thereby reducing the size of the most economic production run.

Quality was, however, thought to be the firm's greatest strength. To preserve this advantage, over the past couple of years both management and labor had been educated in Statistical Process Control (SPC). This systematic way of reducing defects had allowed HTI to remain a leader in the production of quality tools.

New manufacturing technology had also been adopted. Several years earlier the firm had purchased a computer numerical controlled (CNC) machine to replace some older equipment. This machine had been something of a failure. As the plant manager put it, "We bought a Cadillac when what we actually needed was a Chevy." The vice president of operations at the time had purchased the CNC machine on impulse because he had been convinced he was being given a handsome deal. Neither the users nor even the plant manager were consulted on the buying decision. The machine was presently producing a variety of products but at about one-tenth of its potential. A much smaller, less costly CNC machine could have performed much more efficiently and would have matched the plant's actual requirements.

LABOR RELATIONS

Because of the increasingly competitive conditions facing HTI and the hand tool market in general, HTI employees had voiced concerns over job security. These concerns had culminated in the bitter 12-month long strike, which ended without management giving any concessions on the job security issue. Management-labor relations continued to be strained.

HTI'S STRATEGIC CHALLENGE

There were three major areas where HTI needed to excel in order to compete effectively in the North American hand tool market. The first and foremost area, and one in which the firm was strong, was quality. The provision of a quality product (with a lifetime guarantee) at a premium price continued to be an area of constant, reasonable demand and where the competition, particularly from overseas, was less effective.

The second area was the speed at which the firm could get the product to the marketplace. In this era of "just-in-time" delivery systems, there was increased pressure to deliver the product on time. HTI had to work especially hard at improving its performance in this area so it could prove to its customers that it had fully recovered from the strike.

The third and equally important area was flexibility; the ability to produce a variety of products. HTI had several thousand different products with small runs of each product. The ability to switch from one product to another in a timely and economical manner was essential.

PRELIMINARY INVESTIGATION INTO CAD/CAM

HTI's plant management had prided itself on having one of the more efficient plants in the North American hand tool industry. This was partially attributable to the forward thinking approaches of HTI's production management. Both the plant manager and the chief engineer had spent several Saturdays attending trade shows, visiting competitor's plants, speaking with various industry people and scanning the trade literature in an effort to evaluate what of the newly available technology could be of use to HTI.

For many years, the engineering department had expressed an interest in acquiring a computer-aided design (CAD) system. The technology could benefit the firm in a number of ways. First, it would substantially reduce the time it took to design a product. Second, it could reduce or eliminate the time taken to build costly prototypes. Third, it would free up the engineers' time; by eliminating drafting by hand, they could concentrate on producing a greater variety of designs. A fourth advantage of HTI would be a decrease in absolute design time; while the product was being designed from the computer, the necessary tooling could be designed simultaneously. Lastly, CAD could be used for revisions of existing work. This was important, since it was generally accepted that 80 percent of drafting work consisted of modifying existing designs.

The major stumbling block for acquiring a CAD system in the past had been the high cost of both the hardware and software (estimated at $250,000 plus). This was considered by top management to be unaffordable.

Recently, however, management had become more receptive to CAD, due to the availability of less expensive and more versatile systems. The AutoCAD system, for example, was available for microcomputers, and a complete system was available for as little as $25,000–$50,000. At this price CAD had become an affordable option even for HTI.

A second automation option was in the drilling and boring area. The Kingsbury machine could be replaced with two CNC lathes. This would decrease the per unit cost and also make throughput more consistent. The throughput of the Kingsbury was highly variable, and depended on the ability and skill of the operator. Only a limited number of the machine's operators could produce enough volume to make the machine profitable. Replacing the machine, however, would mean a $250,000 capital investment, and finding personnel skilled enough to operate the replacement machine properly.

THE DILEMMA

Despite the difficulties HTI had faced over the past decade, the company remained dominant in the high quality end of the Canadian and the United States hand tool markets.

This dominance would be threatened if new technology gave the competition the ability to achieve economies of scope. Such capability would give larger firms, which normally produced much longer runs and which therefore sought high volume markets, the ability to expand downward into smaller markets by making shorter production runs more economical.

This would mean that, despite its quality, HTI would no longer be able to charge its high prices and still remain competitive. To compete effectively HTI would have to be able to lower its price while maintaining its quality and its profit margins. The replacement for the Kingsbury would allow HTI to do this, thus retaining the company's competitive edge.

Despite relatively efficient production processes and an innovative management team, increasing offshore competition, cash flow problems and tense management-labor relations were all putting pressure on the plant to become even more efficient. This meant a push to longer runs, and that would take HTI away from its productiuon strengths and its markets. What the company really needed was a full order book for about a year, so that changes could be made in an orderly way, and all the problems addressed.

John's prayers had been heard, at last. HTI had just been told that a $2–$2.5 million order would be placed with them shortly. This could be an opportunity for HTI to redeem itself by performing well on a lucrative long-term contract. It could also provide the breathing space sorely needed if any coherent action was going to be taken. The kicker was, though, that performance to the contract's terms would probably require an immediate investment in new machinery, and new people.

CONCLUSION

Although the new technology would help to resolve some of John Smith's concerns, and perhaps make the company more competitive and able to meet its contractual obligations, John still felt deeply disturbed about a number of issues. He listed a few, but he knew that thinking more deeply would surface more:

1. What effect would new technology have on quality and productivity? How should any new technology be implemented? And how to you measure its effectiveness?
2. How could the problems which plagued the acquisition of the last CNC machine be avoided?
3. Assuming that the new technology would not show a positive NPV over the short-term, what arguments could be used to convince a banker that any investment made sense. How could you package a survival argument in terms bankers would understand, and with which they might be sympathetic?
4. How should HTI introduce and integrate the new technology into the existing plant? What specific changes might be considered for HTI, in both the short- and long-term, to realize the full benefits of the new technology? What impact would new technology have internally and strategically?

As he entered his office, Smith realized that the answers to the questions would not be found in his office, and he picked up his telephone to call a meeting of his management team for two hours time. In the meantime, he had to prepare the agenda, and that meant getting the questions right, at least. The first question was, though, where do you start.

Chapter Seven

NEW TECHNOLOGY JUSTIFICATION AND ASSESSMENT

SITUATION 7.1

Economic Justification for CIM[1]

Assessing the economic justification for CIM is one of the most critical tasks facing the management and technical staffs of manufacturing companies throughout the industrialized world. Companies that overlook the importance of this key technology could suffer serious economic and competitive hardship in the not too distant future.

On the other hand, however, companies that act too soon might load themselves with expensive and inflexible installations that might provide little payback and that could quickly become outmoded in a field where the pace of change is so rapid. Worse still, a mistake in system design, equipment choice, application area or project management might rob the company of its opportunity for a very needed, significant and early success.

Obviously management of technology is as important as technology itself. Another widely held belief is that senior management must be involved in the design, acquisition and implementation of CIM. This is for several reasons.

One reason is because the proper adoption of CIM will have such a large influence on the future health of the company. Another reason is because it must be planned, implemented and integrated across departmental lines. If implemented in only one area, as an island of automation, many of the benefits will fail to be realized.

A third reason is that the introduction of CIM is not the same as just purchasing and installing a piece of equipment. CIM is more a way of doing things. It depends heavily on people.

A fourth reason is that conventional methods of economic justification are not

[1]Jack Scrimgeour, *Technology Source*, Volume 1, No. 3, May 15, pp. 4–5. © 1988, CAN-MATE. Reprinted with permission.

working. This view is being increasingly recognized and expressed in the United States and Europe, and explains the widespread and growing interest in the economic justification for CIM.

There are three methods used for economic justification of a new technology. Only one of these three methods requires lengthy and detailed feasibility studies. The three methods or phases, each appropriate under certain times and situations, are:

1. Green fields, faith, pioneering
2. Detailed economic justification studies
3. Routing application, few questions asked

Attention at the present time is focused primarily on method number two because it applies to most people in most companies and currently poses as their chief impediment to CIM implementation.

SPECIFIC EXAMPLES OF ECONOMIC JUSTIFICATION

The following specific examples of economic justification and benefits have been reported by CIM users. They show that the savings are very substantial for those who apply it successfully and can represent an almost overwhelming competitive advantage. Examples cited by CIM users identify benefits such as:

> Fifty to 75 percent reduction in design time; reduction in the number of machines used from 68 to 18; reduction of space requirements from 103,000 square feet to 30,000; reduction in processing time from 35 days to a day and a half; raw material inventories reduced by 60 percent; WIP inventory levels reduced by 40 percent; materials handling labor reduced by 40 percent; an 80 percent reduction in the investment of equipment; overall reduction of 25 percent in annual operating costs; nonbudget and intangible benefits are also a good and frequent basis of justification. These include quality improvement, consistency, reliability, technological progress, cost avoidance, and risk reduction.

CHECKLIST FOR ECONOMIC JUSTIFICATION OF CIM

These and other specific examples of economic justification have been combined to create the following checklist.

1. Savings in time (all leading to shorter delivery times and faster response to market change)
   -Reduced engineering design time
   -Reduced drafting time
   -Reduced tool design time
   -Reduced setup time
   -Reduced process time in manufacturing operations

2. Higher quality product
   - Fewer errors in information handling (often derived from the use of a common database)
   - More uniformity in manufacturing operations
   - More thorough inspection
   - Tighter control of manufacturing operations
   - Reduced installation, service, and warranty costs
3. Better use of materials
   - Optimized engineering designs
   - Improved layout of parts, less scrap
   - Reduced scrap and rework due to errors
4. Labor savings due to:
   - Optimized engineering designs
   - Improved labor productivity
   - Use of better equipment
   - Improved access to information
   - Reduction of injuries and improved worker safety
5. Savings in equipment costs due to:
   - Higher utilization of existing equipment and facilities
   - Fewer engineering change notices
6. Savings in space required due to:
   - Reduced number of machine tools due to higher utilization
   - Reduced space for work-in-process (WIP) inventory
7. Savings in inventory
   - Reduced raw material inventory
   - Reduced work-in-process inventory
   - Reduced finished product inventory
8. Strategic and competitive advantages
   - Greater market share

READING 7.1

Must CIM Be Justified by Faith Alone?[2]

When the Yamazaki Machinery Company in Japan installed an $18 million flexible manufacturing system, the results were truly startling: a reduction in machines from 68 to 18, in employees from 215 to 12, in the floor space needed for production from 103,000 square feet to 30,000, and in average processing time from 35 days to 1.5. After two years, however, total savings came to only $6.9 million, $3.9 million of which had flowed from a one-time cut in inventory. Even if the system continued to produce annual labor savings of $1.5 million for 20 years, the project's return would be less than 10 percent per year. Since many United States companies use hurdle rates of 15 percent or higher and payback periods of five years or less, they would find it hard to justify this investment in new technology—despite its enormous savings in number of employees, floor space, inventory, and throughput times.

The apparent inability of traditional modes of financial analysis like discounted cash flow to justify investments in computer-integrated manufacturing (CIM) has led a growing number of managers and observers to propose abandoning such criteria for CIM-related investments.

Faced with outdated and inappropriate procedures of investment analysis, all that responsible executives can do is cast them aside in a bold leap of strategic faith.

But must there be a fundamental conflict between the financial and the strategic justifications for CIM? It is unlikely that the theory of discounting future cash flow (DCF) is either faulty or unimportant: receiving $1 in the future is worth less than receiving $1 today. If a company, even for good strategic reasons, consistently invests in projects

[2]Robert Kaplan, "Must CIM be Justified by Faith Alone?" March-April, 1986. © 1986 by the President and Fellows of Harvard College. Extracted with permission from *Harvard Business Review*.

whose financial returns are below its cost of capital, it will be on the road to insolvency. Whatever the special values of CIM technology, they cannot reverse the logic of the time value of money.

Surely, therefore, the trouble must not lie in some unbreachable gulf between the logic of DCF and the nature of CIM but in the poor applications of DCF to these investment proposals. Managers need not, and should not, abandon the effort to justify CIM on financial grounds. Instead, they need ways to apply the DCF approach more appropriately and to be more sensitive to the realities and special attributes of CIM.

TECHNICAL ISSUES

The DCF approach most often goes wrong when companies set arbitrarily high hurdle rates for evaluating new investment projects. Perhaps they believe that high return projects can be created by setting high rates rather than by making innovations in product and process technology or by cleverly building and exploiting a competitive advantage in the marketplace. In fact, the discounting function serves only to make cash flows received in the future equivalent to cash flows received now. For this narrow purpose—the only purpose, really, of discounting future cash flows—companies should use a discount rate based on the project's opportunity cost of capital (that is, the return available in the capital markets for investments of the same risk).

It may surprise managers to know that their real cost of capital can be in the neighborhood of 8 percent. (See Part I of the Appendix.) Double-digit hurdle rates that, in part, reflect assumptions of much higher capital costs are considerably wide off the mark. Their discouraging effect on CIM-type investments is not only unfortunate but also unfounded.

Companies also commonly under invest in CIM and other new process technologies because they fail to evaluate properly all the relevant alternatives. Most of the capital expenditure requests I have seen measure new investments against a status quo alternative of making no new investments—an alternative that usually assumes a continuation of current market share, selling price, and costs. Experience shows, however, that the status quo rarely lasts. Business as usual does not continue undisturbed.

In fact, the correct alternative to new CIM investment should assume a situation of declining cash flows, market share, and profit margins. Once a valuable new process technology becomes available, even if one company decides not to invest in it, the likelihood is that some of its competitors will. As Henry Ford claimed, "If you need a new machine and don't buy it, you pay for it without getting it." (See Part II of the Appendix.)

A related problem with current practice is its bias toward incremental rather than revolutionary projects. In many companies, the capital approval process specifies different levels of authorization depending on the size of the request. Small investments (under $100,000, say) may need only the approval of the plant manager: expenditures in excess of several million dollars may require the board of directors' approval. This apparently sensible procedure, however, creates an incentive for managers to propose small projects that fall just below the cutoff point where higher level approval would be needed. Over time, a host of little investments, each of which delivers savings in labor, material, or overhead cost, can add up to a less-than-optimal pattern of material flow and to obsolete process technology (Part III of the Appendix).

Introducing CIM process technology is not, of course, without its costs. Out-of-pocket equipment expense is only the beginning. Less obvious are the associated software costs that are necessary for CIM equipment to operate effectively. Managers should not be misled by the expending of these costs for tax and financial reporting purposes into thinking them operating expenses rather than investments. For internal management purposes, software development is as much a part of the investment in CIM equipment as the physical hardware itself. Indeed, in some installations, the programming, debugging, and prototype development may cost more than the hardware.

There are still other initial costs: site preparation, conveyors, transfer devices, feeders, parts orientation, and spare parts for the CIM equipment. Operating and maintenance personnel must be retrained and new operating procedures developed. Like software development, these tax-deductible training and education costs are part of the investment in CIM, not an expense of the periods in which they happen to be incurred.

Further, as some current research has shown, noteworthy declines in productivity often accompany the introduction of new process technology. These productivity declines can last up to a year, even longer when a radical new technology like CIM is installed. Apparently, the new equipment introduces severe and unanticipated process disruptions, which lead to equipment breakdowns that are higher than expected; to operating, repair, and maintenance problems; to scheduling and coordination difficulties; to revised materials standards; and to old-fashioned confusion on the factory floor.

We do not yet know how much of the disruption is caused by inadequate planning. After investing considerable effort and anguish in the equipment acquisition decision, some companies, no doubt, revert to business as usual while waiting for the new equipment to arrive.

Whatever the cause, the productivity decline is particularly ill-timed since it occurs just when a company is likely to conduct a postaudit on whether it is realizing the anticipated savings from the new equipment. Far from achieving anticipated savings, the postaudit will undoubtedly reveal lower output and higher costs than predicted.

TANGIBLE BENEFITS

The usual difficulties in carrying out DCF analysis—choosing an appropriate discount rate and evaluating correctly all relevant investment alternatives—apply with special force to the consideration of investments in CIM process technology. The greater flexibility of CIM technology, which allows it to be used for successive generations of products, gives it a longer useful life than traditional process investments. Because its benefits are likely to persist longer, overestimating the relevant discount rate will penalize CIM investments disproportionately more than shorter lived investments. The compounding effect of excessively high annual interest rates causes future cash flows to be discounted much too severely. Further, if executives arbitrarily specify short payback periods for new investments, the effect will be to curtail more CIM investments than traditional bottleneck relief projects.

But beyond a longer useful life, CIM technology provides many additional benefits—better quality, greater flexibility, reduced inventory and floor space, lower throughput times, experience with new technology—that a typical capital justification process does not quantify. Financial analyses that focus too narrowly on easily quantified savings in labor, materials, or energy will miss important benefits from CIM technology.

Inventory Savings

Some of these omissions can be easily remedied. The process flexibility, more orderly product flow, higher quality, and better scheduling that are typical of properly used CIM equipment will drastically cut both work-in-process (WIP) and finished goods inventory levels. This reduction in average inventory levels represents a large cash inflow at the time the new process equipment becomes operational. This, of course, is a cash savings the DCF analysis can easily capture.

Consider a product line for which the anticipated monthly cost of sales is $500,000. Using existing equipment and technology, the producing division carries about three months of sales in inventory. After investing in flexible automation, the division heads find that reduced waste, scrap, and rework, greater predictability, and faster throughput permit a two-thirds reduction in average inventory levels.

Pruning inventory from three months to one month of sales produces a cash inflow of $1 million in the first year the system becomes operational. If sales increase 10 percent per year, the company will enjoy increased cash flows from the inventory reductions in all future years too—that is, if the cost of sales rises to $550,000 in the next year, a two-month reduction in inventory saves an additional $100,000 that year, $110,000 the year after, and $121,000 the year after that.

Less Floor Space

CIM also cuts floor space requirements. It takes fewer computer-controlled machines to do the same job as a larger number of conventional machines. Also, the factory floor will no longer be used to store inventory. Recall the example of the Japanese plant that installed a flexible manufacturing system and reduced space requirements from 103,000 to 30,000 square feet. These space savings are real, but conventional financial accounting systems do not measure their value well—especially if the building is almost fully depreciated or was purchased years before the price levels were lower. Do not, therefore, look to financial accounting systems for a good estimate of the cost or value of space. Instead, compute the estimate in terms of the opportunity costs of new space: either its square foot rental value or the annualized cost of new construction.

Higher Quality

Greatly improved quality, defined here as conformance to specifications, is a third tangible benefit from investment in CIM technology. Automated process equipment leads directly to more uniform production and, frequently, to an order-of-magnitude decline in defects. These benefits are easy to quantify and should be part of any cash flow analysis. Some managers have seen five- to 10-fold reductions in waste, scrap, and rework when they replaced manual operations with automated equipment.

Further, as production uniformity increases, fewer inspection stations and fewer inspectors are required. If automatic gauging is incuded in the CIM installation, virtually all manual inspection of parts can be eliminated. Also, with 100 percent continuous automated inspection, out-of-tolerance parts are detected immediately. With manual systems, the entire lot of parts to be produced before a problem is detected would need to be reworked or scrapped.

These capabilities lead, in turn, to significant reductions in warranty expense. Although it may be hard to estimate these savings out to four or five significant digits, it would be grossly wrong to assume that the benefits are zero. We must overcome the preference of accountants for precision over accuracy, which causes them to ignore benefits they cannot quantify beyond one or two digits of accuracy.

We can estimate still other tangible benefits from CIM. John Shewchuk of General Electric claims that accounts receivable can be reduced by eliminating the incidence of customers who defer payment until quality problems are resolved. Consider too that because improved materials flow can reduce the need for forklift trucks and operators, factories will enjoy a large cash flow saving from not having to acquire, maintain, repair, and operate so many trucks.

INTANGIBLE BENEFITS

Other benefits of CIM include increased flexibility, faster response to market shifts, and greatly reduced throughput and lead times. These benefits are as important as those just discussed but much harder to quanity. We may not be sure how many zeros should be in our benefits estimate (are they to be measured in thousands or millions of dollars?) much less which digit should be first. The difficulty arises in large part because these benefits represent revenue enhancements rather than cost savings. It is fairly easy to get a ballpark estimate for percentage reductions in costs already being incurred. It is much harder to quantify the magnitude of revenue enhancement expected from features that are not already in place.

Greater Flexibility

The flexibility that CIM technology offers takes several forms. The benefits of economies of scope—that is, the potential for low-cost production of high-variety, low-volume goods—are just beginning to flow from FMS environments as early adopters of the technology start to service after market sales for discontinued models on the same equipment used to produce current high volume models. We are also beginning to see some customized production on the same lines used for standard products.

Beyond these economy-of-scope applications, CIM's reprogramming capabilities made it possible for machines to serve as backups for each other. Even if a machine is dedicated to a narrow product line, it can still replace lost production during a second or a third shift when a similar piece of equipment, producing quite a different product, breaks down.

Further, by easily accommodating engineering change orders and product redesigns, CIM technology allows for product changes over time. And, if the mix of products demanded by the market changes, a CIM-based process can respond with no increase in costs.

CIM's flexibility also gives it usefulness beyond the life cycle of the product for which it was purchased. True, in the short run, CIM may perform the same functions as less expensive, inflexible equipment. Many benefits of its flexibility will show up only over time. Therefore, it is difficult to estimate how much this flexibilty will be worth. Nonetheless, as we shall see, even an order-of-magnitude estimate may be sufficient.

Shorter Throughput and Lead Time

Another seemingly intangible benefit of CIM is the great reductions it makes possible in throughput and lead time. At the Yamazaki factory described at the beginning of this article, average processing time per work piece fell from 35 to 1.5 days. To be sure, some of the benefits from greatly reduced throughput times have already been incorporated in our estimate of savings from inventory reductions. But there is also a notable marketing advantage in being able to meet customer demands with shorter lead times and to respond quickly to changes in market demand.

Increased Learning

Some investments in new process technology have important learning characteristics. Thus, even if calculations of the net present value of their cash flows turn up negative, the investments can still be quite valuable by permitting managers to gain experience with the technology, test the market of new products, and keep a close watch on major process advances.

These learning effects have characteristics similar to buying options in financial markets. Buying options may not at first seem like a favorable investment, but small initial outlays may yield huge benefits down the line. Similarly, were a company to invest in a risky CIM-related project, it could reap big gains should the technology provide unexpected competitive advantages in the future. Moreover, given the rapid pace of technological change and the advantages of being an early market participant, companies that defer process investments until the new technology is well-established will find themselves far behind the market leaders. In this context, the decision to defer investment is often a decision not to be a principle player in the next round of product or process innovation.

THE BOTTOM LINE

Although intangible benefits may be difficult to quantify, there is no reason to value them at zero in a capital expenditure analysis. Zero is, after all, no less arbitrary than any other number. Conservative accountants who assign zero values to many intangible benefits prefer being precisely wrong to being vaguely right. Managers need not follow their example.

One way to combine difficult-to-measure benefits with those more easily quantified is, first, to estimate the annual cash flows about which there is the greatest confidence: the cost of the new process equipment and the benefits expected from labor, inventory, floor space, and cost-of-quality savings. If at this point a discounted cash flow analysis, done with a sensible discount rate and a consideration of all relevant alternatives, shows a CIM investment to have a positive net present value, well and good. Even without accounting for the value of intangible benefits, the analysis will have gotten the project over its financial hurdle. If the DCF is negative, however, then it becomes necessary to estimate how much the annual cash flows must increase before the investment does have a positive net present value.

Suppose, for example, that an extra $100,000 per year over the life of the investment is sufficient to give the project the desired return. Then management can decide whether it expects heightened flexibility, reduced throughput and lead times, and faster market response to be worth at least $100,000 per year. Should the company be willing to pay $100,000 annually to enjoy these benefits? If so, it can accept the project with confidence. If, however, the additional cash flows needed to justify the investment turn out to be quite large—say $3 million per year—and management decides the intangible benefits of CIM are not worth that amount, then it is perfectly sensible to turn the investment down.

Rather than attempt to put a dollar tag on benefits that by their nature are difficult to quantify, managers should reverse the process and estimate first how large these benefits must be in order to justify the proposed investment. Senior executives can be expected to judge that improved flexibility, rapid customer service, market adaptability, and options on new process technology may be worth $300,000 to $500,000 per year but not, say, $1 million. This may not be exact mathematics, but it does help put a meaningful price on CIM's intangible benefits.

As manufacturers make critical decisions about whether to acquire CIM equipment, they must avoid claims that such investments have to be made on faith alone because financial analysis is too limiting. Successful process investments must yield returns in excess of the cost of capital invested. That is only common sense. Thus the challenge for managers is to improve their ability to estimate the costs and benefits of CIM, not to take the easy way out and discard the necessary discipline of financial analysis.

EXAMPLE OF AN FMS JUSTIFICATION ANALYSIS

With the following analysis, one United States manufacturer of air handling equipment justified its investment in an FMS installation for producing a key component:

1. Internal manufacture of the component is essential for the division's long-term strategy to maintain its capability to design and manufacture a proprietary product.
2. The component has been manufactured on mostly conventional equipment, some numerically controlled, with an average age of 23 years. To manufacture a product

in conformance with current quality specifications, the company must replace this equipment with new conventional equipment or advanced technology.

3. The alternatives are:
   - Conventional or numerically controlled stand alone
   - Transfer line
   - Machining cells
   - FMS
4. FMS compares with conventional technology (see Exhibit 7.1).

Exhibit 7.1 Comparison of Vonventional Equipment with the Proposed FMS

	Conventional Equipment	FMS
Utilization	30%–40%	80%–90%
Number of employees needed (including indirect workers, such as those who do materials handling, inspection, and rework)*	52	14
Reduced scrap and rework	—	$60,000 annually
Inventory	$2,000,000	$1,000,000**
Incremental investment	—	$9,200,000

* Each employee costs $36,000 a year in wages and fringe benefits.
** Inventory reductions because of shorter lead times and flexibility.

5. Intangible benefits include virtually unlimited flexibility for FMS to modify mix of component models to the exact requirements of the assembly department.
6. The financial analysis for a project life of 10 years compares the FMS with conventional technology (static sales assumptions, constant, or base-year, dollars) as shown in Exhibit 7.,2.

Exhibit 7.2 Financial Analysis for the Two Alternatives

Year	Investment	Operating Savings	Tax Savings ITC and ACRS Depreciation	After Tax Cash Flow 50%
0	$9,200	$ 900[a]	$ 920	$ −7,380
1		1,428[b]	1,311	1,370[c]
2		1,428	1,923	1,675
3		1,428	1,835	1,632
4		1,428	1,835	1,632
5		1,428	1,835	1,632
6		1,428		714
7		1,428		714
8		1,428		714
9		1,428		714
10		1,428		714

After-Tax yield: 11.1% Payback period: during year 5.

[a] $ 900 = Inventory reduction at start of project.
[b] $1,428 = 38 fewer employees at $36,000/year + $60,000 scrap and rework savings.
[c] $1,370 = (1,428) (1 − 0.50) + (1,311) (0.50).

7. With dynamic sales assumptions showing expected increases in production volume, the annual operating savings will double in future years and the financial yield (still using constant, base-year, dollars) will increase to more than 17 percent per year.

On the basis of this analysis and recognizing the value of the intangible item (5), which had not been incorporated formally, the company selected the FMS option.

APPENDIX A

Getting the Numbers Right

PART 1—THE COST OF CAPITAL

A company always has the option of repurchasing its common shares or retiring its debt. Therefore, managers can estimate the cost of capital for a project by taking a weighted average of the current cost of equity and debt at the mix of capital financing typical in the industry. Extensive studies of the returns to investors in equity and fixed income markets during the past 60 years show that from 1926 to 1984 the average total return (dividends plus price appreciation) from holding a diversified portfolio of common stocks was 11.7 percent per year. This return already includes the effects of rising price levels. Removing the effects of inflation puts the real (after inflation) return from investments in common stocks at about 8.5 percent per year (as shown in Exhibit 7.3).

Exhibit 7.3 Annual Return Series, 1926–1984

	Mean Annual Returns		
Series	1926–1984	1950–1984	1975–1984
Common Stocks	11.7%	12.8%	14.7%
Long-term Corporate Bonds	4.7	4.5	8.4
U.S. Treasury Bills	3.4	5.1	9.0
Inflation (CDI)	3.2	4.4	7.4

Exhibit 7.3 (Cont'd.)

	Real Annual Returns (Net of Inflation)		
Series	1926–1984	1950–1984	1975–1984
Common Stocks	8.5%	8.4%	7.3%
Long-term Corporate Bonds	1.5	0.1	1.0
U.S. Treasury Bills	0.2	0.6	1.6

These historical estimates of 8.5 percent real (or about 12 percent nominal) are, however, overestimates of the total cost of capital. From 1926 to 1984, fixed income securities averaged nominal before tax returns or less than 5 percent per year. Taking out inflation reduces the real return (or cost) of high-grade corporate debt securities to about 1.5 percent per year. Even with recent increases in the real interest rate, a mixture of debt and equity financing produces a total real cost of capital of less than 8 percent.

Many corporate executives will, no doubt, be highly skeptical that their real cost of capital could be 8 percent of less. Their disbelief probably comes from making one of two conceptual errors, perhaps both. First, executives often attempt to estimate their current cost of capital by looking at their accounting return on investment—that is, the net income divided by the net invested capital—of their divisions or corporations. For many companies this figure can be in the 15 percent to 25 percent range.

There are several reasons, however, why an accounting ROI is a poor estimate of a company's real cost of capital. The accounting ROI figure is distored by financial accounting conventions such as depreciation method and a variety of capitalization and expense decision. The ROI figure is also distorted by management's failure to adjust both the net income and the invested capital figures for the effects of inflation, an omission that biases the accounting ROI well above the company's actual real return on investment.

The second conceptual error that makes an 8 percent real cost of capital sound too low is implicitly to compare it with today's market interest rates and returns on common stocks. These rates incorporate expectations of current and future inflation, but the 8.5 percent historical return on common stocks and the less than 2 percent return on fixed income securities are real returns, after the effects of inflation have been netted out.

Now it is possible, of course, to do a DCF analysis by using nominal market returns as a way of estimating a company's cost of capital. In fact, this may even be desirable when you are doing an after tax cash flow analysis since one of the important cash flows being discounted is the nominal tax depreciation shield from new investment. I have, however, seen many a company go seriously wrong by using a nominal discount rate (say in excess of 15 percent) while it was assuming level cash flows over the life of their investments.

Consider, for example, the data in Exhibit 7.4, which is excerpted from an actual capital authorization request. Notice that all the cash flows during the 10 years of the project's expected life are expressed in 1977 dollars, even though the company used a

20 percent discount rate on the cash flows of the several investment alternatives. This assumption of a 20 percent cost of capital most likely arose from a prior assumption of a real cost of capital of about 10 percent and an expected inflation rate of 10 percent per year. But if it believed that inflation would average 10 percent annually over the life of the project, the company should also have raised the assumed selling price and the unit costs of labor, material, and overhead by their expected price increased over the life of the project.

It is inconsistent to assume a high rate of inflation for the interest rate used in a DCF calculation but a zero rate of price change when you are estimating future net cash flows from an investment. Naturally, the inconsistency using double-digit discount rates but level cash flows—biases the analysis toward the rejection of new investments, especially those yielding benefits five to 10 years into the future.

Exhibit 7.4 Example of a Capital Authorization Request*

Alternative 1 Rebuild Present Machines

Year	1977	1978	1979	1980	1981	—	1986
Sales	$6,404	$6,404	$6,404	$6,404	$6,404	—	$6,404
Cost of Sales:							
Labor	168	168	168	168	168	—	168
Material	312	312	312	312	312	—	312
Overhead	1,557	1,557	1,557	1,557	1,557	—	1,557

Alternative 5 Purchase all New Machines

Year	1977	1978	1979	1980	1981	—	1986
Sales	$6,404	$6,724	$7,060	$7,413	$7,784	—	$7,784
Cost of Sales:							
Labor	167	154	148	152	152	—	152
Material	312	328	344	361	380	—	380
Overhead	1,557	1,4401	1,390	1,423	1,423	—	1,423

*Adapted from Robert S. Kaplan and Glen Bingham, Wilmington Tap and Die. Case 185–124 (Boston: Harvard Business School, 1985).

PART II—MEASURING ALTERNATIVES

Look again at the capital authorization request in Exhibit 7.4. The cash flows from Alternative 1 assume a constant level of sales during the next 10 years; the cash flows from Alternative 5 show a somewhat higher level of sales based on a small increase in market share. The difference in sales is based on a small increase in market share. The difference in sales revenue as currently projected, however, is not all that great. Only if managers anticipate a steady decrease in market share and sales revenue for Alternative 1, a decrease occasioned by domestic or international competitors adopting the new production technology, would Alternative 5 show a major improvement over the status quo.

PART III—PIECEMEAL INVESTMENT

Each year, a company or division may undertake a series of small improvements in its production process—to alleviate bottlenecks, to add capacity where needed, or to introduce islands of automation based on immediate and easily quantified labor savings. Each of these projects, taken by itself, may have a positive net present value. By investing on a piecemeal basis, however, the company or division will never get the full benefit of completely redesigning and rebuilding its plant. Yet the pressures to go forward on a piecemeal basis are nearly irrestible. At any point in time, there are many annual, incremental projects scattered about from which the investment has yet to be recovered. Thus, were management to scrap the plant, its past incremental investments would be shown to be incorrect.

Although none of the usual incremental process investments may have been incorrect, the collecction of incremental decisions could have a lower net present value than the alternative of deferring most investment during a terminal period, earning interest on the unexpended funds, and then replacing the plant. Again, the failure to evaluate such global investment is not a limitation of DCF analysis. It is a failure of not applying DCF analysis to all the feasible alternatives to annual, incremental investment proposals.

READING 7.2

Nontraditional Method for Evaluating CIM Opportunities Assigns Weights to Intangibles[3]

INTRODUCTION

Competitive pressures are prompting manufacturers to consider carefully how they can incorporate computer-integrated manufacturing in their planning. To properly evaluate prospective CIM opportunities, a methodology that includes both strategic and tactical weighted evaluations as well as financial considerations such as net present worth is needed. This article describes such a method (see Exhibit 7.5).

NONTRADITIONAL JUSTIFICATION

Computer-based automation equipment and systems require massive capital investments. Many firms have tended to base their investment decisions on traditional discounted cash flow financial justification methodologies that are better suited to meeting profitability criteria than to evaluating ways of reaching long-term strategic goals. These traditional methodologies, when used in conjunction with the high hurdle (minimum attractive) rates that are prevalent in today's uncertain and capital-scarce environment, often result in rejection of proposed high technology equipment and systems.

The inadequacy of such traditional justification procedures has become apparent. Much of the published literature blames the problem on their inability to quantify and formally consider so-called intangible benefits; other writings point out the shortcom-

[3]John Canada, *Industrial Engineering*, March 1986, pp. 66–71. © 1986 Institute of Industrial Engineers, Atlanta, Georgia. Reprinted with permission from *Industrial Engineering*.

Exhibit 7.5 Recommended Selection Process

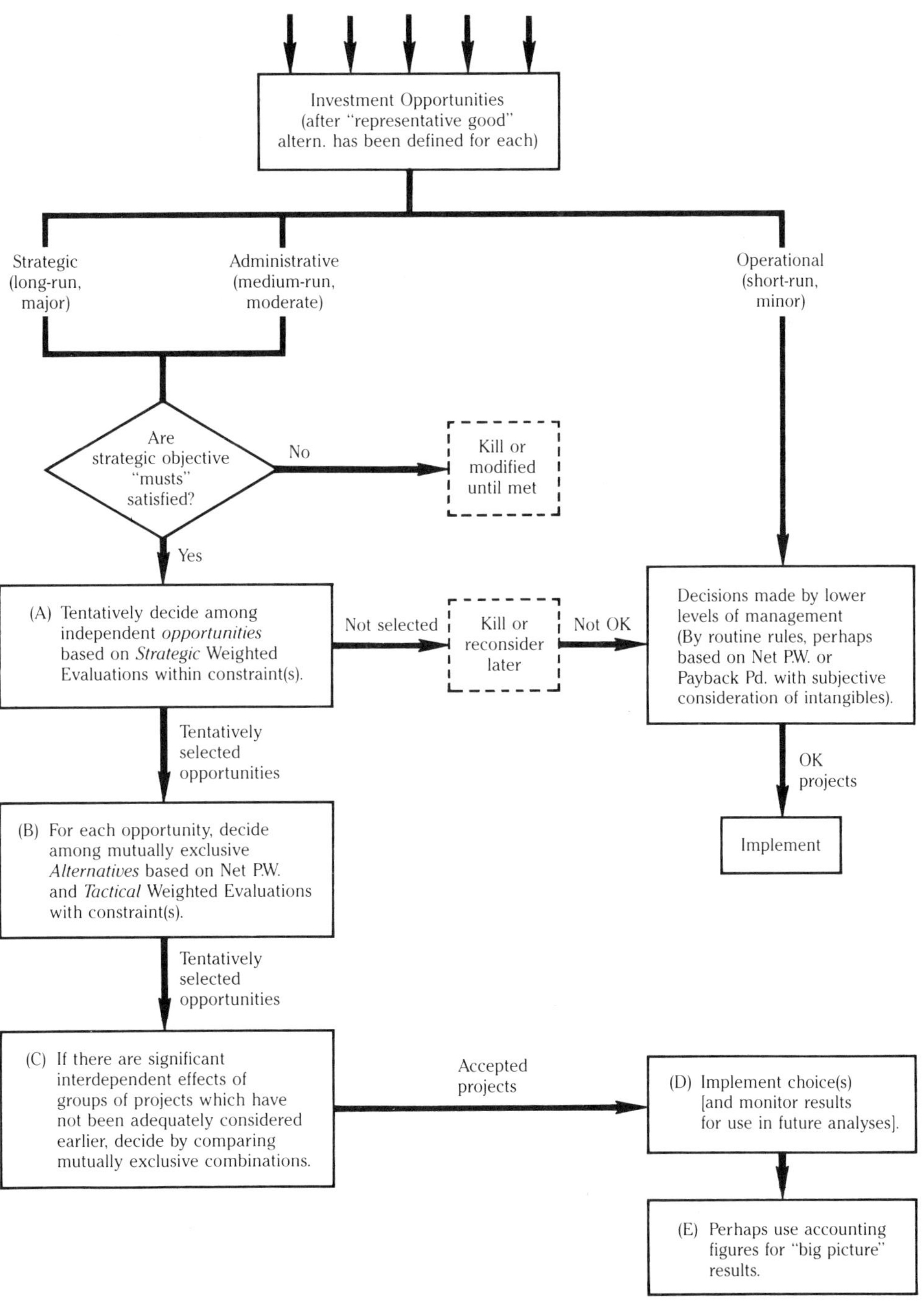

ings of contemporary and allegedly outmoded cost accounting systems that inhibit the use of relevant, but often unconventional measures of performance. Some authors even totally discredit attempts to justify modern automation through traditional capital budgeting evaluation practices on the grounds that such decisions should be made primarily based on strategic considerations.

METHODOLOGY AND EXAMPLES

Exhibit 7.5 diagrams the methodology suggested here. The analysis is based on the common procedure of considering investment projects in two categories:

1. *Opportunities,* which are independent of each other (that is, any number of such opportunities can be chosen within whatever constraints exist without affecting the prospective results of other opportunities).
2. *Alternatives,* which are mutually exclusive (that is, at most one of the alternatives within a given opportunity group can be chosen).

For example, opportunities for a firm could be an automated storage and retrieval system for a finished goods warehouse and a CIM system for a particular manufacturing plant. Within each such opportunity there probably are numerous alternatives, such as different vendor systems. If opportunities happen to be interdependent, so that one increases or decreases the desirability of another, combinations can be considered.

Returning to the top of Exhibit 7.5, first a pool of representative good investment opportunities is compiled and placed into one of three categories as shown in Exhibit 7.6.

Exhibit 7.6 Categories of Investment Opportunities

Category (Length of Decision Impact)	Examples
Strategic (long-term)	CIM systems New product line
Administrative (medium-term)	Replace general purpose equipment
Operational (short-term)	Fixtures and minor equipment Discretionary repairs

Operational decisions are shown as being made by routine decision rules. Investment opportunities in the strategic and administrative categories, because they tend to overlap, are shown to go through the same subsequent steps. They are first screened according to whether strategic objective "musts" are met. As the name implies, these "musts" are criteria or questions which must be satisfied before an opportunity will be eligible for further consideration. Examples are: "Does it maintain or advance the firm's technological capabilities?" and "Does it keep us concentrated in the (blank) business?" and "Does it risk less than (X) percent of the firm's worth?"

OPPORTUNITY SELECTION

Those opportunities which pass the strategic "musts" test are then ranked and tentatively selected within whatever constraints exist according to a method called "strategic weighted evaluation" (see Exhibit 7.5, block [A]).

Exhibit 7.7 lists eight example strategic attributes and describes the potential benefits due to CIM for each. The use of this methodology must determine which of these or any other attributes or criteria are of significant importance to the firm, and those chosen should be as independent of each other as possible; in other words, the outcomes for a given attribute should not be affected by what the outcomes of any of the other attributes happen to be.

Exhibit 7.7 Example Strategic Attributes and Criteria (Potential Benefits Are a Function of Extent of Implementation of CIMS)

Attribute	Potential Benefits Due to CIMS
1. Quality	Greater consistency in manufacture and ease in testing.
2. Flexibility	Increased ability to adapt to changing customer requirements (product or volume) economically.
3. Lead times	Reduction in time to achieve product or process designs and to manufacture and ship.
4. Capacity	Increased manufacturing throughput ability.
5. Inventories	Reduced size due to flexibility, shorter lead times and precise, fast information systems.
6. Controls	Tighter due to reliance on computer programs rather than operators for process and shop actions.
7. Future options	Created through firm's acquisition of new technological capabilities (hardware, software and people) on which it can build.
8. Long life	Maintain capabilities and use rates of facilities due to ability to combine economics of high-volume dedicated automation with the flexibilities of job-shop production.

The strategic weighted evaluation is calculated in exactly the same manner as for the tactical weighted evaluation (to be explained in the following section)—the only difference is that the chosen strategic attributes and their respective weights will typically differ significantly from the chosen tactical attributes and weights.

ALTERNATIVE SELECTION

Next, any mutually exclusive alternatives for each tentatively accepted opportunity (Exhibit 7.5, block [B]) are considered and tentative selections made by consideration, within existing constraints, of:

- Nonmonetary (intangible) factors; ("tactical weighted evaluation.")
- Monetary (quantifiable) facctors; ("net present worth.")

Tactical Weighted Evaluation. Exhibit 7.8 is a form illustrating the identification and weighting of attributes. Note that only four tactical attributes are considered applicable or important. Typically, it is recommended that the most important of these attributes be given a weight of 100, and all other chosen attributes be given lesser weights according to their perceived importance relative to other attributes. Such weights are often so subjective that it is advisable to test various combinations for "consistency of preference" until you are satisfied that the weights are reasonable.

The last column of Exhibit 7.8 shows the formula for normalizing the weights to total 100. This is merely a thinking convenience, as people tend to refer to quantitative weights as parts of 100 or percentages.

Exhibit 7.8 Identification and Weighting of Tactical Attributes

What: ILLUSTRATION OF WEIGHTING FOR TACTICAL ATTRIBUTES

Check One: ___ Strategic ✓ Tactical

Attribute/Criterion	Check if Applicable	Weight	Normalized Weight (=Weight/Tot. Weight)
1. Quality			
2. Flexibility - Product			
3. Flexibility - Schedule			
4. Lead Times			
5. Capacity			
6. Inventories			
7. Controls			
8. Future Options			
9. Long life			
10. Scrap/Rework			
11. Employee satisfaction			
12. Riskiness, LACK OF	✓	63	25
13. Serviceability/Maintainability			
14. Mgt./Engr. Effort Req'd.	✓	37	15
15. Other CIMS AIMS, HOW WELL MET	✓	100	40
16. Other PROFITABILITY, EXPECTED			
17. Other RELATIONS, EMPL./PUBLIC			
18. Other PRODUCIBILITY			
19. Other CONTROLLABILITY			
20. Other COMPATIBILITY			
21. Other SERVICEABILITY	✓	50	20
22. Other			
23. Other			
24. Other			
25. Other			
		Total Weight = 250	Total = 100

Figure 7.9 shows a form for calculating the tactical weighted evaluation for two alternatives. Note that the normalized weights from Exhibit 7.8 are used. Note also that an "evaluation rating" (on a scale of zero to 10) is made to reflect how well each alternative meets each attribute. For example, with respect to the first attribute, "CIMS tactical aims," alternatives P-1 and P-2 scored 7.5 and 9, respectively. These scores could have been based on some quantitative scales, or simply on subjective judgment with some guides—such as, a zero would be "very poor" and a 10 would be "extraordinarily good." The evaluation scores shown for the "CIMS tactical aims" attribute would indicate that alternative P-2 rates close to "extraordinary" with a 9 and alternative P-1 rates somewhat less, probably "very good," with a 7.5.

The right-hand portion of Exhibit 7.9 shows the formula for computation, with the column totals for the two alternatives being the "weighed evaluation" measures—which were 82 and 75, respectively. Note also that the bottom right-hand side provides a place for entering any monetary measure of merit (separately determined).

Exhibit 7.9 Weighted Evaluation of Alternatives

Check One: ___ Strategic
✓ Tactical

What: ILLUSTRATION OF TACTICAL WEIGHTED EVALUATION OF ALTERNATIVES

Project Descriptions:
P-1 ALT. I-A
P-2 ALT. I-B
P-3
P-4

Attribute/Criterion (Ref. FIG IV-4)	Normalized Weight	Evaluation Rating P-1	P-2	P-3	P-4	Weight & Evaluation Rating ÷ 10 P-1	P-2	P-3	P-4
CIMS TACTICAL AIMS	40	7.5	9			30	36		
RISKINESS, LACK OF	25	8	6			20	15		
SERVICEABILITY	20	10	7.5			20	15		
MGT/ENGR'G EFFORT	15	8	6			12	9		
					Total	82	75		
Monetary Measure of Merit, Like Net P.W. (If considered separately)						$300M	$350M		

Exhibit 7.10 Project Monetary Costs and Savings

What: EXAMPLE CALC OF NET P.W.; ALTERN. I-B

Savings Compared to: (If not obvious in "What") NO CIM, KEEP STATUS QUO

Comments ALL NOS. IN $M

Net P.W. @ 20 % = $350

Payback Pd. = ~1.7 YRS

Line	How Calc? (Lines)	1986 0	1	2	3	4	5	Each Yr. 6–10	TOTAL
INVESTMENT, CAPITALIZED									
(1) Equipment Cost		130							
(2) Accessories & Tooling Cost		10							
(3) Other ______		-							
(4) Total Capital Inv.	(1) + (2) + (3)	140							
(5) Investment Tax Credit	10 % x (4)	14							
INVESTMENT, EXPENDED									
(6) Engineering		30							
(7) Installation		13							
(8) Startup		5							
(9) Other									
(10) Total Expensed Inv.	(6) + ... + (9)	48							
(11) Total All Inv. Aft. Credit	(4)+(10)-(5)	174							
OPERATING SAVINGS (COSTS)									
(12) Direct Labor Savings			50	80	100	– SAME AS YR. 3 –	– SAME AS YR. 3 –	150	
(13) Indirect Labor Savings			10	10	10			10	
(14) Material Savings			30	50	60			80	
(15) Maintenance Savings			10	10	10			10	
(16) Other Savings ______			40	50	60			88	
(17) Other Costs			(20)	(20)	(20)			(30)	
(18) Total Operating Savings	(12)+...+(17)		120	180	220			308	
ANALYSIS									
(19) Depreciation	___ x (4)	48	28	28	28			0	
(20) Net Before Tax Savings	(18)-(19)	(48)	92	152	192			308	
(21) Net After-Tax Savings	(20)x(1-.50)	24	46	76	96			154	
(22) Net After-Tax Cash Savings	(21)+(19)	24	74	104	124			154	
(23) Net After-Tax Cash Flow	(22)-(11)	(150)	74	104	124	124	124	154×5	1,170.0
(24) Discount Factor @ 10%		1.000	.909	.826	.751	.683	.621	2.354	
(25) P.W. @ 10%	(23)x(24)	(150)	67.3	85.9	93.1	84.7	77.0	362.5	620.5
(26) Discount Factor @ 20%		1.000	.833	.694	.579	.482	.402	1.202	
(27) P.W. @ 20%	(23)x(26)	(150)	61.6	72.1	71.8	59.7	49.8	185.0	350.0
(28) Discount Factor @ 40%		1.000	.714	.510	.364	.260	.186	.379	
(29) P.W. @ 40%	(23)x(28)	(150)	52.8	53.0	45.1	32.2	23.1	58.4	114.6

Net Present Worth. Exhibit 7.10 shows a good easy-to-use form for calculating the net present worth for an alternative project. The form provides for considering income taxes and after tax cash flows for up to 10 years, and it also includes a discount factor of 10 percent, 20 percent or 40 percent. The example figures happen to be for alternative I-B (which was also shown in Exhibit 7.9). For an after tax discount factor (minimum attractive rate of return) of 20 percent, the net present worth for that alternative is shown to be $350,000 in the right-hand column, next-to-bottom row.

Exhibit 7.11 shows a summary of typical study results for all mutually exclusive alternatives for four different opportunity groups in terms of both tactical weighted evaluation and net present worth. It also provides for information on "resources used" for which there may be constraints (in right-hand columns). In this case, only the

Exhibit 7.11 Alternatives for Top Four Opportunities

Rank by: ___ Weighted Eval. ___ Net P.W. ___ Final Recomm. ✓ Other

What: SUMMARY OF STUDY RESULTS -- ALTERNATIVES FOR TOP FOUR OPPORTUNITIES (NOTE: TACTICAL WGTD. EVAL. NUMBERS ARE NOT NECESSARILY THE SAME AS FOR STRATEGIC WGTD. EVAL.)

Ident.	Opportunity/ Alternative/Combin. Description		✓Tactical / Strategic Weighted Evaluation	Net P.W. (If applic.) IN $M		Resources Used: INVEST, $RO IN $M			
				Amt.	Cumul.	Amt.	Cumul.	Amt.	Cumul.
1	IV - AS/RS WHSE.	ALT. A	85	560		100			
2		" B	↘85	660 ↙		75			
3		" C	75	340		50			
4									
5	II - CIM, PLT II	ALT. A	72	70 ↙		70			
6		" B	↘80	-10		70			
7									
8	I - CIM, PLT I	ALT. A	↘82	300		50			
9		" B	75	350 ↙		150			
10									
11	III - CIM, PLT III	ALT. A	65	320 ↙		80			
12		" B	↘70	200		100			
13		" C	68	100		60			
14									
15									

Total Avail. (250) Total Avail. (____)

Comments:
Other Considerations: ARROWS "↘" AND "↙" DENOTE BEST ALTERNATIVE FOR EACH OPPORTUNITY (GROUP) FOR WGT'D EVAL. AND NET P.W., RESPECTIVELY

Recommended Decision/Reason(s) ____________

investment in year zero was shown as a constraint, and the total of that resource available was shown at the bottom of the column.

Note in Exhibit 7.11 that arrows were used to denote the best alternative for each opportunity group for tactical weighted evaluation and net present worth, respectively. The final choice will depend on the decision maker's preference for tactical weighted evaluation scores versus net present worth. As a typical aid, Exhibit 7.12 shows the best alternative for each opportunity ranked by decreasing tactical weighted evaluation.

Similar ranking according to decreasing net present worth could be done to facilitate thinking regarding final selections within given constraints. If the number of projects and trade-off possibilities is fairly large, the final choosing can be facilitated by graphical comparisons.

Note in Exhibit 7.12 that the choices by decreasing rank are IV-B, I-A, II-B and III-B. To live within the $250,000 total investment constraint, project II-B would have to be dropped. Note, however, that project II-B has a net present worth of $10,000. One might rationally decide it is worth substituting project III-B for project II-B to in-

Exhibit 7.12 Rank Ordering of Alternatives By Weighted Evaluation

Rank by: ✓ Weighted Eval. ___ Net P.W. ___ Final Recomm. ___ Other

What: RANK ORDERING BY WEIGHTED EVALUATION FOR BEST ALTERNATIVE WITHIN EACH OF TOP FOUR OPPORTUNITIES

Ident.	Opportunity/ Alternative/Combin. Description	✓ Tactical / Strategic Weighted Evaluation	Net P.W. (If applic.) IN $M Amt.	Net P.W. Cumul.	Resources Used: INVEST, YR0 IN $M Amt.	INVEST, YR0 IN $M Cumul.	Amt.	Cumul.
1	IV-B: AS/RS, ALT B	85	660	660	75	75		
2	I-A: CIM AT I, ALT A	82	300	960	50	125		
3	II-B: CIM AT II, ALT B	80	-10	950	70	195		
4	III-B: CIM AT III, ALT B	70	200	1,150	100	295		
5								
6								
7								
8								
9								
10								
11								
12								
13								
14								
15								

Total Avail. (250) Total Avail. (____)

Comments:
Other Considerations ____

Recommended Decision/Reason(s) INDICATED CHOICES ARE IV-B, I-A, AND III-B

clude a net present worth of $200,000 rather than $10,000, even though that means having a tactical weighted evaluation of 70 rather than 80. With this substitution, the final choices would be projects IV-B, I-A and II-B with a total net present worth of $1.16 million and requiring a total investment of $225,000 (within the constraint).

INTERDEPENDENT EFFECTS

The previous procedure can be supplemented to consider interdependent effects of opportunity groups (Exhibit 7.5, block [C]). For example, suppose the acceptance of CIM at Plant I would enhance the benefits of CIM at some other plant. Or, possibly the acceptance of an AS/RS finished goods warehouse would decrease the benefits of a computerized administrative information system. Such interactive effects can be considered by detailing out all "mutually exclusive combinations" of projects under consideration and choosing the combination which has the best trade-off of tactical weighted evaluation scores and net present worth.

EPILOGUE

Towards a New Accounting Standard

In many respects, cost accounting systems have failed to keep pace with radical changes in manufacturing brought on by the adoption of new technology (NT). A particularly poignant example of this is the allocation of manufacturing overhead costs on the basis of direct labor hours. When direct labor accounted for 50 percent or more of product cost, this was appropriate. Today, however, with direct labor comprising only about 10 percent of total cost, this allocation method is inappropriate. Specifically, it results in an overallocation to those products in which some of the direct labor has been replaced by an automated process, which in turn results in either overpricing or underpricing of products; the inexorable replacement of direct labor with new technologies exacerbates this problem.

It is clear that change is needed. Some changes already implemented in industry include allocation on such bases as machine hours, materials used, space taken, and output by the machine. The machine life cycle has been suggested as one element of product costing, in the same way as traditional product life cycles are used. This is a valid consideration, and is good for theoretical discussion, but it is very difficult to implement, especially for flexible dynamic machinery, and its use is very rare at best.

There are several barriers to the justification of NT which can be broadly classified as misestimation of costs and misestimation of benefits. The costs of NT extend far beyond the machine, or system hardware alone. A summary of these costs, including both capital costs and operating costs, is presented in Exhibit 7.13. While this list is fairly comprehensive, it is by no means exhaustive. There is also a temporary but virtually inevitable decline in productivity accompanying the technology introduction. As Kaplan (Reading 7.1) noted:

> "...noteworthy decline in productivity often accompany the introduction of new process technology. These productivity declines can last up to a year, even longer when

Exhibit 7.13 Types of Project Costs

A. CAPITAL COSTS
  1. Project Engineering
    (a) project evaluation and justification
    (b) preliminary engineering
    (c) line redesign for optimum utilization
  2. Purchasing
    (a) systems specification
    (b) purchase price
    (c) systems engineering
    (d) line modifications, transfer and fixturing equipment
    (e) added utilities, spare parts, special tools, diagnostic equipment
  3. Installation
    (a) downtime
    (b) installation labor and supervision
    (c) operator and supervisor training
    (d) operator relocation and retraining

B. OPERATING COSTS
  1. higher operator skill level and salary
  2. spare parts stocking
  3. maintenance costs and time off-line

Source: CAIP Corporation (1986), *A Critical Review of Developments in Computer Vision Systems.*

> a radical new technology like CIM is installed. Apparently, the new equipment introduces severe and unanticipated process disruptions, which lead to equipment breakdowns that are higher than expected; to operating, repair and maintenance problems; to scheduling and coordination difficulties; to revised materials standards; and to old-fashioned confusion on the factory floor."

It is notable that this productivity decline, while it probably cannot be completely overcome, can at least be reduced and controlled through proper project management and implementation planning. Thus the cost problem associated with NT investment is two-fold. Either (1) once all the appropriate costs are considered, the project is beyond the company's budget, or (2) the project is undertaken without considering all relevant costs, and consequently the results are far from what was expected.

The benefits of NT, then, can be classified as tangible and intangible. A summary of these benefits are provided in Exhibit 7.14. There is a fundamental misunderstanding among managers (especially in North America) of the benefits provided by NT. By considering only the tangible, quantifiable benefits, the traditional justification systems used today undervalue NT investments. This outlook, being typically short-term, retards the introduction of NT, and thus a somewhat more liberal approach is appropriate. This approach should look beyond the "machine" as the simple sum of its costs, and begin to incorporate strategic considerations, such as improving quality, strengthening the competitive position, and customer satisfaction.

Perhaps the most important of NT's intangible benefits is quality. The effects of quality in reducing scrap, rework, and service and warranty costs have been well-

Exhibit 7.14 The Benefits of CIM Operation

TANGIBLE BENEFITS

Lower inventory
Reduced labor costs
Less scrap and rework
Higher throughput and yield
Fewer engineering prototypes
Reduced changeover costs and time
Improved and safer working conditions
Increased design and drafting productivity
Reduced and more predictable maintenance cost
Eliminated data re-entry and duplicated data processing systems

INTANGIBLE BENEFITS

Centralized database
Better quality control
Faster product introduction
Better competitive standing
Greater customer satisfaction
Improved employee participation
Consistently high product quality
Consistently and tireless operation
Improved on-time product delivery
Redistribution of personnel skills
Versatility and rescue of capital equipment
Better data quality for management purposes
Shortened design and manufacturing lead time
Ability to simulate the total factory operation
Wider variety of designs within a product family
Ability to attract and retain high-quality engineers
Ability to handle increasingly complex product designs
Greater use of standard components, logic circuits, and so forth
Flexibility in design, product mix, volumes, and process routings
Greater control, accuracy, and repeatability of the engineering and production processes

documented, but there are further, more significant benefits which run much deeper in an organization's strategy. It has been suggested that quality is the single most effective strategy that a company can employ to improve its business. It has been noted that companies which deliver quality, relative to their competitors, can be significantly more profitable (up to a 10 percent spread in ROI has been observed).

It is generally agreed that intangible benefits, such as improved quality, flexibility, customer satisfaction, and ability to meet production and delivery schedules, are very significant in the assessment and justification of NT. This, however, creates a dilemma. Intangible benefits are very difficult to estimate accurately, and yet they must be considered.

Some discussion is also warranted on the inability of traditional capital budgeting methods to account for these intangibles. Many intangibles accrue only over the long-term, and take several years to appear on the bottom line. The result of this, of course, is an inability to financially justify the investment.

Kaplan (Reading 7.1) has suggested a solution whereby the justification problem is approached in reverse. That is, rather than attempt to value intangibles at the outset, managers could reverse the process and see, after tangible benefits have been considered, how large the intangibles would have to be to justify the proposed project. While this attempt is a step in the right direction in that it attempts to include the nonquantifiables, the estimation amounts to little more than a "gut feeling" by management. However, "gut feeling" is not sufficient to justify projects to banks and top managers who control the needed funds. Given that they are not as close to the situation and probably lack a practical understanding of the technology, a more tangible approach to justification seems appropriate. While steps are being made in this area, progress is slow. Unless the intangibles can be operationalized and made concrete for other people they are of limited utility, and hence justification will remain a major barrier to NT implementation.

In the meantime, justifying the project in order to obtain financing, particularly from outside sources, still amounts to "selling" it. There are several ways firms attempt to "sell" projects. First, some make use of case studies of similar past investments at other firms which were successful. Others stress the fact that the flexibility inherent in the new technology increases its resale value and provides some security against nonsuccess. It is notable that, while the effect of financing as a barrier to NT investment varies significantly across firms, on average, it is reported to be the number two factor slowing the rate of NT adoption. The number one reason is poor economic conditions, which probably just exaggerate the ability to finance.

There are many problems in the areas of NT assessment, justification, and financing. If North American industry is to overcome these problems, and improve its competitive stance through NT, it must begin to regard NT not simply as production machinery, but as a viable strategic weapon, and take steps to see that this view permeates both the organization and its environment.

CASE 7.1

Zepf Technologies Inc. (B)[4]

In April 1987, Larry Zepf, CEO of Zepf Technologies Inc. (ZTI) was once again considering the company's future. And once again, the future involved the possible purchase of computer-aided design (CAD) equipment.

ZTI was a Waterloo, Ontario-based company, specializing in the design and manufacture of machinery and parts for the packaging industry. Founded as a family firm in 1972, the firm had established a good reputation for quality and design ingenuity. Zepf Technologies Inc. (A) (Chapter 2) outlines the history of the company through early 1984. ZTI had consistently demonstrated an aggressive attitude to the purchase of new technologies, as the presence of two expensive computer numerical control (CNC) machine tools and an advanced CAD system in the company testified. Both purchases had been made on the flimsiest of analyses, and both decisions were proven to be totally justified.

The sales growth that followed the purchase of the equipment had been impressive, and Larry was keenly aware that the $3 million annual sales potential of the present manufacturing facilities would be surpassed within the next five months. (See Exhibit 7.15.) A decision had to be made immediately, therefore, on how ZTI would obtain more capacity.

For the past two years ZTI had been operating out of two sites in Waterloo. The main plant (Exhibit 7.16) held the office area as well as the production and assembly/rebuilding areas. The office area included administration, engineering and design, and the CAD system. The production area was used for machining change parts for packaging machines, and for making the blanks used by the CNC machines. The

[4]This case was written by Professor Hamid Noori with the assistance of John McDale, 1988.

Exhibit 7.15 Zepf Technologies Inc.
Balance Sheet as of August 31, 1986

	1986	1985
CURRENT ASSETS		
Bank	$ —	$ 9,384
Accounts receivable	415,711	368,977
Due from shareholders	18,074	—
Investment tax credit receivable	125,112	2,047
Inventory	583,738	460,887
Prepaid expenses and deposits	21,017	14,031
Current portion of note receivable	—	29,631
	1,163,652	884,957
NOTE RECEIVABLE	—	4,143
FIXED	513,131	424,741
OTHER		
Investment	10	10
Deferred development costs	24,604	—
Investment tax credit receivable	18,106	—
	42,720	10
TOTAL ASSETS	$1,719,503	$1,313,851
CURRENT LIABILITIES		
Bank overdraft	$12,683	$ —
Bank loan	90,000	159,000
Accounts payable and accrued liabilities	321,420	199,244
Customer deposits	139,184	67,919
Current portion of long-term liabilities	124,057	70,774
	687,344	496,937
LONG-TERM LIABILITIES	302,830	333,738
SHAREHOLDERS' ADVANCES	1,500	33,975
	991,674	864,650
SHAREHOLDERS' EQUITY		
Capital Stock	243,834	220,511
Retained Earnings	483,995	228,690
	727,829	449,201
	$1,719,503	$1,313,851

Exhibit 7.15 *(continued)*

Statement of Income as of August 31, 1986

	1986		1985	
SALES	$2,757,459	100%	$2,291,646	100%
COST OF SALES				
Inventory of finished goods (beginning of year)	140,903		126,083	
Cost of goods manufactured	1,631,032		1,355,539	
	1,771,935		1,481,622	
Inventory of finished goods (end-of-year)	115,208		140,903	
	1,656,727	60.1	1,340,719	58.5
GROSS MARGIN	1,100,732	39.9	950,927	41.5
SELLING AND ADMINISTRATIVE EXPENSES— per schedule	938,661	34.0	724,786	31.6
INCOME FROM OPERATIONS	162,071	5.9	226,141	9.9
OTHER INCOME (EXPENSE)				
Interest	2,940		7,424	
Miscellaneous (expense)	(1,179)		315	
Investment tax credit refund	111,173		—	
Gain on sale of fixed assets	—		2,746	
	112,934	4.1	10,485	0.4
NET INCOME BEFORE TAXES	275,005	10.0	236,626	10.3
PROVISION FOR (RECOVERY OF) INCOME TAXES				
Current	97,700	0.7	(2,047)	(0.1)
NEW INCOME	$ 255,305	9.3%	$ 238,673	10.4%

Statement of Retained Earnings as of August 31, 1986

	1986	1985
RETAINED EARNING (DEFICIT) (beginning of year)	$228,690	$ (9,983)
NET INCOME	255,305	238,673
RETAINED EARNINGS (end-of-year)	$483,995	$228,690

assembly/rebuilding area was devoted mainly for the assembly of the converger/diverger machines, the ZTI-designed and built machines which were now the staple product for the company. The total area of this facility was 1,000 square meters.

The second facility (Exhibit 7.17) was located about one kilometer from the main plant and housed the CNC machines which produced timing screws and cams. Timing screws were the key to ZTI's success, for, without ZTI's experienced mechanical design team and the CNC machines, competitors could only compete against 40 percent of ZTI's timing screw designs—and with lower quality products. This facility had a total

Exhibit 7.16 Main Plant Layout

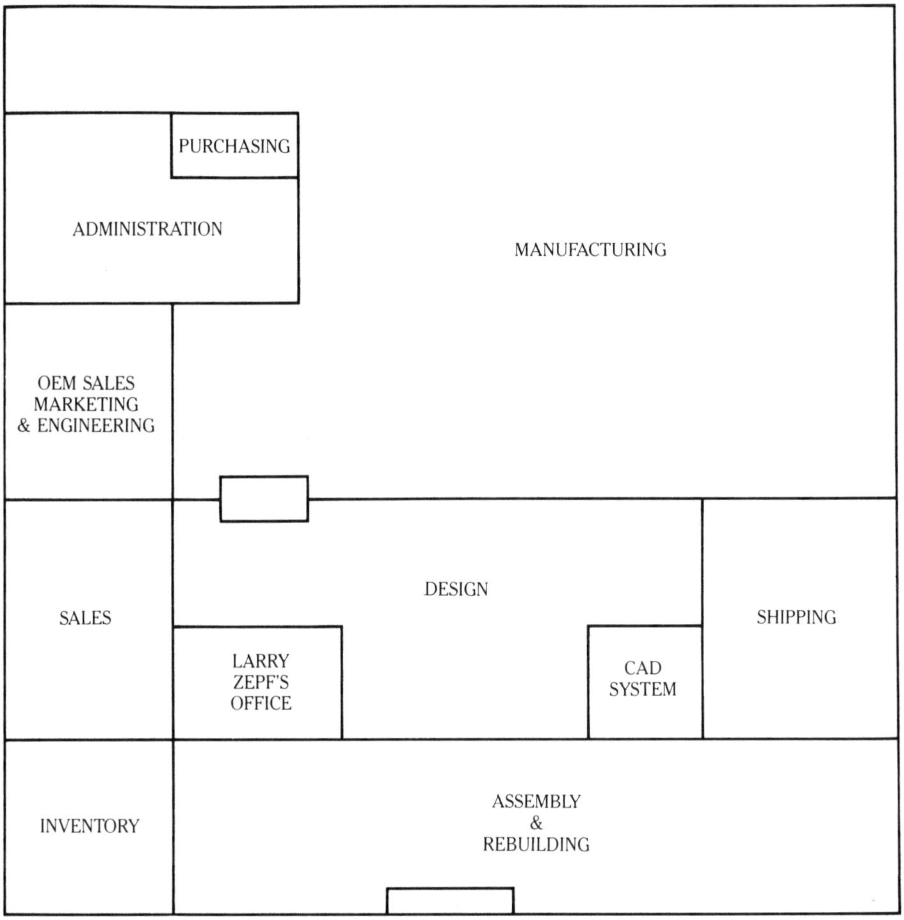

PURCHASING
ADMINISTRATION
MANUFACTURING
OEM SALES
MARKETING
& ENGINEERING
DESIGN
SALES
SHIPPING
LARRY
ZEPF'S
OFFICE
CAD
SYSTEM
INVENTORY
ASSEMBLY
&
REBUILDING

Exhibit 7.17 CNC Plant Layout

PROGRAMMING
MANUFACTURING OF CAMS
& TIMING SCREWS
INVENTORY
&
SHIPPING &
RECEIVING
SHIPPING
&
Q.C.

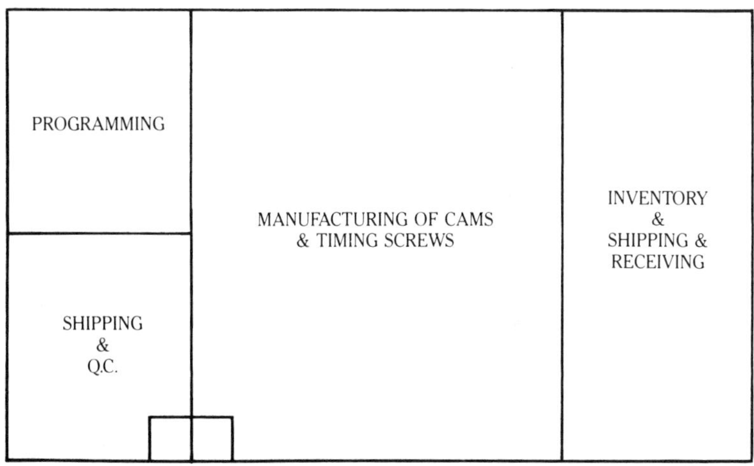

area of 500 square meters. The combined lease costs for both facilities were $52,000 per year.

ALTERNATIVES

Larry felt that there were four feasible alternatives for acquiring more space:

1. ZTI could lease existing space in the area for about the same rate now being paid.
2. ZTI could bid to purchase the building in which the company's main facility was housed. The building's estimated market value was $450,000 and it contained approximately 1,700 square meters.
3. Build a new building in the area. The land and building cost was estimated at $700,000 for 2,000 square meters, with an option to expand to 3,000 square meters.
4. Do nothing—wait, and see if growth occurred.

NEW TECHNOLOGY

The facilities decision could not be made in isolation. Larry also wanted to purchase a new CAD system which would be compatible with the existing system, and would double the design capacity available at ZTI. The cost of this CAD system was estimated at $250,000. This would complement the potential purchase of a new, more advanced CNC lathe which would supplement the two existing machines. This new machine would be 50 percent faster, and more adaptable, than either of the existing machines, and would cost $700,000.

"Our problem," said Larry, "is deciding amongst the various alternatives, as the technology decisions are obviously capacity generating decisions in their own right. The difficulty is that traditional capital budgeting techniques might not be appropriate."

"When we made the decisions on the CNC machines in 1979, and the CAD system in 1984, we made them on the basis that if we didn't purchase we would not survive for long. When we purchased the CNC machines we might not have survived at all if we all hadn't pulled together to get the beasts working. At that it took us three years to iron out all the hidden bugs. And to be quite honest, being stand-alone decisions, and being pretty aggressive about these thing, the hardest part was not making the decision but finding someone as aggressive as us to loan us the money."

"This time it is different. We have a mix of facilities and technology decisions to make, and that means we have to be able to compare them fairly and objectively—and that means some quantitative analysis. How do you quantify the benefits of new technology? How do you put a value on flexibility, quality, ability to service customers, and the like? I know it sounds dumb, but we know less about these technologies now that we have had them for a few years than we did before we purchased them."

"We realize now that there is more potential here than we appreciated at first, and we are also aware that the impact on people and their relationships with each other and with their jobs is more profound than we had thought. How do you quantify the various qualitative impacts on the various stakeholders in the decision? And where do we go to get the answers? This time we have to attempt to analyze this properly, or we may lock ourselves into a future we don't want to experience."

CASE 7.2

Transprovincial Engineering Limited (A)[5]

In early April 1982, Michael Kinnear, manager of Toronto operations for Transprovincial Engineering Limited (TEL), a national consulting engineering and planning firm, had to formulate his input into the decision before the company's Computer-Assisted Drafting and Design (CADD) committee. A feasibility study for CADD applications within the company had been done by a consultant and his report had just come back. It recommended that TEL invest in the new CADD technology and indicated that substantial productivity gains were possible with it. The committee's chairman had called for comments from the committee members about whether the firm should proceed with the implementation of one or more CADD systems and, if so,where the initial system or systems should be located. As managaer of the largest branch and one of the initiators of the study, Mr. Kinnear had considerable interest in the decisions and knew that his opinions would carry a good deal of weight with the committee chairman. Because the systems could have a significant impact on his office, and on the company as a whole, he wanted to be sure that TEL was taking the right step, and at the right time.

THE CONSULTING ENGINEERING INDUSTRY

Consulting engineering was the diverse industry involved with the design of engineered systems and the management of the construction or fabrication of them. In most cases, the work done was project-oriented, consisting primarily of the production of unique designs to meet client specifications. The largest segment of the industry dealt with the construction of new engineered systems (for example, electrical distribution systems, refineries, bridges, roads or pipelines) or the engineered components of architectural projects. Within this segment, consulting engineering firms ranged enormously in size and scope of activities. The size varied from small independent offices with only a single

[5]This case was written by David McCutcheon and John Haywood-Farmer.

engineer or a few partners to the largest engineering and project management companies that were international giants with annual billings in the multibillion dollar range. The scope of activities tended to vary with the dollar range and with the size of the company. Usually, larger firms maintained specialist staffs that had skills that covered a particular area in some depth. These companies might have strengths in either the depth in expertise or the number of various engineering fields covered by their specialist staffs. In addition, larger firms generally had the ability to offer more services to the client beyond the basic production of designs, being capable of handling all phases of the project from initial study through design to management of the construction work.

The consulting engineering business closely followed construction industry trends and thus was subject to large swings in volume.

TEL

TEL was a consulting engineering and planning firm that specialized in civil engineering and municipal projects. It had over a dozen offices spread across Canada from St. John's to Vancouver Island; the offices varied in size from a recently opened two-person branch in British Columbia to the 200-person head office in Toronto. This was an unusual organizational structure for an engineering firm. The competition in most locations would typically be from small, independent firms serving only a local area or from very large firms that might work throughout a large territory but which centralized their operations in a single 300- to 400-person office.

The unusual organizational structure was largely a product of TEL's history; the company had been formed through the merger of a multibranch Ontario-based firm that served Eastern Canada and a similar organization based in British Columbia that served the West. Each company was well-established at the time of the merger in the mid-1970s, both having been in business for over 20 years at that point. The new company, TEL, had one of the widest local office networks in the country, providing representation in seven provinces. Its organizational structure reflected a desire to maintain an equitable east-west distribution of control, with, for example, the Board of Directors composed of nearly equal numbers of eastern and western representatives. TEL was wholly owned by its employees and the number of shareholders in each office was in approximate proportion to its number of employees.

The company's policy for the management of its branches reflected its decentralized nature. Each office was operated independently, with the branch manager responsible for hiring and training staff, obtaining contracts, controlling the design and project work generated, and for the profitability of the office. All branch managers were shareholders and were encouraged to operate their offices as independent local businesses. Unless special expertise was required, work obtained in one area was carried out by that area's resources. Some of the branches were quite isolated from the main offices but the main concentrations were in southern Ontario and in British Columbia, with more than one-half of the offices located in these areas.

Although the company would be considered a large one on the basis of its number of employees, TEL was somewhat specialized to a relatively narrow range of civil engineering fields. Primarily, the company's skills were in the planning and design of transportation services and facilities, municipal and environmental services projects and engineering structures such as bridges, roads, and tunnels. The concentration within these specific fields allowed TEL to offer considerable depth of expertise in them. The company could supply related services such as urban planning and design studies plus complete or partial management of the execution of its designs. As a result, the small TEL branches were backed by many more resources than would typically be available with smaller local competitors; at the same time, the larger branches could find themselves competiting against firms that were considerably bigger and had similar depths of resources in a wider variety of fields.

PROJECT DEVELOPMENT

The work carried out by TEL generally came from three sources. Some large government projects were announced by public calls for tenders. More often, municipal and provincial governments approached those firms with which they were familiar with requests for proposals (RFPs). In both of these cases, the proposals would be based on specifications provided to the companies. Large private companies or developers might seek consulting engineering services either through the RFP route or by selecting a firm with whom they had dealt previously. If it wished to try for the job, TEL would formulate a bid that would include the basic design proposal and an estimate of the cost, based on the expected number of hours and other resources required multiplied by the billing rate for each specific resource.

If, on the basis of the bid or proposal, a TEL office was awarded a contract for the project or service, the work was normally carried out by that particular branch. Usually, a senior engineer whose specialty fitted with the demands of the work was assigned as the project manager. Responsibilities of the project manager included both the administrative aspects of the project (work assignment, budget control, and so forth) and the technical aspects. Like many large project-oriented firms, TEL was reporting going through separate routes. The project manager was provided with a designated team of junior engineers, scientists and technicians that had the special skills needed for the study or design work inivolved. The project team members reported to their respective department heads (for example, a draftsperson reported to the chief draftsperson) for technical direction and to the project manager for direction on the project. In turn, the project manager reported to the branch manager administratively and to the chief engineer of the discipline involved for technical matters. There were 21 chief engineers and planners who established policy either within a functional area (such as graphics) or within an engineering discipline (such as strucural engineering); these senior staff worked out of six different branches and for technical matters, all of them reported to the assistant vice president–technical, who worked in the firm's Ottawa office. On the administrative side, the branch managers reported to one of the three regiuonal vice presidents–operations. Through this network system, the company could maintain local autonomy among the branches while bringing to bear specialist skills from outside any particular office if the need arose.

Once a contract had been landed, the first important criterion for project management was the production of the required studies or designs within the limited time frame established by the contract specifications; the second was the control of the actual time spent by the various members of the project staff carrying out the work. Billing was normally itemized by standard rates for the personnel and the equipment that had been employed. Although it varied considerably from branch to branch, on a company-wide basis, TEL maintained the industry average of about $50,000 annual revenues per employee. Profitability depended on keeping the actual hours spent within the range of the estimate that had been used in calculating the bid, and by maximizing the utilization of the resources within the office.

THE POTENTIAL OF CADD

Drafting is the drawing of architectural or engineering plans and designs in a standardized format. The draftsperson traditionally used ink and drawing instruments to translate the physical layouts and dimensions of those systems designed by engineers, architects, technologists and scientists into highly accurate maps and projections of the designs. Drafting was normally the final step in the design preparation sequence. Sketches might be done to aid the designer in layout or design calculations, but the laborious work involved with final drawings normally dictated that only after the design was stabilized would this part of the project be carried out. Upon completion, the drawings became a major final product for a design project, the essential "illustrations" for construction and a record of the design which, if signed by an engineer, could have legal liabilities attached to it. About 20 percent of the TEL staff was made up of draftspersons or graphic artists.

Although project engineering firms created unique designs and plans for their work, the basic elements of the design process and the mechanical drawing techniques used for committing them to paper were quite standard. This standardized nature made the process appropriate for automation. Since the early 1970s, the capabilities of computer systems designed to automate drafting and design work had increased dramatically.

The earliest developments in this field were in computer-aided drafting. For engineering and architectural drawings, there were well-established standards for sizes, formats, signs and symbols, and for the layout of drawing notes and most of the other features that would normally appear on them. By combining a video display terminal, interactive computer instructions, a memory library of symbols and a large format electronic plotter, drawings that would have otherwise been done by hand could be generated, recalled, modified and printed by a skilled operator working at a terminal. Early versions of the equipment were limited in their capacity and were very expensive, but the technology was rapidly improving.

A major feature that had become available more recently in CADD systems was the inclusion of one or more design-oriented capabilities. Rather than simply reproducing existing outlines or representations, these machines could be programmed to perform highly complex technical analyses of the systems or objects that had been drawn. Alternatively, the computer could be used to assist in the layout of features by allowing objects represented on the video screen to be moved or altered by use of light pens or easy-to-use control boards. For example, the furniture in an office could be displayed in a plan, or overhead view, and the drawings of the chairs, tables and desks could be moved about to find the best layout. For complex engineering situations, such as the design of refineries, the use of these systems could make the design work fast and accurate. Previously, the plans might have been so difficult to draw and check that scale models were sometimes made to ensure that two objectives were not inadvertently planned to occupy the same place.

As with many design firms, the concept of computer-aided design was not a new one for TEL. Many of the TEL offices had small scientific-applications computers that handled a variety of engineering design and analysis programs, each program being quite specific in use. In most cases, the program had been acquired or developed independently by the various branches according to their own particular needs. However, the scope and power of the potential applications, the interactive nature and the close link to the drafting functions that were implicit with CADD systems would be departures from the established methods for TEL, as they would for most similar firms.

Recently, major manufacturers of CADD systems had begun to specialize as they targeted particular fields. Many concentrated on the industrial users, providing systems that were used to draw parts designs and, in some cases, to transfer the designs to computer-controlled manufacturing equipment. By this time, six major firms were competing with systems designed for multidiscipline engineering design and drafting. These systems varied considerably in their capabilities of handling architectural and civil engineering applications specifically. There were other differentiating factors as well. Some companies sold stand alone systems that had specialized terminals, or work stations that could be connected to one or more types of computers. Another main differentiating feature was the capability of handling three-dimensional (3D) representations as opposed to only 2D. There was little compatibility and few standards among the systems being marketed. Operating methods and the stored database of symbols and notes developed on one system would not necessarily be transferable to another. Hardware, including ancillary equipment, was subject to rapid obsolescence. For example, electronic plotters ranged in price from $15,000 to 10 times that amount but could have very low resale value if another type became the industry standard. Leasing the equipment reduced this sort of hardware risk for the firm but did not eliminate the problem of having methods and data incompatible with more modern systems.

At this time, adoption of the equipment had been limited to about 5 percent of the architectural, engineering and technical consulting offices in Canada. Surveys had indicated that high costs and the uncertainties of the technologies were the major reasons why CADD vendors had not made further penetrations into this market.

THE PUSH FOR CADD AT TEL

Despite the mitigating factors, larger firms were investing in the technology. Mr. Kinnear knew that some of their major clients were beginning to differentiate competitng consulting firms on the basis of whether or not they incorporated CADD applications in their design preparation process. Although the clients may not have been prepared to pay more for drawings and designs generated by CADD systems, the use of the computerized methods was a definite marketing advantage—the consulting firms that used them were considered to be progressive and potentially capable of offering better service.

In addiition, many municipal and provincial government departments were using CADD systems or were planning to do so. These departments in partiuclar were beginning to have expectations for similar sophistication in the companies they hired for their outside work, an important consideration for a number of the larger TEL offices.

However, it was the possible increase in productivity for drafting operations that had been the main selling feature for CADD systems. For drafting a new drawing (that is, one that could not be produced by revising existing ones), productivity ratios of 5 or 6:1 for CADD over conventional methods had been cited. Where revision drawings were required, this advantage dropped to about 2:1. A draftsperson, who cost the firm about $20 an hour, was billed to the client at about $40 per hour.

Mr. Kinnear realized that the use of CADD would not be right for every office of TEL. CADD installations were typically run in two or even three shifts in order to utilize the system more fully, decreasing the per-hour cost that would be allocated. Only some of the TEL offices could generate the "critical mass" of drafting requirements on a steady basis that could guarantee that amount of use. As a rule of thumb, an office with 50 or 60 employees would generate enough work for economical use of a four work station system.

It looked as though this consideration could easily be met at TEL. Despite very high interst rates, the Toronto office was very busy and the one in Vancouver had recently expanded to about 150 personnel and had created a new branch office. The Calgary office, with about 100 personnel, and Edmonton, with about 70, were growing. In addition, several other branches might be large enough to ensure adequate loading of a system.

Another consideration was the type of work generated at each office. Some of the branches had expertise in the areas which required the drafting and design work that were better suited for CADD applications.

A unique situation existed at the Toronto head office, where a large minicomputer had been installed recently to handle administrative computing for the firm. It had sufficient excess capacity at this point to take on other tasks. It was possible that a CADD system could be found that had work stations that could be used in conjunction with this existing computer capacity.

With the potential of this situation, Mr. Kinnear was one of several branch managers who were interested in exploring the possibilities of CADD. Eventually, the assistant vice president–technical had been convinced that this issue deserved thorough investigation. A committee was formed to study the idea; the committee, chaired by the assistant vice president–technical, consisted of a dozen senior administrative managers and chief engineers from offices across Canada. The group's work resulted in the hiring in January 1982 of a consultant who specialized in CADD systems; the report of his findings had just been received by the CADD committee members. Excerpts from the report are contained in Exhibit 7.18.

Exhibit 7.18 Transprovincial Engineering Limited (A)
Excerpts from the Consultant's Report

1. EXECUTIVE SUMMARY

A review of the current level of engineering design and drafting at six TEL offices was completed during February and March 1982 to determine the justification for the use of computer-assisted drafting and design (CADD) techniques. The six offices (Victoria, Vancouver, Edmonton, Calgary, Toronto and Ottawa) were selected on the basis of size, staff classification by discipline, and general project activity.

At each office, typical project drawing sets were selected from each major drafting area and were evaluated on the basis of the type of drafting involved. Productivity improvement factors, known from industry experience, were applied to establish an average rating for the different categories of drafting.

Three categories of project drafting are common to the offices but vary in current activity level from office to office:

- highway or roadway
- municipal systems
- structural/mechanical

The structural/mechanical category, including both bridges and buildings, can provide the earliest productivity improvements, in the order of 5 to 1. The other categories will require considerable time (18–24 months) to build up an adequate library of usable symbols, standards, details and background information to show substantial productivity improvement over current drafting practices and techniques. For this reason, the recommendation is to implement a multidiscipline CADD system to commence with structural/mechanical drafting and then selectively schedule the remaining forms of drafting. Over the longer term (three years), both highway/roadway and municipal services drafting will provide productivity improvements in the order of 6 to 1.

Analysis of the drafting review are shown in the following example.

RESULTS OF DRAFTING REVIEW

Note: "Index" refers to the total annual drafting volume in the three categories for each office in proportion to the annual volume produced in the Toronto office in the previous year.

Office Drafting by Type	Index	% of Drawings in Office	Potential Productivity Improvements (after 12months)
Toronto	100		
Mechanical/structural		21.4	4:1
Municipal		11.4	2:1
Highway		67.2	2:1
Vancouver	80		
Mechanical/structural		20.5	5:1
Municipal		51.8	2:1
Highway		27.7	2:1

Exhibit 7.18 *(continued)*

RESULTS OF DRAFTING REVIEW (cont'd)

Office Drafting by Type	Index	% of Drawings in Office	Potential Productivity Improvements (after 12months)
Victoria	44.3		
Mechanical/structural		50.0	5:1
Municipal		24.2	2:1
Highway		25.8	2:1
Ottawa	50		
Mechanical/structural		25.7	4:1
Municipal		20.0	2:1
Highway		54.3	2:1
Calgary	40.1		
Mechanical/structural		30.2	5:1
Municipal		13.5	2:1
Highway		56.3	2:1
Edmonton	51.4		
Mechanical/structural		5.5	5:1
Municipal		15.3	2:1
Highway		79.3	2:1

The results of the drafting review indicate that the implementation and use of CADD are justified in Toronto and Vancouver, based on initial workload of mechanical/structural drafting plus the range of highway and municipal drafting available to initiate CADD systems. The Victoria office has substantial mechanical/structural work and could be served initially with one or more remote work stations and a plotter connected to the Vancouver system. Similarly, Ontario offices could be connected to the Toronto system. Edmonton and Calgary currently do not have enough mechanical/structural work to justify a system until the other forms of drafting are well initiated with other systems.

Based on the drafting review, a multisystem 3D multidiscipline drafting system with limited design capability is recommended. The nature of the drawings make a 3D system advantageous and this is also the type being favored by city and provincial governments.

Alternative to the purchase of a complete system, three choices are:

1. Joint ownership or shared use of a system with other consulting firms.
2. Lease of a work station connected to a CADD service company or another CADD user.
3. Contract use of over-the-counter computer drafting services.

At this time, none of these alternatives is available. A proposal was received from a Vancouver-based firm that offered CADD services but only in 2D configuration.

The approximate cost of a four work station complete system would be \$700,000–\$800,000 and would require space modifications and furniture costs of \$40,000. In addition, monthly operating costs would be about \$11,500. The Toronto office's computer can support a CADD, assuming it is available, installation costs for a system there would be reduced by \$250,000–\$300,000.

Exhibit 7.18 *(continued)*

Projections of costs and revenues from these systems are shown in Sections 2 and 3. Revenues would be dependent upon the shift usage and client billing procedures. Two six-hour shifts per day and 90 percent availability of the system during those shifts were used in the estimates. An average productivity of 65 percent of the eventual level was assumed for the first year.

The successful planned use of CADD by TEL can provide enormous benefits to the company during the 1980s from both an increase in productivity and enhanced image within the consulting engineering industry. Initially, the benefits will result in productivity improvements in drafting. As experience is gained through the use of the system for drafting, benefit will result from the use of the system for design as well. Valid productivity estimates in the order of 10:1 can be realized from the successful use of CADD for both design and drafting.

2. COST PROJECTIONS

The cost to purchase, install and operate a multidiscipline four work station CADD system is summarized as follows:

Capital Costs	Typical System	Toronto System
CADD system (four work stations)	$600,000	$350,000
Second disk drive	40,000	40,000
Plotters (electrostatic and ink pen)	120,000	120,000
Modifications for computer room	30,000	2,000
Miscellaneous additional furniture	10,000	10,000
	$800,000	$514,000

Capitalized over 30 months at 18 percent interest, the monthly cost will be approximately $30,000 for a typical system and $19,500 for the Toronto system.

Operating Expenses (per month)		
Systems Manager	$4,000	$4,000
Assistant	2,000	—
Maintenance	5,000	2,500
Supplies	500	500
	$11,500/month	$ 7,000/month
Monthly Operating Cost (including capitalization)	$41,500/month	$26,500/month

The initial use of the Toronto office's computer provides a reduction of approximately $15,000 per month compared to a typical four work station system. However, two factors must be emphasized: one, not all vendors supply CADD programming for this type of hardware and, two, the expansion of CADD work stations may be limited to six or eight because of other uses for the computer.

Remote Work Stations and Plotters	
One remote work station with communication controller	$ 65,000
Second remote work station	55,000
Plotter	45,000
	$165,000
Capitalized over 30 months @ 18 percent	$6,500/month

Monthly Operating Cost (two work stations and plotter)	
Purchased or leased equipment	$ 6,500
Telephone line & modems (leased)	1,500
Equipment maintenance	1,500
Total	$ 9,500/month

Exhibit 7.18 *(continued)*

3. REVENUE ANALYSIS

A revenue rate (for drafting only) based on the use of a CADD system with four work stations, an electrostatic plotter (for check prints) and an ink pen plotter (for check prints) on two shifts of six hours each is made as follows:

Billing Rate (drafting only)

Work stations	$80 per hour
Operators	40 per hour
Electrostatic plotter	.50 per sq. ft.
Ink pen plotter	20 per hour
Plotter operator	20 per hour

Income per work station (assuming 10 percent downtime of equipment)

Work station:	2 shifts × 6 hour/shift/day × 21 days/month × 90% availability ×$80/hour
Operators :	2 shifts × 6 hour/shift/day × 21 days/month × 90% availability ×$40/hour
Plotting :	1 electrostatic plotter and 1 ink pen plotter as required

Cost/Revenue Analysis

		Typical Four Work Station System		Toronto Four Work Station System
Operating Costs				
System operating expenses		$ 41,000/month		$ 26,000/month
Operator salaries (8×$20/hour × 126 hours/month)		20,160		20,160
Miscellaneous operating expenses		1,500		1,500
		$ 63,160		$ 48,000
	use	$ 65,000	and	$ 48,000
Revenues				
Four Work stations @ 90%		$ 72,500		$ 72,500
Operators (8×$40/hour × 126 hours/month)		40,320		40,320
Plotting		10,000		10,000
		$122,820		$122,820
			and $120,000	

For analysis, assume first year productivity of 65 percent, therefore producing monthly revenue of approximately $80,000 and $120,000 thereafter, the CADD system can provide a return on investment after 23 months. For the Toronto system, with the monthly operating cost of $48,000 and monthly revenues of $80,000 in the first year and $120,000 thereafter, the CADD system should provide a return on investment after 18 months.

The addition of two work stations with a plotter increases the revenue potential of the system by 50 percent ($60,000) while increasing costs by only 30 percent ($20,000). The period for return on investment is reduced by four months.

Exhibit 7.18 *(continued)*

4. PROCUREMENT AND IMPLEMENTATION PLAN

The successful implementation of a CADD system is dependent upon the establishment of a detailed "Procurement and Implementation Plan" to ensure that several activities are properly planned and managed. The following outline lists many of the important activities to be completed as part of the plan and an estimate of the person-days involved in each:

	Estimated Activity Time (Person/Days)	Completion Date (Week)
1. Prepare a detailed specification for required hardware and software.	5	6
2. Evaluate available CADD systems; develop a short list of preferred suppliers. (Visits to suppliers or users may be required.)	10	6
3. Prepare and issue a request for proposal.	5	8
4. Evaluate proposals received, using a benchmark test procedure.	10	12
5. Prepare detailed cost and income justification. Submit and obtain management approval for purchase.	5	16
6. Appoint a systems manager to participate in remainder of procurement and implementation activities.	1	16
7. Complete contract negotiations.	5	16
8. Supervise site preparation.	15	40
9. Attend vendors' "Systems Manager's Training."	5	32
10. Identify and select operators.	5	36
11. Supervise system acceptance tests.	3	40
12. Coordinate training for operators.	3	41
13. Assign operators.	2	42
14. Identify, schedule initial drafting.	5	42
15. Manage system operation.	Ongoing	
16. Plan and schedule additional drafting.	Ongoing	

THE NEXT STEP

The report projected a considerable positive return for CADD systems even without the benefits to TEL's design process being used in the financial assessment. Mr. Kinnear thought that the drafting survey appeared to be accurate and that the consultant's methods for arriving at the basic productivity ratios looked reasonable.

Mr. Kinnear realized that, although any office that had a CADD system setup in it would have the potential marketing and productivity benefits working specifically for that branch, the initial project would be a pilot one, with the expenses born by the company as a whole. With the decentralized nature of the firm, it might be harder for the CADD committee chairman to sell this idea to the board of directors. What was good for a main office was not necessarily transferable to other, small branches which nonetheless had shareholder employees who were anxious to see the overall company operate as efficiently as possible.

In addition to those effects on TEL in general, Mr. Kinnear had particular concerns about how operations within his own branch might be affected if the Toronto office was picked as a site for a system. The consultant's report had outlined an "implementation plan" that would be spread over 42 weeks. Not only would hardware and software have to be purchased or leased but a systems manager and at least two operators per work station would have to be selected and trained. The consultants had suggested that the operators be drawn from the drafting personnel. The selected staff would have to change their daily routines substantially to fit into a schedule where a six-hour stretch would have to be spent in front of a computer terminal. On top of this was the knowledge that a Toronto-based system utilizing the existing computer was an interesting proposition from a cost point of view but one with its own problems; the requirement to fit the CADD setup to the existing hardware would narrow the options for software considerably, the existing computer would allow only limited expansion beyond the four work station configuration, and the future administrative uses of the computer, for which it had originally been intended, would then have to compete with CADD applications for capacity on the machine.

After reviewing the memo (Exhibit 7.19) that had been attached to the consultant's report, he recognized that it was not going to be easy for him to formulate an answer.

Exhibit 7.19 Transprovincial Engineering Limited (A)

MEMORANDUM

TO: CADD Committee

FROM: Asst V-P–Technical DATE: 1982 04 02

RE: Computer Drafting and Design Applications

The attached report by the consultant hired a few months ago presents the results and recommendations from his study of the feasibility of implementing CADD in TEL.

In brief, it appears that there is an excellent potential for CADD in the Toronto and/or Vancouver offices initially and for other offices at a later stage.

Please let me have your comments on the report. It is important that you confirm from your records that the number of drawings by discipline in your branch has been correctly reported. Please advise also the total number of drafting staff in your branch who are engaged in drafting activities relevant to CADD applications. In reviewing the report, you should bear in mind that this is a *feasibility study,* intended to identify if there is an application for CADD systems in TEL and the priorities for implementation. The next step, if approved, will carry out detailed investigations of the costs and benefits for the initial installation.

Your recommendations are also required on the following:

1. Should we proceed with the implementation of a CADD system at TEL? and if so:
2. Where should we install the initial system(s)?
3. Should we retain this consultant to assist in the detailed planning and implementation of this system? (Approximate fee would be about $15,000.)

As we wish to reach a decision shortly on this matter, an early reply would be appreciated and prior to April 23rd at the latest.

Chapter Eight

INTERNAL IMPACT OF NEW TECHNOLOGY

SITUATION 8.1

Magna International Inc.[1]

By mid-1986, annual sales of Magna International, Inc. were projected to top $1.0 billion for the first time. As Canada's largest manufacturer of automotive parts, Magna had just realized one of its corporate objectives of having an average of $100 of its auto parts built into every North American car.

Although company founder Frank Stronach and his management team continuously espoused a "small is beautiful" philosophy, their dreams for Magna were by no means small. Stronach stated in 1985 that he was intent on creating "one of the largest corporations in North America," and that he felt Magna could maintain 30 percent annual growth for many years. By 1986, it was also clear that Magna was committed to a strategy of increased internationalization of its operations. These goals clearly raised questions about the appropriateness of Magna's current operating philosophy and organization for the planned growth.

THE MAGNA "SUCCESS FORMULA"

Some observers, including Magna's management and, especially, Frank Stronach, attributed its success to Magna's unique "corporated culture" whose key elements were embodied in the company's "Corporate Constitution" published for the first time in Magna's 1984 annual report. The stated purpose of the Constitution was to "define the

[1]William Webb under the direction of Professor W. Beamish, 1988. Magna International Inc., School of Business Administration Case 9-88-M002. © 1988, The University of Western Ontario. Extracted with permission.

rights of employees and investors to participate in the company's profits and growth and impose discipline on management." Stronach thought that Magna might be the only company in the western world with a corporate constitution which guaranteed employee rights and imposed discipline on management. Exhibit 8.1 shows some excerpts from the 1985 annual report that demonstrate the Constitution in praactice at Magna.

Other critical components of the corporate culture included a commitment to keeping all Magna plants small with the maximum of about 100 employees each, an emphasis on research and development, and rewards for both management and workers through an attractive profit-sharing plan and a range of social benefits from day care for employees' children to a recently opened company-owned conservation and recreation area.

Organization and Operating Structure

Magna's unique operating structure consists of three levels of responsibility: the operating unit, group management (in charge of an operating group) and executive management.

At the operating unit or individual factory level, maximum employment was kept to 100 workers because of Stronach's belief that management and employees should maintain close working relationships and that smaller units sparked individual initiative and a degree of entrepreneurialism. Stronach felt that a "family relationship" should exist among co-workers and management with each person knowing the name of all his fellow employees.

Every Magna factory was unique in its own right, with its own product mandate, R&D department, and production and profit objectives established by that unit's management team. Every employee had access to management and since each earned shares in the company through a profit-sharing plan, they were likely to come forward with assembly line suggestions to improve quality or cut costs—suggestions that could lead to promotion, more profits to share and increased equity participation. The small scale of each unit's operations and Magna's emphasis on factory-floor technical skills (promoted by in-house technical education and upgrading programs) resulted in a high degree of flexibility and an ability to adapt quickly to changes in manufacturing operations.

Growth at the operating unit level, as for all levels of Magna, was somewhat "organic" in nature, rather than "planned" in the traditional sense. When a particular unit (factory) could no longer keep pace with demand and was running three shifts of 100 people on a 24-hour schedule, the unit's general manager would be allowed to build a second factory. If more factories had to be built for a common product line, these might eventually form the basis of a new management group with the former general manager as group vice president. As this suggests, Magna had a rather unusual and interesting method of delegating responsibility and controls between the executive management, group management and the operating units. Magna's unit general managers were given 100 percent control, authority and responsibility for their units, with the requirement that they clearly identify themselves as part of Magna International when communicating with suppliers or customers.

Although organic, growth was not indiscriminate at the factory level and was monitored by group management which worked within the broad corporate policy set

Exhibit 8.1 Magna International
Excerpts from the 1985 Annual Report Corporate Constitution in Practice

Magna's continued growth is based upon our unique corporate culture which allows the company to make a better product for a better price.

Our culture recognizes that it takes three ingredients to be successful in business, namely: management, employees, and capital. Furthermore it requires that each of these ingredients has a right to share in the profits that it helps to generate. This foremost principle and other operating principles are enshrined in Magna's Corporate Constitution.

We, in management, continuously search for ways to stimulate employees to achieve greater productivity. In recent years this has been partially accomplished through the introduction of new technology. At Magna we continue to emphasize the human capital as we introduce technology in a manner that does not result in the displacement of employees. We are focusing on productivity improvements through new technology as a means of continuing to upgrade wages for production employees in the years ahead while maintaining our competitive position in the marketplace.

Management's primary responsibility is to demonstrate to employees that we care for their well-being particularly with regard to wages, environment, safety in the work place, fairness, and equal opportunity for advancement. We are committed to these principles and intend to strengthen further our Human Resources department to make sure that our standards are maintained. A structure like this can only function through total openness. It is an education process. In our view the employees must fully understand the competitive factors facing the company as well as the facts surrounding our financial structure. I like to see employees reading the financial section of the papers in the morning realizing that they are shareholders of Magna. In fact, at this stage, our manufacturing and office employees own more than $30 million of Magna stock.

Members of management are also large shareholders in the company. The value of their shares amounts to approximately $30 million and accordingly they have an interest in protecting the value of their investments. It is important for a healthy, growing company to have a strong equity base in relation to debt but we are sensitive to the effect of equity dilution on our ability to maintain investor confidence. Accordingly, we try to balance issues of new equity with growth in earnings per share.

Sales growth translates into the need for new production facilities. As a result, Magna's investment in land and buildings continues to increase. Management utilizes Magna's job creation capability to obtain favorable terms when purchasing land. We also seek joint venture partners to assist in the development of those lands. Our objective is to minimize Magna's capital outlay for land so as not to divert capital from our automotive components manufacturing activities.

QUALITY ASSURANCE

Quality is stressed throughout Magna—our success has been built on it—our future depends on it. We continue to train employees at all levels in matters relating to quality including the use of sophisticated measuring devices and statistical process control techniques. As a result of efforts in the area of quality, our operating units received many quality awards from our customers. Magna is dedicated to supplying automotive components and systems which are "world class" in quality and value.

HUMAN RESOURCES

Magna's greatest asset is its motivated work force. We continuously strive to provide a positive, safe and fair environment for all employees.

With this in mind we continue to expand our human resources departments at the group and corporate offices and sponsor seminars which stress the importance of good communications between management and employees. Wherever possible productivity gains are recognized with improved wages and expenditures to improve the working environment.

During the year we introduced "Magna People," a bimonthly newsletter about Magna and its people. Simeon Park, which opened officially in June 1984, saw the introduction of many employee organized functions, both winter and summer. The allocation to our Employee Equity Participation and Profit Sharing Program amounted to $8.3 million in 1985 compared to $6.4 million last year.

by executive management. Executive management consisted of Frank Stronach and a handful of senior executives. Corporate headquarters were housed in a two-story office in a suburban Toronto business park and consisted of a lean, 100 person staff.

Operating units were grouped geographically and by market under one of five group management teams which were destined to divide and form more groups as Magna expanded. Each group was responsible for speciic technologies and product lines and had its own marketing, R&D, and planning responsibilities.

Equity Participation

Frank Stronach maintained that employees had "a moral right to some of the profits they help generate. . . If they get profit, and they put in into the company equity, there's a sort of discipline which helps the employee. We've got some people on machines who've got $30,000 sitting there. That's a lot of money for an average person."

In keeping with Stronach's belief, Magna had a type of deferred profit sharing program for its employees to reward productivity and loyalty. Employees were awarded a point for every $1,000 they earned and a point for each year they stayed with the company. The more points they had accumulated, the greater their share in the fund. Each year, 7 percent of profits before tax were transferred to an employee equity trust fund. Employees received quarterly statements of how many shares they owned and their value. If an employee left within two years, his shares reverted to other employees. After his third year with Magna, he owned a percentage which increased until the 10th year when they became completely his, even if he left. In Magna's earlier years, profit sharing was only available to middle management but was expanded to cover all employees in 1978.

READING 8.1

Designing Organizations to Innovate and Implement: Using Two Dilemmas to Create a Solution[2]

The topic of innovation in complex organizations has become increasinglyimportant to the international manager in almost all industries. The intensified level of present day international competition, both in the domesic United States market and around the world, demands an ongoing process of innovation merely to stay abreast of the game. Product market life cycles have become steadily attenuated, leading to an increased demand for innovation in products and services. Ongoing advances in productivity are now the norm rather than the ideal. Growth in both the size and number of internatinonal firms has led to an enhanced demand for innovations both in process technology and administrative procedure. The added size and complexity of the contemporary international organization lends itself not only to the demand for administrative innovation but also provides a greater opportunity for it—huge process gains can conceivably result from clever organizational design, gains that stem not only from reduced costs but also from the constant augmentation of the firm's ability to compete in a dynamic environment. Put quite simply, proper organization innovation, is not just a matter of having smart managers come up with new ideas. The design of the organization itself is intimately related to the organization's ability to innovate.

While it is far easier to design organizations for innovation than to come up with innovations oneself, a design approach is not without its pitfalls. For the most part, research on innovation has identified those sorts of organizational structures that seem best suited to encouraging the generation, development, or adoption of innovations.

[2]Christopher Gresov, "Designing Organizations to Innovate and Implement: Using Two Dilemmas to Create a Solution." *Columbia Journal of Business*, Winter, pp. 63–67. © 1984 by The Trustees of Columbia University, New York. Extracted with permission.

The next problem, however, (and one that is of increasing importance to the organization with a plethora of operations in a multitude of contexts, each with its own distinctive sets of habits, biases, rules, procedures and climates) is that of the diffusion, or internal marketing, of the innovation generated or adopted. While large organizations are often very good at generating something new somewhere in the organization, the organizational left hand, so to speak, often does not know, or finds it difficult to know, what the organizational right hand is doing.

Similarly, researchers have identified various organizational designs that seem to enhance the ability of the firm to routinely implement changes in a timely and efficient manner. Unfortunately, these sorts of structures tend to rely on a centralization of authority and decision making. They are not aptly suited to the primary process of innovation generation and/or adoption due to the fact that the managers with real decision-making authority are less exposed, as a group, to the wealth of environmental information that acts as a catalyst to the innovative process.

When designing for innovation is thus limited to purely structural choices, the designer faces inevitable trade-offs between innovation and implementation capabilities. As I will discuss below, some of the research literature on innovation has faced this problem. Various structural solutions to this dilemma have been proposed, but upon examination it seems that such solutions are, at best, inadequate—some of them might even aggravate the problem.

Recently, the cultural aspects of organizations have received a great deal of attention from both academics and practitioners. Many authors have expressed the view that a "strong" organizational culture, in which both innovation and efficiency are highly valued ideals in some way serves to modify and complement the existing capability of the organization's structure whether it is slanted towards innovation or implementation.

This cultural approach to design holds a great deal of promise, but previous treatments of the topic have ignored the potential trade-offs between innovation and implementation that are inherent in a purely cultural approach. The cultural approach to design, taken in isolation, results in a design dilemma strikingly similar to that implied by the structural approach taken in isolation.

The suggested course in designing for innovation is to consider both structural and cultural aspects of organizational design, using the strengths of one pattern to offset the weaknesses of the other. Only by taking this approach can the organization hope to constantly augment both its ability to innovate and to implement, rather than striking an unhappy medium between the two. While commonsense has it that two wrongs can never make a right, organizational researchers have often found that two dilemmas can be combined to create a solution.

THE STRUCTURAL DILEMMA OF INNOVATION

At its heart, the notion of an organizational structure is simply the pattern by which information enters or is generated by the organization, flows to focal choice points (decision makers), and reissues from them in the form of directives for action (or inaction). Structure is the pattern of relations by which information is processed and decisions are made. Organizations vary in their propensity to process information or make decisions, and often too little information (or too much) will affect the decision process adversely.

A distillation of the wisdom to be found in the literature on organizational innovation from the 1960s and 1970s[3] suggests that all organizations that are characterized as loosely-structured, "organic," decentralized, complex or heterogeneous, tend to be more sensitive to the existence of innovations in their environment and to generate more innovations for two reasons. First, there is a greater sensitivity overall to different parts of the environment. Thus, information flows into the organization rapidly. Second, the decentralization of authority allows for (in fact, demands) more lateral communication, and hence a greater intensity of intraorganizational stimuli. The result is that ideas ferment more rapidly, and solutions to problems are generated quickly. Unfortunately, the very complexity and "democracy" of these organizations acts against the possibilty of unified action. With so many parts of the organization going in their own direction, top management is at a loss as to how to translate the innovations of one part into useful practice for the others.

Organizations that are "mechanistic," tightly-structured, centralized, highly formalized, not highly differentiated and homogeneous are consequently slower to generate innovations and less sensitive to their existence. They seem better designed to accomplish the sometimes herculean task of implementation, taking an innovation from the initial decision when the actual adoption or generation occurs to the point where it is made routine throughout the other parts of the organization in ongoing practice. Decision makers have wider authority to implement a desirable innovation, but consequently have a smaller pool of innovation to draw from. This wisdom applies with equal force both to those innovations that are technological (product) in nature and those that are administrative (process) in nature. The scope of the problem facing the would-be innovator in top manageament in organizational decision choices is thus amplified.

SOME STRUCTURAL SOLUTIONS

Along the way, innovation researchers have posed several solutions to the ongoing design dilemma from their experience or organizations that have managed to both adopt and implement successful innovations, as those that have not. Victor Thompson writing in the mid-1960s, construed the dilemma as a conflict between innovative and bureaucratic form organizations, and suggested that project teams of innovative managers could be isolated from the surrounding organization to generate and adopt innovations that could be implemented and made routine by more hierarchical bureaucracy.[4] Richard Daft, after studying innovations in the educational system, suggested that a "dual core" might exist, whereby different groups of professionals, in this case educators and administrators, might each respond to and propose the adoption of innovations within their relevant

[3]G. Zaltman, R. Duncan, and J. Holbek (1973). *Organization and Innovations*. Wiley, New York; and T. Burns, and G. M. Stalker (1961), *The Management of Innovation*, Tavistock, London.
[4]V. Thompson, "Bureaucracy and Innovation." *Administrative Science Quarterly*, 10:1, 1965.

specialized knowledge domain.[5] The research literature on professionals in organizations has for a long time been concerned with their role as agents of innovation. Though the organization bound professional is subject to possible conflicts between two sets of institutional norms and guidelines, his access to a second institutional context affords the organization a monitor on changes and emerging innovations in a specialized knowledge domain. Research suggests that those professionals capable of communicating knowledge both across and within organizational boundaries rise rapidly in their organizations, presumably because of the invaluable function they perform.[6] While specific tasks and responsibilities along these lines are rarely written into the formal design of organization, the presence of boundary-spanning professionals constitutes a macro-design option of which many managers are aware.

A frequently used structural solution is the creation of an internal department together and diffuse innovations to the whole organization. The creation of a centralized "data bank" for innovation recognizes that implementing innovations is a function best served by specialists.

Unfortunately, these and other proposed solutions to the dilemma of designing for organizational innovation often compound the problem instead. One of the reasons for this is that innovation research has focused on rates of adoption (adoptiveness) as an organizational trait and its relation to structure at the expense of research on subsequent implementation, partially because the latter is a much more difficult process to track. This "adoption myopia" tends to equate the successfully innovating organization with the quickly-adopting one, and hence the proposed design options have addressed one side of the innovating managers' dilemma at the expense of the other.

Clearly, purely structural solutions to the dilemma are either inadequate or compound the problem, perhaps because the very way we conceive of structure involves a trade-off between a diffusion of authority (and greater adoptiveness) and centralization of authority (and greater ability to implement). Any solution that fiddles only with strucure is bound to augment one of these structural attributes (perhaps even at the expense of the other) but can never augment both. Fortunately, though, thinking in the organizational innovation field is not completely limited to structural concerns.

CULTURE AND INNOVATION

While domestic managers may remain somewhat skeptical about the relevance of "culture" to their concerns, the international manager faces cultural issues on an ongoing basis, and is thus eminently qualified to consider the ramifications of culture in design choices.

The cultural patterns of organizations have been variously described as "a set of shared understandings," "the way we do things around here," and "a set of control mechanisms" that serve to promote identification and elicit organizationally-desirable

[5]R. Daft, "A Dual-Core Model of Organizational Innovation." *Academy of Management Journal*, 21:2, 1977.

[6]M. Tushman, "Special Boundary Roles in the Innovation Process." *Administrative Science Quarterly*, 22:4, 1977.

behaviors when more prosaic forms of bureaucratic controls and guidelines cannot do the job efficiently. What all these definitions seem to imply is that elaborate cultural phenomena serve to facilitate and promote both horizontal and vertical communication across functional lines due to a shared feeling of overarching solidarity and a common language. In considering the relevance of culture to problems of innovation, however, most of the authors simply suggest that innovation be emphasized as a valued ideal. This approach is overly simplistic.

Meryl Reis Louis has described organizations as "culture-bearing melieus,"[7] a concept that embraces both the possibility of the popularly advertised overarching "corporate culture" and the possibility of many subcultures arising from functional or geographic diversity within the same organization. Thus the idea of an organizational culture need not be synonymous with the organization itself. The organization, in Louis's conception, may conceivably play host to, or provide a milieu for, one or more "cultures" that may either be "nested" (circumscribed by organizational boundaries, as in the case of a divisional or subsidiary's culture) or "overlapping" (both within the organization and without, as in the case of a culture derived from a geographical locale or organized professional group).

This concept of organizational culture is at once more complex and more fertile in terms of design options for innovation, as it admits the possibility of cultural heterogeneity as well as homogeneity. If cultural homogeneity binds organizational members together, it is possible that many of the communication problems inherent in the phenomenon of structural heterogeneity can be overcome. The other possibility of course, is that cultural heterogeneity, where it exists in an organization, can alleviate the bureaucratic rigidities inherent in the highly centralized and formalized organization.

When considering cultural issues in isolation, the innovating manager faces a dilemma somewhat similar to that posed by the issue of structure in isolation. Assuming that a unified cultural pattern can be established throughout an organization and across national boundaries, communication across functional or product-divisional lines would tend to be maximized. This cultural context would tend to increase the ability of the organization to diffuse innovation rapidly within itself. In short, the homogeneous organizational culture implements innovations efficiently. The "down side" of this pattern is the "group think" phenomenon that accompanies the lack of cultural heterogeneity—the homogeneous culture becomes insensitive to the potential for innovation, and is consequently slower to adopt changes. As interaction between individuals becomes ritualized, rigidities in thinking as well as behavior may become enshrined in organizational practice.

The possibility for cultural heterogeneity, on the other hand, is always an option for the international organization, requiring only the extension of autonomy to operating arms of the organization in their various geographic locales while allowing the vagaries of local influence to take their toll. The benefits of such cultural autonomy include greater sensitivity and willingness to experiment with the innovations generated out of the immediate local environment. The weakness of this pattern, however, is the resulting

[7]M. R. Louis, "Organizations as Culture-Bearing Milieux." In L. Pondy, P. Frost, G. Morgan, and T. Dandrige (eds.), *Organizational Symbolism*, JAI Press, Greenwich, Connecticut, forthcoming.

inability to implement innovations throughout the entire organization, due in part to the resistance generated by the provincial sectors of the organization against innovations not originating in their ow domain.

USING TWO DILEMMAS TO CREATE A SOLUTION

While it is a cornerstone of common knowledge that two wrongs do not make a right, it is often the case in organizational practice (or any systems design problem) that two dilemmas can be combined to create a solution. In their most fundamental sense, structure and culture can be seen as two different modes of organizing relations between members of a social system. Since both are modes for organizing relations, each mode can be used in design to fine tune and compensate for the shortcoming inherent to the other.

Thus, by considering both modes simultaneously, the designer can choose to compensate for the poorer adoptive capacity of the centralized structure by encouraging and promoting cultural heterogeneity. If, on the other hand, problems have been discovered in implementing innovations in a complex structure despite its proven capacity to generate and adopt them, the designer can seize upon the various devices used to solidify and extend a more homogeneous cultural pattern.

By way of example, suppose that the manager of a structurally heterogeneous organization wishes to increase the implementing capacity of his or her firm, but is satisfied with its current ability to generate innovations. Without increasing structural centralization (which will involve a trade-off with the capacity to innovate), the manager should seek to create a more homogeneous organizational culture. This can be accomplished through a variety of devices. On the one hand, junior and middle managers from a variety of functional and departmental roles can share a similar socialization experience through an intraorganizational executive education program. "Shared understandings" quickly evolve from shared experiences. Another option might involve horizontal transfers of managerial personnel to different countries over the medium term (that is, every two or three years). This option creates an experience whereby the organization as a social entity is more salient to the manager than any national culture in which he or she is located. This option has the added benefit of increasing implementing capacity immediately, since the transferred manager often carries and diffuses a wealth of experiential wisdom and local knowledge from the old context to the new one.

If, on the other hand, greater innovative capacity is desired, it is unnecessary to create greater structural complexity through a cumbersome (and often costly) reorganization. Cultural heterogeneity can be added to the international organization through a variety of options such as longer assignments to particular countries or an announced policy of involving managers more intensively in their local cultures. The tendency of local cultures to "absorb" foreigners or their own members (called "going native") can be counted on to take its course, thus adding to the total cultural diversity in the organization. The resulting increase in diversity of perspective creates a father stimulus to innovation activities.

CONCLUSION

The beauty of using the two modes of design for innovation is that it creates the possibility of ever-increasing levels of innovative capability. In any solution involving a trade-off, the capacity to implement or to innovate may be adjusted up or down, but the overall capacity to do both most always remains the same, holding other inputs such as human, financial, and technological resouces constant. The value of using the two modes of organizing as compensatory design devices lies in the fact that implementing and generating abilities are not traded-off. Compensatory design offers the possibility of retaining strength while repairing weakness.

While using cultural devices to compensate for structural dispositions, with careful design the manager can constantly adjust the innovative capacity of the organization upward. A cautionary note is in order, however. With cultural devices, it is the pattern of culture (or "cultures") in the organization that matters, in information processing terms. The actual content of "shared understandings" or organization-specific values may have little or nothing to do with the capacity to process information. Simply holding up "innovation" or "getting things done—done right and done quickly" as value and exemplars for desirable managerial behavior may elicit motiviation but in all likelihood will do little to augment the existing capabilities of the structural design. The analysis and modification of cultural patterns, on the other hand, may hold great promise for designing the innovative organization of the future.

EPILOGUE

Organizational Impact of New Technology

The effects of new technology stretch far beyond the factory floor. They reach other disciplines such as marketing, human resources, and finance and accounting as well. In fact, new technology promises to have a profound impact on the entire organization. Those firms that are to succeed in new technology applications must also understand and manage these changing roles, for even in the automated environment, the human component is essential. To highlight, we first consider the impact of new technology on some functional areas:

> *Marketing:* The changes in the manufacturing capabilities of firms will dramatically affect marketing. For example, flexible automation will allow marketing to offer the market customized products, even for high volume items. Higher quality products, and more rapid and reliable production and delivery also provide a competitive weapon which the marketing function may utilize. Shorter product life cycles and more volatile and demanding market segments suggest the need for a marketing department which is more flexible and more responsive to market swings.
>
> *Human Resources:* With the accelerating adoption of new technology come substantial human resource concerns. Employees, unions and social groups are all fighting to maintain the integrity of the individual worker in the face of the technology onslaught. Worker education, training, retraining, relocation and dehumanization are only a few of the issues which are gaining prime importance in this area.
>
> *Finance and Accounting:* As discussed in Chapter 7, these areas face some pronounced change in the near future if they are to keep up-to-date with some of the fundamental changes new technology has brought to manufacturing, and to the organization in general. A modified and updated cost accounting system, and revised capital budgeting techniques, capable of explicitly considering some of the idiosyncracies of automation vis-à-vis conventional production methods, are definite priorities.

Just as new technology demands change in individual functional areas, it will also demand substantial change in the way our organizations are currently structured. At present organizations follow one of two distinct organizational structures, the machine bureaucracy and the adhocracy.

The machine bureaucracy is essentially based on centralization of power and control. Decisions are made at the top, and the organization promotes a rigid hierarchy of authority and decision making. It is thought that this is an appropriate structure for the implementation of new technology, since it allows good control and definition of rules, procedures, and policies. Conversely, the tightly controlled atmosphere does little to promote the creativity and autonomy which foster innovation.

The adhocracy on the other hand is based on informal interaction, communication, and decentralized decision making. Due to the looser, more autonomous nature of this structure, creativity and participation help facilitate innovation. On the other hand, the lack of formal control often makes organized implementation of innovations rather difficult.

Clearly then, a problem arises. To be successful with new technologies, an organization must be able to innovate and implement. Neither pure structure is singularly sufficient; both are necessary. A large organization cannot just switch its organizational structure on a whim, regardless of what phase of the technological life cycle it is in. Therefore, what is needed is an organization that is simultaneously flexible and loose enough to generate innovations, while still organized and controlled enough to facilitate implementation. Theoretically, this does not sound too difficult, but in practice it is extremely hard for management to effectively establish and maintain such a structure. This is perhaps one of the main reasons why new technology is promoting renewed interest and investigation into the management of the organization.

CASE 8.1

Cavalier Tool and Manufacturing Limited[8]

Although it was only 7:30 AM on a December morning in 1987, Rick Janisse was already thinking five hours ahead to the meeting of the three partners in Cavalier Tool & Manufacturing Limited (Cavalier)—Rick, Ray Bendig, and Ron Hellenberger. Ron (president and sales manager) had called the meeting at Rick's (vice president–mold making) insistance, and Ray (vice president–machining) would be a key player in resolving an issue involving Cavalier's new CAD/CAM technology. A customer had accepted Cavalier's bid of $85,000 for a complex steel mold, and Rick was convinced that Ron had underbid by at least $15,000. One major consideration of the tender was that the successful bidder use CAD/CAM technology extensively for the project. But what, Rick had asked, was the point of adopting new technology if costs were not going to be covered? Ron had countered by stating that the recent investment of $500,000 in CAD/CAM equipment *had* to have resulted in a marked reduction in the cost of making a mold; had they spent the funds to stay in the same position they have been in a few years previously?

The impasse was troublesome. This was the first order Cavalier had received solely because of its CAD/CAM equipment, and it probably marked the beginning of a significant trend in the industry. At the meeting Ray would outline how the mold would be designed and manufactured. Rick, however, was concerned with how the CAD/CAM technology affected the firm in general. And he had until noon to figure that out, and to decide how to overcome the problems he encountered.

[8]This case was written by Professor Russell Radford. © 1988, University of Western Ontario.

BACKGROUND

Cavalier made steel molds which were used on injection molding machines for the manufacture of plastic products. All molds were made to order for custom molders, and most orders were won through a competitive bidding process. Each mold was unique, as the mold had a longer life than the product it made. Demand for injection molded plastic products had increased steadily for many years in North America, and growth was expected to continue for the forseeable future. Substitution of plastics for metal, development of new plastics and improvements in the properties of existing plastics meant that 1986 sales of $10 billion in Canada would be easily exceeded in 1987 and subsequent years. United States markets exhibited the same growth, and the future looked bright.

MOLD MAKING INDUSTRY

Mold makers would play a major part in meeting this growth challenge. Part of the machine tool and die industry (which in North America had about 32,500 plants and employed about one million people in 1986), the 200-odd Canadian mold makers exported over $239 million of molds and dies in 1986, a 20 percent increase over 1985. Of this total $223 million (or 75 percent of all molds and dies made in Canada) was exported to the United States. Most United States customers were located in the northern states, and the Canadian mold making industry had therefore concentrated in southern Ontario, in particular around Windsor.

The typical mold making firm employed 10–15 people in total, of whom four or five were highly skilled tradesmen who had completed five year apprenticeships in Canada or Europe. Owners tended to be highly skilled artisans who managed the shops themselves. Machinery was typically general purpose and manually operated, although progressively more companies were purchasing numerical control (NC) metal shaping machines. Most firms bid on small, simple molds required for houseware, hardware, furniture, appliance and computer industries; in this, the largest volume segment of the mold making industry, the basis of competition was price. In the medium size, complex mold segment in which Cavalier chose to operate, price was secondary to quality and delivery. The largest customer group in this segment was the automotive industry, and their particular requirements demanded higher skill levels in the work force and more complex manufacturing techniques and controls than were available in the bulk of the mold making plants. The lowest volume segment was the large mold segment; the molds were often less complex than those produced for the medium-size segment, but the heavy specialized equipment needed to move and shape the molds was very expensive, and owned by only a handful of shops.

Relationships in the medium-size segment were cordial, reflecting the high levels of trust required between firms before a long-term relationship could be established. Mold makers worked with approximately four custom molders, and each custom molder worked with about four mold makers. Although the tender process implied a very formal relationship, the normal practice was for the custom molder and the mold maker to suggest changes to mold at any and all stages of manufacture. The relationships between the custom molders and their large customers was very formal, with contracts being awarded to the lowest cost bidder. While this placed the mold maker in the hands of the molder, mold makers themselves affected the unit cost of the injection molded product because individual mold costs were high. Cavalier's molds were priced in the range of $40,000 to $200,000 and took anywhere from four to seven months to make.

TRENDS

The North American automobile industry and its suppliers had been under severe competitive pressure for several years, and Canadian mold makers had felt the effect. Despite expanding markets for injection molded plastics, the number of Canadian mold makers had decreased in the past five years as foreign mold makers started selling into North America, and as demands from the automotive industry became more severe. With the automobile industry demanding shorter lead times on product changeovers, guaranteed and high frequency part resupply, integrated (and therefore more complicated) parts from suppliers, and continually lower prices, the mold makers were pressured to reduce their mold making turnaround time while guaranteeing their quality and, at the same time, reducing their costs on increasingly complex molds.

Automobile manufacturers had decided that computer-aided design (CAD), computer-aided manufacturing (CAM), robots and electronic communication links within and across plants were vital to their survival, and were actively encouraging their suppliers to adopt these new technologies. It would not be long before most contracts would require suppliers to use CAD/CAM technology, and this would extend to second level suppliers such as mold makers.

Along with the change in technology the automotive industry was fostering an assembler-supplier multidisciplinary approach to product and process development called simultaneous engineering. By using the skills available at all stages of the production chain it was assumed that product costs could be lowered and response to change could be improved by the adoption of this "arms around" rather than an "arms length" approach to product development.

CAVALIER TOOL AND MANUFACTURING LIMITED

Located in Windsor, Ontario, Cavalier was founded by its three partners in 1975. Starting with only themselves in rented premises the firm had grown steadily. Now their own building was being expanded to give them 24,000 square feet of manufacturing shop in which their eight mold makers, 17 apprentices, and 28 journeyman machinists would work. Total company strength was 75 employees; company organization is shown in Exhibit 8.2, and financial data are shown in Exhibit 8.3 and Exhibit 8.4.

Exhibit 8.2 Cavalier Tool and Manufaturing Limited Organization Chart

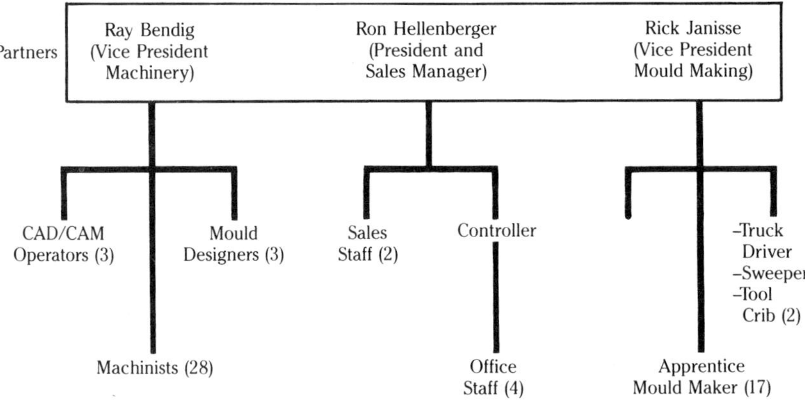

Exhibit 8.3 Statement of Operations and Retained Earnings (Year Ended November 30) ($000)

	1987	1986	1985	1984	1983	1982	1981
Sales	6,140	5,808	4,367	4,323	3,216	2,142	1,762
Cost of Goods Sold							
WIP—year start	946	677	432	402	298	152	342
Material	864	874	666	766	523	358	177
Direct Labor	2,274	1,860	1,862	1,705	1,318	824	712
Overhead	2,247	1,552	1,053	1,044	709	30	649
WIP—year end	1,007	946	677	432	402	298	152
Total Cost of Goods Sold	5,323	4,285	3,579	3,513	2,552	1,572	1,538
Gross Profit	817	1,523	788	810	665	570	224
Selling & Administrative Expenses	693	988	635	562	316	263	283
Net Profit	124	535	153	247	349	307	(58)
Other Income	47	53	64	66	—	—	—
Income Taxes	35	159	40	30	36	28	(7)
Net Income	137	429	177	283	314	279	(51)
Retained Earnings—Start of year	874	445	268	(15)	246	43	94
Dividends Paid	600	—	—	—	575	76	—
Retained Earnings—End of year	411	874	445	268	(15)	246	43

Exhibit 8.4 Balance Sheet (November 30) ($000)

	Assets						
	1987	1986	1985	1984	1983	1982	1981
Current							
Cash	—	—	—	—	—	1	1
Deposits in Trust	540	—	—	—	—	—	—
Accounts Receivable	1,268	1,817	1,065	1,094	715	643	377
Inventory—Raw Materials	50	39	35	32	56	43	35
—WIP	1,007	946	677	432	402	298	152
Prepaid expense	25	17	13	12	3	2	1
Tax receivable	100	60	24	6	—	—	—
Investment tax credit	112	27	62	51	—	—	—
Deposits in trust	539	—	—	—	—	—	—¢
Receivable from employees	—	—	—	—	2	3	1
Total Current	3,101	2,906	1,876	1,627	1,178	990	567
Fixed (Gross)							
Land	75	75	51	51	51	51	51
Parking Lot	47	10	10	10	10	10	10
Building	1,298	420	420	420	423	404	404
Shop Machinery & Equipment	1,951	1,536	978	753	554	407	359
Office Equipment	48	43	37	27	19	12	6
Automobiles	119	100	79	14	14	46	46
Leasehold Improvements	10	10	10	10	—	—	—
Total Fixed (Gross)	3,548	2,194	1,585	1,285	1,071	930	876
Fixed (Net)	2,730	1,521	1,101	869	742	606	687
Total Assets	5,831	4,427	2,977	2,496	1,920	1,596	1,254

	Liabilities						
	1987	1986	1985	1984	1983	1982	1981
Current							
Overdraft	33	122	66	25	28	3	275
Bank Loans	660	644	682	676	507	447	255
Accounts payable	1,038	724	569	526	342	286	177
Management bonus payable	90	435	120	120	45	—	—
Customer advances	440	513	68	203	119	164	24
Equipment loan payable	—	—	—	5	—	—	—
Current portion, long term debt	271	181	135	—	48	76	79
Accrued expenses	—	—	—	—	90	31	15
Payroll deductions	—	—	—	—	41	29	20
Income taxpayable	—	—	—	—	—	3	—
Loan payable—Continental BAnk	—	—	—	—	5	—	—

Exhibit 8.4 Balance Sheet (*continued*)

	Liabilities						
	1987	1986	1985	1984	1983	1982	1981
Total Current	2,531	2,620	1,639	1,554	1,225	1,037	844
Long Term	2,721	800	840	641	687	305	367
Deferred Tax	168	133	53	33	23	8	—
Total Liabilities	5,420	3,552	2,532	2,228	1,935	1,350	1,211
	Shareholders Equity						
Share Capital Issued	.3	.3	.3	.3	.3	.3	.3
Retained earnings	411	875	445	268	(15)	246	43
Total Liabilities and Equity	5,831	4,427	2,977	2,496	1,920	1,596	1,254

Markets

The automobile market on which Cavalier focused was highly seasonal. Most molds were ordered in December or January for delivery in May or June. To keep the plant running at capacity all year, therefore, Cavalier bid on contracts in other, less lucrative industries such as hardware and appliances. In these, and related, industries the molds were generally simple, and the competition came from small shops with little or no overhead as customers were looking for the lowest cost above all else. Success rates on bidding for these simple molds was low, and 80 percent of Cavalier's total volume was automobile industry related.

The Bidding Process

Whether initiated by custom molders or generated by one of Cavalier's two salesmen, an order started with a request for quotation (RFQ) from a potential customer. On receipt of the RFQ one of the salesman prepared a detailed quotation which was reviewed by Ron Hellenberger. Each quotation was prepared in two ways: on a mold-component basis and on a function basis. The quotations were developed using experience, rules of thumb and rough calculations; sometimes the salesmen would consult someone else in the company, and often Ron would consult the register of every job Cavalier had ever done when reviewing bids.

In most instances the two methods of cost estimating roughly agreed with each other; where they differed Ron analyzed the quotation closely to identify the errors. The bid process was complicated because alternative manufacturing processes were often available. Cavalier routinely provided a customer with prices for each of the alternatives, and the customer was responsible for selecting the desired alternative.

Over the years, Cavalier's cost structure has been 14 percent cost of goods sold for materials (including steel), 13 percent for outside contracts and purchased services, and labor and overhead most of the balance. The current labor charge-out rate was $46, of which $12 was Cavalier's average cost of direct labor, $11 was overhead, $11 was selling and administrative costs, and $12 was gross margin.

The cost estimate bore little relationship to the quotation given to the customer, because Ron would adjust his price based on his knowledge of the likely competition, the volume of work in the shop, the order book, and the likelihood of design changes (on which Cavalier's pricing could be more flexible). In the past year Cavalier had issues quotations worth a total of $90 million, and had received orders for $6 million. This understated Cavalier's success rate in winning orders from custom molders, as the custom molders themselves did not win every contract on which they bid.

Mold Manufacturing

Traditionally, Cavalier made molds by duplicating a solid pattern. On the receipt of blueprints from the customer, wooden models were ordered from a pattern maker, and steel blocks from which the molds would be made were ordered from one of two steel suppliers. Wooden models were normally received two weeks after order, and after being checked carefully against the blueprints, were sent to the customer for approval. While the model was away the team assigned to making the mold would decide how the mold was to be made and by whom, and would begin squaring up the steel blocks and machinery ancillary items such as ejector pins and cooling lines.

Following receipt of the approved wooden models, the mold making team used the models to prepare the 3-D fiberglass patterns (called "lay-ups") which would be duplicated using duplicating milling machines. A multistage manufacturing process involving rough cutting, stress relieving, semifinishing, finishing, inspection, and attachment to the mold of cooling lines and mechanisms for operating the mold in the injection molding machine was followed by trials of the mold, customer acceptance of samples prepared during the trials, and delivery of the mold to the customer.

Each mold making project was assigned to a core group of four—a senior mold maker (who managed the project), a journeyman mold maker, and two apprentices. Most of the noncritical machining was done by other journeyman machinists, and the senior mold maker had to negotiate with Ray Bendig for their time and for machine time. In addition to the responsibility for managing and scheduling his team for work on the project, therefore, the senior mold maker was required to spend a considerable amount of time coordinating his team's activities with those of the other teams and with other functions, particularly purchasing. This included a daily meeting of all project managers, at which operations for all molds were coordinated for that day.

Because each project was different and offered different challenges Rick had to be careful assigning mold making teams to particular jobs. To be successful a mold maker had to be aggressive and to be able to accept the challenge of "fighting" with the design to produce a workable (if not elegant) mold to tight tolerances and a tight building schedule. The large capital investment in the shop, long production cycles and capacity constraints and bottlenecks in the shop put pressure on the mold project team to finish the mold as quickly as possible. Speed had to be balanced against quality for any job, and as each project team handled several jobs simultaneously each senior mold maker had to be aware of several deadlines at all times.

Control

When a contract was awarded Cavalier opened a unique project file on the computer. As all employees (except the three partners and the office staff) punched time cards, accurate, detailed direct labor hours were charged for each job. Hours were turned into costs by multiplying hours by an employees' actual hourly pay rate. Overhead was applied at a standard 90 percent of direct labor cost, this percentage being historically stable. There was little indirect labor since almost all design, engineering, inspection, quality control, cleanup, machine setup and minor maintenance was charged to some job. What indirect labor occurred was combined with employee benefits, overtime charges, and miscellaneous supplies (including consumable items such as nuts and bolts) as "overhead." All major materials and purchases were identified with and allocated to specific jobs.

While all creditors expected prompt payment for supplies and services provided, Cavalier could not apply much pressure to its customers. Cash flow management was therfore a critical issue for Cavalier and most other mold makers. The average 26 week build-time for a mold was compounded by the traditional 43 week credit terms the automotive industry had been accorded and to which all firms subscribed. New customers were being expected to advance 33 percent of the contract price when the contract was awarded, 33 percent on receipt of sample parts, and the balance 30 days after receipt of the mold. As automotive molds accounted for 80 percent of Cavalier's business, this new policy had little impact on cash flow. With up to 40 projecs in process, therefore, work-in-process (WIP) inventory hovered around $1 million; the only way to reduce WIP, and reduce working capital requirements, would be to reduce the production time for each mold.

Programmable Automation

Advanced manufacturing technologies seemed one means by which production time could be reduced and cost contained. In 1984 the partners rebuilt a major duplicating milling machine, and fitted computer numerical controls (CNC) to the machine. While initially programmed on-line (the cutter paths being first worked out by the customer's blueprints and then punched into the control panel while the machine was idle), Cavalier had since purchased a computer to allow cutter path programming to be carried out independently of the milling machine.

Despite the lack of readily available software, and the difficulty of developing cutter path programs for the intricate surfaces of the majority of their molds, Cavalier extended the manufacturing automation program. Currently Ray Bendig had three CNC milling machines; two rebuilt pattern duplicating machines (each still capable of traditional pattern duplicating) and one new CNC-only machine. This CAM equipment was proving highly popular with machinists and tool makers, as machining and tool design problems could be identified earlier and rectified quickly and more easily than with the non-CAM machines. The earlier identification of problems allowed production times to be reduced by an average of one week, and allegedly produced better quality. To date, however, the internal enthusiasm had not been shared by customers, only one of whom specified CAM technology.

CAD, the other piece of the CAD/CAM puzzle, was an entirely different kettle of fish. The computer purchased to operate with the CNC milling machines was used for developing cutter paths. That was still the current practice, as Rick knew, although there was some interest from Ray to expand to full computer aided design and draughting with automatic generation of cutter paths for the machines. This step would face some resistance from the shop floor, and perhaps from others.

This was because the introduction of computer-generated cutter paths had not been completely successful. Part of the problem was the software the CAD programmers had to work with, but Rick was aware that the programmers themselves contributed to the problem. CAD programmers needed to be more than computer programmers; they needed to have a good grasp of mechanical engineering design principles, machining, and mold making. Hiring college trained programmers and expecting them to learn about mechanics had not worked; nor had giving mold making apprentices on-the-job programming instruction. Where did you find people with the skills required of a CAD programmer? How did you develop the skills if no qualified candidates would be found? What extra skills would be required of CAD designers? None of Cavalier's management could answer these questions.

Ray Bendig had suggested that CAD would ultimately save one week at the design stage by eliminating the need for subcontracting out the making of the wooden duplicating pattern. But what would a customer verify before approving the start of mold machining? And what other impacts might CAD have? Today's meeting had been called to resolve conflict arising from Cavalier's very first quotation for a fully CAD/CAM mold making project, and while the argument was centered on the quoted price, Rick was aware that the real argument would be about how CAD/CAM would affect internal organization, internal relationships, and the way mold making projects would be handled.

Two other issues complicated Rick's thinking. The first was the way Cavalier had aproached CAD/CAM. At present the system was neither fish nor fowl, with only three milling machines capable of accepting coded cutting instructions, and those from a stand alone computer. Should the company have moved wholeheartedly into CAD/CAM in one step? Should CAD have been purchased first? Was it feasible to consider those alternatives now—and what might their impact be?

And how would customers expect to work with Cavalier in the future? Just as there was potential to "link" the designers directly to the machines (providing the software was available) so there was a potential for Cavalier's manufacturing equipment to be linked directly with the computers of the custom molders or even to those of the automobile manufacturers. What would a large network like this do for (and to) Cavalier? What impact would that have on costs?

CONCLUSION

As he sat at his desk, Rick agreed with Ron's assessment that CAD/CAM was a strategic necessity, and cost justificaiton of the purchase was not a consideration. The impact of CAD/CAM on the company and the way the company operated was a primary concern, both because of the impact on cost structures of the major investments already made (and still to be made) in CAD/CAM equipment, and the impact the technology would have on people and their relationships with each other inside the company. With the pressures of the day already mounting, Rick wished the meeting was a week away.

CASE 8.2

Drew International Inc.[9]

It was January 1985, and Joan Davis, newly-promoted engineering supervisor of Drew International Inc.'s Canadian operations, was having second thoughts about the project she had been assigned to implement. Approval had been received from Corporate Headquarters to install a new automated forming line, but Joan was concerned by the impact this machine would have on Drew's hourly paid workers. Even at the best of times, the prospect of laying off workers because of new technology created tensions in the company. To add to the stress this time, however, 1984 would bring the next round of contract negotiations with the union, and a poorly handled installation would inevitably be reflected in the negotiations and the potential strike. Joan knew that she would be singled out by both senior management and the union as a prime cause of unrest and suspicion, even though Drew's previous brush with automation had caused layoffs, and relationships between management and the union were already poor.

DREW INTERNATIONAL INC.

Drew International Inc. was a worldwide manufacturing organization, with operating companies in over 35 countries. Drew Canada (Drew) began operation in Toronto shortly after the end of World War II, and had relocated to a smaller town some 70 km away in the 1950s. In 1985 Drew's Canadian work force of 170 operated two plants, making a wide range of consumable products for the metallurgical industry. Its 90 hourly workers were members of the United Steel Workers of America, and their current two year con-

[9]This case was written by Professor Hamid Noori, 1987.

tract was due to expire in November. Drew had been peacefully organized in 1972, and all seven contracts had been negotiated without a strike or a lockout. Despite the history, however, there was always the possibility that the "next" round could go sour, and that was compounded by the mater of the new equipment.

PRODUCTS

The metallurgical industry in North America was composed of steel mills, steel, iron and aluminum foundries, aluminum smelters, and nonferrous casters. Although Drew produced cement additives and sealers for the construction industry, the bulk of sales were to the Canadian metallurgical industry, that aggregation of ferrous and nonferrous foundries, smelters, and casters, including the major steel mills and aluminum smelters. The metallurgical products fell into four main categories; refractory boards, refractory sleeves, blended powders, and coatings.

Refractory Boards

The range of flat or slightly curved refractory boards was Drew's highest volume product line. The company currently had an 85 percent share of the Canadian market; interruption for any reason would lose market share which would take years of intensive effort to regain. Refractory boards were sold to 20–25 companies for use in foundaries and steel mills. In foundries, the boards provided insulation and protection to transfer ladles, pouring ladles, tundishes, and other reservoir vessels. Before the vessles were used, the boards were placed on the inside of the shell, and wedged tightly together. The joints were then cemented, leaving the vessel fully lined with a consumable, sealed inner surface. This preparation fully protected the vessel from damage, thermal shock, and deposition of the chilled metal when the hot metal was poured in. When the transfer, or other, cycle was complete, the ladle or tundish would be inverted and the partly consumed boards would fall out. The cycle was continuously repeated under normal operating conditions, with each set of boards being used once only.

In steel mills, the boards were used in three areas. The first was to line the transfer ladles shown in Exhibit 8.5. These were used to transfer and pour the molten steel produced in a steel making furnace into the semifinishing process the mill used—either ingot pouring or continuous casting. The boards were used in the same way as in the ladles in foundries, described previously. The other two uses of boards were in ingot pouring, or teeming, and continuous casting.

In ingot teeming (shown in Exhibit 8.6), the boards tightly lined the top, inside surface of the ingot mold. These boards were exothermic in nature; when the molten steel was poured into the mold, it ignited the boards, causing them to burn slowly. This heat slowed the shrinkage rate of the steel, increasing the yield and improving several metallurgical properties in the ingot. Once the exotherm (or burning) was complete, the remaining board material provided refractory characteristics to the steel.

Exhibit 8.5 Steelmaking Alternative Processes

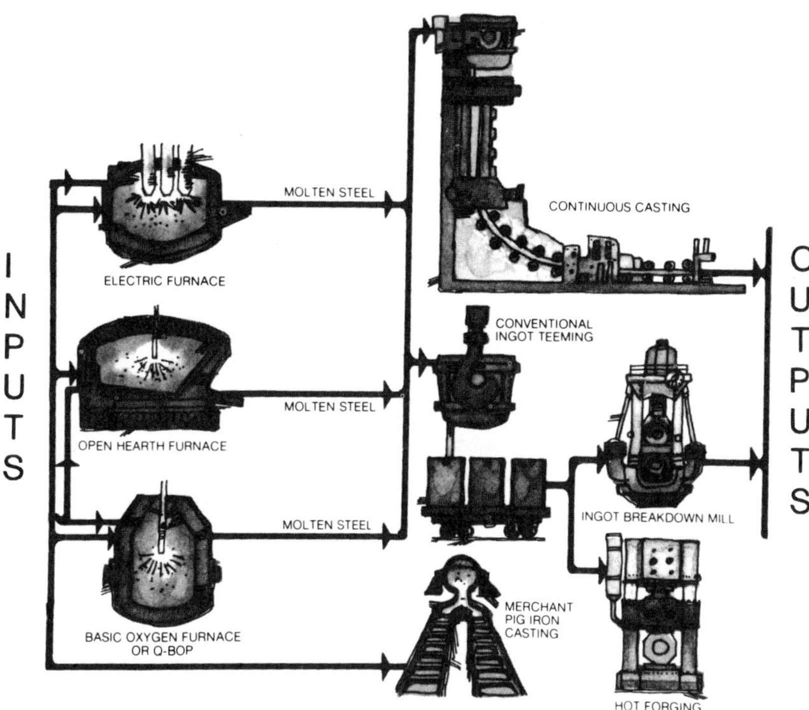

Exhibit 8.6 Cutaway of Continuous Castes Tundish Showing Consumable Liner

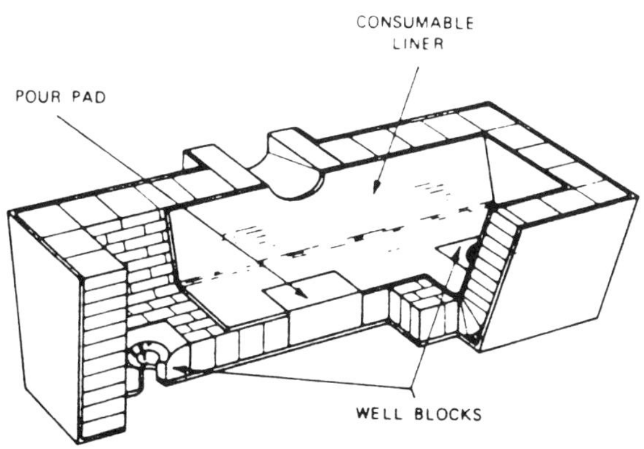

Continuous casting, as shown in Exhibit 8.6, was much more efficient than ingot teeming, because it eliminated an entire step in steelmaking. In ingot teeming the molten steel went through five stages (furnace, transfer ladle, mold, reheat, rolling), while in continuous casting, the steel went through only four stages (furnace, transfer ladle, tundish, rolling). This not only saved the energy required to reheat the solidified ingot, it also saved space, time and transfer equipment. Despite the high capital investments required for "concast," most of the top steel companies around the world had converted to this method. All of North America's major producers were forecast to have at least one such caster in operation by 1987.

The tundish used in continuous casting was a large bathtub-shaped vessel with one or more exit holes in the bottom. The holes were blocked during the pouring of the first few ladles, to allow the molten steel level to rise to a predetermined height. At that point, the exits were opened, allowing the steel to pour out the bottom. More ladles of molten steel were then continuously poured into the tundish, maintaining the depth (the ferrostatic head), which controlled the exit velocity of the steel. The steel strand was allowed to cool slightly for solidification, and was then pulled through a series of vertical, curved and horizontal rolls.

The application of the refractory board in the tundish was different than in the ingot mold, where it was used for only one filling. In the tundish, the board system had to stay in place for the entire pour, which could last up to 20 hours. Its function was to provide insultation and separation of the molten steel from the steel vessel over this period. In order to counter the erosion caused by the motion and heat of the steel, tundish boards had to be of much higher density and strength than ingot mold boards.

Refractory Sleeves

The refractory sleeves were used in foundries, where they guided the flow of molten metal into molds. They were exothermic in nature, and insulated the metal in the risers of the mold to prevent premature cooling and solidification.

Blended Powders

The blended powders encompassed a wide range of applications in both steel mills and foundries. They were thrown into a vessel of molten metal to remove impurities, to aid in cleansing of the metal, or to form an insulating noncrusting layer.

Coatings

The coatings ranged from water or spirit based liquids to various pastes used in the foundry industry. They coated sand cores and molds, in order to produce better surface finishes on the casting.

The proposed new automated forming machine will be used to make refractory boards, which are used in both foundries and steel mills. They insulate the molten metal, and protect the surface of the containing vessels. One variety of boards is also exothermic in nature, to improve the metallurgical properties of the metal itself. This is in addition to offering high temperature refractory characteristics, minimum chill properties, and superb insulation.

THE BOARD MAKING PROCESS

The process by which all of Drew's several hundred different refractory boards were made was relatively straightforward. A batch of raw materials—vqarious types of sand, fiber reinforcements, resin binders, and fuels and sensitizers (in the case of the exothermic boards)—were placed into a large mixer. Water was added, and the ingredients mixed together. The resultant slurry, with a solids content of 25 to 50 percent, was pumped, through transfer lines, to a forming machine. The slurry was deposited into a forming tank, where it was kept in suspension by constant agitation. An open topped mold, or tool, mounted on top of an attached vacuum chamber, was then suspended in the slurry bath. The mold resembled a cookie cutter in the shape of the desired refractory board, and was suspended face-up in the slurry.

Once the mold was immersed in the slurry a vacuum was drawn in the lower chamber. A fine mesh screen separated the tool from the vacuum chamber, the mesh being fine enough to allow only water to be drawn through. Solids, not being able to pass through, were drawn to and held against the screen. The tool was soon filled with solids, the density of the mass being controlled by the degree of vacuum being drawn.

When the mold was completely filled the tool was raised out of the slurry, still face-up. The vacuum continued to be drawn, causing the moisture content to be further reduced. When the desired moisture content was reached (usually less than 15 percent), the tool was turned over, the vacuum turned off, and the "green" board fell out of the tool and onto a drying screen. The board was then dried in an oven, where the heat caused the resin to activate, bonding the board together with much higher strength than it had in the green stage.

MOLDING MACHINES

Drew currently had several manual molding machines, and one automated machine which had been purchased in 1980. The manual forming machines were relatively simple. On all machines an operator sprayed the tool to remove debris from the previous cycle, started the new cycle, put an empty drier screen in place to receive the next green board, and took the most recently made greed board away for drying. Where boards required mounting hardware (used to keep boards in place at the top of ingot molds and the like) an operator put the hardware in by hand. Mounting hardware was required in about 30 percent of all boards.

The existing automated machine used the same sequence of operations as the manual machines, but differed from the manual machines by having two forming tanks, not one, and by incorporating an automated conveyor line on which the molding machine placed the green board, the board then being carried automatically to the drying oven. Only one worker was required in the entire automated system, unloading green boards from the end of the conveyor line and placing them in the oven. One other person was retained for monitoring the machine and to make necessary tool changes between runs of different boards. The automated machine could not be used to make boards which required mounting hardware.

THE PROPOSAL

The scheme which the Board had approved, and which Joan was to install, called for another automatic forming machine to be installed, to replace three manual machines, and to make higher density, and therefore higher margin, refractory boards than the company currently produced. The demand for refractory boards was high; the slump of 1981/1982 was now history, and steel companies were operating at capacity. In addition, the move to continuous casting and away from ingot teeming was changing the product mix to a much greater proportion of high density boards, and to a smaller proportion of boards requiring mounting hardware.

The installed cost of the new machine was $1.17 million. Drew's engineers had estimated that, based on projected sales volumes, and capacities of the present manual and automated machines, the payback period for the proposed machine would be less than two years. The savings would come in several ways. These would be:

1. Direct Labor	$225,000
2. Scrap	40,000
3. Natural Gas	85,500
4. Existing Machine Upgrade	20,600
5. Effluent Disposal	13,300
6. Increased Contribution	237,000
Additional Revenues	182,680
Total	$804,040

Of these costs, the single greatest saving would be reduced direct labor cost, the equivalent of 12 workers. This would also provide the greatest challenge, however, as the unionized work force was still smarting from the introduction of the first automated machine. In addition, most of the hourly work force was wary of automated machinery.

THE WORK FORCE

Drew's work force had little formal skills training. Nearly all the plant's equipment was manually operated and simple to operate. Training was carried out on the job, and a worker was expected to be up to speed in less than a week for most operations. Despite the lack of formal training, however, there were several jobs which required knowledge, skill, and judgment; these jobs were "owned" by longer term workers, even though no formal job classification existed for those prestige jobs.

The first automated forming line, installed in 1980, was much more complex than the manual machines it replaced. Even though the machine performed the same sequence of operations as all the manual machines, the work force was intimidated by the technology. The proposed machine would be even more complex, due to refinements in the base machine, and the introduction of programmable controllers. Joan was even a little awed herself, and she could appreciate how the workers might feel.

Not only had the new technology intimidated the work force; the union felt the machine had been the first move in a struggle to get rid of the union. When the first automated machine was introduced, a formal meeting had been held with two of the union's local executives, to explain the machine's function. No meeting had been held with the membership at large to prepare them for the advent of the machine, and to let them know what impact the machine would have on its operators, and on job security. In fact, in the 3½ years over which the machine had been operating, the monitoring of the machine's operation had been done by the plant supervisory staff, and all tool changes had been performed by the maintenance department. These jobs had not yet been turned over for union classification, nor did the management seem to be in a hurry to abandon its position.

This was like rubbing salt in the wound to the union, for not only had members' jobs been lost to the machine, but the three to five jobs involved in two shifts plus overtime operation of the machine had not been given back to them. In response to a request from the union, Drew's management had indicated that the jobs required special skills and responsibilities which the hourly work force could not handle. However, the past 3½ years had shown the operation to be relatively straightforward, and the union was adamant that any of its members could successfully operate the new machine, given some limited instruction. No formal meetings had yet been held between management and union regarding the second machine. However, Joan was aware that it was common knowledge on the shop floor (from engineering staff activities, contractor visits, and general conversations) that another automated machine, costing $2 million, was going to be installed.

The work force in general believed that 14 jobs were lost to the first automated machine. Everyone begrudgingly conceded that the plant equipment was old and that the company could not remain competitive unless changes were made. But it was also clear that more jobs would be lost, and there were rumors that up to 25 percent of the work force would be made redundant.

To further compound matters the work force no longer believed it was being treated fairly, from a wage perspective. From 1972 to 1982, contracts had been negotiated every two years. In 1982 the company had asked to have a two year settlement on language and only a one year settlement on wages. This was agreed to, under duress, by the union, and low wage settlements had been made in 1982 and 1983—despite high levels of inflation. Now rumors of a new machine had begun to circulate, and several influential workers had suggested this was a ploy to panic the union into accepting another unduly low settlement. Several workers had said that the current negotiations had to be settled in the union's favor—or else. And they wanted the automated machine operator jobs brought into the bargaining unit. Nothing less would be acceptable.

MANAGEMENT

Joan knew that Drew's management had a very different view of the situation. The first machine was seen as a unqualified success; for the first year-and-a-half that it was in operation, it produced a greater number of boards, at higher quality and lower scrap levels than the manual machines were able to achieve. And at lower labor costs, although the union's assessment of 14 jobs was not accurate.

Because business had been better than forecast in 1980, many of the manual machines slated for replacement by the automated machine (and used as part of the project justification) were operated in parallel to the new machine, in order to meet production demands. In the last half of 1981, there had been a downturn in the demand for refractory boards, and the old machines slated for removal in 1980 had at last been scrapped. Demand picked up slightly in the first half of 1982, but plummeted in the second half. Layoffs in both plant and office had been made, and many that stayed were put on reduced work weeks in conjunction with government work-sharing programs. As business started to improve in 1983 some, but not all, of the people were brought back. At present the work force was 14 fewer than it had been as the machine was installed, but it had been even lower in 1982. It would be irresponsible to say that the 14 jobs were lost to the first machine.

There was also good cause for keeping the job classification for both automated machines out of the bargaining unit. By stretching supervisory personnel slighty, the company would be able to accommoate the operation of the machine at little extra cost. This meant that there would be no need for a new labor grade, that would undoubtedly require higher pay standards than those currently in existence. Management was also afraid that the unionized operators would purposely slow down the speed of the machine; this would mean that the payback period would not be met, and the manual machines would not appear to be so vulnerable.

If the jobs were turned over to the work force, management would not be able to handpick the machine operators, but would have to use seniority as the principal selection criterion. With so much money tied up in the new equpment, the company did not want to be told who could, and would, operate the machines. In all probability the issue of who operated the machines would be decided outside the company; the union had filled three separate grievances against Drew as a result of the supervisory staff's continued operation of the first automated machine. These were now ready for arbitration, and the company's legal counsel had advised that the union would probably win.

CONCLUSION

As she walked to the coffee machine Joan began to realize the dubious honor she had received. The double shift operation was running six and even seven days a week to meet demand. Absenteeism was on the rise, and productivity was falling. The extra "temporary" demands placed on the supervisory staff was taking its toll, and quality was down as a result. No better arguments could be made in favor of better, faster machinery. But the last thing the company needed was a crippling strike, which would jeopardize sales for several years. How should she go about installing and operating the new automated forming machine, Joan wondered, and how long would it take? Should she get involved in this project at all?

Chapter Nine

MANAGERIAL ASPECTS OF NEW TECHNOLOGY IMPLEMENTATION

SITUATION 9.1

Human Resource Development for Advanced Manufacturing Technology[1]

Earlier this year our company, Perkins Engines, unveiled Phaser, a new family of four and six cylinder automotive diesel engines hailed as "The next generation of power technology."

It is the most important product development at Perkins for nearly two decades. It has taken five years and more than £30 million to research and develop.

However, designing and perfecting a new range of engines is only part of the battle. The key to success in the 1990s and beyond will be our ability to sell Phaser engines against ever increasing competitive pressure, and that demands considerable investment in new manufacturing facilities.

This investment has been based on a very clearly designed strategic plan, which itself was derived from our overall business plan. As a result, we have installed new facilities in almost every area of the factory. The investments over a wide range of manufacturing processes, ranging from:

- cylinder block and head machining
- crankshaft heat treatment
- automated assembly
- automatic material storage and distribution

and we are continuing to invest.

[1]J. Towers, "Human Resource Development for Advanced Manufacturing Technology." This paper is reproduced from "Planning for Automated Manufacture." Reprinted with permission of the Council of the Institution of Mechanical Engineers. © 1986 Institution of Mechanical Engineers.

Our plan is to spend another £50 million in our factory over the next five years. We believe that such investment is a vital ingredient in Perkins' strategy to remain one of the world's most successful diesel engine suppliers in an intensely competitive market.

You will understand just how competitive when I tell you that in the world today there are 320 manufacturers of diesel engines which between them have a total capacity of nine million units, chasing a current demand of only six million! However, as anyone who has installed AMT facilities will agree, making these investments work well is not a simple case of getting the technology working.

Perkins believes, and experience has proven us correct, that one of the most vital ingredients in the successful introduction of AMT facilities is the team of people who will operate and maintain it. However much you spend on equipment, and no matter how cleaver it is at doing the job, someone must run it and someone must maintain it. If you do not invest in the people as well as the technology, then expensive and sophisticated machinery will always fail to fulfill its potential.

Perkins deliberately sets out to invest in people, and as a result, we believe that the process of introducing AMT facilities has gone much more smoothly than we would have imagined possible when our investment plan began.

Far from Perkins' employees reacting negatively to new technology and seeing it as a threat to their jobs, they have responded with enthusiasm, taking considerable pride in the company's development and seeing it as a way of protecting their own futures.

So, how is it done? What are the basic ingredients to ensure this correct blend of people and technology?

There are four main elements:

1. Is the ongoing communication designed to ensure that everyone at Perkins has a realistic understanding of the company's position in the marketplace, the competitive pressures it is operating under and what the long term future is going to be? For that to be accepted the communication must be frank, open and involves sharing with our employees some very commercially sensitive plans.
2. In establishing a professional and well-plannned timetable for introducing new facilities. This plan maximizes employee involvement upwards of two years before new facilities are likely to be installed on the shop floor.
3. Is the creation of an integrated training program which results in everyone likely to be involved with the facility being comprehensively trained before we press any buttons?
4. Is there continuing involvement of employees long after the facilities have been installed and the production engineer has signed it off? We do this by Improvement Teams.

These teams are autonomous groups of employees who find, analyze, solve, and implement solutions to problems they meet at their work place. The problems can be product, environment, or facility led. We have 18 teams operating at Peterborough, and they are enthusiastically supported by management and operators alike.

Let me now outline the broad structures of our internal communication systems, then go on to show how a major new facility can be successfully introduced using, by way of illustration, the robotic line for the automatic assembly of cylinder heads.

Perkins' internal communications are both extensive and regular and interlock with our training programs.

The cornerstone of the company's communications process is the Team Brief—a monthly update of the current company business situation for employees by their immediate supervisors.

That briefing includes facts on how the business performed in the previous month, with an open declaration of the quality, output and delivery performances actually achieved. Month-by-month, employees are kept fully aware of how many engines or component kits have been dispatched, and what the year's total is to date. There will be comparisons on the daily build rate between the current month, last month and the projection for the months ahead.

The briefing also includes an honest assessment of the market outlook for the three months ahead, and what is being done to secure improved sales.

"Right First Time" quality performance data is given along with a comparison of previous performance. The brief also contains general company or industry information including data on our competition and local information of interest to particular sections. A favorite feature is the "Rumor of the Month" corner, which enables us not only to deal with rumors if they arise, but also to diminish the importance which employees might attach to them. These days it is proving difficult to provide material for the section because rumor mongering has become a laughed-at hobby.

The Team Brief is also a two-way process and constitutes a key vehicle for channeling employee views upwards. Obviously the quality of the Team Brief depends on the communication skills of the supervisor giving it. But surveys conducted within the factory have shown that the brief is consistently regarded as the most effective and most relied upon source of company information. Employees complain if the section next door gets a more comprehensive brief than theirs.

Perkins was one of the first employers in the region to establish its own in-house newspaper. This 12-page tabloid is published monthly and provides employees simultaneously with even more information which they know they can rely upon. The opinion surveys which we carry out have shown that this newspaper is similarly very well received and accepted as a source of information.

Where significant news has to be released before either the Team Brief or the company's newspaper is published, Perkins uses an ad hoc system called "Newsline" to update employees. As well as being posted on notice boards, Newsline sheets are distributed on the tables in the company's restaurants and rest areas. "Special" newslines are communicated by supervision in the same manner as the Team Brief.

Alongside this continuing communication Perkins has also established a series of courses which are a blend of training and information, both giving and receiving. Perkins has gone on to develop video communications. A 20-minute long video, often using professional presenters and interviewers, each covering particular aspects of the company's position. These occur three times a year. They effectively update the "Perkins Tomorrow" program—thus ensuring that employees once having been put in touch with the company's position never lose it.

From this realistic awareness of what Perkins has to deal with, employees are better able to understand the need to invest in new technology for improving quality and productivity, and are more willing to cooperate in making it happen in the knowledge that this is the way to secure and protect their own jobs.

Now, let me turn to one particular project—the introduction of Perkins' robotic assembly machine for cylinder heads, and let me use that example to illustrate the level of employee involvement which we strive to achieve. This facility was installed in 1985 and was the first fully automatic assembly machine ever to be installed at Perkins. The facility is designed to automatically subassemble cylinder heads. It uses eight robots to assemble the valve train on all Perkins' four and six cylinder engines. It is computer controlled and it is no exaggeration to say that, in terms of technology, it is light years ahead of the facilities it replaced. These facilities were totally manual and equipped with only the very basic tooling and fixturing.

As a result of the communication and training I have already described, Perkins employees were given a general understanding why there was a need for such an investment. However, as soon as the project had been authorized, all the operators who would be affected by the facility received a detailed briefing. Remember this was happening up to 18 months before the machine was planned to go into production. Our objective was to secure their support, commitment, and input, right from the start.

Volunteers to operate the facility were sought from appropriate employees and in fact were substantially oversubscribed. That meant that we were in a position to be able to select. However, it must be stressed that we were selecting from existing operators—we did not recruit specifically to fill these new jobs. Each month the Team Brief updated everyone on the progress of the project. I think it is fair to say that everyone at Perkins knew when the site was to be cleared and when the facility was going to be installed. Those selected were involved in the project months before the new facility appeared on the shop floor.

Part of that involvement was to spend at least a week at the supplier's factory in Bristol seeing the machine taking shape. The enthusiasm which was generated in the supplier's factory had to be seen to be believed and was, I am convinced, crucial to developing genuine commitment to the new plant.

Senior management also spent time with the operators in Bristol. They were already talking in terms of "my" and "our" machine. When you work out the cost of this involvement it may seem high initially, but looked at in terms of the total investment the company is making, it pales into insignificance.

In some instances changes were made at the operators suggestion. These were not major but were enormously important in adding to their involvement and belief in the new equipment.

Seeing it take shape helps to remove the mystique of the equipment. They understand it better and lose those lurking fears of the unknown that the prospect of strange new hi-tech equipment can generate in the minds of nearly all of us. Thus, long before the new machinery reached us the operators knew it inside out, and this process of training continued as the equipment was installed and commissioning started.

This whole process was achieved without any blanket regarding of the operators, although, clearly, where new skills were involved, employees were given the appropriate rewards. In tandem with this process was a reorganization of our maintenance operations within the factory. Previously we operated a maintenance department which was centrally managed and provided a service to "client" departments. In its place we have created a blend of maintenance and production personnel so that they now work under a single local manager. This creation of a team who operates and maintains their facility are a vital element in creating collective responsibility.

Maintenance men, like production workers, were also fully involved in the early familiarization process and that was accompanied by an agreed blurring of the demarcation line between maintenance and production activities. There is now a proper acceptance that production workers should carry out routine maintenance work. But the advent of new equipment, much of it computer controlled and involving highly sophisticated electronics, meant that we also had to rethink our entire maintenance structure in another way. In the past, maintenance personnel were split between mechanical and electrical specialists. Perkins became one of the first major engineering companies in Britain to achieve a multiskilling arrangement with its maintenance craftsmen.

Well over a quarter of Perkins' maintenance personnel have been through this six-month multiskilling course which has been run within Perkins' own training department. Today, the Automated Cylinder Head facility is just another routine AMT investment on Perkins' shop floor. But the employees are not finished yet. The Improvement Team in that area is working quietly away making minor modificaitons here and there to further enhance the performance of their equipment.

Investment in high technology is crucial if we are to continue to win the battle to stay on top of an intensely competitive industry. Our experience at Perkins is that even the most modern equipment needs the commitment and enthusiasm of those who will operate and maintain it. We are convinced that our formula for success is a vital ingredient in the introduction of AMT facilities. Investment in people is just as important as investment in technology, and this will continue to be the case long into the next decade.

READING 9.1

Implementing New Technology[2]

Introducing technological change into an organization presents a different set of challenges to management than does the work of competent project administration. Frequently, however, the managers responsible for shepherding a technical innovation into routine use are much better equipped by education and experience to guide that innovation's development than to manage its implementation.

A DUAL ROLE

Those who manage technological change must often serve as both technical developers and implementors. As a rule, one organization develops the technology and then hands it off to users, who are less technically skilled but quite knowledgeable about their own areas of application. In practice, however, the user organization is often not willing, or able, to take on responsibility for the technology at the point in its evolution at which the development group wants to hand it over. The person responsible for implementation—whether located in the developing organization, the user organization, or in some intermediary position—has to design the hand-off so that it is almost invisible. That is, before the baton changes hands, the runners should have been running in parallel for a long time. The implementation manager has to integrate the perspectives and the needs of both developers and users.

[2]D. Leonard-Barton and W. A. Kraus, "Implementing New Technology," November–December. Reprinted with permission from *Harvard Business Review*. © 1986 by the President and Fellows of Harvard College.

Perhaps the easiest way to accomplish this task is to think of implementation as an internal marketing, not selling, job. This distinction is important because selling starts with a finished product; marketing with research on user needs and preferences. Marketing executives worry about how to position their product in relation to all competitive products and are concerned with distribution channels and the infrastructure needed to support product use.

Marketing Perspective

Involving users in a new technology's design phase boosts user satisfaction, but the proper extent, timing, and type of user involvement will vary greatly from company to company. For example, software developers in an electronic office equipment company established a user design group to work with developers on a strategically important piece of applications software when the program was still in the prototype stage. Prospective users could try out the software on the same computer employed by the program's developers. The extremely tight communication loop that resulted allowed daily feedback from users to designers on their preferences and problems. This degree of immediacy may be unusual, but managers can almost always get some information from potential users that will improve product design.

A marketing perspective also helps prepare an organization to receive new technology. Many implementation efforts fail because someone underestimated the scope or importance of such preparation. Indeed, the organizational hills are full of managers who believe that an innovation's technical superiority and strategic importance will guarantee acceptance. Therefore, they pour abundant resources into the purchase or development of the technology but very little into its implementation. Experience suggests, however, that successful implementation requires not only heavy investment by developers early in the project but also a sustained level of investment in the resources of user organizations.

Framework for Information

Just as marketing managers carefully plan the research through which they will gather critical product information, so implementation managers must develop an iterative, almost accordion-like framework to guide decisions about when and how to collect needed information from all groups affected by an innovation. We say "accordion-like" because the process necessarily involves a search for information, a pause to digest it, and then another active period of search, cycle after cycle. What information is important—and who has it—may vary at different stages of the implementation process, but someone must coordinate the iterative work of gathering it—and that someone is the implementation manager.

Multiple Internal Markets

The higher the organizational level at which managers define a problem or a need, the greater the probability of successful implementation. At the same time, however, the closer the definition and solution of problems or needs are to end users, the greater the probability of success. Implementation managers must draw up their internal marketing plans in light of this apparent paradox.

As these managers identify the individuals or groups whose acceptance is essential to an innovation's success, they must also determine whom to approach, when, and with which arguments. Top management and ultimate uisers have to buy into the innovation to make it succeed, but marketing an idea to these two groups requires very different approaches.

Top management, most concerned with an innovation's likely effect on the bottom line, is accustomed to receiving proposals that specify return on investment and paybacks. Many of today's computerized technologies, however, do not lend themselves to justification in traditional financial terms, yet they may be essential to a company's future. Amid growing calls for the accounting profession to provide better means to assess the value of robots, CAD, and computer-integrated manufacturing, some companies are beginning to realize the limitations of traditional capital bugeting models.[3]

Selling top management on the case for new technology—without simultaneous involvement of user organizations in the decision-making process—is not enough. It is equally important for users of an innovation to develop "ownership" of technology. The meaning of this term depends largely on the scope of the project. Although it is patently impossible to involve all users in the choice and/or development of an innovation, that is no excuse not to involve their representatives.

Perhaps even more important is to plan for the transfer of knowledge from the old operations, in which people knew the materials and the product very well, to the new process, which outsiders may initially design and run. The developers of the new process (especially when it is computer software) often know their tools very well, but rarely do they understand the materials and processes to which their software is applied as well as the people on the plant floor who have been working with both for years. At the very least, managers should provide some mechanism and time for such knowledge to flow from experienced worker to developer.

Promotion versus Hype

Many a technology developer will confess bewilderment that innovations do not win automatic acceptance. It may be overly optimistic to believe that an innovation will sell itself, but it is equally dangerous to oversell the new system. Novel and exotic technologies are especially vulnerable to hype.

Articles in the media about robots and artificial intelligence, for example, have raised expectations far higher than the actual performance of current technologies warrant. Potential users quickly grow disillusioned when much touted innovations perform below expectations.

[3]See Donald Gerwin, "Do's and Don'ts of Computerized Manufacturing." *Harvard Business Review*, March-April, 1982, p. 107; Bella Gold, "CAM Sets New Rules for Production. *Harvard Business Review*, November-December, 1982, p. 88; Joel D. Goldhar and Mariann Jelinek, "Plan For Economies of Scope." *Harvard Business Review*, November-December, 1983, p. 141; and Robert S. Kaplan, "Yesterday's Accounting Undermines Production." *Harvard Business Review*, July-August, 1984, p. 95.

Risky Site, Safe Innovation

There are two reasons for conducting a pilot operation before introducing an innovation across the board in a large organization: first, to serve as an experiment and prove technical feasibility to top management and, second, to serve as a credible demonstration model for other units in the organization. These two purposes are not always compatible.

Testing the new technology at the worst performing unit, even though it may be where the innovation is most needed and would show the most spectacular results, is no better a choice. If the project fizzles, the implementation manager will not know how much of the failure was caused by extraordinary problems with the site and how much by the inherent properties of the technology. If the project succeeds, critics will be quick to note that anything would have helped operations at that site.

The solution, therefore, is to be clear about the purpose of the test, experimental or demonstration, and then to choose the site that best matches the need. The customized end of one large computer manufacturer's business suffered from a problem. If customers cancelled orders, the partially built systems were either totally scrapped—that is, broken down into components and sent back to the warehouse—matched with incoming orders to determine if the fit was close enough to warrant retrofitting. When this matching process, which had been done manually, was computerized, the first applications site was an operation with an enthusiastic champion, but it was to be phased out in a matter of months. The site was politically risk free but not useful for a demonstration. Although the first application was successful, the operation closed down before the site could serve as a demonstration for other plants, and the implementation manager in charge of the next site had to start all over.

Even if managers realize that the trial of a new technology is a critical demonstration, they do not always ask the next question: a demonstration for whom? The physical and organizational position of the first site will heavily influence who the next wave of users will be.

Obviously, it is not always possible to site new equipment for everyone's convenience. Even so, the placement of an innovation frequently determined who uses the new technology first and most. If the equipment is located farther away from older or more reluctant potential users, they have a ready excuse for avoiding it. Consequently, managers who do not consider physical layout in their implementation strategies may, by default, select as first users people with little or no influence in the organization.

Often, however, an implementation manager has to create new role models by siting the innovation where the workers, most open to change, can demystify the technology for others by using it themselves. Although it is definitely a mistake to correlate resistance with age per se, it remains true that people with a long-term investment in certain routines and skills often hesitate to give up the security of those habits. Again, it is best to avoid extremes and to site new technology near workers who are fairly open to change but not so different from those whose resistance makes them poor models.

The Many and The One

If an innovation is to succeed, the implementation team must include: (1) a sponsor, usually a fairly high-level person who makes sure that the project receives financial and manpower resources and who is wise about the politics of the organization; (2) a champion, who is a salesperson, diplomat, and problem solver for the innovation; (3) a project manager, who oversees administrative details; and (4) an integrator, who manages conflicting priorities and molds the group through communication skills. Since these are roles more than one person can fulfill a given function, and one individual can take on more than a single role.

Even if all these roles are filled, however, the project can still stall if the organization does not vest sufficient authority in one person to make things happen. One of these individuals, usually the sponsor or the champion, must have enough organizational power to mobilize the necessary resources, and that power base must encompass both technology developers and users.

There are, of course, many ways to mobilize supplies and people. By encouraging ownership of an innovation in a user organization, for example, skillful advocates can create a power base to pull (rather than push) the innovation along. But enthusiasm for a new technology is not enough. New technology usually requires a supportive infrastructure and the allocation of scarce resource for preparing the implementation site. A champion based in the development group with no authority among the receivers must rely on time-consuming individual persuasion to garner the necessary resources. Further, even if prospective users believe in an innovation's worth, they may have to convince their superiors to free up those resources.

LEGITIMATE RESISTANCE TO CHANGE

Overt resistance to an innovation often grows out of mistakes or overlooked issues in an implementation plan. Tacit resistance does not disappear but ferments, grows into sabotage, or surfaces later when resources are depleted. Because the advocates of change have such a clear view of an innovation's benefits, resistance often catches them by surprise. A manager should not shrug such resistance aside on the dual assumption that it is an irrational clinging to the status quo and that there is nothing to be done about it. Clinging to the status quo it may indeed be—but irrational, rarely. And managers can do something about it.

Thus the beginning of wisdom is to anticipate opposition. An innovation needs a champion to nurture it, and any new technology capable of inspiring strong advocacy will also provoke opposition. Where there are product champions, there will also be innovation assassins. Assassins, moreover, can fell a project with just one well-aimed bullet, but champions need to marshal forces and nurture support to implement new technology in the face of resistance. The most common reasons for opposition to a new technology are fear of the loss of skills or power and absence of an apparent personal benefit.

Fear of Loss

As talk about the deskilling potential of new computerized technologies has grown, unions are seeking retraining for their members whom automation would otherwise displace. Many companies are upgrading the status of their workers who are forced to trade hard earned manual skills for the often dreary routine of button pushing. Although the problem is far from being resolved, it has at least merited recognition.

There is, however, another aspect of deskilling that has been much less obvious to implementors: the simple necessity of extending concern about deskilling to foremen and supervisors. They do not, of course, actually have to run the new machinery or to possess the intimate knowledge of the system that daily operators do. Even so, giving subordinates knowledge that supervisors and foremen do not have undermines their credibility. If the foremen or supervisors worked their way up through the ranks, they will know the old machinery well. They served as problem solvers when it broke down and derived no small part of their authority from their experience with it. To train their subordinates and leave them out is to invite hostility.

Another reason for resistance is fear that the innovation will be politically enfeebling and that supervisors and even operators will lose some control by adopting it. A good implementation plan should try to identify where a loss of power may occur so that managers can anticipate and possibly avert any problems arising from that loss.

Personal Benefit

An innovation must offer an obvious advantage over whatever it replaces, or potential users will have little incentive to use it. The more visible the costs of an innovation (financial, convenience, the need to learn new skills), the greater the importance of making potential benefits and rewards apparent. These benefits include expended influence over work (stopping a production line), increased value of work (no in-process inventory), greater recognition (being part of a valued implementation team), solution of a long standing problem (a shop floor control system that gives up-to-the-minute production reports), and preservation of jobs.

It is easy for managers to forget that benefits buried in the system which they can see because of their position, may be totally invisible to the operators on whom the success of the innovation depends. A new technology may pay off for an organization as a whole but not for individuals in any form they can recognize. That is why it is so important to make these benefits visible through encouragement from supervisors as well as through explicit and timely feedback on how the innovation is affecting the workers output. In general, the faster the positive feedback to users, the more visible the benefits will be.

In retrospect, it is clear that all the benefits of the new technology accrued to the organization, not to the individuals who used it. In fact, many potential users thought they would be penalized for using the new methodology, since managers judged their performance on speed and low cost, not on the quality of their output. The organization's rhetoric supported, indeed mandated, use of the new technology but the reward structure militated against it.

Now, contrast this situation with one in which managers gave some thought to the challenge of translating organizational benefits into individual rewards. Before installing a shop floor control system, a major appliance manufacturer conducted informal research into the problems of the hourly work force. They discovered that the current voucher system never permitted workers to know how much their pay would be in a given week. A small modification of the control system's design made it possible for employees to receive a report on cumulative salary with each job they entered. Although this piece of information was not central to the needs of the organization, adding it to the system's design was a low cost way to boost the innovation's benefits to workers. This small feature more than compensated them for the pain of developing new skills and habits, and the advantage of the new system over the old was apparent every time they used it.

A WORD ABOUT HEDGERS

Besides the champions and assassins in an organization, there will always be some "hedgers," individuals who refuse to take a stand against an innovation so that others can address their objections but who also refuse to support the new technology. They straddle the fence, ready to leap down on either side to declare that they had foreseen the value of the innovation all along or that they had known it would fail from the start. These risk-averse managers can affect the future of a new technology when they are a key link in the implementation plan. Because these hedgers are usually waiting for signals to tell them which way to leap, astute implementation managers will see to it that they receive the appropriate signals from those higher up in the organization.

Like product assassins, hedgers can be found at any level in an organization, and dealing with them effectively requires a sequence of actions. The first, and the easiest, is to persuade top management to take some kind of quick symbolic action in support of the innovation. Whether the action takes the form of a memo, a speech, or a minor policy change, it must send a signal that top management will stand behind this technology even in a budget crisis.

The second step, which is harder, is to help managers at all levels send out the right signals. If, for instance, the first step was an announcement of a new drive for quality, the second should be to increase the emphasis on quality throughout the company. If workers hear an announcement about a new quality program but continue with impunity to ship products that they know are inferior, the initial symbolic gesture loses potency. Worse, all future gestures lose credibility too.

The third step is the hardest—and the most necessary. Managers must bring the criteria used to judge the performance of innovation users into conformance with the demands of the new technology. New techndologies often require new measures. If, for example, a new, structured software technique requires more time than did the old, managers must evaluate programmer-analysts less on the basis of the quality of output than on the basis of its quality.

Further, because productivity commonly declines whenever a new technology is introduced, more accurate measurements of productivity in the old sense may lead supervisors to fear that their performance will look worse—not least because, with a fully automated system, direct labor drops but indirect labor grows.

Other adjustments might include a phase-in period for the new technology during which the usual output measurements do not apply. It might also make sense to reward people for preventing rather than just solving problems and for developing work behavior identified with the new technology. Although operators do not respond well when they view technological systems as controlling their behavior, they respond quite well when a system gives them feedback on their performance and the performance of their machines. Information increases the amount of control people have over their environment.

Converting hedgers into believers is not a simple task, but it is one more of the inescapable challenges managers face as they try to implement new technology. Indeed, as the competitive environment changes and as the systematic effects of new technologies become even more pronounced, the work of implementing those technologies will increasingly pose for managers a distinctive set of challenges—not least, the task of creating organizations flexible enough to adjust, adapt, and learn continuously.

READING 9.2

Planning and Implementing Advanced Manufacturing Technology—The Tortoise and the Hare[4]

The title of this paper has probably bemused you. You may well be wondering what Aesop's fable of the tortoise and the hare has to do with implementing and planning advanced manufacturing technology. You will remember that in the fable the tortoise and the hare decided to have a race. The hare, who shot off and fell asleep, lost the race to the steady plodding tortoise.

In the race for manufacturing productivity it is striking that many approach the implementation of advanced manufacturing technology in the same way as the hare approached the start of this race. These companies decide that there must be some advantage to be gained from the new technologies. They allow a pilot project to be set up by an individual or some graduate who must understand the new computer-based technologies because none of the existing engineering staff does.

These companies are surprised that the technology does not live up to expectations. The result of two recent surveys demonstrate just how widespread are these problems:

1. The survey of MRP II (Manufacturing Resource Planning) users caried out by Oliver Wright Associates which found that 60 percent of implementations failed to provide the anticipated benefits.
2. The Engineering Council's survey of 300 companies using CAD/CAM (Computer-Aided Design and Computer-Aided Manufacturing) which found that 33 percent of solid

[4]P. McHugh, "Planning and Implementing Advanced Manufacturing Technology—The Tortoise and the Hare." This paper is reproduced from "Planning for Automated Manufacture." Reprinted with permission of the Council of the Institution of Mechanical Engineers. © 1986 Institution of Mechanical Engineers.

modeling systems typically used in aerospace and shipbuilding do not perform in the way their users hoped.

The Engineering Council through its industry director Graham Anthony commented that the fault lies in the application rather than the technology. The Council is concerned that too few managers understand the demands the CAD/CAM makes on the whole of the company's operations.

This brings us back to the group of enthusiasts endeavoring to install a pilot project. They are almost certain to fail to create a significant change in the business, not simply because their project is concerned with a small part of the business but because management is satisfied that they are taking action and fails to appreciate the wider impact the technology could and should have on their business.

We therefore arrive at the central theme of this paper. Implementation of AMT is a management problem. That is not to say that management has to be slow and plodding like a tortoise but that it must be methodical and retain a sense of purpose and consistent direction in its activities.

Advanced Manufacturing Technology is today a powerful competitive weapon. It is not the purpose of this paper to discuss this in detail, but the results of the 1985 survey into AMT implementation speaks for themselves. It showed manufacturing companies reducing lead times by 72 percent, stock by 60 percent, and increasing added value by 30 percent.

Despite this potential for successfully changing the cost structure of manufacturing companies, it is easy to fail. The following case studies illustrate just how dramatic this failure can be. Obviously in a paper of this nature it is not politics to name the companies and supplies involved so their identities have been deliberately suppressed, however, the general type of industry and the company and case statistics are accurate. Each short case study is introduced by the major issue which it illustrates.

CASE 1—IMPLEMENTATION LONGER THAN TWO YEARS

This company, part of an international group, manufacturers a wide range of pumps and ancillary optional equipment. They employ 3,500 people in design, component manufacture, assembly and test. The production director decided that to gain control over material and deliveries that it should install a sophisticated MRP II (Manufacturing Resource Planning) system. He correctly identified that the DP department should not play the major role in this project so a small user team was set up. The team began their tasks with enthusiasm and drew up the broad phases of the implementation. The production director held monthly meetings to monitor progress. So far, so good; but then things began to go wrong: the user production departments were not fully involved in determining the system specifications. The overall plan was unclear. The implementation of the various phases took longer and longer. The young members of the project team moved off to "greater" things. Today, five years down the road a pilot MRP has just been run. The moral here is simple. Do not plan the implementation of any phase of a project over more than two years. If you do, the momentum of the project will not be maintained, the key staff will leave and you will spend more time building interim solutions than the final system.

CASE 2—PUSHING ESTABLISHED TECHNOLOGY TOO FAR

This company, part of a European group, manufactures gearboxes for industrial, automotive and marine applications. They employ 2,500 in design, manufacturing, assembly and test. It was decided that a new gearbox casing machining facility was needed to meet a projected increase in demand for part of the range used in the automotive industry. The existing plant was judged to be inappropriate for the volumes and flexibility needed. After looking at the automotive industry processes for similar products and discussing the requirements with a number of manufacturers, a turnkey contract was placed. This contract specified a highly flexible transfer line costing £7 million. The problems then began. The transfer line technology was unable to handle the rapid product changes and the control systems, based on relay technology, were inflexible. At the same time the industry moved toward FMS (Flexible Manufacturing System) technology and microprocessor-based control systems. Ultimately the system failed to meet its specification and an expensive court case resulted in the supplier accepting liability and the line being sold to a scrap dealer. The morals again are clear. It is essential to find out how technology is moving, to evaluate the impact of these changes, not to rely totally on turnkey vendors and not to push existing technology too far.

CASE 3—ATTENTION TO FINE ENGINEERING DETAILS

There are many cases of AMT projects failing to perform due to the lack of attention to detail. In this case study the impact of this, on a materials handling robot servicing three machine tools, illustrates the delays and costs which occur to put right this basic fault. The robot handling system concerned was designed as part of a machining cell producing heavy cast iron roller casings. The principle justification being that a man doing the same job would have to lift 60 tons of components a shift. At this point the basic engineering went well and despite some problems caused by the need to interface electrically between four different supplier control systems, the system was ready on time for commissioning. At this point, the problems began. The bearings were required to locate on fixtures permanently fixed to the machine heads. However during the rough and finish boring operations a great deal of cast swarf and dust was generated. With manual loading this dust could be easily cleared from both the fixtures and the components. With the robot, however, this was far from easy. As a result poor location occurred with machine jams and unreliable quality. It took 18 months to bring the system reliability up to specification which was achieved by a multitude of fixed brushes, air-jets and a paraffin wash being introduced in the cycle. This case study illustrates just how important attention is to fine detail both in the case of systems and mechanics.

CASE 4—SET UP THE PROJECT TEAMS AND PLANNING SYSTEMS FIRST

On many occasions Advanced Manufacturing Technology is introduced to create a fundamental change to the cost structure of a manufacturing business. Typically this will involve a charge from the product cost largely being determined by direct labor to it being based or the cost of capital. When this occurs the business involved needs to adapt significantly. This adaption in its own right requires people with experience of managing technology change—a situation which is unlikely to exist in a business based on labor. This was illustrated by one of the largest United Kingdom pharmaceutical manufacturers who produce batches of various medicines and bottles them for distribution. They found that their business was being threatened by smaller, more specialized producers. As a competitive response they determined to reduce their costs significantly through a restructuring of the organization and a move to capital intensive manufacturing. The reduced costs would then force a restructuring of their industry. High level plans were laid which showed how by halving their labor force of 4,000 and introducing a new plant they would reduce costs by £150 million. The labor reduction program went well. However, as they began to prepare specifications for the new plant they found that the planning had not been completed in sufficient detail and the engineering staff was not of the standard necessary to manage such a large change. Consequently, the project was delayed for one year while appropriate staff was recruited and a new project planning system introduced.

CASE 5—GET SENIOR MANAGEMENT COMMITMENT

Despite the technical success of some projects, they often fail to address the critical problems of the manufacturing business and more tragically fail to impact on the areas where they should. Just how this occurs is evident from the experience of one of the largest manufacturers of machine tool systems. These systems, involving mechanical, electrical and electronic assemblies, are designed and built to contracts. Traditionally the industry has engaged high margins and relaxed delivery schedules. In this environment the production engineering department, headed by a forthright and forseeing chief production engineer has made significant investments. They had introduced computer-aided design, process planning, part programming, tool offset registration and interfaces to a number of machining centers through direct numerical control. Today this installation is technically one of the most advanced in Great Britain. It has nonetheless failed to impact on the performance of the company for two reasons. Firstly the real problem facing the company was the planning and control of materials which was unaffected by the new technology. Secondly no designs were put onto the CAD system except by the production engineers because the technical director did not believe he would get a productivity improvement from CAD. At this point the company's market position was weakened by losing a major order on cost grounds. The general manager, seeing that the production engineering team had failed to impact on costs, decided to reduce the staff through redundancy and institute a program of materials control. In this tragic example for the production engineers who felt rightly that they had done a good technical job the moral is clear that senior management commitment must be engaged in from the beginning and that the project must remain strongly focused on achieving business rather than technical objectives.

In what has proceeded we have seen that there are a number of prerequisites for success in planning and implementing advanced manufacturing technology. These are:

- Do not expect a pilot project to impact significantly on your business.
- Have a realistic perception of the impact of AMT.
- Do not leave implementation to a group of enthusiasts.
- Ensure that management priorities are consistent throughout the project.
- Do not plan any phae of the implementation over more than two years.
- Involve the end user departments in the project development phases.
- In any phase of a project, base your plans on known technological capabilities.
- Pay attention to the level of detail of your initial plan if you want the estimates to be realistic.
- Particularly take care of the system's mechanical and electrical interfaces.
- Get the project teams and planning systems in place before you begin development.
- Ensure that the level of awareness in the organization of the technology's potential is there before you begin.
- Get senior management committed from the outset.
- Retain a strong business objective in your projects, do not look soley for technical success.

It is notable how all of these factors for success in implementing AMT relate to the earliest phase of the project, that of mobilizing and planning the resulting work. It is therefore not surprising that the "hare" approach to implementation so often fails. In the remainder of this paper we will be examining a model for successfully completing the early planning stages of a project to implementing AMT and illustrate this by an example.

The staged approach to planning AMT implementation relies on a number of carefully executed steps, some of which can be carried out in parallel. The overall approach is illustrated in Exhibit 9.1.

Exhibit 9.1 The Staged Approach to Implementation Planning

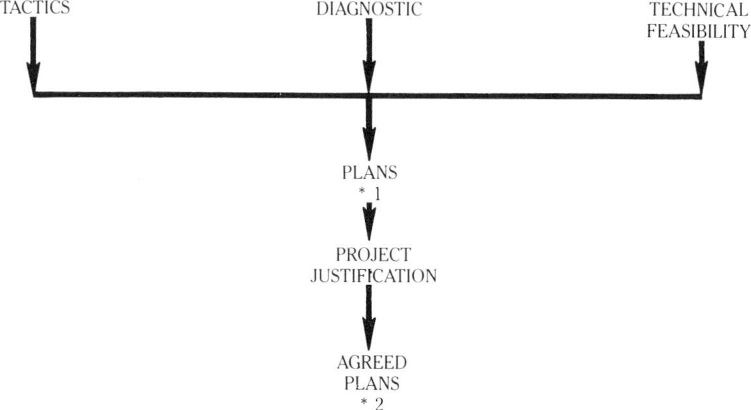

The first three activities are carried out largely in parallel. They are manufacturing tactics, diagnostic, and a technological feasibility study. These are discussed in more detail below.

Manufacturing Tactics

Perhaps more commonly called strategy, however, since strategy is a widely misused word today and has the connotations of being wishful thinking about the total business, "tactics" is more appropriate to AMT implementation. Quite simply this activity means thinking out the fundamentals on which the remainder of the project is to be based. These fundamentals, of which there are likely to be 30 or 40 in a typical manufacturing business, relate to the organization, technical and logistical, and systems building blocks such as:

- There will be only five levels of management between the hourly paid and board level.
- A common computer hardware supplier will be used for all microprocessor-based equipment.
- Batch sizes will be determined by periods of demand rather than any technological constraint.
- System will be packaged based rather than bespoke.

These fundamentals must be thought out, collected into a common document and agreed by senior management before detailed plans may be laid. Often the tactics can be expressed in very simple terms such as those used by Austin Pover "to be the lowest cost automobile producer" of IBM "to be the world leader in assembly automation." Experience shows however that by expressing tactics under a number of headings one is able to set a more balanced and useful target.

Diagnostic

A health check of the current organization without regard for planned improvements. The review should cover all functions from research through design, drafting, production engineering, manufacturing technology, planning systems and inventory control to quality assurance and finance. Its purpose is to highlight those areas of the business where the new systems and technologies will have the greatest impact and hence should be implemented first. As a bonus, a review of this type also enables the business to be measured against international industry norms and provides an opportunity to undertake improvement projects which in their own right can give valuable business gains. In many cases these improvement activities can be carried out without any technology implementation. The purpose of the diagnostic, as well as providing the priorities for AMT, also enables a high degree of management consensus to be obtained on the priorities for the business.

Technological Feasibility

This must be managed in parallel with the definition of tactics and the diagnostic review. Its purpose is to examine the technologies in terms of techniques, systems and hardware which exists on the market and which may be used to move the business from the diagnostic position to that expressed by the tactics.

Experience shows that it is best to carry out this review without cost constraints in order to capture the creativity of technical staff. Cost and other resource constraints can be applied at the later project justification activity. Finally it is important not to make technology forecasts in this study, although newly released products may be assumed to be available. Again this approach is based on experience since products in the research stage are unlikely to have matured to really useful, proven products within the time frame of any AMT project as they generally take up to five years to mature. This fact is soundly reassuring for manufacturing companies as the purchasers of AMT since it enables them to minimize the risk of introducing inappropriate or poorly developed technology. It is generally difficult enough to introduce the technology to an organization, without having to cope with systems and technology failure.

Plan Issue 1

With the tactics, diagnostic and technology feasibility completed, it is possible to draw up plans for developing and implementing the AMT. From what has been said earlier there are some guidelines which should be followed:

- Each phase of the project should be less than two years.
- Plans should be detailed enough to enable reliable resource estimation to be made.
- If you need to enhance the skill level of the organization or to carry out an education program do it before attempting to specify the technology.
- Set up improvement projects in parallel with technology development.

There is a need to recognize that the plans need only address the major 20 percent of problems since these will give on the time honored rules of Pareto 80 percent of the benefits. Finally Murphy's Law applies to AMT, perhaps more than in any other area:

- If something can go wrong it will.
- You won't find what will go wrong until it happens.

Therefore, plans should contain the minimum of preanalysis of error conditions and the maximum of time for debugging and commissioning. Fortunately the microprocessor-based technologies give a great deal of freedom for error correction. It is therefore appropriate to allow for extensive enlargement and modification of the control systems. By using structured programming techniques this can be most easily accomplished.

Project Justification

Of all the areas relating to AMT, that of justification is the most widely discussed. Many papers have addressed the issue and business "gurus" have pronounced on their approach. Generally there are two views of project justification. View one which says that because of its strategic nature AMT cannot be financially justified in traditional terms, and view two which says that traditional techniques of estimates are inappropriate so that some new basis such as asset productivity should be used. In practice project justification requires a combination of these views. One should look at the hard savings, estimate carefully the effect of integration and set the results against the business objectives. This means that a top down and bottom up look at the project should be reconciled by using the experience of other businesses and then the resulting rate of return evaluated against long term objectives. Fortunately there are two great truths about AMT justification, firstly that the resources required are always more than those estimated and secondly so are the benefits. Since both these effects move the resultant return in the same direction by allowing a large (say 15 percent) contingency in resources one can achieve the expected return.

Plan Issue 2

By limiting the plans with the availability of resources such as manpower, skills, capital and revenue, the uncost constrained technical solutions can be modified. The output of this process being a final AMT plan which can be approved and authorized for implementation.

It is useful to illustrate the application of the staged approach the example has been chosen of a supplier of mechanical systems to the aerospace industry. This company employs 1,500 people in design, manufacture and test of complex mechanical systems involving much detailed engineering analysis and machining to tight tolerances with exotic materials. Some years ago a start was made to introduce three dimensional modeling, part programming, process planning, and a production planning system. The company coming under pressure from the MOD for cost effectiveness and realizing that its traditional markets were limited, determined to introduce extensive AMT in order to give it a new advanced capability for the design and manufacture of defense systems.

The company, having determined their strategy, turned to a major computer hardware and systems supplier for the technical feasibility study. The study identified that the objectives of the business could be met by a four phase, £5 million implementation plan which would be executed over five years. In each phase of the project elements of the total system would be laid down or expanded. The complete system is shown in Exhibit 9.2.

In the first phase of the project, for example, it was decided to lay down the basic production planning systems to replace those currently in existence. Then to link the existing 3-D modeling systems to the part programming system so that complex geometry could be automatically transferred. Finally, to provide a DNC link to the shop floor.

The company then asked management consultants, Coopers & Lybrand, to assist

Exhibit 9.2 Final Advanced Manufacturing Technology (AMT) Systems to be Installed in an Aerospace Manufacturer

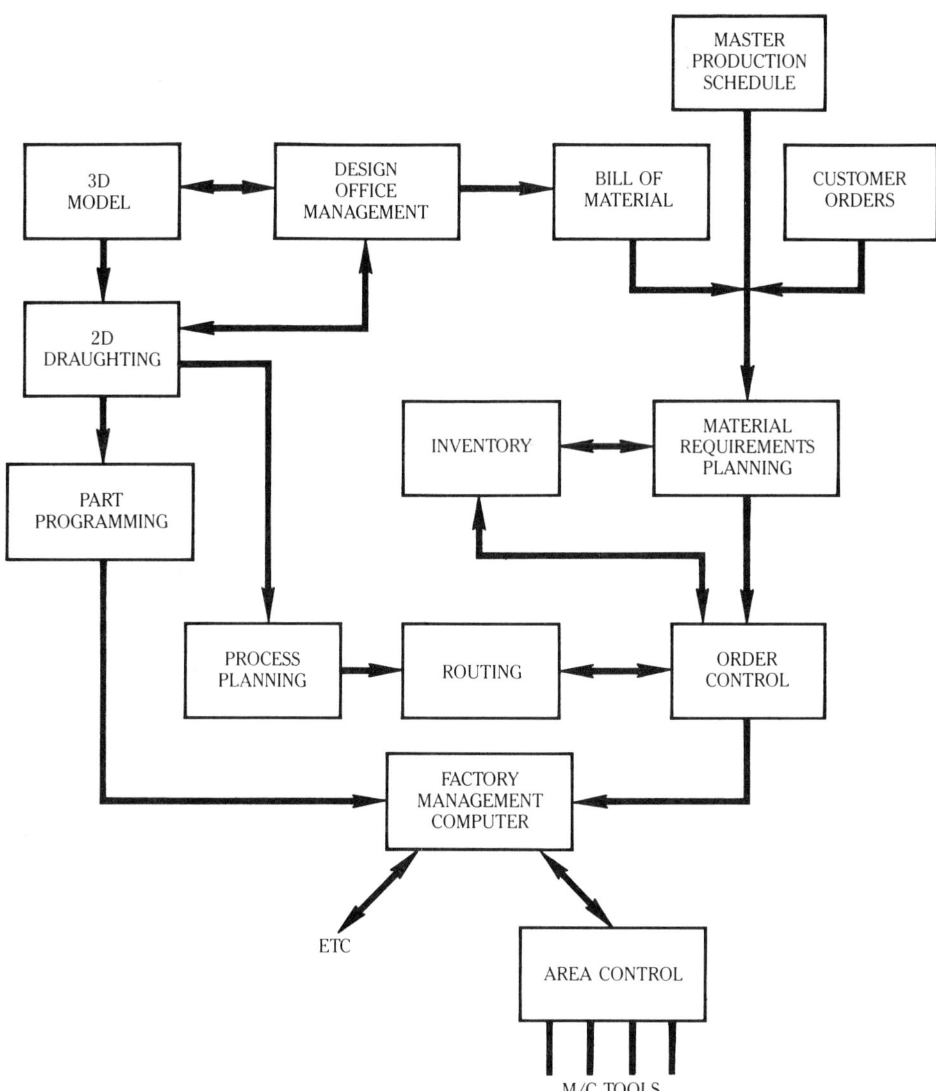

with the diagnostic activity. This was completed in six weeks and involved a wide range evaluation of performance in all areas of the company. The diagnostic findings were presented to senior management who agreed that they should form the basis for the AMT plans.

The plans drawn up as a result of the tactics, diagnostic and technical feasibility modified slightly the four phases given by the original technical feasibility report. The plans also addressed a number of improvement projects to be undertaken as a basis for establishing the latter systems.

In the first phase of the total project for example, 17 subprojects were defined which ranged from short team improvements in stock recording, through program management to the selection and installation of a package-based MRP system.

A project organization was also established at this time as shown in Exhibit 9.3. This organization consisted of a Steering Committee composed of main board members and was chaired by the managing director. To the Steering Committee reported the project manager who coordinated the various task activities. The project manager was also a member of two working committees who work weekly; one for CIE (Computer-Integrated Engineering), the other for MRP (Manufacturing Resource Planning). These working committees were attended by the task leader of each of the 17 subprojects. Each task leader in turn had his own team members who met on a regular basis.

Exhibit 9.3 AMT Project Organization

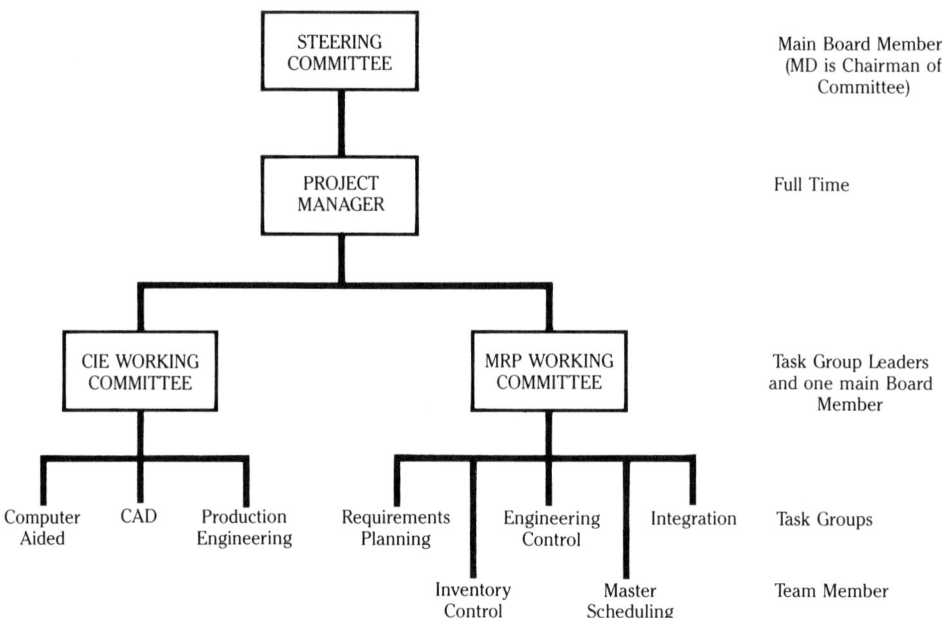

The first issue of the plans was not subjected to a justification process. This was achieved by looking at each area of AMT to be installed and evaluating its hard savings in the primary and secondary business functions affected. The results of this exercise were then compared with experiences in other industries and modified to bring out the synergy benefits which occur in integrated systems. The project justification report took one month to complete with the assistance of a microbased spreadsheet. The result was favorable and showed a four-year return on the investment of £5 million with an internal rate of return of the order of 30 percent. Sensitivity was also investigated by assuming that only a percentage of the benefits would be obtained. Finally the project plans were modified in line with the resource smoothing carried out in the previous step. These final plans were issued in a comprehensive report to top management and approved by the Steering Committee for implementation.

The net result of the planning stage of the project was evident in the forthcoming months. Management was aware of the need to commit their time to the project. More detailed plans and task team mobilization were carried out smoothly. The benefits of the first stages of implementation came in on time. The system being installed met both the business and operational objectives of the organization.

CONCLUSION

The paper has illustrated many of the common pitfalls of planning for advanced manufacturing technology. These pitfalls can be avoided by the adoption of a carefully phased planning stage and not by rushing into development and implementation. The benefits to be gained are significant. Management seeking to change their business by AMT should emulate the tortoise in adopting a steady direct approach to their planning. They should avoid rushing off like a hare in pursuit of some ill-defined objective.

EPILOGUE

Implementation Process—Mixing Man and Machine

Implementation and integration of new manufacturing technologies are perhaps the most important issues facing firms attempting to take up the technological challenge. Realizing the strategic need for new technolgy, and the justification and appropriation of adequate financing are only preliminary steps leading to implementation. This is the most crucial stage, for poor implementation usually means significant waste and major cost overruns. Not only will there be a waste of human and financial resources, there may also be a substantial opportunity cost of gains which could have (and indeed should have) been realized.

Successful implementation requires several things. First, a detailed project plan is critical from the outset. A firm must explicitly consider where it is now, and then outline a detailed step-by-step plan for getting to where it wants to be. This plan should include time and resource allocation schedules, as well as significant "stepping-stone" points along the way. Exhibit 9.4 shows a sample of such a plan.

Whether a company can (or should) move through this implementation process slowly, in stages, or rapidly, in one great leap depends on several factors. It depends on overall corporate and industry norms and strategies; the firm's previous experience (if any) with the technology; the extent of operator training and resistance, and the simple economics of alternate methods.

Secondly, commitment to the project within the firm is the key. This means commitment at upper- and middle-management levels, as well as on the shop floor. Without this commitment, proposed new technology applications will meet substantial resistance. This resistance may come from individuals through habit, fear, or personal insecurity, or it may come from the organization itself through power relationships, vested interests, unions, or structural barriers.

Exhibit 9.4 The Project Plan Elements

1. Overview—A short summary of the objectives and scope of the project. Includes goals, managerial structure and milestones.
2. Objectives—Detailed statements of the goals, including profit and competitive aims, as well as technical goals.
3. General Approach—Includes both managerial and technical approach, including any deviations from standard procedures. Technical approach relates the project to available technologies.
4. Contractual Aspects—Description of all reporting requirements, customer-supplied resources, liaison arrangements, advisory committees, project review and cancellation procedures, proprietary requirements, use of subcontractors, and the technical deliverables and their specifications and delivery schedule.
5. Schedules—Task schedules, with responsible signoffs, and milestone events.
6. Resources—Two parts: budgetary, consisting of capital and expense requirements by task, and cost monitoring and control procedures.
7. Personnel—Expected personnel requirements, including special skills, training required, recruiting problems expected, legal or policy restrictions, security clearances, and so forth. The needs are indexed to the project schedule.
8. Evaluation Procedures—The methods for monitoring, collecting, storing and evaluating the project's progress.
9. Potential Problems—A description of the things that have a significant possibility of negatively affecting the project, such as weather, subcontractor default, technical requirements and resource limitations.

Source: J. Meredith, "Automation Strategy Must Give Careful Attention to the Firm's Infrastructure." *Industrial Engineering*, May, 1986, pp. 68–73.

Much of this resistance may be sidestepped or overcome if the proper people are brought on-side early. People are generally less resistant to implementing a change they feel they have helped create. This may be done in several ways: employee education, communication, opportunities for participation, provision of rewards, or even manipulation and coercion in extreme circumstances.

Management may want to involve production workers early to garner their support, with the dual understanding that since they work closest to the process they may understand it the best and provide some very valid input in the course of the project. Such action may also help gain the support (or at least moderate the resistance) of unions to the implementation effort. It is important that management's involvement of employees not be a mere token involvement, since this has a high likelihood of backfiring. The days of deception, concealment and coercion are gone. Implementation efforts today should ideally be based on trust, respect and open, two-way communication.

Management commitment is also critical. Top management must fully support the project since it is they who allocate the funds which turn the wheels of change in the organization. Middle management has to be on-side because it is they who communicate with, control, and motivate lower level managers and shop floor workers whose commitment is essential. Commitment of lower level managers is absolutely vital, as theirs is often the group most threatened by new technology. In the absence of any of these conditions, new technology implementation will be difficult at best.

At all stages of implementation, management must monitor and alter the process if necessary. Delays may have to be addressed, problems resolved, or further progress modified as the learning process continues during the entire implementation cycle.

Whatever the reason for, and nature of, changes to the implementation plan, they must be communicated quickly and effectively to all parties involved.

Much consideration has been given in the literature to new technology implementation. It is a complex process integrating financial, strategic, operational, technical and human factors. If all these areas are to be managed together in a dynamic environment, sincere commitment, constant communication, and careful planning are critical. Ignoring such key front end factors will inevitably result in underrealization of the available benefits of the new technology.

CASE 9.1

ZBB (A)[5]

In November 1984, Mr. M. Okkerse, works manager at ZBB, was working on an automated bagging project proposed for 1985. ZBB, located at Koog a/d Zaan, about 10 miles north of Amsterdam, was one of Holland's oldest and largest cornstarch producers. Mr. Okkerse wished to review the proposal before submitting it to the executive group.

ZBB

ZBB produced cornstarch, by-products such as corn germs and protein, animal feed in fresh and dry form, and also through further processing glucose and iso-glucose and a variety of other starch derivatives—see Exhibit 9.5.

Cornstarch and starch derivatives were sold to a large variety of customers for a wide range of final products. These included the food and drinks industry in applications such as soft drinks, puddings, candy, sauces, soups, and bakery supplies; the textile industry for strengthening fibers; the paper industry for improving surface smoothness and printability; the glue industry for drilling sealant. ZBB's cornstarch faced significant competiton from other cornstarch/producers, as well as from potato starch. The producers of potato starch had lobbied extensively for government support on the basis that this was in the best interest of Dutch potato growers.

ZBB sold its products in all countries of the world, except North and South America, and was actively trying to increase its market share, so that the factory could be operated at a higher level of utilization.

[5]This case was written by Professor M. R. Leenders and Ir. B. A. A. M. van Baren for the sole purpose of providing for class discussion.

Exhibit 9.5 ZBB (A) The Industrial Processing of Corn

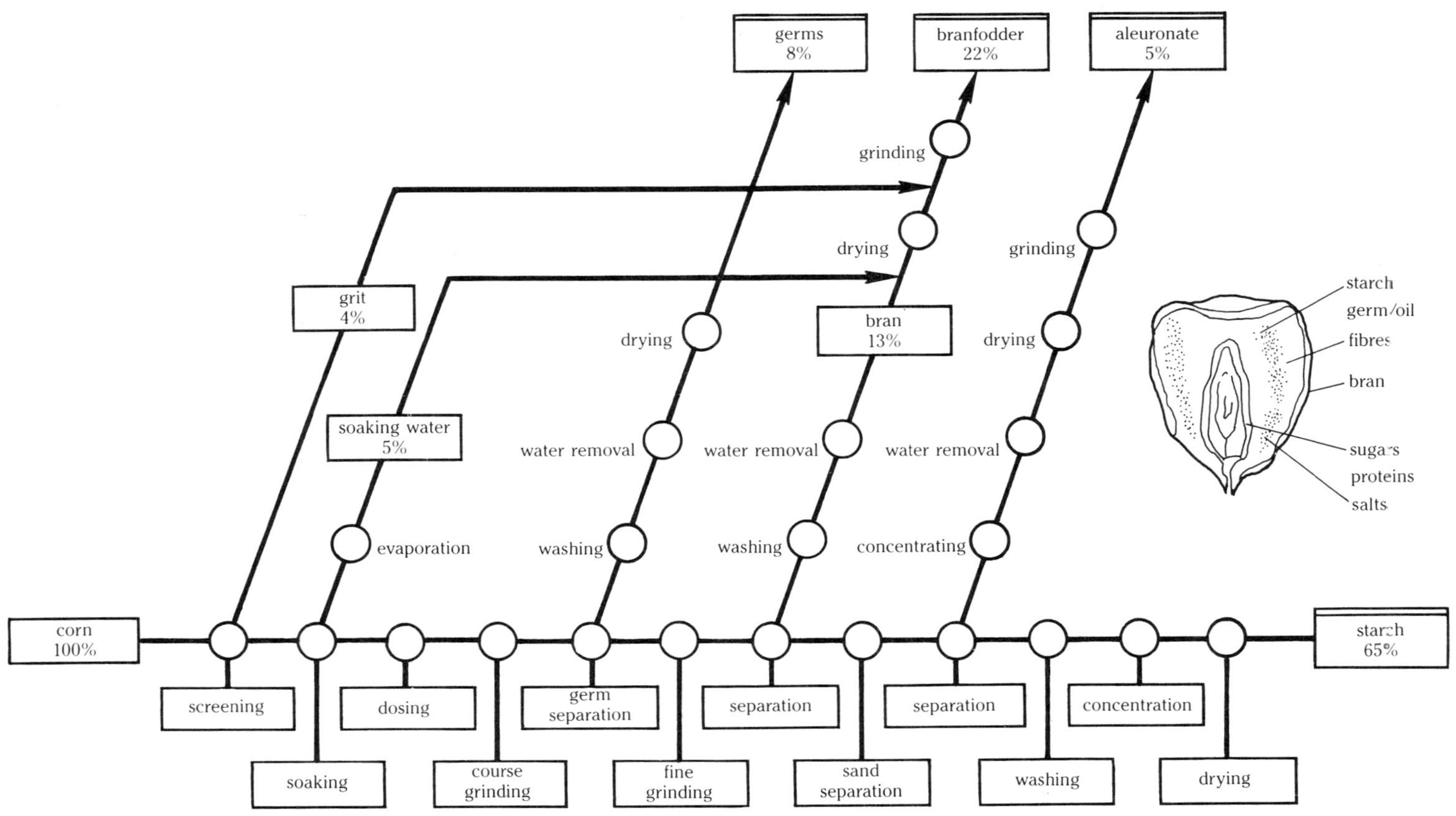

Total sales in 1984 were about *f*216 million[6] and profits about *f*5 million. Total employment stood at 343 full-time and 35 part-time employees. The original cornstarch factory on the ZBB site had been a windmill operation which in 1874 had been converted to steampower. In 1978 the company had gone bankrupt, largely caused by overly ambitious investments outside the Netherlands. Partially because of extensive lobbying by the employees of the Koog a/d Zaan site ZBB was reorganized on that site, and allowed to restart operations. The Dutch government set up a special holding company to hold all shares of the new organization. Three government appointed persons formed the directorate of this holding company. One of the conditions of the reorganization was that all profits and funds remaining after debt and interest repayment be reinvested in ZBB. The executive group of ZBB consisted of four persons, with Mr. M. Okkerse, as works manager, in charge of all manufacturing operations.

THE PROCESS

All corn processed at ZBB was imported from southern Europe or overseas. It was delivered by inland boat and cleaned and transferred to the corn silo. Exhibit 9.6 illustrates the process flow diagram.

Soaking

The process started with soaking: (1) to soften the kernels so that the various components could easily be separated; (2) to remove the largest part of the soluble sugars and proteins; and (3) to clean the kernel as much as possible. SO_2 containing water was added. Soaking required about 42 hours at a temperature of 50°C. The soaking water was subsequently evaporated to a 40–50 percent solids content and added to the animal feed, or sold as a raw material for the fabrication of penicillin.

Rough Milling

After soaking, the corn kernels were rough milled so that the corn germs would be separated from the other components. The corn germs floated to the top of suspension, were skimmed off, washed, and dried. Corn germs contained about 45 percent oil which could be used for cooking, or soap.

After corn germ separation, the corn shells and remaining corn pieces were finely ground and separated into starch, protein and shells.

The Bagging Operation

About half of all cornstarch produced was further processed into other products by ZBB. Of the remaining half about 40 percent was sold in bulk form and the remainder bagged in 50 kg bags.

[6]In 1984 one Dutch guilder (*f*) was worth approximately 30 U.S. cents.

Exhibit 9.6 ZBB (A) Process Flow Diagram

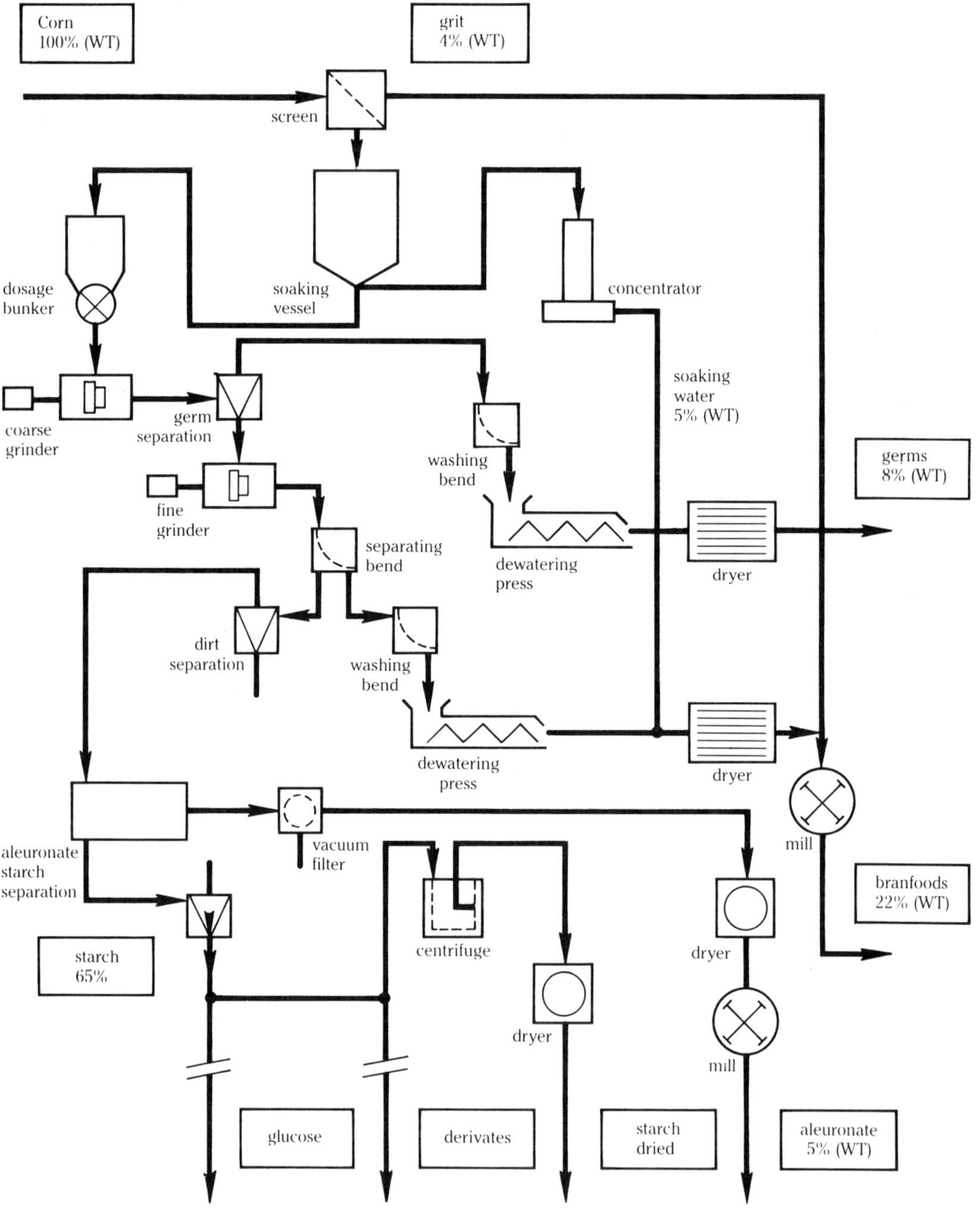

Cornstarch for bagging was moved from the main finished starch silo to a blowtank to delivery silos connected to the two filling stations. One worker per shift handled this semiautomated operation. Seated between two filling spouts, the operator grabbed a bag, pushed it over the spout and started the automatic filling operation. The machine weighed the contents progressively and when the bag was full, the operator pulled it off the filling spout and let it drop on the conveyor belt which took loaded bags to the automatic palletizer located in a nearby warehouse. While one bag was in the process of being filled at one spout, the operator could remove a bag from the other spout and start the filling operation. Total cycle time per bag was about 20 seconds. This gave the bagging operation some extra capacity, in the sense that the operator could replenish bags, have personal time and do some minor other duties during each shift. Silo capacity was such that it was necessary to run the bagging operation each shift that the starch producing operation was working.

The technology for the current bagging operation was about 12 years old. Installed in the early 1970s the bagging operation had not changed substantially since. Although different suppliers had at various times tried to sell automatic bagging units to ZBB management, each time investigation showed the technology not to be sufficiently reliable.

Bags

Depending on the location of the customer for the starch, bags were either three, four, or five walls thick. Overseas customers would require stronger bags than nearby domestic ones. A basic three wall bag cost about *f*0.80 and each additional wall cost about *f*0.10 more. Bags were supposed to be self-sealing, but when the bag did not close properly on removal from the filling spout, the operator would pull the closing flap shut. Bags also had ventilation holes so that the air could escape during filling. About every three months ZBB received an order for about 100 tons of cornstarch to be delivered in plastic bags. Plastic bags were more difficult to fill and handle than paperbags. Paperbags were supplied in lots of 20,000–50,000 from a well-known Dutch manufacturer with whom ZBB had annual contracts.

Although some starch suppliers provided starch in 25 kg bags, and ZBB sold some starch derivatives in 25 kg bags, ZBB sold basic cornstarch only in 50 kg bags. In 1984 a 50 kg bag of basic cornstarch sold for about *f*50.

THE AUTOMATED BAGGING PROPOSAL

In 1984 Mr. Okkerse had encouraged his staff to continue their efforts to look for productivity improvements. Although management and workers had proven that the ZBB operation could be viable since the reorganization, Mr. Okkerse considered the starch industry to be highly competitive with thin margins. He believed that without continuing improvement ZBB would be unable to survive. Opportunities to automate were part of the company's total effort at cost improvement. Other efforts included better methods, energy saving, and getting better utilization of people and equipment. In the opinion of Mr. Okkerse "the obvious automation targets are the boring and repetitive tasks in the plant. We are always on the lookout for ways and means of reducing the number of jobs in that category."

Mr. Okkerse continued: "Right now we are only running the factory at 120 hours per week with three shifts. A continuous operation like ours should obviously be run at a higher level, if market demand permits. I would like to get us to at least a four-shift operation at 136 hours and eventually to a full five-shift operation at 168 hours per week. At that level, we would normally plan on the basis of six persons for each plant position, with five on shift and one reserve for each five. At an annual cost, including fringe benefits, of about ƒ60,000 per person employed in the plant, the reduction of even one plant position starts to have a significant financial impact. In energy saving projects we want to get our savings back within a year at least, because who knows what is going to happen to real savings in energy? However, when it comes to labor savings we are willing to take a longer time like three years to recover our investment, because we feel the long term impact will be more significant."

Again in 1984, as in previous years, the basic starch bagging operation was reviewed as a potential target for automation. ZBB personnel noted with interest that significant equipment improvements had been made. Consequently, a serious investigation was started. There were several options initially. One option was to purchase the equipment from an independent equipment manufacturer. Although this idea was seriously examined, the ZBB project group did not recommend it. The option proposed to Mr. Okkerse was that the equipment be purchased from ZBB's bag supplier B&C N.V. This company had started to import American-made bag filling equipment in the 1960s. Subsequently, it had started making its own equipment and by 1984 it had become a significant domestic supplier. The particular unit proposed by this supplier used a French manufacturer's unit as the heart of the installation. It would be custom designed for ZBB's requirements and would be able to use bags produced by B&C as well as bags from other manufacturers. It would be setup so that both original filling spouts could be left in place, affording ZBB the opportunity to switch back to manual filling any time the machine malfunctioned.

Similar installations had been made by B&C at various nearby plants and the ZBB project team had visited some, including a cement bagging example. The proposed cost, including installation, was about ƒ350,000, and lead time about four months.

CURRENT STAFFING

Current staffing in the bagging area consisted of four persons per shift. Each shift was headed by a chemist who performed a variety of supervisory and quality control duties. The second person was a starch centrifugist. The third was a bag filler whose position would be replaced by the automatic bagger. The fourth person worked in the warehouse at the palletizing operation. The last two positions were considered to be at the lowest skill level in the plant and were, consequently, paid less than the others. In ZBB there were about 15 jobs at this lowest level in 1984.

Mr. Okkerse had made it standard practice that all crews be cross-trained on production tasks. Therefore, each of the four persons in the bagging area could physically perform the bagging operation. Thus, in the absence of the bagger, one of the others would serve as replacement. Mr. Okkerse was also aware that each of the other three persons in the bagging operation had a full set of activities to attend to.

Mr. Okkerse was also fully cognizant that other attempts to automate at ZBB had not always proceeded smoothly. The Dutch culture was such that it was difficult to fire employees. It would, therefore, be preferable to handle technological redundancies through attrition and retraining, rather than straight layoffs. Often, it was possible only after automation, to find out exactly what the human operator contributed to the job. Moreover, the very people who were asked to help implement the automation, were the ones whose jobs were in danger. This frequently meant a signficant period of adjustment and experimentation during start-up to address problems as they arose. How to maintain production and, at the same time, resolve human and technological problems associated with start-up was not an easy challenge. Such extra time and costs were seldom reflected in the original proposal. This was certainly true of the automated bagging proposal which detailed only equipment and installation costs totalling *f*350,000.

CASE 9.2

UWO Voice/Telephone Registration[7]

INTRODUCTION

Mark Hurley was impressed. As the manager of the University of Western Ontario's (UWO) Academic Records Department, he had just finished an hour on the telephone to Humber College, in Toronto, selecting and dropping courses and acquiring a wide range of information and advice—all through the Humber College computers! With the chaos and waiting lines that course registration created each September, the potential for a computer-based registration system at UWO was enormous. But could the complex, time-constrained registration system at UWO be computerized? If so, how, at what cost, and to what benefit would such a system be installed? And here it was, February 1987, with registrations for the next academic year slated to begin in March.

THE UNIVERSITY

The University of Western Ontario (UWO) was the second largest university in Ontario. Located in London, approximately 17,000 full-time and 5,000 part-time students attended classes in the 1986–87 academic year. Typical of other universities, Western was administered in a matrix fashion, with administrative and academic units combining efforts in committees which reported to the Senate and Board of Governors. Policy changes

[7]This case was written by Professor Hamid Noori and Mike Smith, 1988.

were developed at the committee level, presented to the Senate for approval and passed to the Board of Governors for final approval. Changes to the registration process would have to be initially introduced to the Subcommittee on Registration and Timetabling (SURT). After a thorough analysis of all the implications of these changes, SURT could decide to put forward a motion to the Senate. At the Senate the motion might be passed, defeated, or returned to SURT for further clarification. Any motion passed by the Senate was sent to the Board of Governors for final approval; normally, this approval was automatic.

The deliberate nature of the decision-making process ensured that policies were not changed unnecessarily, and that potential impact on all parts of the university was explored before implementation of the change. While minor changes were normally approved within a few months, major policy changes could take well over a year before final approval was given.

The Director of Admissions and Academic Records (DAAR) was a member of SURT and his immediate supervisor, the Academic Vice President (AVP) Student Services and Registrar, was a member of the Senate. Exhibits 9.7 and 9.8 show the organization of the University and the Department of Admissions and Academic Records, respectively.

Exhibit 9.7 Organization Chart—UWO Department of Admissions and Academic Records

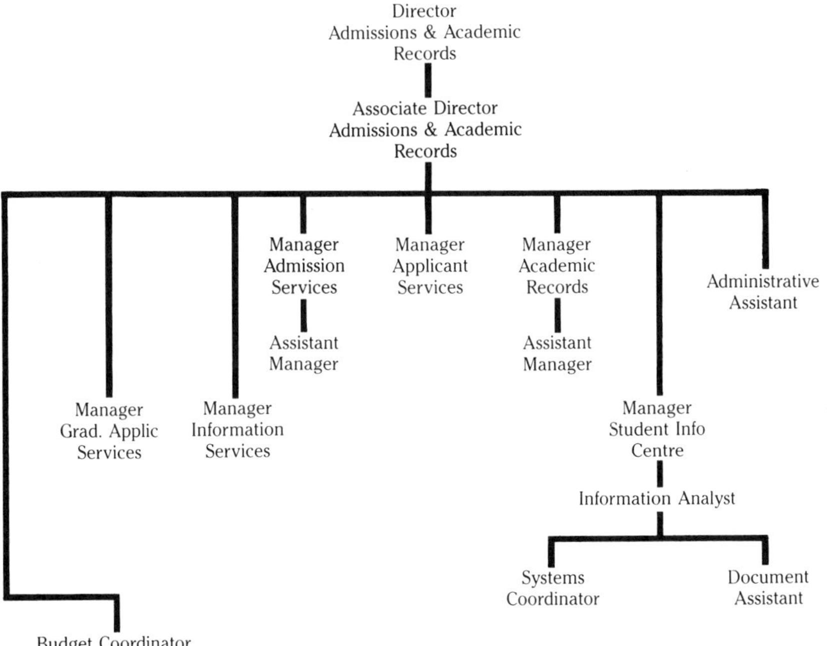

Exhibit 9.8 The University of Western Ontario Organization

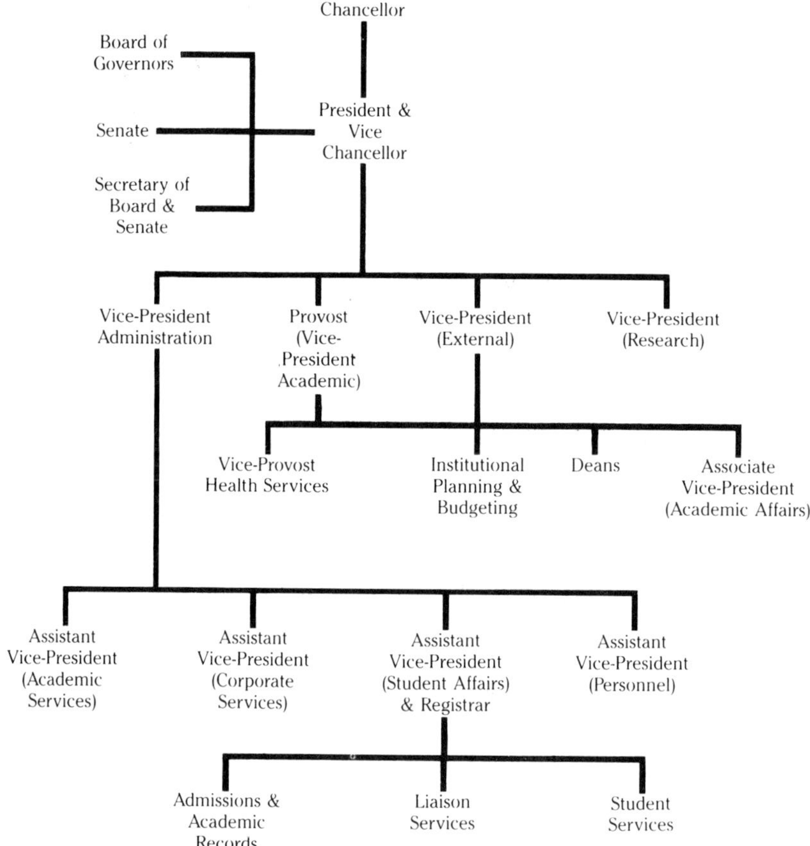

THE REGISTRATION PROCESS

A complex process of registration for undergraduate students had been developed at UWO (see Exhibit 9.9). In place since 1972, the system required upper class students to enter next year's courses during March. Each student received a calendar, a course selection form, an academic record, and a set of instructions from the DAAR. The students had to determine a program of courses for their next academic year and have this program approved by faculty counselors (professors appointed by each department). For example, a student in the third year of a political science program had to have approval from someone in that department. Required courses were initialed individually and the counselor signed the bottom of the form to indicate overall approval of the course selection. Students who were unsure of their choice could receive counseling from the academic counselors within their faculty (for example, Social Science). These counselors could also sign course selection forms.

Exhibit 9.9 Simplified Registration Flow Chart

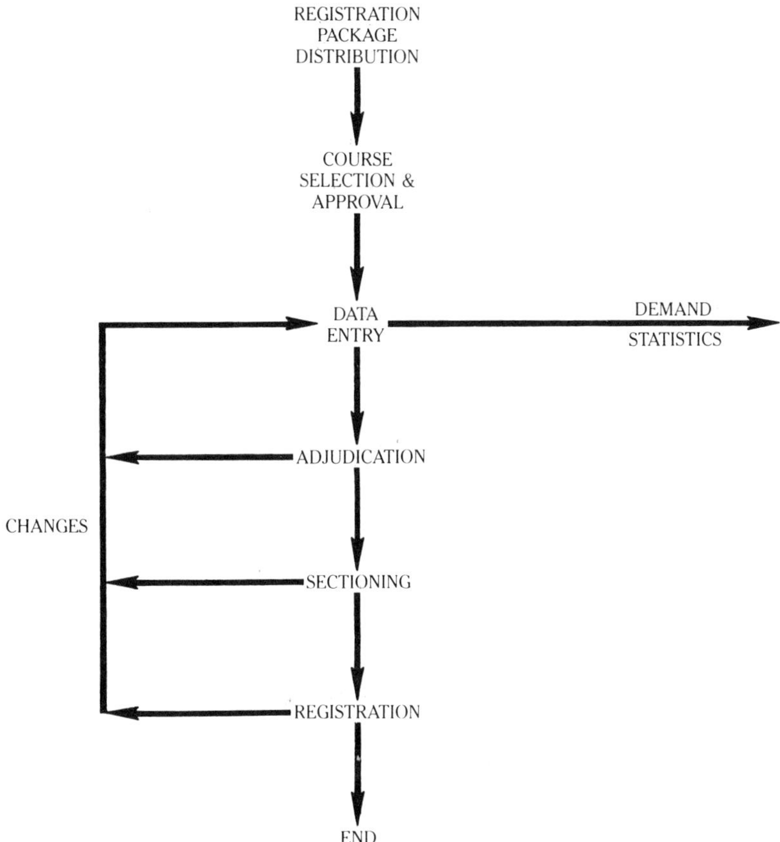

Approved course selection forms were to be returned to the DAAR by the end of the course selection period so that selections could be entered into the computer. This allowed a timetable to be produced for registration in September. For each course, demand statistics were generated from this data in April. This allowed each academic department to make alternative plans for high demand courses.

For students who selected courses in March, a review of their performance in April's final examinations occurred in May. Each student's program was looked at by the academic counselors of his or her faculty. Any students who were judged by their faculty as automatically eligible for a program (that is, marks were at the appropriate level and no critical courses were failed) would have their status changed on the computer to one which allowed them to be sectioned (timetabled) into the indiviudal sections of the courses selected in March.

Students who had a problem (for example, failed course) were sent a course Revision/Registration Form (R&R). Necessary changes were then made on this form and it was subsequently approved again by the student's faculty before submission to the DAAR. Course changes were entered onto the computer system and the student's registration status was updated for sectioning. Approximately 3,000 R&R's were issued in 1987. Failure to return the R&R placed the student in the Late Registrant category.

From mid-June to late August, students were timetabled into their courses using a computerized sectioning algorithm. Problems (for example, incomplete timetables due to data entry errors) would be verified, or corrected manually if time permitted. Approximately 20–25 percent of all timetables remained incomplete due to conflicting or filled courses.

Registration occurred during "Frosh Week," the four days following Labor Day in September. Students paid fees and received their computerized timetables. Those students with incomplete timetables (or blank timetables for Late Registrants) could begin adding courses immediately upon leaving the Registration area. For students with complete timetables, course changes could be made beginning on the following Monday, the first day of classes. Using a Course Change Request form (CCR) the student could add courses, drop courses, or change sections of courses for a specified period of time (for example, addition of courses had to be done within the first three weeks of classes). Each change on the CCR had to be approved by a faculty counselor for the department of the course (that is, History counselors approved History course changes, while English counselors approved English courses). Once students were satisfied with the changes, the CCR was submitted to his faculty (Arts, Science, Social Science, Physical Education) for approval.

An approved CCR was sent to the DAAR for entry of the changes onto the computer. Students could then request a revised version of their own timetables from the DAAR.

Approximately 22,000 course changes were recorded each year; each requiring signatures from departments and faculties. This was a ratio of 1:3 changes per student.

PROBLEMS WITH THE COURSE SELECTION PROCESS

The major problem with the current registration process was duplication of effort. Faculty members and academic counselors were requested to approve course selections in March, May, and September—all for the same student. The number of course changes in the Fall caused considerable frustration to counselors who had spent significant amounts of time approving earlier course selections, only to have the student change the courses in September on some apparent whim. For this reason, a number of faculty members were advocating a return to the older "Bull Ring" system, where students selected courses in one big free-for-all in September. A fixed number of spaces were available in courses under this system. Once a course was full a student had to make a different selection. The disadvantage of the "Bull Ring" was that it required all 17,000 of Western's returning students to line up for courses at the same time, creating a very chaotic situation. Furthermore, no advance notice of demand problems could be obtained and thus little advance planning was done to meet demand for specific courses.

VOICE/TELEPHONE REGISTRATION

The basic idea behind a Voice/Telephone Registration process was to provide a minicomputer which acted as a data link between a touch tone telephone and the mainframe computer system (Student Record System databases) of the university. Students who called the university would hear a taped voice which requested the student to punch a specific number to make course selections. Another number would allow the student to be routed to a telephone switchboard for transfer to an academic counseling office if so desired. Course selection would occur after courses had been processed in May. Therefore, while March course registration would be eliminated, the grades review in May would still be necessary, in order to instruct the computer as to the courses which were required by a student, or restricted to other students. Add/Drop in September would be expected to decrease since students would be making their selections at a later time. This suggested that students were more apt to select courses that were really important to them. Filled courses would be immediately identified to the student for selection of an alternate choice. Any time before September students could change their minds and amend their course selection.

The estimated cost of each system was $200,000, with additional costs for professional voice recording and other "add-ons." Final costs, including training and debugging, were conservatively estimated at $400,000.

SAVINGS TO ACADEMIC RECORDS

The sectioning process in the summer would be eliminated, removing six part-time positions at $5.65 per hour (35 hour week; average job lasting 12 weeks). Current add/drop processing averaged about 850 hours. Clerical salaries averaged $17,000 per year. Course registration used six clerical staff for 630 hours.

PROBLEMS WITH THE NEW SYSTEM

A number of problems would exist under a Voice/Telephone registration process, and while Mark had identified the following list, he was sure other problems would surface later:

1. The problem of advance planning would resurface. The elimination of March course registration would mean no demand statistics for courses would be available to departments in April.
2. The technology was new and unproven. Even if it worked, would the company still be in business to support it next month; next year?
3. How easily would the system interface with the existing computer system? The Student Record system databases were newly developed, in-house systems, and a number of "bugs" were still being worked out.

4. Policies would need to be changed. Who would ensure that students were selecting the correct courses? Would the onus of responsibility shift more to the student and away from the academic counselors? The new system would encourage this approach but a great deal of opposition within departments could be expected.
5. Security. Could the security of the students' records be maintained at the current level. Auditors at the university required three security levels for access to the Student Record System. Could this security be guaranteed when access by 17,000 students was required?
6. The change was radical. Could a radical change be implemented at a conservative, bureaucratic institution such as Western?
7. Timing. How long would it take to get approval? How long would it take for implementation and debugging? Information from the University of Alberta (which had just in-

Exhibit 9.10 Reactions from the University

- Not received with enthusiasm. If this is to be carried out by students the many checks will have to be made to ensure that:
  a. the student is eligible
  b. there is room in the course (section and lab), the limits must not be exceeded
  c. the student drops unwanted courses before entering new ones. If a student wants to take a reduced load this may not be easy to deal with
  d. departments would need frequent feedback to ascertain the status of a course

  If this is to be carried out by departments then special temporary telephone lines would have to be installed and access to student records and class listings would be needed for checking (a), (b) and (c) above.
- I heartily endorse the recommendations, especially those for "long-term implementation;" indeed I hope the long-term is understood to mean "as soon as possible."
- Your memorandum of May 12 regarding Add/Drop, Course Registration and Registratioan has been circulated to all the faculty within the department and the recommendations made are quite satisfactory.
- 1. With the current procedure for registration, whereby students are required to seek departmental approval for courses, a telephone system would be needed in each department. This would necessitate that each department be given access to student records, somewhat compromising the confidential nature of these records. If implemented, however, telephone registration should be restricted to those students for whom registering in person is difficult, for example, handicapped or elderly students, or those with full-time employment.
  2. If the entry of on-line add/drop data were extended to departments, our concern is that too many inexperienced and necessarily fallible operators may seriously muck things up.
- Good idea.
- Yes, I think telephone registration is well worth exploring.
- Very real concern exists over the actual implementation of the long-term proposals. It will be absolutely imperative that, before such a practice be established, a reliable software package with the capability of checking prerequisites and program requirements be devised and thoroughly proofed. At this time in our faculty our staff of counselors spend a great deal of time checking the courses and programs recommended by faculty at the department level. Alas, until a foolproof computer checking scheme is well-entrenched, the long-term recommendations may well be a recipe for disaster.
- Our reaction to the long-term recommendations is strongly negative at this time. Any movement away from personal contact with the student seems undesirable. We have enough trouble giving the students good advice under the present system.

troduced a similar system), suggested a one year period simply to develop all the messages which needed to be taped.

8. Conceptual confusion existed throughout the university. Not many of the academic units truly understood what was meant by a Voice/Telephone registration system. Thus, they were not adequately prepared to evaluate the consequences and merits of the new system.

CONCLUSION

Reactions to any new system would be mixed, Hurley knew. He had read reactions to Senate discussions of the concept, and while Senate had endorsed research into the proposal, Hurley realized that overcoming Faculty and Staff resistance would be a significant part of any implementation plan, see Exhibit 9.10. But what other implementation issues would there be? What impact might the implementation alternatives have? And how should a vendor be selected? In short, where do we go from here?

CASE 9.3

Transprovincial Engineering Limited (B)[8]

In November 1984, Michael Kinnear, manager of Toronto Operations for Transprovincial Engineering Limited (TEL), a national consulting engineering and planning firm, had to decide on the type of computer-assisted drafting and design (CADD) system that he should select for the company's pilot study into this technology. Although the choice had been narrowed to two brands, the selection of the better system and the general plan for bringing it into the branch's operations had yet to be decided.

The company had formed a CADD committee in the spring of 1982 to investigate such systems; its decision was to do nothing at that time about investing in any equipment. The uncertainties of technology at that particular time were considered to be too great, adding to the risks of high costs with unknown potential returns. Standardization and performance: cost ratio improvements were occurring rapidly with the technology and the CADD committee deemed it prudent to wait before becoming involved with CADD equipment.

"Basically," said Mr. Kinnear, "we got cold feet."

A few months after this decision had been made, the general economic recession of late 1982 brought a large part of the construction industry to a halt. Like many professional service operations, reduced business was handled at TEL by reducing staff accordingly. In fact, the major offices in the west were reduced in size to the point that none would have been large enough to generate the amount of drafting work to keep a CADD system operating at anything near an efficient level. It would also have been difficult to justify the expense of such an investment in face of the hard times that most of the branches were experiencing.

[8]D. McCutcheon and J. Haywood-Farmer (1985).

By the spring of 1984, the economy had recovered substantially. The company had also recovered, to the point that total staff was at about 80 percent of the 1982 level. The British Columbia and Alberta branches remained at lower levels of staffing, in some cases at only 50 percent of the 1982 levels.

A SECOND INVESTIGATION

In the meantime, significant technological advances had been made by CADD developers. A new generation of CADD systems was beginning to come on the market which provided better features, greater capacity, and lower cost. In March 1984, the first decided to investigate the possibilities of CADD once again. Mr. Kinnear was prominently involved in getting the study underway.

The CADD consultant hired previously by the firm was asked to do an updated evaluation of current company needs and capabilities. He recommended that the company purchase a package system produced by a leading hardware manufacturer. With a single work station, a 2D/3D system would cost about $350,000, and any additional work stations would cost about $100,000 each.

However, Mr. Kinnear was reluctant to commit the firm to any type until it was more familiar with systems that were already in place. He wanted to learn as much as possible about not only the systems but also the experience of others with the implementation and use of CADD technologies. Since it was now understood that the trial project would be carried out in the Toronto branch, the investigation was done largely by personnel from that office. Mr. Kinnear was in charge, with the investigation involving several others. The general attitude of those investigating the CADD system was quite positive, and Mr. Kinnear found himself playing a role of keeping the investigation in check, concerned that the enthusiasm would reduce the objectivity of the exercise.

An important part of the investigation was to see some of the CADD systems in use by actual operators, a task, made difficult by the relative scarcity of some types of systems and by the concerted efforts of some of the vendors to block direct contact between a potential customer and current users. However, when such visits were possible, they sometimes proved to be very revealing.

"We saw one consulting engineering firm that had gone into CADD in a big way—they got a deal on a big, sophisticated system," said Mr. Kinnear. "It almost bankrupted them. The whole organization was turned upside down; it was unprepared for all the changes that the system forced onto it. It was just too much all at once for the company to swallow—you could see the confusion it had brought on."

"We also visited a company that was just the opposite. The management there had gone about bringing its system in carefully. Even though their CADD system was an older, relatively unsophisticated type that was fairly labor intensive, they had taken care to ensure that the system fit properly into their operation, and now it is working beautifully."

The investigation was conducted over six months. By the end of 1984, TEL had compelling arguments for at least the Toronto office to get involved in a CADD system. The provincial government department for transportation and communication, a major client and influence in the local business, was compiling a list of those consulting firms that operated CADD systems internally, leading to speculation that the department might establish a preferred category for bidding purposes. At least half a dozen major competitors had CADD capabilities and a growing number of important clients (such as the railway companies) had CADD systems.

THE ALTERNATIVES

The search by the team from the Toronto branch had narrowed the choice of established systems to one being marketed by Alpha, one of the major firms in the CADD industry. Towards the end of their search, however, the investigators had also located a system that was about to be produced by Gamma, a relatively new company. Gamma had been established by a leading programmer who had been responsible for much of the CADD software developed by Alpha. The new company's system had the potential of being as good or better than Alpha's and it also had the advantage of being easier to invest in incrementally. A single Gamma work station would cost close to $200,000 with the necessary ancillary equipiment; however, it was capable of expansion, being able to take up to five other work stations that would cost about $150,000, with each additional work station costing about $80–$90,000. (In either case, the plotting equipment would be the same; although expensive, there was a recognized industry standard for this sort of equipment now, so that, if the project was abandoned, the plotting system could be resold relatively easily to recover most of the $200,000 outlay for it.)

The ability to resell the CADD systems being considered were not equal, however. Alpha had a solid reputation and a history of many successful applications. These applications were not exactly what TEL needed, though. Gamma could provide a system that would apparently suit TEL very well but it would be the first application of the system for civil engineering and architectural work. Similar use applications were in place in a few companies but there were no other sites that had requirements like TEL, and Gamma would be custom designing the package if TEL chose it.

There was a potential for problems if TEL were to choose this route but it had the advantage of putting the company on the leading edge of the technology if the new company's package delivered the capabilities promised.

There were several other considerations that would have to be worked out in detail as well. The system brought in would be justified as a pilot project. Any future implementation of CADD beyond this system would be decided on the basis of the success of this project; the way in which this project was organized was likely to affect that success a great deal.

One of the main considerations was the training and development of the systems manager and the operators. If some members of the current drafting staff were willing, they could be trained at a local community college over a period of several months, perhaps partially on company time. The system used for training at the college was an Alpha. As yet, the drafting staff had not been approached about this possibility.

The mandate for the project had been confined to setting up as small a system as was practicable for demonstrating the potential performance of such equipment.

Although the pilot project budget would currently cover only a single work station plus plotters for whichever system was chosen, Mr. Kinnear felt that there would be little difficulty in getting approval from the Board for a second station "for training purposes."

Two immediate decisions that had to be made were to choose which system would be better for TEL and whether or not to go for a second station. More importantly, these decisions would have to be integrated into an entire implementation plan that would ensure that any system brought in would have the greatest possible effectiveness. Ordering any equipment now would give him five to six months during which the preparations could be carried out before the system arrived.

Chapter Ten

SOCIAL IMPLICATIONS OF NEW TECHNOLOGY

SITUATION 10.1

Robot Installation: An Economic Feasibility Study[1]

Expectations concerning productivity improvements are generally the reason for the introduction of automated machinery. In medium to high volume firms, CAD/CAM, flexible manufacturing systems, and robots are the vehicles for achieving this productivity. Robots generally dominate in welding, painting, loading and unloading areas of a company. Originally robots were intended to replace workers in hazardous environments. This purpose has been extended to include the replacement of workers in monotonous, repetitive, nonstimulating jobs.

It is estimated that by 1990 the robot population will be about one million. Initially automation causes significant displacement of workers. In the long term, the application of new technology creates new jobs and leads to higher productivity. Studies have revealed conflicting results. Some say displacement will be widespread. Others indicate that displacement of humans is necessary such as when dealing with hazardous chemicals, even though it is economically undesirable. Generally there is a psychological fear that robotization leads to increased unemployment. Even Japanese workers resist the introduction of robots if the robots take away pleasant easy jobs.

Anil Mital and R. Vinayagamoorthy of the University of Cincinnati conducted a feasibility study to determine the economic effects of robotization on the company, the government, and society.

[1]Based on A. Mital and R. Vinayagamoorthy, "Case Study: Economic Feasibility of a Robot Installation." *The Engineering Economist*, Volume 32, No. 3, Spring, pp. 173–196. © 1987, Institute of Industrial Engineers. Extracted with permission.

BACKGROUND

A medium-sized metal industry in the mid-west was the target of the study. The selected application was a gearhobbing machine center. Within this center four machines operated individually by semiskilled laborers. Operating functions include loading gear blanks, cutting gear profiles, stacking semifinished parts, trimming gears on a shaving machine, cleaning and inspection of pieces. The proposed robot performed all loading and unloading operations. Stacking, inspection and the supervision of the work station was handled by one operator, as opposed to the previous four. The production capacity of the human-operated center had been 800 units/day. The robotized center produced 1,315 units/day. The feasibility and economic analysis was taken from two points of view, the company's and the government's. Some assumptions were made in order to minimize the variables in the study analysis. These include the assumption that the company was unable to meet demands due to low productivity. The additional capacity can be sold without difficulty. All retraining costs will be born by the company, ignoring the effects of inflation. Displaced workers are permanently unemployed. The former employees' sole source of income is government and welfare agencies.

Company Costs

- Robot and accessories (special tools, test equipment)
- Installation costs
- Rearrangement costs (safety fences, conveyors)
- Special training tools
- Change in fixture design (clamps, sensors, limit switches)
- Operating supply cost (annual cost of utilities and services used by the robot)
- Maintenance supply costs
- Launching costs rework stoppages due to installation
- Taxes and insurance

Company Savings

- Reduced scrap
- Increased productivity, increased sales
- Savings in direct labor

For this company the estimated return of investment is greater than the company's marginal annual rate of return desired for new products, indicating the project is good for the company. The payback estimated is three-and-a-half years.

GOVERNMENT ANALYSIS

Three unemployed workers are the result of automation. This alters the cash flow to and from the government. Most changes are due to tax losses such as unemployment compensation and welfare. If the individuals relocate, tax revenues may alter due to changes in incomes. The company's profits increase from selling additional capacity which lead to additional tax revenues to the government. Two probable scenarios occur. These are (1) the displaced workers are permanently unemployed, and (2) displaced workers are relocated.

In the first case where permanent unemployment results, taxes to the government from workers and the company stop. Government expenses increase. The company's increased productivity and labor savings increase profits which in turn causes tax revenue to the government to rise leading to a higher GNP. A further breakdown analysis indicates that the robotized work center is not desirable from the government's viewpoint if displaced workers are permanently unemployed. This applies even if the installation is beneficial to the company.

When displaced workers are relocated, based on the assumption they are transferred to another location in the same company. If no retraining occurs, and the new job requires the same skills, the three workers will earn the same salary. In this case the company's revenues increase due to larger productivity volumes, leading to higher government revenues. Therefore, if workers are relocated the installation is beneficial to the company, the government and society.

These studies indicate that the decision to install robotics may differ depending on whose point of view is taken.

RESULTS AND RECOMMENDATION

The study indicates that policy changes are required at company and government levels. Alteration to the tax structure and company profit policies are required to reduce the adverse consequences of robot installation. There is growing responsibility on the employer's behalf to provide for the continuity of employment for all individuals displaced by automation. This continued employment need not be in the same company. Attention must also be paid to the retraining and relocation of these workers. Training programs should reflect present and future industrial needs. The company also has a responsibility to pass on savings from robotization to the workers.

In terms of governmental changes, the tax structure must be altered in favor of advanced manufacturing investments in order to minimize the impact of unemployment due to robotization. Government policies should influence growth through special tax incentives, loan guarantees or other sources of funding.

READING 10.1

The Factory of the Future: What About the People?[2]

Since the mid-1970s, scare accounts of the human impact of the factory of the future have hit the American public about once a month. These nightmare versions play on human feelings of powerlessness—victims confronting the relentlessness of the unfeeling, never-tiring machine. At best, the image of Charlie Chaplin, all by himelf, fighting his way off an assembly line of machinery painted white in a factory also painted white. At worst, the image is that of the sorcerer's apprentice, unable to let go of the magical brooms and buckets, engulfed in uncontrollable, destructive "productivity."

These fears, however, have little to do with the actualities of the factory of the future. True,there is some bad news to report. Nearly everyone in the factory labor force and all their management are certainly in for a change, and change may be painful. But there is good news, too. Overall, factory automation seems likely to result in relatively favorable trends in employment, job enrichment, and human productivity.

What follows is a qualitative analysis of the forces and trends that bear on factory automation and its impact on jobs. Unlike most other such analyses, however, this one provides a broad perspective that will offer a useful context for qualitative work still to be undertaken.

INSIDE THE FACTORY

Qualitative changes in job content, organization, and work culture inside the factory will be as real and noticeable as reductions in numbers will be. Robotics, word processors,

[2]Homer Hagedorn, "The Factory of the Future: What About the People?" *The Journal of Business Strategy*, Volume 5, No. 1, Summer, pp. 38–45. © 1984 by Warren, Gorham, & Lamont, Inc. Extracted with permission.

CAD/CAM systems, modern materials handling, and manufacturing resource planning have been applied long enough in sufficient settings to provide many clues about the prospective impact of these technical and managerial innovations on the organization. Fortunately, the trends are consistent with the requirements of the information revolution and the preferences of the less submissive work force that is taking over factory jobs.

Job Content

Average skill levels will be higher. General Motors believes that skilled tradesmen, who now number 16 percent of GM's plant work force, will be up to 50 percent by the year 2000. These men and women will not be college graduates necessarily, but they will have received at least a couple of years of post-secondary education, much of it to make them competent to use, operate, monitor and control software that will reside in all manner of computing equipment and will mediate nearly every production activity that goes on within the plant.

The scope of typical production jobs—once just above the level of sweeping and cleaning—will be broad. Nearly everyone in the plant will be comfortable in accessing computerized information and inputting commands as well as data. Nearly everyone will have an integrated understanding of a broad range of operating and support functions. Being only a machinist in itself will not be enough; skilled machinists will be succeeded by workers who understand a good deal about supply, parts inventory control, demand forecasting, scheduling, and finished goods inventory control, as well as tool operations and the maintaining of work quality and quantity. These workers will be monitors more than doers, trouble-shooters more than fixers, and information manipulators rather than object manipulators.

It will be unusual for anyone to improvise a repair by crawling under a machine with a rusty nail, a rag, or a wrench as was once done. Most remedies will be prescribed by decision rules and administered by specialized outsiders. The ability to handle abstract concepts and to think comfortably about how the operating functions fit together will take a higher priority than is now the case. Working groups will be smaller and potentially much closer. Thus, there will be less need for people to relate casually to large numbers of people.

Organization and Work Culture

Some prophets of the information revolution predict that teamwork will become less important. Team makeup will certainly change, along with what is to be accomplished by teamwork. However, the best and most productive work places will still be characterized by effective teamwork. There will be much less need for long-lived production teams on the shop floor. There may be less need for managers to meet regularly for the purpose of information transfer and communication. But a prodigious amount of planning, trouble-shooting, and anticipatory problem-solving will be needed—and the essence of these real problems of all kinds is that they will initially exceed the knowledge energy or skills of any one person. Our best guess is that ad hoc problem-solving teams, and the interpersonal and intellectual skills required to make such teams effective, will be prominent features of the factory of the future.

Organization itself will change accordingly. The table of organization will be much narrower at the bottom, and there will be fewer levels. Spans of control will tend to be narrower in terms of the numbers of subordinates reporting directly but will be broader in apparent, substantive scope for each manager or supervisor.

These simplifications in structure will allow the organization to function more like an informal grouping of colleagues (an accountable network) and less like a bureaucratic, hierarchical army. Much of the precise control that has been attainable only through rigid procedures and detailed supervision will be handled by microchip technology which will surpass accuracy and consistency. The people will not have to be regimented in the same detailed way that an assembly line demands. In fact, those in the factory may come to experience organization and management in a fully automated factory as not regimented at all. Since multiple locations can easily be provided from which to monitor and modify automated production processes, and from which to call up necessary reports, records, and specifications, very few people will be limited to particular physical locations for long periods of time. Most monitorial and trouble-shooting jobs will depend on what is going on in the head of the incumbents. Close and continuous supervision is not practical in the here and now.

Part of the organizational informality that people will experience is also inevitable simply because of smaller numbers. A factory that employs 50 people in the United States is almost always less hierarchical and formal than one that employs 500 people. Even the outline changes because small working teams normally take a very simple form. There is a leader in the middle, surrounded by a cluster of assistant leaders, specialists, and technicians. Nearby, and somewhat intermingled, are other clusters of support and cleanup workers.

Despite greater freedom to roam and a less hierarchical organization, not everyone now working in factories will like the new environment. But there will be fewer dirty and noisy jobs to do. For people able and willing to fix attention on many complex streams of information, working life should be more interesting in general. The problem is that the information they are dealing with will have to be presented in rather abstract form, requiring that they make the initial effort necessary to be able to interpret it. They must also be able to concentrate on abstractions for relatively long periods without faltering in their concentration—certainly for many minutes, sometimes for an hour or more at a time.

Those people fascinated by the process of figuring out what the information means and what to do with it will be the real managers and the real workers, which also implies that the boundaries between what mangaers do and what workers do will be even less clear in a machine shop; or an assembly plant than is now the case. It will be more like the overlapping and interacting among skills and activities that occur in product development, when project engineers, designers, draftsmen, manufacturing engineers, and technically literate marketing personnel work together amicably in a company not too hampered by functional organizational barriers.

OUTSIDE THE PLANT

A host of new people will be needed outside the plant to provide a number of services that either are not now required or will be drastically changed in terms of their importance and the skills they require. The fundamental fact is that the factory of the future will operate as a fully integrated and interdependent system, very capital intensive. In fact, it will operate as a fine-tuned system, incredibly efficient when operating in "resonance," but dramatically decreasing in efficiency with even a small deviation from its ideal operating condition.

Specialized Outside Maintenance

When this happens to a system, redundancy decreases, every path becomes a critical path, and costs and risks of stoppages go sky-high. Part of the remedy is to reintroduce partial redundancy, certainly feasible when other purposes are served as well. In flexible manufacturing systems, for example, one sets up many alternative pathways for work in progress. In one instance, metalworking equipment is linked by parts-carrying "tracks," whose automated "cars" position parts properly for being worked. The metalworking equipment is programmed to shift automatically and swiftly to whatever is required for a particular part. The main objective may be to profit from the flexibility that results from very short setup times, but the robustness that comes with redundancy is an advantage just as important as flexibility. This is only true, however, up to the point at which it costs too much.

In many cases, the efficient use of specialized skills and test equipment will dictate that centralized facilities be developed for module maintenance and for specialized training. These activities may be managed by the same corporation that owns and operates the automated factories, or they may be in the charge of separate companies working under maintenance or service contraacts. The point is that they constitute work and, therefore, jobs that are in addition to the in-plant jobs. Part of the reduction in plant jobs will be absorbed by the kind of jobs on which the plant will depend, even though they are outside the day-to-day plant operations and are not counted in direct factory employment.

Like the technicians in the factory, the service support technologists will have to understand the design, maintenance, and operation of the robots, the jobs the robots do, the materials on which the robots are working, and the tools through which the work gets done; their technical knowledge and the nature of their experience will need to be more extensive, however, to enable them also to carry out complex adjustments and updates, to uncover subtle problems, or to organize and orchestrate million-dollar overnight module changes.

One cannot emphasize too strongly that costs associated with downtime will be very high. Thus, managers of factories of the future will endure the expenses associated with effective outside support services. In particular, the constant stream of updates, major module changes, and their associated recurrent need to replace the basic systems configuration and the overall design of the manufacturing process will enforce the need for high-quality outside specialized support. Even after the stage is reached when certain routine types of preventive maintenance are taken back into the factory, managers will still require specialized support.

TRAINING

The systems will be constantly under improvement and renewal, and keeping them up-to-date implies keeping the people working with them up-to-date as well. The computer-controlled, highly interdependent, costly systems that even now are being built require training specific to the hardware, to the software, and to the application. As more and more steps in the product development, production, and distribution cycle become integrated, most of the people in the factory will need significant retraining at shorter and shorter intervals. People able to provide this training will constitute a class perhaps as numerous as the service support technologists who maintain the hardware and the software. Many of the trainers will be associated with vendors, with training courses, or with academic institutions, although large companies with many manufacturing plants will also expand their internal training and human resources development activities far beyond current levels.

The hours of productive work for factory-related people will be reduced by the severe training requirements associated with sustaining an ever-changing mix of interconnected, interactive, chip-driven systems. In some manufacturing companies, the managerial and professional employees already are reporting the need to spend a few hours a week keeping up with the generalities of their fields. When most employees of a factory are similarly affected and must also have specific updating to keep the systems running, employers will have to bring the training responsibilities into the plant. It just won't be safe or possible to do otherwise.

In both manufacturing and financial services companies heavily engaged in computerized automation, training budgets have doubled despite the recent recession and the drive to eliminate unnecessary overhead. Those training directors who truly understand the information revolution say that they have seen enough to believe that average training requirements will be 10 to 20 percent—four to eight hours a week—by the late 1980s. A result of this requirement will be a further decrease in net jobs lost.

LOGISTICS EXPEDITERS

Distribution and supply functions will also need to be staffed to a depth and at a quality level now tolerated only by those relatively few companies with policies stipulating 100 percent service levels. ("Stock-outs will not be tolerated; customer emergencies must be met.") Granted, computerized logistics can provide the information for efficient problem-solving and expediting, but only when knowledgeable people are available to interpret the implications of the information properly.

Linking one's own computers and data bases to suppliers and customers provides the opportunity to save inventory and, in many ways, to exploit a competitive edge, but interconnection also extends the chain and complexity of critical paths and thereby increases vulnerability to mischance. People "redundancy"—high quality expediters and logistics trouble-shooters, perhaps described as salespeople or purchasing agents—will provide a solution. Their numbers may be relatively small, but they will be extremely important people. They will have a highly specialized function, not now developed in most companies beyond a rudimentary level except perhaps for a "good Joe" salesman or someone like a national sales manager who happens to be located at the intersection of the kinds of information needed and has learned to use the information creatively.

HOW SEVERE WILL JOB DISPLACEMENT BE?

Filling the jobs that do not now exist reduces the overall jobs impact of computer-integrated manufacturing. Although only a tenth of the people that will be required may be on a production line, many others will be doing things outside and nearby that currently do not need doing or that cannot yet be done. Estimates of the net effect of this vary, but we can be reasonably sure that half or more of the apparent increase in labor productivity associated with the factory of the future will be absorbed by the need for the new kinds of support described in the previous section. Remember that the major savings are in direct labor and that even in 1982 and 1983, direct labor tended to be less than 30 percent of total employment across the total range of manufacturing companies. That percentage probably will continue to decrease over the next decade, although we should also remember that the effects of office automation and the drive to cut down overhead or staff operations may become large factors themselves. Indeed, given the 70–30 ratio that currently exists, more industrial jobs in absolute terms may be "lost" to these causes than to the factory of the future.

WHERE WILL THE PEOPLE COME FROM? AN UNANSWERED QUESTION

If many of the people needed to operate and support the factory of the future must be mature, flexible, resilient, and computer-literate to an extent undreamed of before the late 1970s, United States industry can expect to face actual labor shortages in a number of job categories. Not all of the people needed will have to be college educated. However, almost none of the 1984 graduates of United States high schools would be able to step into a production job in the factory of the future without months of training. In fact, they would probably need 10 to 20 months' worth of training. The problem would be more evident by now were it not for the circumstances of recent years. Retrenchment, recession, imports of automobiles and electronic equipment, and offshore manufacturing have thus far obscured the difficulty in getting novices trained and have reduced the need for retraining experienced workers.

Much of the content that will be required in these training programs can be discerned in vendor training programs now available or being developed. Much of the rest is buried in the materials being poured into brand new graduate engineering programs in manufacturing. But there is little ground for believing that we know how to teach these new skills, procedures, principles, and concepts to a large number of average people, and can do it efficiently. Nor is there much reason to believe we know who these pepole will be, how to go about selecting them, or how to motivate them. If it turns out that large numbers of them will have any of the independence and intellectual obsessiveness of computer "hackers," which now seems entirely possible, their training and supervision will indeed require rethinking and reinvestment.

Where these people will come from and how they will obtain necessary skills and knowledge constitute potential major problems. The likeliest scenario is one in which those United States firms that start earliest and drive hardest toward computer-integrated manufacturing will capture the most skilled and trainable labor, thus minimizing their immediate need to invest heavily (order-of-magnitude increases) in training. Other less aggressive and less well-financed firms, however, will be late and will lose out to new foreign as well as domestic competition which by then will be established. These firms will have the automated systems but will not profit from them because they will lack the time and money to train the people they need.

COPING WITH DISPLACED PEOPLE

What will happen to unskilled and semiskilled workers and those whose skills have become antiquated is a different problem, and also a difficult one. Tens of thousands, and probably hundreds of thousands, will be displaced, too many of them in locales already overburdened by industrial decline. Making reliable projections will give labor economists headaches for a long time to come.

The automation timetable is neither rigid nor centralized, and it is subject to an almost infinite number of variables and contingencies. Will the computer generate more jobs than it eliminates? What will be the overall impact of reducing further the dependence of factory location on the location of labor supplies (allowing other logistic and economic factors to predominate more)? Will government, industry, and academia take hold of the training and retraining issues or will the "let alone" scenario prevail?

Most readers are probably familiar with those negative factors that are most certain to make displacement tough to handle. The people displaced will be less than ideal for retraining. They will tend to be among the older members of the labor force. They will be less educated and less mobile than the average worker. They will often be oblivious or resistant to modern technology, rather than enthusiastically eager to embrace it.

On the other hand, industrial demographics serve to mitigate the problem. The 20 million Americans now employed in the manufacturing industry are only about half the number so employed in the immediate post-war period. Three-quarters of retirees (using numbers from just before the onset of the recession of the early 1980s) were blue-collar workers in a rapidly aging blue-collar population; however, only half of those entering the work force were going into blue-collar jobs.

Perhaps the most important contingency with respect to displacement is whether we will have the vision to invent forms of industrial organization that match the requirements of factory automation to the available labor supply well enough not to exceed our aggregate training capabilities, improved or not. The alternative to making a favorable match would appear to be a hardening and perpetuation of so-called structural unemployment.

WHO MUST BE MOTIVATED TO BRING ABOUT THE FACTORY OF THE FUTURE?

The results of interactions among major trends and forces will determine the kinds of experience rank-and-file workers will have with the transition to the factory of the future. In addition, each individual company will have its own transition to work through, which brings us to an entirely different set of human problems—those associated with managing top-to-bottom change. The work of nearly everyone in a manufacturing company will ultimately be affected by the transition, including senior management. Consequently, nearly everyone will ultimately need to change or to allow himself to be changed in what he does, how he does it, or whom he does it with.

Somehow, the pioneers of factory-of-the-future automation must overcome the natural paranoia of the functional organization—the suspicion of other specialists and line managers concerning the plea of a manufacturing specialist who, lacking the data required to meet hurdle rate requirements, argues that spending a lot more money in the way that he suggests will solve major problems facing the firm.

Two other potentailly difficult motivational problems or conflicts are likely to emerge: one is surprising and involves information systems management; the other is quite predictable and involves the unions.

The information systems management problem is partly a jurisdictional dispute and partly a role change. The problem arises because switching to computer-integrated manufacturing makes the manufacturing staff into principal users in the firm of the computer system's capabilities. Redrawing the boundaries and assuring that the people with the data actually make the decision inevitably takes some time, but it can be worked out.

The enforced role change may cause worse troubles. Computer systems people for a generation have been among the leading technical pioneers in nearly every major United States company. To be cast as conservatives when the initiative passes outside the information systems department is confusing for them to deal with and may be quite difficult for computer specialists and especially for system developers.

Since several of the major unions have been living with the onset of computerized automation in the factory for a decade or more, the concern and the position of such major labor unions as that of the machinists have come to be well known: As long as a reasonable provision is made for displaced union members and things are arranged so that union members will share in the benefits, they will not oppose the factory of the future.

CONCLUSION

Nothing about any of these problems is exceptional. As usual, motivation is mostly a matter of recognizing existing interests, analyzing them accurately, and assuring that interested parties are aware of the analysis and working with them accordingly to provide relevant leadership. The implementation of a planned transition of the factory-of-the-future is, of course, like the implementation of any other major strategic change that requires significant internal rearrangement and reorganization. It will upset at least some painfully achieved internal agreements on turf, pecking order, and succession. It also will require some shifts in both material and nonmaterial incentives. Senior management leadership, action, and decision will become essential to making the transition effectively.

The closer one comes to the new technologies themselves—robots, CAD/CAM systems, automated materials handling, and so forth—the simpler the motivational problems. Experience thus far suggests that it is easy for people to get involved in day-to-day work using the new technologies. Intellectually active people generally are exposed to a broader overview of the job, get to know more about what is going on, and interact with more people. Their jobs are more fun. Most people also find that their work goes better and they get more done, which leads to the positive feeling that they are productive.

READING 10.2

The Automated Factory: The View from the Shop Floor[3]

Too often public debate centers simply on figuring out how to automate as rapidly as possible, rather than on finding ways to develop and install the best technology—one that both improves life on the job and provides efficient production.

Along with my M.I.T. colleagues, Steven Herzenberg and Sarah Kuhn, I recently had the opportunity to explore the way automation affects work life. As part of a project by the congressional Office of Technology assessment to study computer-based automation in factories, we visited an automobile plant, a commercial aircraft plant, an agricultural equipment plant, and seven small metalworking shops. These firms differ in many respects, but all are leading and experienced users of automation.

We agreed not to divulge company names and in exchange were allowed a free hand to observe factories and obtain private interviews with everyone from top management to hourly workers. When I presented our findings to engineers who had actually designed many of the kinds of equipment we studied, some were surprised to learn about traps that they had not imagined would occur on the road to automation.

THE INDIVIDUAL MACHINIST

Before the arrival of computer-based automation, the machinist's skill provided the missing link between a blueprint and a finished part. Using intricate fixtures and making careful measurements, machinists would orient parts to be machined in just the right way, and would then turn the necessary cranks and run the cutting tools.

[3]Harley Shaiken, "The Automated Factory: The View From the Shop Floor." *Technology Review*, January, pp. 17–37. © 1985. Reprinted with permission from Technology Review.

In numerical control (NC), a computer punches holes in a paper or plastic tape, and when the tape is fed into a machine tool, these holes control (CNC), a newer form of the technology in which a computer at the machine directly controls its operation. Both NC and CNC (the terms are often used interchangeably) can be far superior technically to manual control. The computer is able to guide the cutting tool through complex arcs and angles that no machinist could duplicate. Furthermore, intricate fixtures to hold parts at special angles are often unnecessary. Since all operations are preprogrammed, NC enables a machine to proceed from cut to cut far more rapidly than is possible with manual control, thereby reducing the time required to make a part. However, the machinist must still set up the work piece to be cut, make adjustments to correct for tool wear, and top the machine if anything goes wrong.

The technology of CNC leaves a wide latitude as to who programs the computer. At one extreme full-time parts programmers sit in front of a screen and determines how a part will be made. At the other extreme, a machinist does the same thing at a minicomputer at the machine.

There are sometimes compelling technical reasons for programming to be done off the shop floor. Devising long, complex programs may require intricate calculations taking several days. In other cases, it may be more efficient for machinists to write programs—particularly for making simpler parts. Operators at the machines are also especially well-situated for debugging flawed programs. For example, in one shop we visited, a program called for making a heavy cut across a block of aluminum—an operation that generates considerable heat—and then boring two holes a precise distance apart. When the steps were carried out in this order, the distance between the holes decreased as the aluminum cooled. The machinist was able to correct the problem by editing the program to drill the holes first.

Managers in the small shops we visited organized production on CNC machines in different ways. In one shop, prototype machinists, who make the initial prototypes of parts, did the programming. Another shop rotated some machinists through the programming department. However, in the vast majority of cases, the responsibility for writing instructions for the machines had been removed from the shop floor and given to programmers working in offices, even when this was far from optimal technically.

Shop owners were also concerned by what they saw as a shortage of skilled machinists and by the leverage of those who were available. "Five, six years ago, we were very dependent on skilled labor, to the point where I spent half my life on my hands and knees begging somebody to stay and do something," said one shop owner. "Machinists tend to be prima donnas. This is one of the motivations for bringing in NC equipment. It reduced our dependence on skilled labor." Another shop owner was so impressed by the power of CNC that he was considering firing most of his 10 employees and starting over with a more amenable group. "Sometimes too much knowledge is dangerous," he said.

In practice, visions of firing the entire shop floor work force and hiring pliable new people off the street are probably not workable. Nor can CNC eliminate the need for machining skill somewhere in the production process. However, managers did report that this technology gave them more control in determining which jobs require that skill.

They could employ machinists with considerably less expertise than they needed to run conventional tools—in effect moving that skill to the programming department.

However, using the lowest level of skill necessary to run CNC machines is not necessarily the way to make production most efficient from a technical standpoint—especially in machining small quantities of intricate parts. Not only can machinists contribute to programming; they must also often intervene in operations even after the program has been debugged, many owners admitted. "In a small business, when you invest a lot of money in a piece of NC equipment you don't want to save $2.00 an hour by putting an unskilled operator on it," said one head of manufacturing engineering. "The higher the operator's skill, the more we get out of the machine."

The paradox is that, though skill and experience are required for operators of some CNC equipment, that very skill and experience may make operators dislike the equipment. Skilled machinists were particularly frustrated by CNC if they did no programming.

Skilled machinists, who had formerly planned production on conventional machines, told us that they would be more interested in using CNC machines if they had responsibility for writing programs. The chance to program would not eliminate boredom during long running times or repeated production of a single type of part, but it would make jobs more creative and could increase productivity. Some machinists said that they already do some programming unofficially and felt that managers should give them formal recognition for it.

SPY IN THE SKY

CNC enhances managerial control of the work place but does not make it complete. This technology affects only what happens when a part is actually being machined—and not, for example, how parts move from one production step to another through the shop. And machinists have a certain measure of control even while a part is being cut. They usually have a dial to override programmed feed rates (the rates at which work pieces are fed into cutting tools) to compensate for special factors such as unexpected hard alloys. Thus, operators can slow down or speed up the work pace.

To secure more control over this aspect of the machinist's job, and to better estimate the efficiency of the operation, the managers at the aircraft company implemented a computerized monitoring system on 66 NC machines. The system categorizes each machine as running, running at less than 80 percent of programmed feed rate, temporarily halted, or down. A panel in a control room above the shop floor displays the status of each machine with colored lights. A supervisor can check these lights and gain further information by glancing out at the floor below. Daily reports tell supervisors not only about production levels, but also about how each worker spends his or her time. Upper management receives weekly and monthly reports. Obviously, such a system has the potential to weave an electronic net of control through the shop.

Thge information that the system produces may also be extremely misleading. One machinist told us that he had to work long and furiously to set up a particularly intricate part to be cut. As a result this machine sat idle most of the day. While he felt that he had never worked harder, his supervisor reprimanded him because the system reported that his machine was idle.

THE DOMINO EFFECT

A common managerial vision is to combine CNC machine tools, automated carts, robots, and other computer-controlled equipment into an entire production unit—a flexible manufacturing system (FMS)—that can run with as little human intervention as possible.

One FMS we visited—in effect, a computer-controlled machine shop—produces transmission cases and clutch housings for a line of heavy-duty tractors. At one end of the system, workers load a large iron casting onto a chain-driven cart. Guided by computers, the cart carries this work piece to one of 12 computer-controlled machine tools. Here it is unloaded, machined, reloaded, and shuttled off to another station. A complex formula ensures that the various operations are scheduled efficiently. Finally, workers unload precision-machined cases and housings—untouched, at least in theory, by human hands.

Three supervisors and 11 production workers are assigned to the day shift, fewer to the other two shifts. One operator is responsible for every three machines, changing tools when the computer indicates it is time, inspecting parts to be sure they are correctly cut, cleaning the area, and solving any problems. The system is intended to minimize operator intervention—particularly in setting the pace of production.

However, there is something of a dichotomy between what the managers of an FMS intend and what actually happens. Though the project manager spoke of not having to rely on people, he also admitted that operators must minister to this complex system with considerable "tender loving care." A tool may wear in such a way that it fails to cut accurately, or the boring head, which turns and maneuvers the cutting tool, may be slightly out of alignment. In both cases the operator has to make sensitive adjustments. Or a cart may jam and have to be unstuck.

Problems inevitably occur in such complex electronic systems, and when they do, they can spread in a domino effect. The planners of the FMS were able to limit this effect to some extent by designing the system with some redundancy. If one machining center goes down, the program and the part can be shuttled to another. However, it is hard to foresee all eventualities. Even the designers of the FMS expected that it might be down as much as 33 percent of the time. Managers' estimates of actual downtime, after the initial debugging period, range from an unbelievably low 4 percent up to 20 percent. Some workers told us that downtime was far higher than that.

Our own research team's experience at the plant, admittedly limited, suggested that downtime is a serious problem. While we were there, an air conditioner malfunctioned, causing a machine control to overheat and the machine to go down. This stopped the entire system. While it was down, the carts drifted slightly, and the computer lost track of their exact locations. Setting up everything again took three-quarters of an hour. On the following night the system was down for several more hours. Although managers scheduled work for the weekend to catch up, problems with the software caused the shift to be cancelled.

High downtime does not necessarily imply that automated systems are unproductive. They work so fast when they are up that they do typically increase total output. However, high downtime does indicate that an automated system is falling short of its potential—a serious consideration, given the cost of the technology.

The robotized welding system that we visited in the body shop of the auto maker shed further light on some of these problems. Before robots were introduced, workers wielded heavy hand-held welding guns. The long black cables that connected these guns to overhead racks looked like vines and gave the body shop its nickname, "the jungle." The welders working in this spark-showered jungle had some of the most unpleasant jobs in the plant. Thus, one might expect that using robots—programmable mechanical arms—to do the welding would improve the work environment even though it eliminated jobs. However, many of the 100-odd workers who remained on the new welding system disliked it because it had intensified the pace and eroded the quality of their work life.

Under the new system, workers assemble the floor, sides, and some roof members of each car and secure them by hammering small metal tabs into slots, much as model tin cars are built. Then a gate, or large metal frame, cradles the body and holds it while robots weld it. This setup is referred to as a "Robogate" system. Mini-Robogates cradle and weld together subassemblies such as floors and sides before they are fed into the main line. Over 60 robots and other welding machines are employed in the entire operation.

Before the company installed the Robogates, workers welded some subassemblies at largely independent work stations. After they had completed the wheel-wells or other body parts, they could either place them on the main assembly line to be put together into car bodies, or store them in piles known as banks. This gave the workers some control over the pace of their work: to break the monotony of the day,they could push ahead quickly, bank a lot of parts, and then have some free time later on. Supervisors did not object to banking because it assured a continuous supply to the main assembly line even if unexpected problems occurred, such as a breakdown of the welding machines.

In contrast, the Robogate system ties subassembly workers directly to the line. They now operate welding machines working side-by-side with robots. There is no bank: when the subassembly is complete, they place it directly on the conveyor to the main line. The Japanese "just-in-time" concept, in which supplies arrive just before they are needed, is the theory behind this new approach. The company's director of manufacturing engineering argues that with fewer parts waiting to be worked on, defects are spotted quickly, and productivity increases.

Promoters of automation often claim that it broadens the scope of maintenance jobs. At both the tractor plant's FMS and the auto maker's Robogate, maintenance jobs did indeed become more challenging. Workers told us that maintaining computerized control systems requires expertise in electronics and broader diagnostic skills than are needed for conventinonal equipment. However, automation puts those responsible for maintenance, particularly supervisors, under extraordinary stress, because a failure of one critical component could paralyze the system and even the entire plant.

The main Robogate line processes car bodies at the rate of more than one per minute, and any number of things can go wrong. The photocells installed to count car bodies may tell the computer to fit too many bodies into too little space. Then the carriers that transport the bodies along the line become jammed, and the robots sometimes keep on welding anyway. The scene that ensues resembles a crash on the freeway more than the effortless grace of automatic production.

The Robogate was initially built with storage areas capable of holding a two-hour supply of bodies at a number of critical points. But because the storage systems proved less reliable than the main system, managers told us they plan to eliminate them. Then, if the main Robogate line goes down, the factory will be able to run for a short time. However, as soon as the storage capacity in the main line is exhausted, the entire body shop, with its millions of dollars worth of equipment and hundreds of workers, will stand idle.

ENGINEERS NEXT

Computer technology can be used as a powerful tool to restructure the jobs of engineers as well as production workers. We discovered this in our visits to the manufacturer of commercial aircraft, a subsidiary of a larger aerospace firm. Only about one-third of the division's 40,000 employees actually "touch" the aircraft during production. Management plans to revamp most of the remaining two-thirds of the jobs through automation.

Engineering is now organized so that knowledgeable people in various departments and levels make decisions, communicating in meetings and by exchanging drawings. For example, the design engineer sends a blueprint of a part to the tooling engineer, who is responsible for figuring out how to make the devices to hold intricate aircraft components during production. The tooling engineer then generally modifies the design engineer's drawing and sends it back for checking.

Introducing computer-aided design (CAD) systems, in which engineers work on computer terminals and video screens rather than on paper, need not mean changing this organizational structure. However, the aircraft company we visited is using computers to give elite engineering teams greater control.

Such teams will soon establish the basic design of an airplane and feed it into the computer system, along with fundamental decisions about tooling and manufacturing. This information will be launched throughout the rest of the company via the CAD network. Tooling and manufacturing departments will still be necessary, but only to work closely with the elite team in fleshing out the details of decisions that have already been made.

The design teams at the source of this stream of information will have broader responsibility, but, for a given volume of work, as many as a third of the engineers and technicians downstream are likely to find their jobs eliminated. Up to 80 percent of the manufacturing engineers, who plan how parts proceed from step-to-step during production, could be eliminated, according to company officials. And the downstream jobs that remain will be more constrained.

Another problem is that engineers working on computer terminals may find themselves mistaking computer simulations for reality. A story has been going around among enginers about a young designer at a British aircraft company, who created an igniter, somewhere along the way a decimal point was moved one place. The computer therefore instructed a machine tool to cut out a part that was 10 times too big. When the machine operator brought the part up to the designer, the designer did not see anything wrong.

TECHNOLOGICAL CONTROL OR HUMANE WORK?

The managerial obsession with technology as a way to establish tighter control over production became an overriding theme in our study of automation. Managers often find it hard to exert close control over a skilled worker such as a machinist, who is making many intricate cuts to produce a complex part. The task is so difficult that a manager must simply rely on the machinist to work at a reasonable pace and to produce a good part. Skilled workers also have substantial bargaining power: if they walk off the job, untrained hands cannot fill in. Thus, managers intent on control seek to remove skill from workers and transfer it to complex machinery. The resulting jobs are tedious, high-paced, and stressful.

Under certain circumstances, managers can increase output while making work more routine and stressful. However, concern for improving production should not outweigh consideration for what workers do on the job. Degrading the work people do ultimately demeans their lives—a cost that is seldom figured into calculations as to which system is more efficient. Computer-based automation holds extraordinary promise for improving life on the job. The emphasis should be on realizing that promise.

EPILOGUE

A Socio-Technical Approach in Technology Adoption

The effects of new technology at the firm level are very significant. However, there are also several social considerations to reflect on. Individual firms must evaluate both the implicit and explicit effects of their actions before undertaking new technology projects. The government also must play a role in monitoring and controlling the actions of firms in the public interest, through the various policy tools it has available.

There are several social impacts which have gained attention over the last few years. First, there has been a great deal of debate over the effect new technology will have on overall employment levels. Some predictions and studies maintain that there will be massive unemployment, others that new technology will result in significant job creation, and still others that there will be no dramatic effect at all. In fact, there are so many factors intervening that it is difficult, if not impossible, to determine which of these assessments is correct.

Employment patterns may also undergo some shifting as a result of new technology. It is likely that the demand for technically skilled individuals, in engineering, maintenance and machine operation, will increase significantly. Correspondingly, the need for unskilled general labor, particularly in manufacturing industries, will decrease. The size of the displacement and reallocation between sectors is difficult to predict. One fact is clear, however; a displaced, unskilled worker will not become a skilled technician merely by wishing it so.

As such, a challenge is presented to workers, managers, and public policy makers. The challenge is to see that, through education, training and retraining, an ample supply of the necessary skills is made available, with a minimal negative social impact. Looking out for workers in this respect will also be an important role which unions must play in the future, primarily through the collective bargaining process.

What is needed, then, is a means of determining the potential impacts of prospective new technologies. Only after these have been identified can workers, unions, management, and public policy makers (if necessary), pursue a course of action which avoids, or at least minimizes, some of the negative impacts.

Often there are two extreme opposing views of new technology, optimistic and pessimistic. Most people will be located on a continuum somewhere between the two, but will lean subjectively, one way or the other. The difficulty is to find an objective, a method of assessment which is not clouded by the inherent biases of the individual parties. An objective framework for evaluating the impact of new technology would overcome the perceptual restrictions of opposing views (see Exhibit 10.1), and thus aid decision making.

Exhibit 10.1 Alternative Views on the Potential Social Impacts of New Technology

Optimistic View	Pessimistic View
• Technology has been changing throughout history—past technological advances had led to increased standards of living—there is no reason why this trend should not continue.	• Because of the speed of today's technological advances and the nature of new technology, it is fundamentally different than previous technological advances—therefore, the past cannot be used to predict the future.
• New technology will lead to increased productivity, resulting in higher wages and lower costs for goods. This in turn will increase demand, and thus, create more jobs.	• Increased demand and consumption will in no way match the increased productivity gains realized through new technology. Therefore, massive unemployment will occur.
• New technology will result in increased skills and higher wages for everyone.	• New technology will lead to a greater split between high-skilled/high-wage and low-skilled/low-wage jobs (that is, an erosion of the middle class).
• Everyone will benefit from the fruits of new technology.	• Only top decision-makers will benefit from the fruits of new technology.

CASE 10.1

J. M. Schneider Inc. and the Ontario Robotic Centre[4]

In mid-January 1985, the Management Committee of J. M. Schneider Inc. received the report of an automation feasibility study conducted by the Ontario Robotic Centre. The report indicated that three elements of Schneider's pork processing lines could be automated. Before a more detailed study could be carried out, however, the Management Committee would have to tell the Robotic Centre which process t investigate. With the impetus from the Board of Directors to automate in the current fiscal year (Schneider's fiscal year was November 1–October 31, the committee members knew that their decision had to be made by early February. And they looked to one of their members, the Kitchener plant manager, for leadershipo in this matter.

J. M. SCHNEIDER INC.

J. M. Schneider Inc. was the largest operating subsidiary of the Heritage Group, a holding company established in 1908 to control a growing company diversifying out of Schneider's core business of meat packing. J. M. Schneider had started in business in the 1880s as a pork packer; the company had grown steadily, expanding to encompass beef and poultry processing, butter and cheesemaking, and nonanimal-based food products manufacture. Schneider's Head Office and the largest plant were located in Kitchener, Ontario. The company's other meat packing plants were in Ayr, Ontario (poultry), Burnaby, British Columbia, and Winnipeg, Manitoba (two plants).

Schneider's diversification had occurred in part because of pressures on the meat

[4]This case was written by Professor Hamid Noori, 1987.

packing industry. Consumers in North America had been moving from red meat products to alternative foodstuffs for both cost and health reasons; while the markets in both Canada and the United States had suffered, the United States market was still bouyant enough to entice Canadian meat packers. The United States market was becoming more difficult to penetrate or survive in, however, because of lower wage rates and higher productivity in the United States, and determined political efforts to restrict meat imports from Canada. And the Japanese market, normally lucrative for Canadian producers, was under siege from heavily subsidized European pork products. Several Canadian producers had closed plants or gone out of business as a result of these enormous competitive pressures, and the remaining companies had invested in more attractive areas.

Despite the emphasis on, and the success of, the diversification efforts, most of Heritage's profits still came from the Kitchener plant. Net earnings for the group in 1984 (see Exhibit 10.2) were less than 1 percent of sales; for Schneider's and the Kitchener plant the returns were lower than the group averages. To remain competitive costs had to be reduced, and this meant productivity had to be improved. And one way to improve productivity might be to automate. The Ontario Robotic Centre had been engaged to see what, if any, elements of the pork processing and packing lines could be effectively automated.

Exhibit 10.2 Selected Financial Data

	1984	1983
Sales	$645,558,000	$590,574,000
Cost of sales, and operating expenses	625,558,000	571,045,000
Of which salaries, etc.?	128,316,000	108,508,000
Net earnings	5,766,000	5,272,000
Working capital	24,336,000	22,487,000
Net fixed assets	56,732,000	54,207,000
Of which machinery and equipment?	21,903,000	20,195,000
Total assets	136,811,000	126,867,000
Long-term debt	19,259,000	19,747,000
Shareholders' equity	61,983,000	57,384,000
Total employees	3,970	3,827

AUTOMATION AT J. M. SCHNEIDER

This would not be Schneider's first involvement with automation. In early 1984 the company had installed a material requirements planning system in Kitchener, and had also automated some parts of the Ayr poultry processing operation. Automation at Ayr was limited to processing steps on the eviscerating line, where a standard sequence of operations was performed with little variation. All inspection, carcass dressing, and trimming operations remained manual. The system, installed at a cost of almost $1 million, immediately increased line throughput. Although 20 work stations had been automated, the displaced workers filled jobs created by both the expanding market for poultry and the increased hourly production rate.

The move was judged to be only reasonably successful, however, for carcasses that were malformed or outside the standard size range were poorly processed. As a result, a consideration percentage of the poultry carcasses were either inadequately processed or damaged by the automated equipment. These losses were acceptable in poultry processing because of the small per unit costs; in pork or beef operations, however, much more significant losses would likely result.

THE PRELIMINARY STUDY

The competitive pressures in the red meat packing industry made the introduction of robots and other automated processes in Kitchener attractive—provided the automation was both effective and improved productivity. Unfortunately, opportunities for automation in meat processing were limited. Animal evisceration and meat cutting, for example, would have to remain a series of manual operations since each animal processed was a different shape, size, and configuration. Computer vision systems were not yet sufficiently developed to replace any of Schneider's visual inspection processes. Nor was it likely that the complex problems would be overcome for a considerable time, making a fully or highly automated meat processing plant a distant dream.

However, this did not mean that no automation opportunities existed for Schneider's production facilities. The Ontario Robotic Centre's preliminary report showed that three operations in Kitchener had definite programmable automation potential:

1. *Processing of bacon from hog bellies.* This was one of the major pork production operations at J. M. Schneider. Pork bellies were currently loaded manually into an automated "Nutridan" press which subsequently "squared" the bacon as an assist to improving slicing in the packaging department. The press cycle time was approximately 10 seconds.
2. *Loading frozen meat into a grinder.* Blocks of frozen meat were manually removed from boxes and plastic overwrap, then placed on a moving conveyor which led to a grinding machine. Since the meat was frozen at this stage, complete removal of the plastic overwrap was difficult. Visual inspection was required to confirm that all plastic was removed, for the plastic overwrap often stuck to the meat and had to be chopped out with a hatchet.
3. *Washing vats from the blending and cutting departments.* Stainless steel vats, used by the blending and the cutting departments, were currently loaded onto a dumper by a fork lift vehicle and washed with a detergent solution. Excess water inside the vats was removed using the dumper.

The Ontario Robotic Centre had used a scorecard to determine the suitability of applying robotics to the three operations. (See Exhibit 10.3.) For each operation under consideration, a number was assigned from "0" to "10," the higher the score the easier or the more desirable automation would be.

Exhibit 10.3 Assessing Robotic Applicability

Application	Task Complexity	Vision Required	Workspace Available	Jobs Eliminated	Environmental Severity	Back-up System Available	Total Score
Loading Hog Bellies	10	10	4	2	5	5	36
Loading Frozen Meat into Extruder	6	5	6	1	2	3	32
Washing Vats	10	9	10	3.5	7	9	48.5

Six parameters were considered in assessing a project, but one parameter (jobs eliminated) was not included in the project's score. The parameters were:

Task Complexity: the difficulty of applying automation in some way to the situation. It was very important to choose an initial application that was simple, and the higher the score, the easier it was to program the situation.

Visual Requirements: the importance of inspection in the process; the higher the score here the less important the inspection function.

Work Space Availability: the ability to install robots without changing the physical work space. Robots generally took up more space than human workers. It was also dangerous to have workers in close proximity to robots during their operation. The higher the score the more space available for robots.

Jobs Eliminated: jobs directly lost to automation was also a very important category. The score showed the number of jobs eliminated if automation was implemented.

Environmental Severity: a measure of the potential harmful effect of the immediate work environment on human workers, based on such factors as heat, cold, dampness, or use of hazardous chemicals. The higher the score the greater the potential environmental impact.

Back-up System Availability: the ability to operate if unanticipated mechanical failure occurred. The higher the score, the easier it was for manual operations to take over the operations of the automated machines until the problem was fixed.

Total Score: obtained by summing the scores for all of the columns except *Jobs Eliminated.* The higher the total score the greater the feasibility of automation.

ONTARIO ROBITIC CENTRE RECOMMENDATION

The Ontario Robotic Centre stated that the vat washing operation presented the greatest potential for automation, followed by the loading of the hog bellies and finally, the loading of the frozen meat into the extruder. However, Schneider's Management Committee would have to address a nubmer of questions before a final recommendation could be made. Among these were:

- How high should a score be before automation was considered? How reliable was the scoring?
- Should more weight be given to categories dealing with social issues such as Jobs Eliminated or Environmental Severity?
- Had all relevant factors in the decision of whether or not to automate been considered?

This last issue had been providing the Committee the most trouble, as the parameters considered in scoring were very narrow. One factor not considered was quality, historically and currently one of Schneider's hallmarks. Could product quality be allowed to suffer as a result of automation? If so, to what extent? And what about the work force?

Schneider's had historically worked very hard to maintain positive employee relations, and had always been a nonunion company. Any decision likely to compromise management-employee relations would be rigorously examined by the Board. Automation at Ayr had been easy because displaced workers had been assigned to other line jobs in the plant. This would be difficult to achieve in Kitchener, especially in the future as the processes became progressively more automated. Should the Company guarantee employment to workers displaced by automation?

Another point was the integration of workers and machines. Had the Ontario Robotic Centre considered this apsect of the proposal adequately? What would be involved in ensuring the system was "appropriate?" What did "appropriate" mean? How could this be established, and what impact would concepts like "appropriateness" have on system costs?

CONCLUSION

As the Committee members filed into their January 31 meeting they were all aware of the complexity of the issue facing them. Rumors of impending automation were currently sweeping the Kitchener plant, and many workers had individually expressed their concerns to their direct supervisors, and to the plant manager. The workers' principal concerns were security of employment,and quality of work life, and while it was unlikely that any of the three projects currently being considered would have any serious effects on the Kitchener plant, the plant manager was aware that attention had to be given now to all the company's relevant policies, even though their impact might not be felt for some time. The meeting promised to be intense, if not lively.

CASE 10.2

University Hospital: The In-Vitro Fertilization Program[5]

In February 1987, the In-Vitro Fertilization (IVF) program of University Hospital, London, Ontario, was the envy of many of the more than 200 such programs in North America. It had achieved more than 100 pregnancies for the 450 couples who had been through it. This success placed it in a very select group among the programs that were attempting to meet the burgeoning demand for infertility treatment. Leslie Pearson, nurse coordinator for the program since its inception in 1984, had established an excellent reputation among other such administrators for program delivery. Recently however, the IVF team had purchased new equipment which could increase program capacity from 10 patients per week to more than 20. Although the increased capacity would certainly help reduce the huge waiting list, there would be no increases in staff and Leslie wondered what impact the new technology would have on both the patients and staff in the IVF program.

THE FEMALE REPRODUCTIVE CYCLE

A woman's reproductive cycle follows a consistent and usually predictable pattern. Each cycle lasts for a period of approximately 28 days beginning with the onset of menstruation and centered around ovulation when one mature egg is usually released for fertilization.

[5]This case was prepared by Christopher Houston and Professor John Haywood-Farmer. © 1987. The University of Western Ontario.

Days 1–5

During this period the lining of the uterus, or endometrium, which has been thickening over the last 28 days, is shed as menstrual fluid. Hormones released from the brain stimulate an ovary to ripen a follicle which usually contains a single egg (see Exhibit 10.4).

Exhibit 10.4 The Reproductive Cycle in Women

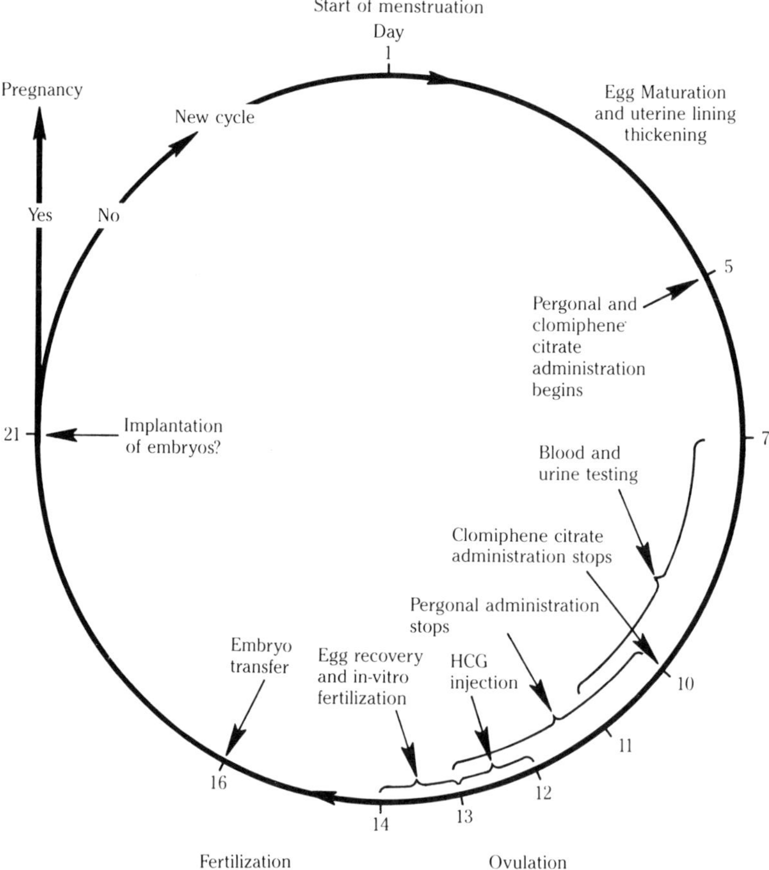

Note: Days of the cycle and normal biological processes are located outside the circle. The IVF steps are located inside the circle. Time periods are approximate and vary from patient to patient. Some of the drug regimens were subjects of controlled experiments and were still being assessed.

Days 6–10

The lining of the uterus, begins to thicken in preparation for implantation of a fertilized egg. The follicle, containing the unfertilized egg, continues to mature and becomes visible on the surface of the ovary.

Days 11–20

Finally the egg is released from ther follicle, and passes down a fallopian tube toward the uterus. The old follicle becomes a gland called the corpus luteum which produces hormones that stimulate maturation of the endometrium. At this point in the cycle, fertilization may or may not occur. Fertilized eggs start to develop, and approximately five days after fertilization, the new embryo, which has now travelled down the fallopian tube, may implant into the now fully-developed endometrium. The resulting pregnancy is sustained by human chorionic gonadotropin (HCG), a hormone produced by the placenta, the organ which attaches the embryo to its mother.

Often, eggs are not fertilized or do not implant; instead they are reabsorbed into the body. As time passes from day 20 to 28, the concentration of hormones which sustained the thickened endometrium decreases and the endometrium is lost as menstrual fluid on or about day 28, when a new cycle begins.

INFERTILITY PROBLEMS

Although the reproductive cycle may seem relatively simple and predictable, there are numerous ways in which it can go wrong. For many couples who discover that they are unable to conceive, the trauma of frustrated parenthood can be very intense. Problems can occur at each step. The ovaries may not produce eggs or the uterine lining may not form properly. There may be structural difficulties whereby eggs released from the ovary never reach the uterus or sperm are blocked from reaching the egg. There may, of course, be an assortment of problems of male infertility such as a low sperm concentration, insufficient sperm motility, or simply no sperm at all.

Serious infertility problems may make pregnancy very unlikely. In such cases, after sufficient time has passed to confirm the physician's diagnosis (usually one year), enrollment in an IVF program may be warranted.

IN-VITRO FERTILIZATION

As the name implies, in-vitro fertilization involves the fertilization of one or more human eggs with sperm, outside the woman's body. The process takes place in-vitro, that is "in glass" (Latin) rather than in-vivo, "in living tissue" (also Latin). In simple terms the process involves three basic stages: egg maturation and 'harvesting;' fertilization and initial development in a culture medium; and embryo transfer and pregnancy. Pregnancies achieved through the process are subject to all the same difficulties and failures of 'normally' achieved pregnancies. As with all technologically complex medical procedures, provision of the IVF service is accomplished through a well-integrated and technically competent team of physicians, nurses, biologists, laboratory technicians, and other support personnel.

THE IVF PROGRAM AT UNIVERSITY HOSPITAL

University Hospital, a leading teaching and research facility adjacent to, and closely affiliated with, The University of Western Ontario, began its IVF program in February 1984. Although the program was backed by a $50,000 pool of seed money from the hospital, it was self-supporting from the start and had never used any of the seed money. The Ontario Health Insurance Plan (OHIP), a comprehensive tax-supported provincial governmental health insurance plan to which almost all residents of Ontario belonged, covered the physician's charge for IVF procedures, but until October 1986 did not cover other costs, such as staff salaries ($68,500), equipment ($6,000), supplies ($14,000), and hospital overhead ($12,000). The program charged its Ontario patients $1,200–$1,400 and non-Ontario patients about $3,000 per treatment cycle to cover these annual costs (parts of which were usually covered by other provincial health plans). American IVF programs typically charged between U.S. $3,500 and $7,000 per treatment cycle.

Although University Hospital employed the program's staff, and was responsible for the costs of equipment, supplies and overhead, the four IVF physicians were all employees of the university with offices in University Hospital. They were members of a group of gynecologists specializing in infertility treatment. Under their contract with the university, they were paid a salary and were allowed to earn up to a certain amount above their salary from clinical practice;clinical income above that level reverted to the university. Each of them was at the income ceiling. They were remunerated for their clinical services on a fee for service basis either through billing OHIP for allowed procedures on covered patients or by billing uncovered patients directly. The IVF program occupied about 25 percent of their clinical work.

In October 1986 the Ministry of Health added IVF treatment to its covered procedures. Under OHIP funding the hospital received an operating grant to support the program and the patient paid nothing directly for treatment. Subsequently, University Hospital was allowed $601,888 per year to treat 425 IVF patients with the provisions that should the program treat fewer patients, the budget could be reduced but if more patients were treated, there would be no corresponding budget increase. A patient usually went through more than one treatment cycle. The annual budget and the number of patients treated were subject to periodic negotiations with the Ministry but the government was clearly trying to control all health care costs. For non-Ontario patients the hospital charged $3,000 per IVF treatment cycle ($4,500 for patients from outside Canada); these funds were retained by the hospital, not the physicians.

ADMISSION TO THE IVF PROGRAM

Candidates for admission to the IVF program at University Hospital were typically referred by other physicians after lengthy treatment for infertility. During the consultation leading up to an approach to the IVF program most prospective patients and their husbands had discussed adoption as an option and most were on adoption waiting lists. The IVF program screened them on the basis of age, length of infertility, likelihood of success and other factors. Typically, a suitable candidate for IVF ovulated, at least on an occasional basis, and had a demonstrated desire and the necessary maturity to begin an arduous process which had a very limited success rate. The program had established a waiting list, which had recently been closed, of several years.

Approximately two months prior to their first IVF cycle, the IVF team invited patients and their partners to an information session where they were introduced to the IVF team and the process was explained to them (see Exhibit 10.5). Every effort was made to make as much information available as possible and patients were encouraged to ask questions. The low probability of success was reiterated frequently. In the next few weeks, patients and their spouses would complete a battery of psychological tests

Exhibit 10.5 Process Flow of the IVF Cycle

Step	Staff Involved[1]	Purpose
IVF Candidates	Physicians	Test for infertility
Admission to IVF Program	Physicians	Admit to the IVF program
	IVF Nurses	Set priority date
Information evening	Full IVF Team	Give patients information and stress the "team" concept
	Instructional Resources	
Assessment day	Instructional Resources	Show instructional video
	Psychologists	Assess susceptibility to stress
	IVF Nurses	Explain patient responsibilities and answer questions
	Physician	Perform physical examination
	Laboratory	Analyze semen
	Pharmacy	Fill clomiphene citrate and pergonal prescriptions
Day 1 of cycle	IVF Nurses	Review IVF cycle and update information
Day 5[2]	IVF Nurse or Family Physician	Start clomid (orally) and pergonal (injections)
Day 11[2]	Hormone Laboratory	Monitor hormones in blood & urine
	Radiology[3]	Count follicles using ultrasound
	Pharmacy	HCG for injection
Day 14[2]	Hospital Admissions	Admit to hospital
	Out-Patient Clinic	
	Operating Room[3]	Egg recovery
	Anaesthetists[3]	Egg recovery
	IVF Physician	Egg recovery
	Biologist/Gamete Lab	Identify and store eggs collect semen and fertilize eggs
Day 16[2]	IVF Physician	Transfer embryos
	IVF Nurses	Transfer embryos
	Gamete Lab	Transfer embroys
Day 21[2]		Pregnancy or a new cycle

[1]Both IVF and University Hospital staff were involved at points in the process.
[2]Times are approximate and vary from patient to patient.
[3]Functions no longer required with the new ultra-sound recovery technology.

Exhibit 10.6 Daily Instruction Sheet for IVF Patients

Phone No. after Day 11 ____________

PATIENT DAILY INSTRUCTION SHEET

DAY 1 ________ Cll IVF Office—(519) 663–2966.
Begin temperature chart. REMEMBER to bring in your temp. chart when we start monitoring your blood.

DAY 5 ________ Clomiphene

DAY 6 ________ Clomiphene Pergonal amp(s)

DAY 7 ________ Clomiphene Pergonal amp(s)

DAY 8 ________ Clomiphene Pergonal amp(s)

DAY 9 ________ Clomiphene Pergonal amp(s)

DAY 10 ________ Pergonal amp(s)
Possibly report to IVF Office, Room 9GE7, U.H.

DAY 11 ________ 7:45 a.m. — Report to London Biochemistry Lab., 245 Pall Mall Street, London, for blood drawing.
Pick up urine collection kit.
____ a.m. Report to IVF Office YES NO
____ a.m. Appointment with nurse YES NO
________ Ultrasound YES NO
Pergonal amp(s) Location: ____________
Time: ____________

DAY 12 ______ 7:45 a.m. — Report to London Biochemistry
Urine collection YES NO Time: ____________
Ultrasound YES Time: ____________ NO
Pergonal _____ amp(s) — Location: ____________
Time: ____________

DAY 13 ________ 7:45 a.m. — Report to London Biochemistry
Urine collection YES NO Time: ____________
Ultrasound YES Time: ____________ NO
Pergonal _____ amp(s) — Location: ____________
Time: ____________

DAY 14, 15, 16, 17 — carry on as directed daily by IVF Office and be available between 2:00 p.m. and 4:30 p.m.

which would be used to measure their ability to cope with the significant stress imposed by the program.

For the patient, the IVF experience differed from the normal doctor-patient interaction in two very significant ways. First, the IVF process was managed by a team and the patient might be seen by several physicians during the process. The IVF surgeons worked on a roster system so that each was on duty about every fourth week. Second, most of the patient's interaction was with the nursing and other hospital staff rather than with a physician.

After the evening information session, a patient and her husband attended an 'assessment day' at University Hospital during which they received an instruction sheet for the IVF cycle (Exhibit 10.6). The assessment involved a physical examination of the patient to calibrate instruments for the embryo transfer and a semen analysis to ensure that the husband was able to produce a satisfactory semen specimen when the recovered eggs were ready to be fertilized.

Again, the couple viewed videotape material which explained the IVF cycle and prepared them for the next stage. They spent an hour with the IVF team psychologist discussing the results of the tests and exploring ways in which they could prepare for the rigors of the next few weeks. Although the results were not used to screen patients out of the program, they provided an essential profile of each patient which the IVF team later used to help them respond to the patient's inquiries. A summary table of a patient's psychological profile is shown as Exhibit 10.7.

At the conclusion of the assessment day, patients received their prescriptions for clomiphene citrate and pergonal, two drugs used to stimulate egg development.

THE IVF CYCLE

On day one of the patient's cycle, she called the IVF office and notified them that her period had begun. At that time, the IVF staff prepared the patient's file. This document (see Exhibit 10.8) provided the base from which the IVF team made most of its decisions. The file included medication protocols ordered by the physicians, results of the psychological tests and other personal history data. As the cycle continued, the file was updated daily through frequent telephone contact with the patient.

On day five the patient started her cycle of medications. Clomiphene was taken orally and pergonal was administered intramuscularly by either the IVF staff or the patient's own doctor. By day 11, blood samples were drawn at a local laboratory and used to monitor the rate of development of the eggs. Urine samples, collected every three hours, were used in the final stages of egg maturation to measure hormone levels and thus to determine the optimal time for egg recovery.

On approximately day 13, after an ultrasound examination determined the number and size of the maturing follicles, the patient received an injection of HCG which would induce ovulation in 33 to 36 hours. The timing of this stage was crucial for the eggs had to be mature but had to be collected before they were naturally released in ovulation. HCG allowed the IVF team to schedule the surgical procedure called laparoscopy, by which the mature eggs would be recovered.

Exhibit 10.7 Summary of Results from Pscyhological Testing

______________	______________
PROFESSION: ______________	PROFESSION: ______________
PSYC. STR: HI AVER LO	PSYC. STR: HI AVER LO
HARM AVOIDANCE: HI AVER LO	HARM AVOID: HI AVER LO
ABIL TO ASK FOR SUPPORT: YES NO	ABIL TO ASK FOR SUPP: YES NO
NEED FOR ORG'N: HI AVER LO	NEED FOR ORG'N: HI AVER LO
NEED TO NURTURE: HI AVER LO	NEED TO NURTURE: HI AVER LO
TEND TO ANGER: HI AVER LO	TEND TO ANGER: HI AVER LO
NEED FOR INFO: HI AVER LO	NEED FOR INFO: HI AVER LO
GEN. ANXIETY: _____ SPEC. ANX: _____	GEN. ANXIETY: _____ SPEC. ANX: _____
LIFE SAT'N: HI AVER LO	LIFE SAT'N: HI AVER LO
MARRIAGE: GOOD OK LO OPEN	MARRIAGE: GOOD OK LO OPEN
PRIVATE: HI AVER LO	PRIVATE: HI AVER LO
AMBITIOUS: HI AVER LO	AMBITIOUS: HI AVER LO
DEPRESSED: _____ SAD: _____	DEPRESSED: _____ SAD: _____

Laparoscopy and Egg Retrieval

Recovery of the mature eggs for in-vitro fertilization required a surgical procedure. Under general anaesthetic, the IVF surgeon recovered one to 15 eggs from the ovaries through a small incision in the patient's abdomen. A technician from the IVF laboratory, who was responsible for the egs as they were recovered, assisted the surgeon. Each egg was stored separately in a carefully controlled atmosphere while being transported from the operating room to the laboratory.

When all the eggs were retrieved, the IVF surgeon concluded the surgery and reported the results to the patient's waiting husband. The procedure took 30 to 60 minutes; the IVF team arranged to schedule egg recovery surgery between 8:00 and 9:00 AM daily. There were many other users of the operating rooms of the University Hospital.

Egg Treatment and Fertilization

Upon return to the laboratory, the biologist prepared the eggs for fertilization. The eggs were stored in a culture medium prepared from a sample of the patient's blood collected

Exhibit 10.8 Information Summary Sheet Prepared for Each Patient

NAME: ____________ D.O.B.: __/__/__ CHART: ______ DAY 1: ______

HUSB. NAME: ______ CITY: ______ PHONE: h) ______ LONDON: ______

TPAL: ____ DIAGNOSIS: ____________ CYCLE LENGTH: ______

MEDICATION PROTOCOL: ____________

CYCLE NO.: ______ # OF TRANSFERS: ______

LAP'Y DATE: ______ CYCLE DAY: ____ # OOCYTES: ____ PHYSICIAN: ______

TRANSFER DATE: ______ # EMBRYOS ____ TENACULUM: YES/NO, EASY/DIFFICULT/CRAMPING

PHYSICAN AT TRANSFER: ______ MENSES — DAY: ____ BETA HCG: ______

MONITORING

CYCLE DAY:		DAY 11	DAY 12	DAY 13	DAY 14	DAY 15	DAY 16
DATE:		___	___	___	___	___	___
ESTRADIOL:	AM:	___	___	___	___	___	___
	PM:	___	___	___	___	___	___
L.H.:	AM:	___	___	___	___	___	___
	PM:	___	___	___	___	___	___

HCG: DATE: ______ TIME: ______ (Cycle Day____)

ULTRASOUND

CYCLE DAY: ______ LEFT ____ % ACCESS RIGHT ____ % ACCESS

DATE: ______

TIME: ______ ( ) ______ ( ) ______

______ ______

URINES

	0300	0600	0900	1200	1500	1800	2100	2400
DAY 13	/	/	/	/	/	/	/	/
i.u./hr	___	___	___	___	___	___	___	___
DAY 14	/	/	/	/	/	/	/	/
i.u./hr	___	___	___	___	___	___	___	___
DAY 15	/	/	/	/	/	/	/	/
i.u./hr	___	___	___	___	___	___	___	___

on or about day 11 of the cycle. After about two hours, the husband produced a semen specimen which, after preparation, was introduced to the waiting eggs. The sperm and egg(s) were incubated together for 24 hours.

Fertilization was a critical stage and although as many as eight or 10 eggs may have been recovered from the ovaries, rarely would more than three or four have reached sufficient maturity to fertilize successfully. The day after fertilization, the couple returned to the Hospital for embryo transfer.

Embryo Transfer

As the couple waited in the day treatment room, the laboratory technician brought in the embryos for transfer. Under the microscope they appeared as clear balls of cells at various stages of development. The clusters of from two to 12 cells had just begun the journey of life; the team members referred to them as "the kids." There was an air of wonderment in the room. The couple may have struggled for years with the deeply felt emotional scars that come with infertility and yet, beneath the microscope lens, was new life and with it, new hope. Perhaps they had never known whether fertilization had ever before occurred and here was proof that "everything works." It was a great moment.

The physician quickly completed the embryo transfer. The small syringe with a flexible plastic tube or catheter which had been calibrated on assessment day, was loaded with the embryo(s) and inserted through the patient's vagina into her uterus where the embryos were deposited. The procedure was simple and required only 15 to 20 minutes. After an hour of bed rest, the patient was ready to go home and begin the two to three week wait to see whether a pregnancy had been achieved.

THE IN-VITRO FERTILIZATION TEAM

The IVF team (Exhibit 10.9) consisted of five physicians, a nurse coordinator, two full-time and two part-time nurses, a biologist and two full-time and one part-time technician in the gamete laboratory, a psychologist, and various other hospital employees. Each interacted with the patient in a different fashion and contributed both essential but diverse elements of the service.

Physicians

Physicians were the initial point of contact for a patient with the IVF team. A group of five doctors, all members of the gynecology department of Unviersity Hospital, decided who would be admitted to the program and where they would be on the priority list. Each doctor's practice included some patients who were potential or accepted IVF candidates. Because of the proximity of the IVF center to their own practice offices, the doctors had been able to fit IVF procedures such as assessment examinations and embryo transfers, unscheduled, into their normal cycle of patients visits.

The primary concerns of the physician group were for the welfare of their individual patients. However, because of the team concept, an IVF patient might be seen

Exhibit 10.9 Personnel Involved in In-Vitro Fertilization at University Hospital

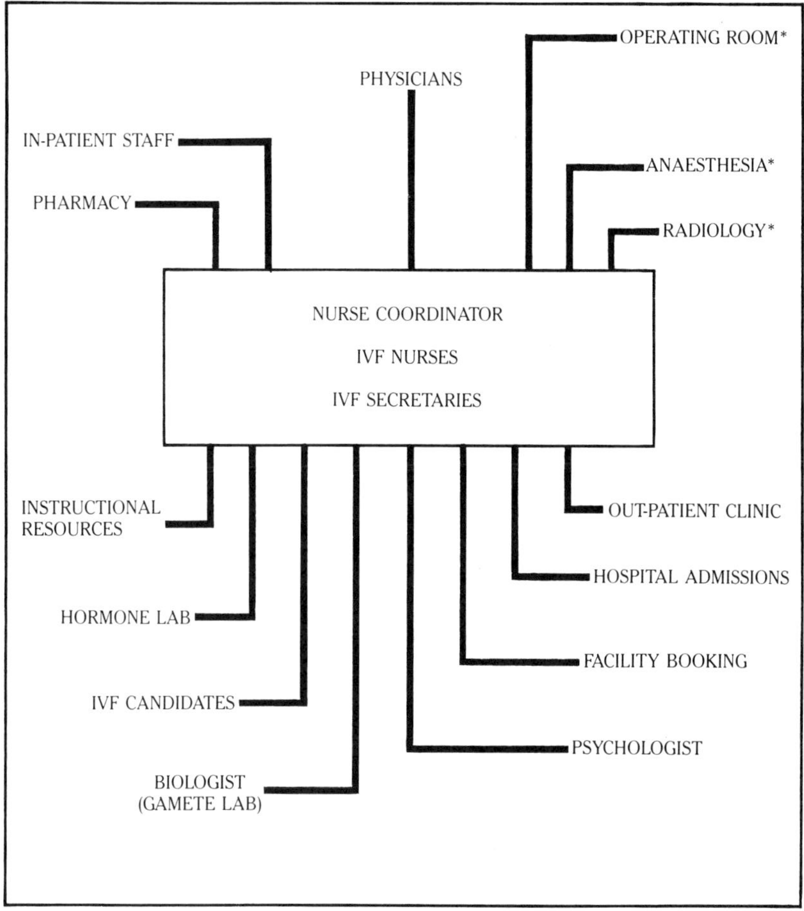

*Note: Hospital facilities/personnel made redundant by ultrasound egg recovery process.

by several physicians, none of whom she had seen before. All doctors had to be familiar with, and skilled in, each IVF procedure. IVF technology was relatively new and much of the work conducted in London was at the leading edge of current technology. Consequently, the physicians were always keen to see more successful treatment procedures. They measured their success largely in terms of the number of patients who became pregnant. Dr. Bill Hamilton, one of the original IVF physicians, commented:

> We physicians want to do everything we can to increase the number of pregnancies and we tend to concentrate on that. However, when I reflect on the situation and when I talk about it, I have to remember that most of the patients are unsuccessful.
>
> We need to keep reminding ourselves that we are doing several things with this program. It is the 'end of the road' for all of these patients. This is the last resort treatment.

> Those that get pregnant receive what they came for. Those that do not, however, also need to receive something of benefit. They come to the program seeking closure. They take this reasonably small chance that they are going to have a baby, but also they come to realize and accept that if they don't get pregnant, they can go on with their lives. The danger is that when we increase the number of patients we will cheat those people. Treatment in IVF is more than just an attempt at pregnancy.

Nurse Coordinator

This portion, although principally administrative in nature, represented the key managerial function in the IVF team. The nurse coordinator acted as a liaison between the physicians, the patients and the rest of the hostpial staff. University Hospital's IVF nurse coordinator, Leslie Pearson, had an unusual role for a nurse. She was responsible for administering and managing the program; for example, several people reported directly to her and she decided how many patients would be treated and when. She also had above average experience in knowing when medical intervention was necessary. Bill explained:

> It happened as a result of my trip to Australia where I saw the way they had set up their program. It centered around the nurse coordinator who was kind of a quarterback to the whole team. The doctors said that they went where they were told! I looked at it then as an organization rather than a doctor-patient relationship. The IVF treatment is a complicated procedure, best organized through nursing staff rather than with physicians because we would not handle the coordinating function well. I think that is evident in most other programs that are doctor-dominated. As a result of visits to University Hospital by other physicians, changes are being made to other Canadian IVF programs. If I tried to do what Leslie is doing, I'd probably do an inadequate job and while I would have more contact with patients, I would probably have a poorer rapport with them.
>
> What we have built up in this program with the nursing staff is a healthier, better relationship for the couple than anything a doctor and the couple could ever hope to build up alone.
>
> It would be more difficult to put the current structure into effect in an existing program. At the beginning, there were very few patients and everybody was keen, interested, and putting in time to develop the patient relationships. The physicians developed close relationships with their patients but as the program got bigger, we physicians moved more and more into a technical role and Leslie took over more and more of the patient-care role. The program was built around the concept of trying to maintain the support of the patient relationship through the nursing staff.

IVF Nurses and Secretaries

The nursing and secretarial staff of the IVF team were the principal contact points for the patients. On the first day of a new patient's cycle, she called the IVF office and the paperwork was set up. Leslie described the role of the secretaries:

> The secretaries are a big help; no other program has given the secretaries as much independence as we have, but we have trained them to do about 80 percent of the initial setup on each patient. When the patient phones up on day one, that very day there is a one-and-one-half hour setup which is now divided into about 20 percent nursing time and 80 percent secretarial time. That all takes a lot of time and I like to get involved. We really individualize the care at this point, and that sets us apart from other programs.

The patient relayed information to the secretaries and nurses daily regarding her condition, and the IVF staff informed the patient about laboratory results and reminded her of procedures. The nursing staff coordinated and planned the information evenings, assessment days, patient laboratory visits, daily pergonal injections, and scheduled the egg recoveries and embryo transfers.

Occasionally a patient did not respond well to the medications and for a variety of reasons there was not much point in continuing the treatment. A poor response included patients who did not develop multiple eggs or displayed abnormal hormonal patterns, in which cases success (pregnancy) was very unlikely, and those who developed far too many eggs, which was dangerous. This kind of news was never good and with the emotional investment each patient had made, telling the patient was difficult. In preparation for the phone call, the nurses or physicians went over the patient's psychological profile to ascertain the kind and intensity of reaction the patient would likely have. Once prepared, the IVF team member could pass on the bad news as compassionately as possible. Telling unsuccessful patients was time-consuming and involved a lot of short-term counseling at intervals over a period of 24 hours or so. Except in cases in which continued treatment would be dangerous to the patient, the program staff did not cancel a patient's treatment unilaterally; although they tried to persuade the patient to cancel, they left the decision to withdraw from a treatment cycle up to the patient and her husband. Bill Hamilton considered that the way in which the bad news was presented was a very important part of the couple's decision.

Central assimilation and dissemination of information was essential to the success of the IVF program. A whiteboard in the IVF office contained details of each patient's condition and from a binder of patient files, any nurse or physician could update the progress of each patient in the current IVF cycle. When a patient telephoned the IVF office, the nursing or secretarial staff was able to advise them of their latest laboratory results and to inform them of any required changes in medications.

The nursing staff was called upon to act as counselors, administrators, lobbyists, educators and, occasionally nurses. They also arranged the patient's interface with the other parts of the hospital. Operating rooms and anesthetists had to be booked for egg retrieval laparoscopies. In order to provide a couple with as much privacy as possible, arrangements were made to assign unused private rooms where possible and without additional charges. Admissions were arranged to allow the IVF team to monitor a patient as she approach ovulation in order to prevent premature release of the eggs from the ovarian follicles. The IVF team had to be prepared to accelerate retrieval by rescheduling the operating room and the surgical team in case the patient showed signs of ovulating without drug therapy.

Psychologist

One psychologist from the University Hospital psychology department was assigned on a full-time basis to the IVF program. For each patient, there was a one hour interview on assessment day to discuss the results of the psychological tests completed by the couple. Each set of tests required about 120 minutes to score, 60 minutes to summarize in a report, 90 minutes of typing, and 20 minutes to discuss the results with the IVF team.

In addition to the testing procedure, the psychologist was also available for counseling, when the couple requested it. Although only about 10 percent of patients in their first cycle made use of this service, the percentage was higher for patients after their second unsuccessful cycle when they realized that the third and final opportunity was now before them. More recently, the physicians in the IVF program had been referring non-IVF patients to the psychologist as a part of their infertility treatment.

The psychological assessment and counseling of each patient played crucial roles in the program. The IVF team members decided how to communicate with each patient during their IVF cycles based on the data provided by the testing procedure. They were essential elements in the customization of the process and contributed significantly to the sense of personal attention. One patient commented: "It was as if the whole program was set up just for me." They also allowed team members to manage patient emotions to avoid long-term emotional scars in unsuccessful patients.

Laboratory Staff

The laboratory staff consisted of a biologist, who was also engaged in research on human reproduction, and technicians. Their function was to take responsibility for the sperm and egg(s) prior to fertilization and to perform the necessary steps to return the maximum number of fertilized eggs for implantation. They had virtually no direct patient contact and remained administratively distinct from the rest of the IVF team. However, the function they performed was both essential to, and integrated with, the research focus of the five physicians.

Other University Hospital Staff

Other University Hospital staff involved in the IVF program included admissions staff for the overnight stays required for the laparoscopies, radiology staff who conducted the ultrasound examinations during the assessment days, pharmacists who stocked and administered the expensive hormone drug treatments, surgicial staff, including anesthetists, who arranged and ran the operating rooms for the entire hospital and instructional resources staff who provided assistance in the preparation of information materials for patients.

THE NEW ULTRASOUND TECHNOLOGY

In February 1987, the IVF program received a new ultrasound unit, recently developed in Sweden. The new technology would allow the physicians to conduct the preretrieval assessments without needing the hospital's radiology unit, and the actual egg retrievals without the need for a laparoscopy. The new retrieval procedure would mean that the patient would need no general anesthetic. The surgical procedure would be replaced by a much simpler egg retrieval using a vaginally inserted needle attached to an ultrasound transducer. The ultrasound picture would allow the physicians to perform the egg recovery by watching the procedure on a television monitor.

Because the ultrasound equipment was located across the hall from the IVF office, the nursing staff could handle all the patient's needs. Under the new procedure, a couple would simply come to the IVF office and wait their turn for egg retrieval. The procedure would take 20 minutes and be followed by a two to three hour recovery. They would be free to return home and, if all went well, return two days later for the embryo transfer.

The capacity of the program could increase from 10 patients cycles per week to 20, as there would be no limit imposed by the operating room schedule. Using ultrasound technology the revenue received by the hospital and the physicians from both OHIP and the directly billed uncovered patients would remain unchanged. Costs would be reduced by an estimated $85 per case for supplies. Costs for the hospital as a whole would not be reduced because the operating rooms were always in demand and operating room time not used by the IVF program would be allocated to other services.

The new technology offered an opportunity to increase substantially the number of patients that could be given some hope for pregnancy and thus to reduce the waiting list. But doubling capacity might have a significant impact on the experience of the patients in the IVF program.

Bill commented:

> The doctor is the one who will be least affected by a significant increase in IVF patients. The nurses will be affected the most and the patient somewhere in the middle.
>
> I don't see how an increase in capacity could not affect the way in which we manage patients. I don't think we give our patients as much tender, loving care as we gave our initial patients when the program began. It's probably more realistic now, though. We are moving all the time towards a "factory process" but we try not to let it appear that way to the patients; so far, we have been successful. There is no question that this program is more patient centered than any other I'm familiar with.
>
> With regard to the proposed capacity expansion, the technical side of it can be done. Certainly the busier you are, the greater the potential for mistakes but that does not worry me because we have enough safeguards. If I make an error, Leslie will catch it. She has no hesitation in coming to me and pointing out mistakes. Even if Leslie misses it, the lab goes over the protocol as well; they are not reluctant to ask what I'm doing either.
>
> I really worry about the effect on staff. If we go up to 20 a week the burnout could be horrendous. People are not going to enjoy their jobs, they are going to be under so many demands and will be running here, there, and everywhere, staying late, coming early, working over noon hour, knowing that they are not satisfying patients, knowing that the job is not going to get finished, worrying about missing something all the time. The people who work in this program have put a lot of pressure on themselves not to make errors, to be the best in the team, and to put everything into it to get these people pregnant. They are very committed people who tend to be perfectionists and hate to make mistakes.

THE DILEMMA

The dilemma that Leslie Pearson and the IVF team faced was not easy to resolve. To increase the size of the program would certainly result in more pregnancies and more couples having an opportunity to have one last attempt to fulfill a very strong desire—getting pregnant. However, with no additional funding available, the quality of service for each couple could be radically altered. Leslie was concerned that any breakdown in the patient-nurse relationship could result in more misinformation being passed around and with the emotionally charged nature of the subject, she had already spent countless hours on the phone calming distraught patients.

Leslie commented:

> The patient network is so incredible that now pretty well everybody knows somebody who is in IVF. Consistency of information is so important. A patient might have to be cancelled in the middle of a treatment cycle. If the story wasn't quite right and she tells a friend who then says, "That's funny, my LH was the same as that and I didn't get cancelled," the patient gets confused and upset. We have to be so consistent and for that reason we spend an awful lot of our time in meetings.

Should the IVF program grow to serve 20 patients per week? If the program managers did decide to increase volume, how long would it take to do so, and how should the staff members prepare for the change? As Leslie contemplated these and other issues, she also wondered what impact her own imminent resignation would have, and whether she should recommend that the capacity increase be delayed for some time in the future. She also wondered what type of person should be found to replace her and how that person should be trained.

Chapter Eleven

GOVERNMENT'S ROLE IN NEW TECHNOLOGY

SITUATION 11.1

Japan Adopts a New Technology: The Roles of Government, Trading Firms and Suppliers[1]

The Japanese have seldom invented major new industrial technologies, nor have they been noted for being particularly fast to introduce new technologies elsewhere. Their strength has been to be relatively early to use technology, to be very effective at working out any bugs associated with it, and (once the new technology is proven) to be extraordinarily quick to use it to replace older technologies. The Japanese government often plays a role in this success, as do trading firms and affiliated firms.

The purpose of this article is to give some sense of the dynamics of their contribution to the introduction of major new industrial technology. This will be done through a description of the introduction of the basic oxygen furnace in Japan. Some contrasts will be made with what happened in the United States and Canada.

Most of the events described here took place in the 1950s when the Japanese steel industry was much smaller in the world context, and when the Japanese Ministry of International Trade and Industry (MITI) was much freer to promote its own industrial policies than it is now. Despite these changes, the patterns described here are still representative of many of the processes occurring today. This point will be taken up again in the conclusion.

THE BASIC OXYGEN FURNACE

The Basic Oxygen Furnace (BOF) was first put into commercial operation by a small Austrian steelmaker in late 1952. By 1970 it had replaced the open hearth as the world's

[1]Leonard Lynn, "Japan Adopts a New Technology: The Roles of Government, Trading Firms and Suppliers." *Columbia Journal of World Business*, Winter, pp. 39–45. © 1984 by The Trustees of Columbia University in the City of New York. Extracted with permission.

most widely used steelmaking process. Steelmakers, however, were not equally quick to recognize the advantages of the new technology. Some continued to build open hearths until about 1960. Nor were the steel industries of different countries equally effective in exploiting the BOF.

The Japanese put their first BOF into operation in September 1957, earlier than all but the steel industries of Austria, Canada and the United States. They were early to use this new technology, but not extraordinarily so. Indeed a small steelmaker in Canada and one in the United States put BOF plants into operation some three years ahead of them. Once the BOF technology was proven to their satisfaction, however, the Japanese industry was extremely quick to make the fullest use of it. By April 1962, all six of the major Japanese steelmakers were using BOFs, compared to only one of the eight major American steelmakers. By 1971, the Japanese had replaced all of the open hearths at their integrated plants. United States steelmakers have yet to do so.

One aspect of the rapid diffusion of the BOF in Japan was an industry-wide effectiveness in evaluating the technology at a time when its superiority was still in question. Between 1954 (when the first commercial BOF was put into use outside Austria) and 1960, the Japanese built nine new steelmaking shops. Six were BOF. The United States industry built 16 new steelmaking shops. Only five were BOF.

In sum, while some United States firms may have been quick to use the BOF, the United States steel industry as a whole was slow to do so. And, while none of the Japanese firms were very early in adopting the new technology, the Japanese steel industry as a whole was very quick to use it.

The Japanese have been noted for an unusual ability to refine technologies developed elsewhere, and in the case of the basic oxygen furnace they excelled. The two most generally applicable advances in BOF technology, the multihole lance and the OG pollution control/energy recovery system were both developed in Japan. The Japanese successes at refining the BOF technology do not stop here. Reports in the literature suggest that Japanese steelmakers have led over the years in computerizing BOF operations and in the development of new operating procedures.

THE OPEN HEARTH "PROBLEM" AND THE SEARCH FOR SOLUTIONS

In the years after World War II, the open hearth was easily the dominant steelmaking process in the world. Competing processes, such as the Bessemer and Thomas, were limited with respect to the raw materials they could refine and the types of steel they could produce. Despite this dominance, however, the open hearths had obvious shortcomings. They were expensive to build and operate. They also required the use of scrap for economical operation, and scrap prices were volatile. In many areas it was sometimes difficult to get scrap at all.

In 1949 two small Austrian steelmakers started research to develop a new technology that would overcome the drawbacks of the open hearth. After they successfully established the world's first commercial BOF in late 1952, they began aggressive efforts to license the technology to steelmakers around the world. Before this, however, a Japanese firm was already evaluating the new steelmaking process.

THE JAPANESE SEARCH LEADS TO THE BOF

In December 1950, nearly two years before the first commercial BOF went into service, an article describing a BOF pilot plant appeared in the German technical journal Stahl und Eisen. The article did not attract widespread interest, but it did attract the attention of engineers at Nippon Kokan (NKK), Japan's third largest steelmaker at the time. These engineers were given further information on the BOF by a Mitsubishi Trading Company engineer who had recently returned from Europe. In June 1951, four NKK engineers embarked on a three month tour of steel plants in Europe to learn more about the BOF and other technologies.

The second Japanese steelmaker to develop an active interest in the BOF was Yawata, then the leading firm in the industry. Yawata had focused much of its attention on the much publicized efforts of American firms to develop a side-blown steelmaking process. The company's engineers had closely reviewed the United States and European technical literature on side-blown experiments. In 1952, they built a pilot side-blown converter. Their experiments convinced the Yawata engineers that this technology was not viable and led them to search for alternatives. Having followed the development of the BOF technology for some time, they replaced the pilot side-blown furnace with a BOF. NKK, Yawata sought further information about the basic oxygen furnace from a trading firm and then sent engineers to Europe.

PROCESSES OF EVALUATION: JAPAN

Yawata, like Dofasco, carried out extensive pilot plant tests. Like Dofasco, Yawata sent engineers overseas to further collect information on several occasions. Yawata, however, seems to have sent its people overseas more often than the Canadians. Yawata's engineers went to Dofasco as well as to the Austrian firms. They sought information not only on technical matters related to the BOF, but also on the patents and other legal rights held by the Austrians. Yawata was assisted in all this by Ohkura Trading Company.

Yawata also used its pilot plant in a program to develop refractory brick, but its approach here was very different from that used at the North American firms. In Japan each of the major steelmakers had one or more refractory firms as an affiliate. Yawata initiated joint research programs with two of its affiliated suppliers. Each program pursued a separate line of development. The affiliate that developed the best solution had its capital doubled by Yawata and built a new plant to supply Yawata with BOF refractories. Interestingly, the ties between Yawata and the affiliate were loose enough that later the affiliate was able to sell brick to other major Japanese steel firms.

The evaluation of the BOF took on the flavor of high drama at NKK. The company's top management was unwilling to risk pioneering this new technology. One member of the executive board argued that the assumption of such risks was the duty of Yawata or Fuji Steel. These two firms were the leaders of the industry and before being separated under the antitrust reforms of the United States Occupation they had been a "public policy company." NKK did make some low-cost efforts to gain further information on the BOF, for example, in July 1953 when it sent several questions to the German firm that had built the first basic oxygen furnaces. The request was rebuffed. In June 1954 NKK managers again visited one of the Austrian BOFs.

These efforts did not satisfy the NKK engineers who had visited Austria in 1951. These engineers formed the core of a group of BOF advocates, a group determined that NKK would pioneer the BOF in Japan.

Without authorization the advocates built a pilot BOF; operated an "underground" technical press, publishing the results of their tests and translations of foreign articles about the BOF; and even made dangerous experiments using the company's steelmaking converters. These activities continued until mid-1955 when NKK learned that Yawata was planning to adopt the BOF. At this point NKK abruptly decided that it would also adopt the BOF. The company was now determined to be general licensee for the technology in Japan.

Many of the concerns NKK's engineers had about the BOF were resolved during the unauthorized pilot plant experiments and from the information collected overseas. NKK had a refractories division that produced some brick for the company. Like Yawata, NKK also was served by affiliated producers of refractories. NKK initially produced its own brick for the BOF. One of its affiliates purchased Austrian refractories technology and also began its own development work. When the affiliate developed a successful brick, NKK spun off its refractories division to be incorporated into the affiliate.

As in the initial search efforts that resulted in the "discovery" of the BOF, we see relatively aggressive efforts on the part of Japan in evaluating the technology. The Japanese steelmakers were helped in their efforts, both by general trading firms and by affiliated suppliers of refractory brick. The North American firms also had an advantage that has not yet emerged from our account. There was a much freer flow of information from firm to firm in the steel industry in North America than in Japan. A J&L engineer reported on his 1953 visit to the Austrian BOFs at the 1954 National Open Hearth Conference—a conference attended by engineers from all the companies. Other reports on plant visits to Austria were later given by engineers from Dofasco and Kaiser Steel. Dofasco shared information with McLouth and J&L, and later sold its BOF pilot plant to U.S. Steel. There were no exchanges of information between the Japanese steelmakers until later, and then only under prodding from MITI. Yawata's engineers knew little about what was happening at NKK, and NKK could only surmise what was happening at Yawata. Much of this North American advantage was to disappear shortly due to patent disputes that made it inadvisable for engineers at many of the American firms to share information.

MITI AND THE BOF

The sharpest contrast between the North American and the Japanese firms was in the legal arrangements that were made to use the technology. And here we see significant involvement by the Japanese government.

In mid-1955 the two Japanese firms sent people to Austria in an effort to acquire license rights to the BOF. NKK was particularly thorough in its background research before approaching the Austrians. It sent two managers to North America to learn about the experiences McLouth, Dofasco and Kaiser engineers had with the Austrians. Extremely valuable information on the Austrians was also provided by Mitsubishi Trading. This information suggested that NKK had several options. It could approach BOT, a Swiss firm that had been established to market the BOF technology, or it could approach either of the firms that had developed the technology. NKK appears to have used this information to gain an unusually favorable draft license agreement. Under this agreement NKK would pay a lump sum of $1.2 million to use the technology.

Yawata also wanted to be the Japanese general licensee for the technology, and had been offered a per ton royalty agreement similar to that held by Dofasco. The result of this emerging competition could have been bidding between the two or perhaps NKK sublicensing the BOF to other Japanese steel firms at a profit to itself (as in Canada). Some of the Yawata engineers wanted to avoid use of the Austrian patents—an outcome that might have led to court battles like those in the United States.

At this point MITI became involved. At that time MITI's approval was required before a Japanese firm could enter into an international agreement involving the payment of royalties. Metallurgical engineers in MITI's iron and steel production division had long been interested in the BOF. It seemed to them that this new technology might help to reduce Japan's dependence on imported scrap. The director of the division had recently published laudatory articles on the BOF.

The presidents of Yawata and NKK met at MITI's Heavy Industries Bureau. Under the arrangements arrived at during the meeting, NKK was allowed to be general licensee for the technology. Yawata, however, would have equal access to guidance from the Austrians and all Japanese steelmakers would be allowed to use the technology under equal conditions. Under the agreement NKK had arranged, the license for the BOF cost $1.2 million and involved no running royalty. It appeared at the time that, given Japanese levels of production, this would entail a cost per ton of about seven cents—considerably below the level paid by the Canadians and asked of the Americans. As it turned out, however, Japanese production so exceeded expectations that the actual cost of the technology during the license period was only a fraction of a cent per ton. Indeed, the Japanese later received in royalties far more for refinements in the technology such as the OG process than they paid for the technology itself. Another aspect of the agreement arranged at the MITI offices called for all users of the BOF technology to share the related technology they developed at biannual meetings. Later users of the BOF were to send their people for training at NKK and Yawata.

This arrangement effectively encouraged the early Japanese users of the BOF to overcome the reluctance of Japanese steelmakers to share technical information with each other. It helped to promote the rapid diffusion of the technology in Japan. And it helped to ensure that Japan got the technology at a very low cost. In contrast, the development of a patent dispute in the United States may have had the opposite effect. An existing inclination to share technical information was somewhat inhibited.

MITI AND THE PROCESS OF INNOVATION

MITI played strategic roles in reducing the royalties the Japanese steelmakers had to pay for the BOF, helped to facilitate the flow of technical information between firms, generally promoted the diffusion of this technology. One reason MITI was able to play these roles effectively is the high level of expertise on the steel industry that it had in-house. In the 1950s the iron and steel production division included more than a dozen people, about half of whom were metallurgical engineers. Some of its engineers were outstanding graduates of the best schools. These people not only had excellent ties with the industry, they commanded its respect. In the 1950s, MITI was able to exercise considerable control over events through its control over the allocation of foreign exchange.

MITI no longer has the level of expertise or control that it did 25 years ago. Neither, however, has it totally vanished. The iron and steel production division is only about half as large as it was, even though Japan's iron and steel production is about 10 times larger. The steel industry no longer warrants the special attention it did in the 1950s when it was seen as one of four priority industries. Nevertheless, there is still concentration of expertise on the steel (and other industries) in MITI that is lacking in the United States government.

MITI also has lost some of the administrative controls it once held. Foreign exchange has largely been liberalized. New devices to promote similar goals, however, have evolved. In the case of the BOF in the 1950s, MITI used its power over technology imports to force the steel firms to cooperate toward technological advance. Since the mid-1960s MITI's Agency for Industrial Science and Technology has helped promote collaborative research between rival firms through its national R&D programs.

CONCLUSION

Three major points seem to emerge from this account: that the Japanese were able to draw on more resources for the collection of crucial technical and commercial information than the North Americans; that the Japanese steelmakers took a stronger lead within the cluster of firms involved in the introduction of this major new technology; and that the Japanese government played a distinctive role in the introduction and diffusion of the technology.

READING 11.1

Government Policies in Support of Automated Manufacturing: Japan, The United States, and Western Europe[2]

The introduction of automated manufacturing systems (AMS) on a timely and cost-effective basis is emerging as a key to international competitiveness in an ever-widening range of industries.[3] The rate and extent of introduction of these systems are a function of industrial management policies and practices and the national economic environment as it affects the demand for and supply of automated manufacturing equipment and systems. Both sets of determinant variables are in turn influenced by government policies as they affect private-sector risk propensities toward capital expenditures for new industrial plant and equipment and investments in capital research, design, and engineering. Government measures in support of a rapid and extensive introduction of automated manufacturing include tax measures, joint funding, government procurement policies aimed at reducing private sector costs and risks, and commercial trade policies aimed at maintaining a competitive environment to reinforce demand for the new industrial systems. This chapter analyzes and compares the government policies and national environments of Japan, the United States, and selected Western European countries (France, Sweden, and West Germany) (see Exhibit 11.1).

There are vast differences between market-driven and Soviet-style planned economies in both government policies and their impact on innovation in general and the introduction of AMS in particular. In the Soviet economy, the risks and rewards

[2]Jack Baranson (1987). *Competitiveness Through Technology: What Business Needs from Government.* In J. Dermer (ed.) Lexington, Massachusetts, Lexington Books, pp. 147–157. © 1987, D. C. Heath & Co. Reprinted with permission.

[3]Automated manufacturing systems (AMS) refers to a broad range of equipment and systems, including computer-aided design, computer-aided manufacturing, robots, flexible manufacturing systems, and integrated machining centers.

Exhibit 11.1 Comparison of Government Policies and Measures

Policies and Measures	Japan	Europe	United States
Industrial policy Trade policies Regulatory measures	Intervention to promote innovation visions Sunrise industries support long-term risk	France: Highly supportive of high technology West Germany and Sweden: Rely more on market forces EEC trade barriers	Rely largely on market forces Adversarial government-industry relations
Economic measures Capital measures Tax incentives Interest rates Growth Employment	Funds to priority sectors Bank leveraging and tax-sheltered corporate reserves Promote savings, low interest rates	France: Tax shelter capital funds in high-tech industries Germany and Sweden: mild limited intervention EEC: Declining growth rates, employment, rising interest rates	Tax incentives to promote capital investments RD&E generally budgetary Deficits raise interest rates, appreciate currency, intensify foreign competition
R&D Procurement	Jointly fund R&D of next-generation technology Credits for AMS leasing	France highly supportive of AMS RD&E West Germany and Sweden: Limited support	Antitrust inhibits cooperative R&D efforts Strong support of defense-related R&D Tax policies neutral

of innovation (enterprise profits and individual earnings) are linked to government policies and organizational structures very different from the market-driven economies of the United States, Japan, and Western Europe. Policy and structural differences stem from differences in the autonomy of the enterprise in production management, supply procurement, industrial investment decisions and R&D activities for new or improved products and processes, and the pricing mechanism governing both factors of production inputs and product output. Study of Soviet-type economies sharpens our perspectives of the forces that drives Western-type market economies and provide critical insights on how government policies can enhance (or inhibit) innovational dynamics.[4]

There are also dynamic contrasts between the market dynamics in the United States and Japan and prevailing conditions in the EEC, the result, once again, of respective government policies and their impact on national market structures. According to the *Economist*, the EEC suffers from a balkanization of national markets.[5] This is, in part, the result of nontariff barriers, which in effect have raised national R&D and production costs and restricted access to one another's markets. Competition is the spur to innovation, but the ability to amortize the substantial funds needed for the new generation of products and production systems also requires access to sizable markets. The immobility of capital and people (relative to the United States economy) also has stifled

[4]The author is currently directing a research project on the economic environment for introducing AMS into the Soviet Union and systemic differences between planned and market economics as they affect the rate of introduction of AMS.

[5]See "How Europe Has Failed" and "Europe's Technology Gap," *Economist*, November 24, 1984, pp. 13–14, 93–98.

the creation of new, particularly small enterprises, which, it is generally credited, are responsible for the introduction of new products and new or improved production systems. In contrast to conditions in the EEC, deregulation in the United States telecommunication and airline industries has given widespread impetus to innovation from a flood of new small enterprises into these sectors. In Japan, the dependence on external markets and the intensification of international competition have been the innovative drives.

IMPACT OF GOVERNMENT POLICIES ON AMS INVESTMENTS

AMS can produce a much wider range of product variations at relatively low volumes and still be cost-effective, maintain high technical standards, and most important, respond to the rapid and frequent changes in product design and production parameters now typical of world markets. The new industrial automation also has another competitive advantage over conventional high-volume manufacturing systems based on extended product life cycles and using expensive special purpose equipment; it avoids the high risks of locking into capital amortization schedules and product designs that may be rendered obsolete by changes in market demand and shifts in competitive cost structures (as has been the case in the substantial decline of the United States automotive manufacturer's shares, despite restrictive import quotas).

In market driven economies, government policies affect the demand for and supply of automated manufacturing equipment and systems in a variety of ways. AMS investments mean substantial outlays and risks longer-term payback perspectives, and consequently, the risk propensities of industrial managers and corporate commitment to long-term growth and technological development are critical. Also important are the effects of government policies and regulations on capital markets, bank lending, and corporate risk management.

Government policies in support of innovation may include tax measures to reduce purchase costs of AMS products, cost sharing of high risks in the development of AMS products, government procurement to reinforce demand when AMS products are introduced into the marketplace, and education and training programs to increase the supply of needed technical and engineering personnel. Special programs to assist small- to medium-sized industry help to reinforce critical component supplier industries and innovative segments of the economy that have special difficulties obtaining required financial resources. Commercial and trade policies have an indirect effect on internal competition among AMS producers or on their competitiveness abroad. Protectionist measures depress domestic demand for the technological upgrading implicit in AMS products. Government-backed credits reinforce international sales of AMS products.

Government policies have an indirect effect on general economic conditions and market structures. For example, deflationary measures combined with high interest rates depress demand for capital goods in general and AMS products in particular. New capital investments in AMS also are influenced by AMS prices relative to the wages or replaced industrial labor. The size of the internal market influences the range and price of AMS products offered for sale. Competitive forces also influence effective demand for technological upgrading among user industries. Included under financial structures are the availability of industrial capital, credit terms, leasing arrangements, and the risk perspectives of suppliers of equity debt capital. Financial resources are also needed to fund research design and equipment expenditures, new or improved plant and equipment expenditures, and new or improved plant and equipment, as well as to reinforce effective demand for AMS capital expenditures.

The introduction of AMS systems implies profound changes in industrial organization and management and high financial risk. Consequently government-industry relations, trade policies, and regulatory functions that affect risk management are critical. There are nonetheless wide differences in viewpoints on the proper role of government in managing technological change.

U.S. GOVERNMENT POLICIES AND MEASURES

Under the Reagan administration, the prevailing philosophy has been that free market forces should allocate resources and make investment decisions in the private sector. Trade and industry policies are confined largely to maintaining domestic competition (supported by antitrust legislation) and promoting two-way international trade. United States national policies contrast dramatically with those of Japan. Aside from government support of R&D and tax, and depreciation measures to encourage investment in general, United States government industry relations continue to be adversarial rather than cooperative, consensual, and orchestrated as they are in Japan. Adversarial confrontation between government and industry, industry and labor, industry and consumers, and among industrial firms themselves drains vital human and financial resources that might otherwise be used to increase United States industrial competitiveness.

Tax Incentives and Regulatory Measures

Antitrust laws, originally intended to deter constraint of trade in the United States economy, in recent years have inhibited United States firms from mergers and/or joint action to share R&D costs or to utilize each others' corporate strengths to improve international market positions. As a consequence, antitrust laws have hampered the efforts of United States firms to meet international competition, since Japan and most Western European countries permit or encourage such joint action.

The Economic Recovery Act of 1981 permitted accelerated depreciation for the cost of new investments in plant and equipment and increased the size of investment tax credits for industry, but the Tax Equity and Fiscal Responsibility Act of 1982 effectively cancelled nearly half of the benefits business received in the 1981 bill.

Government Support for R&D and Government Procurement

The United States government has traditionally supported long-range, high-risk research and technological development (particularly in defense-related areas), leaving the private-sector to fund R&D that has a good potential for near-term return on investments. The

United States government provides a market for the fruits of the R&D it sponsors through its defense procurement policies, thereby minimizing the costs and risks associated with both innovation andn commercialization of new technology. The bias toward military and aerospace projects in government R&D funding and procurement, combined with the emphasis on basic research (with only long-term payoffs for industry), means that little government support is available that directly aids industrial competitiveness and commercialization. Funding of certain R&D projects is the only explicit way in which the government supports the expansion of AMS, but these expenditures are also generally limited to mission-oriented national defense needs.

The military of government R&D on manufacturing technology has two detrimental side effects from the commercial standpoint: (1) neglect of generic, systems approaches, limiting the applicability of results to civilian problems and settings, and (2) the emphasis on hardware and predominance of physical scientists and engineers on program staffs, which results in neglect of social and organizational factors in design of manufacturing systems, making user implementation of the technologies development more difficult. The Defense Departments Manufacturing Technology Program provides hundreds of millions of dollars annually for purchase of advanced manufacturing equipment.[6] But very little pressure is exerted on defense contractors to become cost-effective and internationally competitive through commercialization of technological innovations. In the past, military-funded R&D has led to the development of numerically controlled (NC) machine tools and automatic programmed tool (APT) language, both of which are now in commercial use worldwide, but the commercial spillover effects are not comparable to those realized in Japan.

AMS-Related Trade Policies

Persistent protectionist lobbying in the consumer electronics, steel, automotive, and machine tool industries has buffered certain industries against foreign competition and slowed the adoption of AMS.[7] The United States trade representative has argued that

[6]United States government support for R&D on robots was about $18 million in fiscal year 1982. In recent years the National Science Foundation (NSF) has spent about $4.5 million annually on civilian robots and related research (distributed largely to universities and nonprofit laboratories in small grants of about $200,000 each). NSF primarily supports basic research centering on improved robot dexterity and sensory perception, higher-order robot programming languages, and computerized manufacturing and assembly. The National Bureau of Standards spends about $1.2 million per year on in-house robotics research, generally focused on robotic applications and interface standards. Each of the United States military services spends significant amounts ($1 million to $10 million annually) to support mission-oriented basic and applied R&D in robotics (Science and Technology Program). They also spend $1 million and $5 million a year on procurement to support adoption of AMS by defense industry suppliers (Manufacturing Technology Program). The air force particularly has been active in promoting adoption of AMS by the aerospace industry (ICAM Program). For a detailed description of military involvement in AMS, see E. Martin, *Department of Defense Statement on Robotics Technology*, Subcommittee on Investigations and Oversight of the Committee on Science and Technology, U.S. House of Representatives, June 23, 1982.

[7]The National Machine Tool Builders Association (which represents several AMS producers) has repeatedly lobbied against import penetrations, now near 40 percent, on the grounds of national security.

the potential threat of competition from automated factories abroad necessitates the short-term hardships resulting from reduced protection.

JAPANESE GOVERNMENT POLICIES AND MEASURES

The government-industry relationship in Japan plays a major role in the process of formulation and implementation of Japan's economic and technological development policies. The Japanese government has strong confidence in comeptition and in market forces, but it also perceives a need to intervene from time to time in order to achieve and maintain a high level of economic performance. For example, there has been a sustained effort to encourage the movement of people and resources into sectors with high growth and high productivity. Areas of improving comparative advantage are encouraged to accelerate, and declining or poor performance industries are encouraged to phase down.

The Japanese vision of the 1980s called for steadfast progress toward a "technology-based nation" and "knowledge-intensive" industries.[8] The strong commitment to movement in these directions can be traced back, to the early 1970s, when government-sponsored studies, prepared in cooperation with Japanese industry, predicted the development of information-oriented societies and set out agendas to develop the complementary knowledge-intensive industries. Responsibilities for implementing these guidelines rests largely with the Ministry of Finance (MOF) and the Ministry of International Trade and Industry (MITI). The MOF is the ultimate source of financing, and it guides the industrial lending policies of commercial banks. In order to maintain and expand Japan's industrial growth while minimizing commercial risks, the banks and other investors tend to rely on the MOF-MITI perceptions of what are the most promising avenues of expansion and innovation.

A wide array of Japanese government policies and consultative procedures are designed to strengthen the country's already formidable industrial technology base. The Japanese government, in consultation with appropriate segments of Japanese industry, has established several guidelines and objectives in its efforts to stimulate further the country's technological development; emphasis is placed on the commercial application of current state-of-the-art capabilities and, increasingly, on the development and commercializatioan of next-generation technologies. The Japanese government has entered into cooperative contracts with large corporations leading to technological innovation, particularly in areas enhancing the international competitiveness of Japanese industry. This was the case in the automotive industry during the 1950s and early 1960s and again in the growing computer industry during the 1970s. The 1978 Temporary Law for the Promotion of Specific Electronics and Machinery Industries promoted the aggregation of factories to internationally competitive scale by allowing cartel formation under government surveillance.

[8]J. Baranson and H. B. Malmgren, *Technology and Trade Policy: Issues and Agenda for Action*, report prepared for the Office of the U.S. Trade Representative and the U.S. Department of Labor, October 1981, pp. 6–8, 64–66.

The Japanese government also encouraged and facilitated cooperation among firms in the same industry, thus avoiding the antitrust restrictions typical of the United States. Companies share information on new products under development in order to eliminate repetition of costly research and engineering. This acceptance of industrial cooperation strengthens Japan's competitiveness in the world markets.

Tax and Depreciation Measures

The Japanese fiscal policy has a number of provisions designed to help the nation's technology positions. If a Japanese firms' R&D expenditures for a given year exceed the largest amount of annual R&D expenditures for any preceding year since 1966, 70 percent of the excess may be taken as a credit against the corporate income tax. Firms that are members of research associations can take an immediate 100 percent depreciation deduction on all fixed assets used in connection with research activities.

Government-Funded R&D

Although most R&D work in Japan is performed and financed by industry, government laboratories do conduct a limited, but significant, amount of R&D work in specific, well-targeted areas. These government laboratories are usually working on either basic research or new product conception. Targeted R&D activity by the government has played a substantial role in the dynamic growth of several Japanese industriees, such as electronics and automotive in previous years, and currently in new, high-technology areas such as robotics and biogenetics. In performing these activities, the Japanese government has reduced the risk and cost to Japanese industry of developing new technologies.

The Japanese government also provides direct financial assistance to the private sector to develop its technological capabilities. The various types of government financial assistance represent a form of public subvention of private technology development efforts. Although the absolute amount of subsidization has not been large, it is well-targeted to the promotion of specific industries and products that hold the potential for attaining world technological leadership.[9] Japan spends very little money on defense-related R&D, allowing it to concentrate its funding on projects with greater potential for private-sector commercialization, Japan's fierce competitiveness is based not only on its ability to research and develop new technology but also on its proved proficiency in accumulating and improving technology developed in other countries.

Government Measures Regarding AMS

The government uses a variety of financial and other incentives to encourage companies to enter growing industries, such as robotics. It is felt that domestic competition will

[9]Japanese industrial planning mechanisms set targeted dates for moving to next-generation technology in the very large scale integration (VLSI) area. This involved progressively moving from 4K to 1 million K random access memory. In the floppy disc field, used in office and home computers, the Japanese reduced the size of these discs from 8 inches to 3½ inches. The line widths in VLSI devices are critical, and Japanese industry set goals to move from 6 microns to 1 micron tolerances.

lead to success in the international market, where much of Japan's rapid economic growth has come from. The government is offering support to AMS producers to facilitate the proliferation of companies in the market. Its promotional role has been aimed largely at intensifying competition and reinforcing demand for AMS. In fiscal year 1980, the following measures were implemented: a leasing scheme by the development bank of Japan, computer-controlled industrial robots were added to the list of equipment eligible for special corporate tax depreciation, and special financing for robots was provided by the National Finance and Small Business Finance Corporation for robots with industrial safety features and for the purchase of robotics to modernize small business operations.

EUROPEAN GOVERNMENT POLICIES AND MEASURES

Because of the greater weight of exports in national income earnings and political pressures to maintain industrial employment, technological innovation (including automation) and increased productivity are major goals of West European government. They have addressed this need by formulating national policies specifically directed toward robots and computerized manufacturing process. But national policies vary greatly, ranging from France's designation of the robotic industry as a key sector for future public investment to Sweden's lack of specific measures aimed at AMS industries.

France

In France the Committee for Development of Strategic Industries (CODIS) has identified industrial robots and automated production systems as a key sector of the economy. Basically the government has two goals: to encourage the manufacturing enterprises to invest heavily in automatic equipment (so as to increase productivity and expand market share in France and abroad) and to facilitate the development of a strong French industry in the AMS sector. A key factor in implementing these measures has been the decline of the machine tool industry in France to eighth place worldwide.[10]

Robotics has been designated as a key industry, and approximately $400 million (2.4 billion francs) over a three-year period was budgeted in 1980. The government set a goal for the manufacture of 5,000 robots and the establishment of 410 research positions by 1984 and for the creation of 2,000 qualified jobs over a 10-year period.[11] The Advanced Automation and Robotics Group, consisting of 10 research institutes, has emphasized the development of robotics, advanced remote operations, and flexible production systems. The Mitterand government also planned an increase in procurement of robots, from 50 million francs to 1.2 billion francs over the three-year period. CODIS issued contracts to several French companies.

[10]The French government's first major industrial plan was developed for the machine tool industry. It provided for an expenditure of 4 billion francs four doubling machine tool production, reducing imports by half, and increasing exports over the next three years. The government's objective was to place 16,000 new computer-controlled machines in service by 1985 and thereby end the industry's seven-year crisis.

These restructuring measures reflect a policy change from stimulating demand to bringing together the user industries, the producers, and the government in a comprehensive program. An effort has been made to identify potential areas where robotics could be introduced, and consideration has been given to measures to facilitate acceptance of AMS systems. AMS production in France still has many deficiencies, particularly in the basic components sector. The government's goal has been to complete a robotics industrial chain, centering the robotics industry around a few of the largest enterprises, such as Renault's subsidiary ACMA. The supply end of the chain will be restructured to facilitate the regrouping of the marketing activities of small producers.

Sweden

Swedish government efforts in support of AMS development have been minimal until recently in accordance with traditional laissez-faire policy toward industry except to reinforce market adjustments to economic and technological change. In view of the latter, government financing of AMS research development and utilization has expanded since 1980. In the period 1972–1979, the Swedish Board for Technical Development (STU), which is under the Ministry of Industry, allocated about $800,000 for the development of the robotics industry. In 1980, STU's support of R&D in engineering industries increased significantly to about $40 million, with funds going for advanced R&D at universities, research laboratories, and industrial enterprises. Funding for computer-aided design and manufacturing (CAD/CAM) alone amounted to about $8 million during 1980–1985. The Swedish Association of Mechanical and Electrical Industries was to sponsor a five-year research program through 1985. The Computer and Electronic Commission recommended that the government promote wide diffusion of robotics and CAD/CAM through an information campaign among small- and medium-sized firms, complementary software development loans with conditioned repayment, and the encouragementa of related training programs.

West Germany

Government and industry support for manufacturing technology development (of which robotics is a significant part) has averaged about $100 million annually in recent years. The Federal Ministry for Research and Technology has sponsored a number of robotic manufacturing programs through several organizations. The Association for Fundamental Technology has managed programs in CAD and process control by computer, and the German Institute for Aerospace Research and Experimentation has coordinated and monitored advanced manufacturing technology programs, including the development of sensors and feedback systems for robots. The German Research Society receives about $30 million a year from the federal government and from state governments for research on computerized machine tools and robotics. Other sources of funding include the

[11]In 1980, France imported over 60 percent of the robots in use. The density of robots in use in France is relatively low: only 0.3 robots per 10,000 industrial workers as compared to 11.2 in Sweden, 4.4 in Japan, and 1.6 in the United States. See Jack Baranson, *Robots in Manufacturing: Key to International Competitiveness*, Lomond Press, 1983, p. 12.

Frauenhofer Foundation, a cooperative organization of institutes for applied research; two of its members, the Institute for Production and Automation and the Institute for Data Processing in Technology and Biology, are involved in the development of industrial robots.

CONCLUDING OBSERVATIONS

The key to innovational dynamics is the management of risk within an economy. The innovational thrust in a society depends heavily on a combination of public-sector policy, private-sector initiatives, and the participative role of financial institutions in risk management. The entrepreneurial function in seeking out innovational opportunities and in managing technological change is pivotal, but levels and quality of performance depend heavily on the policy and institutional environment. As part of risk management, public policy must also take on the task of economic and social adjustments to technological change. This may include subsidies to retain or relocate displaced labor force or adjustment assistance to business enterprises that require technological upgrading.

EPILOGUE

Government's Role in Facilitating Technology Adoption

Without question, the effective formulation and implementation of a technology strategy at the firm level is very difficult. Consider then the complexity and difficulty of doing this on a national scale. This will give some idea of the magnitude of the situation which governments face.

Developing and implementing a consistent and appropriate national technology policy through the various policy tools available is perhaps one of the most important tasks of government today, for the effectiveness of the policies developed may, to a large extent, determine the economic future of the country. If, for example, we intend to catch and surpass Japanese industry, unplanned, uncoordinated technology adoption by individual firms and industries will not be sufficient. What is required is a well-planned, well-focused strategy at the national level. This strategy must utilize and integrate the available resources in the best manner to gain national competitive advantage.

Research plays a big role in developing these resources and creating strategic tools. However, as with the overall technology strategy, this research must have a focus. The government, through the operation of its own research aid labs, and through a well-targeted research fund to both firms and universities, can help provide this focus. This is not to say that the government should determine what research is appropriate and what is not; rather its role should be one of support and guidance. Individual firms and industries, being closest to the marketplace, still must maintain some independence and discretion to allow their research to focus where they feel the market lays. The ideal is for industries, universities and the government to collaborate in their efforts, to jointly determine the best course, and then draw upon the resources of the three parties as needed to help them along. At present, however, this does not happen nearly often enough, and a considerable amount of progress still needs to be made.

If the research process is successful, it results in invention and then innovation. Again, government has a role to play, one which is both vital and controversial. A national policy which considers macroeconomic and long-term strategic factors, as well as the inherent resource limitations of a country, can play a very key role in influencing the economic direction and well-being of a country.

The classic controversy here is just how much the government, which is somewhat removed from the realities of the market, should participate in the innovation process. Individual opinions differ but the general consensus appears to be that governments should play a role of support and moderate guidance, rather than a role that is strategically and operationally deterministic. This basically means well-targeted resource support and the establishment of a general economic climate which is conducive to successful innovation at the industry level.

The last step in the technology cycle, once an innovation has been produced, is transfer. This may mean transferring it in any number of ways: from federal labs to industry, from universities to industry, from one industry to another, from firm to firm or between groups within a firm, or even between countries. This is a difficult process to evaluate, since it depends largely on which type of transfer is being discussed. National and individual firm security concerns, and poor education and communication, appear to be the main inhibitors of technology transfer. Some of these bariers are necessary, but others are not. It is appropriate that government, industry and university together consider the issues and concerns which underlie these barriers. Through this, those which are currently proper and functional may be monitored and maintained, while those which are not may be dismantled or avoided. When this occurs, technology will flow in a way which benefits the company and its social and economic well-being.

In research, invention and innovation, and technology transfer, the government plays a support role through the provision of resources. These resources could be *expertise* in a particular area, or *financial resources,* such as grants, tax credits, joint funding and procurement policies. By judicious targeting of the applications of these resources, governments can effectively aid the development and prosperity of a country through guidance and support of the real actors—individuals in industries and universities.

CASE 11.1

Raytheon Canada (A)[12]

As Bob Carpenter, Contracts Administrator for Raytheon Canada Limited (RCL), waited for clearance from Korea on the proposal to use Koshin as a supplier for advanced electronic components, he questioned the countertrade system of offsets. Even if Koshin were selected to fulfill the offset agreement, they were an unknown company in the United States. He had no idea whether their components would sell or whether they could be used internally by RCL. He had no doubt about the desirability of making the sale, but he wondered if the demands were becoming too stringent.

To put the decision regarding the countertrade system of offsets in perspective, this case will first provide the history of Raytheon Canada and its involvement with the Radar Modernization Project (RAMP). It will then discuss how it came to be involved with Ground Controlled Approach Systems in Korea.

CANADIAN OPERATIONS

RCL was incorporated in January 1956 as a wholly-owned subsidiary of its American parent—Raytheon Company. Operations covered the fields of electronics, aircraft products, energy services and major appliances, in addition to several other lines. The company is among the nation's 100 largest industrial companies ranked by Fortune magazine each year. In 1984, sales were $6 billion with just under 50 percent of the total

[12]This case was prepared by Professors J. Alex Murray and David L. Blenkhorn with special assistance from executives of Raytheon, Hyundai and External Affairs Canada. Distributed through the LAURIER INSTITUTE, School of Business and Economics, Wilfrid Laurier University, Waterloo, Ontario, Canada, N2L 3C5.

from the United States government. RCL's sales to customers outside the United States comprised 19 percent of revenues. Exhibit 11.2 gives a summary of the continuing operations for 1982 to 1984.

Exhibit 11.2 Raytheon Company—Business Segment Reporting—Continuing Operations

	Operations by Business Segments					
Years Ended December 31	Electronics	Aircraft Products	Energy Services	Major Appliances	Other Lines	Total
			(in $ millions)			
Sales to Unaffiliated Customers						
1984	$3,399	$723	$ 680	$797	$397	5,996
1983	2,995	642	926	710	358	5,631
1982	2,656	568	1,124	565	304	5,217
Income From Continuing Operations Before Taxes						
1984	431	6	14	61	33	545
1983	385	14	17	53	28	497
1982	319	61	65	22	23	490
Capital Expenditures						
1984	136	188	35	37	18	414
1983	103	83	34	21	13	254
1982	101	34	57	16	16	224
Depreciation and Amortization						
1984	81	27	36	18	12	174
1983	70	17	33	16	12	148
1982	63	10	32	16	10	131
Identifiable Assets at						
December 31, 1984	1,697	959	306	455	183	3,600
December 31, 1983	2,071	741	354	391	172	3,729
December 31, 1982	1,934	643	412	359	151	5,510

	Operations by Geographic Areas		
	United States	Outside United States (Principally Europe)	Consolidated
		(in $ millions)	
Sales to Unaffiliated Customers			
1984	$5,450	$546	$5,996
1983	4,903	728	5,631
1982	4,419	798	5,217
Income From Continuing Operations			
1984	327	13	340
1983	294	15	309
1982	273	30	303
Identifiable Assets at			
December 31, 1984	3,326	274	3,600
December 31, 1983	3,430	299	3,729
December 31, 1982	3,187	323	3,510

The head office of Raytheon Company was in Lexington, Massachusetts, and the firm had 12 major operating subsidiaries and more than 80 plans and laboratories in 26 states. The major overseas subsidiaries and affiliates were located in six countries with a principal one being RCL, which received a world product mandate from its parent company to design, manufacture, and market air traffic control (ATC) systems worldwide. The RAMP project explained below was an integral part of this world product mandate and was to be completed in 1992. A second major commitment for RCL was their international radar program for air defense surveillance radars and ground control approach radars (GCAs). Typically, GCA systems were comprised of three basic units; an Airport Surveillance Radar (ASR), a Precision Approach Radar (PAR) to assure accurate approach on landings, and a Secondary Surveillance Radar (SSR) for systems operations. An International Radar Marketing team had been organized with the President of RCL as team coordinator to sell GCA systems worldwide. Exhibit 11.3 gives an organizational chart for the Marketing Group.

Exhibit 11.3 Raytheon Canada Limited Marketing Organization

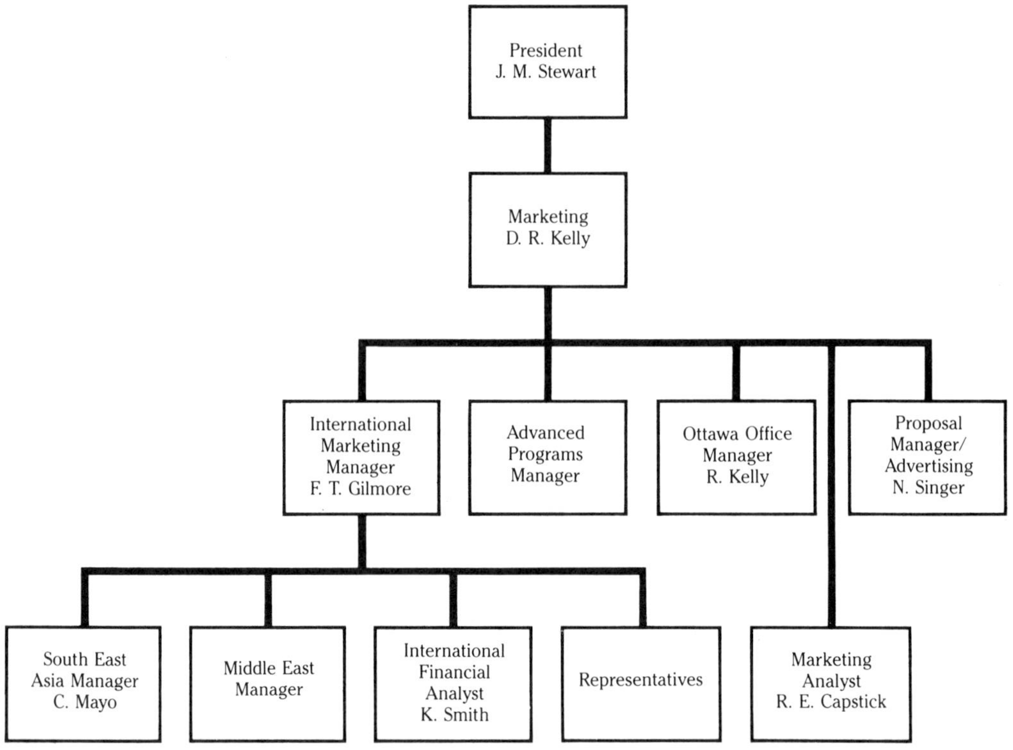

THE RADAR MODERNIZATION PROJECT (RAMP)

In 1978, the Canadian Federal Government developed a formal plan to update the present antiquated radar system in Canada based on a concluison of its specially appointed Dubin

Commission of Inquiry on Aviation Safety, that "radar equipment presently in use at Canadian airports was obsolete." The plan, known as CASP (Canadian Air Space Programs) was massive in scope with an expected cost totaling $3.5 billion by 1992.[13] Two years later, the federal government set specifications for the first of the new systems that made up CASP and made a Request for Proposals (RFP). Six firms responded with proposals for the project; RCL was one of these companies. In order to position itself competitively, RCL had increased its research and development on radar technology and by 1980 was well along on the development of the world's most advanced civil airport surveillance radar. Among other advances it featured solid state technology in the transmitter rather than the more conventional high voltage glass output tubes and this was a factor in winning the contract valued at $390 million. It was the involvement with the huge RAMP project and being at the forefront in airport radar technology that put RCL in good contention for contracts in the international marketplace.

The Canadian Federal Government, through the Minister of Transport, the Department of Supply and Services and the Department of Regional Industrial Expansion were all actively involved with the RAMP negotiations. Canadian air traffic engineers had complained quite vehemently about the outdated system which had been in place for over 22 years. In order to upgrade the system, and at the same time spread the benefits across Canada, three important requirements were included in the Request for Proposal (RFP):

1. The radar system should provide maximum safety for civil air traffic.
2. Many Canadian jobs should be created by the project.
3. Control of the technology should reside in Canada so that Canada could export the radar system to other countries.

Initially, the government had compiled a list of 27 national and international firms to which RFPs would be sent, early enough for international firms to find Canadian partners and qualify for the bidding process. The government established several criteria in order to evaluate different proposals.

1. Demonstrated experience in the field of radar systems.
2. Canadian entity; however, the government would accept a joint venture between a Canadian firm and an international firm contingent on there being an active Canadian component.
3. The financial stability of the company.
4. Evidence of good management.
5. Acceptable pereformance in past government contracts.
6. Present facilities or access to facilities capable of completing a project as large as RAMP.

[13]Called RAMP/RSE (Radar Modernization Project/Radar Site Equipment), this first project covered the radar equipment (sometimes called sensors) at 41 sites and would be followed by an RFP for the RAMP DSE/RDPS (RAMP Display Site Equipment/Radar Data Processing System) about one year later.

THE RAYTHEON PROPOSAL

RCL assembled a team in order to present an integrated package for the proposal. In addition to an advanced engineering and technology system which would cover all the specifications listed by the RFP, RCL planned the following strategy:

1. RCL would own the radar technology.
2. RCL would export this and other technologies to other countries worldwide through world product mandates from their U.S. headquarters, Raytheon Company.
3. Jobs would be distributed throughout Canada so that all areas would benefit, not just southern Ontario. RCL estimated that employment would be created as follows:
   242 person years in the Atlantic region
   1,310 person years in Quebec
   2,310 person years in Ontario
   790 person years in western Canada
4. The United States and the United Kingdom content would be 100 percent offset by Raytheon Company purchases in Canada.
5. The price would be competitive.
6. The building of a working model would cost approximately $1 million and would demonstrate the radar's effectiveness.

The RAMP contract was critical to the future direction of RCL; however, Westinghouse was a strong competitor. Both RCL and Westinghouse had existing products that were similar to that which was needed for RAMP. Their respective proposals, while meeting the rigid specifications of the Canadian government, were considerably different technically, in the management approach and in the countertrade programs (socioeconomic benefits or SEBs). The role of SEBs in awarding the contract to a specified firm was given added weight as a factor in the award. The Canadian government had developed a unique set of offset procedures in which items not produced in Canada had to be balanced with exports of "like" products. It also developed that the Westinghouse bid had an appreciably higher price than the RCL submission.

INTERNATIONAL RADAR MARKETING

RCL was awarded the RAMP project on May 9, 1984. This was the world's largest and most comprehensive civil airport radar system yet implemented. Establishing a bid for this initial phase had required over $5 million of input funding over approximately three years. The major phase of the contract required the construction of 24 terminal surveillance radars at airports across the country. In 1985, RCL expanded its Waterloo, Ontario plant to a 126,000 square foot office and manufacturing facility on a 25 acre site. However, even before the RAMP award, RCL increased its export efforts to demonstrate its commitment to the Canadian government by undertaking the sale of its world mandate products to a number of foreign countries. Marketing strategies were initiated in the Pacific Rim, Middle East, Africa and South America in order to implement a new ATC marketing plan. Of particular interest were Indonesia, Australia, Korea, Thailand and Greece, in which the military was very interested in talking to RCL about its ground approach systems.

GROUND CONTROLLED APPROACH SYSTEMS

In mid-1983, RCL received a world product mandate from its United States parent for Ground Controlled Approach radar systems (GCAs). Such GCA systems consisted of three separate units. The first was the Airport Surveillance Radar (ASR) which provided for primary surveillance up to a range of 60 nautical miles. This unit displayed "blips" corresponding to approaching objects.

The second was the Prevision Approach Radar (PAR) which displayed all approaching aircraft and tracked as many as six aircraft on final approach. It displayed precise locations and other critical information needed to guide an aircraft into a landing. The third was the Secondary Surveillance Radar (SSR) which addressed a transponder on the aircraft triggering a response that included an identification code, speed and azimuth bearing. An integrated system of the above three units was first produced by the parent company as both a guidance for approaching aircraft and a surveillance radar system. RCL identified three immediate overseas markets for the system—Korea, Thailand and Taiwan—because of their need to provide both military surveillance of the skies and landing guidance for their own aircraft. Frank Gilmore, RCL's International Marketing Manager, pinpointed, in partiuclar, the Korean need in 1983 for GCAs. The Korean Air Force had inherited a number of radars from the United States at the end of the Korean War in 1954, and had continued to periodically purchase new or updated equipment. They naturally went to the United States for their radar requirements when it became a priority. The only possible suppliers were those in the U.S. Armed Forces Inventory, that is, Westinghouse, ITT, Raytheon and Texas Instruments. The Korean market appeared to be the most promising in 1983 since a general budget allocation had been designated for such general systems.

Raytheon's GCA systems were already used in South Korea by the U.S. Air Force because of their advanced technology. The Korean Air Force was familiar with the system and this made it preferable as a military defense purchase.

The Korean Government had committed 25 percent of its budget (6 percent of GNP, compared to 1 percent for Japan) to defense, and the military agencies were anxious to obtain the most sophisticated equipment available. Strained diplomatic relations with North Korea, China and the USSR had placed a serious obligation on the government to assure a military alertness only possible with the most advanced systems.

THE REPUBLIC OF KOREA

Korea existed as a part of various personal kingdoms and dynasties until 1910, when it was taken over by Japan. At the end of World War II, the struggle for its control escalated into the Korean "Conflict" when the country was divided, with the Communists ruling North Korea and an elected government in South Korea (The Republic of Korea). In 1961, Colonel Park Chung Hee seized military power and preached that the key to South Korea's economic success lay in exports. This commenced the move toward manufacturing for export, taking advantage of an inexpensive labor force.

Since 1980, Chun Doo Hwan, the current president, had taken a vigorous stand attacking inflation and improving living standards. He succeeded in reducing inflation from 25 percent to 4 percent, while the per capita GNP rose from $100 U.S. to $2,500 U.S. This was accomplished through rigorous fiscal control and zero-based budgeting for all departments of the government.

Korea had enjoyed five years of steady growth and social stability since the turmoil of 1980, when troops crushed an uprising in Kwangjw. Unfortunately, this new-found wealth had not been broadly distributed with the resulting inequality lending support to the opposition efforts of Kim Dae-Jung, who returned from exile a short while later to make significant gains in recently held elections.

CONTRACT NEGOTIATIONS

Preliminary to successfully winning an order from the Republic of Korea for a GCA system, lengthy and involved negotiations were necessary. RCL's negotiation team consisted of two executives—Cy Mayo, Project Manager and Bob Carpenter, Contracts Administrator, both from the Waterloo company.

Mayo had an extensive technical background and could keep all interested parties up-to-date with the capabilities of the equipment. He also could help explain the feasibility and expense of "peripheral" features in a system demanded by the Korean govenrment. Carpenter was an expert negotiator and handled the commercial end of the negotiations.

The Korean negotiating team consisted of a high-ranking officer from each of the Navy, Defense Procurement Agency (DPA), and the Republic of Korea Air Force (ROKAF). DPA was RCL's immediate contact. The three were experienced and patient negotiators. Like negotiators in many Pacific Rim countries, they were not above using the tactic of threatening to cancel negotiations and award the contract to a competitor if certain progress objectives were not met.

The bargaining began when the field was narrowed to RCL and one of its traditional competitors. The other contenders did not have equipment which specifically met the Korean requirements, while RCL had produced such equipment, and its opponent had similar equipment in the developmental stage. RCL had a competitive advantage in that the U.S. Air Force used their system at its Korean bases.

From October 20 to November 17, 1983, representatives from each potential supplier met with the Korean bargaining team for all-day sessions. By mid-November, offers and counteroffers had been proposed, discussed and revised. Three major items of contention had been resolved.

First, there wasd an agreement on price. RCL's price was significantly higher, which was a major problem at the beginning since the Koreans were under a very strict budget and had many other items to procure with a fixed sum. Eventually it was agreed that RCL's price was acceptable. Since its competitors had never actually built the required system, cost overruns could be a problem or quality might suffer in order to meet the cost objectives.

Second, the terms of payment were another major hurdle which was overcome. The original plan called for payments in the first year which would exceed budget and was unacceptable to the Koreans. At the same time, RCL needed to ensure that working capital was coming in as fast as project expenses were going out. Finally an agreement was reached to pay more money up front in return for add-on peripheral components being included in the package.

Third, performance bonds had presented a severe problem in the negotiations but that issue too was eventually resolved. A compromise was struck, whereby complaints would be arbitrated by a panel of three—one independent and one appointed by each side of the contract.

OFFSET AGREEMENTS

In the world of international trade where goods are frequently bartered and countertrade among nations is commonplace, offset agreements are often used. An offset is broadly defined as a commitment by an international seller to do something that favorably impacts the economy of the buying country and describes a wider range of transactions than is usually referred to by the term "countertrade." Offsets may be contrasted to countertrade in that in the case of offsets, the purchaser is a foreign government, the bilateral trade agreement covers a long period of time, and the transactions often include a technology transfer to the buying country as the items involved have a high value. Benefit packages, besides technology transfer, may include industrial spinoffs and guaranteed purchase commitments.

By the time the contract reached discussions of offsets in the spring of 1984, the Koreans were only beginning to develop an operational policy on the items and delivery to be incuded in any offset package.

THE RAYTHEON OFFSET PROPOSAL

When confronted with the offset requirement, John Steward, president of RCL, decided to approach Korean companies presently doing business in Canada. His aim was to initiate importation to Canada of Korean products in order to satisfy the offset requirement. The government provided a list of candidates, of which three were in Toronto. The International Marketing Manager was assigned the task of reviewing the candidates, the first on the list being Hyundai Canada Inc. of Markham, Ontario. They proved to be a $10 billion conglomerate with vast interests that included shipbuilding, construction, manufacturing, electronics, automobiles, and engineering.

Hyundai Canada's parent in Korea, Hyundai Engineering and Contruction Company Limited, was founded in 1947 and grew from a small trucking firm. The company is also a major factor in the Korean financial and service industry including banking, insurance, marketing stocks and bonds, and hotels. The Hyundai motor division is one of the larger components of Hyundai Industries.

First discussions with Mr. Hyo-Won O, General Manager and Director, found that Hyundai was indeed interested, and had plans to import the Hyundai Pony. They were presently negotiating with FIRA (Foreign Investment Review Agency) for permission to import the automobiles, but needed something like the RCL proposal to make it happen. An agreement was signed, and for a fee, Mr. O agreed to make imports of Korean-made products that would satisfy RCL's 100 percent offset requirement. In turn, Hyundai would use the GCA contract to persuade FIRA to approve the import of Ponys. It was clear in the agreement that if insufficient Ponys were in fact imported, Hyundai would import one of its many other products. No difficulty was foreseen in the amount of imports required.

COUNTEROFFERS

By 1984, an offset program had been established by the Korean government, as detailed in Appendix A. The guidelines called for support of high-priority industries and attempted to offset with "like" products. The Koreans were seeking electronic product offsets to match the purchase of electronic equipment as an entry into the North American market. There was also a general feeling on the part of the Koreans, that the Hyundai Pony would have succeeded without the help of RCL. Since the approval of FIRA had been expected, and sales were actually projected to be higher than the levels proposed by Raytheon, the Koreans felt that this was not a very advantageous offset and sought additional ones.

The Defense Industry Bureau (DIB), as the ministry watchdog for promoting Korean high-tech, obviously wanted to negotiate the best offset contract to assist in technology transfers and employment to selected companies, particularly those firms the DIB felt had the most promise. RCL located and contacted Koshin,[14] a supplier to a large United States retailer of branded television sets. They agreed to be part of the offset arrangement. This left only two items on the agenda—the dollar amount needed to satisfy the addiitional offset requirement and the timetable for the offset purchase in order to satisfy the agreement.

By the fall of 1984, Bob Carpenter was ready to go back to the Korean government with these questions. He was prepared to purchase 5 percent of the contract's value (about $1 million U.S.) and take delivery over the next five years. The Koreans demanded 50 percent of the contract price in additional offset purchases (about $10 million U.S.) and delivery within the two-year span of the ASR agreement.

The Koreans said they would consider Koshin as a supplier for the offset, but to Carpenter's surprise television sets could not be the product of the offset. He was told these were not considered "like" products under the guidelines. RCL would have to take elecronic components (for example, integrated circuits) from a specified supplier in order to satisfy the terms of the offset agreement. This was the only line manufactured in Korea which was considered "favored" by the government.

[14]Koshin, as the parent holding company, was in several industries such as pharmaceuticals and banking and, through one of its groups, had become a major exporter of electronic products and components.

APPENDIX A

Summary Guide for Korean Offset Program; Defense Industry Bureau; Ministry of National Defense; Republic of Korea

1. PURPOSE

   The purpose of this "Guide" is to outline definitions, objectives, basic guidelines and procedures in support of Offset Programs, directed by the Defense Industry Bureau (DIB), Ministry of National Defense (MND), Republic of Korea.

2. SCOPE OF APPLICATION

   This "Guide" applies to all agencies under the Ministry of National Defense and Korean industries as well as all foreign contractors incurring obligations under the Republic of Korea Offset Program.

3. DEFINITIONS

   A. Offset Program: The Offset Program is work, or the provision of work, or other compensatory opportunities, directed to the Republic of Korea by foreign contractors as a result of receiving, or in anticipation of receiving, a major order for equipment, material (including spare parts) or services in which the Government of the Republic of Korea is involved. There are two offset categories—direct and indirect. The determination of category, as well as project qualification, will be made by DIB, MND.

      (i) Direct Offset: Activities in the direct offset category are those which are directly related to the original purchase by the Republic of Korea, or foreign equipment, material or services. Direct Offset includes the following:

         (a) Transfer of technology to achieve the capability to manufacture and manage the production of parts and components to meet follow-on logistic support.

         (b) Provision of opportunities to manufacture and export parts and components related to the original purchase.

         (c) Transfer of technology to obtain a maintenance capability for equipment purchased within the Republic of Korea.

         (d) Assistance in obtaining maintenance opportunities in overseas markets for which the Republic of Korea has the technological capability.

(ii) Indirect Offset: Activities in the Indirect Offset category are those activities which are not directly related to the production of equipment originally purchased. Indirect Offset activities include the following:
   (a) Korean Industry Participation (KIP)
      (1) Activities in paragraph 3.A. (i) (a) through (d) which are not directly related to the original purchase.
      (2) Opportunities to participate in major research and development projects.
      (3) Assistance in establishing industrial facilities and developing technological capabilities.
      (4) Assistance in creating new employment opportunities.
      (5) Any approved activity that will further Korean national, political, economic, military, and industrial interests.
   (b) Counterpurchase: Counterpurchase activities include those which are related to the purchase of general commodities and financial assistance. It should be noted that general commodity purchases will not be indiscriminant and credit will only be allowed when a commodity purchase has been given approval from DIB, MND. Counterpurchase activities include the following:
      (1) Direct purchase by the contractor of Korean products or services.
      (2) Assistance in selling, or the direct purchase of, self-defense articles from original Korean sources.
      (3) Assistance in arranging sales to third parties from the original Korean manufacturer.
      (4) Efforts to obtain financial assistance for Korean products.

B. Memorandum of Agreementn (MOA) for Offset Programs: An addition to the basic contract setting forth the obligations and understandings of foreign contractors and the Government of the Republic of Korea with respect to the Offset Program.

4. OFFSET PROGRAM OBJECTIVES

The primary objective of the Offset Program is to assist the Republic of Korea in developing and expanding its manufacturing and industrial capability. The goal of the program is to obtain new technology, provide design and development work, assist under-utilized sectors of industry, selectively stimulate sectors of the economy, and create new employment opportunities. The program is intended to increase technological and industrial capability with an emphasis on the area of National Defense.

5. BASIC GUIDELINES

A. The Offset Program will apply, on a case by case basis, to all major equipment, material and services purchased by the Government of the Republic of Korea for more than $1 million U.S.

B. The national goal for an individual Offset Program will be at least 50 percent of the basic contract value. At least 20 percent of the basic contract value will be in the Direct Offset category.

C. The basic offset proposals will be considered on a competitive basis and foreign contractors will submit Offset Program Proposals to DIB, MND within a specified period of time. Offset Program agreements will be an important factor in awarding the final contract.

D. The Memorandum of Agreement for the Offset Program will be part of, and attached to, the basic contract.

E. In executing the Offset Program, all values that exceed program goals will be credited to the foreign contractor for follow-on contract.

6. EVALUATION CRITERIA
   A. The technological sophistication, the total dollar value and the length of time to complete the Offset Program will be major factors in the evaluation process.
   B. It is expected that Korean equipment, material and services will be used to the maximum extent possible. Priority will be given to those Offset Program Proposals containing a greater amount of Korean material and services.
   C. Some projects will not be approved by MND because they do not meet selection criteria.
   D. The following categories are listed in order of importance: Activities of national high priority which promote political, economic, military and industrial development objectives:
      (a) Participation in advanced technological development projects.
      (b) Transfer of advanced technology and know-how.
      (c) Creation, or improvement of, self-reliance in equipment purchased by providing for:
         (i) Ability to independently produce equipment.
         (ii) Ability to jointly produce equipment.
         (iii) Ability to produce spare parts independently.
         (iv) Ability to maintain equipment independently.
      (d) Creation or improvement of self-reliance in related equipment/industry by providing for:
         (i) Ability to independentrly produce related equipment.
         (ii) Ability to jointly produce related equipment.
         (iii) Ability to produce spare parts independently.
         (iv) Ability to maintain related equipment independently.

CASE 11.2

The Pacific Programmable Controller[15]

On November 7, 1977, Mr. Ian Coombe, Applied Technology Coordinator for the Central Region of the Development Finance Corporation of New Zealand (DFC), received a formal application for financial support from Solid State Equipment Limited (SSE). Ian was anxious to have his recommendations on SSE ready by November 11 for the next meeting of the Applied Technology Program Committee. Ian had been in contact with SSE's managers since early October. He had already concluded that its proposed development project on the PACIFIC programmable controller was eligible for consideration for DFC financial support under the Applied Technology Program (ATP) guidelines. He was not sure, however, if the project could become a technological success and if SSE was capable of making it commercially viable.

THE APPLIED TECHNOLOGY PROGRAM

DFC had evolved from its inception in 1964 into a well-known development bank with assets of over $200 million and annual revenues in excess of $15 million from disbursements of about $50 million per year to New Zealand industry. DFC provided financing as well as advisory and technical services to New Zealand businesses. It also promoted investment in New Zealand industry with a view to improving the balance of payments and the economy in general. DFC was owned entirely by the New Zealand government and, although it was self-supporting, and in practice autonomous, it was required to

[15]This case was prepared by Professor John Haywood-Farmer. © 1982 The University of Western Ontario.

comply with the directives of the Minister of Trade and Industry. DFC was, therefore, an instrument of government economic policy.

The New Zealand government was attempting to restructure the economy to reduce the nation's traditional dependence on the export of agricultural commodities to pay for imported manufactured goods. Manufacturing, introduced to reduce the level of imports, had developed in an insulated environment using largely imported technology, and operated on a relatively small, inefficient scale behind a barrier of trade restrictions. The government was trying to encourage more New Zealand manufacturing, greater primary and secondary product and market diversifications, export a higher level of refinement, and increased exports of manufactured goods. No particular industry was identified for special development.

In late 1976 DFC was directed by an Act of Parliament to undertake the administration of government support programs for industrial R&D. The government had established these programs to promote commercial exploitation of inventions originating within both the private and public sectors and to encourage increased industrial R&D in New Zealand. The government was particularly interested in supporting significant advances in the application of existing technology to areas that were new or in which there were major technical deficiencies. ATP, established by DFC to administer these functions, was to be funded by an annual govenment grant ($2.5 million in 1977) about 15 percent of which covered the administrative costs of the ATP to DFC.

ATP SUPPORT

ATP funding was allowable for a wide range of R&D activities from the end of basic research to the beginning of commercial production. The support was available through grants, loans or equity participation. In addition, ATP clients were eligible for the full range of advisory or referral services available to other DFC clients. The size, composition and repayment terms of ATP funding were diverse. Support packages averaged about $20,000 but ranged from a few hundred dollars to well over $100,000.

DECISION MAKING IN ATP

The ATP Committee reported directly to the DFC Board of Directors and was the only decision-making authority with ATP. The Committee was composed of six senior individuals from government, DFC and science.

The key individuals in the program were the 25 analysts in four regional DFC offices who dealt directly with clients regarding ATP and other DFC business. Normally the client's analyst was its only contact in DFC. The analysts were responsible for collecting relevant data, analyzing it, negotiating with clients, carrying out a variety of day-to-day functions, and making recommendations on clients to the ATP Committee. Analysts prescreened out a high portion of the initial inquiries to ATP and 70–80 percent of potential clients after a plant visit and preliminary research. The Committee accepted analysts' recommendations unaltered 90 percent of the time and with amendments 5 percent of the time. Analysts did not usually attend Committee meetings.

The analysts came from a variety of academic backgrounds; most had first degrees in accountancy, economics, science, or engineering. Most were in their early thirties and had some experience in banking, finance or management. The analysts were looked on as generalists (many had multidisciplinary backgrounds) but some had developed acknowledged skills in certain industries. Ian was responsible for coordinating the activities of the analysts in the Central Region based in Wellington. In addition, he served as an analyst himself for a small number of clients.

In ATP decisions, DFC was looking both for products that were novel and marketable, and for capable management. There were no hard and fast rules or formulae for evaluating projects or managers. The analyst was looking for commitment by the client based on a hard-headed, sound analysis of the project and where it and the client could reasonably be expected to go. Ultimately the analyst's decision was based on his judgment of the information he had obtained from numerous sources on the client and its technology.

THE INITIAL CONTACT

On October 5, 1977 Ian met George Jones and Neil Poletti, the owners of SSE. The two had been referred to Ian by a senior executive of the Department of Trade and Industry to whom they had been directed by a personal friend after a period of business setbacks. At the meeting the two parties exchanged information. Ian described ATP, the available forms of assistance and the types of projects DFC was interested in. George and Neil described SSE, the products it made, and the development that they had accomplished to date on the PACIFIC system. From this information the three men concluded that they were interested in pursuing the matter further. George and Neil subsequently prepared a formal application to DFC for financial support (see Exhibit 11.4). Ian, as a start to his analyses, obtained as much information as he could on SSE and its technology.

THE FOUNDING AND COMMERCIAL HISTORY OF SOLID STATE EQUIPMENT LIMITED

In 1967, George Jones and Neil Poletti were working as scientists in the Physics and Engineering Laboratory (PEL), of the Department of Scientific and Industrial Research (DSIR) located in Lower Hutt, about 20 km from Wellington. Within PEL opportunities arose from time to time for scientists to become directly involved in commercial ventures with outside firms and individuals. As a result of one such opportunity in 1967, Neil did some evening work helping design and build an oscillator for an electronic music studio at Victoria University in Wellington. George, also in his spare time, designed a circuit for a sector harbor light as an aid to marine navigation. This project grew into

Exhibit 11.4 SSE's Application for Assistance from the ATP

Project

The PACIFIC Programmable Controller is a microprocessor-based minicomputer, the first locally designed and built mini in New Zealand. It is a modular system, comprising a set of printed circuit cards in a card frame. Together with a power supply, it fits into a standard 19-inch instrument rack with a height of 7 inches, or can be installed in a cabinet of slightly larger dimensions. We have developed the circuit cards so that the system has powerful input and output abilities, that is, it can be connected to many different kinds of electrical signals and can drive many kinds of electrical machines. Whereas almost all minicomputers have a few inputs and outputs with large computing ability, our system is most efficiently used with many inputs, and a moderate amount of computation. Because it is modular, we can supply systems that are not over-engineered, yet are readily expandable to cater for new or different needs.

The older techniques in electronic engineering were to specifically design a piece of electronic apparatus to do a certain job. If made sufficiently versatile at the design stage it was capable of expansion to a moderate extent. You will be familiar with many examples and I will name a few. A numerical control for a machine tool is designed specifically for this purpose and has the ability to be programmed to make different parts. An automatic system for dipping components into a series of wash and etch baths in an electroplating factory cannot be expended to control a machine tool in spite of the fact that both machines control a pair of motors. It certainly cannot be the office stock control and accounting machine, even though it can count the number of parts it has handled in a day.

The more modern approach is to design a programmable machine and replace some hardware design with software design. Hardware is the electronics that you can see, and software is the program to control it. In most systems, there is a trade-off between hardware and software, for example, to send information from a computer down a telephone line, tones are used. It is possible to generate these directly from the software program or to add tone generators, hardware, to the output stages, thus releasing the central processing unit, CPU, the "brain" of the system, so that it can handle other functions.

Solid State Equipment Limited decided to develop microprocessor-based electronics three years ago when this technology was only about a year old. Since then it has steadily developed the PACIFIC for as wide a use as possible. The first system was developed for the Geophysics Institute, Victoria University, and as they needed a fairly complete set of cards for datalogging, we have since tended to accept jobs that we have already developed cards for. So when, PEL, DSIR, ordered dataloggers for field use, we had most of the cards developed. However we had problems in converting our laboratory prototypes to production prototypes, but have now solved these. Also we have now developed a set of software to handle each of the cards we make. If we develop, for example, a card for interfacing our system with a cassette recorder, we have to have the software to control rewinding, recording, and playback before the development of that subsystem is complete. Then, and only then we can use it in a system. So hardware and software design go hand in hand and together make up the development of that function.

When a customer comes to us we look at his problem and endeavor to configure our system to solve his problem. We then, if we get the order, build the appropriate cards and modify the software to suit his particular needs. It may mean the design of special extra software which will be costed into our price. However, if we need to supply a function that we do not have and could be of general use to us, we may decide to develop the hardware and software to handle it. This may cost a lot more than the customer is willing to pay for, and calls for investment on our part so that we can have an expended ability with the system.

If we decide to branch into a new field of endeavor with our product, we have to build a whole new set of programs using only a few of our present ones. For example, the potentially very high sales in a very small stock control and accounting machine would necessitate no development in hardware but a lot of new software. We would include our already developed cassette-handling routines

Exhibit 11.4 SSE's Application for Assistance from the ATP (*continued*)

as a small part of the program. However, no single customer would be willing to support the cost of this development.

As presently constituted, our system has been developed as a datalogger for scientific research. We wish to further develop the software to add a real time clock (one that tells the time in years, months, days, hours, minutes and seconds, convert the cassette recording system to the international standards, and reduce the time between readings so that very fast data acquisition can be an added feature of our system. Automatic range changing and the ability to recognize an event and record at higher speed would be added features that would be highly desirable and would attract customers.

We are receiving a large number of inquiries about industrial control. For example, if we developed a motor control system our PACIFIC could be used to control an electric hoist, carrying batches of components and dipping them in turn into baths of acid, alkali, wash, and wax. Furthermore, we can provide temperature control of the baths, plus interlocks (like don't lower into solid wax). General Motors, Petone,[16] awaits our go-ahead for this project. With motor control we can control an X-Y table in a metal punching, drilling or milling machine. Keying in the coordinates on a keyboard, storing them on a cassette, would make for a versatile, semiautomatic system, ideal for small runs of more than one unit.

Ashley Wallpapers Limited, Porirua, is extremely interested in ways to reduce their annual $100,000 paper loss. They have approached us for help. We propose a PACIFIC system to monitor the rotation of their printing machines and also accept data from keyboards scattered around their factory. This data will be used in calculating their bonus incentive scheme, and so reduce the administrative overhead in filling and analyzing forms. They also need automatic control of color registration in printing. Two machines already have the mechanics to do this, together with poor electronics. We envisage our system also keeping track of the color registration in these machines. To eliminate the problem of giving the CPU too much to do it is proposed to develop a subsystem (also using a microprocessor) to handle each set of push buttons and numerical display. There will be about 40 of these small systems throughout the factory. This will later be an extremely useful peripheral for our PACIFIC, whenever communication is needed between the operator and the system.

There are a large number of potential uses for our PACIFIC system. We would like to immediately market dataloggers, especially with more sophisticated software. We have to enter into this market promptly especially as in a year or so there will be on the market imported loggers, with similar specifications. Our market edge at the moment is because of the extra ability derived from the intelligence of our system, and from the simple yet extremely versatile controls.

In the industrial control field, we need to develop extra hardware like motor control and remote keyboard and display, together with the software to handle these functions. This field has the greatest potential to help industry in New Zealand because with the increasing cost of labor and the relative age of some of the machines, automation, semiautomation, or better control of industrial processes becomes an extremely economic proposition. Each system is inexpensive enough to have systems distributed throughout a factory. This has also great potential for energy savings with better control of processes. An example of this saving is that in the first month of operation $90 of fuel costs were saved by controlling the heating of a modern office block in central Wellington. Energy waste like having both heating and refrigeration operating at the same time on the coldest day in Wellington's winter[17] can be eliminated from several Wellington office blocks. Automatic power factor correction and loading shedding can reduce our increasing electricity bills.

There is a large potential in small office machines, with the development of the necessary software. Once the programs have been developed, their cost of reproduction is negligible, so we can produce a system for small businesses for stock control and simple accounting at a cost comparable to that of a photocopier. However, we consider this a longer term project and would concentrate on

[16]Petone and Porirua are communities within about 20 km of Wellington and Lower Hutt.

[17]It rarely freezes in Wellington.

Exhibit 11.4 SSE's Application for Assistance from the ATP (*continued*)

loggers and industrial control first because of the higher cost of the software. We estimate that it would take a year to be in a position to consider this field for office machines.

Finance

We are in financial difficulties now because with the general downturn in our bread and butter lines there has not been enough to support the last of the development of the datalogger. An estimate of $40,000 is needed to be spent about equally four ways. About $10,000 would be needed to pay the more pressing of our creditors, about $10,000 would pay our staff over the next three months, about $10,000 would buy the parts to make up a batch of about 10 PACIFIC systems, and the remainder would supply us with much needed development tools, upgrading our ability to produce software, hardware, and the associated metalwork.

About $20,000 would be needed now, and the remainder in a month's time to pay for the parts and capital items. So we have spent a total of about $80,000 over three years on this project and now are confident that we have a good product that there is a good market for. We will do a minimum of advertising; however, we have found that as people find out about our product they have been beating a path to our door. So far we have accepted or quoted for only a small proportion of the inquiries. We believe that we could pick up $100,000 of orders before Christmas without trying. The potential is several millions of dollars, especially in small business machines. After we get more experience and receive feedback from our customers, we will consider export to Australia in particular.

Production

In production we would build up small batches of cards, say 10 or 20 at a time. This is well within our present production capabilities. We would also build the mechanical hardware in batches. We have a precision lathe to do the majority of the work, and the right man to supervise its operation. A lot of testing of the cards is software testing, using special programs that we are developing at the moment. All electronic components used are imported either by ourselves or by wholesaler component suppliers. All metal work is sought by us as sheet or extrusion and we either form it ourselves or arrange for others to process the parts we cannot. We own a program development system and have the expertise to build our own programs. When we need special imported parts we have to wait perhaps 10 weeks for air freight delivery, but most of the parts are generally available ex-stock in New Zealand. It is difficult to estimate labor content in production, however, for a typical datalogger selling for $5,500 there would be about $1,900 in parts at cost plus an estimated $600 of labor at $14 per hour for a run of 10 units. This does not include extra programming.

Commercial Feasibility

In the datalogging field our system is comparable in price, but gives a computer compatible output for easier manipulating of data. It can be very versatile, tuned to the customer's needs, can be easily modified to cater for his continuing needs. For field use it uses extremely low power, with a small 12V battery lasting a couple of months or so. It can also be operated by relatively unskilled or forgetful staff because of its relative intelligence. In opposition are dataloggers with fairly limited ranges of the older type of electronics.

The disadvantage of our system is that we are newcomers in the field without much practical experience and little users' feedback. This is especially true in the industrial control field where we have much to learn. However, we will have little overseas opposition in industrial control because we have the great advantage of being here in New Zealand with the ability to cater for the customers needs much more precisely and to offer after sales service that is sadly lacking in this field. However, there are some New Zealand businesses offering good facilities in this field, but there is plenty of work for all for quite a while yet.

Exhibit 11.4 SSE's Application for Assistance from the ATP (*continued*)

In small business machines we would be able to undercut the imported minicomputer systems because of the larger markups that seem to be common with all computers. Also our system would hit at a larger market because, in general, small businesses cannot afford the expensive systems. Our production costs would be much lower because ours is a small system.

It is difficult to estimatet the total market for our product. But it could be at present $5M per year in New Zealand and expanding at 20 percent per year. We could reasonably expect to sell $200,000 worth (40 units) next year with a growth rate of 100 percent per year. To do this we would have to actively go out and sell. Immediately one of our staff could be on the road, with later a full advertising campaign. However we have to learn to walk first. We would probably start organizing an export sales campaign in Australia in about mid-1978 for dataloggers.

Economic and Social Benefits

One of the benefits for New Zealand as a whole would be import substitution, because of the low imported content of our product. It would also make for more efficient industry in New Zealand, from energy saving to better management decisions based on more accurate and up-to-date information. Relieving the more tedious and repetitive parts of the work of the labor force would be a natural consequence of automation. At the end of this year the first graduates are coming from our universities and technical institutes with microprocessor experience. We are already receiving applications for work from these people. At the moment we are turning them away, but know that they are looking to firms like ours to supply them with careers. We need to prosper to keep these people in New Zealand.

Our products are close to the world markets, because they are readily air freighted. With good marketing expertise added, we can successfully compete in these markets.

the development of a complete and operational light unit. Between 1969 and 1971 George spent his spare time bringing development of the light through to production. A $21,000 contract from a New Zealand Harbor Board for 80 such lights provided the necessary financing for further research in emergency lighting.

In 1969 Neil left DSIR to work in Australia. At the end of 1971 he returned to New Zealand and along with George established Solid State Equipment Limited as a private company specializing in electronic equipment. The company was incorporated with $200 in shareholder's funds contributed equally by the four shareholders, Mr. and Mrs. Neil Poletti and Mr. and Mrs. George Jones. Under the arrangement the Managing Director, George, loaned some of his personal savings to the company to provide Neil with a monthly salary equivalent to his own. Neil was to work full-time for SSE while George remained in the employ of DSIR.

Neil began his work in a spare bedroom in his home, where, with evening assistance from George, he developed an emergency fluorescent light to fulfill a contract with Tolley Industries. During 1972 the company put all its effort into the development of such lighting systems. Soon Neil found that the scale of his operations and the presence of a toddler in the house made his spare bedroom an unsuitable location for operations. The principals remortgaged their private homes and purchased a house in Lower Hutt, which they rented to the company.

1973–1975

During 1973, sales of emergency and navigational lighting totaled $10,000 but the line was not profitable. The company retained its research orientation which both founders found satisfying. In late 1973 SSE employed Jeremy Taylor, the son of a DSIR friend, to help in the manufacture of emergency lighting gear. George left DSIR and became a full-time employee of SSE. With the combined activities of three employees, sales rose rapidly. Both owners regarded 1974 as a frustrating year, however. They spent a lot of time acquiring production equipment, becoming trained in its use, and learning how to manufacture efficiently. At the same time they found running the company to be alarmingly time consuming.

In August 1974 George took a year's leave of absence from SSE to attend to family business in Europe. While he was there he attempted to promote a smokemeter SSE had developed in anticipation of large European sales, however, the smokemeter did not meet Euruopean legal standards and no sales materialized.

1975–1976

Upon his return to New Zealand in August 1975, George found that production capacity at SSE was inadequate. Accordingly, SSE estalbished a facility for the production of safety lights in a rented building about 100 miles away from the head office. Later in 1975 SSE developed a smokemeter for the Mnistry of Transport. Ministry officials had told SSE that the Ministry was in the process of drafting air pollution regulations which would create a need for automobile smokemeters. No additional orders had been received and although SSE lost money in the development work, the project was not a total loss. Both George and Neil considered the work fun and the cash received for the initial order of six smokemeters enough to keep the firm going.

1976

In July 1976 Chubb Alarms asked SSE to rush the development of a top of the line burglar alarm to meet new legal requirements. Under the agreement Chubb was to provide the specifications to which SSE would work. Chubb expected to have an annual requirement of 200 alarms but the agreement specified no price. The increased volume necessitated another move, this time to a location eight km away in Naenae. To take advantage of a volume discount, SSE purchased 200 boxes to house the alarms. When the initial batch of 25 metalwork-intensive alarms reached the market, it became evident that Chubb's stringent specifications had resulted in an unacceptably high selling price with low margins for SSE. Because of the poor sales, Chubb decided not to place any more orders, and SSE was left with unrecovered development costs and 175 metal boxes.

Although the outcome was both disappointing and expensive for SSE, the company remained enthusiastic and became interested in producing a special automobile burglar alarm for Chubb. Chubb expected to sell 500 of the alarms per month and placed an initial order of 150, followed by an order for 1,500. Although SSE had ample physical capacity, and although it had grown over the years, it lacked adequate staff to meet this increase in production. Therefore Neil and George asked their production staff to recommend possible employees. In late 1976 SSE hired several housewives described by George as "intelligent but inexperienced," on a part-time basis, bringing the total staff of SSE to 20. A short time later, after they had been trained, the women left for the duration of the school summer holidays and were replaced by a group of equally inexperienced university students. The employees worked "flat-out" to reach the deadlines. The necessity of reworking several batches that had failed tests hindered their work. SSE subsequently found that at least one faulty batch had reached the marketplace.

By the time the initial orders had been completed, it was clear that sales had not materialized as expected and that the fixed price, fixed quantity orders would not be renewed. Although Chubb paid for the 1,650 alarms ordered and bore the immediate burden of the market failure, SSE once again had been unable to recover its development costs.

1977

By February 1977 when the housewives returned, SSE's production activities were restricted to emergency lighting equipment. In addition, demand for these and other building products had been reduced by a downturn in the building industry. Nevertheless, despite these setbacks and creditors screaming for money, Neil and George were reluctant to lay off any staff. They still hoped that the automobile alarm system would sell and they wished to maintain the intimate family atmosphere of the company.

In early 1977 SSE vacated the Naenae factory and established production in another rented building 25 miles from the company's head office and research laboratory. Excess space in the rented building was sublet to DSIR for storage thereby reducing the rent to a nominal figure. In addition, George and Neil felt that the new facility offered a better production control opportunity.

By August 1977 the company had a backlog of creditors and little production. Eight of the staff had resigned but George and Neil decided that some additional staff had to be laid off. SSE subsequently gave notice to three women. Another woman resigned, leaving SSE with a staff of eight: three electronics engineers (including the two owners), three part-time assembler/technicians, one mechanical engineer/technician, and one secretary/receptionist.

R&D AT SSE AND DEVELOPMENT OF THE PACIFIC SYSTEM

R&D was an on-going activity at SSE. Each of the products described previously had originated as a research and/or development project subsequently brought to manufacture by SSE. In addition to these products, SSE had developed and sold varying numbers of a battery charger, a high power inverter (to invert the waves in electrical signals), a temperature function integrator (to measure the deterioration of frozen products), a tacho sensor for diesel motors, an accelerograph (for earthquake research), a crystaloscillator (for physics research), a digital tachometer (for emergency diesel generators), and an earthquake trigger (to shut off power and fuel in the event of an earthquake).

Since 1974 the major research at SSE had involved the development of products incorporating microprocessors. SSE had developed and built the PACIFIC, New Zealand's first minicomputer, which could be used either as a computer or as a datalogger. The PACIFIC, which had its own month-long power supply, could be adapted to collect electrical information (datalogging) which could be either fast or slow, digital or analogue, under a wide range of climatic conditions. The information thus gathered could be stored, manipulated, displayed or used to control a variety of electrical equipment. Research support had come from DSIR which had placed orders with SSE for datalogging equipment from 1975 to 1977. The company had sold two additional units and had orders for others. The customers were government departments, a university, and a crown corporation.

SSE had recently issued quotes totaling $80,000 for more dataloggers, alarm panels, a sawmill control system, and a factory data acquisition system. The principals expected sales of $50,000 to result from these quotes. They felt that active selling could produce sales of $100,000 in the next year. Earlier, SSE had received inquiries concerning possible use of an etch bath dipping controller, as a fast access TV screen price list system for a chain of small retail shops, as an automatic parts positioner in metal punching, and as an automatic monitor and alarm system in the engine room of an ocean-going vessel. One government department had commissioned SSE to develop a simplified version of the PACIFIC to sell for a few hundred dollars. SSE was about to produce prototypes of this version. SSE felt that the system could be used to control stock, to carry out accounting functions or to monitor and control industrial processes. It felt that the full system with all options was relatively cheap at $4,000 to $6,000 with simple operations available at about half that amount.

The initial work on the PACIFIC system had been completed by Bill Stevens, SSE's only programmer, whose contract provided for a three-month annual vacation to allow him to pursue his mountain climbing interests. Bill's work was followed-up by a Swiss engineer, Mr. Klaus Bauer, who joined SSE on a part-time basis in November 1976. He had come to New Zealand at that time to take a language course. By February 1977 Klaus was engaged full time on the PACIFIC system development. He was later joined by a Swiss friend but in June 1977 both men returned to Switzerland. Their departure left SSE with a product approaching completion, too few qualified employees to carry on the work, and insufficient resources to hire new employees. Both owners felt that the PACIFIC system had great potential and devoted their entire attention to completing the DSIR datalogger order which was already one year overdue. By the end of September 1977 SSE had completed two prototype dataloggers.

TESTS ON A DATALOGGER

Ian sought an independent test of one SSE PACIFIC datalogger from DSIR. The unit was tested for continued operation against temperature variation, vibration, voltage variation, and high humidity. Its performance and construction were rated sound. DSIR suggested that improvement could be obtained by:

1. Adding an external signal processing facility.
2. Providing differential signal input converters.
3. Complying with an international data standard.

MARKET POTENTIAL FOR THE PACIFIC

From his investigations of market potential, Ian concluded that "a significant potential exists in New Zealand and Australia for datalogging equipment alone and primarily in New Zealand for the minicomputer as a control function." Ian found that there were several hard-wired, nonintelligent, nonmicroprocessor based, datalogger models available from a number of manufacturers in the $3,000 to $7,000 range. The newer microprocessor based equipment ranged from a very slow model at $2,000 to $5,000 up to systems from $12,000 to $20,000. Apparently two New Zealand manufacturers other than SSE were offering equipment in this field. New Zealand companies had recently been invited to tender for the supply of equipment for New Zealand's aluminum smelter. It appeared that SSE's bid was most competitive. Ian also recognized potential sales for scientific data monitoring and recording in government departments, hospitals, universities, and similar establishments. The PACIFIC datalogger was the only equipment capable of outdoor applications.

In Ian's view the minicomputer market was well-serviced by overseas suppliers offering a wide range of hardware and general application software packaged. The PACIFIC system would in no way be capable of competing in any but the very low end of the minicomputer market. Its advantage would like in a greater versatility and adaptability than overseas models when performing relatively straightforward process control functions. He also felt that it would be some time before SSE would be in a position to exploit the market but noted the interest shown by several firms in the PACIFIC system as a control device.

CUSTOMER'S VIEWS

SSE had a good technical reputation with its customers. In the view of Tolley Industries Limited, SSE's largest customer (30 percent of SSE's sales), SSE was an industrial development group that would require continuous funding for research on an on-going basis. Tolley felt that New Zealand needed the type of R&D carried out by SSE "on a continuous basis which, when brought to a preproduction stage would perhaps be handed over to others for marketing and production."

GEORGE JONES AND NEIL POLETTI

Over a 15-year period Neil and George had established an excellent working relationship. They considered that their thought patterns were sufficiently similar to allow communication without words. Although George was formally Managing Director of SSE, both men regarded themselves as equals in their devotion to electronics and SSE, and in the time and effort they put into their work. Neil had a good reputation among technical people in the electronics field. In early 1977 George had been tempted to leave SSE to pursue his interests in winemaking and beekeeping and his preference for a rural lifestyle but his fascination with the technology and his faith that there was a bright future for electronics drew him back. Originally, the two chose to work weekends and late into each night; more recently the burden of managing the firm had necessitated such effort.

Both principals had taken a course in small business management at the nearby Central Institute of Technology some years before. The course had posed the question: "Do you want to remain small or become big?" Their response, that small is fun and beautiful, seemed to typify their business orientation and their personal preferences for R&D over production reflected this attitude. Both described themselves as reluctant managers.

The principals viewed SSE's strengths to be:

1. Dedicated staff.
2. Good relationships with customers, suppliers and their bank manager.
3. Small size giving it the ability to react quickly to new technologies.
4. Close links with DSIR.
5. Location close to government departments and distant from competitors.
6. Pioneers of microprocessor technology in New Zealand.
7. Reputation as a successful science-based industry.
8. Good customers who paid promptly.

They also recognized some weaknesses:

1. Severe underfinancing.
2. Deteriorating relationships with suppliers and SSE's bank manager.
3. Sporadic management because of directors' technical workload.
4. Development orientation at the expense of a sales orientation.

In addition to the notes Ian had taken on the PACIFIC system, potential markets, SSE, and its principals, he had collected financial statements (unaudited) from the company, made an independent assessment of SSE's financial position, and obtained information on SSE's sales by product and month for the past year. With this information in hand, Ian sat down to prepare his report. He had to decide whether or not to recommend assistance to SSE, and if so, what support would be needed and what terms and conditions should be attached (see Exhibits 11.5 through 11.7).

Exhibit 11.5 Financial Statements of Solid State Equipment Limited

	INCOME STATEMENTS FOR THE YEARS ENDING 31 MARCH				
	1973	1974	1975	1976	1977
Sales	$ 9,872	$37,806	$63,569	$105,289	$118,230
Materials	3,448	19,681	26,634	50,106	44,056
Wages	362	4,263	16,567	35,974	69,734
Outwork	294	344	2,251	2,654	1,625
Gross Profit	5,768	13,518	18,117	16,555	2,815
Expenses					
Car Running	897	1,225	1,349	1,837	2,832
Depreciation	256	187	525	6,066	2,232
Interest	410	814	879	1,068	2,010
Rent	486	2,170	2,170	2,310	5,340
Salaries	5,157	5,433	0	0	0
Other	1,938	1,847	6,594	6,431	3,778
Net Profit (Loss)	(3,377)	1,842	6,600	(1,157)	(13,377)
Tax	0	0	256	0	0
Tax Paid Profit (Loss)	(3,377)	1,842	6,344	(1,157)	(13,377)

	BALANCE SHEETS AT 31 MARCH				
SHAREHOLDERS' FUNDS					
Paid in Capital	200	200	200	200	200
Accumulated Profits	(5,502)	(3,656)	2,688	1,530	(11,847)
Total	(5,302)	(3,456)	2,888	1,730	(11,647)
REPRESENTED BY					
Sundry Debtors	1,900	6,296	14,651	11,719	16,307
Stocks on Hand	5,700	8,368	15,119	11,117	40,570
Other Current Asssets	394	381	0	1,417	1,283
Total Current Assets	7,994	15,045	29,770	24,253	58,160
Less					
Sundry Creditors	1,477	4,272	8,378	7,249	40,866
Bank Overdraft	0	0	3,320	2,212	12,681
Other Current Liabilities	0	0	1,253	0	2,032
Total Current Liabilities	1,477	4,272	12,951	9,461	55,579
Working Capital	6,517	10,773	16,819	14,792	2,581
Fixed Assets (Net)	866	1,346	3,376	8,256	9,716
Other Assets	632	250	0	0	0
Total Assets	8,015	12,369	20,195	23,048	12,297
Shareholders' Advances	13,318	15,825	17,307	21,318	23,944
	(5,302)	(3,456)	2,888	1,730	(11,647)

Exhibit 11.6 Financial Position of SSE on October 7, 1977 as Assessed by DFC

	1976			1977									
	Oct.	Nov.	Dec.	Jan.	Feb.	March	April	May	June	July	August	Sept.	Totals
Car alarms	$10,946	$ 936				$5,570							$17,452
Mail alarms	5,900												5,900
Navigation lights	390	416		$ 796			$ 410				$ 960		2,973
Tolley chargers	1,072	1,094	$ 732	2,502			5,078	$1,366	$13,520	$1,068	4,682	$2,431	33,544
Tolley repairs	102												102
Chubb	88							170		264			522
Hetchcraft	20												20
Tachosensors		5,876										2,200	8,076
Fluorescent light fixtures			6,000		$ 3,500		441	4,032	4,877	500	3,021		22,371
Repairs			218	162				522	137	212	1,076	47	2,375
MOT assembly		512											512
CA[4]				2,360			6,358	140					8,858
Earthquake trigger				903									903
Door switches				375									375
Dataloggers					7,800			3,000				5,075	15,875
Slaves					1,500								1,500
12V units					420								420
Clocks						1,910			456				2,366
BCNZ boards						2,294							2,294
Charger						59							59
Computing time						273		640					913
Clock boards						720							720
Pace assembly time							256		656				912
MacEwans parts and repairs									241				241
Power supply									300				300
Speed sensor										5,300			5,300
UK RAM										1,786			1,786
Flasher unit											600		600
AC voltage regulator											926		926
MO2												880	880
Spare parts												585	585
Domes												283	283
Control cards												99	99
Miscellaneous		109			9	183	61			118	36		517
Totals	$18,518	$8,431	$6,950	$7,609	$13,229	$11,009	$12,604	$9,870	$20,187	$9,248	$11,301	$11,599	$140,556

Case writer's note: Some sales are identified by product and others by customer; some products may be referred to by more than one name; MOT = Ministry of Transport; BCNZ = Broadcasting Corporation of New Zealand. Numbers may not add to Totals because of rounding.

Source: Company records

Exhibit 11.7 Sales by Product and Month

	Actual Current Value
Fixed Assets:	
Plant, furniture, fitting, vehicles	$10,000
Current Assets:	
Debtors	13,000
Stock (valued on "fire-sale" basis)	7,000
Bank	0
Intangible Assets:	
Valuation of Minicomputer/Datalogger development potential (actual company expenditure $80,000)	40,000
Total Assets	70,000
Current Liabilities	
Creditors (Trade)	26,000
Bank (O/D)	14,000
	$40,000
Shareholders Funds	$30,000

Current sales revenue is ranging between $4,000–$10,000 per month.

Note: The intangible assets valuation is an arbitrary assessment of its potential for development and cannot be realistically used to assess a share valuation.

Chapter Twelve

A DYNAMIC ANALYSIS OF ADOPTING NEW TECHNOLOGY

SITUATION 12.1

Butler Metal Products

INTRODUCTION

Butler Metal Products, a large manufacturer of automotive parts for such companies as GM, Chrysler and Ford, faced and still faces many obstacles in the successful implementation of new technology (NT). These obstacles, along with methods to overcome them, are briefly described and analyzed in the following report.

CURRENT SITUATION

Growth, automation, and specialization are the company's current strategies for prosperity in a crowded market. Butler has hired 230 people over the past year and is now completing a three-year, 100,000 square foot plant expansion part of a $26 million upgrading program. It is speculated that the company may add another 50 employees this year. In addition, the purchase of 95 welding robots, which cost $40,000 and $100,000 each depending on their size, makes Butler an industry leader in robotics (Strathdee 1988, B12)

PAST IMPLEMENTATION EXPERIENCES

As a result of Butler's advanced position in the automotive industry, they have few, if any, companies to look to for ideas in creating solid and successful NT implementation strategies. In the past, and still today, Butler's implementation plans have been based on what they have learned from their own implementation experiences. In effect, much of their planninig for NT rests on a type of trial and error methodology.

Many of Butler's first NT implementation efforts have been described by some company representatives as "not highly successful." According to Ray Pederson, Director of Human Resources and Purchasing, there are three reasons for this lack of success: poor timing, customers' dictation of technology, and lack of adequate employee preparation.

Poor Timing

Poor timing was in the past, and still is today, one of the major implementation obstacles faced by Butler Metal Products. As a manufacturer in the automotive industry, an industry experiencing such a rapid rate of change that it is almost impossible to keep pace with the technology, Butler has had to, and still must, implement NT before properly being prepared. This lack of adequate planning has resulted in many unforeseen and detrimental consequences.

Customers' Dictation of Technology

A second major obstacle to successful implementation of NT experienced at Butler is the customer's dictation of the technology process they want Butler to use to produce their products. Only one of Butler's current customers allows for the flexibility of Butler's manufacturing process, by allowing its product design to fit more easily with Butler's current manufacturing process. On the other hand, Butler's other customers demand that Butler produce their products in a particular way, permitting no deviations—even if this means manipulating the manufacturing process to suit their product design. Manipulation of process has had and still has vast implications for profitability and productivity since innovations in technology or production cannot be implemented during the entire OEM model year.

Employee Preparation

The final reason stated for Butler's lack of success in past implementation efforts is inadequate employee preparation. Hagedorn (1985) contends that "the more sensitive management is to people issues, the more successfully a company can introduce NT and automate" (Hagedorn 1985, 72). However, a brief announcement was the only step taken to inform employees of Butler's NT projects in the past. Lack of employee skill, preparation and full commitment was the consequence of such negligence.

PRESENT IMPLEMENTATION EFFORTS

Learning from past mistakes has improved many of Butler's present implementation strategies. These improved methods of implementation are briefly described below.

Project Team

The company now uses a project team approach when implementing and selecting NT. A project team made up of representatives from various departments and levels, from laborers to management executives, creates a more integrated approach to the implementation of NT at Butler. No longer is planning left entirely up to production and/or engineering departments. The introduction of NT into any production facility has many implications for several parts of the company which are not directly concerned with manufacturing. A single flaw in the NT environment is often multifaceted. Consequently, all areas of the company, such as labor relations, production, finance and sales, and so forth, need to be fully integrated into the planning process if the outcome is to be successful.

Present Employee Preparation

Butler's project team representatives recognize that introducing technological change in the past without acknowledging the importance of the human element was one of their gravest errors. Thus, to avoid falling victim to such an omission again, Butler's project team has developed methods to combat the main areas of employee resistance as well as procedures to improve employee technical skill. It is also hoped that these new approaches, focusing on the human element, will shorten the length of the learning curve, as well as increase worker commitment and productivity levels.

Employee/Management Meetings

According to Hagedorn (1985), resistance to change must be viewed as legitimate, appropriate, and something to be expected otherwise resistance will only ferment and develop into sabotage of the system later on. Management must seek ways to consult employees about changes that affect them and to assure them that management will make every effort to avoid, defer, or minimize layoffs from higher productivity to ensure employee commitment. Participation affords an opportunity to confront the change directly and to provide the group with needed information. With this in mind, labor/management meetings were arranged by Butler team representatives to deal with employees' questions and fears concerning the impact of technological change on their jobs. The first fear/concern addressed at these meetings was the fear of job displacement—one of the strongest reasons for employee resistance and lack of commitment in the past.

It was also mentioned at these meetings that the NT (specifically robots) would have a favorable impact on the quality of jobs. Management stressed that the newly implemented robots would do a lot of dirty and dangerous jobs such as welding, which workers hate. In effect, management at Butler not only promises to safeguard jobs but to create higher quality jobs for their workers as well. Such promises have produced higher employee acceptance, commitment, and satisfaction, which in turn have resulted into lower employee turnover rates.

Training

Butler has also setup an in-house training program. In their initial training sessions Butler made an all out effort to sell the two or three most receptive laborers in the company first and then involved them in the training sessions. It was believed that these new converts would sell the most skeptical laborers faster—as employees are often less suspicious of and more receptive to messages given by peers than to messages provided by management. In-house training also has many attractive features in dealing with the preparation of such high-tech implementations.

Education Upgrading

Education upgrading is also part of Butler's strategy to increase employee commitment and technical skill. Butler anticipates that by upgrading employees' education, workers will become more flexible, multifunctional, highly skilled technicians with developed conceptual skills that will help them better program, monitor, and maintain computerized robotic equipment. It is assumed that such improvements in employee's technical and conceptual skills will shorten the present length of the learning curve as well as increase the number of trouble-shooters that are so desperately needed at Butler.

Productivity Improvement Program

A Productivity Improvement Program is also part of Butler's current strategy to increase employee commitment, satisfaction and productivity levels. This particular program encourages employees (through such incentives as company jackets) to provide input into how the company can cut costs and improve productivity.

CURRENT IMPLEMENTATION PROBLEMS

Robot Vendor Selection

Networking difficulties for equipment purchases from different vendors is one of the most pressing problems currently experienced at Butler. Many robot vendors supply specific robot components, few supply them all. In addition to this dilemma, studies have also shown that vendors can no longer afford the time and expense to help potential clients. There used to be enough time for a technology to evolve so that vendors could recover this cost, as it was more directly related to their free standing equipment. However, amidst rapidly changing system technologies, salesmen can rarely afford the time to deal with customers. Thus, tying individual components supplied by various vendors into an integrated system has become one of Butler's largest tasks.

Management Issues

Managers of today's "high-tech" factory must anticipate risks, identify potential problems and overcome them so the system performs to specifications. No longer does the manager just meet short-term production goals and cost budgets like managers of the not so distant past. Many of Butler's managers find such new expectations highly stressful. In addition to these higher expectation levels for managers, managers have little, if any, time to solve present or even past problems. The need to stop growth, in order to effectively plan and solve current implementation problems, is not a strategy permitted by Butler's customers. It is a "grow or die" reality which managers find very stressful. As a result of such high stress levels experienced by managers, turnover rate is much higher for those in management positions than those in labor related positions.

CONCLUSION

As a result of Butler's advanced position in the automotive industry they have few, if any companies, to look to for guidance in the successful implementation of NT. As previously noted, Butler's past and present implementation efforts rests on a type of trial and error methodology. However, learning from past mistakes has improved many of Butler's present implementation strategies. These improved methods of NT implementation have been briefly described and analyzed throughout this report.

READING 12.1

Production Policy and the Acquisition of New Technnology[1]

INTRODUCTION

New technology (NT) is likely to significantly affect national economies, organizations, and management structures. Perhaps the best description of these effects is by Schon (1973) who argues that high levels of technology change have brought a fundamental "loss of stable state" in the last 50 years. All societal institutions are now changing and it is likely that an increasingly important future concern of organizational policies will be adapting to changes.

This paper reviews the impact of NT and examines reasons for its introduction into organizations. The literature on technology within the organizational system is surveyed and important production policy questions which concern the adoption process are addressed. The central thrust of the paper is to argue that the acquisition of NT should not be based on economic benefits alone and that it ought to be considered according to a much more comprehensive framework.

The effectiveness of firms in adopting NT is viewed as a function of four sets of factors: (1) why the technology is needed? (2) when to introduce it? (3) where should it be introduced? and (4) how to introduce it? Based on these factors, a conceptual framework is developed to guide management in the acquisition of NT and to clarify the relationship of technological considerations and organizational policy.

[1]Hamid Noori (1987). *Engineering Management International,* Volume 4, pp. 187–196.

NEW TECHNOLOGY–AN OVERVIEW

Before attempting to explore the implications of NT, let us consider exactly what is meant by the term technology. In this paper, we adopt the following definition of technology:

> The collection of plant, machine tools, and recipes available at any given time for the execution of the production task and the rational underlying their utilization.

This definition includes both "hardware" aspects (machines and techniques) of manufacturing and "software" aspects (rational) of manufacturing. It should be noted that the term "technology" applies to all types of organizations although our focus in this paper will be on the manufacturing aspect of it.

With respect to the history of manufacturing technology, our starting point is Frederick Taylor, who applied the modern technological principles to manual work in order to imitate man's physical skills (Drucker 1970, 79). This went under the name of "scientific management."

The immediate result of scientific management was to drastically reduce the costs of manufactured goods and to permanently change the structure and composition of the work force. Numerous skilled laborers were replaced by fewer machine operators who were paid the wages of highly skilled workers. Taylor's work rested on the assumption that "knowledge," rather than "manual skills," is the fundamental resource. This resulted ultimately in a complete shift in the focus of work from labor to knowledge. Following this lead, today's technology attempts to imitate man's mental skills in addition to his physical skills.

Thus, today's new (manufacturing) technology refers to the intellectual organization on the programmability feature of technology, and is typified by the microprocessor, numerically controlled machine tools, robotics, computer-aided design and manufacturing, automated materials-handling equipment, and computer-integrated manufacturing. As an illustration, an advanced flexible manufacturing system would begin with product design on a computer-aided system that conveys information to a central database. Using the database and directed by a computer, a parts carrier then brings raw materials to the production line. Remote terminals allow management to oversee the production process without physically being in the plant. A robot then loads and unloads the machine tool and places finished parts on a conveyor that transports them to an assembly robot. This robot assembles the product, and a welding robot joins the parts together. The product is then automatically inspected and placed on a cart that carried it off to the shipping area. Human involvement is limited to the design and control of the process, which consists of watching and adjusting the machines.

REASONS FOR INTRODUCING NEW TECHNOLOGY

There can be little doubt that the key motivation for today's NT is economic—see for example (Crozier 1980; Noori and Tampler 1983; Munro and Noori 1986; Tanner 1982; and Tlusty and Crozier 1981). Cost reduction has been the determining factor in nearly all the decisions to adopt NT. This applies as much to the machinery of industrial revolution and the introduction of computers nearly two decades ago (Roberts 1965) as it does to the introduction of microelectronics today in manufacturing facilities (Thomas 1983). In addition, as Roberts mentions, some organizations have found that adopting NT stabilizes total costs when the volume of production is changed, since automation typically increases fixed costs relative to variable costs.

The increasing cost of labor, declining product quality, loss of market share, and declining productivity were the four most important reasons given by the responding companies in previous surveys (Noori and Templer 1983; and Munro and Noori 1986). From these studies, it appears that most companies do not take much account of wider social and environmental issues in their decisions to automate. These findings contradict the conceptual argument that technology should be viewed in terms of an overall organization policy. As Schon emphasizes, NT displaces old technology already in place and supported by the system: "There is no clear grasp of the next stable state (for individuals within the system)—only a clear picture of the one to be lost."

Given the existing perception among the top management for acquiring NT, it appears that a conceptual framework that helps recognize the important policy questions is desirable. Before this, however, we review the way that technology has been treated in the literature.

TECHNOLOGY AND ORGANIZATIONAL STRUCTURE—A BRIEF LITERATURE REVIEW

The literature on the role of technology in organizations and the degree to which it determines their structure reveals two opposing views. The first group of researchers, we call them the "technological imperative group," treat technology as an independent variable and views organizations as open systems in which technology plays a key role in determining structure (for example, span of control, number of hierarchical levels, and so forth) and influencing policy. An open system is one in which the structure of an organization is viewed as something to be explained, at least in part, by the operation of external forces and is not completely under the control of system participants (Scott 1975, 23).

The empirical research of Woodward (1970; 1970; 1958) first called attention to technology as a general determinant of organizational structure. In her initial research, production type was found to be the most important factor in shaping organizational structure and relationships among personnel. Harvy (1968) and Zwermann (1970) later came to the same conclusions as Woodward. Zwermann concluded that: (1) a relationship exists between mass production and hierarchical authority in organizational structures; (2) the number of employees in a firm is not related to organizational structure; (3) a strong correlation exists between structure and production technology, with each production type having its own organization structure; and (4) the ratio of managers to other personnel is related to the type of technology. These findings are subsequently supported by others, among them are Burns and Stalker (1961), Mahoney and Frost (1979), Perrow (1967), Thompson (1967), and Udy (1965).

While the technology imperative group views the organization as an open system and treats technology as an independent variable, a second group of researchers (the "antitechnological imperative group") dismisses the open system approach and considers technology as a dependent variable. This group argues that only a moderate, little, or no relationship exists between technology and structure. The researchers in this group examined variables describing the bureaucratic strategy of control of the organization (for example, rules, definition of tasks, and level of decision-making).

Briefly, the "antitechnological imperative group," led by the Aston University group (Pugh et al. 1963) and Hickson et al. (1969), assert that their research shows technology to be much less important than other variables such as number of employees. Furthermore, they found that technology is the strongest determining factor only at the operating level, in that structure is more affected when it directly depends upon the technology of the work flow. Consequently, the smaller the organization, the more its structure shows the effects of technology; the larger the organization, the more these effects are related only to employees who are directly linked to the work flow. Therefore, in larger organizations, work flow factors do not affect administrative activities and the more remote hierarchical levels.

In summary, the "technological imperative group" and "antitechnological imperative group" represent the two extreme views on the relationship between organizational structure and technology. As Child and Mansfield (1972) point out, both size and technology are factors in determining organizational structure.

In dealing with the debate over technology and structure, Gillespie and Milete (1977) argue that ". . . Technology has been elusively defined, refined, treated soley as an independent variable, applied holistically to organizations, confused with structure, crudely measured, and studied mainly in manufacturing firms." This confusion has given rise to a third view, namely that technology and the prevailing social system jointly determine structure (Tanner 1982; Jelinek and Golhar 1982; and Walker 1962). The key focus in this view is on adaptability and obtaining the best fit possible between the various subsystems of the organization. This view is at least compatible with both the technological imperative and antitechnological imperative groups.

A FRAMEWORK FOR ACQUISITION OF NEW TECHNOLOGY

From the previous literature review, it is evident that the adoption of NT can, along with other factors, influence the organizational structure. It can also be generally stated that serious negative impacts may occur from the introduction of NT if a total systems view of the organization is not taken into account. This is so because a total system view allows for a comprehensive reassessment of whether or not acquisition of NT is consistent with the company's objectives and cultures.

A useful framework for evaluating the acquisition of NT will have to incorporate the theoretical findings mentioned previously, and will have to be practical. The framework should first of all conform to the open systems concept of the organization and indicate the processes involved and guide managerial decision-making in acquiring NT. This can, perhaps, best be done through impact analysis (Porter et al. 1982).

Impact analysis is a useful tool for assessing NT since it assists companies in performing "what if" analyses before implementing NT. It assists in thinking about possible responses to important questions dealing with acquisition of NT and opens up new and better ways of doing things which might not otherwise surface. A framework such as the one illustrated by Exhibit 12.1 can be developed to conduct the necessary impact analysis by addressing the following four fundamental questions about introducing new technology into an organization: why, when, where, and how to introduce NT. The following section describes the framework in detail.

The proposed framework structures the decision to introduce NT around the four major questions under two types of environment. The first environment includes the market, the economy, government, unions and culture. The second is the sociotechnical environment in the organization that immediately surrounds the production system. The framework stresses that NT is introduced into the supporting system that currently surrounds the "old" technology (Burns and Stalker 1961; Udy 1965; Jelinek 1981; Jelinek and Burnstein 1982; and Kim and Utterback 1983), and that production technology and organizational design choices interact (Jelinek and Burnstein 1982; Lawrence and Lorsch 1969; and Thompson and Bates 1957, 1958). This interaction is represented as a joint matching process in the model. Also, the framework proposes that the eventual outcome variables are both economic and social, that is, an effective production technology is measured in terms of joint consideration of social and technical variables (Beer 1980).

As indicated, the proposed framework is based on four general questions. The first and most obvious question to ask is why should we consider introducing NT? This question deals with environmental pressures, including competitive pressures. Dominant factors to be considered are such economic indices as rising production and labor costs; labor shortages and employee unwillingness to work in certain hazardous or unpleasant environments; needs for production flexibility in the face of declining available lead times; employee morale and employment issues; and the cost and availability of alternative production technology. The why question is typically asked first, but the other three following questions need to be considered simultaneously when contemplating the reason for introducing NT.

The second question to ask is when should NT be introduced? Subcomponents of this question have been addressed by various authors, see, for example (Abernathy and Wayne 1974; Cohn 1981; Ettlie 1982; Kiechel 1981, and Malpas 1983). None however, have drawn ideas together to produce a practical checklist of factors to be considered. The key to this question is an analysis of the organization's need for and readiness to accept NT, including a consideration of technical, production, managerial and social readiness. Dominant factors to be considered are managerial and employee acceptance of NT, likely economies of scale such as improved technical processes for high volume production, cost and benefit analysis, the industry cost structure, the positioning of competitors on the production "learning curve," and culture-dominant coalitions in the organization.

The third question to ask is where should NT be introduced? Some good studies have addressed this question, but they are all based on specific experiences with technology introduction and are hard to generalize from. In the main, however, the

Exhibit 12.1 The Making of the Compatible Organization

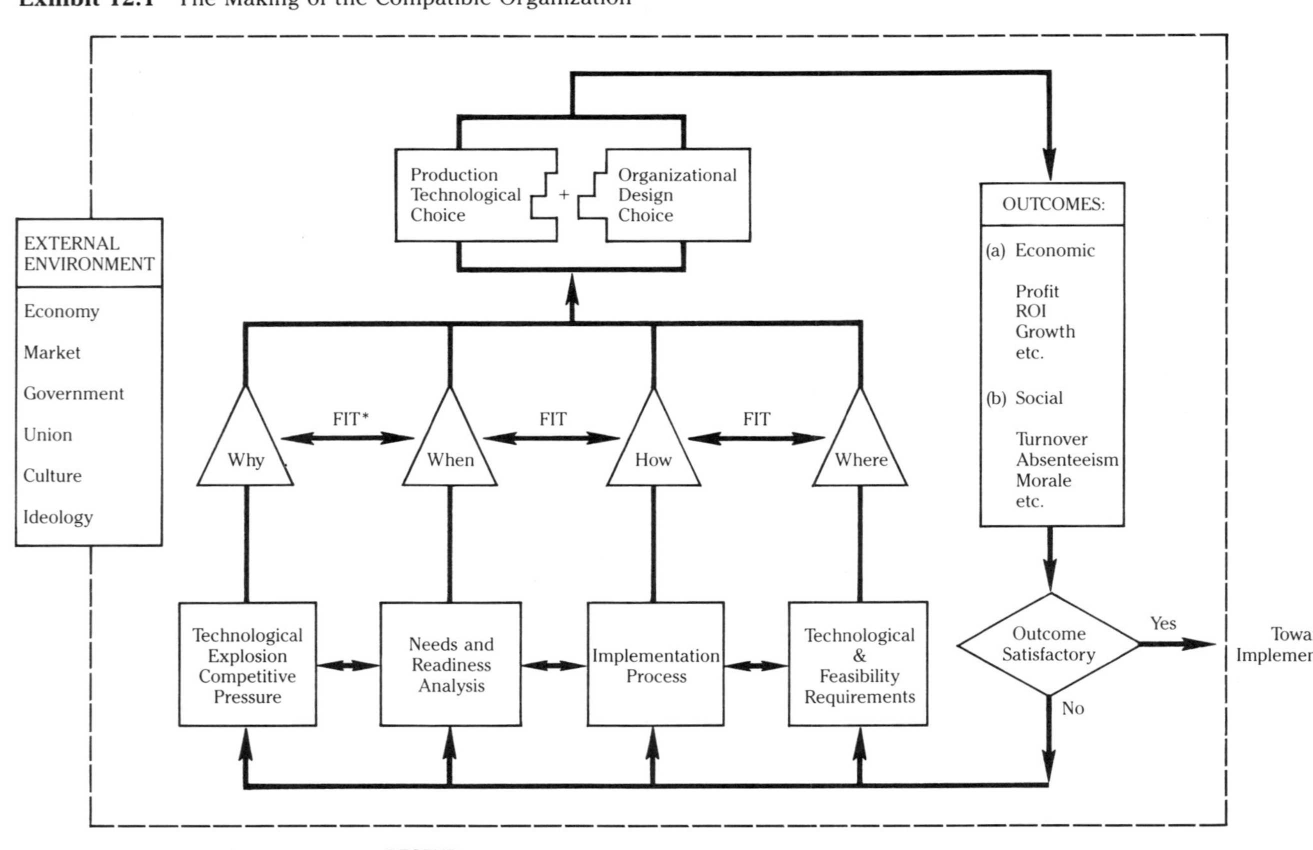

LEGEND

*FIT: Goodness of fit between pairs of components in each of the four categories of questions.

key to this question is an analysis of the technological feasibility and point of greatest impact of the proposed NT. Dominant factors to be considered are: departmental differences in readiness and enthusiasm, available technologies, product life cycle differences, and geographic and locality differences. Thus, it might be feasible only to introduce NT on a partial basis in the more receptive areas of an assembly operation.

The fourth question to be asked related to process: how should NT be introduced? The process of implementing technology underlies the where and when questions, for they cannot be answered without considering the way in which major changes, such as new forms of technology, will be introduced. The focal point here is the integration of technology, people, and organization. In general, the dominant factors to be considered are social and technical interfaces with workers and management, union participation in the implementation process, and implications of the NT on employment levels.

Exhibit 12.2 provides an extensive list of variables and decision alternatives to be considered when adopting NT, together with detailed considerations for each of the four groups of questions.

It is considered that the particular contribution of this framework is its focus on the four implementation questions. This focus makes it possible for the model to achieve its stated intention to combine theoretical accuracy within a framework for guiding managerial choice of production technology. On the basis of the premises of the proposed framework a decision flow chart for the acquistion of NT is illustrated in Exhibit 12.3.

Generally, NT cannot be effectively introduced unless it is part of a predetermined organization policy and production policy. These policies must take into account a wide range of relevant variables and are assessed against the multiobjective criteria of economic and social outcomes. The introduction of NT is usefully considered in terms of the four sets of questions set out in the framework, and not just the initial query: Why should we introduce the NT? The process of introducing NT is extremely important and may even have a greater impact on eventual success than the actual technology chosen. The model spells out that this success is a function of a careful analysis of organizational readiness, technological feasibility, and a sociotechnically designed implementation process.

CONCLUSION

Through the examination of the effects and possible implications of NT and through the use of concepts developed in previous models of the organization, a broad systems framework is developed for practical use. The framework discusses the fitness between four basic categories of questions: why acquire NT, when, where and how to introduce NT, in order to successfully implement. A comprehensive list of variables and decision alternatives for each of these questions is also suggested. The proposed framework is useful in guiding, implementing and evaluating future acquisitions of NT.

Future research is needed to expand the proposed framework and to address questions such as: Is this framework sufficiently inclusive? that is, are all relevant variables

Exhibit 12.2 A List of Variables and Decision Alternatives to be Considered When Adopting New Technology

DECISION AREA	DECISION CONSIDERATIONS	DECISION ALTERNATIVES
WHY should new technology be considered?	Increased technological availability	Seize opportunity; or retain existing processes.
	Degree of NT adoption by competition	Respond to competitions; or maintain current processes.
	Labor cost considerations	Reduce labor costs by seeking to improve existing work force productivity; or substitute NT applications for direct labor requirements.
	Flexibility requirements	Introduce a complete flexible manufacturing system; or supplement existing process with NT applications; or existing process.
	Quality level	Utilize recent developments in NT providing precision and consistency; or apply manual statistical quality control; or implement quality circles.
	Degree of operating leverage	Increase application of NT; or decrease greater labor emphasis: or pursue existing policies.
	Dependability	Achieve shorter lead times (resulting from increased efficiency of NT applications); or change inventory policies; or reassess capacity constraint.
	Total system emphasis	Increase integration and interaction (among functional areas within firm utilizing NT applications); or apply traditional organizational methods.
	Information accessibility requirements	Bridge information gap (traditionally found between upper management and operations function through automation of informaiton systems); or address information requirements via existing organizational structure.
	Engineering and design	Utilize CAD system or traditional manual approach.
	Economies of scale	Achieve similar benefits at lower volumes—with product diversity—by applications of NT; or expand plant capacity with existing processes.
	Distinctive competence	Utilize NT to establish distinctive competence/retain such in face of environmental pressures; or pull strategic levers utilizing current process emphasis.
WHEN should NT be introduced?	Competitive pressures	Adopt reactive; or proactive strategy.
	Social pressures/implications	Coordinate timing (so as to minimize negative social impacts/maximize positive social impacts); or base timing on internal factors to the firm only.
	Market considerations	Time NT acquisitions in response to market demands or independent of market demand.
	Corporate culture	Base timing considerations in adherence to traditional corporate policies; or irrespective of past practices.
	Management and technical preparedness	Introduce NT applications at point in time when management and staff have developed capability; or do not postpone acquisition based on such considerations.

Exhibit 12.2 A List of Variables and Decision Alternatives to be Considered When Adopting New Technology (*continued*)

DECISION AREA	DECISION CONSIDERATIONS	DECISION ALTERNATIVES
	Cash flow considerations	Acquire NT when incoming revenues can accommofdate purchase; or base acquisitions on other criteria (debt financing).
	New product introductions	Time NT acquistions in accordance with or irrespective of new product introductions.
	Recency of the technological innovation	Acquire NT applications immediately after market introduction; or postpone acquistion until developed further.
WHERE should NT be?	Plant and equipment condition	Introduce NT as a means of replacing dated equipment and facilities; or introduce irrespective of existing condition.
	Departmental/functional adaptability	Restrict the base of NT introductions on suitability of process; or seek to alter given processes to broaden adaptability.
	Impact ramifications	Focus NT introduction on specific processes which have greatest potential for benefit; or adopt an encompassing approach.
	Product life cycle stage	Introduce NT applications particular to specific products (which display adequate remaining sales potential); or allocate priorities based on other criteria.
	Availability of labor	Introduce NT specifically into areas lacking sufficient labor resource base; or adopt a policy of even dispersion coupled with retraining redistribution of displaced workers.
	Growth implications	Incorporate NT acquisitions into areas of anticipated growth; or utilize NT applications to maintain consistent and broad support.
HOW should NT be introduced?	Speed of introduction	Adopt gradual; or swift approach.
	Employee/union participation	Involve employees in decision-making process; or conduct decisions independent of employee output.
	Impact on employee levels	Consider whether immediate and long-term effects on employment play a considerable role; or insignificant role in implementation decisions.
	Utilization of support services	Heavy reliance on government/consultant support services during implementation; or reliance on in-house expertise.
	Pre-generation of concept acceptance	Initiate measures to encourage positive disposition among employees regarding NT applciations; or allow employee reactions to run their course.
	Degree of prior orientation	Preclude NT implementation with training and orientation of personnel as well as process testing; or implement NT and learn by doing.

Exhibit 12.3 A Decision Flow Chart for Adopting New Technology

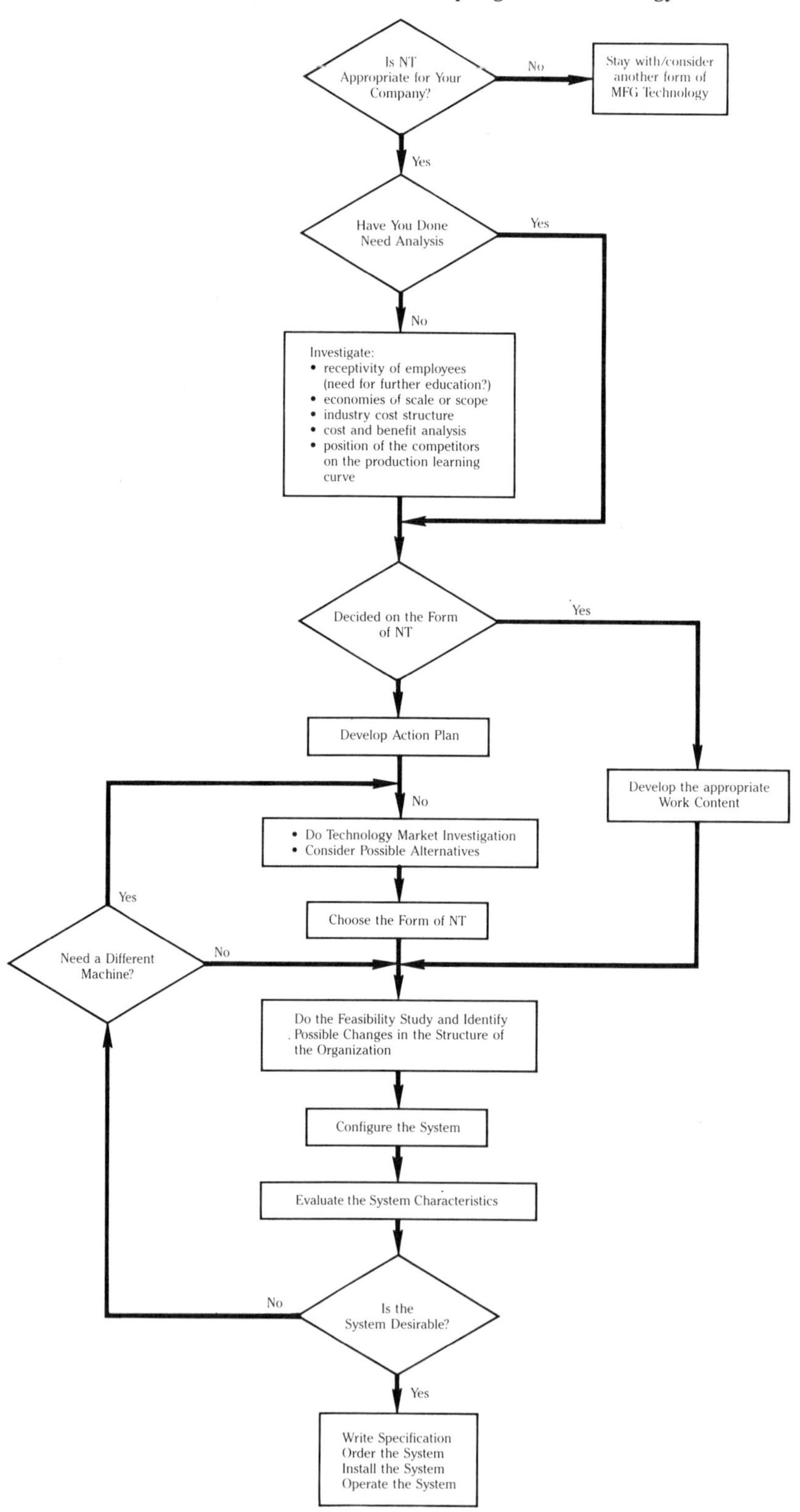

at least assignable to a place in the model? Are the proposed questions sufficiently comprehensive? Is the multiobjective emphasis a true reflection of reality and are the dual outcomes meaningful criteria for effectiveness? And, how useful is the framework for guiding the implementation of NT?

REFERENCES AND BIBLIOGRAPHY

ABERNATHY, W. J. and K. WAYNE [1974]. "Limits of the Learning Curve," *Harvard Business Review*, Volume 52, September-October, pp. 109-119.

BEER, M. [1980]. *Organizational Change and Development: A Systems View*. Goodyear, Santa Monica, CA.

BURNS, T., and G. M. STALKER [1961]. *The Management of Innovation*. Tavistock Press, London.

CHILD, J., and R. MANSFIELD [1972]. "Technology, Size and Organizational Structure," *Sociology*, Volume 6, pp. 369-393.

COHN, S. F. [1981]. "Adopting Innovations in a Technology Push Industry," *Research Management*, Volume 24, pp. 26-31.

CROZIER, J. E. [1980]. A survey to identify the attitudes and awareness of numerical control users and the technological and economic strengths and weaknesses of machine tool part programming. Canadian Institute of Metal Working, Technological Innovation Studies Program, November.

DRUCKER, P. F. [1970]. *Technology, Management and Society*. Harper and Row, New York, NY.

ETTLIE, J. E. [1982]. *Performance Grap Theories of Innovation*. De Paul University, Chicago, Illinois.

GILLESPIE, D. F., and D. S. MILETI [1977]. "Technology and the Study of Organizations: An Overview and Appraisal," *Academy of Management Review*, Volume 2, No. 1, pp. 7-16.

HARVEY, E. [1968]. "Technology and Structure of Organization," *American Sociological Review*, Volume 33, No. 2, April, pp. 247-259.

HICKSON, D. ET AL. [1969]. "Operations Technology and Organization Structure: An Empirical Reappraisal," *Administrative Science Quarterly*, Volume 14, No. 3, pp. 378-379.

JELINEK, M., and M. C. BERSTEIN [1982]. "The Production Administrative Structure: A Paradigm for Strategic Fit," *Academy of Management Review*, Volume 7, No. 2, pp. 242-252.

JELINEK, M., and J. D. GOLHAR [1982]. "The Interface Between Strategy and Manufacturing Technology," *Columbia Journal of World Business*, Volume 18, No. 1, Spring, pp. 26-36.

JELINEK, M. [1981]. "Technology, Organizations and Contingency," in M. Jelinek, J. Litteres, and R. Miller (eds.), *Organization by Design: Theory and Practice*. Irwin-Dorsey, Georgetown, Ontario, pp. 219-229.

KIECHEL, W. [1981]. "The Decline of the Experience Curve," *Fortune*, Number 105, October, pp. 139-146.

KIM, L., and J. M. UTTERBACK [1983]. "The Evolution of Organizational Structure and Technology in a Developing Country," *Management Science*, Volume 29, No. 10, October, pp. 1185-1197.

LAWRENCE, P. R., and J. W. LORSCH [1969]. *Organizations and Environment*. Richard D. Irwin, Illinois.

MAHONEY, T. A., and P. J. FROST [1974]. "The Role of Technology in Models of Organizational Effectiveness," *Organizational Behavior and Human Performance*, Volume 11, pp. 122-138.

MALPAS, R. [1983]. "The Plant After Next," *Harvard Business Review*, July-August, pp. 122-130.

MUNRO, H., and H. NOORI [1986]. "Reflecting Corporate Strategy in the Decision to Automate," *Business Quarterly*, Volume 50, No. 4, pp. 115-120.

NOORI, H. A., and A. TEMPLER [1983]. "Factors Affecting the Introduction of Industrial Robots," *International Journal of Operations Management*, Volume 3, No. 2, pp. 46-57.

NOORI, H. A., and A. TEMPLER [1983]. "Robots in Canadian Industry: The Impact of New 'Steel Collar' Workforce," Wilfrid Laurier University, School of Business and Economics, Waterloo, Ontario.

PERROW, C. [1967]. "A Framework for the Comparative Analysis of Organizations," *American Sociological Review*, Volume 32, No. 3, April, pp. 194-208.

PORTER, A. L., F. A. ROSSINI, S. R. CARPENTER, and A. ROPER [1982]. *A Guidebook for Technology Assessment and Implementation*. Elsevier, Amsterdam, The Netherlands.

PUGH, D. S. et al. [1983]. "A Conceptual Scheme for Organizational Analysis," *Administrative Science Quarterly*, Volume 8, pp. 289-315.

ROBERTS, R. S. [1965]. Management Decisions to Automate. Monograph No. 3, U.S. Department of Labor Manpower/Automation Research, Washington, DC.

SCHON, D. A. [1973]. *Beyond the Stable State*. Nortran and Company, New York, NY.

SCOTT, R. W. [1975]. "Organizational Structure," *Annual Review of Sociology*, No. 1, pp. 1-20.

TANNER, J. A. (ed.) [1982]. *Robotics in the Canadian Manufacturing Industries.* National Research Council, January.

THOMAS, D. [1983]. "The Unemployment Crisis," *Canadian Business,* February, pp. 61–71.

THOMPSON, J. D. [1967]. *Orgnaizations in Action.* McGraw Hill, New York, NY.

THOMPSON, J. D., and F. L. BATES [1957/58]. "Technology, Organization and Administration," *Administrative Science Quarterly,* Volume 2, pp. 325–343.

TLUSTY, J., and J. E. CROZIER [1981]. *A Robotics Application Study.* Canadian Institute of Metal Working, National Research Council, March.

UDY, S. H., JR. [1965]. "The Comparative Analysis of Organization," in J. D. March (ed.), *Handbook of Organizations.* Rand McNally, Chicago, Illinois.

WALKER, C. R. [1962]. *Modern Technology and Civilization.* McGraw-Hill, Toronto, Canada.

WOODWARD, J. [1970]. *Industrial Organization: Theory and Practice.* Oxford University Press, Oxford, U.K.

WOODWARD, J. (ed.) [1958]. *Management and Technology.* Her Majesty's Stationary Office, London.

ZWERMAN, W. L. [1970]. *New Perspectives on Organization Theory.* Greenwood Press, Westport, CT.

READING 12.2

Managers' Misconceptions About Technology[2]

By any realistic measure, the record of technological innovation by American industry is a magnificent human achievement in the face of immense uncertainty, grinding anxiety, and low odds of success. Nonetheless, unrealistic expectations have kept that technological capability on a roller coaster of corporate funding. For 20 years after World War II, companies and public opinion gave technological innovation virtually universal support. During the next 10 to 20 years, however, it was increasingly seen as a villain that pursued the wrong objectives, was socially unresponsive, and, worst of all, was ineffective.

The scientists and engineers most closely associated with the work of innovation are painfully aware of the consequences of misconceptions about the rate, direction, and character of technological progress. But even they find it difficult to specify what technology can provide, what forces drive and constrain it, and how quickly innovation capacity can respond to those forces. Indeed, to cite but one example, judging correctly when a major technical discontinuity is on the horizon or when extensions of conventional technology will prevail remains a crucial, difficult decision for business people and scientists alike.

After 29 years of experience in nurturing innovative activity at General Electric, I am still amazed by how fragile and improbable a process innovation really is. More to the point, I am convinced that only if we have a genuinely realistic understanding of the gauntlet an innovation must run in order to succeed will be more appreciative

[2]Lowell Steele (1983). "Managers' Misconceptions about Technology." Reprinted with permission from *Harvard Business Review*, November-December, pp. 133–140. © 1983 by the President and Fellows of Harvard College.

of the achievement, less vulnerable to disappointment, and better able to manage the process.

Let me, then, identify the most common misconceptions about managing technology and point out their unfortunate consequences.

MISCONCEPTION 1

The criterion for determining the implementation of technology should be "best possible," not "good enough."

> "Good enough" may not be elegant, but it accurately reflects the often overlooked fact that social and economic considerations should and do determine the priorities for a technology's application and set the appropriate level of performance. Technology that is not wanted has little market value and so it is not worth creating. Similarly, better technical performance than customers desire nearly always incurs a cost penalty. The proper target, therefore, is to create not the best possible technology, but technology that is good enough.
>
> A number of years ago, in an attemmpt to gain insight into new program opportunities for corporate R&D at GE, I queried engineering managers about their most critical problems. Virtually everyone responded that the principal barriers were not technical—some peformance capability they were unable to achieve—but economic.
>
> Familiar definitions of industrial R&D hold that the work inevitably contains risk and uncertainty as to whether the goal can be attained.

These definitions rarely make clear, however, that the goal in question includes cost as well as performance targets for the product or process. True, a small fraction of industrial R&D explores technical feasibility with little concern for economic constraints, but all large expenditures mut be concerned with both. Especially in a business setting, cost barriers are technical barriers.

Every product on the market is the result of a series of compromises among cost, performance, and product life. Obviously, if these compromises do not reflect the values that customers want, the product does not sell. When, for example, consumers did not care about energy efficiency, materials recycling, or the environment, technologists put their efforts into achieving lower costs in areas that did matter very much to customers. The technology existed at that time to make electrical appliances more energy efficient, but at a cost that would have priced them out of the market.

Attempts to sell customers on a higher level of performance than they want are also highly problematic. In the late 1940s, GE mounted a campaign to increase public interest in preserving the environment. The response was underwhelming, to say the least. Ford's efforts in the 1950s to push safety-related features met with similar results. In fact,much of what R&D does is develop solutions that are less than technically elegant but that reflect a value for which customers are willing to pay.

When social values change, technology responds, but managers often overestimate the speed of that response and the level of improvement that can be achieved in the short run. Driven by their enthusiasm, technologists themselves may lend credence to these overexpectations. They sometimes forget that trying to make something work correctly all the time at a cost-effective price is an excruciatingly detailed task. I well recall the wonderment of one of my associates when charged with putting into operation a new process he had been working on for several years. "Son of a gun," he said. "When my boss tells me to 'make it work,' he means 24 hours a day, 7 days a week, 52 weeks a year!"

Technologists working in the field, may underestimate the magnitude of improvement they can achieve over the long term. After all, their reputations are on the line. Given the inherent uncertainty of their work, it is not surprising that they often give conservative estimates of what is possible.

MISCONCEPTION 2

"Good enough" is determined by careful rational choice, not by convention—that is, by what consumers have learned to accept or expect.

What R&D produces is rarely as good as what the present level of knowledge about physical laws allows. Instead, it is in Herbert Simon's words what "satisfices"—that is, what meets social expectations.

In health care, for example, where expectations are boundless, science and technology have made nonstop efforts for improvement supported by ample funds from the political system. By contrast, environmental deterioration and energy efficiency were for many years of little concern and so received scant attention from technologists.

Widely shared beliefs, even if mistaken, do much to shape technical effort. At times, what is good enough for the market is actually better than what is physically required to achieve the desired goal. With modern detergents, for instance, cleaning ability is relatively independent of water temperature. Even so, belief in the virtue of hot water in ensuring cleanliness has been slow to change, despite the energy saving that results from using cold water.

Or consider the consequences of the American consumer's view that small household appliances are mainly gifts or impulse purchases. This perception necessarily affects the price, the method of merchandising, and the levels of performance and durability established as design specifications. Technology that is good enough must yield a cost acceptable to mass market for gift items. In Canada and Europe, however, these appliances are regarded as important additions to household capital, and consumers demand—and are willing to pay for—products that have a longer life and that meet higher performance standards.

Sometimes "good enough" is based on erroneous assumptions about costs. Targets for product quality usually derive from the belief that high volume always incurs a penalty in quality and that, beyond some point, the costs of quality are greater than the savings it generates. The Japanese, by questioning these assumptions, have demonstrated that our beliefs about quality are no more than conventions—and mistaken conventions at that.[3]

[3]David A. Gardin, "Quality on the Line." *Harvard Business Review*, September–October 1983, p. 64.

MISCONCEPTION 3

Most innovations are successful—and should be. This distorted perception arises to some extent from the natural tendency of both companies and individual managers to publicize successes while allowing failures to die quietly. In addition, the data needed to analyze a failure—even for an internal study—are usually skimpy and difficult to assemble.

In reality, the failure rate of innovations is high. This fact reflects the intricacy and interdependence of modern advances in technology. To be successful, any attempt to introduce a technical capability must demonstrate that the capability really does offer substantial advantages. Most of the time, however, a new technology either is not enough of an improvement over the old to warrant the effort and the risk it entails, or it has problems and deficiencies that were not apparent initially. As with a jigsaw puzzle, adding a piece to a simple two-dimensional puzzle is not difficult, but fitting a new piece into a complex, three-dimensional puzzle is.

Consider, for example, the interlocking relationships among such products as fabrics, detergents, and washers and dryers, each of which is produced by a different industry. Wash-and-wear fabrics forced the redesign of washers and dryers and the reformulation of detergents. If the advantages of the new fabrics had not been so dramatic, they would not have induced these related changes.

When a single dramatic advance like X-ray tomography or xerography leads to a new level of capability much desired by customers, success is likely to follow. Many technical advances, however, face extended barriers to success.

The need for lower costs in making photovoltaic solar energy available for instance, is spread uniformly over the entire process—production of high-purity silicon, wafers, and solar cells; assembly into barriers; methods of installation on roofs; and control systems for the resulting electrical output. Hence, no one dramatic improvement can have more than a limited impact on total system costs.

A second reason for the high failure rate of innovations is that the jigsaw puzzle in quesiton changes when threatened with a new piece, thus making a good fit more difficult to achieve. The manufacturers of photoflash bulbs delayed for 20 years the widespread adoption of the electronic flash for amateur use by producing lower cost and more conventient flash bulb systems. The threat to the photoflash business was a powerful stimulus to innovative effort designed to hold off the commercial effects of advances in electronic flashes.

New technology constantly chases the moving target of conventional technology, which is itself goaded to accelerated improvement by the threat. The new technology rarely catches up. In fact, one of the most important economic benefits of innovative activity is the stimulus it gives to conventional technology. For instance, advances in magnetic tape for audio and video recording have prevented the development of thermoplastic recording. Similarly, advances in existing technologies for interrupting high power circuits have proved an insurmountable barrier to the use of vacuum interrupters, despite their technical elegance and attractive features.

The current competition between videotape and video disk is a good example of one very new technology, videotape, establishing a market position before another.

Improvements in the recording length, ease of use, and miniaturization of the tapes have made them a formidable, and moving, obstacle to the success of video disks.

MISCONCEPTION 4

What do you not know about a new technological advance is probably good; Murphy's law rarely applies.

The attractive features of a new discovery must become apparent rapidly, or it will receive no further attention. But, as Alec Guinness demonstrated with painful hilarity in the film *The Man in the White Suit*, our ignorance is usually greater than we realize, and even exciting new discoveries can have undesirable attributes.

Sometimes it is possible to discover a fatal birth defect quickly. GE's corporate R&D invented a new fiber that looked and behaved more like wool than any other synthetic material known. Unfortunately, the fiber disintegrated in dry cleaning solvents, and the R&D staff was unable to solve this problem.

Sometimes a limitation elicits, but does not respond to, extended efforts to eradicate it. GE eventually abandoned its program on hydrogen-oxygen fuel cells after years of trying to avoid using platinum as a catalyst. Without platinum, fuel cell life was too short; with platinum, operating costs were uneconomic, and known world supplies of platinum were inadequate to permit its extensive use.

Sometimes, however, a limitation creates immense anxiety but eventually yields to creative effort and luck. It was almost impossible to mold PPO, the key material in Noryl (one of GE's most important engineering plastic), with the technology available at the time. Had GE not discovered PPO's remarkable alloying properties, Noryl would not have survived.

There are also times when a limitation provides application engineers with an excuse not to use the new invention. Solid-state electronic power devices are vulnerable to voltage surges. Before the development of new circuit techniques and specialized resistors, engineers often cited that vulnerability as a reason not to use such devices.

Achieving consistent, predictable, and cost-effective performance requires a concerted effort to understand how and why an innovation works and to remove or find ways around its undesirable features. All this takes time and costs money. Frequently, the necessary skills are not those of the original inventor, who may be, for instance, an organic chemist with little knowledge of or interest in plastics molding or a solid-state physicist with little knowledge of power circuits and applications.

Understandably, potential users tend to remain skeptics until they have evidence of a technology's successful application to their own needs. Identifying the key leverage point can be critical. For example, the excellent but little noticed dimensional stability of GE's polycarbonate Lexan proved to be far more attractive to early users, who were beset with plastic warpage and swelling, than did Lexan's dramatic impact resistance. By contrast, the inability to identify an application for the unique information density of thermoplasatic recording proved fatal to the technology. The virtues of such pioneering applications cannot, alas, be demonstrated by careful analysis and paper studies. Actual market tests and experimentation are essential.

GE once viewed railroad locomotives as an attractive initial market for heavy-duty gas turbines. The limitations were such that this application still has not proved successful. Not until the turbines were redesigned for lower-cost full-factory—rather than on-site—assembly did they demonstrate their special ability to provide rapid, incremental additions to peaking capacity for electricity generation. It took great skill and ingenuity to shoehorn a package of delicate machinery onto a single railroad car, but there was little doubt that it could be done. Management had to hang tough for many years until it finally became clear what was impeding market acceptance.

As one who has participated in many attempts to match newly discovered technical capability with market pull, I have no patience with those who say, "They should have known better." The market-pull approach, if not used carefully, becomes a meaningless tautology. By definition, innnovations that succeed have found market pull. In practice, the pull is usually no more than a barely perceptible tug, which you strain with all your wits to sense and interpret.

MISCONCEPTION 5

In most instances, radically new technology will turn out to be more desirable than advances and extensions of conventional technology.

Despite all the talk of dramatic technological breakthroughs in efforts to attain higher energy efficiency and to reduce environmental damage, most R&D money is going into extensions of conventional technology. Evolutionary advances are less risky, give promise of more timely application, and are, on balance, more cost-effective—that is, they are "good enough."

History may indeed prove me wrong, but I predict that intensification of oil and gas exploration, production in more hostile environments, enhanced recovery methods, cogeneration, combined cycles, and increased attention to efficiency in use will continue to be the most productive responses to our energy problem. Synfuels still wait in the wings, and exotic solar, ocean thermal, and fusion technologies will be many decades in coming along.

We consistently underestimate how much room for improvement is left in a conventional technology. At the same time, we often criticize those who take the opposite course. The people who support evolutionary improvements are not opposed to new technology. Naturally, since they have to bear the odium of being wrong and of seeing an investment prove worthless, they support the development of a technology that promises to be adequate as well as less likely to fail.

After careful study, GE concluded that it knew too little about graphite-reinforced composites, despite their attractive properties, to risk using them in jet engines for wide-bodied aircraft. Consequently, GE decided to use conventional metal alloys. Rolls Royce went ahead with the graphite fibers, and their limitations forced a costly redesign of the RB211 engine.

As I noted earlier, the demands on today's technology are unforgiving; a close fit is not good enough. Much publicity has surrounded the promise of alternatives to the present automobile engine: the Sterling engine, electric cars, gas turbines, rotary engines, and hybrid electrical/internal combustion engines. Each of these types suffers from inherent limitations in operation performance, life, cost, or maintenance that have not yet yielded to persistent efforts at improvement. In other words, there are sound technical and economic reasons for the adoption—and the long-term survival—of the Otto cycle engine for automobiles.

Enthusiasts predicted for years that AC adjustable drives would replace DC motors, but Exxon's abortive excursion into electrical motors demonstrated once again that such change is difficult. Similarly, enthusiasts have long been predicting that electronic controls would replace electromechanical controls in appliances. The transition has not yet occurred. Pneumatic control devices, highly touted during the 1960s, have found only limited application. Much the same is true of thermoelectric cooling.

Sometimes, of course, a new technology proves irresistible. The Pilkington float process for making plate glass is an example. So, too, is the substitution of radial tires for bias-ply tires. But these are exceptions. In, for example, the emerging competition between electronic photography and silver-halide emulsion-based photography, I predict that silver emulsion will prove hard to dislodge.

MISCONCEPTION 6

The success of a new technology rarely depends on the adequacy of available infrastructure.

Inventing a new substance with dramatic new properties does little good if there are no sources of raw materials, if the means to fabricate it do not exist, or if engineers do not know the design rules for using it.

Here, the history of frozen foods is illuminating. Clarence Birdseye had his flash of insight in 1912, but his development of a satisfactory quick-freezing process was only the first in an excruciatingly drawn-out series of steps. Dietetic information had to be developed on the properties of different frozen foods, and new methods were needed for gathering produce. These changes, in turn, required the location of processing plants closer to sources of supply; new techniques and equipment for transporting, storing, and displaying frozen foods; and willingness on the part of both retailers and homeowners to buy adequate storage systems. Even so, the real catalyzing event was the government's decision after World War II to decontrol the price of frozen foods before that of canned goods. In all, it took some 30 years before all the pieces were in place for a major new technology to flower!

Obviously, not all innovations call for so complex and time-consuming an effort, yet often only large enterprises with their extensive financial reserves and ability to marshal diverse skills can stay the necessary course. Before color television could succeed, to cite a familiar example, more or less simultaneous advances had to happen in studio and broadcast equipment, home TV equipment, and the development of appropriate programs.

Today, those observers who postulate the rapid introduction of solar energy or electric automobiles or paperless offices usually ignore the constraints imposed by infrastructure. A good practice is to assume complete technical success and then ask, "Now what has to happen to get this technology widely adopted?"

Labor practices and application skills can be constraints too. The silicone industry developed a long-lived roofing material that could be applied over old roofs even at very low temperatures. The necessary skills in preparing and applying the material were different from those of customary trade practice, which reflected the hot, dirty, low-skilled work long associated with installing built-up roofing. Territorial boundaries among construction trades precluded the use of painters, whose skills better matched the application requirements. For their part, roofing contractors lacked experience with sophisticated silicone-based materials.

It took additional time and money to train contractors in the application of the new material and to verify that they were indeed following prescribed practice. These considerations held up rapid deployment of the technology, imposed additional costs, and so affected both the size of the potential market and the new product's rate of market penetration.

For a company to make needed investments in infrastructure, not only must it be able to assemble the resources, it must also perceive sufficient opportunity or threat. In the early 1950s, GE scientists invented a polymer with remarkable high temperature properties. Neither the equipment nor the know-how to fabricate the material existed, and GE lacked the capability to develop them. It did not even have effective enough relationships with equipment builders and plastics molders to stimulate action on their part. There was no engineered materials industry at the time, and GE was a novice in plastics.

Because sales were small and the business was peripheral to the company's major growth areas, GE reluctantly abandoned work on the new polymer. DuPont, with its large stake in nylon and long experience in process development and in working with plastics molders, saw the opportunity for a high-performance molded material in a very different light.

A few years later, when Lexan and Noryl came along, GE faced quite a different situation. Both materials presented challenging problems for those seeking to commercialize the technology, but molders were now comfortable with high temperature materials, new equipment had been developed, and the company had ample experience in designing plastic parts for engineering applications. Both Lexan and Noryl became major businesses, thanks in large part to the infrastructure that had meanwhile developed.

MISCONCEPTION 7

Making a technology effective does not involve developing routines and standards, achieving greater precision, and working under constraints.

The engineering group in GE's large steam turbine-generator business has a well-deserved reputation for being the best in the world at what it does. The engineers are not easy to work with; they are hard-nosed, doubting, conservative, unforgiving of mistakes, and demanding. To the extent they are resistant to change, scarred as they are from personal encounters with the misconceptions I have been discussing, their resistance helps minimize flawed innovations and costly mistakes. In today's complex technical environment, only the closest attention to detail and the most rigorous insistence on routines and standards make engineering design cost effective.

In software engineering, for example, programmers have been operating with virtually no constraints on their personal idiosyncracies or on their preference for "elegant" solutions. The result has been a vast duplication of effort and a proliferation of programs that, save at great expense, only their creators can maintain or modify. This lack of control has led not only to needless cost in writing and debugging software but also to a maddening diversity for the user. Anybody who has struggled with the endless shifts in symbology and keyboard usage that are required by various software packages for personal computers can attest to this Tower of Babel effect.

We must, therefore, learn how to modularize software, to rely on packages already familiar to users, and to impose rules and standards on the free spirits who are writing software. Admittedly, doing so may take some of the fun out of it, but a more systematic and constrained approach will significantly shorten preparation time, reduce errors, simplify future changes, and simplify the user problems.

An inevitable consequence of imposing structure and order on a technology, however, is that the technology itself becomes increasingly resistant to change. It becomes specialized to the task at hand and develops complex interdependencies with other technologies. But it also becomes more precise, efficient, and comprehensive in the solutions it provides.

TAKING STOCK

Where does a sophisticated understanding of these seven misconceptions lead? First of all, it leads to greater conservatism in predicting success for and in deploying new technology. On a probabilistic basis, if you bet "no" most of the time, you will win. Even with the discovery of an important new capability, a whole series of ancillary changes must often occur before market applications can succeed. Do not hesitate to ask, "Even if this new technology is as good as they say, what else has to happen before it can be deployed" or "How much leverage on the total system does this advance exert?"

From the perspective of the innovator, this understanding focuses attention on the crucial role of a technology's first applications. Because the greatest barriers to innovation are diffusion of effort and uncertainty over performance, there is no substitute for real-life demonstrations in high-leverage applications. Indeed, unless the technology promises a great improvement, it is unlikely even to be tried. Diluting effort by aiming at several potential applications, or seeking refinement of properties without a specific application in mind, is an invitation to failure. To let the learning curve begin to work, you have to get on it.

For those supporting an innovation or debating its potential value, the success of the first application is a crucial bit of information. Once a technological advance has demonstrated its utility and value, the probability that it will "take" soars. In fact, after a technology has begun to demonstrate its value, we have been more prone to underestimate than to overestimate its potential.

Managers must see the process of innovation accurately, not as colored by varied misconceptions. Although the odds are very high that any given innovation attempt will fail, companies must innovate in order to survive. And the benefits of the occasional successes are enormous—not only in direct rewards to the innovator and of gains to society, but also in the ripply effects generated by the process itself. It goads conventional technology into improvement, stimulates adaptability to change, leads a company toward greater self-awareness of its strengths and weaknesses, and responds to one of the most powerful human drives—the urge to try something new.

EPILOGUE

An Integrative Approach to Technology Transfer

Implementing new technology is a very difficult process. Firms which approach it in a haphazard manner, without proper planning and control, may find things do not go quite as anticipated. Often, this is not the fault of the technology itself, but rather that of the people implementing the system. To avoid mishandled implementations, and to ease the process of introducing and integrating new technologies, we present a five step action plan. While this plan is not absolutely comprehensive, it does provide a very useful guide for implementation and can be supplemented by individual insight and experience.

1. INITIATION AND STRATEGIC PLANNING PHASE

Objective: To identify those areas of the business where new technology will have the greatest impact and hence should be considered first.

Actions: A review of current marketing status and national/international competition.

An evaluation of all functional areas including design, engineering, and manufacturing systems and methods

An examination of existing manufacturing systems and methods.

An identification of the company's technical requirements.

Results: Formulation of a management consensus on the priorities of the business. This should enable the company to measure its position vis-à-vis the domestic and/or international competition. Subsequently, improvements may be carried out with no additional technology requisition.

Realization of the extent to which current organizational structure and boundary lines inhibit the response which is perceived as necessary.

Commitment and support of the senior management, establishment of the team, and emergence of the project champion or coordinator.

Decision if full feasibility study is necessary.

2. FEASIBILITY STUDY AND JUSTIFICATION PHASE

Objective: To examine the characteristics of the available and potential technologies in terms of software/hardware.

Actions: An assessment of financial situation and justification plan.

A desire to carry out the review without cost constraints at first.

A review of organizational changes needed, and an evaluation of the technical and training aspects of the technology.

A top-down and bottom-up look at the project utilizing the experience of other businesses.

A participative management style and encouraging staff involvement. Selection of the project team.

An effort to simplify the process and the products whenever possible.

Examine proposed technology for consistency with existing infrastructure.

Evaluation of the potential sources of resistance to technological change within the organization.

Results: Formation of business plan to include new products, new buildings, and so forth.

Development of the necessary technology specifications.

Determination as where the equipment can be sited with particular reference to integration requirement and environmental consideration.

Capturing the potential of new technology and the creativity of the technical staff.

Provision of backup facilities.

If deemed infeasible at present, firm has at least discerned what technology goals should be.

3. SYSTEM SELECTION/DEVELOPMENT PHASE

Objective: To develop a contract (or plan) which is unambiguous and to determine what exactly should be ordered (or done).

Actions: Setting out a timetable.

Writing up a 'firm' technical specification and defining the precise requirements.

A review of potential suppliers and drawing up a list for detailed investigation.

Selection of a short-list of suppliers who will be asked to quote.

Obtaining quotation and making a detailed logical evaluation.

Choosing the most suitable proposal, paying particular attention to the availability of backing a tuition and to that extent the advantage of a local supplier.

Results: Selection of the most (strategically) relevant technology and the most reliable supplier.

4. THE IMPLEMENTATION PHASE

Objective: To provide an environment for a smooth implementation of the technology, and to avoid negative transfers of learning and experience from one technology to another, which increase the error probability and reduce the productivity and reliability of the new system.

Action: A definition for the pace of change contingent upon the training already done, employee resistance, and the simple economics of alternate methods.

Preparation of a detailed schedule for implementation including key dates and performance measures.

Having all the installation procedures ready and clarify detailed individual responsibilities.

Paying particular attention to the integration of the new technology into the rest of the system.

Preparation of a detailed manual describing every step in the operation of the new system.

Have all parts of the new system checked and make judgment about its readiness.

Ensuring all necessary training is completed.

Result: An optimally functional system.

5. POST IMPLEMENTATION PHASE

Objective: To ensure the continuity of the operation and to begin preparing for the next cycle of change.

Actions: Availability of the project coordinator as a 'backstop' for inquiries.

A detailed post-installation audit which closely monitors key result areas to uncover problems which a subjective evaluation would not.

Result: A continuous upgrading of the manufacturing and technology strategy and an easy transition to the forthcoming stage.

CASE 12.1

Northern Telecom Canada Limited: Harmony(C)[4]

By March 1983 Northern Telecom's new telephone, "Harmony," had literally taken shape, and Station Apparatus Division's (SAD's) first basic electronic telephone set was a reality. Harmony, a basic residential telephone set, had been conceived with SAD in an attempt to forestall the London plant's closure in the early 1980s. The concept had been accepted throughout Northern Telecom, with SAD authorized to develop and manufacture the set. Northern Telecom Canada Limited, Residential Telephones (A) provides more detail on product concept testing and development; Northern Telecom Canada Limited, Residential Telephones (B) provides more detail on project organization. Harmony was to be the first of a family of four sets—a basic residential telephone (Harmony), a full-feature residential telephone (Signature), and two business telephones, basic (Unity I) and full-service (Unity II).

Marketing strategies for the full family were still sketchy. Production of Harmony was due to start in November 1983, and if the set was to be, and remain competitive, the manufacturing decisions to be made in the next few days would be critical. And the experience gained from Harmony production would be reflected in design and manufacture of the two business telephones (launch scheduled for first quarter 1985), and Signature (launch date fourth quarter 1985). Jim Baker, Project Engineering Manager for Harmony knew he and the project team had to quickly define the Harmony manufacturing strategy for at least the next three years. Until that was accomplished, none of the manufacturing policies needed to support the strategy could be decided, and implemented.

[4]This case was prepared by Professor Russell Radford.

Jim Baker

Jim Baker had joined Northern Telecom in the spring of 1968 after graudating in electrical engineering from the University of Waterloo's co-op program. In his work phases of the program Jim had been in several of Northern's plants between Ontario and the Maritimes. His first position was a capacitor manufacturing engineer in the London plant. Apart from a three month appointment in Turkey to establish a capacitor manufacturing faciity, Jim's career with Northern had been in London.

In 1975, Jim had moved into project engineering, and had been project engineer on the basic digipulse[5] technology in 1976, and on the digipulse retrofit of the 2500 set in 1977. This was followed by a move into engineering management, and responsibility for managing assembly of the Vantage 12 telephone. As the manager of new product engineering, Jim had been approached about Harmony early in 1982 by Doug Clark, new products manager responsible for NTC's line of residential telephone sets. By the middle of 1982 Doug and Jim had handpicked the biggest group of innovative nonconformists they could find to be the nucleus of the Harmony development team; the team was progressively augmented through 1983 as the task expanded and suitable candidates were identified. By the time Jim Retallack arrived late in the year as Harmony project manager, Jim Baker was firmly established as the manufacturing engineering mastermind for Harmony.

COMPANY BACKGROUND

In 1983 Northern Telecom Limited (NT) was the second largest designer and manufacturer of telecommunications equipment in North America. Its revenues reached almost $2.6 billion in 1981, up from $2.1 billion in 1980, and $1.9 billion in 1979 (see Exhibit 12.4). The company expected audited 1982 revenues to exceed $3 billion. Bell Canada held approximately 52 percent of the company's outstanding common shares, while the remaining shares were widely held. NT's operations were organized through five principal subsidiaries, including Northern Telecom Canada Limited (NTC).

Exhibit 12.4 Financial Data ($000's)

Fiscal Year	Total Assets	Working Capital	Shareholder's Equity	Revenue	Net Income
1981	$2,147,300	$501,500	$853,400	$2,570,900	$120,700
1980	1,985,606	452,739	728,314	2,054,561	121,396
1979	1,884,519	556,925	917,615	1,900,522	113,472
1978	1,344,154	367,273	632,566	1,504,560	94,384
1977	810,897	344,595	468,601	1,268,645	81,833

[5]Digipulse technology allowed standard rotary telephones to be equipped with a dialing "keypad," while still retaining the then standard pulse dialing components in the telephone set. Users of telephones which have digipulse keypads hear the conventional "clicks" of the rotary dial when they make a call; users of touch-tone telephones hear the unique electronic tone for each key as they dial.

NTC was responsible for the manufacture, marketing, and servicing of telecommunications products in Canada. It was headquartered in Islington, Ontario, and was organized into four main operating groups, operating 27 manufacturing plants and 14 associated research and development laboratories. Each group came under the direction of a group vice-president, and was comprised of several operating divisions. One of the main operating groups, the Subscriber Equipment Group, manufactured residential and business telephone equipment, and repaired and refurbished telecommunications equipment. This group was comprised of five divisions, including SAD (see Exhibit 12.5). SAD manufactured telephone sets for residential markets in Canada, the United States, and the rest of the world. Telephones for single line business markets were also manufactured by SAD (Station Apparatus Division–London Plant).

The London plant was built in 1959 when the then Communication Equipment Division of Northern Electric (the company's name before 1975) became constrained for space at its Montreal facility. Production of terminals (telephone sets) began at a pilot assembly plant on Ashland Street in March 1959. The equipment and the locally trained work force were transferred to the present plant in February 1960. By the late 1960s the plant was manufacturing most of its own parts and undertaking R&D work.

In its early years, plant operations were affected by the pronounced seasonal demand for telephones. This seasonality, associated with the frequency of spring household moves (especially the May move in Quebec) was not accounted for in advance by the telephone operating companies—they inevitably tried to pressure the London plant into producing high volumes during the summer when line operators were on vacation. By the mid-1970s the telephone operating companies began forecasting their quarterly demand more effectively, and even started to carry some inventory to meet their demand peaks. This allowed the plant to follow a more level production strategy on its main product, the 500 series telephone.

Until the early 1980s, all of Bell Canada's leased telephone sets came from the London plant. The plant also supplied the largest number of telephones for other Canadian distributors, and sold into the United States,Caribbean and Central American markets. During the 1970s, Northern Telecom became a multinational, aggressively entering foreign markets and setting up telephone manufacturing and assembly plants in the United States, Ireland and Turkey.

The London plant, now the center of an international network of manufacturing facilities, produced a complete line of telephone sets, most of which utilized the same traditional electro-mechanical technology. The 500 series formed the backbone of the product line. From its introduction in the 1950s this basic rotary dial set had been profitable because of high volume production and continuous cost improvements. Style and feature lines were added to the basic production line, and were produced in smaller quantities because their features changed frequently in response to changing consumer tastes and demands. A number of specialized, limited production models (such as sealed, explosion proof sets for grain elevators, railway sets and telephone booth sets) were produced on demand. By the late 1970s the 500 series, due to falling volumes, rising costs, and consumer resistance to price increases, was providing steadily falling contribution per set, and very low return on investment (ROI) for the model family. (See Exhibit 12.6 for a photograph of typical 500 series sets.)

Exhibit 12.5 NT Organizational Chart

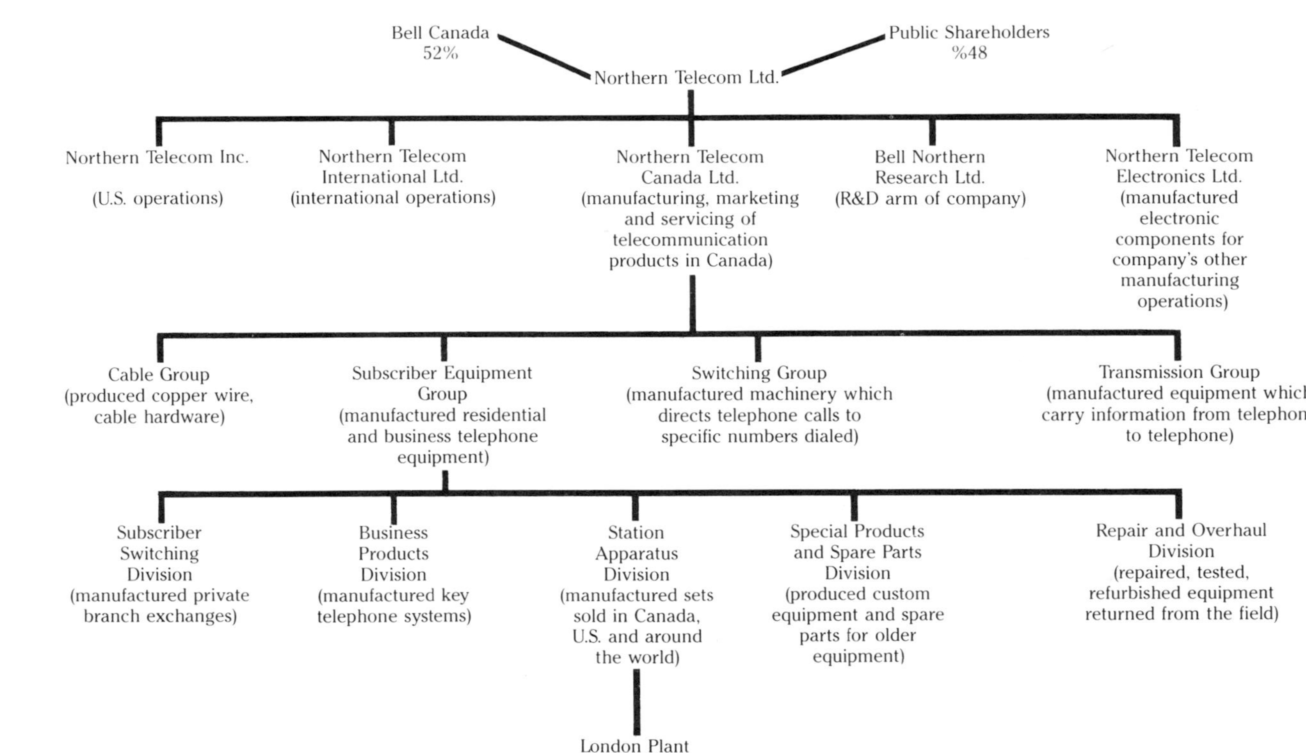

Exhibit 12.6 Picture of Basic Set

PRODUCT CHALLENGE

In 1980 plant management had recognized that, with the existing product line and manufacturing systems, the plant was no longer competitive. The major problems they identified included:

1. A company portfolio of high cost, low margin sets.
2. Basic sets (65 percent of the plant's business) were generating negative return on investment (ROI).
3. Existing products were not suitable for automated manufacture.
4. Style and feature sets faced increasing competition, particularly from foreign competition.
5. The basic sets were mature, commodity products, not suitable for adaptation as electronic componentry. (The abortive digipulse retrofit had proved that.)
6. Tariff barriers made basic sets uncompetitive on price in any but Canadian domestic markets.
7. The basic set's shape was considered outdated in export markets.
8. Style models (for example, Imagination and Contempra) faced heavy competition in both the retail and lease markets, lacking push digipulse dialing and with unfashionable shapes—Contempra was 15 years old and Imagination 6 years old.

Increasing competition in retail markets resulting from deregulation, a flood of cheap, foreign sets into the domestic market, and the plant's labor-intensive manufacturing operations, left the managers facing three options:

1. Reduce the costs of the existing sets even further.
2. Close the plant and either:
   (a) buy telephones from other manufacturers, or
   (b) manufacture in Asia.
3. Develop a new product line which met market demand and corporate profit objectives.

Even though the project team knew that several people at Group and higher levels in the company were constantly questioning the viability of progressing with the third option, within the plant there was seen to be really no choice. Harmony was the first product in the fight back.

PLANT ORGANIZATION

At its peak the plant had employed about 2,200 people on a three shift operation, producing most of the parts for assembling the 500 series sets. Of the 50,000 square meter manufacturing area, about 20 percent had been devoted to metal parts fabrication, and contained a large number of presses and associated equipment. A similar sized area was occupied by injection-molding equipment for plastic parts. Much smaller areas contained equipment used in manufacturing the various cables used in the telephones; these cables were then sheathed in plastic in another small area. But the largest amount of floor space (about 35 percent of the manufacturing area) was devoted to final assembly.

Final assembly was, in reality, a misnomer, as every assembly operation employed in combining the approximately 325 discrete parts (made from 108 different raw materials) into a telephone set was carried out in this area. Several assembly lines were used, with parts being built into components, then components into assemblies, with assemblies ultimately being assembled together to produce the complete product. The assembly lines were completely manual; the assembly labor content of a 500 series set was 30 minutes.

Supporting the various manufacturing operations were a large experienced maintenance staff, an engineering department which included industrial engineers, electrical and mechanical process engineers, a technology department which included telecommunications engineers, and a large materials management organization. Materials management included purchasing, warehousing, and materials handling. The purchasing department ordered materials from a large number of suppliers, based on informatioin supplied by production planning to the plant's material requirements planning (MRP) system. Whether the suppliers were discrete orders or part of a blanket order, they were subject to a strict sampling-based inspection program, stored in the central warehouse if accepted, and issued in weekly lots according to MRP release schedules.

MARKETING STRATEGY

The long-term marketing strategy called for Harmony to be an international set. It was clear that, in the short term at least, the Canadian market would be the most important, but the size of the United States market, and the international potential, made the development of a longer term, international strategy important. Because of market conditions, the company planned to use one marketing strategy in Canada, and a different strategy elsewhere.

Canada

In Canada, Harmony was to be offered only to the operating companies (of which Bell Canada was the largest), who would then lease the set to residential customers. This philosophy would apply to all four telephones in what was to be called the 8000 series. The market researchers had discovered, to the surprise of many observers, that the majority of Canadians wanted quality telephones, and wanted to lease them from the operating companies.[6]

Because the Harmony telephone was being offered to the operating companies only, these companies were expected to provide NTC with forecasts for the sets. The initial forecasts were, in fact, being used to decide planning production volumes. To keep forecasts simple, Harmony was to be offered in five colors only. These color differences would affect only the plastic cover of the base, the two-piece exterior of the handset, and the cord which connected the base to the handset. By using nothing but numbers, letters, and symbols on the telephone, the only written (and therefore bilingual) information would be in the instruction booklet that accompanied the telephone, and on the individual shipping boxes.

United States

Northern Telecom faced a very different market in the United States (and the rest of the world) as the company was not recognized there as a telephone set manufacturer. Having to compete against Western Electric (AT&T's manufacturing arm) for sales to operating companies would be difficult. And with the large number of telephone manufacturers trying to sell "throwaway" telephones the retail market would also be difficult to penetrate. Still, the results of market research showed that retail customers were prepared to pay for quality and reliability, and the company was confident it would succeed, despite the level of competition. However, forecasting sales was, and would continue to be, difficult. If the United States market called for a quite different marketing posture, what impact would that have on manufacturing?

Europe

Northern Telecom currently had assembly operations in Ireland and Turkey, and had an increasing installed base of switches and exchanges in the United Kingdom and Eire,

[6]Research in the United States also showed that a surprisingly large percentage of customers would continue to lease quality telephone sets from their local telephone operating companies. However, the availability of a wide range of inexpensive retail telephone sets, and the onset of deregulation, resulted in a smaller percentage of United States survey respondents favoring the lease option than was the case in Canada.

the remainder of Western Europe, and Asia Minor. In these locations the majority of domestic telephones were leased sets; this policy was the norm for commercial customers as well. Any sales would therefore have to be to the operating companies, and the big question was would Harmony be accepted in Europe? What changes would have to be made? In Turkey, for instance, letters on buttons would be meaningless at best, and could influence the acceptance of the set. Would the set need to be modified to meet regional differences? What would that mean for manufacturing? And how volatile would markets and forecasts be?

MANUFACTURING

Location

Initial cost assessments, made in late 1982, indicate that manufacturing Harmony in London, Ontario would be less expensive than manufacturing in Northern Telecom's Malaysian facility on the island of Penang, and shipping the product to Canada. The manufacturing costs in Penang were $124.35 lower per 100 sets than costs of manufacture in London; freight and duty added $452.66 to Penang's costs, however. This was good news for the London plant's remaining employees (already there was over 500 jobs fewer in the plant than at the peak in 1979). Now the project team had to make the assumptions that underlay the cost comparisons hold.

Costs

In order to keep manufacture in London, set costs could be no more than 58 percent of the costs of the 500 series set—yet meet the same federal standards and the exacting specifications set by Northern Telecom and the operating companies for (among other things) robustness.

Design would help, of course. The 10 groups (each consisting of one design, one test, and one manufacturing engineer) responsible for designing the new set had value-analyzed each component in an effort to reduce material and manufacturing costs. Already the final product was expected to contain only 156 identifiable parts, made from 48 raw materials. The design plan called for a total "vertical build" concept, where each successive module would be placed on from the top (or bottom) and no elements would have to be inserted between horizontal layers. This change in philosophy would make for more simple assembly, either manual or automated. Deciding what and when to automate might present the greatest challenge, and what influences that, at least in part, was the nature and source of materials and components.

Parts Sourcing

Plastics

Sourcing plastic parts would be relatively simple. The reputation the London plant had within the company for quality plastic parts production, and the advantage of in-house production had in its ability to absorb overhead, meant that all injection-molded parts could be made on site. While two-shot injection molding required for the buttons was available on site, however, it seemed likely that the volumes required would be more economically obtained by the company first purchasing the necessary tooling, and then leaving the tooling with the tool maker, who would supply the buttons as required. In addition, the marketing decision which created the need to use two-shot molding (buttons should be dark with lighter colored numbering), could easily be reversed in the future, wasting further investment in two-shot molding machinery.

Metal Conductors

While the number of metal parts in Harmony would be much fewer than in the plant's other products, some simple metal structures (like the conductor element in the jack, and the line switch which was opened when the handset was placed back onto the base after a call was completed) were required. All these pieces could be made within the plant, if necessary.

Electronic Components

Unlike the mechanical components, none of the electronic components could be made in the plant without a great deal of investment. For many items, such as the stock circuit elements like capacitors and resistors, projected volumes strongly indicated that these components be purchased from brokers or wholesalers. The commodity-like nature of these products, and the fact that nearly all manufacturers built to the same general construction and operating standards, meant that price could be used as the principal purchasing criterion. There were six electronic components, however, for which special purchasing action would be needed. These were the microphone, receiver, alterer disc, and three circuit boards.

Microphone

Built into the transmitter which would be inserted in the handset mouthpiece, the microphone element was the critical component in the transmission of the user's speech. A last minute challenge to the transmitter design team to rethink the transmitter layout completely had resulted in a new board layout and acceptance of a different microphone to that originally favored in London. The change resulted in an arguably "better" transmitter; more important, 40 percent was cut out of the transmitter cost, and about 4 percent cut out of the total set cost. The change also meant that the set would use a microphone designed within NTC several years earlier, and licensed to a United States company. There was still only one source for the replacement microphone. The Dallas, Texas based manufacturer of electronic components built the device in its factory in Japan for use in a wide range of recording devices. The manufacturer was prepared to ship as often as Northern required.

Receiver

The receiver was also to be built into the handset, to translate the incoming electronic impulses into sound waves. A Station Apparatus Division design, the first prototypes of the receiver had been built in the London plant. However, volume production of the receiver would be carried out in the company's Malaysian plant on Penang Island because, even with freight and duty added, assembly costs in Penang were much lower than projected costs for manual assembly in London. And to automate the process in order to make assembly in London attractive would require an investment of $2 million.

Alerter Disc

The alerter disc, in the base, replaced the bell in the conventional telephone. A simple product, the disc could be made by several local companies. The question was, how many sources should be used?

Circuit Boards

The same question was being asked of circuit board manufacturers. Three circuit boards would be needed, a main board in the base, a board in the handset transmitter, and a board for the keypad. All would be single sided, and relatively simple affairs. Many Canadian companies could produce the boards, but few could provide the total volume required. How many manufacturers should be used? Purchasing wanted to buy from several vendors in order to spread the risk. The designers, on the other hand, wanted to minimize the number of vendors; they felt that design changes could be made much more quickly with fewer vendors, and quality would likely be higher with only a couple of manufacturers involved.

And while purchasing wanted cost to be the overriding criteria for all purchases, the board designers were adamant that board vendors be selected on potential, not current, performance. What was the point of selecting the low cost producers if they could not improve their performance? Because it was inevitable that there would be constant pressure on the plant to continually reduce the cost of the set, the designers felt that only board manufacturers who were now and would continue to be innovative could help with reducing costs.

BUILD OR BUY

"If that's the case," asked one of the corporate finance team who had listened to one of the frequent design/purchasing arguments, "why not build some of the parts in-house? We know building the receiver here is out of the question—it is, at least, being built by the company and in the least cost location. And the microphone might be more than we could hope to achieve. But surely we could build a simple thing like the alerter disc in London?

"And the circuit boards—I can't believe the discussion I hear over such simple items. If all there is to making the bare printed circuit board is some inexpensive technology and a couple of experts, why don't we go out and spend the dollars to buy the gear and the people? We have the space in the plant for the processes. We have the need. And with what I keep hearing about the inevitability of electronics in everything we do, all our equipment will probably require circuit boards. Why can't London be our sole source for our less complicated boards? We already source most of our injection-molded plastic parts from here for all our Canadian operations, so its not as though its a novel idea. And besides, we can recover some overhead if we build this stuff ourselves.

"The problem with that sentiment," said Jim, "is that it assumes we know what we will be going in three years time, and with a great deal of certainty. Sure, we know that we will need about 500,000 of each board for now. But that is not volume as the bigger PCB manufacturers know it. How can we guarantee getting other boards from within the company to make a PCB operation here really cost effective?

"And another thing—how long do we intend to be using PCB's anyway? If we have to continue driving costs down as Head Office requires, we are bound to look at newer technologies. PCB's are old hat, especially single-sided boards. What if we find we have to move to double-sided boards? Or surface mounted components? We use these technologies now in other parts of the company—why not here?

"Anyway, we have absolutely no competence in this area. How would we go about gaining that competence without a great deal of investment and learning? Why not let others, who know how, assume the technological risk?"

ASSEMBLY OPERATIONS

Because of the modular build principle being employed the assembly operations were to consist of a series of separate but integrated operations. Exhibit 12.7 lays out the assembly process flow.

Main Circuit Board Assembly

In this stage of the operation electrical components would be added to the main printed circuit board. After all components were installed the components were to be soldered

Exhibit 12.7 Assembly Process Flow

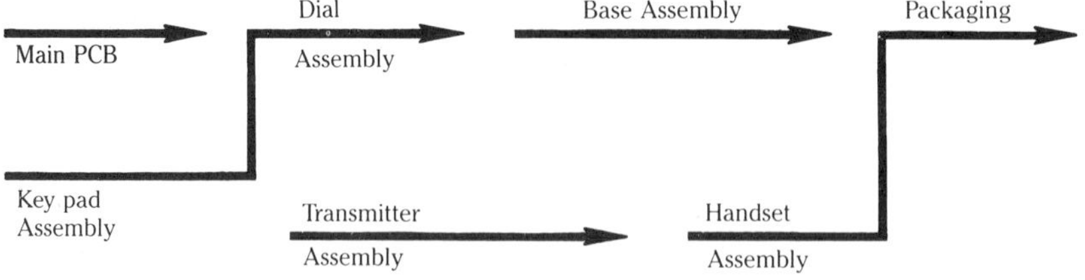

to the board, and the board then put through a series of tests which would check for individual component and full circuit integrity, and for any short circuits caused by component breakdown or bridging from improper soldering.

Keypad Assembly

In this simple operation, the frame for the 12 push buttons was to be turned upside down, and the buttons dropped into their positions. A shaped elastomer rubber pad which was to provide both insulation for the individual buttons, and also the elastic response to return the button to its correct position after finger pressure was released, was to be inserted, followed by a circuit board which was to be connected, ultimately, to the main circuit board. After being electronically checked for circuit integrity and visually checked for the correct location of all buttons, the keypad assembly was to be fused together, and sent to dial assembly.

Dial Assembly

The keypad assembly was to be placed on top of the main circuit board, and the two boards connected by a ribbon connector. At this stage the electronic circuits in the telephone would be essentially complete, lacking only a handset to make the telephone viable.

Base Assembly

Completed dial assemblies were to be set into a plastic base, and secured. Following this the alerter disc was to be dropped into a prepared recess, glued into position, and its two wires attached to the main circuit board. A cover was to be placed over the completed base unit, screwed down, and then the four rubber feet inserted. Once complete the base was to be tested.

The only variation in a set was in the color of the cover, the handset and the cords. While the assembly of components need not be coordinated, therefore, once a base was complete it needed to be matched with a handset as soon as possible if smooth production was to be insured.

Transmitter Assembly

The first stage of manufacture of the handset was to be assembly of the transmitter. A small microphone was to be inserted into the small transmitter circuit board, along with a resistor and the jack to connect the handset by cord to the base. The components were to be soldered in position, and a protective plastic cover placed over the microphone. The cover would contain a cloth insert, to provide acoustic protection to the microphone. The assembly was then to be tested, and the completed units taken and placed in the handset.

Handset Assembly

Handset bodies were to consist of two pieces, the base which touched the telephone user's ear and mouth and contained the electrical components, and the cover. The base would be laid down, and the transmitter and receiver dropped in and secured. Two wires were then to be placed between the transmitter and receiver and soldered to them, care being taken to insure the wire did not touch. The cover was to be placed on, and the two plastic body pieces screwed together.

Packaging

After being tested separtely first a base, then a handset, would be placed in a shipping box. Once the base and handset were in the shipping box the two cords (wall jack to base and base to handset cords) and the instruction booklet were to be placed in the box and the box closed. Boxes were then to be placed on pallets and plastic wrapped before going into a finished goods inventory.

AUTOMATION

The "design for manufacture" principle adopted during the value engineering studies had resulted in a telephone set that could be easily assembled manually or by automated equipment. Jim knew that the feeling in management was to automate. The UAW local, on the other hand, wanted the assembly operations to be completely manual. There was, however, a great deal of uncertainty about what could or should be automated, and the type of automation to be used. Preliminary studies had been carried out on manual and automated assembly. Some results are shown in Exhibits 12.8 and 12.9.

For some years the automobile manufacturers had been experimenting with flexible automation, and it was now commonplace to see flexible automation in frame assembly and painting areas in auto assembly plants. Neither Jim nor any of the people he consulted were aware of flexible automation being used in the ways required for Harmony, however—small, delicate components being assembled at fast rates. Jim had seen robots in vendors' laboratories performing these types of operations. None, however, had been subjected to the rigors of a real manufacturing facility. There were no doubts with items such as the basic insertion machines, or with hard automation like automatic insertion machines; these were already in use in different situations within the London plant. But with anything else the problem became more difficult. And to compound the problem, none of the vendors at the laboratory testing stage had any track record at all with flexible automation and transfer technology.

The pressures on the plant to have the first sets delivered to customers in about 10 months were not helping. Marketing's production ramp from start-up to maximum production was nine months—but that depended on assumptions about demand patterns. What if demand pressures from the operating companies meant ramping-up more rapidly? Or producing more than was anticipated? What if there were pronounced cyclical demand

Exhibit 12.8 Assembly Options

Manual Labor

For all assembly operations, 70 operators would be required per shift. This number would not include support staff, such as materials handlers or supervisors. Hourly rate per employee, including benefits, was approximately $13.00.

Automation

Main Circuit Board Assembly	Total Equipment Cost	Operators Replaced
a) Two pick and place robots with axial and radial component insertion machines	$30,000–$60,000[1] per robot	2
b) Six or seven pick and place robots inserting components not able to be handled by the semiflexible insertion machines	"	7
c) Two pick and place robots with the in-circuit and functional test sets.	"	2
		11
Keypad Assembly		
a) Fully automatic, synchronous assembly line. This includes vision test equipment for button placement and all tooling.	$400,000	14
b) Pick and place robot		
Base Assembly		
a) Fully automatic, synchronous assembly line. Including placing tested set in shipping box, and all tooling.	$400,000	16
b) Pick and place robot		2
Transmitter Assembly		
a) Dedicated Harmony synchronous assembly line. Includes all tooling.	$440,000	10
b) Two pick and place robots		
Handset Assembly		
a) Fully automatic, synchronous assembly line including five robots and all tooling.	$600,000	10
b) Pick and place robot		2
Shipping Line		
a) Fully automatic packaging process, including pick and place robots.	$200,000	5
Total Costs	$3,000,000	

[1]IBM robots were half the price of the more expensive machines. The more costly robots operated at three times the speed of the IBM machines, were more robust, and could handle slightly heavier loads. All pick and place robots lie in this range.

Exhibit 12.9 Option Comparison

Manual Assembly	Automated Assembly
Staffing: 70 operators per shift	Staffing: 18 direct per shift
Total assembly time per set: .635 hours at start-up; .28 hours at standard	Total assembly time per set: .17 hours Cycle time of bottleneck operation: .004 hours

patterns (which the operating companies did not seem to ever forecast, but which seemed to appear in all products)?

There was a recognition that to respond to market fluctuations would require some flexibility in the assembly process. The question was, what types of flexibility applied to Harmony manufacturing, and how should that flexibility be gained? While the company was seriously investigating automated assembly equipment, were there other ways to achieve the necessary flexibility, without the expense and the drawbacks of expensive equipment? And the solution had to accommodate all the 8000 series sets, not just Harmony.

All four sets were to be built in London, at least initially. Should one line be designed that would accommodate all four sets? If there should be more than one line, how should the lines be focused—business sets on one line, domestic on the other? Or some other way? Should the plant prepare for full flexibility right now? Analysis of transmitter assembly automation showed that a line dedicated to one specific transmitter design would cost approximately $330,000. Extra equipment to allow the process to build more than one transmitter could be incorporated into the design now for an extra $460,000. If that equipment was installed later, the extra cost for rearranging the process would be about $70,000—plus a two week delay in getting back to full production.

And as Jim was well aware, while the basic product concept for Harmony was agreed, the detailed design was not due until September 1983—less than two months before production was due to start. In addition, the chances of design changes after the telephone went into full production were high, based on experience with past sets, knowledge of the designers' passion for tinkering, and the speed with which Harmony was being pushed through the system. This applied even more to the other three sets in the family. They were only concepts themselves at this stage. Should a flexible automation assembly process be designed for them before the sets had even been sketched out? Would the flexible automation place constraints on the designs for these sets? Would those constraints be impossible for the marketers and designers to live with?

Should an automated assembly line be designed for a product if high rates of design changes were expected? At what stage should your line be automated—before, during, or after other changes had taken place? And what type of change would be happening at the time the line was being set up? What should the automation timetables look like, and what backup should be available?

OTHER PROBLEMS

System Design

As if the assembly was not enough, Jim knew that system design decisions might influence costs in other ways. The documents just sent to Head Office implied there would be marked reductions in overhead. This would mean condensing the assembly space to reduce the square footage overhead allocation—but that was the easy part. The heart of the reduction was associated with inventories. The plan called for a reduction in WIP stock to 18 days (including component manufacture), finished goods inventory of 16 days, and purchased materials stocks in the central stores of 50 days. Getting down to these physical levels would result in inventories of about $3 million. What did this dollar value really mean? Was it too much or too little? Inventory represented one of the best ways of compensating for uncertainty. If the company was to deliver, was not buffering a reasonable way of helping achieve that goal?

Design Changes

One aspect of uncertainty that impacted on production was design change. Some change was inevitable, but how should it be handled? Should engineering changes be allowed to disrupt a line? How should they be introduced? Should they be incorporated into all sets in the plant, or only in those yet to be built? Resolving those issues would have an impact on organization structure, and on the relationships among design, engineering, and the like. And it would have an influence on quality, if the old dictum was right—increase the number of changes, reduce the quality.

Quality

There were several considerations to be made concerning quality. The first was the cost of inspection. How could the cost be minimized? A partial answer was to build quality into the set. But what did the term "quality" really mean?

One major quality related issue was at that moment a cause of concern to the project team. The decision not to test the completed telephone, and therefore implicitly to sell separate bases and handsets, meant that the acceptance test limts for these components had to be individually tighter than would otherwise be necessary. The manufacturer of the microphone element guaranteed the sound pickup performance characteristics within a range of plus or minus two decibels. This range would be too great for the company to accept if the handset had to meet the more rigorous test requirements; a range of plus or minus one decibel would be necessary.

Those requirements were based on the understanding that user perceptions of the faithfulness of voice reproduction would heavily influence perceptions of set quality. One way of resolving the microphone problem lay in compensating for the range, and the cloth insert in the microphone's plastic cover provided one possible solution. The acoustic resistance of the cloth could be altered slightly, by varying the area of the small hole in the center of the insert; matching the hole to the microphone would solve the sound pickup and clarity problems.

To balance the microphone and the insert, though, required each microphone to be tested, and the results of the test used to decide the appropriate sized hole which would be placed in the insert. This process required flexibility and coordination of the highest order. How could this coordination be achieved, and was it really necessary?

The Future

As he thought about his options, Jim was aware of more imponderables. Decisions on whether the plant should retain a level production strategy, and the number of 8-hour shifts to be worked each week still had to be made. In addition, it was clear that the decision to build the 8000 series in London would be reviewed at very regular intervals, with production moved out of the plant as soon as it lost its cost advantage. Should the local management accept that loss as inevitable from the start, or should the plant strive to constantly reduce costs? In what areas would any cost savings occur? How might adopting a longer-term, cost-reducing manufacturing strategy affect the basic manufacturing process decisions?

The series of interrelated decisions to be made in a very short time reflected the uncertainty the plant was facing. Nothing could be considered stable, yet Harmony's success would depend on the decisions on manufacturing processes and their implementation. How should Harmony be built? It was now clear to Jim why the Chinese could use "may you live in interesting times" as a curse.

CASE 12.2

Matai Mills Limited[7]

In April 1983, Rod Baker-Clemas, executive vice president and general manager of Matai Mills Limited sat is his office in Pokeno, New Zealand, 40 km south of Auckland, evaluating new wood veneer slicing and drying equipment. Matai's parent, the Huron Group of the United States, had developed a new upstroke veneer slicing machine, the first prototype of which had been built in the United States and installed in Huron's California mill in January 1983. By the end of March the slicer's operating crew, assisted by a three-person development team from the head office, had the new equipment operating at up to 90 percent of design speed for periodsof up to four hours; best weekly (single shift) performance was 70 percent of design capacity.

Evans Manufacturing, which had built the prototype slicer from Huron designs, had independently developed a new (and as yet untried) veneer drying technique which was expected to produce flatter veneer at a faster drying rate. Both Huron Group and Evans Manufacturing were keen to install an in-line combination of the new slicer and dryer, and to close-couple them with a short, constant speed, conveyor. Mr. Baker-Clemas was now contemplating whether he should accept the offer of this untried combination of technologies. A decision had to be made in less than a month, or the equipment would be offered to other Huron affiliates.

COMPANY BACKGROUND

Founded in 1947, the Huron Group currently operated manufacturing facilities on four continents. Huron's principal product was hardwood veneer. In addition, the company

[7]The case was prepared by Professor Russell Radford. © 1987, The University of Western Ontario.

produced (albeit reluctantly) sawn lumber from logs which would not provide acceptable veneer. Total Group sales exceeded $400[8] million per year, of which 85 percent came from sales of 2–3 billion square feet[9] of veneer per year.

Huron was represented in Australia by Potter Veneer and Lumber Company Limited, based in Perth, Western Australia, and Matai Mills Limited headquartered in Pokeno, New Zealand. The two companies (operating one veneer mill each) each had a production capacity of approximately 250 million feet of commodity veneer per year if a 21-shift week was worked. Because Huron believed open competition stimulated thought and creativity, the two companies competed against each other in many Australasian and South East Asian markets. Where relevant, all companies in the Group traded veneer at market prices. The one function Huron kept centralized was research and development engineering.

The Pokeno plant, founded by Henry Robertson as the Fern Leaf Veneer Company Limited, began producing veneer in 1957, but quickly encountered financial difficulties when it tried to produce and sell 18 mm plywood in a market controlled by the larger New Zealand and Australian firms. In 1963, the plant was purchased by Humberside Timber Company Limited (which had been supplying particle board for the plywood cores), and continued to operate as a wholly-owned subsidiary producing both hardwood veneer and plywood.

In 1973, Huron, after selling another New Zealand facility, purchased a 50 percent interest in the Pokeno plant from Humberside, and Matai Mills Limited was formed as a jointly-owned private company. Huron purchased Humberside's share in late 1975 and promptly sold all the plywood equipment. Rod Baker-Clemas joined Huron as the general manager of Matai Mills in late 1976 when annual sales were roughly $7 million. In 1978, $4 million was spent installing a fourth slicer, expanding the local warehouse, and opening a warehouse in Sydney, Australia and a sales office in Melbourne, Australia. In 1980, two more slicers and a new dryer were installed, and the warehouse further expanded. All the new installations had been handled well, without any assistance from the head office or other Huron affilitates. Although the two plant engineers, both long-serving and qualified tradesmen, continued making minor improvements to the manufacturing equipment, no major capital expenditures had occurred since 1980.

COMPANY ORGANIZATION

Rod, as general manager, oversaw the four principal company activities of marketing, purchasing, manufacturing and administration. The marketing manager was responsible for all sales and marketing activities, and for the stockpiled cut veneer. Purchasing was responsible for all purchases, of which log buying was the most critical, and for all inventory management other than veneer. The administration function was under the control of the company secretary, who supervised personnel, accounting, legal, financial,

[8]All dollar figures are in Canadian dollars.

[9]One square foot is approximately 0.1 square meters.

and secretarial activities. Manufacturing was under control of the mill manager; to him reported the shift superintendents, each of whom managed manufacturing department foremen, and the support personnel in the boilerhouse, maintenance, engineering, and materials handling departments on each shift. The heads of each of these support departments reported to the mill manager.

Most of the managers were long service employees who had started as hourly employees and been promoted through the ranks. The two major exceptions were Rod and the company secretary, the latter being in the third year of a four year secondment from the Huron Group's head office. All managers were very capable, and Rod was pleased with the overall performance of the company, given the state of the markets.

PRODUCTS

Veneer is a thin layer of wood of uniform thickness produced by peeling, slicing or sawing logs. Sliced veneer was the most sought-after veneer for use in expensive furniture and paneling. Matai Mills produced sliced veneer either by vertical or half-round slicing. Different slicing techniques yielded different wood grain patterns and varied with wood type and market demand. While there were thousands of suitable species worldwide, Matai Mills concentrated on New Zealand native timbers such as rimu, matai, totara, and tawa, and on locally grown non-native species, especially ash and walnut. The company also cut imported logs, such as teak and mahogany, and provided custom cutting services on request.

Rimu accounted for 85 percent of veneer production in 1982, being essentially a commodity business. Raw material availability and the volatility of demand for higher priced veneers largely determined the product species mix. Exhibit 12.10 gives production and sales data for 1980–1982. Veneer could be sliced anywhere from 1.5 mm to 0.3 mm thick. Domestic (Australasian) markets preferred 0.9 mm veneer, as most of Matai's customers did not have equipment which could handle thinner veneers. Export customers in South East Asia, Japan, and Western Europe preferred 0.7 mm veneer for its flatness, ease of use and lower shipping costs. Many Asian buyers, in fact, were demanding thinner veneer on the order of 0.3 mm thick. Thinner slicing generated higher yields—more square feet of veneer per board foot[10] of lumber—so high quality logs tended to be cut for export. Demand was also increasing for flatter, smoother, veneer, which required greater than normal care in manufacturing.

MARKET

Ninety percent of veneer sales were made to furniture, wall panel and cabinet makers, most of which were small independent manufacturers producing specialty products. In 1982 there were more than 1,000 furniture makers in Australasia alone. Buyers tended to have unique requirements based on personal taste and the aesthetic preferences of their customers. The demand for veneer was closely tied to the economic health of the

[10]One board foot is 12 inches long, 12 inches wide, and one inch thick.

Exhibit 12.10 Production and Sales Summary 1980–1982

SALES

Region	1980	1981	1982
New Zealand Square Feet (000)	45,577	56,938	46,692
$000	4,628	6,061	5,294
Australia Square Feet (000)	9,855	15,544	31,097
$000	826	1,598	3,259
Export Square Feet (000)	128,725	105,805	103,944
$000	12,590	10,053	10,126
Total Square Feet (000)	184,157	178,297	181,733
$000	18,044	17,712	18,679

PRODUCTION (Thousdands of Square Feet)

Species	1980	1981	1982
Rimi	185,316	152,031	157,847
Matai	5,838	12,729	5,366
Tawa	5,163	7,723	6,080
Walnut	3,568	4,247	4,722
Other	12,373	11,358	10,843
Total	212,258	188,088	184,868

construction and furniture industries. In the period 1978–1980 strong demand allowed all grades of veneer to be sold profitably. The economic downturn of 1981–1982 had affected the veneer market, however, and even in 1983, sales volumes were still far below the record levels of 1980.

The market was also undergoing changes. In Europe, where historically 20 percent of disposable income had been spent on furniture, consumers were now placing more emphasis on automobiles, recreation and vacations. In Australia and New Zealand, plastic and print panels were capturing increasing shares of the market. The increase in furniture made from these panels exhibited at the semiannual Sydney furniture show, suggested that the demand for high quality furniture was shrinking. Buyers were purchasing more panel length veneer (2,500 mm) and sales of veneer longer than 3,600 mm were declining.

SALES AND PRICES

In 1982, 28 percent of Matai's sales were made in New Zealand, with 17 percent in Australia, and the remainder to Asia and Europe (see Exhibit 12.11). Matai Mills sold through sales offices in Auckland, Sydney, and Melbourne, as well as through agents and brokers in Asia and Europe. The company's six salesmen spent roughly 50 percent of their time on the road, visiting established accounts regularly and continually working on developing new accounts. They also gathered the market and price information needed to remain competitive. The remaining 50 percent of a salesman's time was spent selecting samples to show to individual customers. It was senseless to take a customer $0.12[11] rimu when the salesman knew the buyer wished to pay no more than $0.08.

Exhibit 12.11 Some Representative Veneer Prices ($ Per Square Foot)

	Minimum	Maximum	Average
Rimu	0.01	0.13	0.08
Tawa	0.01	0.75	0.15
Matai	0.01	0.75	0.18
Totara	0.01	0.11	0.065
Walnut	0.01	1.50	0.20

The Marketing Department at Pokeno set base prices for each sliced log, below which salesmen could not sell without written permission. Exhibit 12.11 shows the price variability of selected species. Salesmen were paid a base wage of roughly $1,000 a month, plus commissions of 1 percent of veneer from Matai Mills and 0.5 percent on brokered veneer. Matai Mills had more than 250 active accounts, the six largest accounting for roughly 10 percent of sales.

LOG BUYING

Matai's log buyers could purchase logs from around the world, but bought primarily from small landholders and timber companies in the northern half of New Zealand's North Island. The three buyers, each working exclusive territories, purchased 90 percent of their logs from sawmills, which generally sold 20–30 percent of their better logs for veneer. While there were many log buyers vying for veneer logs, Matai Mills had built a solid network of suppliers based on a long-standing reputation of providing a steady, continuous market even during industry downturns, and promptly paying for logs purchased by the log buyers. General market information from the sales force allowed Matai Mills to make reasonably accurate three month demand forecasts and cursory six month projections.

The "average" veneer log price range had traditionally been very volatile, as shown in Exhibit 12.12. This was caused by the uncertainty of demand for veneer, uncertainty of supply volume for some timber species, and the number of companies bidding for logs in the market. Matai's buyers, therefore, had to be constantly aware of what other firm's buyers were offering. In addition, buyers had to be aware that a log's purchase price was not as critical as the price received for veneer from the log. It was false economy to pay less but get poor quality logs; the Waikato buyer, for instance, had consistently paid 50 percent more than the North Auckland buyer for the same species, but generated consistently higher profits. This could have been due to tighter scaling, darker grain or generally higher yielding logs. Buyers were paid a basic wage of roughly

[11]The price per square foot of the veneer.

Exhibit 12.12 Representative Log Costs*

Species	$ Per Thousand Board Feet
Rimu	1,241–1,365
Tawa	1,878–2,374
Matai	2,691–2,829
Totara	418– 712
Walnut	3,623–3,733

*These are two year averages, not the extremes of the price range.

$1,500 per month to which bonuses were added on the basis of overall profit generated and, more importantly, profit per thousand board feet purchased.

MANUFACTURING

Upon arrival at Pokeno, logs were regarded, scaled,[12] tagged for identification, cut to length and stacked in an area of the yard called the log deck. The log deck contained about six month's supply for the slicers. Scaling, which was checked and adjusted, became important later in yield and profit calculation. During the summer and autumn, logs in the log deck were kept wet from overhead sprinklers to prevent splitting.

Veneer manufacture at Matai Mills was an uninterrupted process from the log deck through drying. Once a log entered debarking, it required all operations be completed in a timed sequence to maintain quality and yield. Ninety-five percent of the logs sliced were to Matai's specifications. The rest were custom cut.

Preprocessing

Logs were taken from the log deck, on a first-in first-out basis, debarked (without damaging any of the sapwood), and cut, lengthwise, into pieces called "flitches" on a large ripsaw. A flitch represented a quarter, third, or half of a full log, depending on log diameter, species, and wood structure. Sawyers exercised considerable judgment in insuring that the maximum possible yield and quality were obtained from each log. For instance, a log with a couple of knots would be cut, if possible so that both knots were in the same flitch. In this way the other flitches were "clear," resulting in higher yields of quality veneer. Flitches were regrouped by log, banded and coded with a plastic tag.

Bundled flitches were loaded into soaking pits, where the wood was steam heated. Following a 24 hour preheat, the approximately 4,000 board feet of flitches in a pit were cooked for 36–48 hours at 75°C–81°C, saturating the wood fibers to insure easier and cleaner slicing. After cooking, the bundles were separated, and each flitch cleaned and prepared for slicing. Computer coding sheets, used to keep track of each log, were attached to each flitch.

[12]Scaling is the determination of log volume.

Processing

After being prepared, flitches, in log lots were moved by roller conveyor to any one of the five vertical slicers.[13] If there was any delay before a flitch could be cut, it was covered with plastic sheets to maintain the temperature and restrict moisture loss. When the slicer became available, the flitch was picked up and maneuvered into place using an overhead crane, positioned against a backing plate, and held in position by retractable clamps in the backing plate itself.

When satisfied the flitch was securely mounted and the operator started the slicer. During slicing on the downstroke machines, the backing plate (and hence the flitch) moved downward past a heated knife, and the veneer slice dropped, knifeside face down, onto a table. After each slice, the backing plate was raised and moved a predetermined distance closer to the knife, and the cut slice was moved and turned mechanically by Huron-designed equipment to insure that the edges did not curl. The slicers in a flitch were always stacked in their original orientation.

Two workers, called stackers, inspected each slice after it had been turned, removed unacceptable slices (those with cracks, cuts and loose knots), and piled the good veneer, in sequence, on a small rail cart. The slicer operator controlled the speed and thickness of slicing which, along with wood temperature, moisture content, and knife temperature and sharpness, largely determined veneer smoothness. Average saleable commodity veneer output from a vertical slicer was 50,000 square feet per 8-hour shift, obtained from slicing 40 to 60 flitches. This represented a yield of 52–53 percent on a volume basis.

Piled veneer was hand loaded, in slicing sequence, from the rail carts into any one of the five dryers within an hour of slicing. The one exception to the rule was walnut, which required three days predryer curing to obtain its characteristic deep rich color. The veneer, which at this stage weighed between one-and-one-half and two times its after-drying weight, was first steam heated to equalize the pressure in all the wood cells, and then dry heated to remove the excess moisture without cracking and splitting the slices.

It took 30 to 45 seconds for veneer to pass through the dryers and reach operators, called unloaders, who piled the pieces in order in flitch lots. Domestic veneer was dried to 6–8 percent moisture content and export veneer to 12–16 percent. The higher moisture content reflected ocean shipment time; also, most customers outside Australasia repressed and dried veneer to their own specifications.

Changing slicer settings to alter slice thickness was a simple operation which took about 10 minutes, and which wasted only about 5 percent of one flitch in confirming the new setting. Changing the dryer settings was more tricky, as it took time for the heating zones in the dryer to stabilize after changing. In general, it was not necessary to change the dryer setting if there was no change in veneer thickness or timber species, and if the veneer was all for either domestic or export markets. The real difficulty came

[13]Matai also operated one rotary slicer, on which flitches were rotated through the knife positions. This slicer, used to highlight unusual grain patterns, was used on average for 16 hours per week.

in moving from commodity to premiuim[14] veneers, when dryer adjustments took roughly three hours as operators satisfied themselves that the dryer was completely stable. Moving from premium to commodity veneers did not require the same degree of stability, as the minor changes in veneer smoothness caused by temperature fluctuations did not seem to influence commodity veneer price. Consequently, for the premium to commodity change, the dryers were usually available 10–15 minutes after the 10 minute dial-setting process was finished.

Domestic veneer, unless it was to be clipped, was shipped to the on-site warehouse after drying. Three slices per flitch, selected by the unloaders, were taken to the sample room for pricing and customer viewing. All export veneer was taken to the clipping room where edges and ends were trimmed of bark and some sapwood to reduce package weight and volume. Export bundles consisted of 16, 24, or 32 sheets of veneer, depending on the amount of clipping required.

Slices from the outer edge of a flitch tended to be packed in bundles of 16, because the width of the sapwood strip along the edge of the slice changed more between slices at the outer edge than in the middle. Slices from the center of the log were usually in bundles of 32. Export buyers generally examined and purchased by the bundle, while domestic buyers selected flitch lots based on the two or three samples taken. All bundles were stored in the warehouse, with their location recorded in computer files.

COSTING

Costs and profits were accounted for on a log parcel basis. Manufacturing and other marginal costs were allocated to each parcel per square foot of saleable veneer produced; these allocated costs were historical, being based on the previous four months actual costs divided by that period's actual total veneer production. Clipping costs, where applicable, were added on the basis of total clipping shop costs in the previous four months, divided by the square footage clipped. All costs for each parcel, from log buying through to clipping, were summed to give the total cost which was then subtracted from revenue to yield contribution per parcel. Manufacturing costs, on a per unit basis, varied from as little as 5 percent within species, to as much as 50 percent between species.

All activities following clipping were considered overhead. Sales were assigned warehouse and frieght costs, with veneer inventory expected to turn at the historical rate of twice per year for export veneer and once per year for domestic veneer. Exhibit 12.13 gives the average cost composition of selected veneers.

Because of labor-saving improvements and poor market conditions, employment levels in the plant had declined from 350 in 1980 to 150 in 1984. Employees were organized by the Northern Timber Workers Union (NTWU). Wages ranged from a base rate of $6.50/hour to $9.00/hour for skilled tradesmen; approximately 50 percent of

[14]The difference between "commodity" and "premium" veneers was often subtle. Expensive logs, such as walnut, were expected to produce high-priced or "premium" veneers, and were treated accordingly. Some lower-priced species, such as rimu, would show outstanding grain formation on being cut, and would be designated "premium" logs. All "premium" logs, however identified, were handled with care, so that the maximum selling price could be realized. This was especially true in drying.

Exhibit 12.13 Average Cost Composition—Selected Species

Species	Log Cost	Manufacturing Cost	Warehouse Selling Cost	Sales Price
A) CLIPPED EXPORT VENEER				
Rimu	35%	37%	6%	100%
Tawa	42%	32%	6%	100%
Matai	50%	22%	6%	100%
Totara	10%	27%	6%	100%
Walnut	65%	26%	6%	100%
B) DOMESTIC VENEER				
Rimu	26%	27%	1%	100%
Tawa	22%	17%	1%	100%
Matai	20%	9%	1%	100%
Totara	6%	16%	1%	100%
Walnut	29%	11%	1%	100%

the employees were paid at the base rate. The labor contract with the NTWU was due to expire in mid-1985.

The mix of labor trades in the mill reflected the mill's history, and the slow rate of change in processes. In addition to the timber workers, the mill employed two electricians, two boilerhouse attendants, two plumbers, one motor mechanic, four millwrights (responsible primarily for tool setting and sharpening), and the two plant engineers. All these people had been apprentices in the mill, and all their work experience was with Matai.

Unskilled labor was readily available locally. Qualified tradesmen could be hired from Auckland, but would need to be paid a 10 percent premium on local wages for working outside the city, and would have to receive $0.20 per km travel allowance and either one hour's pay each time they made the one-way trip, or have travel time included in the eight hour working day.

MANUFACTURING EQUIPMENT

Matai's plant was aging. The boiler, within five years of the end of its life, released considerable fly ash into the air and would have been condemned had it been near a major city. The Number 1 slicing line, which the new slicer and in-line dryer would replace, utilized the plant's largest downstroke slicer, capable of slicing a flitch up to 5,200 mm long. Huron was prepared to offer capital assistance at a 10 percent annual interest rate, and New Zealand government assistance would be available, through energy self-sufficiency subsidies, for boiler plant improvements. Although the new line would cost $2.25 million, total capital cost would likely exceed $7 million once the boiler plant and improvements in the sawmill were included.

The new upstroke slicer was still being debugged at Huron's California plant.

Upstroke slicing, unheard of until 1980, was now being developed by a number of equipment manufacturers since it was faster and, because the veneer fell knifeside up, did not require the veneer to be turned to maintain the sequence. This allowed the veneer (in theory at least) to fall onto a conveyor and be moved immediately into a dryer. Upstock slicers would be heavier machines than their downstroke predecessors, as the upstroke cut required the machine to work against gravity and the resistance of the knife blade. There were advantages to this, however, in the smoothness of cutting action and the reduction of edge crushing as the flitch met the edge of the blade on each cut.

Huron Group's R&D personnel had improved on other upstroke slicers, such as an Italian model, by adding electronic and computerized controls. Evans Manufacturing had also entered the upstroke slicer race, by purchasing slicing technology patents from a French firm which had gone out of business. The result was a slicer which could operate at 120 strokes/minute as opposed to the current Number 1 slicer rate of 80 strokes/minute. The new electronic controls and monitors, which at this stage required an electronics technician to trouble-shoot and service them, would improve cut accuracy and smoothness, and reduce flitch loading time. Huron wished to build the slicer to cut flitches up to 4,700 mm in length. The new dryer would have greater capacity than the current Number 1 dryer, to meet the 120 slices/minute capacity of the new slicer. This increase, in turn, would require greater steam generation capacity.

Earlier attempts at in-line drying had been fraught with problems. It was particularly difficult to match slicer and dryer operating speeds. If the slicer slowed or stopped for more than a minute, the dryer would over cook the next slices entering it. This was not a real problem between flitches, but drying variations within a flitch affected between-slice consistency, and reduced the potential veneer selling price. The higher operating speeds of both the new dryer and the new slicer would compound this potential problem.

Despite its problems, however, in-line drying with the new equipment had significant potential. The current Number 1 line utilized eight employees while the new line, once operational, would use only four. All species but walnut could be sliced on the line, but some species might cause problems. (Walnut could, of course, be cut by the slicer, but could not then be fed directly into the dryer). Rod Baker-Clemas considered rimu, matai, totara, and tawa to be the species best suited to the proposed line. The present line cut all species.

Rod's primary concerns centered on the dryer. He was still uncertain whether the dryer would produce consistently flatter veneer, and keeping it fully loaded might be difficult. While Evans was confident the dryer would work properly, and adjustments to temperature would be at least as rapid as with the existing dryers, Rod knew that this was based on the assumption that the drying load, and hence the amount of heat leaving the dryer, would be reasonably uniform. Coupling the dryer to one slicer might invalidate this assumption. If the load was not uniform, the veneer might not be as consistently flat as Evans claimed it would be. Because the dryer was expected to account for 50 percent of the veneer quality improvements, half the potential sales price increase was in some doubt.

A third option existed, and it seemed to be worth investigating, if only as a compromise solution. This was to purchase another downstroke machine, from an Italian firm, and to use the existing Number 1 line dryer. The combination would employ one more person than the upstroke option, would operate at only 85 slices per minute, and would not improve veneer quality. However, it had the advantages of being less expensive, technologically proven, would require only minimal operator and maintenance training requirements, and would need shorter installation and start-up periods. Huron Group's Board of Directors were currently insistent on a minimum blade length of 4,700 mm, and the Italian slicer's blade would only be 3,700 mm long. Exhibit 12.14 provides some comparative data on the equipment alternatives.

Exhibit 12.14 Capital Equipment Alternatives

	Present[1] Equipment	Italian Downstroke Slicer	Huron/Evans Upstroke Slicer
Capital Cost ($000)	700	850	2,250[2]
Operators Required	8	5	4
Cutting Strokes Per Minute	65[3]	85	120
Equipment Operating Cost[4]		Not Collected	

[1]For comparison purposes only.

[2]Of this, $1 million would be for the new dryer.

[3]As installed. This equipment could now operate at 80 slices per minute.

[4]While these data were not collected, the manufacturers of both new slicers stated the operating cost per square foot of veneer would not exceed that of the old machines and could be as much as 5 percent lower.

MARKET CONDITIONS

One problem which needed to be resolved before the technology decision was made was the market any new machine would serve. The new Huron/Evans equipment held the potential of smoother, flatter veneer and increased capacity. Better veneer would allow the company to realize prices close to the maximum for the timber species involved. The case required to produce premium veneers would reduce effective capacity by 30 percent, however, as the dryer would need to be slowed down in order to attain temperature uniformity.

Neither commodity nor premium veneers would make full use of the new installation's production capacity in the short term. If commodity veneers were run, prices would be only $0.01–$0.02/square foot above the median for the particular species. The market for commodity veneers in Australasia was saturated, as many producers attempted to utilize capacity added during the 1979–1980 boom. There was a 50 percent chance that no premium could be charged at all, even if the mill sold only as much veneer next year as it had this last year. Rod was confident that the higher quality, attributable equally to the upstroke slicer and the dryer, would soon increase market share, and the slicer would be operating at three shift capacity in two to three years.

Even at the slower operating rates required for premium veneers, the markets would absorb only 70 percent of the slicer's 80-hour week capacity on a two shift operation in the first year of operation. This assumed retention of the company's current sales volume of premium veneers, and running all but walnut through the new slicer; selling price was forecast to be $0.115 per square foot, on average, for rimu, and $0.30, $0.35, and $0.095 for tawa, matai, and totara respectively. Species mix would probably change, with rimu representing about 80 percent of veneer sales by volume, the rest being evenly split among matai, tawa, and totara.

The international demand for quality veneer was expected to increase only at the growth rate of GDP, forecast to be approximately 4 percent in Matai's current markets. Market share could be purchased by reducing prices or increasing promotion, but outside Australisia Matai was at the mercy of others. In Australasia market share gains in the premium veneer markets were expected to cost approximately $0.02 per square foot in marketing expense in the first year, and $0.005 per square foot to maintain in subsequent years. The same market share gain could be realized if the selling prices were lowered to an average of $0.105, $0.25, $0.28, and $0.09 for rimu, tawa, matai and totara respectively. Marketing was confident that the markets would take all veneer produced by the upstroks slicer in a 4,000-hour operating year.

CONCLUSIONS

As the minutes passed, Rod realized the apparently straightforward decision had broad implications. How would new technology affect the marketing strategy? How would customers, competitors, and even head office react to Matai's efforts? What would the impact be for Rod Baker-Clemas? What else might Rod do? Rod switched on his computer, and began to work.[15]

Exhibit 12.15 Initial Thoughts

Sustained Capacities

Current downstroke (per machine)—at designed 60 strokes/minute	41,000 square feet/shift
—at current 80 strokes/minute	50,000
Italian, at 85 strokes/minute	53,000 square feet/shift
Huron/Evans, at 120 strokes/minute	75,000 square feet/shift
Note above are commodity rates.	For Huron/Evans on premium, 70% commodity rate; therefore 52,500 square feet/shift

Last year all veneer sales 182 million square feet; premium veneer for all species except walnut 18.5 million.

Personnel

California employs one electronic technician for the equipment—we might need one on hand at all times. Wages in Auckland for this trade currently $10.25 per hour. This person is in addition to the operating crew. What else do we need?

[15]Some of his initial work is shown in Exhibit 12.15.

CASE 12.3

City Central Hospital—Pharmacy Department[16]

INTRODUCTION

On March 5, 1987 Gail Addison, Director of Pharmacy emerged from a meeting of the Computer Planning Group at City Central Hospital (City) with a sense of price and accomplishment. She had spent much of the last several weeks researching and preparing a proposal for the computerization of her department to present at that meeting (see Exhibit 12.16 for the Executive Summary of the 18 page proposal). The directors of three different departments (laboratory, diagnostic imaging and pharmacy) had been competing to be first in Phase Two of City's automation program, slated for the 1987/1988 fiscal year. The Planning Group had just voted 6–3 to automate the pharmacy department (three had voted for the laboratory), but had given Gail until March 31 to develop a detailed implementation plan.

Although she had suggested to the Planning Group that her department had the necessary resources to implement this major technological change, Gail had not yet thought much about a plan for implementation. This could come back to haunt her; automation was her first major challenge as department head, and it had to be done properly. And it was no comfort to know that the laboratory director was shocked at his department not being selected for automation this year, and that he would continue lobbying to have the decision changed in his favor.

[16]This case was written by Professor Hamid Noori and Peter Cummins, 1988.

Exhibit 12.16 Executive Summary

City Central Hospital has decided to implement a hospital-wide patient information system in order to handle huge amounts of patient data more efficiently, facilitate informatimon flow, and produce accurate statistical data for management. The system will also have the potential to improve the level of patient care.

The Pharmacy Department proposes that computerization of the pharmacy will provide several potential benefits to the hospital. They include the following:

- Reducing clerical workload and increasing productivity in the pharmacy while reducing the potential for errors originating in the pharmacy.
- Accurate workload measurement.
- Improved financial management of the department.
- Increased influence on drug use through Drug Utilization Reviews.
- Easier formulary preparation and maintenance.
- Several benefits to nursing staff due to better coordination of pharmacy and nursing records.
- Favorable cost/benefit ratio.

In addition, the department offers the necessary departmental resources necessary to implement the Pharmacy Module. They include numerous professional and personal contacts with other users of this module, a high degree of computer literacy, and a staff that shows interest and initiative in the application of computer technology to the pharmacy.

Finally, the department maintains that implementation of the Pharmacy Module is consistent with the hospital's position on the use of new technology, and the department's desire to provide progressive programs that protect the interest of the patient, and are consistent with current standards of practice.

CITY CENTRAL HOSPITAL

City Central Hospital, located in a city of approximately 80,000 people, was a medium-sized (396 bed) community hospital that offered a full range of acute and chronic care services. The hospital, employing about 1,050 employees, was organized into four main groups. These groups, Patient Care Services, Support Services, Finance, and Special Programs, were themselves organized into several departments. Staff in Housekeeping, Maintenance, Food Services, Diagnostic Imaging, Laboratory and Clerical staff were unionized. The large majority of staff, including the Pharmacy and Nursing staff, did not belong to unions.

The largest department in the hospital, with over 400 staff, was the Nursing department. The nursing staff was responsible for the majority of the direct patient care, and this required nurses to deal with most hospital departments on their patients' behalf on a daily basis. In return, the nursing staff relied heavily on support departments to provide timely, accurate and reliable service. Given the responsibility of the individual nurse and of the Nursing department it was not surprising that the director of nursing services was the only department director appointed at the Assistant Administrator level.

The physicians on City's medical staff were not employees of the hospital. They were, in essence, independent, self-employed professionals, using City's facilities to treat their own patients. The physicians were controlled through a set of several committees, the Medical Advisory Committee being the main committee to which all other medical staff committees reported. The list of medical staff committees is included as Exhibit 12.17. The fact that such a powerful group were not direct employees was a source of frustration to City's management. Medical staff, by nature, were used to relative autonomy as individual practitioners, and generally did not like to be "managed." The Chief Administrator, however, was held accountable by various government departments and bodies for the level and quality of all services provided at and through City, and for the financial performance of the hospital, and the hospital's results were profoundly infuenced by the physicians.

Exhibit 12.17 Medical Staff Committees

Medical Advisory Committee	Disaster Committee
Admission and Discharge Committee	Emergency Committee
Credentials Committee	Medical Day Care Committee
Medical Records Committee	Laboratory/Radiology Liaison Committee
Medical Audit and Tissue Committee	Medical Education Committee
Infection Control Committee	Operating Room Committee
Bylaws Committee	Pharmacy and Therapeutics Committee
Cardiorespiratory Committee	Psychiatric Committee
Chronic Care Committee	Intensive Care Committee

THE COMPUTERIZATION PROCESS

The process of computerization at City had started in October 1984 with the recognition that it would be essential to automate the handling of the increasingly large volume of patient data being generated each year. Manual methods of dealing with the information were becoming increasingly cumbersome and slow, and inthe hospital setting it was essential to have access to accurate and timely information. After several months of investigation a consultant had presented a report to the hospital recommending a phased approach to implementation of a hospital wide computer system.

The Planning Group issued a Request for Proposal (RFP) to several software vendors in April 1985, and on the basis of the criteria established selected software developed by DataMed of Boston, Massachusetts, whose software was already in use in over 200 installations of various sizes in North America. DataMed's principal advantage was their ability to offer a fully integrated patient information system, with modules for every functional department City wished to automate.

City decided to phase-in implementation, and contracted with DataMed for one phase at a time. In the first phase, conducted in the summer of 1986, DataMed installed an Admission, Discharge and Transfer (ADT) system and a Medical Records system. These two modules had already sped up the admissions process at City, and currently provided interested users with important, current information (location, diagnosis and demographic data) on all patients in the hospital. In this phase 55 terminals and 38 printers were installed throughout the hospital. All affected departments, including Pharmacy, had received at least one terminal and printer. Although not one of the phases in implementation, plans were in place to install an electronic mail package in June of 1987, and a demonstration package was already being run within the Information Systems (IS) department. IS had started to run informal training sessions for interested staff on the messaging system; the classes were not compulsory for any particular user or department.

THE PHARMACY DEPARTMENT

The pharmacy department at City was relatively well staffed when compared to pharmacy departments in other nonteaching hospitals of similar size in the area. The director of the department, Gail Addison, had been at City for just over five years. She had started as an intern, was a staff pharmacist for almost four years, and was then made director in March of 1986. Her academic training included a Bachelor's degree in Pharmacy, and she had been taking business courses in the evening at a nearby university for three years. Gail expected to graduate with an MBA within one year, and to use the degree to further her career in hospital administration.

Seven of the full-time staff reporting to Gail were also pharmacists. Their job involved some routine technical work and a considerable amount of work requiring their professional expertise. They had a large degree of freedom in how they chose to spend their time in providing professional pharmaceutical services to patients, physicians, and staff. Over 50 percent of a pharmacist's time was spent on nonroutine tasks. Every pharmacist had completed a minimum of four years of university training, one year of internship, and had passed Federal and other licensing exams. Three of the eight pharmacists were male; all but one was less than 35 years. old.

The other 11 staff in the department were called pharmacy assistants, and their job was almost totally routine; there was little room for them to use their own judgment in the completion of their tasks. Assistants had completed at least grade 12; some had completed a one year college program, with the others being trained solely on the job. All of the assistants were female, and all but two were less than 35 years old. A few of the staff had some training on pharmacy computer systems, or were familiar with microcomputers. The majority, however, had little experience with computers. Most staff could see how computers could help them in their work, but they were all somewhat apprehensive about their ability to master the system, and the effect that it would have on their jobs.

THE DRUG DISTRIBUTION SYSTEM

The pharmacy department was responsible for providing comprehensive pharmaceutical services to the patients and staff of the hospital (see Exhibits 12.18, 12.19, and 12.20 for a departmental Mission Statement and Job Descriptions). Although the department was responsible for a variety of clinical and professional services, its principal respon-

Exhibit 12.18 Mission Statement—Pharmacy Department

Pharmaceutical services of the hospital are developed to be compatible with the Mission Statement of City Central Hospital as an organization.

Progressive programs are developed, operated and maintained that utilize the abilities and training of pharmacy personnel to promote optimal drug use in the hospital. Services are designed to protect the best interest of the patients and the public, and should be consistent with the current professional, legal, ethical and technical standards of practice.

Goals

1. To accept responsibility for implementing and maintaining policies and procedures which ensure safe and appropriate drug use in the hospital.
2. To establish, review and revise procedures which, as far as possible, protect the patient from medication errors, adverse drug reactions, and therapeutic misadventures.
3. To maintain a superior unit-dose drug distribution system that is as efficient and effective as possible.
4. To establish and maintain policies and procedures that ensure necessary documentation of the operational and professional activities of the department. All patient related documentation should be handled in such a way as to maintain the appropriate level of confidentiality.
5. To establish and maintain policies and procedures which ensure the safety of personnel handling hazardous pharmaceuticals, and to protect the environment from pollution by these agents.
6. To provide and administer a pharmaceutical service that is as economical and efficient as possible, while ensuring quality.
7. To ensure personnel of the department respect the patient by maintaining confidentiality of information they are exposed to in the course of professional activities.
8. To maintain a good working relationship with other disciplines involved in direct patient care. This facilitates communication that may result in improvement of services provided by the department.
9. To develop programs of an educational nature that promote optimal drug therapy directly to medical and paramedical personnel, and to the patient.
10. To promote self-development and maintanence of professional competence of department personnel by participation in formal, and informal, continuing education programs, seminars and conferences.

sibility was to maintain an effective drug distribution system. City was one of the few hospitals that had a "unit dose" drug distribution system in the wards, having almost completely replaced the traditional "ward stock" system in 1974 (Emergency still used the ward stock system). The adoption of the unit dose sysem had been undertaken despite the strenuous objections of the director of nursing services, who had seen the new system undermining the authority of the hospital's nurses. Over the years the nursing staff had learned to live with the new system, which had reduced the nurses' medication preparation time significantly. Unit dose had not yet achieved the reductions in drug costs and in distribution errors that the proponents of the unit dose system had guaranteed would result from its adoption.

In any hospital the drug distribution system encompass all drug dispensing, recording and reporting operations, from the receipt of a doctor's order, or prescription, to the administration of the drug to the patient. In the unit dose system the phar-

Exhibit 12.19 Job Description—Staff Pharmacist

DEPARTMENT:	Pharmacy
JOB TITLE:	Staff Pharmacist—registered
QUALIFICATIONS:	Must be currently registered with the College of Pharmacists
RESPONSIBLE TO:	Department Head

FUNCTIONS:

1. To evaluate the appropriateness of individual medication orders received in the department, and as far as is possible, to insure that drug use is rational and complies with the approved hospital policies.
2. To take responsibility for communicating with the prescriber if any modification of medication orders is indicated.
3. To write a covering order of clarification, and to notify the medication nurse of any amended order resulting from (2).
4. To endorse as correct, and take responsibility for, all entries by pharmacy assistants on patient profiles.
5. To perform a final accuracy check regarding individual patient medications and ward stock supplies on designated carts prior to their delivery to nursing units.
6. To accompany pharmacy assistants to nursing units with medication carts in order to assist in cart changing, check for missed doses, and to discuss matters relating to patient orders with nurses.
7. To supervise, guide and check other activities of pharmacy assistants as designated.
8. To dispense medications for home care patients and those patients receiving therapeutic passes.
9. To provide drug information services and to assist in keeping an up-to-date index system of current articles compiled from assigned journal reading.
10. To prepare extemporaneous sterile parenteral products following approved procedures.
11. To aseptically manufacture custom total parenteral nutrition solutions as required.
12. Following approved procedures, to prepare unit-dose, sterile preparations of cytotoxic medications for in-patient chemotherapy.
13. To compound products for use in bulk manufacturing following approved procedures.
14. To participate in investigational drug studies, drug utilization reviews, adverse drug reaction reporting programs, and any other clinical programs established in the department.
15. To participate in scheduled in-service and patient teaching programs such as diabetic and coronary class.
16. To act as a liaison between the pharmacy department anad the assigned nursing unit.
17. To provide after hours on-call service for the department as scheduled.
18. Other duties as assigned by the Director.

Exhibit 12.20 Pharmacy Assistant

DEPARTMENT:	Pharmacy
JOB TITLE:	Pharmacy Assistant
QUALIFICATIONS:	Successful completion of a college diploma course for Pharmacy Assistants or a minimum grade 12 education with one year's related experience in community or hospital pharmacy practice.
RESPONSIBLE TO:	Department Head
FUNCTIONS:	1. To prepare and maintain individual patient medication profiles. 2. To fill new medication orders as received when the medication is required prior to the next scheduled cart delivery. 3. To deliver these orders, when checked, to the nursing unit or the appropriate delivery system. 4. To fill individual patient cassettes with the appropriate medications (unit-dose packages). 5. To check and fill ward stock according to the relevant procedure. 6. To deliver the cassettes, with a pharmacist, to the nursing units at the arranged cart times, to exchange them, and to return the emptied cassettes to the pharmacy. 7. To package medications extemporaneously when needed. 8. To maintain a reserve inventory of prepackaged unit dose medications. 9. To insure appropriate control of lot numbers and expiry dating of packaged unit-dose stock. 10. To fill pass medications for patients as required. 11. To assist in keeping stock in the department neatly organized, and all bin areas, equipment and fixtures sanitary. 12. A pharmacy assistant is designated to distribute and complete an ongoing audit of all narcotics and controlled drugs in the perpetual inventory. 13. A pharmacy assistant is designated as the purchasing clerk. The assistant is responsible for completing all forms related to the purchasing process. Also, the assistant is responsible for assisting the director in inventory control as well as receiving the drugs from their respective supplier. 14. Other duties as assigned.

macy prepares all individual drug doses for all patients. The only drugs kept on the wards are a maximum of 24 hour's supply for each patient, and a few emergency drugs. All doses are individually packaged in disposable containers or packaged by the pharmacy staff, rather than sending several days' supply in prescription vials as is done in the ward stock system.

The pharmacy at City dispensed just over one million such doses to about 80,000 different patients each year. They also had to maintain accurate manual records on all of these patients and their drugs. The drug ordering process started at any one of City's 10 nursing units. Here physicians evaluated their patients and either wrote or gave a verbal order to a nurse for a medication. The nurse interpreted the order and transcribed it onto the Medication Administration Record (MAR). A ward clerk then processed the order and filled out the necessary laboratory requisitons. A copy of the order was sent to pharmacy through the internal delivery service. If the order was urgent the nurse either phoned pharmacy, or used a communication device called the Talos to notify pharmacy. Telephone or Talos messages were matched to the original orders when the orders arrived in the pharmacy.

All orders received in the pharmacy were screened by an assistant and/or a pharmacist, and any drugs required prior to the regular daily drug delivery were sent through the internal delivery service. The order was entered manually by the assistant onto a patient profile. All entries were subsequently checked by a pharmacist. The required 24 hour supply of drugs was then placed in a small drawer reserved for that patient. All drawers for patients on a specific ward were kept in a mobile cart, which the ward nurse would wheel to the patients' bedsides when administering medications. A duplicate set of carts and drawers were kept in the pharmacy; while the nurse used one set the pharmacy staff would be filling the other. Carts were exchanged once a day, 365 days a year.

THE NURSING/PHARMACY RELATIONSHIP

The relationship between the pharmacy and the nursing staff was not generally very good, but problems were still encountered. If the pharmacy did not get a particular drug to the nursing staff when they thought they should have it, the nurses became frustrated with the pharmacy staff and with the distribution system. Most disagreements between nurses and pharmacy were ultimately traced to a discrepancy between the ward records (the MAR) and the pharmacy's records (the patient profile). On occasion a physician would have to be called in to resolve the confict. Each disputed dose was reported by the ward staff as a medication error using City's Incident Report, even if the pharmacy had not received instructions from which to upgrade the relevant patient profile.

Although the pharmacy was legally responsible for the accuracy of the contents of the unit dose container, and for insuring the contents agreed with the current patient profile, nurses were responsible for administering the correct drugs to each patient at the correct time. Any detected errors were reported on an Incident Report. Copies of medication-related Incident Reports were sent to the Directors of Nursing Services and Pharmacy, and to the Chief Administrator. A joint pharmacy-nursing committee reviewed the reports for possible trends, and to assess individual and department performance. City normally allowed a nurse three minor medication errors before a competency review was started; a major error immediately initiated a review. Discipline ranged from verbal warnings to dismissal. A similar process, with a similar graduated discipline scale, was established in pharmacy; no pharmacy personnel had been suspended or dismissed for medication-related errors since the unit dose system had been introduced. There were no clear standards describing what consistuted an error, or what constituted major or minor errors.

Several published studies showed that unit dose distribution systems had medication error rates of three to five errors per 100 drug administrations; that amounted to about 10–15 errors per bed, per year,lower than the average of 50 errors per bed believed to be common under ward stock distribution systems. These were averages, however; Gail had analyzed several months' reported medication errors, and error rates ranged from zero to 17 errors per 100 administrations per mointh across the various wards.

As the unit dose sysem had reduced medication preparation time, so automtation promised a reduction in nursing staff time spent preparing and altering MARs. The new system would allow pharmacy to automatically upgrade and print MARs, and the new MARs could be delivered to the wards overnight, reflecting all orders in the system up to 9 PM, the closing of the pharmacy each day. Any orders written after that time would not appear until the pharmacy was able to print a special label to add to the MAR. The nursing staff would be able to record all necessary drug administration information on the new MARs, which would become a permanent part of the patient's chart.

OTHER RELATIONSHIPS

The relationship between pharmacy and nursing was not the only important external relationship pharmacy had; so was that between pharmacy and the physicians, and between pharmacy and the supplying drug companies. Many of the physicians attending at City relied upon the pharmacy for information about and advice on available drugs; the pharmacy currently carried about 2,000 drugs or chemicals in inventory, and had access to many more through the drug companies. Physicians were not compelled to follow the pharmacy's recommendations, and the pharmacy could not alter a physician's prescription without either the physician's approval or, in extreme circumstances, the approval of the Chief of Medical Services. Questions concerning prescriptions were rare, and Gail hoped they would become even less frequent when the physician had the ability to review the patient's records, medical history, MAR and pharmacy profile at the computer terminal in the ward office. Even with electronic communication from physician to ward office, the ability to alter profiles would still only be available to pharmacy; pharmacy staff would still be required to check for known patient allergies to particular drugs, and for potential drug interactions. All changes to a patient profile would still need a pharmacist's approval before the record was upgraded.

Automation would also improve inventory control and record keeping, reduce waste due to shelf life limits, improve forecasting, generate purchase orders on drug companies, and thereby reduce the $2 million annual drug and related pharmaceutical supplies costs to the City—or so DataMed claimed, thought Gail. Drug companies were currently supplying most solid drugs in plastic strips, each tablet or capsule being individually sealed on the strip. Some solid drugs and most liquid drugs came in bottles or containers representing several doses; these were less expensive than the individual dose strips, and if automation increased accuracy and reduced pharmacy record keeping labor, might not costs be reduced by reducing inventories and returning to the less-costly bulk drug containers? What impact would this have on pharmacy staff, and on the relationships with the drug companies' detailers? Most drug orders were currently prepared by hand and given to the relevant detailers during their regular calls on City's pharmacy; would it be practicable to electronically generate and transmit drug orders in the future?

CONCLUSIONS

As she walked back to her office, Gail realized that there would be major changes in her department in the next few months, particularly in the way drugs were ordered and handled. But there were also inevitable changes in other aspects, such as pharmacy's relationships with other departments and outside agencies. Had she recognized all the important factors involved? How should she and the department approach the change? Who should be involved in planning and implementing the change? How long should she allow for implementation, and what should the plan be? One thing was clear; if this was not handled properly, it would likely be Gail's last major decision at City Central.

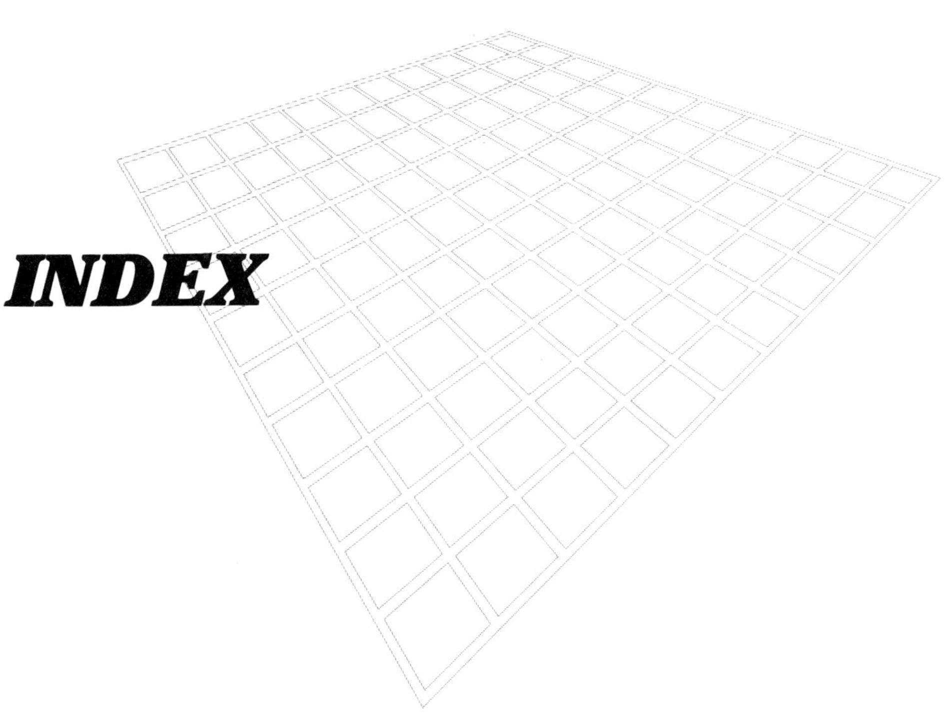

INDEX